computers

Concepts and Applications for Users with BASIC

SECOND EDITION

Robert C. Nickerson
SAN FRANCISCO STATE UNIVERSITY

HarperCollins*Publishers*

Sponsoring Editor: Rick Williamson
Development Editor: Trish Nealon
Project Coordination: Business Media Resources
Text and Cover Design, Illustrations: Seventeenth Street Studios
Photo Research: Roberta Knauf
Production Manager: Michael Weinstein
Compositor: Rad HM Proctor
Printer and Binder: R.R. Donnelley & Sons Company
Cover Printer: The Lehigh Press, Inc.

For permission to use copyrighted material, grateful acknowledgment is made to the copyright holders on pp. 735–736, which are hereby made part of this copyright page.

Computers: Concepts and Applications for Users with BASIC,
Second Edition

Library of Congress Cataloging-in-Publication Data
Nickerson, Robert C., 1946–
    Computers: concepts and applications for users with BASIC/
  Robert C. Nickerson.—2nd ed., instructor's annotated ed.
    p. cm.
    Includes index.
    ISBN 0-673-46553-5 (Student Edition)
    ISBN 0-673-46677-9 (Inst. Annot. ed.)
    1. Computers. 2. Computer software. I. Title.
QA76.5.N5123 1992b
004—dc20   91-36536 & 91-39115
                          CIP   CIP

92 93 94 95 9 8 7 6 5 4 3 2

BRIEF CONTENTS

iii

DETAILED CONTENTS

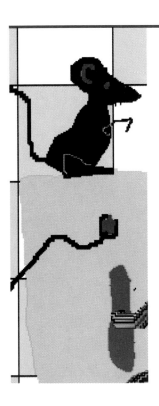

PART 2/HARDWARE

CHAPTER 3   THE CENTRAL PROCESSING UNIT AND PRIMARY STORAGE   52

CHAPTER 4   INPUT AND OUTPUT DEVICES   78

CHAPTER 5   SECONDARY STORAGE   111

CHAPTER 6   DATA COMMUNICATIONS   141

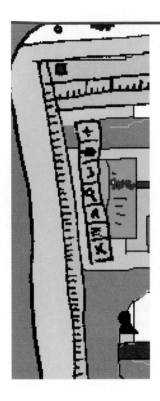

PART 3/SOFTWARE

CHAPTER 9   SPREADSHEET SOFTWARE 226

CHAPTER 12   DEVELOPING CUSTOM SOFTWARE   293

CHAPTER 13   COMPUTER PROGRAMMING LANGUAGES   321

PART 4/INFORMATION SYSTEMS

CHAPTER 14 INFORMATION SYSTEM CONCEPTS AND APPLICATIONS

CHAPTER 17   DEVELOPING INFORMATION SYSTEMS

PART 5/COMPUTERS AND SOCIETY

CHAPTER 18   THE COMPUTER'S IMPACT ON SOCIETY   462

PREFACE

Every year, the role of users in computer applications grows. Today, the user not only interacts with the computer but also develops his or her own applications. To do so, the user needs a solid foundation in computer concepts and a thorough understanding of computer applications. Students today know they will use computers more in the future and want to be prepared to get the most out of their computer usage. *COMPUTERS: Concepts and Applications for Users, Second Edition* provides students with the necessary preparation for a world in which computer use is continually expanding.

  COMPUTERS is a carefully written introduction to computer concepts and applications for present and future computer users. Its language communicates complex and difficult ideas in a simple, straightforward style supported by well-planned illustrations. During the development of the book, the author, editors, and reviewers continually questioned whether a user truly needed to have a working knowledge of a given topic. The subject matter was included only if it was of direct relevance to computer users or if it provided a foundation to understand important concepts. The ultimate goal of this text is to provide the student with just the right background and balance of knowledge to be an *effective computer user.*

CHANGES IN THE SECOND EDITION

The second edition of *COMPUTERS* is the result of a thorough review of the previous edition. The complete text has been reviewed to improve clarity in the writing and the illustrations. All technical topics have been checked for currency and updated if appropriate. More than half of the "Computer Close-ups" have been replaced, but those that the reviewers of the previous edition especially preferred have been retained. New end-of-chapter questions have been added, and answers to half of the review questions are now provided at the back of the book.

  Some topics have been shifted for improved organization. Basic computer concepts have been moved from Chapter 2, "Computer System Basics," to Chapter 1, "Using Computers Every Day," to provide a better basis for understanding the applications discussed there; data organization has been moved from Chapter 2 to Chapter 5, "Secondary Storage," where it ties in with secondary storage; and microcomputer communications software has been moved from Chapter 11, "Graphics and Other Application Software," to Chapter 6, "Data Communications," so that all data communications topics are together. Chapter 7, "Operating Systems," has been substantially reorganized to put more emphasis on operating systems from a user's perspective. Chapter 11 has been modified to more greatly emphasize graphic and related software because of the increased use of this type of software.

A number of new, current topics have been added. These include note-book and pocket computers in Chapter 2; trackballs and page scanners in Chapter 4, "Input and Output Devices," database servers in Chapter 6; graphical use interfaces in Chapter 7; cooperative processing and executive support systems in Chapter 15, "Types of Information Systems"; object-oriented databases in Chapter 16, "Database Processing." Coverage of numerous topics has been expanded because of increased interest in them. For example, more information is now covered on optical disks in Chapter 5; on desktop publishing in Chapter 8, "Word Processing Software"; on spreadsheet software functions in Chapter 9, "Spreadsheet Software"; on presentation graphics and computer-aided design software in Chapter 11; and on viruses and computer ethics in Chapter 18,"The Computer's Impact on Society."

The BASIC appendix, available in one version of the book, has been completely rewritten to eliminate reliance on GOTO statements. Decisions are now implemented using IF-THEN or IF-THEN-ELSE statements, and loops are implemented using WHILE/WEND and FOR/NEXT statements, thus bringing the material into line with modern programming practice. Other changes include the shifting of certain topics for better organization. For example, the coverage of strings has been shifted into Section 2, "Essential Elements of BASIC," and the coverage of subroutines, modular programming, and built-in functions has been moved into Section 5, "Subroutines and Modular Programming." This latter section has been written so that any of its topics can be covered after completing Section 2, thus providing flexibility for the instructor. Complete sample programs developed using the five-step structured programming process are now found in all sections (except the introductory first section). Coverage of pseudocode has been added in parallel to that of flowcharts; the instructor can choose to emphasize one or the other of these tools. Material on program testing and test data design has been added to Section 3, and coverage of program debugging techniques has been added to Section 4. Review questions have been updated, and answers to half of the review questions are now provided at the end of the appendix.

KEY EMPHASES AND FEATURES

Every feature of *COMPUTERS* is designed to be especially useful. Currency, however, is a key strength. Every effort has been made to incorporate the most up-to-date topics in the field. For example, pocket computers are discussed in Chapter 2, "Computer Systems Basics"; erasable optical disks are covered in Chapter 5, "Secondary Storage"; graphical user interfaces are described in Chapter 7, "Operating Systems"; object-oriented programming is covered in Chapter 13, "Computer Programming Languages"; and expert systems are presented in Chapter 15, "Types of Information Systems."

Microcomputer hardware and software are emphasized throughout the book, but not at the exclusion of larger computers. Hardware and software for both IBM PC compatible computers and Apple Macintoshes are mentioned at appropriate points. Minicomputer, mainframe computer, and supercomputer hardware and software coverage is integrated with the discussions of microcomputers.

Extended examples are used in several parts of the book to tie together related material within groups of chapters. An example in Chapters 8 through 11 shows how a sales manager uses microcomputer software for a variety of purposes. Chapters 14 through 17 use an extended example involving a bicycle business to illustrate important concepts about information systems.

The chapters are constructed upon important pedagogical features. Each chapter begins with an outline and a list of objectives. Throughout each chapter, full-color diagrams and photographs illuminate ideas as well as applications and processes. Illustrations are carefully coordinated with the text discussion. Each chapter has a summary of important concepts and a list of all boldfaced terms presented in the chapter. Every term in this list is defined in a chapter-referenced glossary at the end of the book. Finally, each chapter concludes with two types of review questions—fill-in and short-answers, and some experiential projects designed to push the student into new areas. Answers to one-half of the review questions are provided at the back of the book.

The "Computer Close-Up" is another key feature integrated into every chapter. These special readings—two per chapter—focus on real-world applications and go beyond the topics in the chapter, presenting interesting new examples and ideas. Some "close-ups" are taken from popular and professional computer publications, and others are custom-tailored to the book.

CONTENT AND ORGANIZATION

COMPUTERS is organized into five parts. Part 1 provides a basic foundation and helps the reader see how he or she is already an active computer user. Chapter 1 introduces basic computer concepts and motivates the student by providing numerous examples of computer applications. Chapter 2 explains the fundamental technology of computer systems, including the essential concepts of hardware and software. After completing Part 1, the class may follow alternative paths through the other parts of the book.

Part 2 covers computer system hardware and some closely related software and data concepts. Chapter 3 describes the central processing unit and primary storage, explaining the characteristics of these components that affect the user the most. The emphasis is on the CPU and the primary storage characteristics of microcomputers, but minicomputer, mainframe computer, and supercomputer components are also examined. Chapter 4 covers input and output devices, again stressing microcomputer devices without bypassing input/output devices for larger computers. Chapter 5 describes secondary storage devices, including magnetic disk, magnetic tape, and optical disk, and covers data organization and file concepts. Data communication hardware and software are described in Chapter 6.

The chapter emphasizes topics that are relevant to the user, such as micro-to-mainframe communications and local area network communications.

The third part of the book examines computer software, including both packaged software and custom software. The part begins with a discussion of operating systems and software interfaces in Chapter 7. The chapter describes user-relevant operating system concepts, including the general characteristics of common operating systems such as PC DOS, OS/2, the Apple Macintosh operating system, and UNIX. It also introduces menus, icons, windows, and graphical user interfaces, among other topics. The next four chapters cover the generic features of the main microcomputer software packages that users will commonly encounter. Chapter 8 describes word processing software, Chapter 9 examines spreadsheet software, Chapter 10 explains file and database management software, and Chapter 11 introduces graphics and integrated software. These chapters also discuss related software—including desktop publishing software, presentation graphics software, computer-aided design software, personal information management software, and hypertext software. Part 3 concludes with two chapters that deal with software development. Chapter 12 explains the software development process, emphasizing the points at which the user may be involved. Chapter 13 describes common programming languages, including fourth-generation languages and object-oriented languages.

Part 4 covers the essentials of information systems from a user's perspective. Chapter 14 presents information system concepts and common applications. Chapter 15 lays out the range of different types of information systems—management information systems, decision support systems, expert systems, office automation systems, and executive support systems. Database processing and its use in information systems is outlined in Chapter 16. The chapter emphasizes relational databases and discusses SQL. Finally, Chapter 17 explains how information systems are developed, emphasizing the user's role in the development process.

The last part of *COMPUTERS* reviews the place of computers in our society. Chapter 18 provides a look at the present and possible future impact of computers. Finally, for interested students, Chapter 19 examines careers in the computer field. It functions as a practical guide to getting started in a computer career, but it also reminds students that computer usage is part of many job situations.

The book has three appendices that may be studied at any time in the course. Appendix A demystifies the process of selecting a personal computer. Appendix B discusses the history of computers. The material is both complete and illustrated, but it is placed at the back of the book to provide an option for the instructor. Number systems are discussed in Appendix C.

A fourth appendix covering structured programming in BASIC is available in one version of the book. This appendix provides a solid introduction to structured computer programming in the BASIC language. The emphasis is on the process of developing well-structured programs in BASIC to solve a variety of problems. This appendix is divided into sections with review questions and programming problems at the end of each section. A separate glossary and index augments the BASIC appendix.

SUPPLEMENTS PROGRAM

Great care has been taken to provide a comprehensive set of supplementary materials to accompany the text.

Instructor's Manual

The instructor's manual contains for each chapter an overview and summary, lecture outlines, lecture tips, answers to in-text discussion questions, class projects, and additional review questions.

Test Bank

A manual of over 2500 true/false, multiple-choice, and completion questions is available for the instructor. The questions have been thoroughly class-tested and are also available in computerize format, with the HarperCollins TestMaster program.

Color Transparencies

More than 100 four-color transparency acetates of illustrations from within and from outside the text are available.

Study Guide

A comprehensive study guide helps students to retain terms and concepts and to do better on exams. A computerized version of the study guide, SuperShell II, allows the student to study while sitting at the PC keyboard.

Software Tutorials

A new, inexpensively priced modular series of software tutorials covers the fundamentals of microcomputer systems, DOS, and popular releases of WordPerfect, Lotus 1-2-3, dBASE III+ and dBASE IV. The applications software modules come in beginner and intermediate versions.

Integrated Software

The *new Version 3.1* of *PFS: First Choice* is available at a substantial educational discount with the textbook. This powerful, integrated software package provides new and experienced computer users with word processing, spreadsheet, database, presentation graphics, and electronic communications capabilities.

ACKNOWLEDGMENTS

Many of the ideas for this edition of the book came from reviews by users of the first edition. I greatly appreciate their efforts. The manuscript reviewers did a thorough job, and their comments were especially useful. My colleagues at San Francisco State University provided much useful advice and encouragement. Professors Sultan Bhimjee, David Chao, Sam Gill, Gary Hammerstrom, Ron Henley, Hugo Moortgat, and Richard Wiersba were particularly helpful, but many other colleagues contributed in some way.

Finally, I would like to thank my family for their support and help during the writing of this book.

REVIEWERS

The following professors and instructors have provided valuable input in the development of the second edition of *COMPUTERS* either as book users or as reviewers of the revised text. They gave practical input on content, depth of coverage, organization, and accessibility to the student.

William Burkardt	*Carl Sandburg College*
John Cary	*George Washington University*
Jason Chen	*Gonzaga University*
Sandra Cunningham	*Ranger Junior College*
Douglas Goings	*University of Southern Louisiana*
Cheryl Kiklas	*Anoka Ramsey Community College*
Carroll Kreider	*Elizabethtown College*
Linda Lindeman	*Black Hawk College*
Gene Lewis	*Colorado State University*
Jeanne Massingill	*Highland Community Colleage*
Brenda Parker	*Middle Tennessee State University*
Carl Penziul	*Corning Community College*
Pauline Pike	*County College of Morris*
Tom Rosengarth	*Westminster College*
Maria Rynn	*Northern Virginia Community College*
Steve Silva	*DeVry Institute*
Richard Stearns	*Parkland College*

The following professors and instructors reviewed the previous edition of *COMPUTERS: Concepts and Applications for Users.*

Virginia Bender	*Harper College*
Al Campbell	*Golden West College*
Paul Cheney	*Texas Tech University*
D. Epperhart	*Weatherford College*
Richard Fleming	*North Texas State University*
Jeff Frates	*Los Medanos College*
Arthur Geis	*College of DuPage*

Jan Harrington	*Bentley College*
Sharon Harvey	*Normandale Community College*
Colin Ikei	*East Los Angeles College*
Peter L. Irwin	*Richland Community College*
Jim Kasum	*University of Wisconsin—Milwaukee*
Penny Kendall	*Northern Illinois University*
Linda Knight	*Northern Illinois University*
Delores Knott	*Eastern Illinois University*
Robert Lind	*University of Texas—El Paso*
Margaret Marx	*St. Joseph's College*
Stu Myers	*Rancho Santiago Community College*
Bernard J. Negrete	*Cerritos Community College*
George Novotny	*Ferris State University*
Ray Panko	*University of Hawaii*
Ken Ruhrup	*St. Petersburg Junior College*
R. D. Schwartz	*Wayne State University*
Sumit Sircar	*University of Texas—Arlington*
Gregory Smith	*Colorado State University*
Sandra Stalker	*North Shore Community College*

Robert C. Nickerson

computers

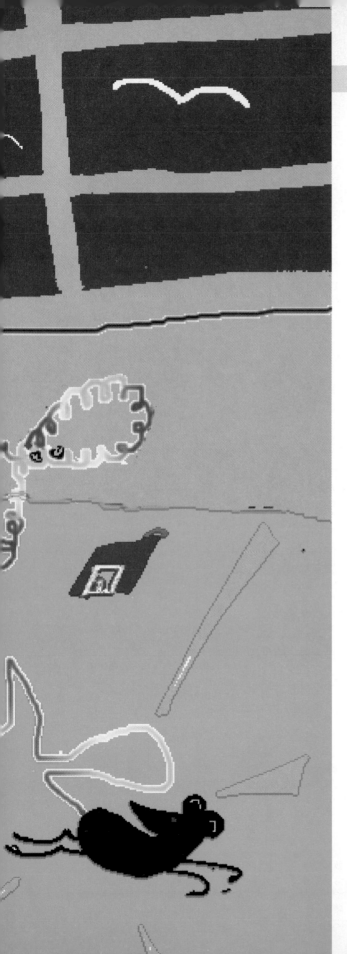

PART ONE

INTRODUCTION

1

USING COMPUTERS EVERY DAY

CHAPTER OBJECTIVES

• After completing this chapter you should be able to:

1. Give the general characteristics of a computer and describe the cycle of input, processing, and output.

2. Describe several ways people use computers in their personal lives.

3. Describe several ways people use computers in their work lives.

4. Explain who a computer user is and describe how and why people use computers.

5. Explain what a computer application is and identify the uses of typical applications.

DID YOU BUY groceries at a supermarket or clothes at a department store today? Did you get money from a cash machine at a bank or pay a bill with a credit card? Did you check a book out of the library, register for a class, or buy supplies at the bookstore? If you did any of these or many other things, you used a computer today. You may not have seen the computer you used, and you may not have known that you were using one at the time. But unless you live far away from the modern world, you used a computer today.

Although you used a computer, you may not have thought you were doing so. Someone else may have decided that what you needed to do required a computer. But often you have to decide for yourself whether or not to use a computer for a certain purpose. You may have made such a decision today. For example, you may have decided to use a computer to type a letter or report, to help analyze your expenses for the month, or to look up information stored in the computer. Whenever you have the choice of using a computer, you need to make an informed decision about why and how to use it.

This book teaches you what you need to know to use computers effectively. It teaches you not only what happens on the outside, that is, between you and the computer, but also what occurs behind the scene, that is, inside the computer. What you learn will help you make better use of computers and better decisions about when to use them.

This chapter gets you started by introducing some basic concepts about computers that you will use throughout this book. Then it examines some of the many uses of computers. These uses are drawn from our personal lives and from our work lives. Not everyone may use computers in the ways described, but there are many uses of computers. Finally, the chapter explains how and why people use computers, and what it means to use them effectively.

BASIC COMPUTER CONCEPTS

Before we discuss computer uses, you need to know some basic concepts. You may already have heard many terms, and you may be familiar to some extent with computers. But it is important that you know precisely what each computer term means and that you understand in detail each concept. The background given here will be used not only in this chapter, but throughout this book.

Let's start at the most obvious beginning: What is a computer? There are many devices that calculate or compute. For example, an abacus, an adding machine, and a pocket calculator all perform computations of some sort (Figure 1–1). In this book, however, we want to consider only a particular type of computing device—the type people typically call a computer. For us, a **computer** has three characteristics that distinguish it from other computing devices.

Figure 1–1   Some Computing Devices

(a)   Abacus

(b)   Adding Machine

(c)   Pocket Calculator

(d)   Computer

First, a computer is *electronic*. That is, it does its computation by electrical means. One important consequence of this characteristic is speed. A computer computes rapidly because it operates at electronic speed.

The second distinguishing characteristic of a computer is that it can remember, or more correctly, *store*, things. One thing a computer can store is **data**,[1] which are facts, figures, numbers, and words that are used by the computer. A computer can store data for immediate use or for future use.

The final characteristic that distinguishes a computer from other computing devices is its ability to store and follow a set of instructions that

---

[1] The word *data* is most correctly used as a plural noun. The singular of *data* is *datum*. A common practice, however, is to use the word *data* in a singular as well as plural sense.

Figure 1–2 The Input-Process-Output Cycle

Input   Process   Output

tells it what to do. Such a set of instructions is called a **program**. The computer stores the program along with the data. The program tells the computer what to do with the data, that is, how to *process* the data.

You can see from this discussion that a computer is more than just a simple computing device. In addition to performing computations, a computer stores data and programs, and processes data by following the instructions in a program.

Before a computer can store and process data, you must put the data into the computer. Data that you put into a computer is called **input data**, or simply **input**. A common way of entering input is by typing it on a keyboard similar to that of a typewriter. After the data is processed, you need to get the results of the processing out of the computer. Data that you get out of the computer is called **output data**, or simply **output**. Output is often displayed on a screen similar to that of a television, or printed on paper.

In summary, then, input data goes into the computer, where it is stored. Then the stored data is processed to produce the output data that comes out of the computer. This is commonly called the **input-process-output cycle** (Figure 1–2).

Some computers can be used by only one person at a time. The person enters the input, which is stored and processed by the computer, and then that person receives the output. The term **personal**

Figure 1–3 A Personal Computer

Figure 1–4   A Multiple-User Computer

computer or **PC** is commonly used for this type of computer (Figure 1–3). Most personal computers are small enough to fit on a desk or to be carried.

Other computers can be used by many people simultaneously. Each person enters his or her own input data, which is stored and processed along with the data from other people. After processing, each person receives his or her own output. We call this type of computer a **multiple-user computer** because multiple people use it at the same time (Figure 1–4).[2] Multiple-user computers are usually much larger than personal computers; some fill an entire room. Whether you use a personal computer or a multiple-user computer, however, the same input-process-output cycle applies.

USING COMPUTERS IN OUR PERSONAL LIVES

Figure 1–5
Using an Automated Teller Machine

Now that you know some basic concepts, let's look at the uses of computers. People use computers in their personal lives in many ways. Here are a few examples that you may recognize.

Computers in Personal Banking

One of the most common ways people use computers today is for personal banking. The most obvious example is the use of an **automated teller machine** or **ATM** (Figure 1–5). An ATM is a device that allows a person to deposit and withdraw money from a bank account and to

---

[2] You could also call a personal computer a *single-user computer,* and a multiple-user computer a *shared computer,* but the terms used in the text are more common.

perform other banking transactions without the aid of a human teller. The person using the ATM inserts an ATM card into the machine. He or she then presses keys to enter a secret code, which assures that the wrong person is not using the card. Next, the ATM gives the person several options, such as depositing money, withdrawing money, or transferring money from one account to another. After the person selects the desired option, he or she enters the amount of money to be deposited, withdrawn, or transferred. Several transactions can be completed at a time. After the last transaction is finished, the ATM prints a summary of all the transactions on a strip of paper. Then, the person withdraws this paper and his or her ATM card from the machine.

An ATM is not a computer by itself. It is connected to a computer that performs the tasks requested by the person using the ATM. The computer looks up the person's account in its records, keeps track of the transactions requested by the person, and adjusts its records to reflect these transactions. The computer is connected electronically to many ATMs that may be located some distance from the computer. For example, a bank's computer in one city may be connected to many ATMs for that bank located throughout the state. Thus, a person can use any ATM connected to that computer for his or her banking transactions.

When you use an ATM you are using a computer. When you insert your card and press keys on the ATM, you are entering input into the computer. The computer processes the input to perform the banking transactions you requested. You receive output in the form of a paper summary and (a unique output) cash. The computer is a multiple-user computer because different people use it through many ATMs at one time. When you use an ATM, you are using the computer to help with your personal banking needs.

Computers in Schools

Many students in elementary schools, high schools, and colleges use computers to help with their studies (Figure 1–6). Usually, computers used in schools are personal computers that fit on a desktop.

In elementary schools, students use computers for practice in basic subjects such as mathematics, reading, and spelling. Junior high and high school students use computers to help them learn subjects such as history, science, and foreign languages. These uses of computers fall into a category called **computer-assisted instruction** or **CAI**. In general, CAI cannot replace a regular teacher, but it can provide additional instruction and practice.

High school and college students use computers to study behavior of something that cannot be observed directly, a use called **computer simulation**. For example, in a chemistry class, a computer can be used to simulate a dangerous experiment without actually doing the experiment. In an economics class, the computer can be used to simulate how the economy might behave if certain policy decisions were made.

Students in high school and college also use computers for **word processing**, which means using computers to prepare written documents such as papers and reports. The student uses a keyboard to type

Figure 1–6 Using Computers in Schools

the document, and sees the words on a screen (Figure 1–7). He or she can easily make changes by first pressing keys that electronically erase words, and then typing in the new words. Whole sentences and paragraphs can be moved around within the document by pressing special keys. After the document is in its final form, the computer can print it out on paper.

Students may also use computers to help with other aspects of document preparation. For example, a student may use a computer to organize notes on the subject of a report. He or she can prepare an outline of the report using the computer. Once the report is typed, the student can use the computer to check for spelling, style, and grammatical errors.

Figure 1–7 Using a Computer for Word Processing

Another use of computers by students is to research topics. Many libraries have computerized services for locating books and articles. If a student wants to find recent articles on a particular subject, he or she can have the computer do the search. Some books and other types of written material are accessible by a computer. For example, the complete works of Shakespeare are available in a computerized form. If a student wants to locate specific quotations from Shakespeare, he or she can have the computer search for the information.

Whenever you use a computer in school, you must interact with it. You enter input data by pressing keys on the keyboard. The computer stores and processes the data. You observe the output data on a screen. You use the computer as an aid in studying and doing schoolwork.

Computers in Homes

Many people use computers in their homes (Figure 1–8). A home computer is a personal computer that costs between a few hundred and several thousand dollars. People use home computers to do schoolwork, to do work brought home from an office or business, and to assist in running a home business. People also use home computers for personal use, including entertainment, self-improvement, and personal financial management. Here we will just concentrate on these personal uses of home computers.

Many entertaining games are available for home computers, including common card games such as blackjack (twenty-one) and board games such as chess. In these games the computer acts as the opponent; you play against the computer. Another type is an adventure game in which you must find your way out of a maze filled with unexpected pitfalls. Some games that are not thought of as games in the traditional sense are also available. In one popular game the computer simulates an airplane. You play by giving the computer instructions about how to take off, fly, and land the airplane. You win or lose depending on the success of your flight. Besides games, you can use home computers for other forms of entertainment, including composing music and drawing pictures.

Figure 1–8 Using Computers in the Home

Home computers can be used to help improve useful skills. For example, you can learn to type, increase your reading speed, and practice taking standard tests such as the SAT. You can use a computer at home, just as in school, to teach yourself many subjects, using computer-assisted instruction.

A home computer can help with personal financial management by keeping track of personal expenses each month and comparing the expenses to a budget. You can also use a home computer to help with income tax preparation. Some people keep track of their investments in stocks, bonds, and real estate on their home computers. People also use home computers to write letters, using word processing.

Whenever you use a home computer, you enter input data by pressing keys and you receive output on a screen. The computer processes the input to produce the output. You use the computer to play a game, teach yourself a useful skill, help with personal finances, or do something else that provides you with enjoyment or benefits your personal life.

USING COMPUTERS IN OUR WORK LIVES

The uses of computers in people's work lives depend on the type of work they do and the type of organization for which they work. Here are several examples of the way people use computers in their jobs.

Computers in Sales

People who work in sales in stores frequently use computers in **point-of-sale**, or **POS**, **systems**. A POS system is a computerized system for recording sales as customers pay for their merchandise. Several types of stores use POS systems, including department stores and supermarkets.

Many department stores use POS cash registers (Figure 1–9). Such a cash register is not a computer but is connected to a computer in the store. When a customer purchases an item, the clerk at the cash register runs a device called a *wand* over a special tag attached to the merchandise. The tag contains a code that indicates what item the customer purchased. As the wand passes over the tag, it senses the code and sends it to the computer. The computer determines the price of the item and records the fact that the item has been sold. The cash register receives the price from the computer and uses this price to compute the amount that the customer owes. The computer uses the sale information to adjust its records regarding the quantity of that item in stock. All the POS cash registers in the store are connected to the same computer, so it usually does not matter which cash register a customer uses to pay for merchandise.

Another example of a POS system is a computerized supermarket checkout system (Figure 1–10). This system includes checkout counters with special devices that sense a code marked on the merchandise. This code is called the *Universal Product Code* or *UPC*. The sensing device in a checkout counter is called a *scanner* and uses a laser beam to sense the UPC on the merchandise. As with a POS cash register, the code is sent to

Figure 1–9
Using a Point-of-Sale Cash Register

Figure 1–10
Using a Computerized Supermarket
Check-Out Counter

a computer to determine the item's price, which is then sent back to the cash register at the checkout counter. The computer also adjusts its records to accurately reflect the quantity of each item in stock.

If you work as a salesperson or clerk in a store that uses a POS system, you use a computer to help you do your job. Each time you pass a wand over a sales tag or run an item past a scanner, you send input data to the computer. The computer, which is a multiple-user computer, processes this data and sends output back to you at your cash register or checkout counter.

Computers in Offices

Many people work in offices in various capacities. Clerks, secretaries, office managers, sales representatives, marketing coordinators, magazine editors, journalists, and many others work at a desk in an office at least some of the time. All these people use computers in some way on their jobs (Figure 1–11). Usually, the computers they use are personal computers.

Office computers are often used to prepare letters and written documents by using word processing. A person types the letter or document into the computer. Then he or she corrects errors and makes changes in the document before having the computer print it on paper.

Office computers can be used to send messages to other people in the organization, a use called **electronic mail** or **E mail**. With electronic mail, letters and memos that normally would be sent on paper are transmitted electronically from one computer to another. The sender keys the mail into his or her computer just as in word processing. Then he or she tells the computer to send the mail to any number of other computers. The receiver can read the mail on his or her computer's screen or have the computer print it on paper.

Figure 1–11   Using Computers in an Office

Some people use office computers to keep track of information in a **database**. A database is composed of data stored in a computer. For example, a sales representative may keep a list of customers in a database. Then the sales representative can periodically check the list to see which customers should be contacted next.

Many people who use office computers also have computers in their homes so they can do some of their work away from the office. Some people take work home at night or over the weekend. Others have arrangements with their employers that allow them to work at home some of the time.

If you work in an office you will probably use computers. Whether you use a computer for word processing, sending electronic mail, storing data in a database, or some other function, you are entering input data into the computer, which stores and processes the data and sends output back to you. You are using a computer to help you perform your job better.

Computers in Business Management

Computers are used extensively by business managers, who are mainly concerned with making good decisions about the business. To make a good decision, a manager needs information related to the decision. Computers used in business management help provide the required information.

Many business managers use computers to look up information in a database. For example, a manager may look up information about the recent sales of certain products made by the business. The information may, for example, help the manager decide whether a new advertising campaign is needed to improve sales. Small databases can be stored in personal computers, but larger databases are usually stored in multiple-user computers.

Business managers, especially those who decide how to use the business's money, often need to analyze data to help in their decision making. Many such managers use a **spreadsheet** to assist them in their work. A spreadsheet is an arrangement of data into rows and columns (Figure 1–12). Calculations are done on the data in the spreadsheet, and the results of the calculations help the manager make decisions. Spreadsheets are almost always used on personal computers.

Some business managers use computers to analyze the sales the business has generated. In such a *sales analysis system*, information about the sales made by each salesperson is recorded in the computer, which is usually a large computer operated by computer personnel, not by the business manager. The information recorded includes codes to identify the salesperson, the region where the salesperson works, the customer who purchased the item, and the item purchased. Also included are the price and quantity of the item purchased.

Periodically, such as every week or month, the computer prints reports that summarize the sales. These reports are given to the manager. For example, one sales analysis report gives the total sales for each sales region (Figure 1–13). This type of report helps the manager decide in

Figure 1–12 A Spreadsheet

| File | Edit | Formula | Format | Data | Options | Macro | Window | ✓ | 14:10:10 |

Normal

| | G173 | | 27.43 | | | | | |

CI '89 TRAVEL EXPENSES

	A	B	C	D	E	F	G	H	I	C
1	ABC PHOTOGRAPHY, LTD. CY 1989 TRAVEL EXPENSES									
2	*NOTE: This form only includes expenses paid in cash/travelers' checks.*									
3	TRIP	LOCATION	DATE	FOR DAY		FOOD	ROOM	XPTN TYPE	XPTN $	CO
4	*End Lines:*	*Singapore=36*	*Taiwan=45*			*S.Korea=62*	*Japan=69*	*Phoenix=94*	*S.Korea=132*	
5	GRAND TOTAL 1989 CASH TRAVEL EXPENSES:									
6			$12,317							
160	*Textbook Photography to illustrate the Traditional South*									
161	CI-S.C.	ORD–CHARLST.	23 Aug 89 Wed	CI	1	$41.92	$34.00	Taxi to ORD	$12.00	T
162	CI-S.C.	CHARLESTON	24 Aug 89 Thu	CI	2	$43.98	$34.00	Fuel/Parking	$10.46	
163	CI-S.C.	CHARLESTON	25 Aug 89 Fri	CI	3	$46.32	$34.00	Rental Car	CC	
164	CI-S.C.	CHARLESTON	26 Aug 89 Sat	CI	4	$35.71	$34.00	Fuel/Parking	$12.00	
165	CI-S.C.	CHARLST.–ORD	27 Aug 89 Sun	CI	5	$8.86	$34.00	Fuel	$4.15	
166	CI-S.C.	ORD	27 Aug 89 Sun	CI	6			Taxi		
167	*TOTAL cash expenses, CI–S. Carolina, in U.S. $:*					$176.79	$170.00		$38.61	
168	*U.S. $ Subtotals for this year to date:*					$3,023.72	$1,001.20		$1,499.13	
169		*Column Subtotal*								
170										
171	Textbook Photography to illustrate Alternate Energy									
172	CI-WISC.	ROCKTON, IL	16 Sep 89 Sat	CI	1		$44.21	Fuel+tolls	$16.48	
173	CI-WISC.	RICHLAND C., WI	17 Sep 89 Sun	CI	2	$37.20	$27.43			
174	CI-WISC.	en route home	18 Sep 89 Mon	CI	3	$3.99			$1.20	
175			19 Sep 89 Tue	CI	4					
176	*TOTAL cash expenses, CI–Wisconsin, in U.S. $:*					$41.19	$71.64		$17.68	
177	*U.S. $ Subtotals for this year to date:*					$3,064.91	$1,072.84		$1,516.81	
178		*Column Subtotal*								

which regions sales were poor so that additional steps could be taken to improve sales. Other sales analysis reports give the total sales for each salesperson, the total for each customer, and the total for each item.

If you are a business manager, you may use a computer in some of the ways described here. If you are using a computer for database or spreadsheet work, you will probably key input data and receive output directly from the computer. If you are using a sales analysis system, you may not be pressing keys or entering information into the computer. Nevertheless, you are still using the computer because it provides you with information to help increase the sales of the business.

Figure 1–13 A Sales Analysis Report

```
                    XYZ CORPORATION
                    SALES BY REGION
                     JUNE, 19XX

           REGION                 SALES

             A                $1,152,385
             B                $1,890,021
             C                  $352,898
             D                $3,745,200
             E                $2,018,316
             F                $1,476,553

           TOTAL    $10,635,373*
```

A DAY IN YOUR LIFE WITHOUT COMPUTERS

What would happen if every computer suddenly stopped working? What effect would it have on people and companies, and how would the world fare? Here is a fanciful account of a day in the life of a New York reporter, a day that never happened, a 24-hour worldwide computer stoppage.

In the morning, I stopped off at the Abraham & Straus near my apartment in Brooklyn to speak with the vice president of operations for the big New York department store chain. I was running late because my alarm clock hadn't gone off—in fact, it wasn't working at all.

The selling floor of A & S was bustling with customers as usual, but the lines at the cash registers seemed unusually long. I was surprised to see the salespeople writing out receipts by hand. On each register was a hastily drawn sign: "Cash sales only today." The elevators were out of order, and I had to take the stairs to the administrative offices.

The vice president took a moment out from his frenzied organizing to explain that all his computers had gone out—and in every one of his 16 stores. I asked why he didn't seem upset by this calamity. He said

that what he'd seen so far this morning had borne out a theory of his about computers. "People allow the machine to communicate for them. This [loss] has opened up a lot of person-to-person communication . . ."

I thanked him for his time and observations and left, annoyed at my tape recorder and camera for not working during the interview.

Outside, I headed for the subway to lower Manhattan, where I was scheduled to meet with the director of the computing unit for the mayor's office. At the subway entrance, a line spilled out onto the sidewalk. Someone muttered something about signal trouble, so I figured I'd hoof it. I tried to call ahead, to say I'd be late, but the public phone didn't work. Nor did the one next to it. In fact, no phones were working.

Not being a morning person, I hadn't yet seen the connection between these inconveniences. So, along with what must have been hundreds of other people, I walked toward the Brooklyn Bridge. It seemed that the only cars on the road were big-finned monsters. Crossing the East River, I saw a tanker collide with a pier.

The bizarre occurrences of the day began to pique my curiosity, but none of my fellow travelers had a newspaper; those with Walkmans said they couldn't pick up any radio stations. With a mind influenced by too many science fiction stories, I suddenly conjured up a vision of a world without computers, a world where communications and transportation were thrown back decades, and where, for the day at least, they were stymied almost completely.

The scene around City Hall was chaotic—but it had always seemed that way, so it didn't faze me. I found the director in her office, giving instructions to a messenger. She told me what I already had guessed; the computers were down and the phones were dead. "I'm lining up typewriters," she explained. She was sending messengers to office equipment rental agencies, "trying to corner the market before anyone else does."

I wondered how the Mayor would react to the developing news media blackout as I made my way to Greenwich Village for my next interview. I was due at New York University to meet with a senior research scientist. I found the professor with his feet on his desk and a smile on his face. "Quite frankly," he said, "a 24-hour loss of computer access is not a disaster." He'd figured out what was going on and sent his students to the library. "It'll do them a lot of good. It'll improve their scholarship," he said.

Taking his feet off his desk, the professor said he planned to go to the library himself to do fundamental research. Then he remembered that without the computer-based library catalog system, he'd have to use the card catalogs. But these were no longer updated and hence were incomplete, so he would be forced to search the shelves.

And anyway, he said, a proposal was pending. "The normal way we do them is on computer," he explained. "And the fact of life is you do them right up to the last minute." Now, he said, it was "back to kindergarten."

"Then we have to find a way to get it to Washington." Someone told him the airlines weren't running and the trains were going 10 miles per hour. "This is going to be a disaster," he admitted.

I left him looking for carbon paper and started uptown for my next appointment,

with a senior information executive at Citicorp. Later, I found out from a Boeing Co. spokesman that almost all commercial airplanes can fly without computers (as evidenced by the day's incredibly few crashes), but that no airport would dispatch one that wasn't already off the ground. Tracking systems, of course, were out. Railroads were running, but at a much slower rate, as switching went manual and communications were impaired.

All this walking had made me hungry. With only a subway token and some change on me, I stopped at a cash machine and put my card in the slot. Of course, nothing. I would have laughed if it hadn't been so annoying.

I was still 30 blocks from the Citicorp building on East 53rd Street, but the walk was not boring. I narrowly missed being squashed by a satellite that had fallen when it ceased receiving telemetry to adjust its orbit.

I trudged up about 30 flights of stairs. Inside, the offices were hot and stuffy—the heating, ventilation, and air conditioning system was on the fritz. The executive greeted me with a wry smile. I asked him how his day was going.

"We have contingency plans with very strict standards," he said. "We opened up the branches—did a manual fallback. People will go see real-life human beings. Manual banking services will go on. We're just stacking up the transactions." But, he points out, "We have a lot of middle managers with nothing to do."

Electronic funds transfer would be done by airborne courier, he said—if he could find the planes.

Citicorp's investment banking arm, which relies on the telephone, was stymied. The institutional banking was likewise at a loss. "I'm sure the bicycle and sneaker business has increased," said the executive.

He glanced at his watch, which I enviously observed was an old-fashioned analog model—my nifty new Japanese timepiece was frozen. "By now," he said, "I imagine a trader would be drumming his fingers wondering how he's supposed to place an order.

The traders are probably trading among themselves or playing cards."

Suddenly, a man with a whistle around his neck and anxiety in his eyes stuck his head through the doorway to deliver a warning. It seemed that an intricate balancing system to keep the building from swaying was controlled by computer and, to prevent occupants from getting motion sickness, we had to evacuate the premises.

It was getting late, and I was grateful that it appeared there would be no blackout. A Con Edison spokeswoman later explained to me that although the utility did have four computers for switching, routing, and monitoring, it "all could be done manually."

As I walked along, I began to notice crowds gathering around cigar shops and stationery stores. I asked someone what was going on and he told me it was Super Wednesday, the last day on which entries could be submitted for the state's record $50 million lottery jackpot. Lotto's computer was down, and as the realization rippled through the crowd that they would not get a crack at the money, they turned ugly. My father always taught me to run away from mob scenes, and over my shoulder I saw magazines flying, windows shattered, and a computer terminal smashed. It was the first of the now-famous Lotto riots.

That night, my fiancée told me that things at the hospital where she works were bewildering. Patient monitoring systems, operating-room surgical equipment tracking systems, nurse station and patient admissions systems—all blinked out. We tried to calculate how many people the computer stoppage had affected (most in the developed nations, a minority in the third world, we figured). We realized gratefully that for as long as the computers were out, missile guidance systems would not work and there was no threat of nuclear annihilation. We also realized that without sophisticated military defense systems, there was an outside risk of conventional war.

We looked forward to an evening of reading and perhaps some Scrabble, but we did not look forward to missing *The Honeymooners* on TV or remaining ignorant about the next day's weather.

What kept coming back to me as I thought about the day was a common thread of almost perverse pleasure expressed by the computing professionals I had talked to. It had less to do with resentment of their work than with their expert understanding of the limitations of their technology. All thought that the world depended on computers but had also needed a day without them to engender an appreciation of this powerful technology and a better understanding of its benefits and its hazards.

Figure 1–14 Using Computer-Aided Design (CAD)

Computers in Design

Many people do work in which they prepare drawings, diagrams, pictures, or other graphic images. Some people, such as architects and engineers, use graphics to design something (such as a building or automobile) to be built by others. Other people—such as graphic designers, advertising layout persons, and television station personnel—design graphic images that convey information (such as in an advertisement) to others. Today, computers are used extensively to assist these people in their design work. Usually, the computers that are used are powerful personal computers that can show designs on large, colored screens.

Architects, drafts persons, and engineers often use computers for **computer-aided design** or **CAD** (Figure 1–14). The person using a CAD system can draw diagrams on the computer screen, easily alter the diagrams, try different designs, and plot the final design on paper. Some CAD systems provide for three-dimensional diagrams that can be rotated and viewed from different angles.

Graphic designers often use computers to design product packaging, company symbols, book covers, and so forth (Figure 1–15). People who work in advertising use computers to lay out ad pieces for magazines and newspapers. Television station employees use computers to prepare on-screen graphics for news broadcasts, weather forecasts, and program promotions. Film production personnel use computers to prepare graphic images for films.

If your job involves design work, you may use a computer. When you do, you enter input that describes the diagram, picture, or layout you want. The computer processes your input to produce graphic output. You are using a computer to help in your design work.

Figure 1–15   Using a Computer in Graphic Design

COMPUTER USERS

The examples in this chapter have described people who use computers. These people are not technically trained computer professionals such as computer programmers and operators. Rather, they are nontechnically oriented people who gain some benefit from using computers in their personal or work lives. These people are called computer **users**.

A computer user performs a task in his or her personal or work life with the aid of a computer. For example, a person using an ATM is a computer user because he or she performs various banking transactions by using a computer. Similarly, a person using a computer for word processing is a computer user because he or she prepares a letter or report with the help of a computer. All the examples have included computer users.

Computer professionals also use computers. For example, computer programmers and operators use computers in their technical jobs. We don't think of these people, however, as users as the term has been used here. In this book, a user will always be a person who uses a computer for some noncomputer-related activity. Sometimes this type of user is called an **end-user** to distinguish him or her from computer professionals.

Some computer users are more familiar with the computers and programs they use than are other users. These users may customize the programs for their particular needs and develop sophisticated uses of the computers. These types of users are sometimes called **power users** because they fully utilize the most powerful features of the computer and its programs.

How Do People Use Computers?

A computer user uses a computer by entering input into the computer and receiving output. Many users use a computer *directly* by pressing keys or by operating a piece of equipment that sends input to the computer. The computer receives the input and does the required processing. After the computer has completed its processing, it sends output back to the user, often displaying it on a screen or printing it on paper. People who use ATMs, school computers, home computers, POS systems, office computers, and computers for graphics work are all direct computer users.

A computer user may also use a computer *indirectly*. In this case, the user may have someone else enter the input and receive the output, which is then given to the user. The sales manager who receives periodic sales analysis reports is an indirect computer user.

One person may use a computer directly, and another may use the same computer indirectly. For example, the sales analysis system could be used directly by some managers and indirectly by others. Sometimes many users use a computer at the same time. A multiple-user computer connected to ATMs is used by many people doing their banking. Often, however, only one user uses the computer. A personal computer used for word processing is used by only one person at a time.

Why Do People Use Computers?

People use computers for three main reasons. The first is *speed*. Computers are very fast at what they do. As a consequence, a user can get the results he or she needs from a computer quickly. For example, if a person uses an ATM for banking transactions, he or she can withdraw, deposit, or transfer money more quickly than with a human teller.

The second reason people use computers is *accuracy*. Computers do not make mistakes like people do. For example, a POS system is much more accurate than a human salesperson in recording the prices of items purchased by a customer. Sometimes you hear about computer errors, but usually these are the results of mistakes made by humans, not by computers.

The third reason people use computers is *capacity*. Computers can easily handle a large amount of data. For example, to do sales analysis, the computer may need to examine data about thousands of sales in order to calculate the required totals. A computer can do this process more easily than a human.

COMPUTER CLOSE-UP

1-2

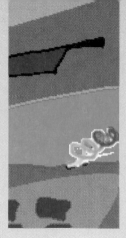

NO ESCAPE FROM COMPUTERS

I have begun to feel like I am permanently attached to my computers—physically and perhaps even emotionally. I'm beginning to wonder if I can function without them as part of my daily life.

My electronic mail, magazine articles, tax returns, telephone numbers and most of my nonpersonal relationships with the outside word exist—nay, live—inside my computers.

There are two main computers in my office—an IBM Personal Computer and an Apple Macintosh. Both are hooked into larger systems so I can retrieve information from more than one place at a time. Of course my own brain cannot handle this data once it is received, but I sleep better at night knowing that such a capability exists at my fingertips.

In addition, my laptop computer usually sits between these two machines, waiting either for my next business trip or for some moment when I can't access my PCs.

I have memory for storing 160 million characters of information on these machines. This is more than most humans need and perhaps more than most deserve. Yet I don't always feel as though it's enough. Call it storage greed; call it memory gluttony. If these were biblical times, you'd probably call it a sin. Nonetheless, when I feel as if I'm running low on memory, I go visit my fiancee.

She can store 40 million characters on her own system.

Such computer addiction does not stop at my office. It extends into my house, right into my yard. Last week, my landscaper came over for a consultation. This didn't involve blueprints or huge sheets of paper extensively marked up with pencil. Instead, the landscaper popped a program into my Macintosh, which gave me a three-dimensional layout of my yard and house, and a view of how new shrubs would look once installed. I just sat there watching, somewhat in awe, although I could see myself on the screen—a little wire-frame stickman positioned inside a little 3-D house on a computer screen. Franz Kafka probably would have had something to say about this turn of events.

This fever even extends to my friends and family. My father just sent me a copy of his most current project—tracing our family lineage. As I opened the bound book I fully expected to see line after line of carefully calligraphic names traced lovingly to faded sepia pictures pasted on yellowing pages. Instead, there were crisp Helvetica fonts (in bold and italic) wrapping around photographs that had been scanned into a program specifically designed for building family trees. Dad will be publishing regular editions as new additions come into our family. This used to take years of labor before computers.

I even attempted a safari in Africa last year to get some respite from computer overload. Turns out the guide was an ex–IBM programmer who decided to do research on native African birds and was recording his findings in a portable PC that he powered off the generator of his Land Rover. He does this more than 1,000 miles from the nearest IBM product center.

To get a little further away from all of this computer omnipresence, I relax by playing and recording music. Sitting down to the synthesizer keyboard, I hook my keyboard's computer interface into one of my PCs, and every single keystroke, each lush arpeggio and trill, is recorded onto sequencing software that will play it all back on command, exactly like a player piano. Only now you don't have those big rolls of floppy paper on a spindle; you have a compressed piece of magnetized plastic on a floppy disk.

When I mentioned that I feared becoming emotionally attached to my computer, I'm not sure I was joking. When it recently contracted a virus (a program that damages other programs and data), I stayed up for two straight days feeding the PC vaccines (programs that find and eradicate viruses). I treated it as tenderly as one would treat a sick relative. Sure, sick relatives don't hold all your business records for the past five years as well as your comprehensive financial statements, contact lists and the latest version of Beyond Castle Dracula, but that's beside the point. I would care for them even if they could do all that for me.

I recently addressed a group of financial managers in London. No simple automated teller machines for these business people. An informal poll of the 200 members of the audience showed that more than half were already investing in intelligent technologies such as expert systems or knowledge bases for their companies.

I personally have not seen a single human being regarding my bank account in almost two years. Sometimes I wonder if anyone still works there.

Now I am writing this at close to 40,000 feet over the Atlantic Ocean. My computer is on my lap, and I am flying over Iceland. In my attempt to find an escape from computing for just a moment, I envision the icy expanse below without any computers. I am enjoying the reverie until I realize that the last expedition up Mount Everest managed to take a portable PC with them up that mountain's snowy heights. Somewhere below, I now admit to myself, there is an ice castle—on-line.

COMPUTER APPLICATIONS

You have seen several familiar uses of computers in this chapter. Each use is a **computer application**. For example, using a computer through an ATM to help with banking transactions is a banking application. Using a computer to prepare letters and documents is a word processing application. Using a computer to look up information is a database application. Using a computer to help identify poor sales is a sales analysis application.

There are many computer applications besides those described so far. Here are a few unusual applications that you may not have thought of:

- A ski resort in New England uses personal computers to monitor snowmaking.
- A beauty salon in California uses a computer to show clients how they will look with different hairstyles and colors.
- A mountain-climbing expedition to Mount Everest used a portable computer to keep track of expedition supplies.
- An ecologist in an airplane uses a portable computer to record data about sea turtles in the Gulf of Mexico.
- An adoption agency uses a personal computer to keep track of clients and to speed up the adoption process.

As you can see, there are many different ways computers are used. Throughout this book you will see numerous examples of computer applications.

USING COMPUTERS EFFECTIVELY

It should be clear from this chapter that many types of people are computer users and that there are many computer applications. Most likely you are a computer user in your personal life and, if you have a job, in your work life. Although there are interesting applications of computers in our personal lives, this book will concentrate on those in our work lives. These applications are the ones for which organizations and businesses use computers and that you may encounter in your job.

You can use a computer in your job with little understanding of computers, but to be an *effective* user, you need to understand some basic concepts about computers and computer applications. An effective user is one who is able to make the best use of computers and make informed decisions about when and how to use them. The purpose of this book is to give you the understanding necessary to be an effective computer user.

Chapter Summary

- A **computer** is an electronic device that stores **data** and **programs**, and processes data by following the instructions in a program. **Input data** is entered into the computer where it is stored and processed to produce **output data**, which comes out of the computer.

- People use computers in many ways in their personal lives and in their work lives. Some examples of computer use in our personal lives include performing banking transactions with an **automated teller machine**, studying a new subject with a computer in school, and playing a game with a home computer.

- Our use of computers in our work lives depends on the type of work we do. A salesperson could use a **point-of-sale system** to record sales to customers, a secretary might use a computer for **word processing** to prepare a letter, a business manager could use a computer to look up information about recent sales in a **database**, and an engineer might use **computer-aided design** to help design an automobile.

- A computer **user** (sometimes called an **end-user**) performs tasks with the aid of a computer. Users enter input into the computer and receive output from the computer. Some users use computers directly by pressing keys or operating pieces of equipment that send input to the computer. Other users use computers indirectly; they receive output from computers without operating any equipment. People use computers for their speed, their accuracy, and their capacity to handle large amounts of data.

- A **computer application** is a way to use a computer. The users of an application are the nontechnically oriented people who gain some benefit from using computers.

Terms to Remember

Review Questions

Fill-In Questions

1. Data that goes into a computer is called _____; the result of processing that comes out of a computer is called _____.

2. A small computer that is used by one person at a time is called a(n) _____.

3. A device used for performing banking transactions without the aid of a human teller is a(n) _____.

4. Using a computer to prepare letters, reports, and other written documents is called _____.

5. A computerized system for recording sales to customers as they pay for their merchandise is a(n) _____.

6. A business manager might look up information about customers in a(n) _____.

7. A nontechnically oriented person who gains some benefit from using a computer in his or her personal or work life is a(n) _____.

8. A use of a computer is called a(n) _____.

Short-Answer Questions

1. What is a computer?
2. What are some uses of computers in schools?
3. What are some uses of computers in homes?
4. What are some uses of computers in offices?
5. What are some uses of computers in design work?
6. What is the difference between using a computer directly and using one indirectly?
7. Give three reasons why people use computers.
8. What does it mean to be an effective computer user?

Projects

1. Find several other computer applications not mentioned in the chapter. Write a brief description of each application, list the users of the application, and describe what the users do.

2. Pick an industry or field in which you are interested or are working (for example, the airline industry or the health care field), and find as many computer applications as you can. Make a list of the applications and give a one-sentence description of each.

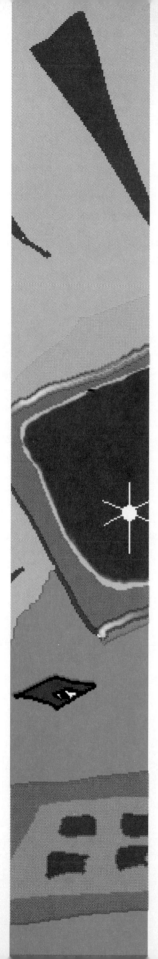

2

COMPUTER SYSTEM BASICS

CHAPTER OBJECTIVES

- After completing this chapter you should be able to:

1. Describe and give examples of the main components of a computer.

2. Explain how the components of a computer communicate.

3. Identify the four general types of computers.

4. Briefly explain how a computer executes a program.

5. Distinguish between application software and system software and identify two sources of programs.

CHAPTER ONE introduced basic concepts about computers and programs. But what exactly makes up a computer? And how does a program function? You need to know the answers to these questions before you can understand how to use computers. This chapter contains a brief overview of computer systems, concentrating on the essentials you will need to know throughout this book. Later chapters will cover many of these topics in greater depth.

COMPUTERS

A computer consists of several interconnected devices or components, as shown in Figure 2–1. In this diagram, symbols represent the components of the computer, and arrows show the paths taken within the computer by data and program instructions. There are five basic components: the input device, the output device, primary storage, the central processing unit or CPU, and secondary storage.

The physical equipment that makes up a computer is called **hardware**. All the components diagramed in Figure 2–1 are computer hardware.

Input and Output Devices

An **input device** accepts data from outside the computer and converts it into an electronic form that the computer understands. The data that is accepted is the input data. For example, if a computer is going to

Figure 2–1 The Organization of a Computer

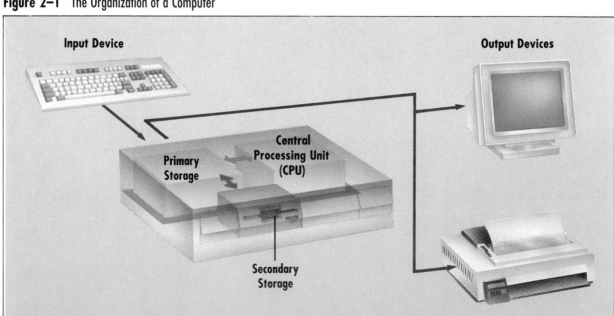

compute the pay for each employee in a business, the input data would include the employees' names, pay rates, and hours worked. An input device would accept this data from the user and transfer it into the computer.

An example of a common input device is a **keyboard**, which is similar to the one found on a typewriter (Figure 2–2a). Each time the user presses a key on the keyboard, the electronic form of the symbol on the key is sent into the computer. The user enters input data by pressing the keys that correspond to the data.

An **output device** performs the opposite function of an input device. It converts data from an electronic form inside the computer to a form that can be used outside the computer. This converted data is the output data. For example, the output from a payroll computation would include employees' names and pay. An output device would produce this data in a form usable outside the computer.

One common output device is a **screen** on which the output is displayed as video images (Figure 2–2b). Another common output device is a **printer** (Figure 2–2c). This device converts data from the computer into printed symbols to produce a paper copy of the output. This type of output is often called computer *printout*.

An input device may be combined with an output device to form a device called a **terminal**. A common type of terminal consists of a keyboard and a screen (Figure 2–3). Terminals are commonly used as input and output devices with multiple-user computers.

Most computers have several input and output, or *I/O,* devices attached at one time. For example, a multiple-user computer may have

Figure 2–2   Input and Output Devices

Figure 2–3   A Terminal

(a)   A Keyboard

(b)   A Screen

(c)   A Printer

Figure 2–4   Part of a Computer with Central Processing Unit and Primary Storage

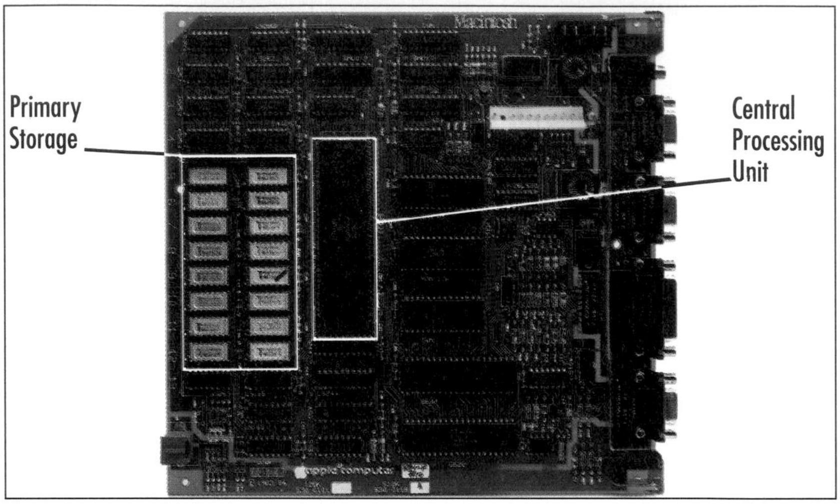

many terminals plus several printers. Most personal computers, how-ever, have only one input device (a keyboard) and one or two output devices (a screen and a printer).

The Central Processing Unit and Primary Storage

Between the input and output devices are two components of the com-puter that work together to do the actual computing or processing. These are the central processing unit and primary storage (Figure 2–4). The **primary storage**, also called **internal storage**, is the "memory" of the computer. An input device converts input data into an electronic form and sends the data to the primary storage, where the data is stored. The data is then used in calculations and for other types of pro-cessing. For example, data used in payroll computations, such as em-ployees' pay rates and hours worked, would be stored in the primary storage and used to calculate each employee's pay. After the processing is completed, the results are sent from primary storage to an output device, where the data is converted into the final output. The primary storage also stores instructions in the program currently being per-formed. For example, in a payroll computation, the instructions neces-sary to calculate an employee's pay would be stored in the computer's primary storage.

The **central processing unit** or **CPU**, which is also just called the **processor**, carries out the instructions in the program.[1] Among other things, the CPU contains electronic circuits that do arithmetic and per-form logical operations. The computer brings data from primary stor-age to the CPU, where it is processed by these circuits, and the results

[1] Some people consider primary storage to be part of the central processing unit rather than a separate unit. Other people use the terms as they are used in the text.

are sent back to primary storage. A computer can do the basic arithmetic tasks that a human can do; that is, a computer can add, subtract, multiply, and divide. The logical operations that a computer can do are usually limited to comparing two values to determine whether they are equal or whether one is greater than or less than the other. Complex processing is accomplished by long sequences of these basic operations. In a payroll computation, fairly simple arithmetic and logical operations are needed. For example, an employee's pay is computed by multiplying the hours worked by the pay rate. Logical operations are needed to determine how much income tax should be paid by each employee.

The CPU also contains electronic circuits that control the other parts of the computer. These circuits perform their functions by following the instructions in the program. The program is stored in the computer's primary storage. During processing, each instruction in the program is brought from primary storage to the CPU. The CPU analyzes the instruction and sends signals to the other units based on what the instruction tells the computer to do. Performing one instruction may involve actions in any of the other parts of the computer. After one instruction in the programmed sequence is performed, the next is brought from primary storage to the CPU and performed. These steps are repeated until all the instructions in the program have been carried out.

Secondary Storage

The final component of a computer is **secondary storage**, also called **auxiliary storage**, which stores data not currently being processed by the computer and programs not currently being performed. Its function differs from that of primary storage, which stores the data and instructions that are currently being processed by the computer. For example, if the computer is currently doing payroll processing, then the employee data and the payroll computation program would be stored in the computer's primary storage. Other data and programs that are not currently being used, such as would be needed for sales analysis, would be stored in secondary storage. Primary storage is *temporary storage*, and anything stored in it is lost when the power to the computer is turned off. Secondary storage, however, is *permanent storage*; anything stored in secondary storage remains there until it is changed even if the power is turned off.

Data and programs are stored in secondary storage as **files**. A file is any collection of related items stored together in secondary storage. There are several types of files. A **data file** is a collection of related data, such as data about employees in a business. A **program file** is a collection of instructions that make up a program. Other types of files include *text files*, used in word processing, and *worksheet files*, used in spreadsheet applications. All types of files, however, are stored in secondary storage until they are needed. Then program instructions or data from the required files are transferred to primary storage for processing.

A common type of secondary storage is a **magnetic disk**, or simply **disk**, which resembles a phonograph record (Figure 2–5a). Disks come in different sizes—some as small as 3 ½ inches in diameter and others

Figure 2–5
Magnetic Disk Storage

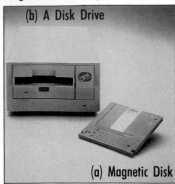

(b) A Disk Drive

(a) Magnetic Disk

Figure 2–6 Magnetic Disk Storage

(a) Magnetic Tape

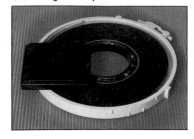

(b) Tape Drives

as large as 14 inches across. Some disks are made of plastic with a metallic coating; others are made of metal. No matter what type of disk is used, data is recorded on the surface of the disk by patterns of magnetism. A **disk drive** is a device for recording data on magnetic disks and for retrieving data from the disks (Figure 2–5b).

Another type of secondary storage is **magnetic tape**, or simply **tape**, which is much like audio recording tape (Figure 2–6a). Magnetic tape comes in reels of different sizes and in cartridge form. Data is recorded on the surface of the tape by patterns of magnetism. A **tape drive** is a device that records data on magnetic tape and retrieves data from the tape (Figure 2–6b).

Most computers have several secondary storage devices attached to them at one time. For example, a computer may have four disk drives and two tape drives. Other types of secondary storage also can be used, but disk and tape are the most common.

Secondary storage and input and output devices are often called **peripheral equipment** because they are located outside the central part of the computer, that is, the CPU and primary storage. In fact, the word *computer* is sometimes used just for the CPU and primary storage, and *computer system* is used for the computer with its peripheral equipment.

Hardware Communication

Figure 2–7
Cables Connecting Hardware

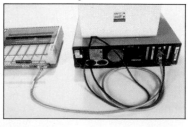

The components of a computer system communicate with each other by sending electronic signals over wire cables that connect the hardware (Figure 2–7). For example, a computer communicates with a printer over a cable that plugs into sockets in the computer and the printer. A keyboard sends signals over a cable that leads from the keyboard to the computer. The computer communicates with the screen over a similar cable. Disk and tape drives also communicate over cables.

Figure 2–8 A Network

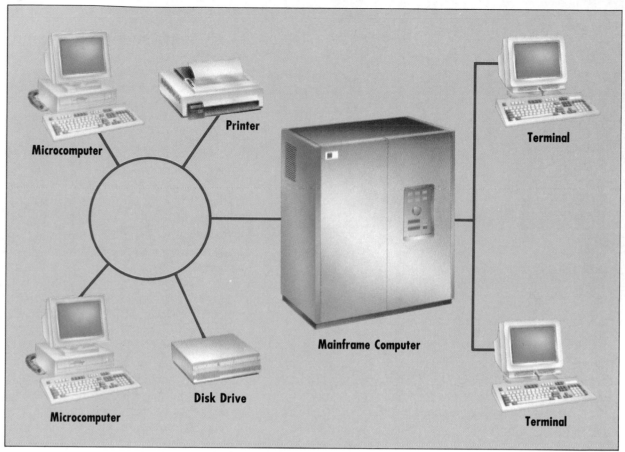

Connecting hardware with cables is simple when the components are located next to each other, such as with a personal computer. Sometimes, however, hardware needs to be connected over considerable distances. For example, a user at a terminal at one location may need to communicate with a multiple-user computer at another location. Such distant communication requires techniques that fall into an area called *data communications*. If the distance is not too great, such as within an office building, it may be possible to connect the terminal directly to the computer with a special cable. When the distance is beyond a certain limit (such as 1000 feet), direct connection is not possible. A common method of long-distance communication involves the use of telephone lines. The terminal and the computer communicate by sending signals back and forth over the lines.

Sometimes it is desirable for several computers, terminals, and other hardware devices to be connected with each other. A configuration of devices connected so they can communicate is called a **network** (Figure 2–8). The network may be constructed from cables that directly connect nearby hardware, or telephone lines may be used to connect hardware over long distances.

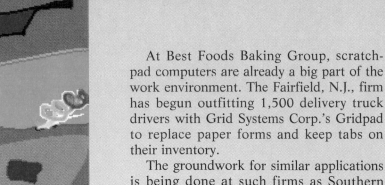

USERS WRITE RIGHT ON CUE

Is the pen mightier than the keyboard? Many hardware developers, software programmers and venture capitalists certainly think so.

Spurred by a series of recent technological leaps, the arrival of notepad-size computers that allow users to enter data by writing rather than tapping keys has many conjecturing that the "scratch-pad" or "pen-based" computer could have an impact on the industry unlike anything since the advent of Apple Computer, Inc.'s Macintosh.

Two scientific achievements in particular have been instrumental in shoving scratch-pad computers into the marketplace: low-cost, powerful microprocessors and screens with electromagnetic sensors able to detect the motion of a metal stylus.

The key breakthrough, however, is that programmers have developed the software necessary to translate printed letters into data that a computer can understand.

Most of these packages work in one of two ways. Some applications act as a huge database where the written image is compared to a library of stored letters and words. The computer then makes the closest match and digitizes the information. In other cases, the software is customized and later adapts to the writer's penmanship.

At Best Foods Baking Group, scratch-pad computers are already a big part of the work environment. The Fairfield, N.J., firm has begun outfitting 1,500 delivery truck drivers with Grid Systems Corp.'s Gridpad to replace paper forms and keep tabs on their inventory.

The groundwork for similar applications is being done at such firms as Southern Pacific Transportation Co., Gillette Co. and Marion Merrill Dow, Inc.

Although scratch-pad computers are relatively new, most computer industry analysts feel they represent a huge growth area because the technology could make a computer approachable to someone who does not ordinarily type or who is put off by computer technology. A scratch-pad computer could slip easily into the routine of workers ranging from delivery truck drivers keeping tabs on inventory to police officers visiting the scene of an auto accident or lawyers updating their files without disturbing the quiet of the courtroom.

Ultimately, the scratch-pad computer is expected to perform all the functions of laptops with keyboards, including organizing columns of numbers, scanning large databases and communicating with computers of every size.

Although expectations are high, there are still concerns. Because the technology is still developing, "one of the biggest problems is overblown expectations about what the machines can do," said E. Gray Glass III, an analyst at research firm Prudential-Bache Securities, Inc.

One problem is that writing on a pen-based computer is unlike the handwriting most people do every day. With most people, letters and numbers are seldom written the same way each time, and some people's handwriting is simply illegible.

With a pen-based computer, letters must be carefully crafted, often in capital letters, one at a time and with adequate spacing because computers cannot pick up the nuances and inconsistencies of the average person's penmanship. Computers that recognize cursive script are years away.

Developers said the market is in a crucial period where it must go beyond simple writing recognition.

"If these machines are more hostile than pen and paper and do nothing more, people will be unaccepting," said Vern Raburn, chairman of Slate Corp. "Ultimately, when people use a computer, all they want to know is, will I get out at 5 or do I have to stay until 5:30?"

In general, any device in a network can communicate with any other device in the same network. One computer can send data to another computer. Several computers can retrieve data from the same disk drive, or print output with the same printer. A terminal can use any computer connected to the network. Networks are very versatile.

Types of Computers

All computers have the basic hardware components diagramed earlier in Figure 2–1. Still, computers vary considerably in storage capacity, speed, and cost. Some of the ways computers differ are in:

- The number of I/O devices and the speed at which each device can transfer data to and from primary storage.
- The number of secondary storage devices, the storage capacity of each device, and the speed at which each device can transfer data to and from primary storage.
- The storage capacity of primary storage and the speed at which it can transfer data to and from the CPU.

- The speed at which the CPU can perform its operations.

All these factors affect the cost of the computer. In general, the more devices, the greater the storage capacity, and the faster the speed, the more the computer will cost.

Computers are often classified into four general types based on their storage capacity, speed, and cost. These types are microcomputers, minicomputers, mainframe computers, and supercomputers. The classifications are somewhat arbitrary. For example, one computer may be called a microcomputer while an equivalent computer may be called a minicomputer.

Microcomputers.   A **microcomputer** is a small computer usually costing less than $10,000 (Figure 2–9). A typical microcomputer has a keyboard for input, a screen and a printer for output, and one or two disk drives for secondary storage. The components of most microcomputers are usually low in storage capacity and slow in speed compared to other types of computers. Most microcomputers can process only one program and can be used by only one person at a time. Therefore, they are personal computers. In fact, the term *personal computer* is used to mean a microcomputer. Individuals and all types of organizations and businesses use microcomputers. One common use of microcomputers is for word processing (see Chapter 1).

The most widely known microcomputers are made by International Business Machines (IBM) Corporation and Apple Computer, Inc. IBM's first microcomputer was the IBM Personal Computer or PC. The company developed various models of the PC over the years, including the XT and AT, which are no longer available. The current IBM microcomputers

Figure 2–9 Microcomputers

(a) An IBM PS/2

(b) An Apple Macintosh

are the IBM Personal System/2 or PS/2, which comes in several models (Figure 2–9a), and the more recent Personal System/1 or PS/1.

Apple's original microcomputer was the Apple II. It came in several models and is still available. The most recent Apple microcomputer is the Macintosh, which comes in several models (Figure 2–9b). People often refer to the Macintosh by the nickname "Mac."

Many other companies besides IBM and Apple make microcomputers. Numerous companies make computers that act just like IBM computers; people call these computers IBM *compatibles* or *clones*. Some companies that make IBM clones are Compaq Computer Corporation, AST Research, and Dell Computer Corporation, but there are many more such companies. Some companies make computers that are different from those made by IBM and Apple. Two well-known companies of this type are Atari Corporation and Commodore International. Another company that makes some IBM clones and some different types of computers is Tandy Corporation, which sells its computers through Radio Shack stores.

Most microcomputers are designed to sit on a desk and not be moved. These are called **desktop computers**. Small microcomputers, designed to be easily carried, are also available. These are called **laptop computers**. Even smaller microcomputers fold up to the size of a notebook and fit in a briefcase. Not surprisingly, these are called **notebook computers** (Figure 2–10). The smallest microcomputers are called **pocket computers** or, sometimes, *palmtop* or *hand-held computers* (Figure 2–11). They weigh less than one pound and fold up to fit in a coat pocket.

Very powerful desktop microcomputers are commonly called **workstations**. Workstations have capabilities beyond those of ordinary microcomputers, especially in their ability to produce graphic diagrams and pictures on the screen. An example is the NeXT Computer, made by NeXT, Inc. (Figure 2–12).

Figure 2–10
A Notebook Computer: This is a NEC
Ultralite

Figure 2–11   A Pocket Computer: This is a Hewlett Packard 95LX

Minicomputers.   Medium-sized computers are commonly called **mini-computers** and cost between $7500 and $200,000 (Figure 2–13). These computers usually have several terminals for input and output, a printer for output, one or more disk drives, and sometimes a tape drive for secondary storage. Minicomputer components are greater in storage capacity and faster in speed than those of microcomputers. Most minicomputers can process several programs at a time and can be used by several people simultaneously. Therefore, they are multiple-user computers. Small to medium-sized organizations and businesses use mini-

Figure 2–12   A Workstation: This is a NeXT Computer

Figure 2–13   A Minicomputer: This is a Digital VAX

computers for their data processing needs. Larger businesses use them for special applications, such as for controlling computerized checkout stands in a supermarket (see Chapter 1).

The most well-known minicomputers are made by Digital Equipment Corporation (DEC). DEC makes the VAX line of computers (Figure 2–13). There are many models in the VAX line; the smallest are really microcomputers, and the largest are mainframe computers (a description follows shortly). The majority, however, fall into the minicomputer range. Other companies that make minicomputers include Hewlett-Packard Company, Data General Corporation, and IBM.

Mainframe Computers.   Large computers are called **mainframe computers** and cost between $100,000 and $10 million (Figure 2–14). Usually, a mainframe computer has many terminals, several printers, and several disk and tape drives. The components of a mainframe computer have greater storage capacity and are faster than those of minicomputers. A mainframe computer can process numerous programs concurrently and can be used by many people at one time. Thus, they are multiple-user computers. Mainframe computers are the principal computers used by medium- and large-sized organizations and businesses for their data processing needs. For example, the computer used by a bank to process data from automated teller machines probably would be a mainframe computer (see Chapter 1).

IBM makes the most widely known mainframe computers. The company has a range of models that have evolved from a line of computers developed in the 1960s. Current models include the 3090 series (Figure 2–14). Some companies make mainframe computers that act the same

Figure 2–14 A Mainframe Computer: This is an IBM 3090

Figure 2–15 A Supercomputer: This is a Cray Y-MP

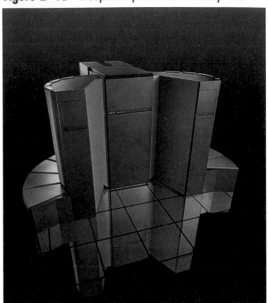

as IBM's. One such company is Amdahl Corporation. Other companies that make mainframe computers different from IBM's include NCR Corporation and Unisys Corporation.

Supercomputers.   The most powerful computers are called **supercomputers** and cost between $5 million and $20 million (Figure 2–15). These computers are designed for very fast processing speeds. They may not have as many terminals or as much secondary storage as mainframe computers, but their CPUs can operate much faster. Because they are so fast, supercomputers are mainly used for complex mathematical calculations, such as those needed in scientific research.

Cray Research, Inc., developed the first supercomputers that were commercially successful. One of this company's current models is the Cray Y-MP (Figure 2–15). Only a few other companies make supercomputers.

PROGRAMS

A computer program is a set of instructions that tells the computer what to do. A computer can do nothing without a program. For example, to calculate the payroll for a business, the computer must have a program that tells it how to do the calculations. Even to do word processing, a computer needs a program to tell it what to do. Every step that the computer goes through must be outlined in an instruction in a computer program. The computer will do whatever it is told, even if this leads to an incorrect result.

SOME USES OF SUPERCOMPUTERS

Some Modeling Taxes Even Supercomputers

Meteorology is an example of an area so complex that it's dependent on supercomputing.

The global climate is a closed system, so in theory, if we put all of the data about worldwide weather into a computer, we should be able to perfectly predict weather. But the problem is putting everything into the computer.

The weather is so complicated that meteorologists split the world up into two pieces: the oceans and the atmosphere.

Dr. Arthur Miller, an oceanographer at the Scripps Institute, attempts to predict the effect of greenhouse gases on ocean temperature. A simple model of this process breaks up the world into squares, each 250 kilometers square. Each square in the grid has 10 levels, modeling the ocean's depth.

In order to run the model for one year of world climate, for example, Miller needs 24 hours of CPU time on a Cray supercomputer. And to predict changes due to greenhouse gases, he needs to run 50 years worth of the model. So, to examine the effects of just one set of parameters can easily take two months of CPU time on the world's largest computer.

The problem is that a model of the ocean with 250-kilometer squares is not good enough for a realistic simulation of the interaction of multiple parameters. To model the ocean accurately, you need a much finer granularity—you need to look at a grid of 30 kilometers, with a depth of 27 layers. This means that there are over $10\frac{1}{2}$ million points, each one of which carries a half-dozen different parameters.

Even if you develop a realistic model of the ocean, you still need to take into account the atmosphere, which runs in a separate, equally large model. Given the overwhelming complexity of the project, only a supercomputer could master this task.

Visualizing a Cure for Alzheimer's Disease

At the University of California at San Diego School of Medicine, Dr. Mark Ellisman is putting a Cray supercomputer to work searching for leads into the cause of Alzheimer's disease, an ailment with no known cure.

In order to investigate the disease, scientists must look inside the neuron, the cells that provide most of the brain's functioning. In traditional research a piece of brain tissue is put into an electron microscope, which provides a two-dimensional slice of the neuron.

Using a 30-foot-high electron microscope, Ellisman and his team were able to collect data from the brain and enter it into a supercomputer. The system then rendered a three-dimensional (3-D) representation of the neuron.

The 3-D information generated by the Cray was then moved to a graphics workstation, where it was displayed. Examination of the neuron structure showed not only excessive neurofilaments, which are linked to Alzheimer's, but several other clues as well.

First, it revealed that diseased neurons were missing another type of filament, called the microtubular structures. Another neuron structure, called the Golgi apparatus, was also shown to have moved much farther than normal from the cell's nucleus.

Although this data is still in the early stages, it has provided important leads for further research.

Creating a "Virtual Chicken"

Why would you need a Cray supercomputer to simulate something smacking into a bird?

When an airplane engine is developed, engineers have to ensure it will not explode when faced with the occasional flying goose in its flight path. At the San Diego Supercomputer Center, the Cray was used to develop a bird-strike simulation, to replace the popular eight-chicken gun traditionally used in aircraft testing. The Cray is used to model the aircraft engine, complete with the effects of different types of poultry.

Aerospace designers need to model large numbers of factors to produce realistic models. Wind tunnels are sufficient to a point, but it's hard to test the effect of high wind, high altitude, and a host of other parameters in a wind tunnel.

Besides, it's not easy to fit a Boeing 747 into a wind tunnel.

The bird strike simulation allows the aerospace designer to see the effect of birds (and other factors) on the engine, without having to use actual chickens as the eight-chicken gun required. A workstation is used to visualize the results and make adjustments to the design.

Computer programs are called **software**. Software is any program that can be used with a computer. In contrast, *hardware* is the actual computer equipment.

Program Execution

To illustrate the idea of a computer program, assume that a computer user wants to determine the sum of two numbers. To solve this problem, the computer must go through a sequence of steps. First, the computer must use an input device such as a keyboard to get the two numbers that the user wants to total. Then, the computer must add the numbers to find their sum. Finally, it must send the sum to an output device such as a screen so that the user can see the result. Thus, to solve this problem, a computer program would contain three instructions:

1. Get two numbers from the input device.
2. Add the numbers to find the sum.
3. Send the sum to the output device.

To perform or *execute* a computer program, the instructions in the program must be in the computer's primary storage. Between executions, however, the program usually is stored in secondary storage. Thus, to execute the program, it must first be transferred from secondary storage to primary storage, a process called *loading* a program (Figure 2–16).

Once the program is in primary storage, the computer executes it by going through the instructions one at a time in the sequence in which they are stored. The computer brings each instruction in turn to the CPU, which analyzes it and sends signals to the other units that cause the instruction to be executed. For example, execution of the instructions in the

Figure 2–16 Loading a Program into Primary Storage

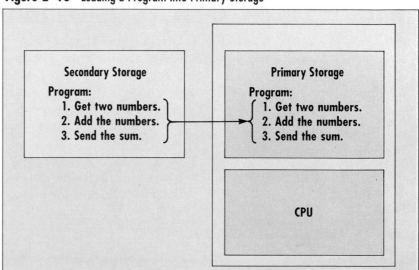

Figure 2–17   Executing a Program

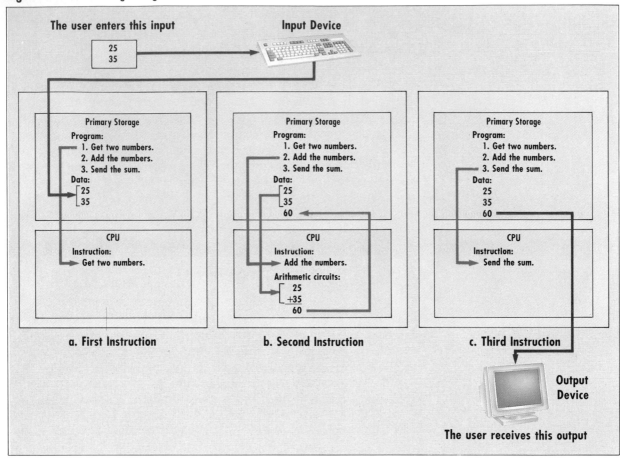

example program to find the sum of two numbers would proceed as follows (Figure 2–17):

1. Get two numbers. The CPU sends a signal to the input device that
causes two numbers (input data) to be transferred to primary
storage.

2. Add the numbers. The CPU sends a signal to primary storage that
causes the two numbers to be sent to the arithmetic circuit in the
CPU. Then the CPU adds the numbers and sends the sum to primary storage.

3. Send the sum. The CPU sends a signal to primary storage to transfer the sum to the output device. Then the output device displays
the sum (output data).

This example illustrates two important concepts. First, primary storage
stores both program instructions and data. All instructions in the pro-

gram are stored in primary storage before the program begins execution. Data is brought into primary storage as the program is executed.

Second, the instructions in the program are executed in the sequence in which they are stored. The sequence must be in a certain order so that, when executed, the problem is correctly solved. If the instructions are out of order, the computer cannot figure out what the right sequence should be. In such a case, the computer would follow the instructions in the order in which they are given and would thus produce an incorrect result.

Programming Languages

The instructions in the example in Figure 2–17 are not in a form that a computer can understand. A program must be written so that a computer can interpret it. Every instruction must follow specific rules that form a language. Humans use *natural languages* such as English and Spanish to communicate with each other. To communicate with a computer through a program, you use a **programming language**.

There are many different programming languages. Some of them will be discussed in later chapters. Figure 2–18 shows an example of a program written in a language called BASIC. This program determines the sum of two numbers. It is in a form that a computer can understand and would execute in a way similar to the example in Figure 2–17.

Types of Programs

There are two main types of programs or software: application programs and system programs. **Application programs** or **application software** are programs designed for specific computer applications. For example, a program that prepares the payroll for a business is an application program. Similarly, a program that analyzes sales and one that keeps track of what items a business stocks are examples of application software. Also, a program used for word processing is an application program.

System programs or **system software** are general programs designed to make the computer easier to use. A system program does not solve a problem for a specific application, but rather makes it easier to use the necessary application program. An example of system software is an **operating system**, which is a set of programs that controls the basic operation of the computer. The operating system does many things. For example, it determines where an application program is stored in the

Figure 2–18   A BASIC Language Program to Determine the Sum of Two Numbers

```
10 INPUT A, B
20 LET S = A + B
30 PRINT ''THE SUM IS''; S
40 END
```

computer's primary storage. The operating system is always in control of the computer when some other program (such as an application program or another system program) is not executing.

Sources of Programs

If you need a program for a particular purpose, you have two main ways of getting it. One is to purchase an existing program; many companies sell computer programs. You can purchase application programs and system programs. Purchased programs, which are often called **packaged software**, are available for all types of computers, from microcomputers to supercomputers.

The other way you can get a program is to prepare a new program from scratch, a process called **programming**. Programs acquired in this way are often called **custom software**. You can prepare custom programs yourself or have a **programmer** do it for you. Custom programs can be prepared for all types of computers.

System programs almost always are purchased. For example, you would purchase an operating system. Application programs may be purchased or prepared from scratch. Packaged software is usually used for microcomputer applications. For example, to do word processing on a microcomputer you would purchase a word processing program. You can also prepare custom software on a microcomputer, although this is done less often than using packaged software. On larger computers, both packaged and custom software are used.

Chapter Summary

- The main components of a computer are the **input device**, the **output device**, **primary storage**, the **central processing unit** (**CPU**), and **secondary storage**. An input device accepts data from outside the computer and converts it to an electronic form understandable to the computer. A **keyboard** is an example of an input device. An output device converts data from an electronic form inside the computer to a form that can be used outside the computer. A **screen** and a **printer** are examples of output devices. Primary storage stores data and program instructions currently being processed. The central processing unit carries out instructions in the program. Secondary storage stores data and programs not currently being processed. **Magnetic disk** and **magnetic tape** are types of secondary storage.

- If the components of a computer are located near each other, they communicate by sending signals over wire cables that connect the components. For communication between distant devices, a telephone line may be used. A **network** is a configuration of several computer devices that are connected so that all can communicate with each other.

- A **microcomputer** is the smallest type of computer. It usually consists of a keyboard, screen, printer, and one or two disk drives. A **minicomputer** is a medium-sized computer. It usually has several terminals, a printer, one or more disk drives, and sometimes a tape drive. A **mainframe computer** is a large computer. It has many terminals, several printers, and numerous disk and tape drives. A **supercomputer** is a computer designed for very fast processing speeds. It may not have as many terminals or disk or tape drives as a mainframe computer, but its CPU is very fast.

- To execute a program, the instructions in the program first must be transferred from secondary storage to primary storage. Then the computer performs the instructions in the sequence in which they are stored. To do so, the computer brings one instruction at a time to the CPU and performs the actions required by that instruction.

- **Application software** is any program designed for a specific computer application such as preparing payroll for a business. **System software** is any general program designed to make the computer easier to use, such as an operating system. Programs may be purchased, or they may be developed from scratch. Those that are purchased are called **packaged software**; those that are developed from scratch are called **custom software**.

Terms to Remember

Review Questions

Fill-in Questions

1. A computer accepts input data with a(n) _____; it produces output data with a(n) _____.

2. A device that is a combination of an input and an output device is a(n) _____.

3. The components of a computer that work together to do the actual computing or processing are the _____ and the _____.

4. Two common forms of secondary storage are _____ and _____.

5. A collection of related items stored together in secondary storage is called a(n) _____.

6. Secondary storage and input and output devices are also called _____ because they are located outside the central part of the computer.

7. A configuration of computer devices connected so they all can communicate with one another is called a(n) _____.

8. A small microcomputer that is designed to be easily carried is called a(n) _____. A powerful microcomputer with special capabilities for producing graphic diagrams and pictures on the screen is called a(n) _____.

9. A program must be in _____ storage before it can be executed.

10. A set of rules for instructing a computer is called a(n) _____.

11. A system program that controls the basic operation of the computer is the _____.

12. The process of preparing a computer program from scratch is called _____; it is done by a person called a(n) _____.

Short-Answer Questions

1. What are the five basic components of a computer?

2. Name one common input device and two common output devices.

3. What does the central processing unit in a computer do?

4. What is the difference between the functions of primary storage and the functions of secondary storage?

5. What happens to anything stored in primary storage and in secondary storage when the power to the computer is turned off?

6. What are two types of files stored in secondary storage?

7. What are the four general types of computers?

8. What happens in the computer during the execution of a program?

9. What is the difference between application software and system software?

10. Describe two ways of acquiring a program. What are programs called that are acquired in each way?

Projects

1. Contact one of the major computer companies and request information about the computers they sell. Write a brief summary of the company's computers. Try to identify the components of each computer, and state which of the four types of computers each one is.

2. Go to a computer store and look at the packaged software available on the shelves. Write down five different types of software (for example, word processing software) that the store sells. Also, write down how many different packages of each type the store sells.

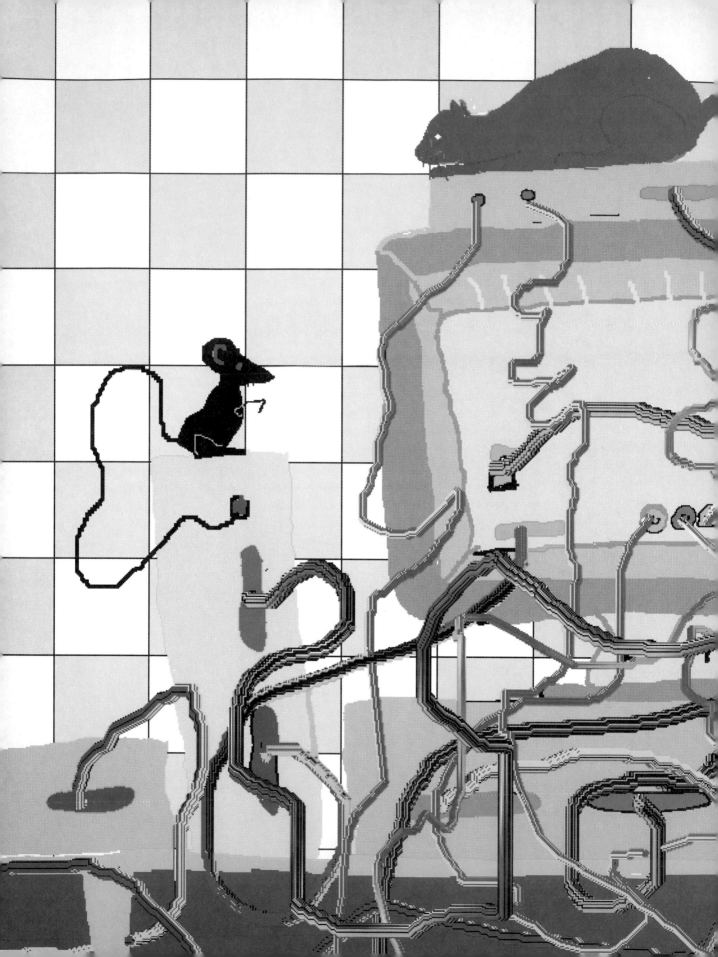

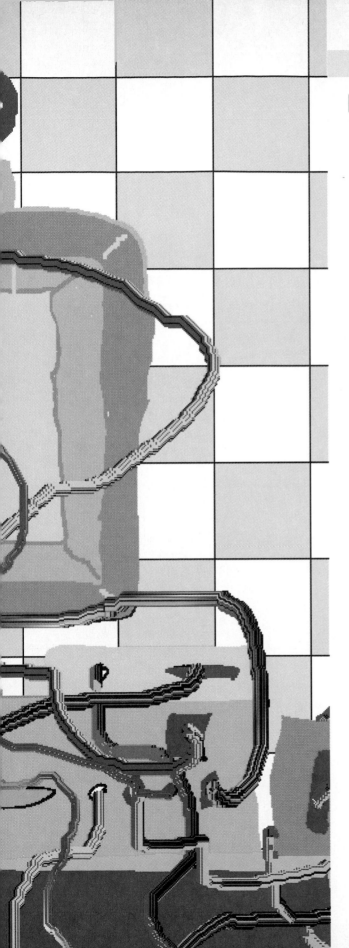

PART TWO

HARDWARE

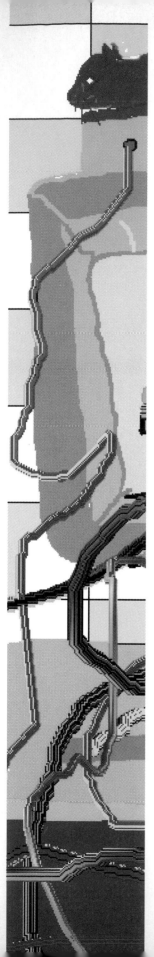

3

THE CENTRAL PROCESSING UNIT AND PRIMARY STORAGE

CHAPTER OBJECTIVES

• After completing this chapter you should be able to:

1. Identify three processing problems for the user and explain what the user should be aware of to solve each problem.

2. Explain how data is stored in primary storage and why data may be incompatible between different computers.

3. Describe the organization of primary storage and explain how primary storage capacity is measured.

4. Describe the structure of the central processing unit and the functions of the units in it.

5. Explain why machine language programs may be incompatible between different computers.

6. Explain how the central processing unit design affects computer speed.

T HE CENTRAL processing unit and primary storage are the main components of a computer. All computing and processing done by the computer takes place in these components. Different computers may have different types of I/O devices and secondary storage, but their CPUs and primary storages have basically the same structure. This chapter provides you with a closer look at these components and what they do.

PROCESSING PROBLEMS FOR THE USER

Why is it important that the user know something about the CPU and primary storage? It might seem that all the user is interested in is getting his or her work done, so any computer should work. But that is not true. Although all computers have the same basic structure to their CPU and primary storage (Figure 3–1), certain characteristics of these components vary, and these variations can create problems for the user.

The first problem is primary storage *capacity*; the amount of primary storage in different computers varies. Recall that primary storage stores programs and data currently being processed by the computer. If there is little primary storage, then only programs and data that require a small amount of space can be used. If the user wants to execute a large program that requires much data, a large amount of primary storage is required.

A second problem for the user is CPU *speed*. Recall that the CPU does arithmetic calculations and makes logical decisions. The speed at which the CPU does its processing varies with different computers. Although all computers seem to be fast, their speed may not be fast enough for the user. If a user has a program that requires many calculations, for example, then a slower CPU will take longer to complete the calculations than a faster one will. The difference in time can be a few seconds to many minutes or even hours. A user may not be satisfied with waiting for the computer to complete the calculations on a slower CPU.

A final problem is *compatibility*, which applies to both primary storage and the CPU. The way data is stored in primary storage is not the same for all computers. If a user wants to use data stored in one computer on another, he or she may not be able to do so if the computers are not compatible. Similarly, the CPUs of different computers use different types of instructions for their programs. A program written for one computer may not be able to be executed by the CPU of another computer.

These three problems make it important for the user to understand some of the characteristics of the CPU and primary storage. If the user needs to select a computer for a task, he or she should investigate solutions to the problems of capacity, speed, and compatibility before making a final decision. In this chapter, you will learn what you need to know in order to solve these problems.

Figure 3–1   The CPU and Primary Storage

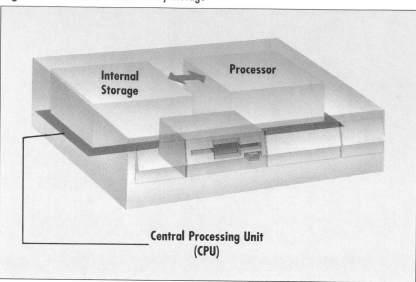

THE COMPOSITION OF THE CPU AND PRIMARY STORAGE

Figure 3–2
A Chip

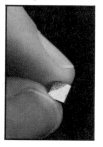

Figure 3–3
A Microprocessor Chip

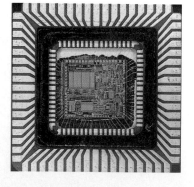

THE COMPOSITION OF THE CPU AND PRIMARY STORAGE

The CPU and primary storage contain electronic circuits that store and process data and program instructions. The circuits are formed from pieces of silicon, a substance found in sand. Each piece of silicon is about ¼ inch square and contains thousands of circuits. A piece of silicon containing electronic circuits is called an *integrated circuit* or, more commonly, a **chip** (Figure 3–2).

The computer needs chips for the CPU and chips for primary storage. The chips in the CPU are sometimes called *processor chips*. With some computers the entire CPU is contained on one processor chip. This type of chip is called a **microprocessor** (Figure 3–3) and is used in microcomputers and in some larger computers. With many minicomputers, mainframe computers, and supercomputers, however, the CPU requires several processor chips.

Primary storage usually is composed of numerous chips. For example, a microcomputer may have sixteen chips for primary storage. Larger computers may have hundreds of primary storage chips. Each chip in primary storage, often called a *memory chip*, is capable of storing a certain amount of data. The amount varies with different types of chips, ranging from 1,000 to 128,000 characters. All the memory chips together make up primary storage.

Each chip is enclosed in plastic and mounted on a board called a *circuit board*. With microcomputers, the microprocessor chip and the memory chips are mounted on one board, called the **motherboard**. For example, Figure 3–4 shows the motherboard for a microcomputer containing a single microprocessor chip and numerous memory chips.

Figure 3–4 The Motherboard for a Microcomputer

Figure 3–5
Circuit Boards for a
Mainframe Computer

With larger computers many boards may be required for the computer's chips (Figure 3–5).

The chips in the CPU and primary storage are connected by a set of wires called a **bus**. Data is sent back and forth between these components over the bus. Thus, the bus is the communication path between the CPU and primary storage.

Other chips and circuit boards are used in a computer besides those needed for the CPU and primary storage. For example, chips are needed to control input/output devices and secondary storage. These chips communicate with the other components over the bus. Sometimes these additional chips are mounted on the same circuit board as the processor and memory chips, and at other times they are found on separate boards. On microcomputers these separate boards, which are called *add-on boards* or *cards*, are plugged into sockets on the motherboard (Figure 3–6). These sockets, which are called *expansion slots*, are connected to the other components by the bus. Thus, the bus serves as a general-purpose communication link between the parts of the computer.

Figure 3–6   Cards Plugged into the Motherboard of a Microcomputer

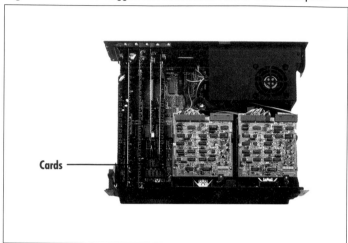

Cards —

PRIMARY STORAGE

Primary storage, which is also called *internal storage* or *memory*, is the part of the computer that stores programs and data currently being processed. Later you will learn how programs are stored; for now, you will just see how primary storage stores data.

Primary Storage Structure

Primary storage is composed of silicon chips containing millions of electronic circuits. Each circuit can be in only one of two states—on or off. In a way, a circuit is like a light bulb, which also can be only on or off. You can think of primary storage as being composed of millions of light bulbs—each either on or off.

The computer stores data in primary storage by turning some circuits on and others off in a pattern that represents the data. For example, using the light bulb analogy, Figure 3–7 shows a pattern that represents a person's name. Later you will see the types of patterns that computers use. For now, just imagine that patterns like the one in Figure 3–7 represent data.

Figure 3–7   Storing a Name in Primary Storage: The Light Bulb Analogy

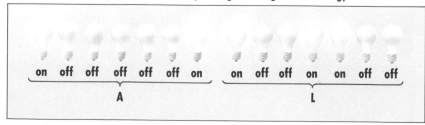

Once data is stored in primary storage, it stays there until the computer changes it. To change the data, the computer changes the pattern in the circuits by turning some circuits on and others off. When the computer changes the data, the original data is destroyed and replaced by the new data. To retrieve data from primary storage, the computer senses the on-off pattern in the circuits. It can transfer this pattern to another part of the computer such as the CPU, an output device, or secondary storage. When data is retrieved, the old data is *not* destroyed; it remains in primary storage and can be retrieved again.

Primary storage circuits, like light bulbs, need electricity to stay on. If the power to the computer is turned off, all the circuits will turn off, and all data in primary storage will be lost. When the computer is turned back on, the data will not reappear; the data is lost forever (unless it is stored in some other form). Because of this characteristic, primary storage is called **volatile storage**.

The type of primary storage described so far is called **random access memory** or **RAM**. The words *random access* simply mean that data in any part of the primary storage can be retrieved (accessed) in any order (that is, randomly). RAM is the main type of primary storage used with computers and, as you know, it is volatile. Many computers also have a type of primary storage called **read only memory** or **ROM**. ROM is **nonvolatile storage**, which means that when the power to the computer is turned off, anything stored in ROM is not lost. ROM, however, can store only preset programs and data put in ROM by the computer manufacturer. Programs and data in ROM can be retrieved (read) as many times as needed, but new programs and data cannot be stored in ROM. ROM is used to store special programs and data needed for the basic operation of the computer. A special type of ROM is *programmable read only memory* or *PROM*. Programs or data can be stored once in PROM but never changed. Another type of ROM is *erasable programmable read only memory* or *EPROM*. EPROM can be completely erased using a special device, and then new programs or new data can be stored in it.

Data Representation

Data is made up of **characters**, that is, letters, digits, and special symbols (such as $ and -). People represent data by using a group of characters, such as a group of letters to represent a name, or a group of digits to represent a quantity. Computers, however, cannot represent data in the same form that people use. There are over one hundred common characters. If a computer circuit were used to represent any character, that circuit would need over one hundred states, one for each character. But as you have seen, each computer circuit has only two states—on and off. Thus, it is not possible to represent any character with a single circuit.

How, then, do computers represent data? The answer is that computers use different patterns of on/off states in a series of electronic circuits for different data. A computer stores data by converting the data to this two-state representation.

Data stored in a two-state manner is said to be in a *binary represen-tation*. For ease of showing data in a binary representation on paper, the digit "1" is used for the "on" state and the digit "0" for the "off" state. The characters "1" and "0" are called **binary digits** or **bits**. For example, the bits that represent the data in Figure 3–7 are:

10000011001100

All data is stored in the computer as patterns of bits.

Character Representation—ASCII and EBCDIC.   Characters are stored in a binary representation by using a code for each character. Over the years many codes have been developed. Each code uses a certain number of bits to represent a character. Early codes used six bits per character; current codes use seven or eight bits per character. Two common codes are **ASCII** and **EBCDIC**.

The name ASCII is pronounced "as-key" and stands for *American Standard Code for Information Interchange*. An industry group that in-cluded many computer manufacturers developed this code as a stan-dard code to be used on all computers. In ASCII, each character is represented by 7 bits. There are 128 combinations of 7 bits, so 128 characters can be represented in the code. Table 3–1 lists the ASCII representation of some characters. As an example, the name JOHN in ASCII is:

1001010 1001111 1001000 1001110

Notice that 28 bits are needed for the name, 7 for each character. ASCII is used on all microcomputers, including those made by IBM and Apple, and on many minicomputers, mainframe computers, and super-computers.

Although ASCII is an industry standard code, it is not used on all computers. IBM minicomputers and mainframe computers, and some mainframe computers that are similar to IBMs, use the EBCDIC code. The name of this code is pronounced "eb-si-dick" and stands for *Extended Binary Coded Decimal Interchange Code*. It was developed by IBM for use on its computers. In EBCDIC, each character is repre-sented by 8 bits. There are 256 combinations of 8 bits, so 256 charac-ters can be represented in EBCDIC, twice as many as in ASCII. Table 3–1 lists the EBCDIC codes of some characters. The name JOHN in EBCDIC is:

11010001 11010110 11001000 11010101

Notice that 32 bits are needed for the name, 8 for each character.

Number Representation.   ASCII and EBCDIC are used for storing characters in primary storage. All types of characters, including nu-meric characters, can be represented in these codes. The codes can be used for numbers by representing each digit in the number by one code. For example, in ASCII the number 45 is:

0110100 0110101

Table 3-1   ASCII and EBCDIC Representation of Some Characters

Character	ASCII	EBCDIC
0	0110000	11110000
1	0110001	11110001
2	0110010	11110010
3	0110011	11110011
4	0110100	11110100
5	0110101	11110101
6	0110110	11110110
7	0110111	11110111
8	0111000	11111000
9	0111001	11111001
A	1000001	11000001
B	1000010	11000010
C	1000011	11000011
D	1000100	11000100
E	1000101	11000101
F	1000110	11000110
G	1000111	11000111
H	1001000	11001000
I	1001001	11001001
J	1001010	11010001
K	1001011	11010010
L	1001100	11010011
M	1001101	11010100
N	1001110	11010101
O	1001111	11010110
P	1010000	11010111
Q	1010001	11011000
R	1010010	11011001
S	1010011	11100010
T	1010100	11100011
U	1010101	11100100
V	1010110	11100101
W	1010111	11100110
X	1011000	11100111
Y	1011001	11101000
Z	1011010	11101001

Fourteen bits are required for the number; the first 7 bits are the code for the digit 4, and the last 7 bits are the code for 5. This number is represented in EBCDIC as follows:

11110100 11110101

In EBCDIC, 16 bits are needed for the number, 8 for each digit.

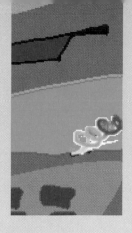

UNIVERSAL COMPUTER CODE DUE

A group of leading computer companies today announced an ambitious effort to develop a lingua franca for the electronics age, a universal digital code that could be used by computers to represent letters and characters in all the world's languages.

A consortium has been formed to develop and promote the new code, known as Unicode. Its 12 members include many top computer companies that are often fierce rivals, like IBM, Apple Computer, Microsoft, Sun Microsystems and Xerox.

If the code becomes a worldwide standard, it would be easier for people in different countries to communicate by electronic mail. The code would also make it easier for software companies to develop programs that can work in different languages.

Right now, for instance, an American computer often cannot understand the codes used by a French computer to represent accented characters, so a message sent electronically from France to the United States might arrive without the accents or with mistaken characters.

But with the new code, any computer anywhere could understand and display everything from French accents to Chinese ideographs, not to mention letters in Bengali, Hebrew, Arabic and other languages.

Computers represent all information as a series of zeros and ones, or as digital bits. What is at issue is the specific sequences of zeros and ones used to represent letters, numerical digits, punctuation marks, as well as other symbols like dollar and yen signs or arithmetic symbols.

The most widespread system, the American Standard Code for Information Interchange, or ASCII, was approved as a standard in 1967. ASCII (pronounced AS-kee) represents each letter and symbol as a sequence of eight zeros and ones. The letter Y, for instance, is represented by the sequence 10111001.

But the International Business Machines Corporation has used a different code in some computers, in which Y is represented by 11101000. That means messages sent from a non-IBM computer to an IBM machine must be translated.

And because ASCII cannot handle special characters used in other languages, other countries have had to design their own codes. Europe has its own 8-bit code, and Asian countries like Japan and China have their own codes to represent the thousands of different characters in their languages.

ASCII cannot be used to represent characters in all these languages because there are only 256 different 8-bit sequences of zeros and ones.

The proposed standard, Unicode, would represent letters and symbols by a sequence of 16 zeros and ones, instead of eight, allowing for 65,536 different combinations. That is enough to give each character used in all the living languages of the world its own unique sequence, with enough combinations left over to eventually include obsolete scripts like cuneiform and hieroglyphs as well.

With each character having a unique code, software programmers would no longer have to worry about which standard was being used or have to translate from one system to another. That would make it easier, for instance, to develop a word-processing program that works in many languages.

"You can now develop international software from the very beginning," said David E. Liddle, the president of Metaphor Computer Systems, a software company in Mountain View, Calif. The company's offices are serving as the headquarters of the consortium, called Unicode Inc.

He said the American computer and software companies were able to put aside their differences to work on the standard because all of them see their overseas markets becoming more important. "How many things are there in the world where you can get Sun, I.B.M., Microsoft and Apple to agree?" he asked.

Unicode has been under development since 1989 by an informal group, and the proposed standard, which now includes sequences for 27,000 characters, is expected to be completed this spring.

Unicod's developers said they have done extensive research and consulted with linguists. One challenge was trying to represent all the Chinese ideographs that are also used in Korean and Japanese.

But Unicode researchers found that the languages have more then 11,000 symbols that are the same, allowing Unicode to represent all the Chinese ideographs with only 18,739 unique characters, instead of the more than 31,000 that would otherwise have been required.

The proposed code still faces hurdles. The consortium needs to attract support from foreign companies, and an international standards organization is developing a competing code. Using 16 bits instead of eight to represent each character would also mean that computers would require more memory and disk-storage capacity.

Problems could also arise in achieving compatibility between computers using Unicode and those using older codes.

Although computers can use ASCII or EBCDIC to represent numbers, they must convert any number to a **binary number** before using it in a calculation. A binary number is made up of only the binary digits 1 and 0. As an example, the binary number that is equivalent to the number 45 is:

101101

Notice that only six bits are needed to represent the number 45 as a binary number. Using ASCII, however, 14 bits are needed, and in EBCDIC, 16 bits are needed. See Appendix C at the back of the book for an explanation of how to convert numbers to binary numbers.

Data Compatibility

You can now see the cause of one of the problems of compatibility between computers: Different computers use different methods for representing data in primary storage. Some computers use ASCII to represent characters, and some use EBCDIC. Even computers manufactured by the same company use different codes. For example, IBM microcomputers use ASCII, and IBM mainframe computers use EBCDIC. Some computers represent numbers using ASCII, some use EBCDIC for numbers, and some store numbers as binary numbers. Even the ways binary numbers are stored vary among different types of computers, and some computers store numbers in several different ways.

Data incompatibility between computers can create problems for the user. For example, assume that a user wants to use data stored in one computer on another computer that stores data in a different form. To do so, the data must be converted to the form acceptable to the other computer. The conversion may not always be possible. If it is, the conversion is usually done by special computer programs. Often, a program on the first computer converts the data from that computer's form to ASCII because it is an industry standard code. Then, a program on the second computer converts the ASCII data to that computer's form. This process can be a time-consuming nuisance for the user.

Primary Storage Organization

As you know, primary storage is composed of many electronic circuits, each of which can be either on or off. In other words, each circuit can store one bit. The bits in primary storage must be organized so that they can be used to store characters and numbers and so that the stored data can be retrieved. This organization is accomplished by arranging the bits into groups. Each group is called a **storage location**.

The number of bits in each storage location depends on the type of computer being used. Most computers have eight or nine bits per storage location, although some computers have more. Computers with eight- or nine-bit storage locations use either ASCII or EBCDIC and store one character in each location. Although ASCII is a seven-bit code, an eighth bit is usually added to provide for special codes. In addition, computers, whether they are ASCII or EBCDIC, often add a

Figure 3–8   Primary Storage Organization

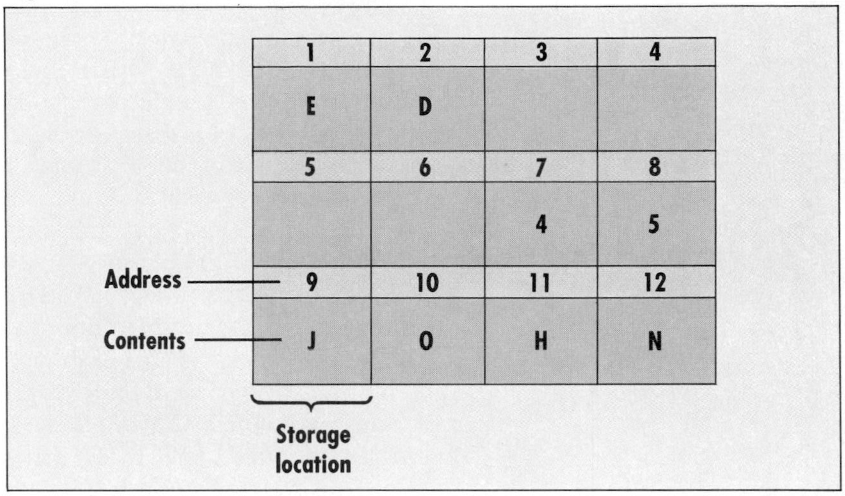

1	2	3	4
E	D		
5	6	7	8
		4	5
9	10	11	12
J	O	H	N

Address —— (9)
Contents —— (J)

Storage
location

ninth bit, called a **parity bit**, which is used to check if there are any errors in the other bits.

A group of bits used to store one character is called a **byte**. Usually, a byte is eight or nine bits. Most computers organize primary storage so that each storage location is one byte.

To store numbers as binary numbers in a computer, several bytes are used together. For example, a computer may use two bytes or 16 bits for a binary number. If the number does not require all 16 bits, then extra bits are set to zero. Some computers use two bytes (16 bits), other use four bytes (32 bits), and still others use eight bytes (64 bits) for binary numbers. A group of bytes used together is called a **word**.

The computer keeps track of storage locations by giving each location a unique number called an **address**. A simple analogy is that of post office box addresses. Think of primary storage being organized into boxes just like the boxes in a post office. For example, Figure 3–8 shows part of primary storage organized into 12 boxes—that is, storage locations. Each storage location in primary storage, like each post office box, has an address to identify it. The contents of each storage location in the computer is data just like the contents of each post office box is mail. To locate a specific post office box, you search through the boxes until you locate the one with the desired address. You can store mail in the box or retrieve mail from the box. Similarly, the computer locates a specific storage location by its address and stores data in or retrieves data from that location.

Primary Storage Capacity

The storage capacity of a computer is measured in terms of the number of bytes in primary storage. Often, the capacity is stated in **kilobytes** or **K bytes** (**KB**). One kilobyte is 1,024 bytes (2^{10} bytes), but most people round this number off to 1,000 bytes. For example, a computer may have 640 K bytes of primary storage. This is exactly 655,360 bytes, but usually people just think of it as 640,000 bytes.

The primary storage of some computers is measured in terms of **megabytes** or **M bytes** (**MB**). One megabyte is 1,048,576 bytes (2^{20} bytes), but again, people round this number off to one million bytes. Thus, 4 M bytes of primary storage would be about four million bytes. An even larger measure than megabytes is **gigabyte** or **G byte** (**GB**). One G byte is approximately one billion bytes. Although computers do not have gigabyte primary storage capacity yet, they may some day.

As you know, the primary storage of a computer stores programs and data. Thus, the storage capacity of a computer determines how big a program can be executed and how much data can be stored in the computer at one time. For example, assume that you have a computer with 640 K byte capacity. If a program requires 360 K bytes, then 280 K bytes (640 minus 360) would be left over for data. If, however, your program requires 512 K bytes, then only 128 K bytes would be left for data. Thus, you must trade off between program size and the amount of data that can be stored. In addition, the program may be too big for the computer. For example, if a program needs 1 M bytes of primary storage, it cannot be executed on your computer with only 640 K bytes.

THE CENTRAL PROCESSING UNIT

The central processing unit (CPU), which is also called the processor, is the part of the computer that carries out the instructions in the program. In doing so, the CPU sends signals to other parts of the computer that tell them what to do. In addition, the CPU does arithmetic and makes logical decisions. This section explains how the CPU performs these tasks.

CPU Structure

The CPU is composed of one or more processor chips containing thousands of electronic circuits. These circuits are organized into two main units, called the **arithmetic-logic unit**, or **ALU**, and the **control unit** (Figure 3–9). The ALU contains circuits that do arithmetic and perform logical operations. The control unit contains circuits that analyze and execute instructions.

The Arithmetic-Logic Unit. The ALU contains arithmetic circuits that can add, subtract, multiply, and divide two numbers. More complex operations, such as finding the square root of a number, are done by sequences of these basic operations. In addition, the ALU has logic circuits that can compare two numbers to determine if they are equal or if one number is greater than or less than the other. Finally, the ALU contains temporary storage locations, called *storage registers*, for storing numbers used in calculations and for storing the results of calculations. The number of storage registers in the ALU depends on the type of computer used, and ranges from 1 to as many as 32.

Figure 3–9   The Structure of the Central Processing Unit

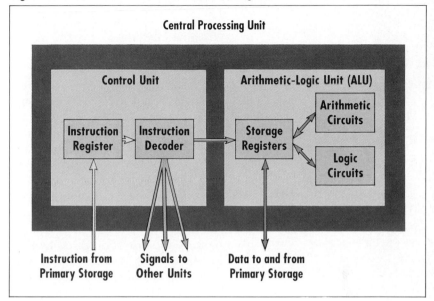

To perform a calculation or logical operation, numbers are transferred from primary storage to storage registers in the ALU. These numbers are then sent to the appropriate arithmetic or logic circuit, and the results are sent back to the storage registers. Then, the results are transferred from the storage registers to primary storage.

The Control Unit.   The control unit also contains a temporary storage location, called an *instruction register*, for storing the instruction being executed. Instructions in the program are brought one at a time from primary storage to the control unit, and stored in the instruction register. The control unit contains circuits, called the *instruction decoder*, that analyze the instruction in the instruction register and cause it to be executed.

The control unit executes *each* instruction by following the same basic sequence of steps:

1. The next instruction in the program is retrieved from primary storage and stored in the instruction register.
2. The instruction in the instruction register is sent to the instruction decoder, where it is analyzed.
3. The decoder sends signals to the ALU, primary storage, I/O devices, and secondary storage, that cause the actions required by the instructions to be performed.

These steps are repeated for each instruction in the program until all instructions have been executed. The sequence of steps is often called a *machine cycle* and is broken into two phases: the *instruction* or *I phase*, consisting of steps 1 and 2; and the *execution* or *E phase*, consisting of Step 3.

Machine Language

The CPU functions by executing instructions in a program. But what form do the instructions take in the computer? The basic language of a computer is called **machine language**. Each instruction in a machine language program consists of an *operation code* or *op code* and one or more *operands*. The op code is a number that tells the computer what operation to perform. There are many op codes, including ones that tell the computer to add two numbers, to subtract one number from another, to retrieve data from primary storage, and to store data in primary storage. The operations the computer can perform and the op code used for each operation depend on the type of computer being used.

The operands of an instruction tell the computer on what data to perform the operation given by the op code. Operands are usually addresses of storage locations in primary storage where the data to be processed is stored, but they may also be codes for storage registers in the ALU. The number and use of each operand in an instruction depends on the type of computer being used.

As an example of a machine language instruction, assume that the op code for addition in a particular computer is the number 23. The operand for the addition instruction is an address of a storage location in primary storage. The following is a machine language addition instruction for this computer:

2346258

The first two digits (23) form the op code; the other digits (46258) are the address of a storage location. This instruction tells the computer to add the number in storage location 46258 to another number that is in a storage register in the ALU. (Although regular numbers have been used for the instruction in this example, a binary representation would be used in the computer.)

A machine language program consists of a sequence of machine language instructions, each similar to the example. The instructions in a program are stored in consecutive storage locations in primary storage. Data to be processed by the program are stored in other storage locations. Notice that instructions are numbers and that they look just like data. In fact, to the computer, there is no difference between instructions and data in primary storage. Once the instructions in a program are stored, the computer executes the instructions by going through them one after the other.

Program Compatibility

Now you can understand the cause of another problem of compatibility between computers: Different CPUs use different machine language instructions for their programs. Each type of CPU has its own set of instructions, which may be different from that of other CPUs. The instruction sets may differ in the types of operations that can be performed, which op codes are used for each operation, and which operands are needed in each instruction. This incompatibility means that a machine language program for one CPU may not be executed on a different CPU.

Two different CPUs are *compatible* if the machine language instructions for one are identical to those of the other. Thus, a machine language program for one compatible CPU can be executed on the other and vice versa. Sometimes, different CPUs are *upward compatible*. This means that the instructions for one CPU may be used on another, more complex, CPU, but the second CPU may have additional instructions that cannot be used on the first CPU. Thus, a machine language program for the first CPU can be executed on the second, but not necessarily vice versa.

CPU Design

The way CPUs are designed varies with different types of computers. Often, you hear that a computer uses an 8-bit, 16-bit, or 32-bit processor as its CPU. An *8-bit processor* can process only 8 bits, or one byte, at a time. A *16-bit processor* can process 16 bits (2 bytes) at a time, and a *32-bit processor* can process 32 bits (4 bytes) at a time. In general, the more bits that can be processed, the faster the computer will be.

CPU design also affects the types of instructions that can be executed by the CPU. In general, 32-bit processors have more complex instructions than 16-bit or 8-bit processors. For example, a 32-bit processor may have instructions to do addition, subtraction, multiplication, and division, whereas an 8-bit processor may have instructions to do only addition and subtraction. Such simple processors do multiplication by successive addition, and division by repeated subtraction—methods that are much slower than in processors that have multiplication and division instructions.

Finally, CPU design affects the maximum capacity of primary storage. This capacity is determined by the size of storage addresses used in instructions. Eight-bit processors have instructions with small storage addresses. Computers with these processors or CPUs can have a maximum of only 64 K bytes of primary storage. Sixteen-bit processors have larger storage addresses. They can be used in computers with up to 1 megabyte of primary storage. Finally, 32-bit processors have large storage addresses and can be used in computers with 32 or more megabytes of primary storage.

In recent years, new types of CPUs have been developed that are designed to be faster and much less expensive than older ones. These types are called *RISC* processors. RISC stands for *Reduced Instruction Set Computer*. A RISC processor has a smaller set of instructions than an older type of processor, which makes it less expensive, but it can execute its instructions very rapidly.

COMPUTER CLOSE-UP

3-2

THE COMPUTER WITH MANY HEADS

In the quest for ever faster computers, researchers are turning to the oldest computer design around: the human brain.

Though engineers have sped up computer circuits by more than 1000 times over the past 40 years, they know their efforts are finally reaching the end of the line. Chips can't get much smaller, and even electricity has a speed limit. Besides, no amount of tinkering will alter the fact that the fastest conventional computer works on a problem by processing pieces of data one by one—which is a little like moving a sand dune grain by grain.

The circuits of the brain, however, work in parallel—that is, all at the same time. The new computers work that way, too. At its simplest, a parallel processor consists of a few computers linked together to jointly tackle a problem. But at the other end of the spectrum is a new computer design that more closely mimics the structure of the brain. Called a neural network, it uses vast numbers of extremely simple processors— the counterparts of the brain's nerve cells. Like the human brain, neural networks are not programmed but rather taught through examples.

Parallel processing is especially good at those real problems that require keeping track of millions of interacting snippets of data. Examples include predicting the weather, figuring out the distribution of stress on a beam used in construction, or searching through a huge data file for a particular piece of information. Even on high-tech, super-fast—and superexpensive—computers, those problems can be time-consuming.

A faster and cheaper alternative may be to use less complex computers working in concert, says Gordon Bell, a pioneer in computer design. "With a Ferrari, you can quickly shuttle 10 people, one at a time, across town," he says. "But you could also do the job all at once with 10 Volkswagens."

Researchers have followed two basic paths in designing parallel computers. In the "coarse grained" approach, a small number of computers, each typically more powerful than a home computer, are linked together. In the "fine grained" approach thousands of much simpler processors are tied together.

Though it is fairly easy to physically connect a bunch of computers, making them do something useful is not. The biggest obstacle is figuring out how to distribute the problem among the many processors. In coarse-grained computers, the processors act like a team of workers building a house. A carpenter might frame a wall while a plumber installs a sink; so different processors work on different parts of the problem at the same time. One advantage of a coarse-grained system is that, since it has only a few processors, it is easier to adapt a program from the vast store of software already written for conventional computers.

Still, some kinds of problems don't always split up neatly into parallel paths. In the same way that you have to plaster a wall before you can paint it, many problems have a few equations that depend on the solutions to other equations, meaning one set of calculations has to be done before the other.

So while the bulk of a problem may be split up among several processors, the machine still has to wait around while one of the processors takes care of the stepwise part of the calculation. "When you are running a relay race with a tortoise and a hare," says

Bell, "the tortoise is going to have the greatest influence on your time."

Most researchers originally assumed that in any problem at least half a percent of the work would have to be done step by step. The slowdown from doing that stepwise part of the calculation—plus the communication congestion that results when the processors trade data back and forth—was thought to limit the speedup of parallel computers to about 200 times, no matter how many processors were joined together.

Researchers at Sandia National Laboratories in Albuquerque proved that assumption wrong. Using a 1,024-processor machine, they solved three classic engineering problems more than 1,000 times faster than a single processor working alone. One of the problems, calculating the stress patterns on a construction beam, would have taken a conventional computer 20 years to solve. Sandia's did it in a week.

While the Sandia researchers used the kind of powerful processors found in coarse-grained parallel computers, they achieved their speed breakthrough using a programming strategy more typical of fine-grained machines. Instead of each processor doing a different kind of computation, all the processors do the same type of computation but on different parts of the data. That's like all the workers on a house teaming up to do the carpentry, then moving on as a team to the plastering, and so on.

Sandia's approach may be applicable to many similar problems that involve handling vast amounts of data. One such problem is creating a topological map of a terrain by comparing stereo images taken overhead by aircraft. On the Thinking Machines Connection Machine, for example, each of its 65,536 processors is responsible for a tiny piece of the map. The processors—each no more powerful than the computer chip in a typical videogame—work simultaneously to put together the entire drawing. The Connection Machine can make 7000 contour maps in an hour; a conventional machine makes 15 maps per hour.

CPU Speed

As you have seen, CPU design affects the speed of the computer. In general, the more bits that can be manipulated by the CPU at one time, the faster the computer will be. But this is only one factor that determines computer speed. Another factor is the amount of data that can be transferred between the CPU and primary storage at one time. Data is transferred between these components over the bus. Some CPUs can transfer only 8 bits (1 byte) at a time; that is, the bus with these CPUs can handle only 8 bits of data at a time. Others can transfer 16 bits (2 bytes) or 32 bits (4 bytes) at a time. In general, the more data that can be stored in or retrieved from primary storage at a time, the faster the computer will be. The number of bits that can be transferred may not be the same as the number of bits that can be manipulated in the CPU. For example, the CPU used in the original IBM PC could transfer 8 bits at a time over the bus but could process 16 bits in the CPU.

The speed at which a computer can transfer data is measured in fractions of a second. The first computers could transfer data to and from primary storage in **milliseconds**. One millisecond is one-thousandth of a second. Later computers stored and retrieved data in **microseconds**. One microsecond is one-millionth of a second. Today's computers transfer data between primary storage and the processor in **nanoseconds**. One nanosecond is one-billionth of a second.

Another factor that affects CPU speed is *clock speed*. CPUs are synchronized to run at the speed of an internal clock. With each tick of the clock, a CPU performs one step in executing an instruction. If the clock ticks faster, then the CPU runs faster. Clock speed is measured in **megahertz** or **MHz**. One megahertz is one million cycles (ticks) per second. For example, the CPU in the original IBM PC ran at 4.77 MHz, or 4,770,000 cycles per second. The CPUs in some models of the IBM PS/2, on the other hand, run at 33 MHz, which means that many more operations can be performed in a second on these computers than on an IBM PC.

The speed of a computer is sometimes stated in **MIPS**, or *Millions of Instructions Per Second*. Microcomputers usually execute less than 5 MIPS. Minicomputers fall into the 5-to-20 MIPS range. Mainframe computers execute 20 to 100 MIPS. Supercomputers can execute 100 to over 1,000 MIPS.

Common CPUs

CPUs in all computers have basically the same structure. As you have seen, they all contain a control unit and an arithmetic-logic unit. CPUs differ, however, in the machine language instructions they can execute and in the number of bits they can transfer and process at one time.

Microcomputer CPUs. As you know, a microcomputer uses a single-chip processor, called a microprocessor, as its CPU. The first microprocessor was developed by Intel Corporation in the early 1970s and was called the Intel 4004 (Figure 3–10). It was a 4-bit processor used in

Figure 3–10   The First Microprocessor: The 4-Bit Intel 4004

calculators. Subsequent development led to the Intel 8080, which was an 8-bit processor used as the CPU in some early microcomputers. At the same time that the 8080 was developed, MOS Technology developed the 6502 microprocessor. This also was an 8-bit processor, but was not compatible with the 8080. It was used as the CPU in the Apple II and in microcomputers developed by Atari and Commodore. Updated versions of the 6502 are still used in the latest models of the Apple II.

Development of microprocessors at Intel led to the 8088, which was used as the CPU in the original IBM PC and in the later XT, and is used in some IBM clones. It is a 16-bit processor, but it can transfer only 8 bits over the bus at a time. A compatible 16-bit processor is the Intel 8086, which can transfer 16 bits over the bus. Thus, it is a little faster than the 8088. The 8086 is used in many IBM clones and in some models of the IBM PS/2. Another compatible microprocessor is the Intel 80286, usually just called the 286. It is a 16-bit processor that can transfer 16 bits over the bus and is faster than the 8086. It was used in the IBM AT and is used in several IBM PS/2 models, in the IBM PS/1, and in IBM clones. Another is the Intel 80386, or simply the 386, which is a 32-bit processor that can transfer 32 bits at a time. It is faster than the 80286 and is used in various IBM PS/2 models and in several other computers. A final compatible Intel microprocessor is the 80486, or simply the 486. Like the 386, it is a 32-bit processor with 32-bit data transfer ability, but it has additional capabilities that make it faster and more powerful than the 386.

The Intel line of microprocessors are used in IBM and related microcomputers. The Apple II uses the 6502 microprocessor. The Apple Macintosh, however, uses a microprocessor for its CPU developed by Motorola, Inc., called the 68000. This microprocessor is not compatible with the Intel microprocessors or with the 6502. It is a 32-bit processor that can transfer 16 bits over the bus at a time. Enhanced

Figure 3–11   An Advanced Microprocessor: The 32-Bit Motorola 68030

Motorola microprocessors—called the 68020, 68030, and 68040—are also 32-bit processors, but they can transfer 32 bits at a time (Figure 3–11). They are compatible with the 68000 and are used in some models of the Apple Macintosh.

Table 3–2 summarizes the characteristics of the common microprocessors. As you can see, microcomputer companies use microprocessors developed by other companies. For example, the IBM microcomputers and clones use Intel microprocessors. Several microcomputers may use the same microprocessor. In so doing, the computers are compatible with one another. Thus, many computers using the Intel 8088 are compatible with the IBM PC. These computers are called IBM clones. A microcomputer that uses a different microprocessor, however, is not compatible. For example, the Apple Macintosh, which uses the Motorola 68000, is not compatible with the IBM PC.

Minicomputer and Mainframe Computer CPUs.

Minicomputers and mainframe computers usually use CPUs developed by the computer manufacturer. The CPUs developed by one company typically are not compatible with those of another company. Within a line of computers manufactured by a company, however, the CPUs usually are compatible.

The DEC VAX line of minicomputers illustrates this idea of CPU compatibility. This line ranges from small models, which are almost microcomputers, to very large models, which are nearly mainframe computers. The models use several processors for their CPUs that provide different speeds and storage capacities. All are 32-bit processors, and all are compatible. Thus, machine language programs for small DEC VAX computers can be executed on larger models in the line.

The same concept applies to the IBM mainframe computers. In the early 1960s IBM developed a compatible line of mainframe computers called the System/360. The line ranged from small, slow speed computers to large, fast computers. In the early 1970s the line was updated

Table 3–2 Characteristics of Common Microprocessors

Microprocessor	Manufacturer	Processing Capability (Bits)	Data Bus Capability (Bits)	Common Computers
8088	Intel	16	8	IBM PC, XT, clones
8086	Intel	16	16	IBM PS/2, clones
286	Intel	16	16	IBM AT, PS/1, PS/2, clones
386	Intel	32	32	IBM PS/2, clones
486	Intel	32	32	IBM PS/2, clones
68000	Motorola	32	16	Macintosh
68020	Motorola	32	32	Macintosh
68030	Motorola	32	32	Macintosh
68040	Motorola	32	32	

and became known as the System/370. Today, the models in this line of computers are identified by the numbers such as 9300 and 3090. All computers in the line, however, are compatible with each other. Each uses a different 32-bit processor for its CPU that is compatible with all others in the line. These processors, however, are not compatible with those used in the DEC VAX line. Thus, a machine language program for an IBM mainframe computer cannot be executed on a DEC VAX.

Supercomputer CPUs. Like minicomputer and mainframe computer CPUs, supercomputer CPUs are developed by the computer manufacturer. Thus, the CPU used in one supercomputer usually is not compatible with that of other supercomputers.

To obtain great processing speeds, supercomputers often use 64-bit processors for their CPUs. In addition, special chips that are designed for high-speed processing are used. For example, supercomputers often use high-speed chips for arithmetic calculations. Another technique used is **multiprocessing** (also called *parallel processing*), which involves using several CPUs in the computer. For example, a supercomputer may have four CPUs, which means four operations can be performed at one time, making the computer four times as fast as one that has only a single processor. All these techniques are designed to make the computer as fast as possible.

PROCESSING SOLUTIONS FOR THE USER

This chapter began with a list of three processing problems for the user: capacity, speed, and compatibility. You now understand what a user needs to know to solve each of these problems.

Capacity is determined by the number of bytes of primary storage, expressed in kilobytes or megabytes. You need to know how much primary storage is available for the computer being used and how much will be required by the program and data you want to process. If the available storage is not sufficient for your needs, you will have to use a computer with more storage capacity. For example, if your programs and data require one megabyte of storage and your computer has only 640 K bytes, you will need a larger computer.

Speed is determined by the CPU. The more bits that the CPU can manipulate at a time, the more bits it can transfer to and from primary storage on the bus at a time, and the greater the clock speed, the faster the computer will be. It is very difficult to judge processing speed without executing a program. Usually, you have to execute a program; if it does not execute fast enough, you need to use a computer with a faster CPU.

Compatibility is the most complex problem. If you have data from one computer that you want to process on another computer, you have to make sure the data representation (ASCII or EBCDIC) for the two computers is the same. In addition, if you have a program for one computer and want to use it on another, you have to be sure the CPUs are compatible. These factors are the minimum that need to be considered; in fact, many other factors affect compatibility, and the only way to be absolutely sure that two different computers are compatible is to test them.

As you can see, the processing problems do have solutions. As long as you understand the basic concepts about the CPU and primary storage, you can find solutions to these problems.

Chapter Summary

- Three processing problems for the user are primary storage capacity, CPU speed, and data and program compatibility. The user needs to be sure there is adequate primary storage for the programs and data being processed. The user needs to use a CPU that is fast enough for the program being executed. The user also needs to be sure that the data and programs are compatible with the computer being used.

- Data is stored in primary storage in a binary representation, that is, as patterns of **binary digits** or **bits**, which are the digits "1" and "0." Characters are represented by using a code, such as **ASCII** or **EBCDIC**, for each character. Numbers may be represented by using a code but must be converted to **binary numbers** for use in calculations. Data for different computers may be incompatible because the data representations used by the computers may be different.

- Primary storage consists of many electronic circuits, each capable of storing one bit. The bits are organized into groups, which, on most computers, are called **bytes**. Each byte is capable of storing one character of data. The primary storage capacity of computers is measured in terms of **kilobytes** (thousands of bytes) or **megabytes** (millions of bytes).

- The central processing unit consists of the **arithmetic-logic unit** (**ALU**) and the **control unit**. The ALU performs arithmetic operations and makes logical comparisons. The control unit analyzes and executes instructions in a program.

- The basic language of a computer is **machine language**. Different computers use different types of machine language instructions. Hence, machine language programs for different computers may be incompatible.

- The design of a central processing unit determines the number of bits that can be manipulated by the CPU at one time. In general, the more bits a CPU can manipulate, the faster the computer will be. Thus, a 16-bit processor will be faster than an 8-bit processor, and a 32-bit processor will be even faster.

Terms to Remember

Review Questions

Fill-In Questions

1. A piece of silicon containing electronic circuits is commonly called a(n) _____.

2. The main circuit board in a microcomputer is called the _____.

3. A set of wires through which parts of a computer communicate is a(n) _____.

4. A bit is a _____ or a _____.

5. An industry standard code for representing characters is _____. It uses _____ bits for each character. A code developed by IBM is _____. It uses _____ bits for each character.

6. Numbers must be converted to _____ before they can be used in calculations.

7. A group of bits used to store one character is a(n) _____.

8. Each storage location in the computer is identified by a unique number called a(n) _____.

9. A kilobyte is about _____ bytes. A megabyte is about _____ bytes. A gigabyte is about _____ bytes.

10. The basic language of a computer is _____.

11. A millisecond is _____ of a second. A microsecond is _____ of a second. A nanosecond is _____ of a second.

12. A 386 microprocessor would be used in a microcomputer manufactured by _____, whereas a 66030 would be used in one manufactured by _____.

Short-Answer Questions

1. What are three processing problems that a user should be aware of when evaluating a computer?

2. What are two uses of chips in a computer?

3. What is the difference between volatile and nonvolatile storage?

4. What is the difference between RAM and ROM?

5. Write each of the following in ASCII:

   a. MARY

   b. 27

6. Write each of the following in EBCDIC:

   a. SAM

   b. 38

7. The following are written in ASCII. What does each represent?

    a. 1001010 1001111 1000101

    b. 0110011 0110110

8. The following are written in EBCDIC. What does each represent?

    a. 11010010 11000001 11101000

    b. 11110001 11111001

9. What do we mean when we say data is stored in a binary representation in a computer?

10. What are the main units in the CPU, and what does each do?

11. What do we mean when we say two CPUs are compatible? What do we mean when we say one CPU is upward compatible with another?

12. What is the difference between a 16-bit and a 32-bit processor?

13. A computer salesperson tells you that one microcomputer has a 10 MHz CPU and another has a 20 MHz CPU. What does this mean?

14. What is multiprocessing, and why is it used?

Projects

1. If you are using a computer for a class or have access to a computer, find out everything you can about the computer's CPU and primary storage. How much primary storage does the computer have? What code is used to represent data in primary storage? What CPU does it use? What is the CPU's speed? With what other computers is it compatible?

2. Many other chips besides those identified in the chapter have been developed. Contact a company that makes chips (called a semiconductor company), and find out what models and types of chips it has made over the years. Write a brief summary of the company's products and for what purpose each is used.

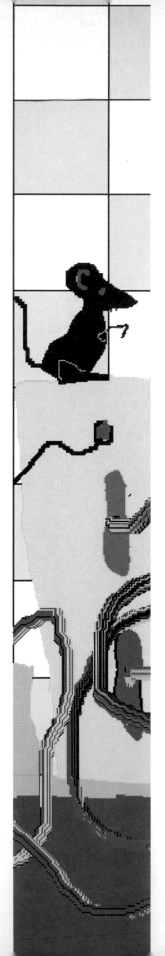

4

INPUT AND OUTPUT DEVICES

CHAPTER TOPICS

Common Microcomputer Input and Output Devices
- Keyboards
- Mouse
- Screens
- Desktop Printers

Video Display Terminals

Other Input Devices
- Touch Input Devices
- Optical Scanning Input Devices
- Magnetic Scanning Input Devices
- Voice Input Devices

Other Output Devices
- High-Volume Printers
- Plotters
- Voice Output Devices
- Computer Output Microfilm Devices

Data Preparation Devices

Ergonomics

CHAPTER OBJECTIVES

• After completing this chapter you should be able to:

1. Describe the main characteristics of common microcomputer input and output devices.

2. Describe video display terminals and their use.

3. List at least three other types of input devices.

4. List at least three other types of output devices.

5. Describe several data preparation devices.

6. Explain the importance of good ergonomic design of computer hardware.

A COMPUTER USER communicates with a computer through input and output devices. The user enters input data into the computer through input devices and receives the results of the computer's processing through output devices. These devices form the hardware interface between the user and the rest of the computer.

Many types of input and output devices make up the hardware interface. This chapter explains what you need to know about these devices. It describes common input and output devices that you use directly, including microcomputer devices as well as devices used with minicomputers and mainframe computers. This chapter also describes less common input and output devices, some of which you may use directly and others that computer professionals use in processing input and output for you.

COMMON MICROCOMPUTER INPUT AND OUTPUT DEVICES

Most input and output devices that users encounter are those found on microcomputers. This section describes common microcomputer input and output devices and explains how to use them. Users also may encounter some of these devices when using minicomputers or mainframe computers.

Keyboards

The most widely used input device on microcomputers is the keyboard. Each time you press a key on the keyboard, an electronic signal is sent to the computer. The signal is a code, usually in ASCII, for the character on the key. You enter data into the computer by pressing the keys for the characters that make up the data.

A computer keyboard includes keys for letters, digits, and special symbols. In addition, other keys commonly found on a typewriter are included. There are Shift keys for capitalization, a Tab key for tabulating, and a space bar. A key marked Caps Lock or Alpha Lock locks the keys for alphabetic characters into capitals but does not affect the other keys. Also included is a Backspace key (sometimes marked ←), which erases the last character keyed in. Sometimes a Delete key is used instead of the Backspace key. Figure 4–1 shows a typical computer keyboard with some of the keys mentioned here.

In addition to the common keys, keyboards include many keys for special purposes (Figure 4–1). The most important of these is the Enter or Return key. This key, which may be marked with the word Enter or Return, or with the symbol ↵, is used to indicate the end of data entry. Usually, after a group of characters representing some data is entered, the Enter key is pressed. This key tells the computer to go on to the next input or to begin processing the data.

Figure 4–1 An Example of a Keyboard

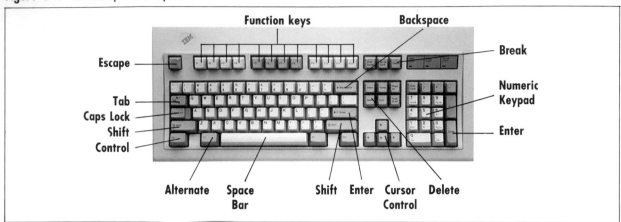

Another important special key is the Control key. This key, which may be marked Ctrl, is used like a Shift key: the Control key is held down and another key is pressed. When this is done, a special code is sent to the computer, the meaning of which depends on the computer and on the program that is executing at the time. For example, with some computers, the program currently executing stops when the Control key is held and the letter C is pressed. This combination is called a "control C" and may be written CTRL/C or ^C.

Some other special purpose keys are the following:

- *Escape key.* This key, which may be marked Esc, is often used to indicate the end of some step during the processing of a program.
- *Break key.* This key is sometimes used to stop the execution of a program.
- *Alternate key.* This key, which may be marked Alt, is found on some keyboards. It is used like the Control key: the Alternate key is held down and another key is pressed. A special code is then sent to the computer, the meaning of which depends on the computer and the program.

Notice that the effect of the special keys often depends on the type of computer being used and the program that is executing.

All computer keyboards have a row of numbers across the top. In addition, many keyboards include a separate set of numbers on the right, called a **numeric keypad**. The numbers in the keypad are laid out like an adding machine so that entry of numeric data is easier.

Another group of keys that are usually found on computer keyboards are called **cursor control keys**. These keys may be in a separate keypad or may be part of the numeric keypad. They are used to move the cursor on a screen. The **cursor** is a mark that indicates where the next output will be displayed or the next input will be entered. This mark may be a box, a line, an arrow, or some other symbol, and may blink on and off or be steady (Figure 4–2). The cursor can be moved

Figure 4–2 Types of Cursors

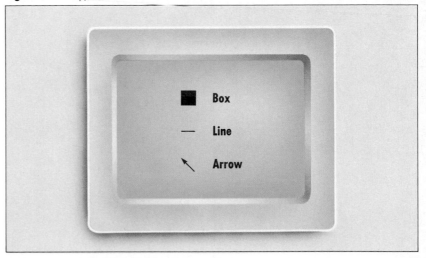

around on the screen by pressing the cursor control keys. Usually, there are four cursor control keys marked with arrows. The → key moves the cursor one position to the right, the ← key moves the cursor one position to the left, the ↑ key moves the cursor up one line, and the ↓ key moves the cursor down one line. Also, a key marked Home may be present that moves the cursor to the upper left-hand corner of the screen, and a key marked End may be included that moves the cursor to the bottom of the screen.

A final set of keys that are found on many computer keyboards are called **function keys**. These keys may be located on one side of the keyboard or across the top. Often, there are 10 or 12 keys marked F1, F2, F3, and so on. The purposes of these keys depend on the program that is executing; different programs may assign different meanings to these keys or may not use the keys at all. For example, with one program, pressing the F1 key may cause the output to be printed, whereas with another program pressing this same key may cause a line on the screen to be erased. You must be familiar with the meaning that different programs assign to each function key.

Mouse

After keyboards, the most common input device encountered on microcomputers probably is a **mouse**. A mouse is a small device with wheels or rollers on the bottom and one or more buttons on the top (Figure 4–3). It is connected to the computer by a cable. You hold the mouse in your hand, roll it over the surface of a table, and press the buttons on the top of the mouse (you "click the mouse").

A mouse has two purposes. The first is to move the cursor on the screen. As you roll the mouse over the surface of a table, the cursor moves. Rolling the mouse to the left or right moves the cursor to the left or right; rolling the mouse forward or backward moves the cursor

Figure 4–3 A Mouse

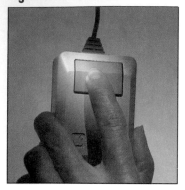

Figure 4–4 Controlling What the Computer Does Next with a Mouse

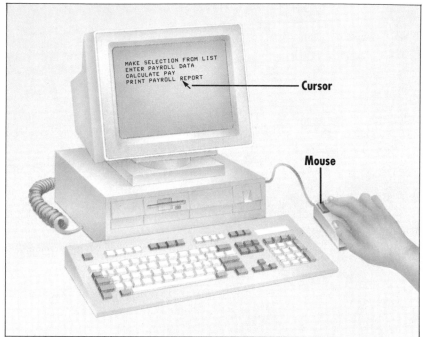

up or down. The mouse can be rolled in any direction, and the cursor will move in that direction on the screen. Often, the cursor used with the mouse is in the form of an arrow, so moving the cursor with the mouse is like pointing at things on the screen.

The second purpose of the mouse is to select what the computer does next. You roll the mouse until the cursor points at something on the screen that indicates what the computer is to do. For example, the computer may display a list of tasks on the screen; you roll the mouse until the cursor points at that task in the list that you want the computer to do next (Figure 4–4). Then, you press one of the buttons on the top of the mouse. This action sends a signal to the computer that tells it to do the task to which the cursor is pointing.

A mouse takes the place of cursor control keys and function keys on a keyboard. The advantage of a mouse over keys is that using the mouse is like pointing, something that everybody knows how to do. Thus, little training is necessary for a user to understand how to use a mouse. A mouse requires you to take your hand off the keyboard, however, which can slow you down.

An alternative to a mouse is a **trackball** (Figure 4–5). This device consists of a base with a ball on top of it and several buttons around the ball. You roll the ball with your hand to move the cursor, and press one of the buttons to select what the computer does next. The advantage of a trackball over a mouse is that you do not need as much desk space to use it.

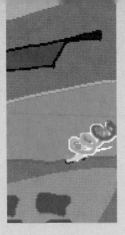

IS IT TAPS FOR QWERTY?

The familiar typewriter keyboard used around the world for more than a century may be replaced in the microelectronic age by a faster, simpler arrangement that lets many touch typists cruise at speeds of 100 words a minute or more.

Directory assistance operators across the country already are using the new system. State governments in Oregon and New Jersey have begun converting their typing operations, and federal agencies such as the Department of Agriculture are experimenting with the new keyboard. Many insurance firms and large manufacturers are boarding the bandwagon.

Efficiency experts have argued for decades that the standard keyboard, know as "QWERTY" after the first six letters of the top row, is slow and unproductive. Indeed, it was designed that way.

Christopher Latham Sholes, father of the typewriter, laid out the QWERTY keyboard in the 1870s. His first machines kept jamming when typists went too fast. To slow things down, he spread the most common letters—E, T, O, A, N, I—all over the board and ensured that frequent combinations (such as "ed") had to be struck by the same finger—the slowest motion.

By the 1930s, typewriters were fast enough mechanically to keep up with most typists, but the purposely inefficient QWERTY held sway because nobody pushed hard for a change; nobody, that is, except August Dvorak, a University of Washington psychologist who devoted his life to an anti-QWERTY crusade.

Dvorak, a pioneer of "ergonomics"—the study of the interaction between man and machine—designed a keyboard built for speed, putting all five vowels and the five most common consonants on the center, right under the fingers.

With the letters on Dvorak's home row—AOEUIDHTNS—the typist can produce about 3000 common English words. The home row on the QWERTY keyboard—ASDFGHJKL—makes fewer than 100 common words.

Dvorak's design also permits a much faster two-handed rhythm by splitting the strokes evenly between the right and left hands. With QWERTY, the left hand does almost 60 percent of the typing; on Dvorak's keyboard each hand types 50 percent of the letters.

"When you see Dvorak typists, it looks like their hands aren't even moving," said Patricia Kaplus, a supervisor in an Oregon government office that has made the switch. "You don't have to jump from row to row, so it's faster and more accurate."

QWERTY is not quitting quietly. Industry officials estimate that there are 30 million standard QWERTY keyboards in use today, and about one-tenth as many with Dvorak capability.

Most typing schools still concentrate on QWERTY, although office managers are starting to look for Dvorak-trained secretaries.

Professor Dvorak died in 1975—just before the breakthrough that has made his keyboard accessible to every home and office.

The invention of electronic keyboards controlled by a programmed microchip has made it possible to switch from QWERTY to Dvorak, and back with the touch of a key. "Ever since they put the chip into a keyboard, there's been a ground-swell (for the faster version)," said Virginia Russell, founder and head of the International Dvorak Federation in Brandon, Vt.

Many computer firms, including Apple, are building in Dvorak conversion capability as standard equipment on their keyboards today, and plenty of low-cost programs are available to reprogram keyboards on other computers.

For older keyboards that convert to Dvorak, a typist can buy stick-on letters to mark the key tops or new key tops to snap on over the old ones. Keyboard makers such as Keytronics and Wico are producing boards that have both the QWERTY and Dvorak letter stamped on each key top—often in contrasting colors.

For the tens of millions whose fingers are trained to QWERTY, Dvorak devotees say the conversion is not particularly difficult.

Eventually, Russell said, Dvorak will prevail because it will become familiar to the thousands of typists banging out new stories at magazines and newspapers everywhere. They will spread the Dvorak gospel.

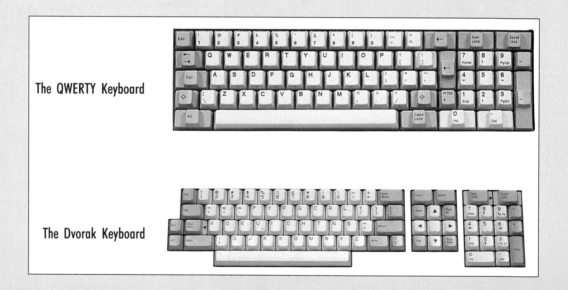

The QWERTY Keyboard

The Dvorak Keyboard

Figure 4–5   A Trackball

Screens

The most widely used output device on microcomputers is a screen on which characters are displayed. To display a character, the computer sends an electronic signal to the screen. The signal is a code, usually in ASCII, for the character. The screen displays the character that corresponds to the code.

To form characters on a screen, individual dots are arranged in patterns that represent each character. The dots are called picture elements or **pixels**. Figure 4–6 shows how pixels can be arranged to form the letter S. The more pixels that are used and the closer they are together, the more the image on the screen looks like the desired character.

Figure 4–6   The Letter S Formed from Pixels

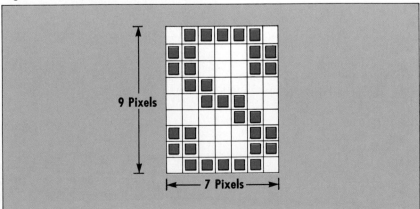

Diagrams and pictures also can be displayed on screens. In general, output that consists of diagrams, charts, pictures, and so forth, is called **graphic output** (Figure 4–7). To display graphic output, pixels are arranged in patterns that represent the diagram.

The number of pixels that can be displayed at one time on a screen is called the **screen resolution** and determines how closely the graphic output resembles a diagram or picture. The more pixels that can be displayed, the more the image on the screen looks like the desired output. A low-resolution screen uses the fewest pixels; a typical low-resolution screen allows 320 pixels horizontally by 200 pixels vertically. A high-resolution screen uses the most pixels; for example, a very high-resolution screen uses 1,000 by 750 pixels. Medium-resolution screens fall in between—for example, 720 by 350 pixels.

A screen is connected to the computer by a cable that plugs into a socket in a circuit board. Often, the circuit board is a special card, called a *display adapter*, that is plugged into the computer's motherboard. The display adapter determines many of the characteristics of the screen output. For example, the display adapter determines the maximum resolution of the screen. Often, a different display adapter can be used to get better resolution on the screen.

CRTs.   The most common type of screen is a **CRT**, which stands for Cathode Ray Tube. A CRT is a tube similar to a television (Figure 4–8). In the tube, a beam of electrons is directed from the back of the tube to the inside surface of the screen. This surface is coated with phosphorus, which glows when hit by electrons. By directing the beam

Figure 4–7   Graphic Output on a Screen

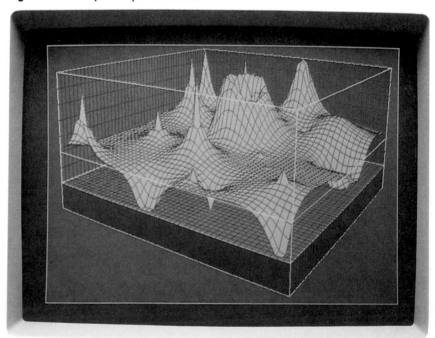

Figure 4–8 A Cathode Ray Tube (CRT)

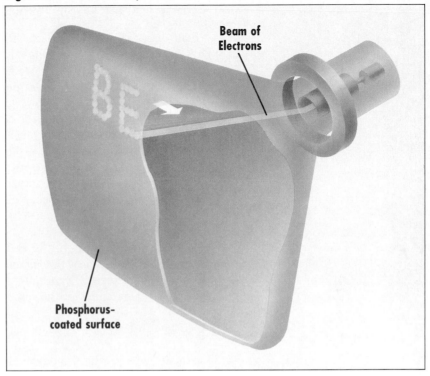

of electrons at different points on the surface, patterns that represent characters and diagrams can be displayed on the screen.

Several types of CRTs can be used with a computer. A standard TV set, either black and white or color, can be used. The resolution on a TV screen, however, is very low, and therefore the screen cannot display much output. A TV set normally should not be used for computer output except in some home computer applications.

A CRT designed for computer use is called a **monitor**. There are two types of monitors: monochrome and color. A *monochrome monitor* displays an image in one color on a contrasting background. The color is usually white, green, or amber, although the last two colors are considered the easiest on the eyes. These colors are displayed on a black background, but some monochrome monitors display a black image on a white background. A *color monitor* displays images in color. The number of colors that can be displayed depends on the monitor and other hardware; sometimes only two colors can be displayed, and other times hundreds of colors can be displayed.

CRT screens vary in size. The most common size is 11 or 12 inches, measured diagonally. Some larger screens are 14 to 17 inches across.

Flat Panel Screens.   CRTs, although very good for displaying output, have one main disadvantage: they are bulky. To display the image on the screen, a CRT must be deep. The larger the screen, the deeper the

CRT, which makes CRTs big and heavy. Although size is usually not a serious problem with desktop computers, it is a problem with portable computers.

To overcome the problem of CRT bulk, **flat panel screens** are used. These screens are thin and lightweight. They are incorporated into portable computers or used in locations where CRTs cannot be used.

There are several types of flat panel screens. One uses a *liquid crystal display,* or *LCD*. LCD shows a dark image on a light background and is used in digital watches, clocks, and calculators. Computer screens using LCD display output in a form similar to a CRT, although with lower resolution (Figure 4–9a). LCD screens are thin and lightweight, but they can be hard to read in low light or at an angle.

Another type of flat panel screen is a *plasma screen* (Figure 4–9b). This type of screen uses a special gas that glows when affected by electricity in a certain way. Plasma screens can be built with very good resolution, but they are expensive.

Flat panel screens are useful in certain situations. Research and development in the area of flat panel screens should produce better and less expensive screens. Eventually, these types of screens may make up a significant percentage of the screens used with computers.

Desktop Printers

As you know, a printer is a device that produces output on paper. Many types of printers are used with computers. Some are relatively fast and are designed for situations in which a high volume of output is produced. Others are comparatively slow and are used when the volume of output is low. Microcomputers generally use slow, low-volume printers, called *desktop printers,* because they are usually small enough to fit on the top of a desk or table.

Printer Classifications.   All computer printers can be classified into one of two general types: impact and nonimpact. An **impact printer** makes an

Figure 4–9   Flat Panel Screens

(a)   A Liquid Crystal Display, or LCD, Screen

(b)   A Plasma Screen

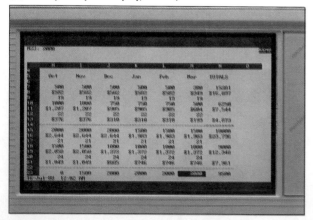

image on paper by striking the paper with a metal or plastic mechanism. A typewriter works in this way, and some computer printers are similar to typewriters. A **nonimpact printer** makes an image in some way other than by striking the paper. An example of a nonimpact printing device is a copier (such as a Xerox machine). Some computer printers use a technique for printing similar to that of a copier.

Computer printers also can be classified by how many characters are printed at one time. Many printers print one character at a time, like a typewriter, and are called **serial printers**. The speed of a serial printer is measured in *characters per second,* or *cps*. Some printers print one line at a time and are called **line printers**. Their speed is measured in *lines per minute,* or *lpm*. Finally, some printers print an entire page at a time, like a copier, and are called **page printers**. Their speed is measured in *pages per minute,* or *ppm*. Until recently, all desktop printers have been serial printers, and faster, high-volume printers have been line and page printers. Now, however, desktop page printers are available.

A final way of classifying printers is in terms of the quality of the image that the printer produces. The printers that produce the best images are called **letter-quality printers**. The output from these printers is as clear as that of a good-quality typewriter, which is important in a business letter. At the other extreme are **draft-quality printers**, which produce output that, although readable, is not of the quality that would normally be acceptable for a business letter. Between these extremes are **near–letter-quality printers**, which produce output that may be acceptable for business letters in some situations but is not as good as letter-quality output.

Speed and quality of output are the most important factors that determine the cost of a printer. In general, the faster a printer prints and the better the quality of the image produced by the printer, the more the printer will cost. Table 4–1 summarizes the characteristics of the printers that will be described here.

Desktop Impact Printers.   Two main types of desktop impact printers are used: fully formed character printers and dot-matrix printers. A **fully-formed-character printer** prints each character by striking a ribbon and the paper with an element shaped like a character (Figure 4–10). Desktop printers of this type are always serial printers. Often,

Table 4–1   Desktop Printer Comparison

Printer	Type	Method	Quality	Speed	Cost
Fully-formed-character	Impact	Serial	Letter	10–90 cps	$400–$5,000
Dot-matrix	Impact	Serial	Draft to near-letter	30–400 cps	$200–$2,000
Laser	Nonimpact	Page	Near-letter to letter	8–28 ppm	$1,000–$10,000
Thermal	Nonimpact	Serial	Draft to near-letter	11–80 cps	$200–$1,500
Ink-jet	Nonimpact	Serial	Draft to near-letter	35–400 cps	$500–$2.000

Figure 4–10 Printing with a Fully-Formed-Character Printer

(a) Fully-Formed-Character Printing with a Daisy Wheel

(b) A Fully-Formed-Character (Daisy Wheel) Printer

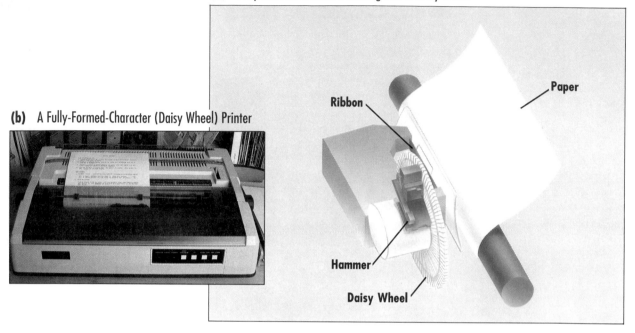

the character elements used in this type of printer are arranged in a circle at the ends of metal or plastic fingers. This arrangement is called a *daisy wheel* because it looks like a daisy. Printers that use daisy wheels are called *daisy wheel printers.*

Fully formed character serial printers are letter-quality printers. In fact, this type of printer usually produces better-quality output than most other types of printers.

A **dot-matrix printer** prints each character by striking a ribbon and the paper with a group of pins (Figure 4–11). Each pin causes a dot to be printed on the paper. The dots are arranged in a rectangular pattern or matrix. To form a character, some pins are raised and others are not so that only certain dots in the matrix are printed. Figure 4–12 shows how the letter S is printed in a 5-dot–by–7-dot matrix of dots. Dot-matrix desktop printers are always serial printers.

Dot-matrix printers print draft-quality to near–letter-quality output. The quality can be improved in several ways. One is to use more dots in the matrix. A printer that uses a 7-dot–by–9-dot matrix prints better quality than one that uses a 5-dot–by–7-dot matrix. Some dot-matrix printers use a matrix as large as 36-dot–by–24-dot. Another way that the quality can be improved is to print each character twice, with the dots shifted slightly the second time. This technique fills in the spaces between the dots and makes the image appear more like a fully formed character.

Figure 4–11   Printing with a Dot-Matrix Printer

(a)   Dot-Matrix Printing

(b)   A Dot-Matrix Printer

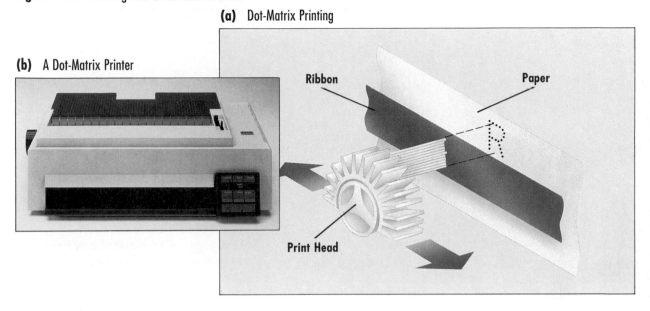

Desktop Nonimpact Printers.   Three main types of nonimpact printers are used as desktop printers. They are laser printers, ink-jet printers, and thermal printers.

The most common type of nonimpact printer is a **laser printer** (Figure 4–13). A laser printer is a page printer that prints by using technology similar to that of a copier. First, an image of the page to be printed is recorded on the surface of a metal drum by a laser. Then, the image is transferred from the drum to paper. Finally, the image is fixed to the paper using the same techniques as a copier.

The image on a laser printer is actually made up of dots, like on a dot-matrix printer. Laser printers, however, can print far more dots in a space than most other printers. Many desktop laser printers, for example, print 300 dots per inch (dpi). As a result, laser printers can print near–letter-quality to letter-quality output.   ·

Figure 4–12   Dot-Matrix Output

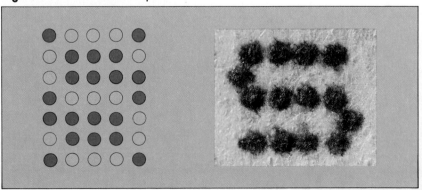

Figure 4–13 Printing with a Laser Printer

(a) Laser Printing

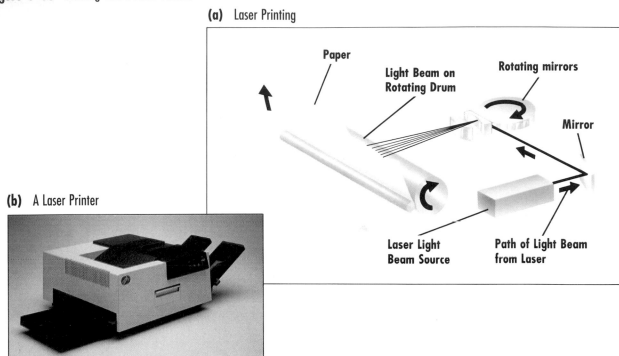

Paper

Light Beam on Rotating Drum

Rotating mirrors

Mirror

Laser Light Beam Source

Path of Light Beam from Laser

(b) A Laser Printer

Laser printers have become very common in recent years because their prices have decreased. They are used by many individuals and organizations, replacing fully formed character and dot-matrix printers.

Another type of nonimpact printer is an **ink-jet printer**, which creates an image by spraying drops of ink on the paper. The drops form characters much like dots form characters with a dot-matrix printer. Desktop printers of this type are always serial printers. The quality of the image of these printers varies from draft-quality to near–letter-quality output.

A final type of nonimpact printer is a **thermal printer**, which uses wires to apply heat to special paper or to a special ribbon. In a sense, the image is burned into the paper. The image is formed from individual dots as in a dot-matrix printer. Desktop printers of this type are always serial printers. Their quality varies considerably. Some produce poor draft-quality and others produce near–letter-quality output. Some are very compact and are used with portable computers. Thermal printers require either special heat-sensitive paper or special ribbons, which are more costly than regular paper and ribbons.

Other Printer Characteristics. The type style that a printer uses is called the **font** (Figure 4–14). Many printers provide some way of varying the font that a printer prints. With some printers the printing elements can be changed to get a different font. Daisy wheel printers are an example of this approach; different daisy wheels can be used for different fonts. With other printers, the font can be changed with commands from the computer. Laser printers have this capability. Some printers can print in

Figure 4–14 Some Fonts

Century Old Style
Palatino
Helvetica
Times Roman
Optima

Figure 4–15 Portrait versus Landscape Orientation

(a) Portrait Orientation   **(b)** Landscape Orientation

a smaller type, called *condensed print*, to get more on a page. Dot-matrix printers often have this capability.

Some printers, such as laser printers, can print sideways. Normal printing is called *portrait orientation*, and sideways printing is called *landscape orientation* (Figure 4–15). Landscape orientation is useful for printing wide documents, such as those with many columns of data.

In addition to being able to print characters, some printers also can produce graphic output. Usually, graphic output is created by printing dots close together in a pattern that looks like a chart or diagram. Most of the types of printers discussed earlier have this capability, although not all models of these printers are designed for graphic output.

A few printers can print in color. Color output can be useful for conveying information, especially in graphs and charts. Color printers are more expensive than regular printers. Still, you can expect their use to increase in the future.

Printer Connection.   A printer is connected to a microcomputer by a cable that plugs into a socket in a circuit board. Often, this circuit board is a card that is plugged into the computer's motherboard. The socket on this card is called a **port**. The CPU sends codes for characters to be printed, usually in ASCII, to the port, where they are sent along the cable to the printer.

There are two types of ports: a serial port and a parallel port. In a *serial port* (not to be confused with a serial printer), one bit at a time is sent along a single wire to the printer. If the ASCII code is used for characters, then seven bits need to be sent in sequence by using a serial port before the character can be printed. In a *parallel port*, all the bits for one character are sent to the printer at one time along multiple wires. For example, to send the ASCII code for a character to a printer using a parallel port, seven wires are needed so that all seven bits can be sent at the same time. Before connecting a printer to a computer, you must know what type of port it needs and whether the computer has the required type.

Figure 4–16 A Video Display Terminal (VDT)

VIDEO DISPLAY TERMINALS

In addition to using microcomputers, users often use minicomputers and mainframe computers. Many of the I/O devices for these larger computers are the same as those used with microcomputers, including keyboards, screens, and printers.

Often with a larger computer, several I/O devices are combined to form a terminal. For example, a screen or a printer may be combined with a keyboard to form a terminal. Other types of input and output devices may also be connected to create terminals.

The most common type of terminal is a **video display terminal,** or **VDT**. It consists of a keyboard and a screen, which is usually a CRT (Figure 4–16). These terminals may have any of the characteristics of keyboards and screens discussed earlier. Some VDTs produce only character output, whereas others, called *graphic display terminals*, produce graphic output.

Some VDTs can only send input to the computer and receive output from the computer. This type is called a *dumb terminal* because of its limited capabilities. Other VDTs have computer processors built in, and in addition to being able to send and receive data, can perform some basic data processing such as allowing you to correct errors in input data. This type is called an *intelligent* or *smart terminal*.

Microcomputers can also be used as terminals. To do so requires data communication technology discussed in Chapter 6. The result, however, is a very smart terminal because the terminal is a computer. The microcomputer can do much of the data processing normally done by the larger computer, plus act as an I/O device for the other computer. Because of these advantages, you can expect to see more use of microcomputers as terminals in the future.

OTHER INPUT DEVICES

The input and output devices described so far are the ones most commonly encountered by users. There are many other I/O devices, however. This section describes other types of input devices.

Touch Input Devices

Several types of devices allow users to enter input by touching something either with a finger or with another device (Figure 4–17). Touch input devices are found on all types of computers, although they are most common on microcomputers. One such input device is a **touch screen**, which is a screen with the capability of sensing where it is touched by a person's finger. A touch screen is usually used to control the functioning of the computer. The screen shows a list of the tasks the computer can do, and the user touches one of the tasks in the list to indicate what is to be done next. This process is much like using a function key on a keyboard.

Another type of touch input device is a **touch pad**, which can sense where it is touched. This device sits on a desk and may be part of the keyboard or may be connected separately to the computer by a cable. Some touch pads are touched by a finger and others by a penlike device. Normally, a template is placed over the touch pad that indicates what function is performed by the computer if the pad is touched in different places. Also, the cursor may be controlled by touching the pad in certain places.

A **light pen** is another touch input device. It is a penlike device that can sense light at its tip. The pen is attached to the computer with a cable. When the person touches the screen with the light pen, the computer can sense where the screen is touched. This type of device is often used to help draw diagrams on the screen.

A final touch input device is a **digitizer tablet**, also called a *graphics tablet*. The user touches the tablet with a pen called a *stylus*. The tablet can sense where it is touched and sends this information to the computer. This device often is used for drawing diagrams and pictures.

Touch input devices have an advantage in that they are used by pointing and touching, an action familiar to users. A disadvantage, however, is that the user must take a hand off the keyboard, and this can slow down the work.

Optical Scanning Input Devices

Some input devices recognize data by scanning symbols or codes with light (sometimes with laser light). The symbols or codes are "read" much like you read data with your eyes. Hence, these devices are called *optical scanning input devices*. These devices are used by users and by computer professionals. Usually, optical scanning input devices are found on minicomputers and mainframe computers, although some are available with microcomputers.

Figure 4–17   Touch Input Devices

(a)   A Touch Screen

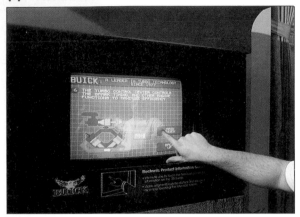

(b)   A Touch Pad

(d)   A Digitizer Tablet

(c)   A Light Pen

One of the most common optical scanning input devices is a **bar code scanner**. This device recognizes a *bar code*, which is a series of bars of different widths (Figure 4–18). The width and placement of the bars represent a code that identifies something. For example, bar codes are used on the outside of packing boxes to give the code number of the item inside the box. Another example of a bar code, discussed in Chapter 1, is the Universal Product Code, or UPC, which is found on grocery merchandise.

Figure 4–18 A Bar Code

Figure 4–19 OCR Characters

ABCDEFGHIJKL
MNOPQRSTUVWXYZ
1234567890
> $ / - # "

Figure 4–20
A Card with a Magnetic Strip

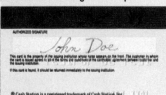

Figure 4–21
MICR Characters

1 2 3 4 5
6 7 8 9 0

A bar code scanner is a device that can recognize the code represented by a bar code. One type, often used with point-of-sales cash registers in department stores, is a hand-held wand, which is passed over the bar code by the user. Another type, used in supermarket checkout counters, is a fixed scanner. The user passes a package or item with the bar code on it past the scanner. In either type, the code is recognized by the scanner and sent to the computer.

An advantage of bar code scanners is that you don't have to enter the code by using a keyboard. As a result, the code is entered into the computer more quickly and more accurately. A disadvantage of these types of devices is that codes must be placed on each item to be scanned.

In addition to bar code scanners, optical scanning input devices are available that can recognize other types of input. One example is an **optical character reader,** or **OCR**. This device recognizes *OCR characters*, which are symbols printed in a special style (Figure 4–19). An optical character reader can recognize the characters printed in this style. As with bar code scanners, an OCR can be hand-held or fixed. The hand-held type is sometimes used with point-of-sales cash registers in department stores.

Another example of an optical scanning input device is a **mark-sense reader**. This device senses marks made on forms such as those used to take multiple-choice tests. A mark-sense reader recognizes where the marks are made on the form and is used often in test-scoring situations.

Finally, there are optical scanners that can sense the image on an entire page. These are called **page scanners**. The user puts a page into the page scanner, which scans the entire page. The page may contain characters or graphic images. The image on the page is sent to the computer by the page scanner.

Magnetic Scanning Input Devices

Another type of scanning input device recognizes magnetic patterns. Data, recorded in a magnetic form, is sensed by a magnetic scanning input device. These devices are mainly found on minicomputers and mainframe computers.

One example of a magnetic scanning input device is a **magnetic strip reader**. This device recognizes data recorded in small magnetic strips that are used on credit, debit, and ATM cards to store the card number, and on some price tags to store the item's price (Figure 4–20). The magnetic strip reader senses the data as the strip is passed through the reader or as it is scanned by a wand. Users who work in stores often use one magnetic strip reader to scan price tags and another to check customer credit cards. Also, an automatic teller machine has a magnetic strip reader that reads the customer's account number from the ATM card.

Some advantages of magnetic strip readers are that few errors are made in entering data and that the data can be entered very quickly. One disadvantage is that the magnetic strip can be easily damaged.

Another example of magnetic scanning is **magnetic-ink–character recognition**, or **MICR**, which is an input technique used in the banking industry to process checks. MICR characters are special characters printed at the bottom of checks (Figure 4–21). These characters indicate the bank, the check number, and the customer's account number. The amount of the check is printed on the check after it is received by the bank.

The check with MICR characters is processed by an *MICR reader-sorter*. This device first magnetizes the characters, then reads the magnetized characters and sends the data to the computer for checking-account processing. The reader-sorter also arranges the checks so that they can be sent to other banks or to the customer. MICR reader-sorters are used with mainframe computers and operated by trained computer personnel.

Voice Input Devices

A type of input that is becoming more common is voice input. In this form of input, the user speaks into a microphone that is attached to the computer (Figure 4–22). Special computer hardware and software are needed to convert the person's voice into a form that the computer can understand—a process called *voice recognition*. This type of input device is available on all types of computers, including microcomputers.

Currently, the main purpose of voice input is to tell the computer what to do. The user speaks words into the computer that cause it to perform various tasks and even to move the cursor. To use this type of input, the computer software first must be *trained* to recognize the user's voice. The training is done by speaking each word several times so that the software can learn how the user says the words. Then, when using the computer, the user must be careful to speak each word in a fashion similar to the way in which the software was trained.

Figure 4–22   Voice Input

One advantage of voice input is that it is the easiest form of communication for most people. A disadvantage is that it currently has limited capabilities.

OTHER OUTPUT DEVICES

This section describes output devices other than the common ones encountered by users. They include high-volume printers, plotters, voice output devices, and computer output microfilm devices.

High-Volume Printers

Printers designed for high volumes of output are used mainly with minicomputers and mainframe computers. These printers require special training to operate and are almost always operated by computer professionals.

Two main types of high-volume printers are used: impact line printers and nonimpact page printers. Serial printers, whether impact or nonimpact, are rarely used for high-volume output because they are too slow. Table 4–2 summarizes the characteristics of the printers described here.

Table 4–2   High-Volume Printer Comparison

Printer	Type	Method	Quality	Speed	Cost
Fully-formed-character	Impact	Line	Draft	to 3,600 lpm	to $100,000
Dot-matrix	Impact	Line	Draft to near-letter	to 900 lpm	to $20,000
Laser	Nonimpact	Page	Near-letter	to 215 ppm	to $375,000

Line Printers.   Line printers use either fully formed character or dot-matrix printing techniques. In fully formed character line printers, a band containing all the characters moves rapidly past the ribbon and paper (Figure 4–23a). As characters on the band pass positions to be printed, hammers in the printer strike the band, causing the character to be printed. The band moves so quickly that it appears as if the entire line is printed at one time. In some printers the characters are on a chain or a drum instead of a band. Dot-matrix line printers print one line of dots across the page at a time. They move down the page, printing lines of dots until characters are formed. Fully formed character line printers, however, are more common than dot-matrix line printers.

Line printers mainly print draft-quality output, although some of the slower, dot-matrix ones can print near–letter-quality output. Fully formed character line printers are probably the most widely used printers on mainframe computers. Figure 4–23b shows a typical line printer.

Page Printers.   High-volume page printers are laser printers that use a similar printing technique to desktop laser printers. The difference is that they are much faster and much more expensive than desktop models. These printers print near–letter-quality output. High-volume page printers are used when large amounts of printed output are needed, such as in a utility company that prints hundreds of thousands of bills each month. Figure 4–24 shows a typical page printer.

Plotters

A **plotter** draws graphic output on paper (Figure 4–25). It uses one or more pens to draw images with ink. This technique is different from that

Figure 4–23   Printing with a Line Printer

(a)   Line Printing

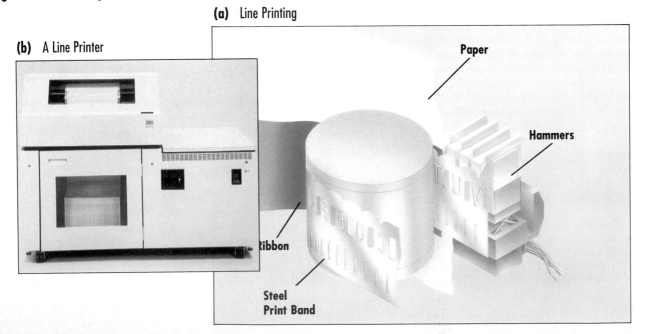

(b)   A Line Printer

Paper

Hammers

Ribbon

Steel
Print Band

Figure 4–24 A Page Printer

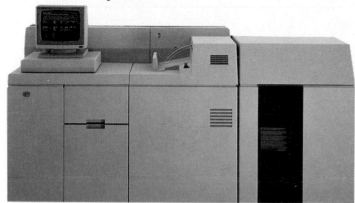

Figure 4–25 A Plotter

of a printer, which produces graphic output by printing dots close together in the pattern of a diagram or chart. In general, a plotter produces better quality graphic output than a printer. Some plotters draw with one color (usually black), and other plotters can draw with several colors. The first type uses only one pen, whereas the second type requires several pens, one for each color.

Plotters vary in the size of output they can produce. Small plotters can plot only on letter-size or slightly larger sheets of paper. These plotters range in price from $700 to $4,000. They are commonly used by users with microcomputers for drawing business graphs and charts. Large plotters can plot on paper as wide as 50 inches. These plotters can cost over $100,000. They usually are found with minicomputers or mainframe computers but may be operated by users or by computer professionals. They are most commonly used for producing engineering and architectural drawings.

Voice Output Devices

A form of output becoming more common is voice output. In this form of output, a human-sounding voice speaks the output to the user through a speaker or earphone. This type of output is available on all types of computers, including microcomputers. An example of voice output is telephone directory assistance. In this system, a human operator takes the request for a telephone number, but the required number is spoken by a computer-generated voice.

Voice output is produced in two ways. One way is for the computer to play stored words over a speaker. The words are stored in a special form in secondary storage and then played back when required. The second way of producing voice output is to create the voice with special computer circuitry, a process called *speech synthesis*. This circuitry is designed so that it can produce signals that sound like a human voice over a speaker. The computer tells the circuitry what words to speak, and the voice is synthesized electronically.

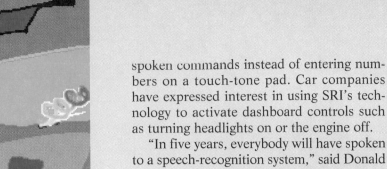

COMPUTERS GAINING A WAY WITH WORDS

In the movie Star Trek IV, chief engineer Montgomery Scott visits the 20th century and is shocked that computers won't respond to his spoken commands. Scotty's problem may be solved soon.

After 40 years of research, computers are finally beginning to understand human speech well enough to respond in a productive way. The machines are years from replacing secretaries and court stenographers, but speech-recognition technology is already appearing in commercial products—and smarter systems are on the way.

SRI International of Menlo Park, California, for example, has developed a prototype airline reservation system that can understand a broad range of spoken questions about air travel. A computer workstation writes the question out and answers it by displaying flight information on the screen.

The nonprofit research and consulting firm hopes such systems eventually will be used by airlines and travel agents. It also is working on language instruction systems that use the same technology, as well as telephone-based banking systems that would allow callers to complete transactions using spoken commands instead of entering numbers on a touch-tone pad. Car companies have expressed interest in using SRI's technology to activate dashboard controls such as turning headlights on or the engine off.

"In five years, everybody will have spoken to a speech-recognition system," said Donald Bell, director of SRI's sensory science and technology center. "If it's done right, they won't have realized it."

"In the past two years we've seen phenomenal progress," added Anita Bounds, president of the San Jose–based American Voice Input/Output Society, a clearinghouse for information in the field.

Among the signs of the times:

- Dragon Systems, based in Newton, Massachusetts, has introduced software and accessories that allow personal computers to take dictation and respond to spoken commands. Its products, priced from $3,100 to $9,000, can understand up to 30,000 words and take down 40 or more words per minute. Customers include the handicapped and journalists with repetitive-strain injuries that prevent them from typing.

- Regional phone companies are introducing voice-activated systems for controlling some operator functions, such as accepting a collect call by answering "yes" in response to a recorded message. In one of the biggest tests so far, Spain's telephone company plans to answer questions about the 1992 Olympics through a system that requires customers to speak numbers (in Spanish) into the phone.

- Computer makers are studying ways to add voice-command systems to make their machines easier to use. Apple Computer, for example, is studying such technologies in a new group under Kai-Fu Lee, a well-known expert in the field from Carnegie-Mellon University. "It seems the natural next step," he said.

Much work remains to be done, however. Understanding the nuances of language, including the differences between speakers' pronunciations and the meaning of similar-sounding words, is a staggeringly complex computing problem.

For example, if someone says "sales are up" the mind of the machine might think of yachting.

To try to solve such problems, researchers developed special software formulas, or algorithms, that break up spoken words into individual sounds and sort them using statistical data about their potential meaning. The progress has accelerated with the introduction of powerful microprocessor chips and workstations that can do the complex calculations quickly and at relatively low cost.

"Speech technology rests on the shoulders of computer technology," said George Doddington, a Texas Instruments expert in the field conducting research at SRI. "We always need more power."

Current speech-recognition systems take shortcuts, and thereby fall short of the industry's ideal—the ability to understand rapid speech by any speaker on any subject.

Dragon's dictation system, for example, requires that users speak slowly, with a definite pause between each word. It is designed for dictation by one person only; users start speaking into the system and gradually teach it their pronunciation by correcting the errors it makes. After eight hours or so of use, the system writes the correct spoken word 95 percent of the time or better, said chief executive Jim Baker.

SRI's system, called Decipher, is good at understanding any user and "connected" speech—with no artificial gaps between words. But the vocabulary totals just 1200 words and the subject matter is limited, making it easier for the system to figure the right meaning of a question from the context, said Hy Murveit, an SRI scientist who helped develop it.

Wearing a headset-microphone, this reporter asked SRI's airline-reservation proto-type simple questions, such as "Show me the flights from Pittsburgh to Philadelphia?" The words as spoken appeared on the workstation screen, along with a translation of the words into a form understood by the system's database. The flight information requested was then displayed.

In a couple of cases, the system made errors in recognizing spoken words. But it nevertheless interpreted the meaning of the question correctly and displayed the right answer.

SRI and other institutions have developed prototype reservation systems as part of research funded by the Defense Advanced Research Projects Agency since 1985. The most advanced DARPA-financed systems now make recognition mistakes just 3.6 percent of the time, down from 20 percent in 1987.

"We've come an enormous distance, yet there is plenty of room for improvement," said Charles Wayne, program manager for DARPA's spoken language system.

The Pentagon wants speech-recognition for several uses. Jet pilots could issue commands to cockpit instruments while their hands and eyes are otherwise engaged. Troops carrying tiny computers could relay written information without keyboards and generals in specially equipped command centers could call up battlefield data without the help of a technician. Speech-recognition also could transcribe intercepted voice communications, though Wayne said that is not a focus for DARPA.

Bell, who has led SRI's speech-recognition effort since 1982, predicts that commercial systems that can recognize speech on limited subjects such as air fares will hit the market soon. SRI is considering spinning off its technology to for-profit companies since its charter bars it from directly making a profit.

Many of the most promising applications involve requesting information over the telephone, such as from banks and brokerage houses. Paradoxically, phone companies may not be quick to replace operators with machines, because of pressure from organized labor and competitors.

"There is an image associated with personal service," noted David Roe, a scientist in Bell Labs speech research department. "It's a question of cutting costs versus company image."

Figure 4–26 Microfilm and a Microfilm Reader

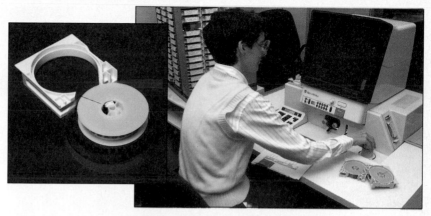

The advantage of voice output over other forms of output is that it is in a form with which humans are most familiar. Voice output, however, is not permanent. Generally, voice output is best for a small amount of output.

Many microcomputers have a speaker that can produce sounds but not voice output. These sounds—beeps, tones, and so forth—are used to alert the user and to play music. This type of output is useful, but it is much less sophisticated than voice output.

Computer Output Microfilm Devices

A technique for saving large volumes of printed output for future reference is called **computer output microfilm** or **COM**. In this technique, the output is miniaturized and put on microfilm, which is a reel of photographic film (Figure 4–26). In the COM device the image of each page to be printed is displayed on a high-resolution screen. A camera takes a small photograph of the image on microfilm. Images of hundreds of pages can be put on each microfilm, thus saving much storage space. Some COM devices use microfiche, which is a sheet of photographic film.

COM devices are used mainly with mainframe computers and are operated by computer professionals. Users, however, may need to read the microfilm pages. This can be done by a microfilm reader that magnifies the image on a screen (Figure 4–26).

DATA PREPARATION DEVICES

Some devices are used to prepare data in a form acceptable to a computer. Data is entered into these devices, which convert the data into a code such as EBCDIC or ASCII. The coded data is stored until it is needed for processing by the computer. Then the data is transferred to the computer.

An example of a data preparation device is a *key-to-disk unit* (Figure 4–27). With this device, a person enters data at a keyboard, and the

Figure 4–27 A Key-to-Disk Unit

Figure 4–28 A Portable Data Preparation Device

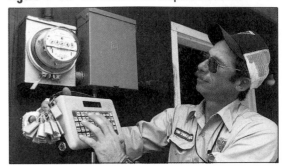

device stores the data on a magnetic disk. Later, the disk can be transferred to the computer, which can access the data on the disk. A *key-to-tape unit* works in a similar way except that the data is stored on a magnetic tape.

Some data preparation devices are portable. These devices use a keyboard, a hand-held scanner, or some other mechanism to enter the data (Figure 4–28). The data is stored in the device and later transferred to the computer. For example, gas company meter readers sometimes use a keyboard-operated device to record gas consumption for each house or business. At the end of the day, data from the device is sent to the computer over the telephone line by using data communications.

ERGONOMICS

As people work with computers more and more, researchers have learned that the design of the hardware can affect how well a person works. **Ergonomics** is the study of how machines should be designed for effective human use. If a machine is poorly designed, the user becomes easily tired, often makes mistakes, and sometimes suffers physical problems such as backaches and eyestrain. A well-designed machine can prevent or at least reduce these problems.

Ergonomics in the area of computer design applies principally to input and output devices. By properly designing these devices, many work-related problems can be reduced or eliminated. Some of the ways that a screen should be designed are as follows:

- A monochrome screen should display output in a green or amber color, which is easier on the eyes.

- The user should be able to adjust the contrast and brightness of the screen.
- The screen should be designed so that glare is minimized.
- The user should be able to rotate and tilt the screen for the best viewing angle.

Some of the ways that a keyboard should be designed are as follows:

- A keyboard should be separate from the screen so that it can be moved to the position most comfortable for the user.
- The user should be able to adjust the angle of the keyboard.
- The keys should have a good "feel" when pressed and should give some indication that they are pressed correctly—for example, by producing a slight clicking sound.
- A separate numeric keypad and separate cursor control keys should be provided.

Similar sorts of guidelines apply to other I/O devices.

In addition to the design of the hardware, other aspects of the work environment should follow a good ergonomic design:

- There should be adequate lighting that the user can adjust.
- The table upon which the keyboard and screen are placed should be at an appropriate height. The keyboard should be at a slightly lower height than a standard table; the screen should be at eye level or slightly below.
- The chair that the user sits on should be adjustable in height and should provide good back support.

These and other ergonomic factors can improve how effectively a person works with a computer.

Chapter Summary

- Common microcomputer input devices are keyboards and a mouse. A keyboard has keys for letters, digits, and special symbols, as well as other keys such as Shift keys, a Backspace key, an Enter or Return key, and a Control key. A keyboard may have a **numeric keypad**, **cursor control keys**, and **function keys**. A **mouse** is a small device with one or more buttons on top, which is rolled on a table top to move the **cursor** on the screen and to select tasks for the computer to do. Common microcomputer output devices are screens and desktop printers. A screen can display characters or **graphic output** by forming the symbols or images out of many dots. Screens may be either **CRTs** or **flat panel screens**. Desktop printers may be **impact** or **nonimpact printers**, **serial** or **page printers** (rarely **line printers**), and **letter-**, **draft-**, or **near–letter-quality printers**. **Fully-formed-character** and **dot-matrix printers** are common types of impact printers. **Laser**, **ink-jet**, and **thermal printers** are common types of nonimpact printers.

- A **video display terminal** (**VDT**) is a combination of a keyboard and a screen used as an I/O device for a minicomputer or a mainframe computer.

- Some other types of input devices are touch input devices (**touch screens**, **touch pads**, **light pens**, and **digitizer tablets**), optical scanning input devices (**bar code scanners**, **optical character readers**, **mark-sense readers**, and **page scanners**), magnetic scanning input devices (**magnetic strip readers** and **MICR** devices), and voice input devices.

- Some other types of output devices are high-volume printers (line printers and page printers), **plotters**, voice output devices, and **computer output microfilm** (**COM**) devices.

- A key-to-disk unit is a data preparation device that records keyed data on a magnetic disk. A key-to-tape unit records keyed data on a magnetic tape. A portable data preparation device allows data to be keyed or scanned away from a computer and later transferred to the computer.

- **Ergonomics** is the study of how machines should be designed for effective human use. Good ergonomic design of computer hardware is important so that users will become less tired, make fewer mistakes, and not suffer physical problems because of using the computer.

Terms to Remember

Bar Code Scanner　p. 96

Computer Output Microfilm
　(COM)　p. 105

CRT　p. 86

Cursor　p. 80

Cursor Control Key　p. 80

Digitizer Tablet　p. 95

Dot-Matrix Printer　p. 90

Draft-Quality Printer　p. 89

Ergonomics　p. 106

Flat Panel Screen　p. 88

Font　p. 92

Fully-Formed-Character
　Printer　p. 89

Function Key　p. 81

Graphic Output　p. 86

Impact Printer　p. 88

Ink-Jet Printer　p. 92

Laser Printer　p. 91

Letter-Quality Printer　p. 89

Light Pen　p. 95

Line Printer　p. 89

Magnetic Ink Character
　Recognition (MICR)　p. 98

Magnetic Strip Reader　p. 98

Mark-Sense Reader　p. 97

Monitor　p. 87

Mouse　p. 81

Near–Letter Quality Printer
　p. 89

Nonimpact Printer　p. 89

Numeric Keypad　p. 80

Review Questions

Fill-In Questions

1. The mark on a screen that indicates where the next output will be displayed or where the next input will be entered is the _____.

2. An alternative to a mouse is a(n) _____.

3. Character and graphic output are formed by patterns of _____ on a screen.

4. Two types of screens are _____ and _____.

5. The speed of serial printers is measured in _____. The speed of line printers is measured in _____. The speed of page printers is measured in _____.

6. A(n) _____ prints each character by striking a ribbon and the paper with an element shaped like a character. A(n) _____ prints each character by striking a ribbon and the paper with a group of wires.

7. A type of nonimpact desktop page printer is a(n) _____.

8. The type style that a printer uses is called a(n) _____.

9. A printer is connected to the CPU of a microcomputer by plugging the printer's cable into a socket called a(n) _____.

10. A device for recognizing the Universal Product Code, or UPC, on grocery merchandise is a(n) _____.

11. A device that can sense the image on an entire page is a(n) _____.

12. The technique used by banks to process checks is _____.

13. A(n) _____ is a device for drawing graphic output on paper.

14. A technique for saving printed output on microfilm is _____.

Short-Answer Questions

1. What are some of the special-purpose keys found on a computer keyboard?

2. What determines the purpose of each function key on a keyboard?

3. What are the two purposes of a mouse?

4. What is meant by screen resolution?

5. What is the difference between impact and nonimpact printers?

6. What are the three types of printers in order from poorest- to best-quality print?

7. What is a video display terminal, and what is it used for?

8. Name three touch input devices.

9. What are the two main types of high-volume printers?

10. What are two ways that voice output can be produced?

11. How is a data preparation device used?

12. Why is it important to have good ergonomic design of computer hardware?

Projects

1. If you are using a computer for a class or have access to a computer, find out everything you can about the computer's input and output devices. What special keys are on the keyboard? Is a mouse available, and how is it used? What other input devices are available? What type of screen is used, and what are its characteristics (e.g., resolution)? What type of printer is available, and what are its characteristics (e.g., speed)? What other output devices are available?

2. New types of input and output devices are continually being developed. Identify as many I/O devices as you can, other than those described in the chapter. Write a brief summary of how each device is used.

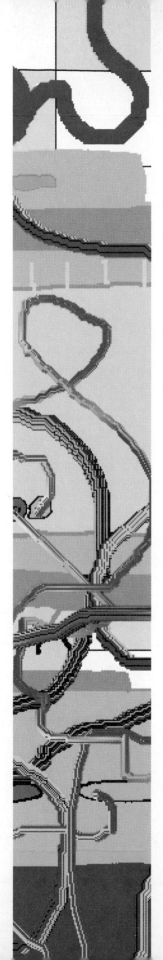

5

SECONDARY STORAGE

CHAPTER OBJECTIVES

• After completing this chapter you should be able to:

1. Give two reasons why secondary storage is used.

2. Describe the organization of data in secondary storage.

3. Explain how data is recorded on a magnetic disk and how data is stored and retrieved by a disk drive.

4. Distinguish between sequential access and random access.

5. Explain how data is recorded on a magnetic tape and how data is stored and retrieved by a tape drive.

6. Explain how data is recorded on two types of optical disks.

7. Describe three types of file organization and state what form of secondary storage and what type of access can be used with each.

T HE SECONDARY STORAGE component of a computer stores data not currently being processed and program instructions not currently being executed. As you know, this type of storage is different from primary storage, which stores data and instructions being processed at the time by the computer. There are several types of secondary storage. Two types—magnetic disk and magnetic tape—were introduced in Chapter 2. There is more to know about each of these, however, and there are other types of secondary storage. This chapter explains what you need to know about secondary storage.

THE NEED FOR SECONDARY STORAGE

Why is secondary storage used to store data and programs? Why isn't everything stored in primary storage? There are two answers to these questions: permanency and cost.

As you saw in Chapter 3, primary storage is volatile, which means that when the power to the computer is turned off, everything stored in primary storage is lost. If lost data or programs are needed again, they must be reentered. Secondary storage, however, is nonvolatile. Any data or programs stored in secondary storage stays there, even with the computer's power turned off, unless someone purposely erases them. Thus, secondary storage is a permanent form of storage.

Permanency is not the only reason to use secondary storage. The other reason is that it costs less than primary storage. Because it is less expensive, you can have a lot of secondary storage for the price of a little primary storage. In fact, computers usually have just enough primary storage for the data and programs they need to process at one time, and plenty of secondary storage for all other data and programs.

The reason secondary storage is less costly than primary storage has to do with speed. As you know, the computer transfers data and instructions between primary storage and the CPU. These transfers take place constantly, and hence primary storage must be designed so that the transfers can be done rapidly. Similarly, the computer transfers data and instructions between secondary storage and primary storage. These transfers do not have to be done as rapidly as those between primary storage and the CPU because they do not happen as often. As noted in Chapter 3, computers transfer data between primary storage and the CPU in nanoseconds (billionths of a second). Transfers to and from secondary storage take milliseconds (thousandths of a second), which is considerably slower than nanoseconds (Figure 5–1). In general, slower speed in a computer is less expensive than faster speed. Therefore, secondary storage is less expensive than primary storage.

Figure 5–1   Data Transfer Speeds

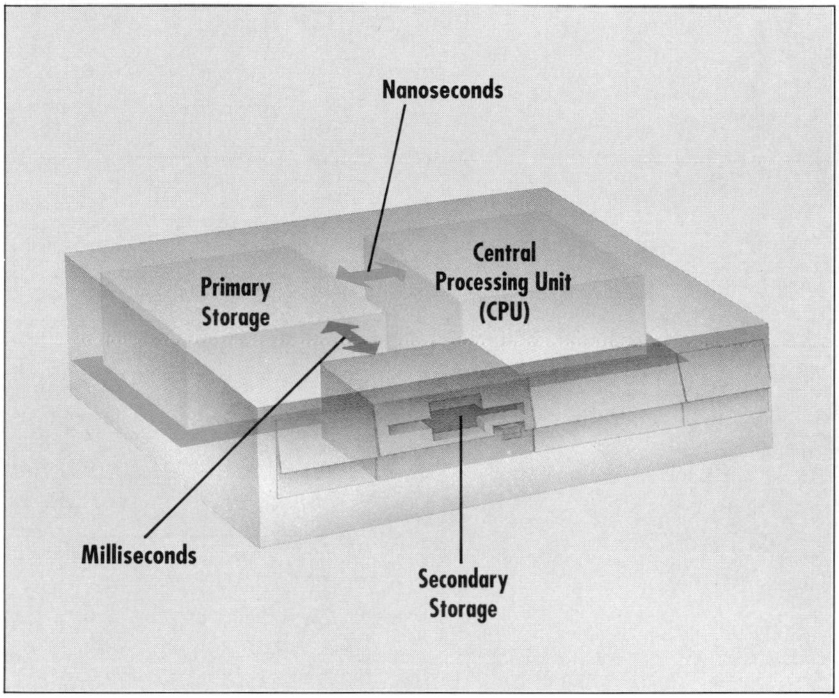

DATA IN SECONDARY STORAGE

As you know, both data and programs are stored in secondary storage. In this chapter, however, we are interested mainly in the storage of data. To be easy to process, data must be properly organized. Figure 5–2 shows the way data is organized in secondary storage.

At the most basic level, data is composed of **characters**—that is, letters, digits, and special symbols. A blank space is also a character and is often important in computer data processing.

Although a single character can represent data, groups of characters are more often used. A group of related characters, representing some piece of information, is called a **field**. For example, a person's name is a field; it is a group of characters that conveys specific information. A social security number is also a field, as are a person's address, pay rate, and age. A field usually contains several characters but can consist of a single character. For example, a one-character code field can be used to represent a person's marital status (M stands for *married*, S for *single*).

Fields are grouped together to provide information about a single entity such as a person or an event. Such a group of related fields is called a **record**. For example, all the fields containing payroll information about a single employee (such as the employee's name, address, social security number, and pay rate) form an employee payroll record.

Figure 5–2   Data Organization in Secondary Storage

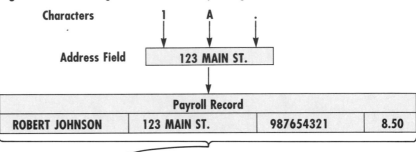

Characters

Address Field

123 MAIN ST.

Payroll Record			
ROBERT JOHNSON	123 MAIN ST.	987654321	8.50

Payroll File			
ROBERT JOHNSON	123 MAIN ST.	987654321	8.50
MARY JONES	876 SOUTH ST.	135792468	11.00
SUSAN ANDREWS	55 FIRST AVE.	564738291	7.25
JAMES MILLER	4567 BAY ST.	293847560	10.75

Employee Database

Payroll Data			
ROBERT JOHNSON	123 MAIN ST.	987654321	8.50
MARY JONES	876 SOUTH ST.	135792468	11.00
SUSAN ANDREWS	55 FIRST AVE.	564738291	7.25
JAMES MILLER	4567 BAY ST.	293847560	10.75

Job Skill Data	
ROBERT JOHNSON	CARPENTER
MARY JONES	PROGRAMMER
SUSAN ANDREWS	DRIVER
JAMES MILLER	OPERATOR

Work History Data		
ROBERT JOHNSON	1/23/84	LOS ANGELES
MARY JONES	5/19/86	BOSTON
SUSAN ANDREWS	11/26/84	SAN FRANCISCO
JAMES MILLER	8/5/85	HOUSTON

All the records that are used together for one purpose are called a **data file**, or simply a **file**.[1] For example, all the employee payroll records for a business make up the employee payroll file. The file contains one record for each employee in the business.

Finally, related groups of data, such as related files, can be combined to form a **database**. For example, an employee database may contain employee payroll data, employee job skill data, and employee work history data. All these data are related because they contain information about employees who work for the same business, and therefore they form a database of employee information.

To summarize, data is composed of characters. A group of related characters is a field. A record is a group of related fields, and a file is a group of related records. Finally, related groups of data form a database.

MAGNETIC DISK STORAGE

The most widely used form of secondary storage is magnetic disk. Disk technology was developed in the 1950s, but it has undergone many improvements over the years. Today it is available on all types of computers from microcomputers to supercomputers.

Magnetic Disk

A magnetic disk is a flat, round platter (like a phonograph record) made of metal or plastic and covered with a metallic coating, which can be magnetized at different spots. You probably remember that a magnet has a north end and a south end. When a spot on a disk is magnetized, imagine that a magnet is placed there. The magnet may be aligned with the north end up or with the south end up. To store data on the disk, let one way of aligning the magnet (north end up) represent the digit 1 and the other way (south end up) represent the digit 0. Thus, each spot of magnetism represents a binary digit or bit on the surface of the disk.

Millions of bits (magnets) can be recorded on the disk. The bits are organized into concentric circles called **tracks** (Figure 5–3). Think of the tracks as being like the grooves of a record except that they do not spiral in. The number of tracks on the surfaces of disks vary with different types of disks; some have as few as 40 while others have more than 500 tracks.

The bits along tracks are grouped to form bytes in the same way that the bits in primary storage form bytes. Each byte stores the code for one character of data in either ASCII or EBCDIC. The same code that is used in primary storage, however, is also used in secondary storage.

The number of bytes in a track varies with different types of disks. The capacity of a disk depends on the number of bytes per track and

---

[1]As noted in Chapter 2, the term *file* is used to refer to any collection of related items stored in secondary storage. The term *data file* is used for a collection of related data organized into records. Most people, however, commonly use the term *file* when they mean a *data file*.

Figure 5–3 Tracks on a Magnetic Disk

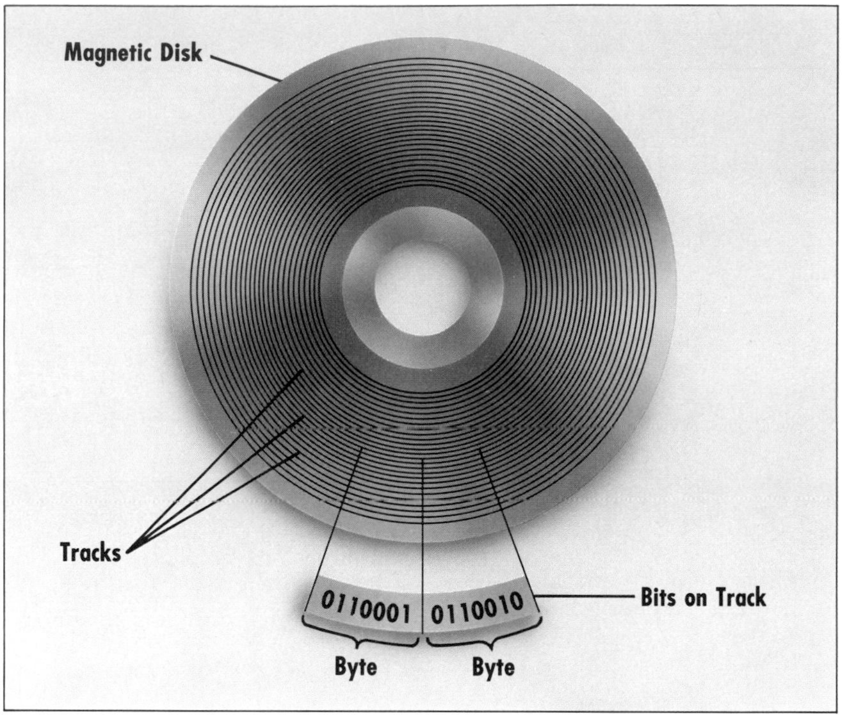

the number of tracks. Some disks can store only a few hundred thousand bytes. For example, the disk used with some microcomputers can store 360K bytes (360,000 bytes). Some disks can store millions of bytes. Many mainframe computers have disks that can store 300M bytes (300 million bytes) to over 1G byte (one billion bytes).

Data may not be compatible between computers because different codes are used to store data on a disk. For example, if data is stored in ASCII on the disk of one computer, it cannot be used with another computer that stores data in EBCDIC unless the data is converted to EBCDIC. This problem of compatibility can be a serious hindrance for a user who wants to use data from one computer on another, incompatible computer.

Because data is stored magnetically on a disk, the data remains on the disk even when the power to the computer is turned off. This characteristic explains why data is permanent on a disk, unlike data in primary storage. The data may be changed, however. If the magnetic spots are realigned, the bits will change and new data will be stored. This can be done purposely by the computer, but it can also be done inadvertently. For example, if a strong magnet is brought near a disk, the bits on the disk can change. Thus, one of the rules about handling disks is to never get them too close to a magnet.

Disks come in various forms and sizes (Figure 5–4). **Floppy disks** are made of flexible plastic with a metallic coating, and can be 3½ or 5¼ inches in diameter. (An 8-inch size is rarely seen today.) A 3½-inch disk

Figure 5–4   Magnetic Disks

(a)   Floppy Disks

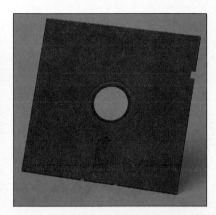

(b)   Hard Disks

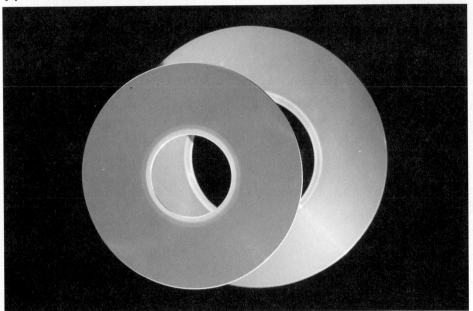

is enclosed in a plastic jacket to protect it, and a 5¼-inch floppy disk comes in a paper jacket. **Hard disks** are made of a nonflexible material such as aluminum, and range in size from 3½ to 14 inches in diameter. Hard disks are enclosed in protective plastic cases. Sometimes a single hard disk is used, and at other times several disks are stacked on top of each other with space between the disks. This latter arrangement is called a **disk pack** (Figure 5–5). Some disk packs contain more than ten disks.

Usually both sides of a disk are used to record data. With floppy disks you sometimes hear about "single-sided" disks, which allow data to be recorded on only one side, but they are rarely used today. Normally with a disk pack, both sides of all disks are used. Thus, a disk pack with ten disks has 20 surfaces on which data can be recorded.

COMPUTER CLOSE-UP

5-1

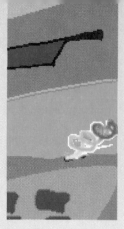

HANDLING FLOPPY DISKS:
SOME DOs AND DON'Ts

DOS

- ■ • Insert the disk carefully into the disk drive.
- • Store the disk in its protective envelope.
- • Write on the disk label with a felt tip pen only.
- ■ • Keep the disk away from magnets and magnetized objects such as telephones.
- ■ • Keep the disk out of direct sunlight and away from high heat.

DON'TS

- ■ • Do not touch the surface of the disk.
- • Do not bend the disk.
- • Do not use a paper clip on the disk.
- • Do not put heavy objects on the disk.
- ■ • Do not use an eraser on the disk.

• Applies to 5¼" disks.
■ Applies to 3½" disks.

Figure 5–5   A Disk Pack

Figure 5–6   Disk Drives
(a)   A Floppy Disk Drive

(b)   A Hard Disk Drive

Disk Drives

A magnetic disk is the medium on which data is stored. To use the disk, however, it must be in a disk drive (Figure 5–6). This device both stores data on a disk and retrieves data from a disk. The disk drive rotates the disk at a speed ranging from 300 to 6,000 revolutions per minute, depending on the type of disk. While the disk rotates, an *access arm* comes out of the side of the disk drive. At the end of the access arm is a *read/write head* (Figure 5–7). The access arm can position the read/write head over any track on the disk. As the disk rotates, data can be stored on the track by sending electronic signals to the read/write head. That is, the read/write head can *write* data on the disk. Similarly, as the disk rotates, the data stored on a track can be retrieved by the read/write head. That is, the read/write head can *read* data from the disk. When data is written on a disk, any data in the same place is destroyed. When data is read from a disk, however, the data is not destroyed.

A disk drive has one access arm and read/write head for each side of a disk that is used to store data (Figure 5–8). The arms move back and

Figure 5–7   Magnetic Disk in a Disk Drive

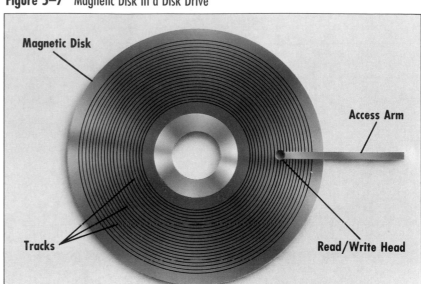

Figure 5–8   Access Arms, Read/Write Heads, and Disks

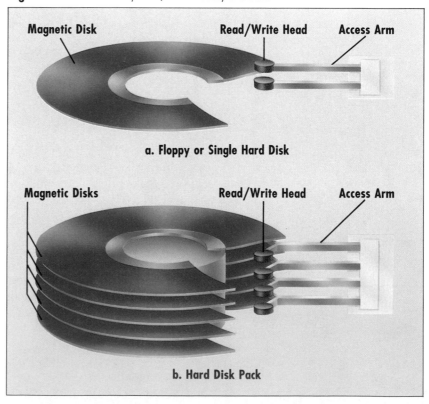

Figure 5–9 Contaminants on a Disk Surface

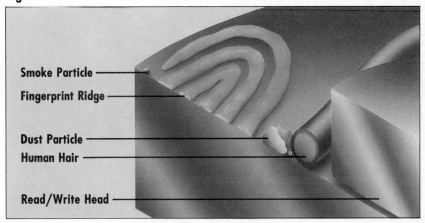

Smoke Particle

Fingerprint Ridge

Dust Particle

Human Hair

Read/Write Head

forth in unison, and both sides of each disk can be read from or written on. On a floppy disk the read/write heads touch the surface of the disk, whereas with a hard disk the heads do not touch the surface but ride on a cushion of air very close to the surface. Sometimes you hear about a *head crash*, which is what happens when a read/write head accidentally touches the surface of a hard disk, causing damage to the head and the disk.

Floppy disks can always be removed from the disk drive, but hard disks may be removable or nonremovable. An advantage of removable disks is that they allow unlimited storage capacity; if you use all the space on a disk, you just remove it and insert another disk. Nonremovable disks, which are sometimes called *Winchester disks*, have the advantages of being more reliable, faster at transferring data, and greater in storage capacity. They are more reliable because they are enclosed in a case with filtered air that contains few contaminants. With a removable disk, a human hair, a dust particle, a smoke particle, or another contaminant can cause damage to the disk (Figure 5–9). Nonremovable disks are faster at transferring data because they rotate faster than removable disks. Finally, they have greater storage capacity because they can store more bits on a disk.

Disk Data Storage

As you know, data in secondary storage is stored in files. A file consists of many records. Each record has many fields, and each field consists of one or more characters. On magnetic disk, each byte on a track stores one character (Figure 5–10). The bytes are grouped to form fields. All the fields in a record are grouped together on a track. One record is stored after another along a track, and each track can hold several records. When a track is full, another track is used.

Floppy disks and many hard disks are organized into **sectors**. A sector is a section of track. For example, Figure 5–11 shows a disk in which each track contains six sectors. The number of sectors in a track

Figure 5–10 Disk Data Storage

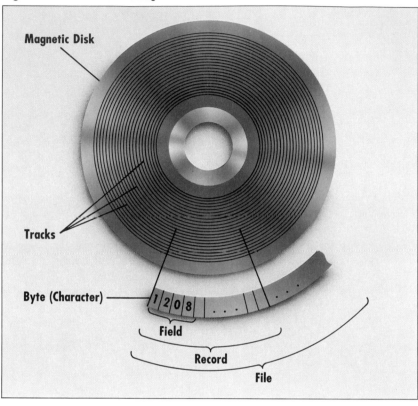

varies with different types of disks. Each record is stored in a separate sector. Once all the sectors on a track are full, the next track is used.

Before a disk can be used, the tracks and sectors must be marked on the disk. This process is called **formatting the disk**. It is done by a special computer program that comes with the computer. Formatting each disk has to be done only once, but all disks, floppy or hard, must be formatted before they can be used. Some disks are preformatted by the manufacturer, but most disks require the user to do the formatting.

Disk Data Access

Data is read or written on a disk one record at a time. To write a record on a disk, instructions in a computer program tell the computer to send the data for the record from primary storage to the disk. Any data in the space where the record is written is destroyed when new data is written on the disk. To read a record from a disk, program instructions tell the computer to bring the data in the record from the disk into primary storage. When data in a record is read, the original data in that record on the disk is not destroyed.

When the disk drive reads or writes a record in a file, the drive can position the read/write head at the first track of the file and read or write the data in sequence, one record at a time, moving the read/write head

Figure 5–11 Sectors

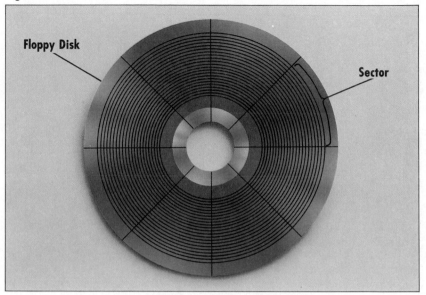

from track to track. This method is called **sequential access** because the disk drive goes through the records in the file in sequence (Figure 5–12a). It is also possible for the disk drive to move the read/write head to any track in a file, and read or write a specific record on that track without going through other records in the file. This method is called **random access** or **direct access**. The records in the file are read or written in random order by moving the read/write head forward and backward to any track in the file (Figure 5–12b).

The speed at which disk data can be accessed depends on three factors. The first is the amount of time it takes to move the read/write heads to the desired track. This time is called the *head movement time* or *seek time*, and it is the slowest of the three factors. The second factor is the amount of time it takes for the disk to rotate until the desired record is under the read/write head. This time is called the *rotational delay* or *latency*. The final factor is the amount of time it takes to read or write the record. This time is called the *data transfer time*, and it depends on how many bytes are in the record. The sum of the three factors is the total time it takes to read or write a record. This sum can be as fast as a one-hundredth of a second and as slow as several seconds.

Disk Compatibility

Not all disks can be used with all computers. There are three factors that determine disk compatibility. The first is the type and size of disk. A 5¼-inch floppy disk is not compatible with a 5¼-inch hard disk. A nonremovable 3½-inch hard disk is not compatible with a removable 14-inch disk pack. The second factor is the format. The number and location of tracks on the disk varies. Some disks are formatted into sectors, and some are not. Even the number of sectors varies. As a result, two disks of the

Figure 5–12 Disk Data Access

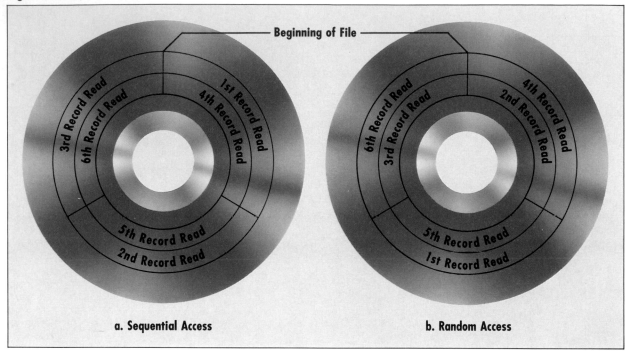

a. Sequential Access   b. Random Access

same type and size—such as two 5¼-inch floppy disks—may not be compatible. The last factor is the code used to store data, which can be ASCII or EBCDIC. All these factors must be considered in determining disk compatibility.

Disk Usage

Magnetic disk is the main form of secondary storage on most computers because it enables large volumes of data to be stored or retrieved rapidly. In addition, data may be accessed randomly or sequentially. Because of these characteristics many computers use magnetic disk as their sole form of secondary storage.

Microcomputers usually have one or two floppy disk drives. In addition, a microcomputer may have a nonremovable hard disk. Larger computers usually have one or more removable hard disks. Some mainframe computers have dozens of hard disk drives. Some minicomputers and mainframe computers also have nonremovable hard disks.

MAGNETIC TAPE STORAGE

The next most widely used form of secondary storage after magnetic disk is magnetic tape. Tape technology was developed before disk technology. Today, however, it is not as common as magnetic disk. Although tape can be used on all types of computers including microcomputers, it is most commonly found on minicomputers and mainframe computers.

Figure 5–13 Tracks on a Magnetic Tape

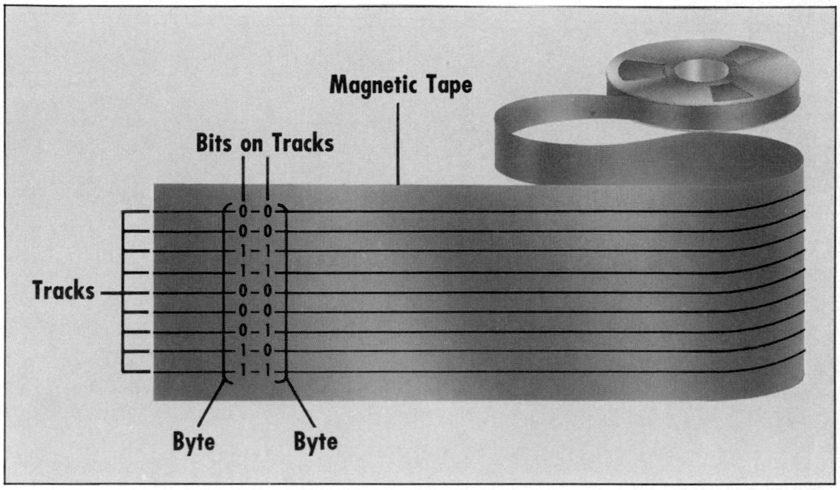

Magnetic Tape

The magnetic tape used with computers is similar to audio recording tape. It is made of a plastic material covered with a metallic coating, which can be magnetized at different spots. The spots of magnetism are like those on a magnetic disk; you can think of each spot as a magnet aligned with the north end up, representing the digit 1, or the south end up, representing the digit 0. Thus each spot represents a bit on the surface of the tape.

The bits on a tape are organized into lines called tracks (Figure 5–13). The number of tracks on tape varies, but 9-track tape is the most common. Bytes are stored on the tape by recording one bit of the byte in each track across the tape. Each byte stores the code for one character in either ASCII or EBCDIC, depending upon the computer. Although these codes require fewer than nine bits, 9-track tape is still used. With ASCII (a 7-bit code) the extra tracks record a parity bit, which is used to check for errors in the other bits, and an additional bit for special codes. With EBCDIC (an 8-bit code) the extra track records a parity bit.

The capacity of a tape is measured in terms of the number of bytes that can be stored, and depends on the *tape density* and the length of the tape. Tape density is measured in *bytes per inch*, or *bpi*. Common tape densities are 800, 1600, and 6250 bpi. Tape length ranges from 200 to 2,400 feet. With these figures you can determine the capacity of different tapes. For example, a 2,400-feet, 6,250-byte tape has a capacity of 180 million bytes (2,400 feet x 12 inches per foot x 6,250 bytes per inch). Note that, unlike disks, only one side of the tape is used to store data.

The problem of data compatibility that exists with magnetic disk also occurs with magnetic tape. If data is stored in one code on the tape of one computer, it cannot be used with another computer that stores data in another code unless the data is converted to the other code.

Figure 5–14   Open-Reel and Cartridge Tapes

As with magnetic disk, data stored on a tape remains there when the power to the computer is turned off, because the data is stored magnetically. The data can be changed, however, by changing the magnetic spots on the tape and thus changing the bits that are stored.

Tapes come in various forms and sizes (Figure 5–14). The most common is open-reel tape, which is ½-inch wide and usually comes on reels that are 10½ inches in diameter. Cartridge tape that is ¼-inch wide is also used.

Tape Drives

A magnetic tape is the medium on which data is stored. To use the tape, however, it must be in a tape drive (Figure 5–15). This device is used both to store data on a tape and to retrieve data from the tape. In the tape drive, the tape is fed from a supply reel, past a mechanism that includes a *read/write head*, and onto a take-up reel (Figure 5–16). As the tape moves, data can be stored on the tape by sending electronic signals to the read/write head. That is, the read/write head can *write* data on the tape. Similarly, as the tape moves, data stored on the tape can be retrieved by the read/write head. That is, the read/write head can *read* data from the tape. As with disks, writing data destroys existing data, but reading data does not.

Magnetic tape can always be removed from the tape drive. Thus, tape provides unlimited storage capacity. When a tape is full, it can be removed and replaced by another tape. Some organizations have thousands of tapes in a *tape library*.

Tape Data Storage

Data is stored in files on tape just as it is stored in files on disks. Each byte on the tape stores one character (Figure 5–17). The bytes are grouped to form fields, and all the fields in a record are grouped together on the tape. One record is stored after another along the tape.

Tape does not move continuously through the tape drive. Rather, the tape stops moving after each record and starts up again for the next

Figure 5–15 A Tape Drive

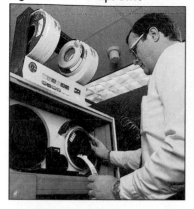

Figure 5–16 Magnetic Tape in a Tape Drive

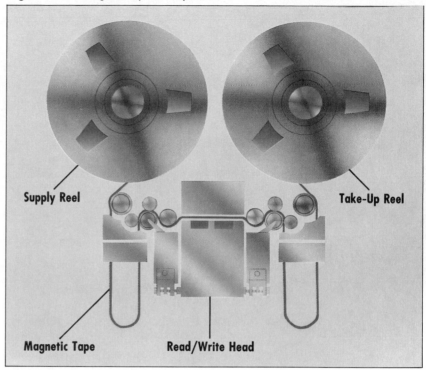

record. To provide space for the tape to stop and start, a gap of about 0.6 inches is left between each record. This gap is called an *interblock gap,* or *IBG.*

Tape Data Access

Data is read or written on a tape one record at a time. To write a record on a tape, program instructions tell the computer to send the data for the record from primary storage to the tape. To read a record from a tape, program instructions tell the computer to bring the data in the record from the tape into primary storage.

When reading or writing the records in a file, the tape drive starts with the first record in the file and reads or writes the records in sequence. As with magnetic disk, this method is called *sequential access* (Figure 5–18). It is not possible to go forward without reading or writing records along the way, and it is not possible to go backward. Thus, unlike magnetic disks, records in a tape file cannot be accessed in random order.

The speed at which tape data can be accessed depends on where in the file the data is located. For example, accessing the first record in a file is much faster than accessing the last record, because to access the last record all previous records must be accessed. The average time to access a record is the time it takes to access *one-half* of the records. Thus, if a tape file contains ten thousand records, the average access time is the time it takes to access five thousand records. Depending on the tape drive, this time can be up to several minutes.

Figure 5–17 Tape Data Storage

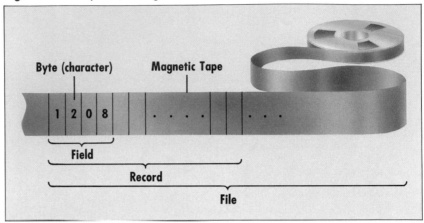

Tape Compatibility

As with disks, not all tapes can be used with all computers. Again, there are three factors that determine compatibility. The first is the type of the tape. An open-reel tape is not compatible with a cartridge tape. The second factor is the tape density. An 800 bpi tape cannot be used with a tape drive that is designed for 6,250 bpi tapes. Thus, even the same types of tape may not be compatible. The last factor is the code—ASCII or EBCDIC—used to store data. All these factors must be considered in determining tape compatibility.

Tape Usage

Only rarely is magnetic tape used as the main form of secondary storage on a computer. Tape data can only be accessed sequentially, and usually a computer needs to access data randomly. Hence, tape is not often used by itself but rather is used along with magnetic disk. Tape is much less expensive, however, than disk, so when data needs only to be accessed sequentially, tape may be used. Tape is also used for storing copies of disk data or other tape data, called **backup copies**, in case the data is lost or destroyed.

Figure 5–18 Sequential Access of Tape Data

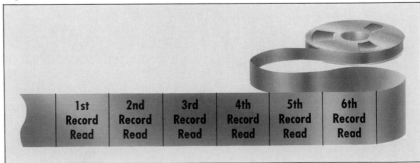

Open-reel tape is used mainly with minicomputers and mainframe computers. A large mainframe computer may have several tape drives, but a minicomputer may have only one. Cartridge tape is used on all sizes of computers. It is popular with microcomputers for making backup copies of disk data.

Mass Storage

One problem with magnetic tape is that, once processing of a tape is finished, a person must change the tape in the tape drive, which can take considerable time. An alternative is a **mass storage system**, which stores data on thousands of magnetic tapes that can be changed mechanically. In one type of mass storage system, each tape is contained in a cartridge and there is space for 9,440 tape cartridges (Figure 5–19). Each tape can store about 50 M bytes of data, so the total capacity of the system is 472,000 M bytes or 472 G bytes.

To access the data on a tape, a mechanical arm locates the required cartridge and inserts it into a special tape drive. This process is much faster than having a person find the tape and put it into the tape drive. In addition, the data on the tape in the cartridge is transferred to magnetic disk, making access to the data even faster. The storage capacity of the tape in a cartridge is not as great as that of a regular magnetic tape, but the total capacity of all the tapes in the mass storage system is much greater. Mass storage is used when very large volumes of data need to be quickly available to the computer. These systems are used only with large mainframe computers.

OPTICAL DISK STORAGE

In addition to magnetic disk and tape, other forms of secondary storage are used. One that is becoming increasingly common is optical disk storage, which comes in several forms.

Optical Disk

An **optical disk** is a round platter on which small holes are used to store data (Figure 5–20a). Each hole represents the binary digit 1; the absence of a hole represents the binary digit 0. Thus, the surface of the disk is covered with bits that are organized to represent data in the same way as bits on a disk or tape. This system of storing data is similar to that used for storing music on audio compact disks (CDs).

To record data on an optical disk, the disk is put into an **optical disk drive** (Figure 5–20b). In the drive, a laser burns the holes into the disk's surface as the disk turns. Data can be recorded only once because there is no way of erasing the holes after they are burned into the disk. To retrieve data from the disk, another laser is used to sense the holes on the disk's surface. The data may be accessed sequentially or randomly and can be retrieved as many times as needed.

Figure 5–19   A Mass Storage System

Optical disks come in several sizes, from over 12 inches in diameter to less than 5 inches across. The latter are called **compact disks** or **CDs**. The capacity of optical disks is very large because the bits can be placed very close together. For example, CDs can store more than 500 M bytes of data.

Most optical disk drives for compact disks can only retrieve—that is, read data from disks. This type is called a **CD-ROM** system, which stands for *Compact Disk–Read Only Memory*. The disks used for CD-ROM must be purchased with prerecorded data. This system can be used to gain access to generally available data such as a computerized encyclopedia or census data. CD-ROM is used mainly with microcomputers.

Some optical disk drives can store—that is, write data once and read the data many times. This type is called a *WORM* system, which stands for *Write Once, Read Many*. This system can be used to store data that is not likely to change in the future, such as old business records. Once the data is stored, it can be retrieved repeatedly. WORM systems are found on all sizes of computers.

Figure 5–20 Optical Disk Storage

(a) An Optical Disk

(b) An Optical Disk Drive

Erasable Optical Disk

Another type of optical disk, called an **erasable optical disk**, is also available. An erasable optical disk actually stores data in a magnetic form, like a magnetic disk. Because the data is stored magnetically, it can be erased and changed.

To record data, an erasable optical disk drive uses a laser beam and a magnet. The laser beam heats the spot on the disk where a bit is to be recorded, which makes the spot easier to magnetize. The magnet then magnetizes the spot in a 1 or 0 pattern. Any spot can be changed to a different pattern by repeating the process. To retrieve data from the disk, another laser beam is reflected off the spot. The pattern of light that is reflected depends on whether the spot is a 1 or a 0. Because an erasable optical disk uses both magnetic and laser (optical) techniques, it is sometimes called a *magneto-optical*, or *MO, disk*.

FILE ORGANIZATION

Secondary storage, whether it is disk, tape, or some other form, stores files of data.[2] To process data in a file in secondary storage, the records in the file must be accessed, which can be accomplished only if the data is properly organized. This section describes how files are organized in secondary storage.

To illustrate file organization, consider a file of inventory data for a bicycle business. Inventory is the stock of goods that a business has on hand. A business that sells bicycles has an inventory consisting of a

---

[2]Databases can be used also to store data in secondary storage. Database processing is discussed in later chapters.

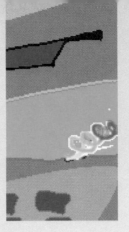

MOLECULES LIGHT UP PATH TO ENHANCED OPTICAL STORAGE

Does anyone really want to know that the Internal Revenue Service is looking into new technologies that will make it easier to store tax records and retrieve information come tax reporting time?

Probably not, but researchers at the Department of Energy's Oak Ridge National Laboratory (ORNL) said they have come up with a way to cram more data onto optical disks—a technology that the IRS, among others, is particularly interested in, they said.

The new optical data storage method would enable the IRS to store a year's worth of completed tax returns using just half of the available storage space on a 12-in. optical disk. It now takes 150,000 reel-to-reel 9-track tapes to store an equivalent amount of information, according to Guven Yalcintas, director of technology applications at ORNL.

In addition to packing more data onto a disk, the technology, developed by Tuan Vo-Dinh, a scientist in the health and safety research division of ORNL, can also be used to devise disks with security features that would make them difficult to read or copy without authorization.

The research lab's technology, called Surface-Enhanced Raman Optical Data Storage (SERODS), is based on the principle that the enhanced light-emitting properties of molecules embedded in an optical medium can be altered to store information. When they are close to a rough metal surface, certain molecules emit a strongly enhanced light, called Raman light, which is a characteristic of their vibrations. This emission is called the surface-enhanced Raman effect.

Conventional optical disks store data in the form of microscopic pits that have been burned by laser into a reflective aluminum disk. In playback, another type of laser reads the stored data by distinguishing between the laser light scattered by the pits and that which is reflected by the areas between them.

A SERODS optical disk contains a substrate of silver-coated microparticles and an "optical layer." Currently, the optical layer is being constructed of silver molecules, but other materials may be used in the future. Like standard optical disks, SERODS disks are recorded and played back by lasers.

The interactions between optical-layer molecules and the substrate are modified by the laser, changing their light-emitting properties, so that they are encoded to store information as bits. A laser and signal detector, tuned to the frequency of the Raman emissions, are used to retrieve the information.

Theoretically, the SERODS storage technology could be used to make disks or even three-dimensional blocks of transparent material with 10,000 times more capacity than current optical disks, researchers said.

Sensitive or classified data can be stored and protected from snoops, who would have to be able to tune the detector to the exact frequencies of the Raman emissions.

ORNL has filed for a patent on the technology. The government-funded lab intends to license it to commercial vendors.

stock of bicycles. Each type of good stocked is called an item in the inventory. Thus, for a bicycle business, each type of bicycle represents an inventory item. An inventory file contains data about the items stocked. Each item is identified by an item number. The business needs to keep track of each item's number, description, unit cost (how much the item costs the business to purchase or manufacture), unit price (how much the business sells the item for), and quantity on hand. The data is stored in an inventory file with one record for each item. Figure 5–21 shows a list of the records in the file. Each line in this figure is a record. Each record contains fields for the item number, item description, unit cost, unit price, and quantity on hand.

The records in a file should be identified in some way, usually by including a field that uniquely determines the record. Such a field is called a **key field**, or simply a **key**. In the inventory records, the key field is the item number. Each record in the inventory file has a different value in its key field. Then, if the value of the key field is given, the corresponding record can be located in the file.

Key fields are usually numeric code fields. Thus, item number, customer number, social security number, and similar fields are used as key fields. The reason numbers and not names or descriptions are used for key fields is that numbers usually are unique. Name and description fields, although easier to remember, are often duplicated in a file and thus cannot be used as key fields.

The way a file is organized determines how a key field is used to locate a record in a file. There are three main file organizations: sequential file organization, direct file organization, and indexed file organization. A file organized in one of these ways is called a sequential file, a direct file, or an indexed file, respectively. Each organization method has its uses, advantages, and disadvantages.

Figure 5–21   An Inventory File

ITEM NUMBER	ITEM DESCRIPTION	UNIT COST	UNIT PRICE	QUANTITY ON HAND
1208	RACING BICYCLE	205.50	259.95	25
2501	TOURING BICYCLE	184.00	239.95	8
2905	RECREATION BICYCLE	76.25	109.95	41
3504	MOUNTAIN BIKE	188.75	229.95	6
4360	TRICYCLE	51.50	69.95	32
4389	TANDEM BICYCLE	256.00	340.50	12
5124	JUNIOR BICYCLE	69.75	99.95	0
5908	LEARNER BICYCLE	62.00	89.95	17
6531	PORTABLE BICYCLE	112.50	179.95	2

Sequential File Organization

In a **sequential file**, the records are organized in sequence, one after the other in the order in which they are stored in the file. The first record stored in the file is the first record in sequence, the second record stored is the second record in sequence, and so on. For example, Figure 5–22 shows the inventory file stored as a sequential file. Records in this figure have been numbered in the order in which they appear in the file. Each record immediately follows the preceding record. (On magnetic disk the records would be stored one after the other along the tracks on the disk surface: see Figure 5–10. On magnetic tape the records would be stored one after the other along the tape's surface: see Figure 5–17.)

The records in a sequential file can be retrieved only in the order in which they are stored. The computer must first retrieve record number 1, then record number 2, and so on. It is not possible to retrieve records in a sequential file in any other order. Thus, a sequential file can only be accessed sequentially, never randomly.

The key field in the records in a sequential file identifies which record was retrieved. When the computer retrieves a record, it simply gets the next record in sequence, not a record with a particular key field value. Once a record has been retrieved, the computer can examine the value of the key field in that record to see exactly which record it is. The records in a sequential file are often arranged in increasing sequence by key field to make locating records easier.

A sequential file can be stored on magnetic disk, magnetic tape, and other types of secondary storage. If stored on disk, it must be accessed sequentially even though disk storage allows random access. Only sequential access can be used with magnetic tape, and a sequential file stored on tape is accessed sequentially.

Figure 5–22   A Sequential Inventory File

RECORD NUMBER					
1	1208	**RACING BICYCLE**	205.50	259.95	25
2	2501	**TOURING BICYCLE**	184.00	239.95	8
3	2905	**RECREATION BICYCLE**	76.25	109.95	41
4	3504	**MOUNTAIN BIKE**	188.75	229.95	6
5	4360	**TRICYCLE**	51.50	69.95	32
6	4389	**TANDEM BICYCLE**	256.00	340.50	12
7	5124	**JUNIOR BICYCLE**	69.75	99.95	0
8	5908	**LEARNER BICYCLE**	62.00	89.95	17
9	6531	**PORTABLE BICYCLE**	112.50	179.95	2

Direct File Organization

In a **direct file**, which is also called a **random file**, the records are not necessarily stored in sequence. For example, the first record stored may be the eighth record in the file, the second record stored may be the first record in the file, and the third record stored may be the fifth record in the file. Figure 5–23 shows part of the inventory file stored as a direct file. Again, records are numbered in this figure. Notice that some of the spaces for records in the file have no data in them, a common characteristic of direct files.

Where a record is stored in a direct file is determined directly from the value of the record's key field. Many different methods are used to determine where a record is stored. For the inventory file, the computer uses the last two digits of the item number (the key field) as the record number where the item's record is stored. Thus, the record for item 1208 is stored as record number 8, the record for item 2501 is stored as record number 1, and so on.

One problem with direct files is that they can waste storage space. For example, using the method for storing records just discussed, the computer would need spaces for 100 records to account for all the possible values of the last two digits of the key (00 through 99). If there are only 40 records with data in the file, however, most spaces for records would have no data, which is why there are spaces with no data in Figure 5–23. Another problem with this method is that two different keys may give the same record number. For example, 1208 and 5908 both produce record number 8 when using the method described here. Resolving this type of problem requires a complex computer program.

A computer can access records in a direct file randomly. Given the value of the key field, the computer can use the previously mentioned method to find the number of the corresponding record. Thus, if you want the data for item 1208, the computer would determine that the data is found at record number 8. Then, the computer would retrieve

Figure 5–23   A Direct Inventory File

RECORD NUMBER					
1	2501	TOURING BICYCLE	184.00	239.95	8
2					
3					
4	3504	MOUNTAIN BIKE	188.75	229.95	6
5	2905	RECREATION BICYCLE	76.25	109.95	41
6					
7					
8	1208	RACING BICYCLE	205.50	259.95	25
9					

the record at that number directly. In so doing, the computer does not have to go through the other records in the file in sequence.

Although the records in a direct file can be accessed randomly, it may be difficult to access them sequentially. Because the file may have spaces for records with no data, a complex program is required to skip these spaces when accessing the records in the order in which they are stored.

Because the records in a random file are accessed randomly, a random file can be stored only on magnetic disk (or some other form of secondary storage that allows random access). It is not possible to store such a file on magnetic tape, because random access cannot be used with tape.

Indexed File Organization

An **indexed file**, which is also called an **indexed sequential file**, is actually two files: a data file and an index file. The *data file* is organized as a sequential file with records in increasing order by key field. The *index file*, or simply the *index*, is a file that has one record for each record in the data file. Each record in the index file contains the value of the key field of a record in the data file plus the number of that record in the file.

Figure 5–24 illustrates the idea of an indexed file. In the example, the inventory file is stored as a sequential file. The records in the file are in increasing order by key field, which is the item number. The index contains the key field and the number of the corresponding record for each record in the data file.

The records in an indexed file can be accessed either sequentially or randomly. For sequential access, the computer retrieves the records in the data file one at a time in the order in which they are stored. The index is not used for sequential access. To access the records randomly, the computer locates the key field of the desired record in the index, which can be done rapidly because the index is small. Then, the corresponding record number in the index indicates where the record is stored in the

Figure 5–24 An Indexed Inventory File

Index file		Data file					
KEY FIELD	RECORD NUMBER	RECORD NUMBER					
1208	1	1	1208	RACING BICYCLE	205.50	259.95	25
2501	2	2	2501	TOURING BICYCLE	184.00	239.95	8
2905	3	3	2905	RECREATION BICYCLE	76.25	109.95	41
3504	4	4	3504	MOUNTAIN BIKE	188.75	229.95	6
4360	5	5	4360	TRICYCLE	51.50	69.95	32
4389	6	6	4389	TANDEM BICYCLE	256.00	340.50	12
5124	7	7	5124	JUNIOR BICYCLE	69.75	99.95	0
5908	8	8	5908	LEARNER BICYCLE	62.00	89.95	17
6531	9	9	6531	PORTABLE BICYCLE	112.50	179.95	2

data file. The computer retrieves the record directly without retrieving any other records in the data file. (This process is like using an index of a book to locate a subject without reading the entire book.)

An indexed file can be stored only on magnetic disk (or some other type of secondary storage that allows random access). Because the records in an indexed file can be accessed randomly, it is not possible to store such a file on magnetic tape.

Comparison of File Organizations

Table 5–1 compares the three types of file organizations. This comparison is based on access speed, storage utilization, and program complexity.

Access speed refers to how quickly records can be accessed in the file. The speed depends on whether sequential access or random access is used. A sequential file can be accessed sequentially the fastest, and a direct file can be accessed randomly the fastest. An indexed file is slower than a sequential file for sequential access and slower than a direct file for random access. Storage utilization has to do with how much secondary storage space is needed beyond that required for the records in the file. A sequential file uses little or no extra space, but a direct file can use a lot of extra storage because there may be many unused spaces for records in the file. An indexed file requires some extra storage for the index. Finally, program complexity refers to how complex the programs are that process a file and thus how difficult they are to prepare. Programs for sequential file processing are relatively simple, but direct file processing programs can be very complex. Indexed file processing programs fall in between.

You can see from Table 5–1 that each file organization has its advantages and disadvantages. Sequential files are usually used when only sequential access is needed. They are the least expensive in this situation because they can be processed the fastest, they use the least amount of secondary storage space, and they are the simplest to prepare programs for. Files for payroll processing are normally sequential files.

When very fast random access is needed, direct files are often used. They can be expensive because they use a lot of secondary storage space and require complex programs. But if fast random access is important, their use is called for. Direct files are often used to rapidly

Table 5–1.   File Organization Comparison

| File organization | Access speed | | Storage utilization | Program complexity |
	Sequential	Random		
Sequential	Fastest	Slowest*	Best	Simplest
Direct	Slowest*	Fastest	Worst	Most complex
Indexed	In between	In between	In between	In between

*Sequential access of a direct file and random access of a sequential file are not possible. With a complex computer program, however, these processes can appear to be done.

look up information. When bank tellers use terminals to look up customer account data, the files they use are often direct files.

Indexed files are used when both sequential access and random access are needed. They are a compromise between the two other file organizations, but the compromise is often necessary. Their cost is between that of the other two forms of files. An inventory file may be an indexed file. Inventory data can then be accessed sequentially or randomly.

Chapter Summary

- Secondary storage is used because, unlike primary storage, data and programs can be stored permanently in it, and it costs less than primary storage.

- Data in secondary storage is composed of **characters**—that is, letters, digits, and special symbols. A group of related characters, representing some piece of information, is called a **field**. A **record** is a group of related fields, and a **data file**, or simply a **file**, is a group of related records. Sometimes related groups of data are combined to form a **database**.

- Data is recorded on a magnetic disk by spots of magnetism representing bits. The bits are grouped to form bytes, which are recorded along concentric circles on the disk's surface called **tracks**. A disk drive stores data on a disk by moving the read/write head at the end of the access arm to the appropriate track, and writing the data on the track as the disk rotates. A disk drive retrieves data from a disk by moving the read/write head to the appropriate track and reading the data recorded there as the disk rotates.

- **Sequential access** is the process of reading or writing records in a file in sequence—that is, in the order in which the records are stored. **Random access** is the process of reading or writing records in a file in any (random) order.

- Data is recorded on magnetic tape by spots of magnetism representing bits. The bits are recorded along lines on the tape's surface called **tracks**. A group of bits across the tracks of the tape forms a byte. A tape drive stores data on a tape by moving the tape past a read/write head and writing the data on the tape. A tape drive retrieves data from a tape by moving the tape past a read/write head and reading the data recorded on the tape.

- Data is recorded on one type of **optical disk** storage by small holes that represent bits. The holes are created by a laser. Once the data is recorded, it cannot be changed because the holes cannot be erased. With **erasable optical disk**, data is recorded by spots of magnetism that represent bits. A laser and a magnet are used together to record the data. Because the data is stored magnetically, it can be changed.

■ In a **sequential file** the records are organized in sequence, one after the other in the order in which they are stored in the file. A sequential file can be stored on tape or on disk, but may only be accessed sequentially. In a **direct file**, the records are stored at locations determined directly from each record's key field. A direct file can be stored only on disk (or on some other random access device) and may only be accessed randomly. An **indexed file** consists of two files: a sequential data file and an index file or index. The index contains the key field and the location of each record in the data file. An indexed file can be stored only on disk (or on some other random access device), but it can be accessed sequentially or randomly.

Terms to Remember

Backup Copy   p. 128

CD-ROM   p. 130

Character   p. 113

Compact Disk (CD)   p. 130

Database   p. 115

Direct (Random) File   p. 135

Disk Pack   p. 117

Erasable Optical Disk   p. 131

Field   p. 113

File (Data File)   p. 115

Floppy Disk   p. 116

Format a Disk   p. 122

Hard Disk   p. 117

Indexed (Indexed Sequential) File   p. 136

Key Field   p. 133

Mass Storage System   p. 129

Optical Disk   p. 129

Optical Disk Drive   p. 129

Random (Direct) Access   p. 123

Record   p. 113

Sector   p. 121

Sequential Access   p. 123

Sequential File   p. 134

Track   p. 115

Review Questions

Fill-In Questions

1. Concentric circles of bits on a disk are called _____.
2. Flexible plastic disks are called _____, and nonflexible disks are called _____.
3. Several disks stacked on top of each other with space between them is a(n) _____.
4. A section of a track on a disk is a(n) _____.
5. Records in a magnetic disk file can be accessed _____ or _____.
6. Records in a magnetic tape file can only be accessed _____.
7. A copy of disk or tape data that is kept in case the data is lost or destroyed is called a(n) _____.
8. A type of secondary storage consisting of thousands of magnetic tapes that can be accessed mechanically is a(n) _____.

9. A type of secondary storage on which data is stored and retrieved using a laser is _____.

10. A field that uniquely identifies a record in a file is called a(n) _____.

11. A(n) _____ file can be stored on disk or tape, but a(n) _____ file and a(n) _____ file can be stored only on disk.

12. The best type of file organization to use when only sequential access is needed is _____.

13. The best type of file organization to use when very fast random access is needed is _____.

14. The best type of file organization to use when records need to be accessed sequentially and randomly is _____.

Short-Answer Questions

1. What are two reasons secondary storage is used?

2. Explain the differences between fields, records, and files.

3. How is data recorded on a magnetic disk?

4. How does a disk drive store and retrieve data on a magnetic disk?

5. Give one advantage of removable disks and three advantages of nonremovable disks.

6. What is meant by formatting a disk?

7. What is the difference between sequential access and random access?

8. Give three reasons why disks may not be compatible.

9. How is data recorded on a magnetic tape?

10. What is the capacity of a 1600 bpi tape that is 1200 feet long?

11. How does a tape drive store and retrieve data on a magnetic tape?

12. Can data on an optical disk be changed? Explain.

13. Why are key fields usually numeric code fields rather than names or descriptions?

14. Explain the differences in the organization of a sequential file, a direct file, and an indexed file.

Projects

1. If you are using a computer for a class or have access to a computer, find out everything you can about the computer's secondary storage. What type of magnetic disk is available? What is its capacity? What type of magnetic tape is available? What is its density? What other types of secondary storage are available?

2. New types of secondary storage are continually being developed, and existing forms are constantly being improved. Identify as many new or improved forms of secondary storage as you can. Write a brief summary of each, and explain why each is better than existing forms.

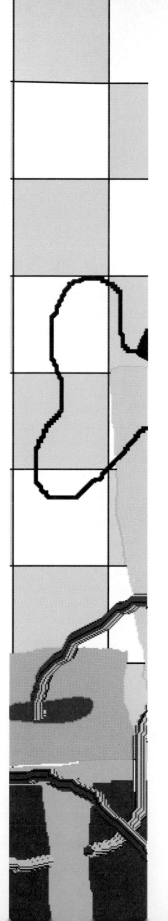

6

DATA COMMUNICATIONS

CHAPTER OBJECTIVES

• After completing this chapter you should be able to:

1. Describe the main characteristics of communications channels.

2. Describe the function of a modem and list several other channel interface units.

3. Describe the main functions of communications software.

4. List the communications hardware and software needs for terminal, micro-to-micro, and micro-to-mainframe communications.

5. Explain the difference between local area networks and wide area networks, and list the microcomputer communications hardware and software needs for each.

COMPUTERS and their components, such as I/O devices and secondary storage, need to communicate with each other. When the hardware is nearby, communication takes place over cables. Longer-distance communication, however, requires other techniques that fall into the area of data communications. This chapter explains what you need to know about data communications.

DATA COMMUNICATIONS FOR THE USER

Users need data communications in several situations (Figure 6–1). The first is when an I/O device operated by the user needs to communicate with a distant computer. Often, the I/O device is a terminal through which the user enters input into the computer and receives output from the computer. Data communications is needed in this situation to transmit data between the I/O device and the computer.

The second data communications situation encountered by users involves two computers communicating with each other. The user, at one computer, needs to transmit data to and from the other computer. The user's computer is almost always a microcomputer, but the other computer may be a microcomputer or a larger computer. When both computers are microcomputers, the situation is called *micro-to-micro communications*. When a microcomputer and a larger computer are involved, the situation is called *micro-to-mainframe communications*.

The last situation in which users need data communications involves sharing computer resources among several users. Often, some resources—such as high-volume printers, large-capacity disk drives, or high-speed computers—are available to many users. Each user has a terminal or a computer, which is usually a microcomputer. These user devices are connected in a network to the shared resources. Data communications is needed in this situation to transmit data to and from the shared resources over the network.

COMMUNICATIONS HARDWARE

For data communications you need special hardware that allows the computer devices to communicate over long distances. Two main types of hardware are needed (Figure 6–2). First is a **communications channel**, which is the link over which data is sent. An example of a medium that is used for a communications channel is a telephone line, but you will see later that there are other media used for channels. Second are *channel interface units*, which connect computer devices to channels. There are several types of interface units, as you will see.

Figure 6–1 Data Communications Situations

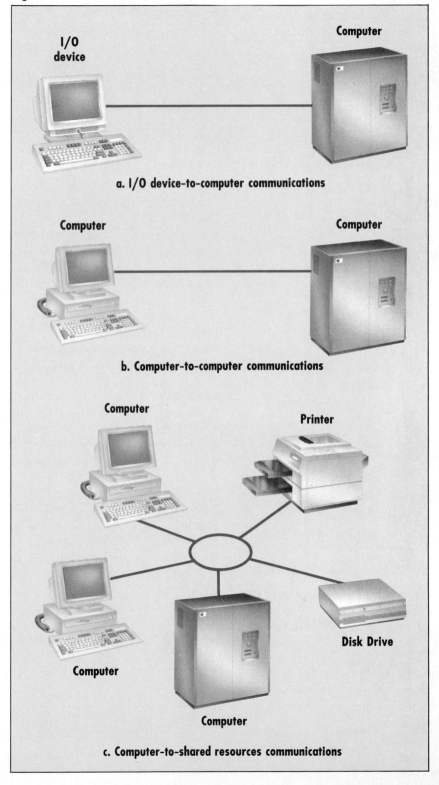

a. I/O device-to-computer communications

b. Computer-to-computer communications

c. Computer-to-shared resources communications

Figure 6–2 Data Communications Hardware

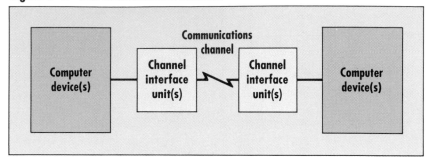

Communications Channel Characteristics

A communications channel is the link over which data is transmitted when using data communications. Different media are used for channels, but before discussing these media, we need to examine the general characteristics of channels. Data is transmitted over a channel as bits; one bit is sent after the other over the channel (Figure 6–3). The bits are grouped to form bytes that represent characters using ASCII, EBCDIC, or some other code. The way in which the bits are sent determines four characteristics of the channel: signal type, data rate, data flow, and transmission method.

Signal Type. Bits can be sent over a channel as either a **digital signal** or an **analog signal** (Figure 6–4). A digital signal is one that transmits bits as high and low pulses. In a digital signal, a high pulse represents a 1 bit and a low pulse represents a 0 bit. An analog signal, however, transmits data by a wave pattern that varies continuously. A human voice is an analog signal because it varies continuously from high to low.

Some channels can transmit only digital signals, and some can transmit only analog signals. A computer uses digital signals to send data between its components. Thus, a computer can transmit data over a digital channel without changing the signal type. A telephone line is an analog channel. To transmit computer data over a telephone line, the data must be converted from a digital to an analog form, a process that will be discussed later.

Figure 6–3 Sending Bits over a Communication Channel

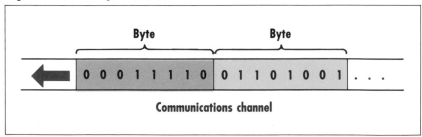

Figure 6–4   Signal Types

(a) A Digital Signal

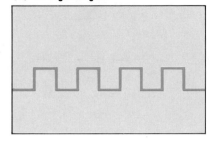

(b) An Analog Signal

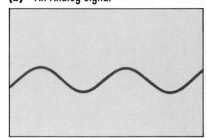

Data Rate.   Data rate has to do with how fast the bits can be sent over the channel. The rate is measured in *bits per second,* or *bps*. Each type of channel has a maximum data rate. Some slow-speed channels, called *narrowband channels*, can only transmit fewer than 300 bps. Medium-speed channels can transmit up to 9600 bps. These are called *voiceband channels* because they are the type that are used for telephone lines; thus, they carry voice communications. High-speed channels, called *wideband channels*, can transmit 50,000,000 bps or more. Note that it is always possible to transmit at a slower rate than the maximum allowed by the channel.

Sometimes the term **baud rate** is used to express the data rate. For example, someone might say he or she is transmitting at "1200 baud," meaning 1200 bps. This term is not exactly correct, however. *Baud rate* refers to the number of times per second that the signal on a channel changes—for example, in changing from a high to a low pulse. Depending on the channel, each signal change can represent one, two, or more bits. If the channel is such that each signal change represents one bit, the baud rate and bps are the same. But if the channel is such that each signal change represents more than one bit, then the baud rate will be less than the bps. Hence, baud rate and bps may or may not be the same. To be safe, the data rate should always be stated in bps.

Because data is transmitted on a channel in a code, each character requires a certain number of bits (seven bits for ASCII, eight bits for EBCDIC). As you will see later when we discuss transmission method, other bits are sent with the code for each character. As a rough rule of thumb, you can assume that each character requires ten bits. Hence, you can estimate the data rate in characters per second by dividing the bits per second by ten. For example, a 1200 bps channel can transmit approximately 120 characters per second.

Data Flow.   The direction that data can flow in a channel can vary (Figure 6–5). With **simplex transmission**, data can flow only in one direction. In a **half-duplex transmission**, data can flow in both directions but in only one direction at a time. With a **full-duplex transmission**, data can flow in both directions simultaneously.

Simplex transmission is rarely used today. An example of its use is for transmission to a stock-quotation terminal that receives only data. Half- and full-duplex transmissions are used for most data communications.

Figure 6–5 Data Flow in Channels

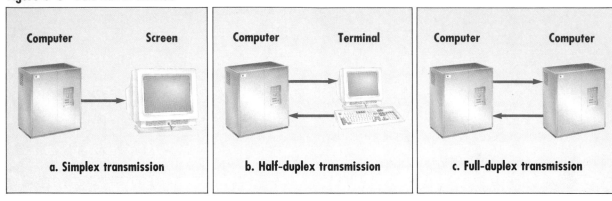

a. Simplex transmission

b. Half-duplex transmission

c. Full-duplex transmission

In some situations full-duplex is faster than half-duplex. When a person is communicating with a computer through a terminal, however, the difference between half- and full-duplex is not significant. For transferring large volumes of data between computers, full-duplex may be better.

Transmission Method.   Two methods are used to transmit characters on a channel: asynchronous transmission and synchronous transmission (Figure 6–6). In **asynchronous transmission**, one character is sent at a time. A solid stream of 1 bits is sent between characters. When a character is going to be transmitted, a 0 start bit is sent. Then, the bits in the code for the character are sent, followed by a 1 or 0 parity bit, which is used to check for errors in the other bits. Following this bit comes a 1 stop bit to signal the end of the character transmission and the beginning of the stream of 1 bits between characters.

In **synchronous transmission**, the codes for several hundred characters are sent together in a block, rather than one character at a time as in asynchronous transmission. In addition, start, stop, or parity bits are

Figure 6–6 Transmission Methods

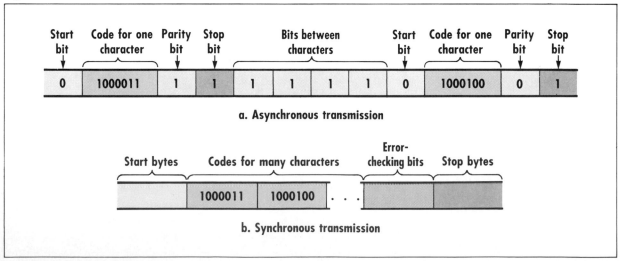

a. Asynchronous transmission

b. Synchronous transmission

not provided for each character. Instead, a group of start bytes are sent before the block, a group of error-checking bits follows the characters in the block, and a group of stop bytes comes at the end.

Asynchronous transmission requires less expensive equipment than synchronous transmission. The latter, however, is faster for sending large amounts of data. For human communications with a computer, which usually involves only small amounts of data, the asynchronous method is less expensive and usually satisfactory. For communications that involves transferring large amounts of data, however, the synchronous method is the preferred technique.

Communications Channel Media

Different media can be used for communications channels. In fact, a channel may consist of several different media connected in sequence. The choice of the media affects the speed and the cost of communications. This section describes some of the common media used for communications channels.

Wire Cables.   Wire cables are the oldest media used for electronic communications. They have been used since the first telegraph machines in the 1800s. Data is transmitted over a wire cable by sending an electrical signal along the wire. Today, two main forms of wire cables are used for data communications: twisted-pair wiring and coaxial cable.

Twisted-pair wiring consists of two wires twisted together. Most telephone lines use this medium for local voice communications, but it can also be used for data communications. It is relatively inexpensive, but its data transmission rate is slow compared to other media (up to 80,000 bps). *Coaxial cable* consists of copper wire heavily insulated with rubber and plaster. It is the type of cable used with cable television systems. It is more expensive than twisted-pair wiring but can transmit data at a much greater rate (up to 50,000,000 bps).

Fiber-Optic Cables.   An alternative to wire cable is *fiber-optic cable* (Figure 6–7). A fiber-optic cable consists of bundles of glass or plastic fibers. Each fiber is 1/2000" thick—about the size of a human hair. Data is transmitted by a laser that pulses light through the fiber. Each pulse represents a bit, so data is transmitted in a digital form. The laser can pulse about one billion times per second, meaning data can be transmitted at about one billion bps, a very fast rate. For long-distance communications, fiber-optic cables are less expensive than wire cables.

Most telephone companies use fiber-optic cables for some voice communications. Because a voice is an analog signal, the voice must be converted to digital form (bits) for transmission over a fiber-optic cable and then converted back to analog form at the receiving end. Computer communication using fiber optics, however, does not require conversion because computer signals are already in digital form.

Microwave Systems.   *Microwaves* are special types of radio signals that are sent through the air from one microwave antenna to the next. Microwave transmission is "line-of-sight," which means that there must be

Figure 6–7 Fiber-Optic Cables

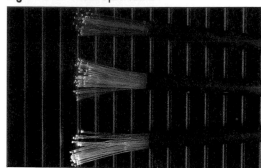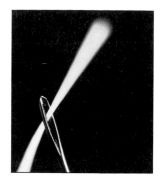

nothing between the antennas. (Microwaves cannot bend around objects.) Both voice and data can be transmitted by microwaves. Microwave systems are very expensive, but they do not require direct cables, and they can transmit data very rapidly (up to 45,000,000 bps).

Two types of microwave systems are used (Figure 6–8). The first is a land-based system, in which data is sent from one microwave antenna to the next. Because microwave transmission is line-of-sight and because of the curvature of the earth, land-based microwave antennas must be no more than about 30 miles apart. The second type of microwave system is satellite-based. In this system, data is sent from an earth microwave antenna up to a satellite and then down to another earth antenna. The satellite is about 22,300 miles in space. At that altitude, the satellite revolves around the earth at the same velocity as the earth rotates, so it appears to be in a fixed position in the sky. Satellite-based microwave systems can transmit data over a much greater distance than land-based systems.

Communications Channel Sources

Communications channels are provided in two main ways. One is by purchasing and installing the necessary hardware, which forms a *private communications system*. The other is by purchasing time on hardware owned by another company, which is called a *public communications system*.

Any organization can purchase the necessary hardware to set up a private communications system. When the communication is limited to a small geographic area, this approach is common. For long-distance communications, private systems are rare. Stringing long-distance wire or fiber-optic cables, setting up a system of microwave antennas, or launching a satellite is very expensive. Such expense is warranted only when the organization has significant communication needs.

Most organizations use public communications systems for long-distance communications. These systems are called *public* because anyone who is willing to pay the fee can use them. The main public system is the telephone network, which is owned by many companies called *common carriers*. Local telephone companies (such as Pacific Bell in California) handle short-distance communications. Long-distance communications is handled by other companies such as AT&T, U.S. Sprint, and MCI.

Figure 6–8 Microwave Systems

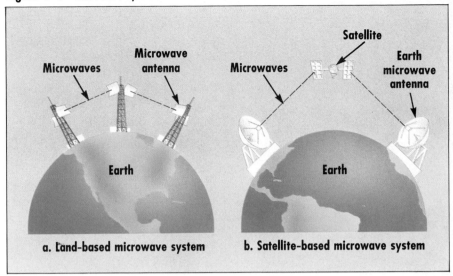

a. Land-based microwave system   b. Satellite-based microwave system

When using the telephone network, two types of telephone lines are available. The first is **switched** or **dial-up lines**, which are the standard lines used by any telephone customer for everyday telephone calls. Using these lines, any number can be called from any other number. Each time a call is placed, a different line may be used. The other type of line is a **leased** or **dedicated line**, which is used only by the customer who leases it. A leased line can be *conditioned*, which improves its quality so that data can be transmitted faster and more accurately over it.

Channel Interface Units

Usually you cannot connect computer devices directly to a channel. Rather, you need special units between the channel and the computer. These channel interface units allow the computer devices to send and receive data over the channel.

Modems.   Computers transmit data using digital signals. If a communications channel is a digital channel, the computer can send data over the channel without changing its signal type. If an analog channel is used, however, the digital signals from the computer must be converted to analog form for transmission, a process called *modulation*. The analog data, when it reaches the other end of the channel, must be converted back to digital form, which is called *demodulation*. Modulation and demodulation are performed by a device called a **modem**, which means MOdulator-DEModulator. There must be a modem at each end of the channel—one to modulate the signal and one to demodulate it (Figure 6–9). Because the most common source of analog communication channels is the telephone network, most modems are designed to connect computer devices to telephone lines and to modulate and demodulate signals sent over those lines.

In addition to providing conversion between digital and analog signals for a channel, modems determine other characteristics of the channel. First, the modem sets the data rate of the transmission. Modems can be purchased with different data rates: 300 bps, 1200 bps, 2400 bps, and even higher. In general, the faster the modem, the more expensive it is. The speed of the modem must be less than or equal to the maximum speed allowed by the channel. Second, the modem determines the data flow: half-duplex or full-duplex. (Simplex is rare.) Most modems can be switched between half-duplex and full-duplex either by a switch on the modem or by special software. Finally, the modem determines whether the transmission is asynchronous or synchronous. Modems can be purchased for either method; usually synchronous modems are more expensive than asynchronous modems. Note that the characteristics of the modems at both ends of the channel must match; that is, they must both use the same data rate, data flow, and transmission method.

A modem can be either internal or external. An *internal modem* is housed in the computer, usually on a circuit board. An *external modem* (Figure 6–10) is housed in a separate case and connected to the computer by a cable plugged into a port. (See Chapter 4 for a discussion of ports.) Whether internal or external, a modem is connected to a telephone line with a modular plug. (An older type of modem is connected to the telephone line by placing the telephone handset in a device called an *acoustical coupler*. Signals are then sent through the telephone mouthpiece and received through the earphone.)

Communications Control Units. Two computer devices may be connected over a channel with no other devices sharing the channel, an arrangement called a *point-to-point configuration*. An alternative is to have several computer devices share a channel. For example, several terminals could communicate with a computer over a channel at the same time. This arrangement is called a *multipoint* or *multidrop configuration*.

To create a multipoint configuration, special **communications control units** are needed. These units control the communications traffic over channels much like traffic police control auto traffic on city streets. For example, when several terminals share a channel, a device is needed to keep the communications from getting mixed up.

Figure 6–9 Use of Modems

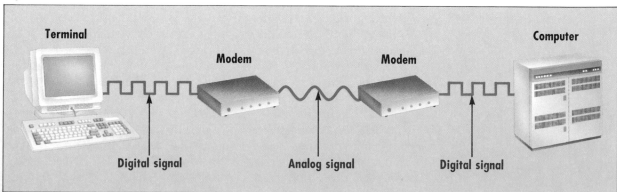

Figure 6–10 A Modem

There are several types of communications control units. One is a *multiplexer*, which takes the signal from several slow-speed computer devices and combines them for transmission over a high-speed channel. At the other end of the channel another multiplexer breaks the high-speed signal from the channel into the separate signals from each device. Another type of communications control unit is a *controller*. This unit allows several computer devices to communicate over a channel by storing signals from each device and forwarding them when appropriate.

Many computer systems have a separate computer that handles communications control. This computer is called a *front-end processor* because it is between the channel and the main computer. It performs the functions of a multiplexer and controller, as well as other functions, thus reducing the work load of the main computer.

Figure 6–11 shows how the communications control units described here may be used for data communications. In this figure, several terminals at the user's local site are managed by a controller. This controller and other terminals send signals to a multiplexer, which combines the signals and forwards them to a modem. The modem modulates the signal from the multiplexer for transmission over a high-speed communications channel. At the remote site, where the main computer is located, another modem demodulates the signal and sends it to the front-end processor. Also at the remote site, the front-end processor receives signals directly from other terminals and from another controller. The front-end processor sends signals from all sources to the main computer. To send signals back to the terminals from the computer, this process is reversed.

Protocol Converters.   When people talk with each other, they follow unstated rules about how to communicate. For example, they agree to talk in the same language, they say "hello" when they meet and "goodbye" when they part, and when one person talks the other person is quiet. These rules are necessary to ensure proper communication.

When computer devices communicate, they also must follow rules. These rules are called **protocols**. The protocols state what language the communication will be in (ASCII or EBCDIC), what signal will start the communication and what signal will end it, and how one device will know whether the other is communicating so that it does not try to communicate at the same time.

Figure 6–11 Use of Controller, Multiplexer, and Front-End Processor

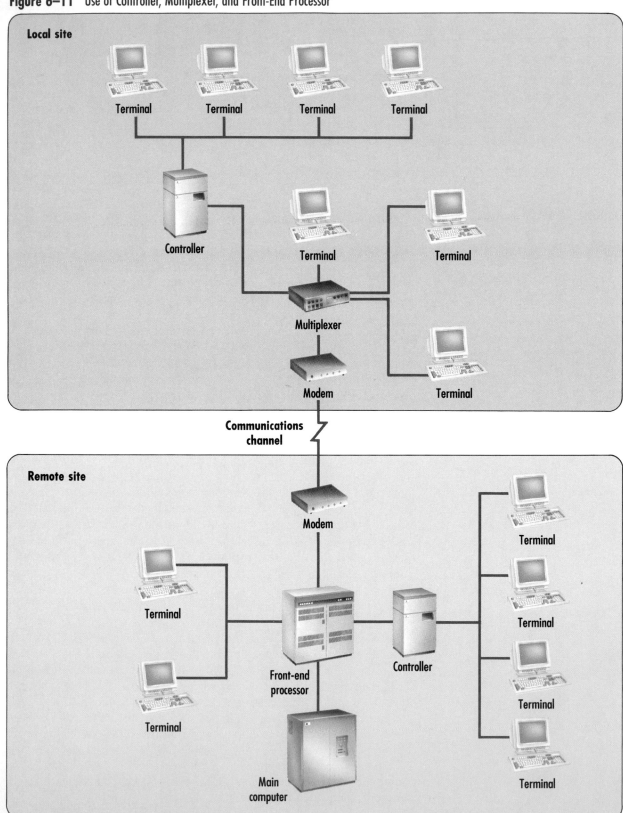

Unfortunately, not all computer systems use the same protocols. Often, computer devices manufactured by different companies use different protocols. If you want two devices with incompatible protocols to communicate, you need some way of converting the protocols of one device to those of the other device. This function is performed by a unit called a **protocol converter**. The converter connects one device with the channel that goes to the other device. With the appropriate type of protocol converter, a computer device manufactured by one company can communicate with one that uses different protocols manufactured by another company.

Data Encryption Devices.   One problem with data communications is the security of the data transmitted over a channel. It is sometimes possible to tap into a communications channel and intercept data sent over it. One way of solving this problem is to code the data in an unintelligible form before it is transmitted. This process is called **data encryption** and can be done by a special data encryption device. The data is coded by the device and then sent over the channel. At the other end of the channel, a similar device is used to decode the data after it is received. The coding and decoding requires the use of a special *key*, which is a number entered into the data encryption device at each end of the channel. If the channel is tapped and the key is not known, the coded data cannot be interpreted correctly.

Network Interface Devices.   When computers communicate using some types of networks, special interface units may be needed to connect the computers to the channel that forms the network. These **network interface devices** allow a computer to send data to and receive data from other computers in the network. Each computer needs an interface device. These devices send data over the network's channel and receive data from the channel. In microcomputers these interface devices usually are special cards that are plugged into the computer's motherboard.

COMMUNICATIONS SOFTWARE

In addition to communications hardware, you need **communications software** for data communications. Each computer that communicates must have communications software (Figure 6–12). This software receives data from the channel interface units and passes the data on to other programs in the computer for processing. The communications software also gets the results of processing from other programs and sends this data to the channel interface units.

Minicomputer and Mainframe Computer Communications Software

The specific functions of the communications software depend on the type of computer and the type of communications. With minicomputers and mainframe computers that communicate with many terminals, the

Figure 6–12
Communications Software

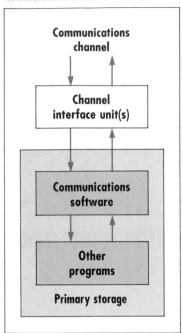

Figure 6–13   File-Transferring

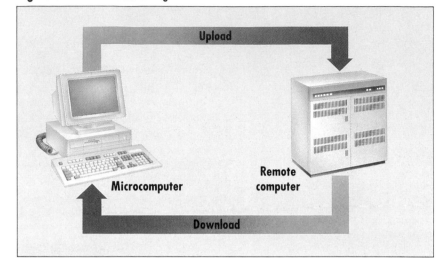

communications software, which is often called a *teleprocessing moni-tor*, keeps track of which terminal sent which data and decides to which terminal the results of processing should be sent. The communications software may also provide some protocol conversion such as converting ASCII to EBCDIC.

Microcomputer Communications Software

With microcomputers that communicate with other microcomputers or with larger computers, communications software provides two main functions: terminal emulation and file transfers. **Terminal emulation** makes the microcomputer act like a terminal. This is necessary because most computers with which a microcomputer can communicate expect a terminal at the other end of the channel, not a computer. The communications software in the microcomputer makes the other computer "think" it is communicating with a terminal. Then a user can use the microcomputer exactly as if he or she were using a terminal connected directly to the other computer.

The other function provided by microcomputer communications software is **file transfer**, which involves sending data from a file at the microcomputer to the other computer and vice versa. When data is sent from a microcomputer to a remote computer, the process is called **uploading**. When data is sent from a remote computer to a microcomputer, the process is called **downloading** (Figure 6–13). Microcomputer communications software allows a user to both upload and download files with another computer.

File transfer is accomplished by following certain rules called **file-transfer protocols**. The protocols specify how data will be transferred and how errors will be checked. There are several file-transfer protocols in use, and the same protocol must be used by the communications software at both ends of the channel. Most microcomputer communications programs allow a user to select the desired protocol.

There are many microcomputer communications programs. Some for the IBM PC and IBM clones are Crosstalk, Smartcom, and PC Talk. Programs for the Apple Macintosh include White Knight, Smartcom, and Microphone. Microcomputer communications programs cost between $70 and $250.

TERMINAL COMMUNICATIONS

In the first section of this chapter you were introduced to three situations in which users use data communications. Now that you have an understanding of communications hardware and software, you can see what is needed in each situation. The remainder of this chapter discusses these three situations in detail.

The first situation involves communication between an I/O device and a distant computer. Most often the I/O device is a terminal at the user's local site. The channel is usually a telephone line and may be switched or leased. What communications hardware and software is needed for a terminal to communicate with a distant computer? Figure 6–14 summarizes the needs.

At the terminal end, the user must have hardware to connect the terminal to the communications channel. At a minimum, a modem is required. The user must set the modem to the same characteristics as the modem at the computer's end of the channel. Thus, the data rate (bits per second), data flow (half-duplex or full-duplex), and transmission method (asynchronous or synchronous) must be the same for both modems. In

Figure 6–14   Communications Hardware and Software Needs for Terminal Communications

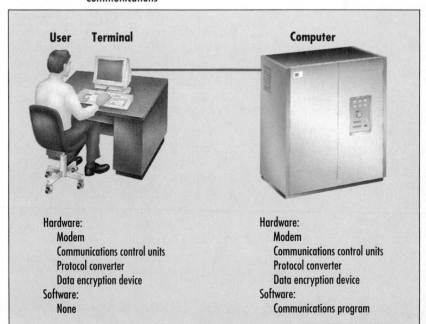

Hardware:	**Hardware:**
Modem	Modem
Communications control units	Communications control units
Protocol converter	Protocol converter
Data encryption device	Data encryption device
Software:	**Software:**
None	Communications program

addition to a modem, a protocol converter and various communications control units may be needed. A protocol converter is required if the terminal's protocol is not compatible with that of the computer. The communications control units are not usually the user's concern, although they may be present to help with the communications. Finally, a data encryption device is needed if data encryption is used.

At the computer's end, communications hardware is needed to connect the computer to the channel. In addition to a modem, various communications control units may be used. A protocol converter may be needed unless protocol conversion is provided at the terminal end. A data encryption device is needed if data encryption is used.

Communications software is not needed with the user's terminal because a terminal is not a computer. The distant computer, however, needs communications software to manage communication with the terminal.

With terminal communication to a distant computer, the user can use the terminal exactly as if it were connected directly to the computer. Typically, the user enters input data into the computer for processing and receives the results of processing through the terminal.

MICROCOMPUTER COMMUNICATIONS

The second data communications situation encountered by users involves communication between computers. Because the user's computer is most often a microcomputer, this situation usually involves communication between a microcomputer and another computer. The other computer may also be a microcomputer, or it may be a larger computer such as a mainframe computer.

Micro-to-Micro Communications

Two microcomputers can communicate by using a direct connection or a telephone line. For a direct connection, the microcomputers must be nearby, usually within a few feet of each other. Then, a wire cable is plugged into a port in each computer and used as a channel. The microcomputers communicate by sending signals over the cable. No modems are necessary. Communications software, however, is required in each microcomputer.

Figure 6–15 summarizes the hardware and software needs for micro-to-micro communications over long distances. In this situation, a telephone line usually is used as a channel. Then a modem is required for each microcomputer. Both modems must be set for the same characteristics (rate, flow, and method). As in the direct connection case, both microcomputers need communications software.

When two microcomputers communicate, a user at one microcomputer can transfer files to and from the other microcomputer. A common example involves transferring files to and from an **electronic bulletin board**, which is a microcomputer system operated by a business or an individual that can be accessed using data communications. An electronic

Figure 6–15 Communications Hardware and Software Needs for
Micro-to-Micro Communications ·ภในแนน

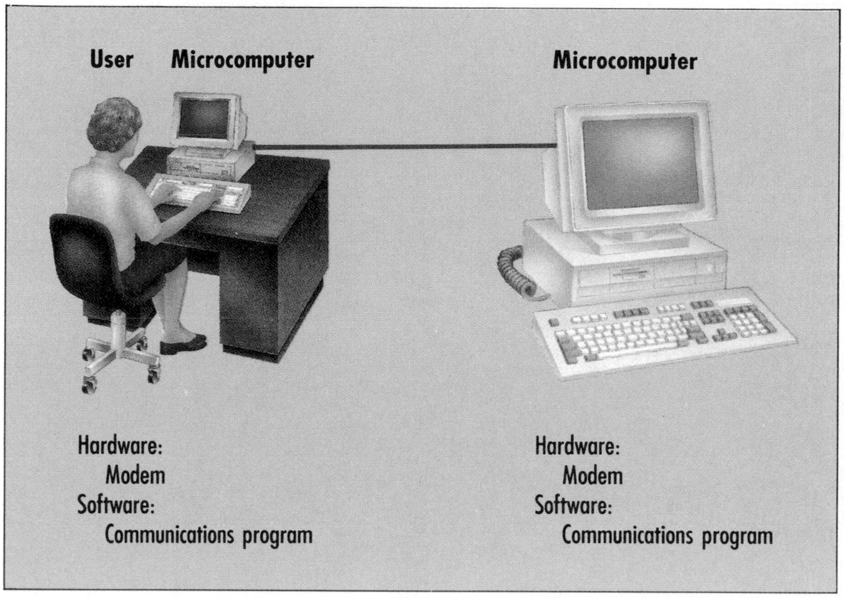

bulletin stores information of interest to certain types of users. For example, one electronic bulletin operated by a bicycle shop provides information about bicycle races. The user can use his or her microcomputer to communicate with the electronic bulletin board's computer over a telephone line. Then, the user can transfer files to and from the computer.

Micro-to-Mainframe Communications

When microcomputers communicate with larger computers, the situation is called micro-to-mainframe communications, even though the larger computer could be a minicomputer, a mainframe, or (rarely) a supercomputer. The microcomputer may be connected directly to the other computer if the distance is not too great, or may use a telephone line for longer-distance communications. Figure 6–16 summarizes the hardware and software needs in the latter case. A modem is needed at the microcomputer end of the channel and at the mainframe end. The characteristics (rate, flow, and method) of these modems must match. Also at the mainframe end may be various communications control units. Data encryption devices may be needed at both ends if data encryption is used.

One of the biggest problems with micro-to-mainframe communications is that many mainframe computers use synchronous transmission while most microcomputers use asynchronous transmission. In some situations, conversion between the two methods is done by a protocol converter at the mainframe computer. Usually, however, the microcomputer has a protocol converter, which is often a circuit board in the microcomputer. This board is connected to the modem. It converts between asynchronous and synchronous transmission, between ASCII and EBCDIC, and between other protocol characteristics.

Figure 6–16 Communications Hardware and Software Needs for Micro-to-Mainframe Communications

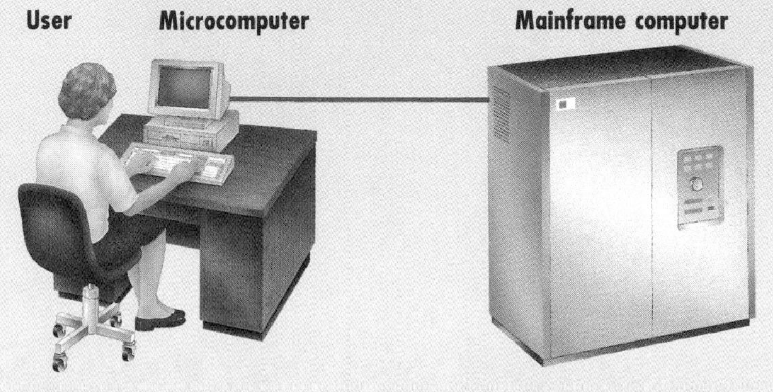

User   Microcomputer   **Mainframe computer**

Hardware: Hardware:
    Modem   Modem
    Protocol converter   Communications control units
    Data encryption device   Protocol converter
Software: Data encryption device
    Communications program   Software:
                                            Communications program

Both computers in micro-to-mainframe communications need communications software. The mainframe software functions like the communications software used in remote terminal communications. The microcomputer software provides terminal emulation and file-transferring capabilities.

When a microcomputer communicates with a mainframe computer, the user can use the microcomputer as a terminal exactly as in remote terminal communications. The user can also transfer files to and from the mainframe computer.

Micro-to-mainframe communications is used in businesses so that users can access the company's main computer. The user can process data with the main computer or transfer data between the microcomputer and the main computer. Another use of this form of communications is to access mainframe computer systems at **information utilities**. These are companies such as CompuServe, The Source, and Dow Jones News/Retrieval, which have computers that store information of interest to a variety of users. Some information utilities store information for the general public, such as stock prices, airline flight schedules, and recent news. Other utilities store information useful to certain types of businesses, such as legal data used by law firms. Some information utilities also provide services such as *electronic shopping* to purchase merchandise, *electronic banking* to perform banking transactions, and *electronic mail* to send messages to other people who have access to the utility.

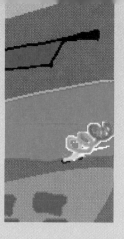

COMPUTER NETWORKS: THE HOTTEST THING TO HIT HOLLYWOOD SINCE THE PHONE

"Cookie! You bring me Tom Hanks and Morgan Fairchild for *Romeo & Juliet, Part II*. I've got goose bumps. Do I love this man? Listen, let's do some E-mail."

The industry that raised schmoozing to an art form is going electronic. William Morris Agency, Inc., a large talent agency in Beverly Hills, Calif., installed 200 NeXT, Inc. workstations alongside 100 personal computers in a coast-to-coast wide-area network.

Agents in New York, Nashville and Beverly Hills can access the network and electronically thumb through a database containing a literal *Who's Who* in entertainment. The pairing of entertainment and computer industries is a natural, said Alex Henry, information systems manager at William Morris. Both are based on the power of information.

A talent agent's challenge is to remember who is available for which project at what price. Henry said William Morris' philosophy is that every agent represents every client.

Without near-immediate access to shared information, that premise could be lost in a world-wide corporation. Common access and the ability to send or receive requests through electronic mail have snagged new admirers, including former "technophobes," he said. "We have agents who have never touched a computer, and they say, 'My assistant can have one,'" Henry explained. "We come back two or three weeks later, and they say, 'Give me one, too.'"

In demonstrating the network, Henry paged past some surprising personalities: Hanks, former U.S. Surgeon General C. Everett Koop, game show host Bob Barker, author Tom Clancy and comedian Andrew "Dice" Clay. Every night, information on them and others in publishing, movies, video, music and stage are updated.

"I have heard agents say they are 30% more productive. I can tell you how loud they scream when the machines are down," Henry said.

Henry could be a computer executive in almost any company. The former consultant at Deloitte & Touche exhibits none of the smarm and flash of most show business intimates, aside from a minor tendency to drop major names.

He oversees a system that grew out of a small network in the Nashville office's music department. In classic Hollywood fashion, the idea came from an unknown, a temporary employee named Mia Bain, who had seen networks used in other offices. Today, Henry said, she is system manager of that network.

The Nashville office, which concentrates on the music industry, continues to rely on PCs, as do the music departments in both New York and Beverly Hills. Employees in Beverly Hills operate 164 NeXT workstations tied via a network to 12 NeXT file servers. New York has 17 workstations and two file servers, and another 75 workstations have been ordered, Henry said.

Figure 6–17 Network Organization with Each Node Connected to All Other Nodes

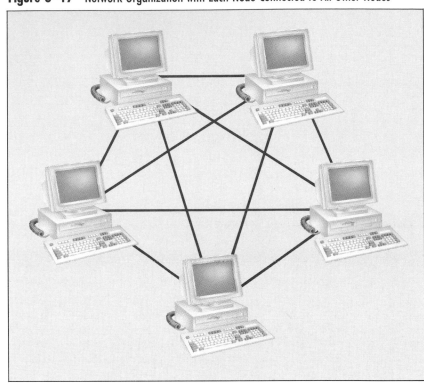

NETWORK COMMUNICATIONS

The last data communications situation encountered by users involves communications with shared resources over a network. There are two main types of networks: local area networks and wide-area networks. The hardware and software needs for these types of networks are different.

Network Organization

Before discussing networks in detail, we need to examine how networks can be organized. Each computer or other component (such as a terminal) connected to a network is called a *node* in the network. One way of organizing the nodes in a network is for each node to be connected to all other nodes in the network (Figure 6–17). The problem with this approach is that as more nodes are added to the network, many more connections are needed. (With 5 nodes, 10 connections are needed; with 6 nodes, 15 connections are needed; with 7 nodes, 21 connections are needed, and so forth.) To solve this problem, several common organizations are used for networks (Figure 6–18).

Star Network.   In a **star network** each node is connected to a central computer node (Figure 6–18a). For two nodes to communicate, data must be sent from one node to the central computer, and then the central computer sends the data on to the other node. The primary advantage of this approach is that the "distance" that data has to travel is short; data has to travel only through the central computer to get from one node to another. The main disadvantage is that if the central computer stops working the entire network cannot function.

Hierarchical Network.   A **hierarchical network** consists of nodes organized like a family tree (Figure 6–18b). The top node is a central computer that is connected to several other nodes, which may also be computers. Each of these nodes may be connected to several other nodes, and so forth. Two nodes can communicate by sending data from the first node "up" the hierarchy to a common node, which then sends the data "down" to the second node. This approach is more reliable than a star network because failure of any one node does not mean the entire network cannot function. It is more complex than a star network, however, and data may have to travel a greater "distance" to get from one node to another.

Bus Network.   In a **bus network**, each node is connected to a single, common communications channel (Figure 6–18c). To transmit data from one node to another, the first node sends the data and information that identifies the node that is to receive the data in both directions over the bus. Each node on the bus examines the identifying information and, if it is the receiving node, takes the data from the bus. This approach is very reliable because there is no central computer, and failure of any node does not affect the function of the network. Communication speed can be slower than other types of networks, however.

Ring Network.   A **ring network** consists of nodes connected to form a loop (Figure 6–18d). Data travels from node to node in the ring, usually in one direction only. To send data from one node to another, the first node sends the data and information about which node is to receive the data to the next node in the ring. This node either keeps the data if it is the receiving node or forwards the data on to the next node. This process continues until the data reaches the receiving node. Most ring networks are as reliable as bus networks because if a node fails the data usually can be sent past the failed node and hence the function of the network is not affected. Like a bus network, communication can be slower on a ring network than on other types of networks.

Local Area Networks

A **local area network**, or **LAN**, is a network located in a single building or in several nearby buildings. LANs usually are organized as bus or ring networks using coaxial cable or twisted pair wiring as a communications channel medium. Users most often use the LAN through microcomputers. Figure 6–19 summarizes the microcomputer hardware and software needs for LAN communication. Each microcomputer is connected to the channel by a network interface device in the microcomputer, which is usually a card plugged into the microcomputer's

Figure 6–18 Network Organization

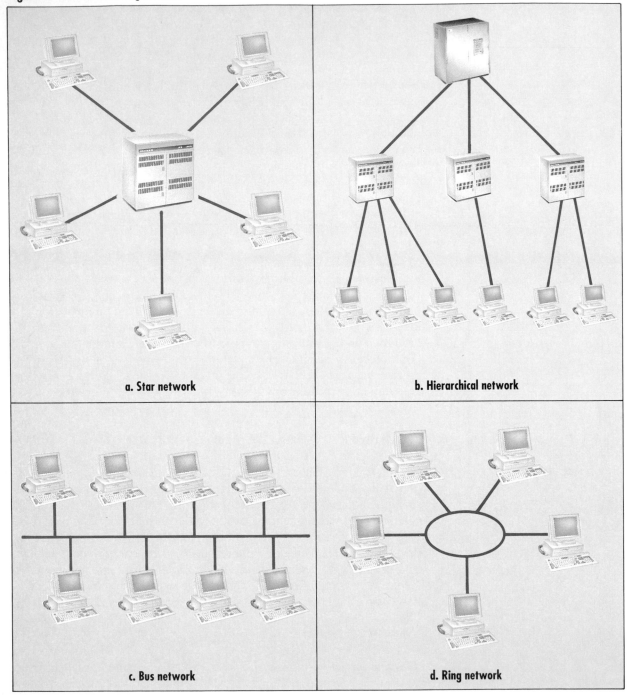

a. Star network

b. Hierarchical network

c. Bus network

d. Ring network

Figure 6–19   Microcomputer Communications Hardware and Software Needs for Local Area Network Communications

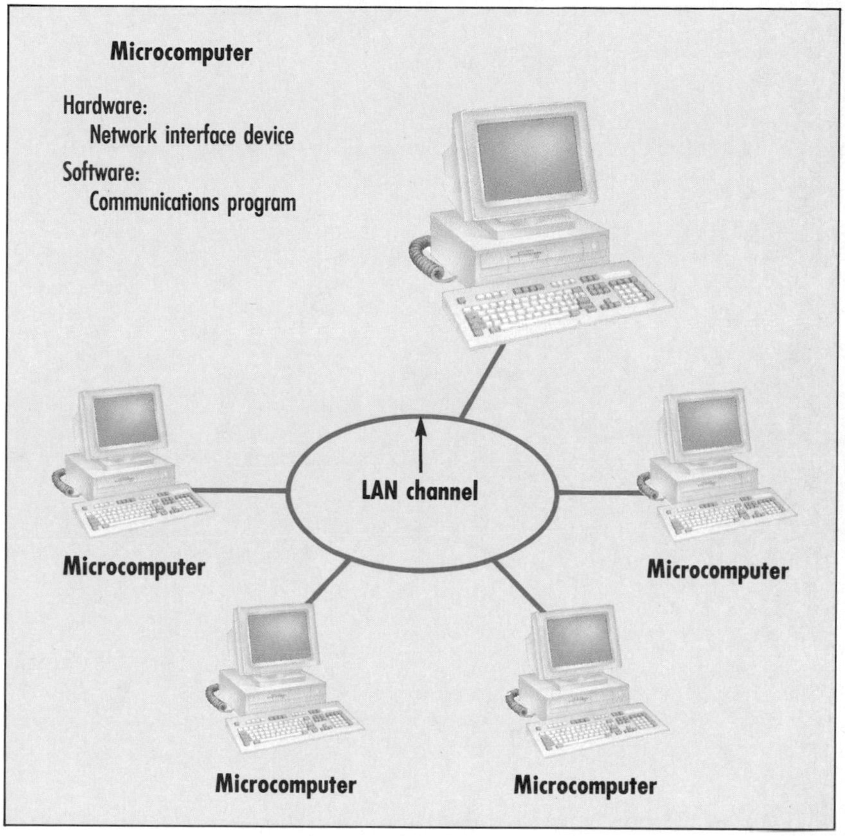

Microcomputer

Hardware:
  Network interface device
Software:
  Communications program

LAN channel

Microcomputer

Microcomputer

Microcomputer

Microcomputer

motherboard. The LAN cable or wire plugs into this device. A microcomputer also needs communications software to allow the computer to send and receive data over the network's channel. This software is often referred to as the *LAN operating system*.

A LAN usually includes many user-operated microcomputers plus several special microcomputers, called **servers**, that control shared resources (Figure 6–20). A **print server** is a microcomputer with a printer that can be used for printing by other microcomputers connected to the LAN. A **file server** is a microcomputer with a secondary storage device, usually a large hard disk drive, that can be used for file storage by other computers in the LAN. (Often one microcomputer is used as both a print server and a file server.) A **database server** is a microcomputer with secondary storage that can be used for database processing by other LAN computers.

Larger computers, such as minicomputers and mainframe computers, may also be connected to the LAN. A LAN may also include a **bridge**, which is a connection to another similar LAN, and a **gateway**, which is a connection to a different type of network outside the LAN. All these components are connected to the LAN's channel.

With a LAN, a user can use any of the shared resources. For example, when the user needs to print output, he or she can transmit the

Figure 6–20 A Local Area Network

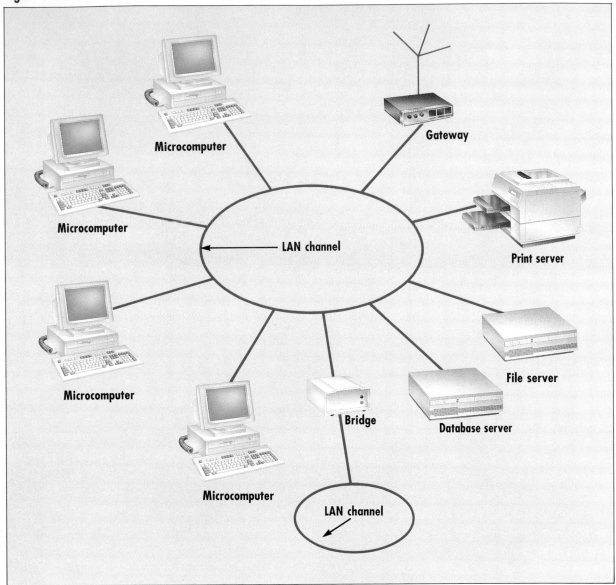

Microcomputer

Microcomputer

Microcomputer

Microcomputer

Gateway

Print server

File server

Database server

Bridge

LAN channel

LAN channel

data to the print server. To store or retrieve common data, the user can communicate with the file or database server. To do specialized processing, the user can send data to larger computers in the network. To communicate with other networks, the user can transmit data through a bridge or gateway. The user can use any of the shared resources in the LAN by transmitting data over the LAN.

One common use of local area networks is for **electronic mail**, or **E mail**. This consists of letters, memos, and other messages entered into the user's computer. The electronic mail is sent over the network to one or more other user's electronic mailbox, which is a special file on a file server. The other user can look in his or her electronic mailbox, read any mail that is there on the screen, and send a reply to the sender's electronic mailbox.

Wide Area Networks

A **wide area network**, or **WAN**, covers a large geographic area. Some WANs cover a part of a country or an entire country (Figure 6–21). Other WANs extend into several countries.

Figure 6–21   A Wide Area Network

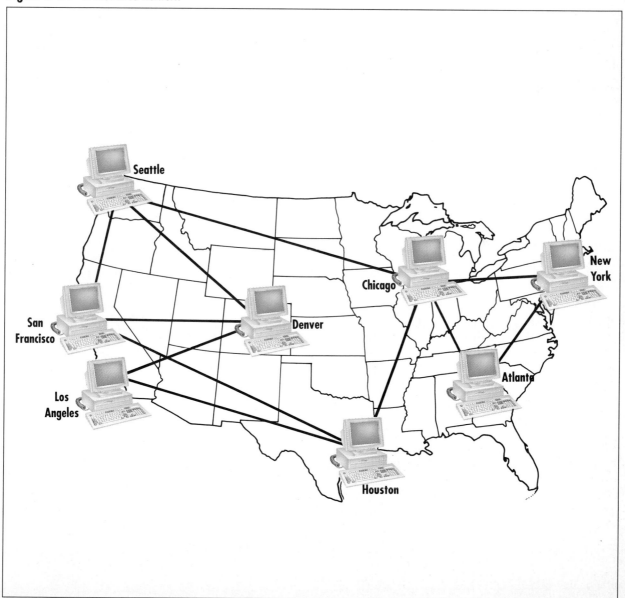

L.A. TIMES USES WIDE AREA NETWORK TO LINK ITS BUREAUS

The *Los Angeles Times*, one of the country's major daily newspapers with news bureaus all over the world, uses what may be one of the widest of the wide area networks in existence. The Coyote system, used to connect the bureaus to the newspaper's central computing system, is a model of simplicity.

The *Los Angeles Times* uses Coyote, based on minicomputers, to manage the flow of text from input copy to edited text through page layout and on to the actual printing. Coyote nodes are located in the *Times*' main office in Los Angeles and at two satellite facilities in Washington and in Orange County, California, said Wayne M. Parrack, deputy systems editor and the person in charge of editorial computing systems.

Reporters located at the news bureaus write their articles on personal computers that are connected by leased line to one of the three regional nodes. Offices in New York and at the U.S. Senate dial in to the Washington node, for example, while reporters in the southern end of Southern California dial in to the Orange County node.

For international bureaus, the wide area network becomes a very wide area network.

Foreign communications go through one of three communications centers, all of which are located in England. All three communications centers communicate directly with the Washington node.

"The same communications protocols are used in the United States, London, and Japan," said Russell D. Francis, editorial communications manager at the *Times*. This makes it easy for reports to use the system, he said, since no modification of the system or of the means of connecting with the system is required.

The basic framework provides a wide range of services. A reporter in Israel, for example, can send a message to a reporter in Japan. The node in Washington handles the messaging functions and facilitates the relaying of messages between bureaus.

Further, reporters can file stories, then call them up from the system during editing. The system, as implemented by the *Times*, provides interactive communications between bureaus and between the bureau and the editorial computer system.

Short of hiring Clark Kent, who can deliver his stories anywhere in the world in minutes, the wide area network system developed by the *Los Angeles Times* appears to be an excellent method of tying a worldwide network of bureaus into a sophisticated computing system.

WANs often consist of nodes that are interconnected in no particular pattern, although sometimes they are organized as star or hierarchical networks. Users use a terminal or a microcomputer to communicate over public or private communications systems with other microcomputers or mainframe computers in the network. Depending on the devices in the WAN, the hardware and software needs may be the same as terminal communication (Figure 6–14), micro-to-micro communication (Figure 6–15), or micro-to-mainframe communication (Figure 6–16).

Wide area networks are used by many businesses that have offices and other facilities at distant locations. For example, airlines use WANs for their reservation systems so that reservation clerks at airports and also travel agents can communicate with central computers. Another example is banks, which use WANs to connect automatic teller machines (ATMs) with the bank's computers. Many organizations use WANs for sending electronic mail. Some WANs extend beyond international boundaries and use satellites for communications.

Chapter Summary

- The main characteristics of **communications channels** are signal type, data rate, data flow, and transmission method. A channel may transmit using a **digital signal**, which is a series of pulses, or an **analog signal**, which is a wave. The data rate of a channel is measured in **bits per second**, or **bps**. With **simplex transmission**, data flows in one direction; in **half-duplex transmission**, data flows in both directions but only in one direction at a time; with **full-duplex transmission**, data flows in both directions simultaneously. In **asynchronous transmission**, one character is sent at a time over the channel. In **synchronous transmission**, a block of characters is sent over the channel.

- A **modem** converts digital signals to analog signals (modulation) and converts analog signals to digital signals (demodulation). Other channel interface units include **communications control units**, **protocol converters**, **data encryption devices**, and **network interface devices**.

- Communications software transfers data between the channel interface units and programs in the computer. On minicomputers and mainframe computers the communications software keeps track of which terminal sent which data, and where to send the results of processing. Microcomputer communications software provides **terminal emulation**, which makes the microcomputer act like a terminal, and **file transfer**, which allows data from a file to be sent between computers.

- For terminal communications to a distant computer, a modem and possibly a protocol converter, a data encryption device, and various communications control units are needed at the terminal end, but no communications software is needed. At the computer end, a modem is needed and possibly various communications control units, a protocol converter, and a data encryption device. In addition, a communications program is needed for the computer. For micro-to-micro communications over a telephone line, each microcomputer must have a modem and a communications program. For micro-to-mainframe communications, the microcomputer requires a modem, possibly a protocol converter and a data encryption device, and a communications program. The mainframe computer must have a modem and possibly various communications control units, a data encryption device, and a protocol converter. In addition, the mainframe computer must have a communications program.

- A **local area network**, or **LAN**, covers a small area such as a single building or several nearby buildings. A **wide area network**, or **WAN**, covers a large geographic area. For local area network communications, a microcomputer must have a network interface device and LAN communications software. For wide area network communications, a microcomputer requires the same communications hardware and software as are needed for micro-to-micro or micro-to-mainframe communications.

Terms to Remember

Analog Signal   p. 144

Asynchronous Transmission   p. 146

Baud Rate   p. 145

Bridge   p. 163

Bus Network   p. 161

Communications Channel   p. 142

Communications Control Unit   p. 150

Communications Software   p. 153

Database Server   p. 163

Data Encryption   p. 153

Digital Signal   p. 144

Downloading   p. 154

Electronic Bulletin Board   p. 156

Electronic Mail (E mail)   p. 164

File Server   p. 163

File Transfer   p. 154

File Transfer Protocol   p. 154

Full-Duplex Transmission   p. 145

Gateway   p. 163

Half-Duplex Transmission   p. 145

Hierarchical Network   p. 161

Information Utility   p. 158

Leased (Dedicated) Line   p. 149

Local Area Network (LAN)   p. 161

Modem   p. 149

Network Interface Device   p. 153

Print Server   p. 163

Protocol Converter   p. 153

Protocols   p. 151

Ring Network   p. 161

Server   p. 163

Simplex Transmission   p. 145

Star Network   p. 160

Switched (Dial-Up) Line   p. 149

Synchronous Transmission   p. 146

Terminal Emulation   p. 154

Uploading   p. 154

Wide Area Network (WAN)   p. 165

Review Questions

Fill-in Questions

1. A data communications link between computer components is called a(n) _____.

2. The data rate over a communications channel is measured in _____.

3. Data flow in only one direction in a channel is called _____. Data flow in two directions in a channel but in only one direction at a time is called _____. Data flow in two directions simultaneously in a channel is called _____.

4. Transmission of one character at a time in a channel is called _____, whereas transmission of a block of characters together in a channel is called _____.

5. A telephone line that can be used by any customer is a(n) _____. A telephone line that is used by only one customer is a(n) _____.

6. The rules that describe how computer devices communicate are called _____.

7. Changing data to a form that is unintelligible unless a special key is known is called _____.

8. Two functions provided by microcomputer communications software are _____ and _____.

9. Transferring data from a local computer to a remote computer is called _____. Transferring data from a remote computer to a local computer is called _____.

10. A(n) _____ is a microcomputer system that can be accessed using data communications and that stores information of interest to certain types of users.

11. A network in which each node is connected to a central computer node is a(n) _____ network. A network that consists of nodes organized like a family tree is a(n) _____ network. A network in which each node is connected to a single, common communications channel is a(n) _____ network. A network in which the nodes are connected to form a loop is a(n) _____ network.

12. A(n) _____ is a microcomputer with a printer that can be used for printing by other computers in a network. A(n) _____ is a microcomputer with a hard disk drive that can be used for file storage by other computers in a network. A(n) _____ is a microcomputer with a hard disk drive that can be used for database processing by other computers in a network.

Short-Answer Questions

1. Describe three situations in which users need data communications.

2. What is the difference between a digital signal and an analog signal?

3. What is meant by *baud rate,* and is it the same as bps?

4. List several common media used for communications channels.

5. What does a modem do?

6. List several devices other than modems that are channel interface units.

7. What communications hardware and software are needed with a terminal so that it can communicate with a computer?

8. What communications hardware and software are needed for two microcomputers to communicate over a telephone line?

9. What communications hardware and software are needed with a microcomputer so that it can communicate with a mainframe computer?

10. What is the difference between a local area network and a wide area network?

11. What communications hardware and software are needed with a microcomputer so that it can use a local area network?

12. What communications hardware and software are needed with a microcomputer so that it can use a wide area network?

Projects

1. If you are using a network or have access to one, find out everything you can about the network. What type of network is it? How is the network organized? What medium is used for the network channel? At what rate is data sent over the channel? What computers and other devices are connected to the network?

2. Contact an information utility (e.g., CompuServe, The Source, or Dow Jones News/Retrieval), and find out what services it provides, how much it charges, and what hardware and software you would need to use it. Write a brief summary of your findings.

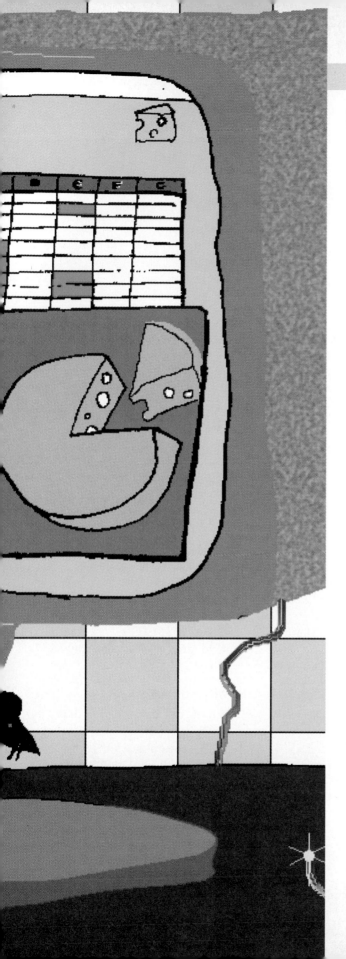

PART THREE

SOFTWARE

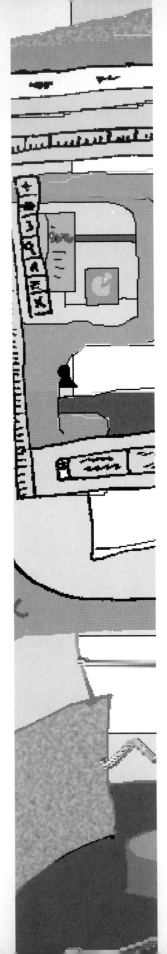

7

OPERATING SYSTEMS

CHAPTER OBJECTIVES

• After completing this chapter you should be able to:

1. List the main functions of an operating system and describe its overall organization.

2. Describe some ways that users can tell an operating system what to do.

3. Describe some of the characteristics that distinguish operating systems.

4. Identify several common microcomputer operating systems and the computers with which they are used.

5. Describe several ways that users can control software.

6. List several ways that users can enter input data into and receive output from a program.

7. Explain the general characteristics of graphical user interfaces.

M ANY TYPES of software are used with computers. Word processing, spreadsheet, and database software are some of the best-known types. However, the most fundamental software that is used is the *operating system* of the computer. Recall from Chapter 2 that an operating system is a set of programs that controls the basic operation of the computer. All other software works in association with the operating system. This chapter describes operating systems and their effect on how the user uses a computer.

Most software, including operating systems, allows the user to interact with it in various ways. How the user interacts with the software depends on the *software interface*, which is the link between the user and the program. This chapter also explains what you need to know about the software interface.

OPERATING SYSTEM CONCEPTS

As you know, a computer needs a program before it can do anything. When an application program is executing, that program is in control of the computer. But when one application program finishes, the computer cannot automatically go on to the next application program. The computer needs another program to take control between application programs. This is one purpose of the operating system.

An operating system is a group of programs that manages the operation of the computer. It is in control of the computer whenever another program is not executing. As soon as one program stops executing, the operating system takes control of the computer. It then begins execution of the next program. Thus, the computer is never without a program.

Functions of an Operating System

An operating system has three main functions: process management, resource management, and data management. To understand the first function, *process management*, think of the execution of a program as a process that the computer performs. The operating system must keep track of all processes—that is, all program executions. It must schedule programs for execution, start the execution of programs when needed, and monitor the execution of a program in case any errors occur. In other words, the operating system must manage the execution of programs, or processes.

The second main function of an operating system is *resource management*. A computer has many resources, including primary storage, input and output devices, and secondary storage. The operating system must assign the required resources to each process. The operating system determines where in primary storage a program will be stored, what input and output devices will be used by the program, and where in secondary storage program and data files will be stored.

The final main function of an operating system is *data management*. The operating system handles all movement of data between the main components of the computer. Any time input data is entered or output data is produced, a data-management routine in the operating system controls the transfer of the data between primary storage and the appropriate input or output device. Any transfer of data between primary storage and a data file in secondary storage is handled by a data-management routine in the operating system. Thus, the operating system manages the data used by the computer.

Organization of an Operating System

An operating system is usually made up of not just one program but several. One program in the operating system is stored in a section of primary storage whenever the computer is running. This program is called the **supervisor**. It may also be called the *monitor, executive,* or *kernel,* depending on the operating system. It is the part of the operating system that is in control of the computer when another program (such as an application program) is not executing.

The supervisor occupies part of primary storage. The rest of primary storage is used to store one or more other programs. To start the execution of a program, the supervisor passes the control of the computer over to the program in primary storage (Figure 7–1a). When the program finishes executing, it returns control of the computer to the supervisor. Then, the supervisor can start the execution of another program by passing the control of the computer over to it (Figure 7–1b). This process continues for all the programs to be executed. Thus, the supervisor is in charge of the computer whenever another program is not executing.

Another function of the supervisor is to bring programs into primary storage when they are needed. As you know, a program must be in primary storage before it can be executed. Usually, nonexecuting programs

Figure 7–1   Executing Programs

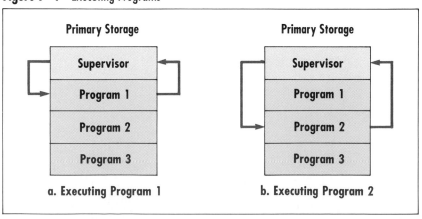

a. Executing Program 1   b. Executing Program 2

are stored in secondary storage. When a program is needed, the supervisor *loads* it into primary storage. Once the supervisor has loaded the program, it can start the execution of the program.

An operating system contains other programs besides the supervisor. These other programs are stored in secondary storage and loaded into primary storage by the supervisor when they are needed. These programs perform functions that are used less often than those of the supervisor. An example is a program that copies the contents of one disk to another disk. This program is not used often, so it is stored in secondary storage and loaded only when it is needed.

Using an Operating System

You have just learned that the supervisor is stored in primary storage whenever the computer is running. But when the computer is turned off, everything in primary storage is lost. Thus, when the computer is turned on again there is nothing in primary storage. How does the supervisor get into primary storage when the computer is turned on if there is no program to bring it in?

The process for loading the supervisor is called **booting**; someone "boots the computer" or the computer "boots up." The supervisor is stored in secondary storage. A special program for loading the supervisor into primary storage is stored in ROM, which as you know from Chapter 3 is nonvolatile, read-only memory. When the switch for the computer is turned on, a special circuit is activated that causes the program in ROM to execute. This program then loads the supervisor into primary storage and transfers control of the computer to it. Then the supervisor can start the execution of other programs.

With some computers, more than just the program to load the supervisor is stored in ROM; some computers have part of the supervisor in ROM. This part of the supervisor is executed automatically when the computer is turned on, and the rest of the supervisor is then loaded from secondary storage. Some computers have the entire supervisor in ROM, in which case the loading step is not needed.

Before you use a computer, someone must turn the computer on and load the supervisor (that is, boot the computer). With a microcomputer, the person who does this is usually the user. With minicomputers and mainframe computers, however, this function is performed by computer professionals. Larger computers are often left running 24 hours a day, so this process is done infrequently.

With a microcomputer, you usually can use the operating system right after the computer has been started. With minicomputers and mainframe computers, however, you normally have to go through a process called *logging in* before you can use the operating system. This process, which connects the user's terminal to the operating system, is needed because large computers are used by more than one person at a time, and the operating system must have a way of distinguishing the users. The actual log-in procedure depends on the computer, but typically it involves entering a *user identification number* or *account number*, followed by a special word called a *password*. The identification number and password normally are supplied by the computer staff and are designed to prevent unauthorized use of the computer. If the log-in procedure is followed correctly, the user's terminal is connected to the operating system. After using the computer, the user must disconnect his or her terminal by following a procedure called *logging out*.

Controlling an Operating System

An operating system needs to be told what to do. It must be told what program to load into primary storage, what program to execute, and what other functions to perform. The way a user tells an operating system what to do determines, to a large extent, how the user uses the computer.

One common way of telling an operating system what to do is by typing in instructions called **system commands**. Every time a user enters a system command, the supervisor interprets the command and performs some function for the user. The actual system commands depend on the operating system. For example, Table 7–1 lists some of the system commands used with an IBM PC operating system called DOS. The system commands used with mainframe computer operating systems are sometimes called **job-control language,** or **JCL,** because they control jobs, which are just programs, or groups of programs. JCL can be very complex and difficult to use.

System commands are sometimes divided into two groups, the first of which is called **internal commands**. These system commands are interpreted by the supervisor, which contains the instructions necessary to perform the functions required by the commands. The second group is called **external commands**. These system commands cause other programs in the operating system to be loaded from secondary storage and executed. When the supervisor receives a system command it first determines if it is an internal or external command. If it is an internal command, the supervisor performs the requested function. If it is an external command, the supervisor loads the required program into primary storage and executes it.

Table 7-1 System Commands for the IBM PC Operating System DOS

Command	Purpose
DIR	Display list of all files stored on a disk
COPY	Make a copy of a file on a disk
DISKCOPY	Copy the contents of one disk to another disk
RENAME	Change the name of a file on a disk
ERASE	Delete a file from a disk
TYPE	Display the contents of a disk file on the screen
FORMAT	Format a disk

Some operating systems are not told what to do by system commands that the user enters. Instead, the operating systems may show the available functions on the screen as small pictures called **icons**. For example, Figure 7–2 shows some icons that may be used with the Apple Macintosh operating system. The user selects the function by using the mouse to move the cursor to the icon and then clicking the mouse (pressing the button on top of the mouse). The operating system then performs the necessary action.

Characteristics of Operating Systems

Not all operating systems are alike. Different operating systems have different characteristics. A description of some of the characteristics that distinguish operating systems follows.

Single- versus Multitasking.   Some operating systems allow only one program to be executed at a time. The operating system will not begin the execution of the next program until the current program is finished. You can think of this process as *single-tasking* because only one task (program) is done at a time. With a single-tasking operating system only one program (and the supervisor) is in primary storage (Figure 7–3a).

Other operating systems allow **multitasking**, which means that more than one program can execute at a time. With these operating systems all programs being executed are in primary storage (Figure 7–3b). (If the operating system uses virtual memory, which will be discussed later, this may not be entirely true.) Although the CPU can execute instructions from only one program at a time, the operating system can jump from one program to the next without waiting for the first program to finish. Thus, the computer can execute a few instructions in

Figure 7–2 Icons for the Apple Macintosh Operating System

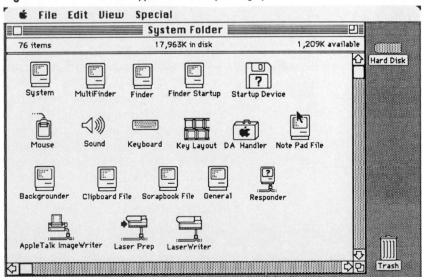

Figure 7–3 Single- Versus Multitasking

Primary Storage

| Supervisor |
| Program |

a. Single-tasking

Primary Storage

| Supervisor |
| Program 1 |
| Program 2 |
| Program 3 |

b. Multitasking

the first program, then a few instructions in the second program, then some in the third program, and so forth.

One reason that multitasking is used is that a user often wants to jump from one program to another without losing the work done by the first program. A user may begin executing one program, then decide to execute another program, and later go back to the first program. Multitasking is accomplished in this situation by letting the user interrupt the execution of a program whenever he or she wants to execute another program, usually by pressing certain keys on the keyboard. The operating system remembers where the first program was interrupted so that the user can go back to where he or she left off in that program and continue execution.

Another reason multitasking is used is that programs often have to wait for some other process to take place in the computer. For example, a program may have to wait for a user to enter data or for output to be printed. During the wait, another program can be executing. The way that multitasking is accomplished in this situation is through **multiprogramming**. In this technique each program is given a priority level. When a program with a higher priority has to wait for some other process such as input or output, the operating system executes a lower-priority program. When the higher-priority program needs to execute, however, the operating system interrupts the lower-priority program and gives control back to the higher-priority program. (Do not get multiprogramming mixed up with *multiprocessing*, a topic discussed in Chapter 3. Multiprogramming is a technique for executing several programs with a single CPU. Multiprocessing is a technique for increasing computer speed by using several CPUs.)

Single- versus Multiple-User.   Some operating systems allow only one user to use the computer at a time; they are *single-user operating systems*. A user can decide which program he or she wants to execute, and no other users can interfere. These operating systems usually allow the user to execute only one program at a time. Some, however, are multitasking systems, so the user can have several programs executing simultaneously.

Other operating systems allow more than one user to use the computer at a time; they are *multiple-user operating systems*. These operating systems are multitasking because each user could be executing a different program. A technique that is used with multiple-user operating systems is called **time-sharing**. With this technique the operating system allows each user a small amount of time to execute his or her program before going on to the next user. For example, each user may be given one-fourth of a second to execute his or her program. Although this is a short period of time, computers are so fast that they can execute thousands of instructions in this time. The operating system goes from one user to the next and eventually gets back to the first user. If there are four users and each user gets one-fourth of a second, the operating system will be back to the first user in one second. This is so fast that the user probably will never know that his or her program stopped executing for a period of time.

Batch versus Interactive.   Early operating systems were *batch operating systems*, which meant that the data for a program had to be prepared in a batch before it could be processed on the computer. The computer executed the first program and processed all its data in a batch, then went to the next program and processed its data, and so on. These operating systems did not allow the user to enter data as the program executed.

Modern systems are *interactive operating systems*, which means they allow interaction with the users as programs execute. A user can enter input data and get the results of processing that data before going on to the next input. Interactive operating systems usually also allow data to be prepared in a batch and processed without user interaction. But the interactive aspects of the operating system are of special interest to the user.

Interactive operating systems may be single-user or multiple-user, single-tasking or multitasking. When an operating system interacts with multiple users, each user sometimes has to wait a few seconds for a response. Some systems, called *real-time operating systems*, respond immediately to high-priority requests for processing. The "users" of these operating systems usually are machines or equipment that must get a response immediately—that is, in "real time." For example, an operating system for a computer that monitors patients in an intensive-care unit of a hospital must respond immediately to any abnormal change in a patient's condition.

Real versus Virtual Memory.   One of the limitations of computers is the amount of primary storage available for storing programs. A program may be too large for primary storage, or several programs that need to be in primary storage at one time may require more space than is available. Some operating systems can only execute programs that can fit into the available primary storage or *real memory*. Other operating systems, however, can execute programs that are too big for primary storage. They accomplish this by using secondary storage to make the computer appear as if it has more memory than the real memory. The memory the computer appears to have with these operating systems is called **virtual memory**. For example, a computer may have real memory of 1M byte (one million bytes) and virtual memory of 32M bytes. Thus, programs larger than 1M byte can be executed. If the operating system is multitasking, several programs that together require more than 1M byte can be executed.

A virtual-memory operating system executes large programs by leaving some of the program in secondary storage and loading into primary storage only a part of the program at a time (Figure 7–4). When a part of the program that is not in primary storage is needed, the operating system brings it in from secondary storage, replacing another part of the program already in primary storage. This process is handled automatically by the operating system without the user knowing it is going on.

Utility Software

In addition to the basic functions described so far, most operating systems provide additional capabilities performed by other programs that accompany the operating system. These other programs are called **utility programs** because they perform useful functions. For example, most operating systems have a *sort utility*, which is a program for rearranging data in a file into a specified order. There may also be a *merge utility* for merging two files into one, a *print utility* for printing the contents of a file, and a *copy utility* for copying the data from disk to tape or vice versa. Using utility programs can make it easier to perform common processing functions on the computer.

Figure 7–4 Virtual Memory

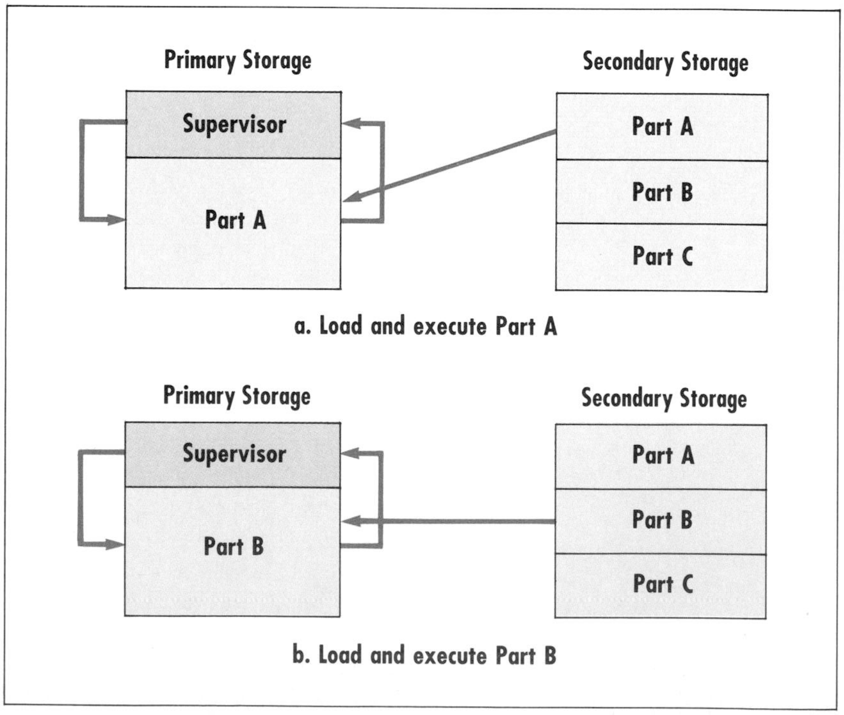

a. Load and execute Part A

b. Load and execute Part B

COMMON OPERATING SYSTEMS

There are many operating systems in use. For some computers, only one operating system is available, but for many computers several different operating systems can be used. Operating systems for microcomputers are usually simpler than those for minicomputers and mainframe computers. First we will discuss common microcomputer operating systems, then we will examine operating systems for larger computers.

Microcomputer Operating Systems

There are several common operating systems for microcomputers. Most are single-tasking, single-user, interactive, real-memory systems, although some have other characteristics.

IBM PC DOS.   Perhaps the best-known microcomputer operating system is DOS for IBM personal computers and IBM clones. DOS stands for Disk Operating System. On the IBM personal computers (PC, XT, AT, and PS/2), this operating system is called PC DOS. On IBM clones it is called MS DOS. The letters MS stand for Microsoft, which is the name of the company that developed the operating system.

DOS is a single-tasking, single-user, interactive, real-memory operating system. When it is ready for the user to enter a system command, DOS displays a letter followed by a "greater than" sign on the screen (for example, A>). The letter identifies a disk drive; the first disk drive is labeled A, the second B, the third C, and so forth. The system command entered by the user applies to the disk drive identified by the letter. For example, to delete a file stored on the disk in disk drive A, the user would type ERASE followed by the name of the file after A>. Some of the commands used with DOS were listed earlier in Table 7–1.

IBM OS/2.   For IBM PS/2 computers, another operating system is available besides PC DOS. This operating system is called OS/2 for Operating System/2. It is similar to PC DOS, using many of the same commands. Like PC DOS, OS/2 is a single-user, interactive, real-memory operating system. Unlike PC DOS, however, OS/2 allows the user to have multiple programs executing at one time, switching from one program to another. Thus, it is a multitasking operating system.

Another difference between PC DOS and OS/2 is that with OS/2 larger programs can be stored in primary storage. With PC DOS, primary storage is limited to 640K bytes. All programs must either fit into this space or be divided into segments that fit and are executed by loading a segment at a time.[1] With OS/2, however, this limit does not exist, and hence large programs can be stored in primary storage.

---

[1]There are expanded memory systems for DOS that allow programs to be larger than 640K bytes.

COMPUTER CLOSE-UP

7–1

DO WHAT I MEAN

If you are the type to get angry with inanimate objects, you probably have on occasion wanted to take a sledgehammer to your computer keyboard. Perhaps, desiring a directory of the files stored on a disk, you meant to type the disk operating system command "dir," but typed "dor" instead. When you do that, DOS spits back the message "Bad command." Why can't the computer figure out that the only three-letter command that begins with a d and ends with an r is the one that lists the files? Why, if microprocessors are so smart, are they so stupid in some ways?

What you need is a fuzzy DOS, which would understand imprecise commands. Such a product is evidently not yet on the market, but perhaps one will be someday soon, if a new type of user-friendliness takes hold. The approach is called DWIM, for "do what I mean."

DWIM-inspired software accepts misspelled and imprecise names or commands or even scribbles, making plausible guesses about what the user intended. Among the companies selling or developing programs with DWIM features are Axon, which is working on sketch-making software; Frank-

lin Electronic Publishers, which sells a "Friendly Finder" program that hunts a database for the name that most closely approximates the incorrect one you typed out; and Go Corp., which is developing software to read handwriting.

Seattle-based Axon, the creation of Jeremy Jaech, is developing a drawing program for the sloppy drawer. There are, to be sure, a multitude of drawing programs available. But most are too powerful, too precise for the casual user to master. If you draw a ragged circle with a mouse on one of these programs, that's what you get, a ragged circle. Or, you can order up a perfect circle, but in doing that you quickly become entangled in a confusing blur of "tools," pull-down menus, and double-clicking mouse commands. Jaech's idea: a program for the unartistic, one with less flexibility but more tolerance. It will automatically transform a rough sketch into a polished one, smoothing jagged arcs, aligning boxes that aren't aligned and connecting boxes into organizational charts. Similarly: Vellum, a design program from Ashlar in Sunnyvale, California, calculates midpoints of lines and assists an engineer with tasks such as drawing perfectly equilateral triangles. You can be sloppy, but it will be precise.

This all fits into a concept called "constraint-based programming." In Jeremy Jaech's words: "If the computer program knows there are only certain things that can be done in a given context, then it will shepherd you in that direction."

Sometimes the user doesn't want to be shepherded. One unsuccessful word processor, called Mindreader, guessed what word you were typing as you were halfway through typing it. This backseat driving proved to be too intrusive, and the feature never caught on.

Mitch Kapor, the man behind Lotus 1-2-3 and founder of On Technology, a Cambridge, Massachusetts developer of software for the Apple Macintosh, says the administrator of a large Unix installation will sometimes write a program to capture bad commands that don't execute. Every week or so the administrator will check to see what common mistakes his users made, then incorporate those mistakes into the system's set of understandable commands.

But, Kapor adds, "DWIM is tricky. If you want to draw a squiggle and your system converts it into a straight line, then it has defeated your purpose. These systems can quickly become the sorcerer's apprentice of software.

On the leading edge of tolerant software is Go Corp., the Foster City, California startup that is working on a "slate" computer. This is a hand-held machine that uses a drawing pen instead of a keyboard, allowing a user to write on a screen and have the computer translate the scrawl into computer text. Like a competent secretary, it will do more than match letters to patterns; it will make judgments based on the context in which those letters appear. A literal-minded machine might say that your intended "6" is closer to a "b"; a DWIM program, noting that the character is in the middle of a telephone number, will read it as a number.

Most computers are and will be built from extremely precise logic circuits. But with an overlay of programs that forgive mistakes and even carry actions out to the next step, the computer may, finally, become a friendly device. Put away that sledgehammer. Help is on the way.

Apple Macintosh Operating System.   The operating system on the Apple Macintosh is quite a bit different from DOS and OS/2. First, it does not have a name, although it is sometimes called System followed by a number, such as System 7.0. More importantly, the operating system is used through another program called Finder. This program displays icons on the screen through which the user selects functions. For example, to delete a file, the user uses the mouse to point the cursor at an icon for the file on the screen, presses the button on the mouse, moves the cursor to an icon that looks like a trash can, and releases the button on the mouse (Figure 7–5). In other words, the user deletes a file by throwing it away into the trash.

The basic Macintosh operating system is a single-tasking, single-user, interactive, real-memory operating system. A multitasking version of it is also available. It is used through a program called Multifinder. With this operating system, a user can have several programs executing at one time and can switch from one program to another. Each program can use a different section of the screen for its display so that the user can see several applications at once.

UNIX.   Some powerful microcomputers use an operating system called UNIX. This operating system was developed for minicomputers in the early 1970s by Bell Laboratories. Since its original development, it has undergone many revisions. Today, versions of UNIX are available for some microcomputers.

UNIX is a multitasking, multiple-user, interactive, virtual-memory operating system. Thus, it has characteristics that other microcomputer operating systems do not have. Because it is a multiple-user operating system, microcomputers running UNIX can be used by more than one user at a time, provided the computer has the necessary hardware. Its virtual memory capability allows it to execute large programs. UNIX has a number of special features, but many people consider it difficult to use.

Other Microcomputer Operating Systems.   Some microcomputers use operating systems different from the ones already described. For example,

Figure 7–5   Using the Apple Macintosh Operating System to Delete a File

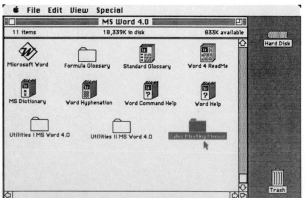
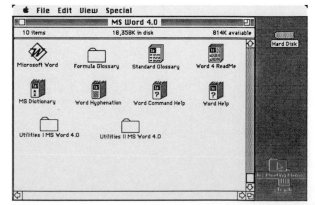

the Apple II line of microcomputers uses an operating system called ProDOS. Some older-style microcomputers use an operating system called CP/M. Non–IBM-compatible microcomputers made by Atari, Commodore, and Tandy have their own operating systems.

Minicomputer and Mainframe Computer Operating Systems

The first operating systems for large computers were single-tasking, batch, real-memory systems. As computers became more powerful, their operating systems became more sophisticated. Today, most minicomputers and mainframe computer operating systems are multitasking (multiprogramming), multiple-user (time-sharing), interactive, virtual-memory systems. These operating systems have many more features than microcomputer operating systems have. For example, they often have complex security features to prevent unauthorized use of the computer. They are also more complex to use than microcomputer operating systems. Some examples are VM (Virtual Machine) for IBM mainframe computers, MVS (Multiple Virtual Storage), also for IBM mainframe computers, and VMS (Virtual Memory System) for the DEC VAX line of minicomputers.

Most operating systems for minicomputers and mainframe computers, such as those listed in the previous paragraph, are designed to be used on a specific computer. For example, VM can be used only on IBM mainframe computers. Versions of UNIX, however, are available for many minicomputers and mainframe computers. As discussed earlier, UNIX is also available for some microcomputers. When it is used on different computers, including microcomputers, users do not have to learn how to use a new operating system when changing from one computer to another. Some people think UNIX will be one of the most common operating systems in the future.

THE SOFTWARE INTERFACE

Operating systems as well as other types of software interact with the user through a software interface. This interface consists of those parts of a program that communicate with the user through the hardware interface—that is, through input and output devices. These parts of a program contain instructions that accept input from the user and produce output for the user. For example, when a user uses a keyboard to type input data, instructions in a program tell the computer to take the data entered at the keyboard and to store it in primary storage. Similarly, a user sees output on a screen because instructions in a program tell the computer to transfer data from primary storage to the screen and to display the data. These input and output instructions create the software interface that communicates with the user through the hardware.

How the software interface appears to the user varies greatly between programs and varies with different types of hardware. One important characteristic, however, of a software interface is that it should be easy for the user to use. What makes software easy to use is not clear. Some software is easier to use than others, but there are no definite rules for an easy-to-use software interface. Often, you hear the term *user-friendly software*. This is supposed to refer to software that is very easy to use. Unfortunately, people sometimes use this phrase for software that is not so easy to use.

There are two main reasons a user interacts with software: to control the software and to enter input and receive output. The user needs to control the software so that he or she can make the software perform certain functions. For example, if a payroll program is executing, the user needs to tell the program which payroll function to perform next—accept the payroll data, calculate the pay, or produce the payroll report. The user needs to enter input data to be processed and receive the output from processing. For example, when a payroll program is accepting payroll data, the user must enter the data at the keyboard. When the program produces the payroll report, the user receives this output.

Controlling Software

A user needs a way of controlling software so that the software does what the user wants. Two common approaches are to use commands and to make selections from menus.

Commands. A **command** is a word or phrase that tells the program to do something. The user enters a command by typing in the word or phrase. This approach is used commonly with system software including many operating systems. As noted earlier, the commands for an operating system are called *system commands*. For example, with DOS, the operating system used on IBM PCs, typing the command DIR (for directory) causes the operating system to display a list of all the files stored in secondary storage. This approach is not used as frequently with application software.

Before a program can be given a command, it must tell the user it is ready to accept the command, which usually is accomplished by displaying a **prompt** on the screen. The prompt means that the program is ready for the next command. For example, the prompt used by DOS is a letter followed by a greater-than sign—for example, A>. Prompts take on many forms; Figure 7–6 shows some examples. Many times, a prompt is just a symbol or a single word, and the user must recognize what it means. At other times, the prompt is a phrase or question that explains what the user is to do. In all cases, the user must know what commands can be entered after the prompt. The acceptable commands depend on the software.

Menus. A **menu** is a list of options for a program displayed on a screen (Figure 7–7). The program displays the menu and then waits for the user to make a selection. After the user enters his or her selection, the program performs the required processing.

A menu may be displayed vertically or horizontally on the screen. Once the menu is displayed, the user can select from it in several different ways. In one approach, each item in the menu is given a code, which usually is a letter or number, and the user types in the appropriate code after a prompt (Figure 7–7). Sometimes the codes are the first letters of the menu items, so the user just has to look at the items to know the codes. In another approach, the user makes a selection by pressing one of the function keys. In still another approach, the user highlights the desired menu item by pressing the cursor control keys and then presses the Enter or Return key (Figure 7–8). The user can also use a mouse to move the cursor until it points to the desired item. Then the user clicks the mouse (presses the button on top of the mouse) to select the menu item (Figure 7–9). Finally, touch screens, touch pads, and other touch input devices can be used for menu selection.

Often, selecting an item from a menu causes another menu to be displayed. The first menu is usually called the *main menu*, and the other menus are called *submenus*. Figure 7–10 shows an example of a main

Figure 7–6 Examples of Prompts

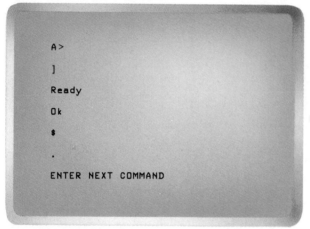

Figure 7–7 A Menu

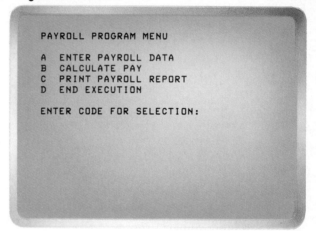

Figure 7–8 Selecting an Item from a Menu by Highlighting the Item

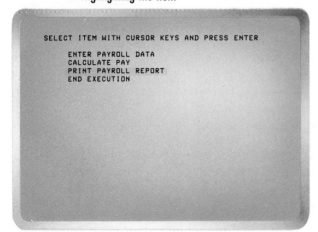

Figure 7–9 Using a Mouse to Select an Item from a Menu

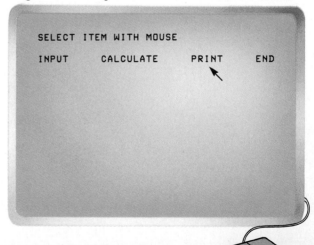

Figure 7–10 A Main Menu and Three Submenus

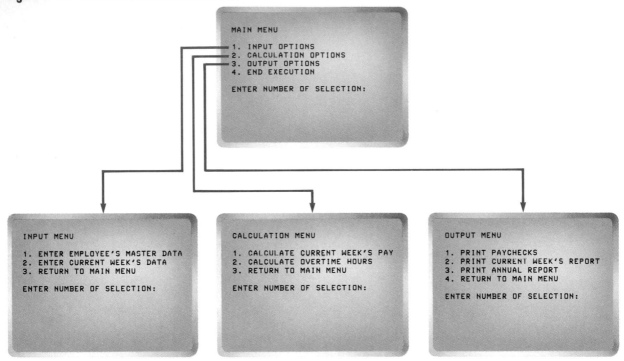

menu and three submenus. Each submenu can also have its own submenus. Usually one of the items in a submenu is an option to return to the previous menu. In the main menu there usually is an item that allows the user to stop the execution of the program completely.

Sometimes a list of menu titles, called a *menu bar*, is displayed across the top of the screen. Then a menu is displayed under a menu title when that title is selected with the cursor control keys or a mouse (Figure 7–11). The menu appears on top of the other items displayed on the screen and disappears after it is used. This type of menu is called a **pull-down menu** or a **pop-up menu**. The menu bar stays on the screen, and the menus are pulled down when needed.

Menus and submenus are most often used with application software. An advantage of menus over commands is that the user does not have to remember commands. A disadvantage is that using menus can be slower than using commands if the user knows the commands. Some software allows the use of either commands or menus.

Icons. The items listed in a menu usually consist of words or phrases that describe each task the software can do. Sometimes **icons** are used instead of words. Recall that an icon is a small picture that represents some function the software can perform (Figure 7–12). For example, a picture of an eraser may represent the function of erasing something on the screen. The function is selected by using the mouse to move the cursor to the icon and then clicking the mouse.

Figure 7–11   A Pull-Down Menu

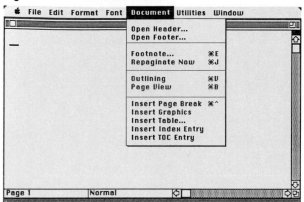

Figure 7–12   Icons

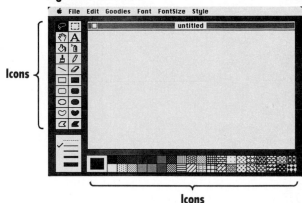

The advantage of icons over words and phrases is that the user can quickly grasp what the icon means. When a menu contains words, a lengthy description may be necessary for each menu item. (Remember the saying that a picture is worth a thousand words?) Some users do not like icons, however, and prefer the other approach.

Icons are used with both system software and application software. For example, the Apple Macintosh operating system uses icons to represent functions (refer back to Figure 7–2). Many application programs for the Macintosh also use icons.

Help Screens.   Users often find it difficult to remember all the options that are available with a particular program. Even with menus or icons it may be hard to remember what each item means. Consequently, many programs have **Help screens** that provide additional explanations of how to use the software. A Help screen is activated by pressing a special Help key that may be one of the function keys, or by making a menu selection. Sometimes the user just types the word HELP to get an explanation of what to do next.

The way a Help screen works depends on the software. Commonly, when the user requests help, the program figures out where the user is stuck and provides a screen of explanations that help the user at that point. For example, if a menu is displayed on the screen and the user requests help, a brief explanation of each option in the menu is displayed. Alternatively, if the user selects an option from the menu and then requests help, a detailed description of just the selected option is displayed.

Data Input and Output

In addition to being able to control software, a user needs to enter input data and receive output from a program. How data input and output are accomplished depends on the program.

Data Input.   The user can enter input data in several ways. With some software the user can enter data in an unrestricted format, called

Figure 7–13   Freeform Input

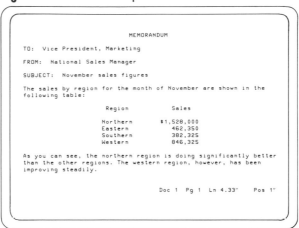

```
                              MEMORANDUM

TO:   Vice President, Marketing

FROM:  National Sales Manager

SUBJECT:  November sales figures

The sales by region for the month of November are shown in the
following table:

                        Region            Sales

                        Northern        $1,528,000
                        Eastern            462,350
                        Southern           382,325
                        Western            846,325

As you can see, the northern region is doing significantly better
than the other regions. The western region, however, has been
improving steadily.

                                    Doc 1  Pg 1  Ln 4.33"     Pos 1"
```

freeform input. This is the case when using a computer for word processing, which was discussed in Chapter 1. Word processing uses software that allows the user to type whatever he or she wants in any form on an almost blank screen (Figure 7–13).

Most software requires the user to enter data in some prescribed form, called *fixed-format input* (Figure 7–14). Usually, the data to be entered consists of fields (groups of characters), and each field is entered separately. The program may provide a prompt for each field. With such *prompted input*, the program displays a prompt, the user enters the input data, and then the program displays the next prompt. Alternatively, the program may display a form on the screen, which really is just prompts for all the fields shown at once. Then the user enters data for each field in the form. Often, this type of *form input*

Figure 7–14   Fixed-Format Input

(a)   Prompted Input

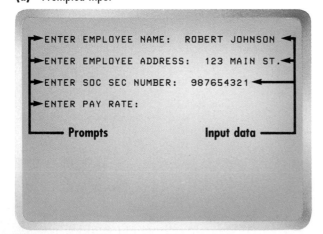

```
►ENTER EMPLOYEE NAME:   ROBERT JOHNSON◄

►ENTER EMPLOYEE ADDRESS:   123 MAIN ST.◄

►ENTER SOC SEC NUMBER:   987654321◄

►ENTER PAY RATE:
```
Prompts   Input data

(b)   Form Input

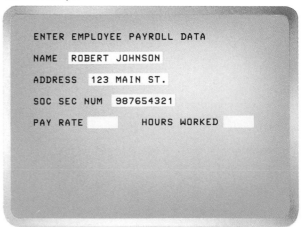

```
      ENTER EMPLOYEE PAYROLL DATA

   NAME   ROBERT JOHNSON

   ADDRESS   123 MAIN ST.

   SOC SEC NUM   987654321

   PAY RATE            HOURS WORKED
```

allows the user to go back and change the value of any field before going on to the next form.

Another way input data may be entered is to provide a menu of choices for the user (Figure 7–15). *Menu input* can be used only in specialized situations in which the possible input data values are limited. The user selects the appropriate value from the menu by using one of the techniques discussed earlier.

Data Output.   Output data can be presented to the user in several ways (Figure 7–16). Most software provides some form of *screen output* that displays a small amount of data. A program also may produce *report output*, which is a larger amount of data arranged in lines, each containing many items. Usually, a report is printed on paper (sometimes called *hard copy*), although it may be displayed on a screen (called *soft copy*). *Graphic output* is another way that the results of processing can be presented to the user. Graphs may be displayed on the screen or produced on paper by using a printer or a plotter.

Windows

Sometimes the software interface is designed so that different parts of the screen can be used for different purposes at the same time. For example, one part of the screen may be used for a menu, another part for data entry, still another part to display a report, and a final part to display a graph. This display may be the result of a single program executing in the computer or of several programs executing at the same time.

In this situation the screen is usually divided into sections called **windows** (Figure 7–17). Each window is surrounded by a border and contains one type of display. Usually, each window can be increased in size, decreased in size, or eliminated from the screen. One window may overlap another, or the windows may be nonoverlapping. The advantage of windows is that the user can view multiple inputs and outputs at one time.

Figure 7–15   Menu Input

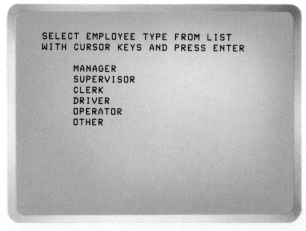

```
SELECT EMPLOYEE TYPE FROM LIST
WITH CURSOR KEYS AND PRESS ENTER

      MANAGER
      SUPERVISOR
      CLERK
      DRIVER
      OPERATOR
      OTHER
```

Figure 7–16 Forms of Output

(a) Screen Output

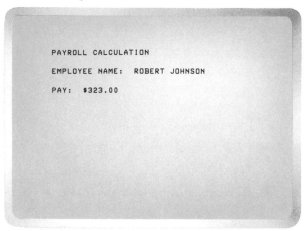

(b) Report Output

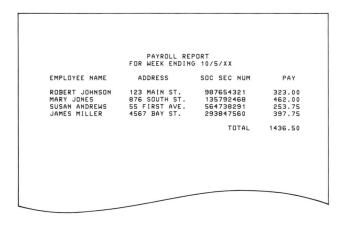

(c) Graphic Output

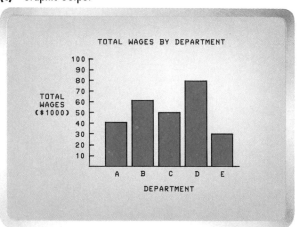

Figure 7–17 Windows

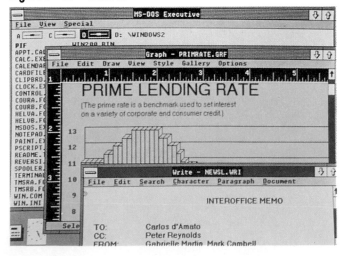

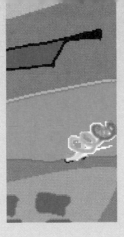

MACS TALK TO THE VISUALLY IMPAIRED

Graphical user interfaces have opened new horizons for most personal computer users, but for blind and visually impaired people, visual windows and icons bring up a new series of obstacles that most cannot surmount. These users rely on character-based screen systems on IBM-compatible PCs to transform on-screen words into speech, braille or scanned output.

That state of affairs left the Apple Computer, Inc. Macintosh's screen virtually off-limits to visually impaired users. However, Berkeley Systems, Inc., a software firm that produces Macintosh system utilities, sells a program that can "read" the Mac's on-screen icons and transform them and the applications they represent into spoken words.

The program, called Outspoken, is aimed at the small community of visually impaired computer users believed to be just a fraction of the 500,000 blind people in the U.S. "We've tried to keep the interface very consistent with the Mac's visual interface," Berkeley Systems President Wes Boyd said.

The unique feature of Outspoken, which "speaks" with a built-in voice-synthesizer that is on-board all Macs, is its linkage to the Mac operating system. Having mastered the ways of Outspoken, even sightless users can buy any new Macintosh program and run that application software without needing to adapt it.

Berkeley System's Marc Sutton, who is sightless save for a perception of light and dark, said the program allows him to access electronic databases, use off-the-shelf spreadsheet and word-processing packages and store notes in electronic files. Using the numeric keypad rather than a mouse, Sutton uses the Mac as quickly as a sighted user.

"There's a real satisfaction that you can conceptualize what's on-screen," said Sutton, who is the technical-support manager for the product. "In everything I do, whether I'm working in an office, eating in a restaurant or walking around the house, I go through a lot of mapping in my mind. Now, I can navigate around the Macintosh screen, even though I can't see it. It's not abstraction anymore." Documentation comes in braille, on audio tape and as embossed images of screen icons.

Sounds substitute for visual cues. As the cursor travels across the Mac's screen, Outspoken users hear a series of words describing objects the cursor touches. For example, the Mac voice might say, in somewhat flattened, electronic tones: "Microsoft Word," "icon" or "database file." When the cursor crosses into another window, a slight beep is heard. As words are defined, a slight background noise is heard.

One user at a California aerospace firm feels a new sense of independence because of the Outspoken package. "Before this, I had people helping me by setting up special Hypercard stacks so I could read them from left to right in a straight line," said the user, who has partial vision. "Now, I can go out and buy any new package, install it myself and start working with it right away."

Graphical User Interfaces

Many new programs are being designed with software interfaces that combine a number of features already discussed. In general, the interface is called a **graphical user interface,** or **GUI** (Figure 7–18). A program with a graphical user interface usually displays icons on the screen and allows the user to select icons with a mouse. The icons and organization of the screen may remind the user of a desktop or some other work environment with which the user is familiar. Pull-down menus may also be used. Similar icons and menus are used for different programs so that the user does not have as much to learn when using a new program.

The screen of a program with a graphical user interface is normally divided into windows. The user can change the size and position of windows and even close (delete) old windows or open (create) new ones. This allows the user to customize the interface to the way he or she wants it. A graphical user interface on a color screen allows the user to select colors for backgrounds, icons, windows, and so forth, thus customizing the interface even more.

The Apple Macintosh operating system has a graphical user interface. Programs that run on the Macintosh also have such an interface. DOS for the IBM PC does not have a graphical user interface. Several programs that work with DOS, however, do. For example, a program called Windows by Microsoft Corporation creates a graphical user interface for IBM PCs. Using Windows, the user does not have to communicate directly with DOS. Programs designed to work with Windows, such as word-processing programs, also have graphical user interfaces.

Many users find a graphical user interface easier to work with than other software interfaces. You can expect more and more software to have this type of interface in the future.

Chapter Summary

- The main functions of an operating system are process management, which involves managing the execution of programs; resource management, which involves managing primary storage,

Figure 7–18   A Graphical User Interface

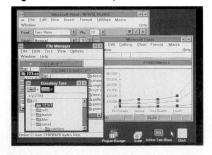
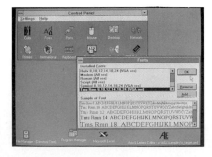

I/O devices, and secondary storage; and data management, which involves managing the flow of data between the main components of a computer. An operating system consists of several programs. One program, called the **supervisor**, is always stored in primary storage. Other programs in the operating system are stored in secondary storage and loaded into primary storage when needed.

■ Some operating systems can be told what to do by giving them instructions called **system commands**. The user enters the system command for the function he or she wants the operating system to perform. Still other operating systems display available functions as **icons** on the screen. The user selects a function by using a mouse to move the cursor to the icon for the function and then "clicking the mouse."

■ Some operating systems can execute only one program at a time, and others are **multitasking**, which means they can execute more than one program at a time. Some can be used by only one user at a time, and others can be used by multiple users simultaneously. Early systems were batch operating systems, which meant that all data had to be prepared in advance in a batch. Current operating systems are interactive, which means they allow interaction with the users as programs execute. Finally, some operating systems are capable of executing only programs as large as the actual primary storage or real memory of the computer, and other operating systems allow programs to be larger than real memory by using secondary storage to store parts of programs. With these operating systems the computer has **virtual memory** that is larger than the real memory.

■ Some common microcomputer operating systems are PC DOS, which is used with the IBM personal computers; MS DOS, which is used with IBM clones; OS/2, which is used with IBM PS/2 computers; and the Apple Macintosh operating system, which is used through a program called Finder. The UNIX operating system is used with some powerful microcomputers. Other microcomputer operating systems include ProDOS for the Apple II line of computers, CP/M for older style microcomputers, and operating systems for non–IBM-compatible computers made by Atari, Commodore, and Tandy.

■ A user can control software by entering **commands**. Each command is entered after a **prompt**. A user can also control software by selecting options from a **menu**. A menu item may be selected by typing in a code number or letter, pressing a function key, highlighting an item with cursor control keys, or using a mouse to move the cursor to the item and then "clicking the mouse." Some menus, called **pull-down menus**, appear on top of other items displayed on the screen when selected, and disappear after use. Finally, a user can control software by selecting an **icon**. The user selects an icon by using a mouse to move the cursor to the icon, and then "clicking the mouse."

■ Users can enter input data into a program in a freeform style or a fixed format. In the latter case, the user may enter each input item after a prompt or may fill in a form on the screen. The user can also select input items from a menu. Users can receive output from a program in the form of a short screen display, as a long report printed on paper or displayed on a screen, and in graphic form displayed on a screen or produced on paper by a printer or a plotter.

- **Graphical user interfaces** combine a number of features to make programs easy to use. These include displaying icons on the screen and allowing the user to select icons with a mouse, creating a screen that looks like a desktop or other work environment, using pull-down menus, and organizing the screen into **windows**. The user can usually customize a graphical user interface to make it exactly the way he or she wants.

Terms to Remember

Booting p. 177

Command p. 188

External Command p. 178

Graphical User Interface (GUI) p. 196

Help Screen p. 191

Icon p. 190

Internal Command p. 178

Job-Control Language (JCL) p. 178

Menu p. 188

Multiprogramming p. 180

Multitasking p. 179

Prompt p. 188

Pull-Down (Pop-Up) Menu p. 190

Supervisor p. 176

System Command p. 178

Time-Sharing p. 181

Utility Program p. 182

Virtual Memory p. 181

Window p. 193

Review Questions

Fill-In Questions

1. Loading the supervisor is called _____.

2. Before you can use a minicomputer or mainframe computer you must _____. After you have finished you must _____.

3. The set of system commands used with a mainframe computer operating system is called _____.

4. Small pictures displayed on a screen that represent functions a program can perform are called _____.

5. A technique used by some operating systems that allows multiple users to use the computer at one time is called _____.

6. Some operating systems allow programs to be larger than primary storage by creating _____ that is greater than the primary storage.

7. A word or phrase entered at a keyboard that tells a program to perform a function is called a(n) _____.

8. A(n) _____ is a symbol, word, or phrase displayed on a screen to indicate that a program is ready to accept input.

9. A(n) _____ is an explanation, displayed on a screen, of how to use some function of a program.

10. A section of a screen surrounded by a border and containing one type of display is a(n) _____.

Short-Answer Questions

1. What are the three main functions of an operating system?

2. What does the supervisor of an operating system do?

3. Explain the difference between internal and external system commands for an operating system.

4. What is multitasking, and what are two reasons it is used?

5. Name some common microcomputer operating systems.

6. What operating system can be used on some microcomputers as well as on some minicomputers and mainframe computers?

7. What is meant by *user-friendly software*?

8. What are the two main reasons users interact with software?

9. What is a menu? What is a pull-down menu?

10. Describe several ways that users can enter input into a program.

11. Describe several ways that users can receive output from a program.

12. What is a graphical user interface?

Projects

1. If you are using a computer for a class or have access to one, find out everything you can about the computer's operating system. What is the name of the operating system? Is it multitasking? Is it a single-user, or a multiple-user, operating system? Is it a virtual-memory operating system? How does the user control the operating system? What are some of its system commands?

2. Investigate a microcomputer program you have never seen before. Write a description of its user interface.

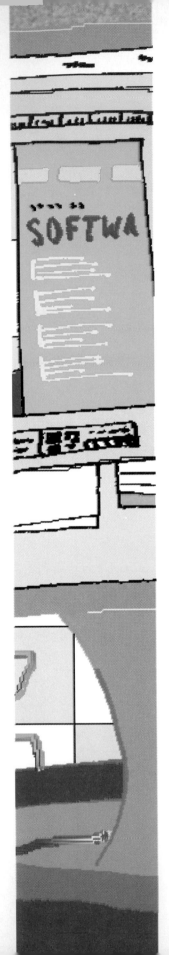

8

WORD PROCESSING SOFTWARE

CHAPTER OBJECTIVES

• After completing this chapter you should be able to:

1. Describe the types of situations in which word processing is more efficient than using a typewriter.

2. Explain the main functions of word processing software and describe several techniques used to control them.

3. State the microcomputer hardware needed for word processing.

4. List several additional features of word processing software.

5. Identify several common word processing programs and the computers with which they can be used.

6. Explain what desktop publishing is and give some of the special features of desktop publishing software.

T HE TYPE of software that users encounter most frequently is application software. As you know, application software is designed to help solve specific problems. Users use some application software for only one particular purpose, such as preparing payroll. Other application software is more general, and users can use it for many purposes.

Most general application software is found on microcomputers. Typically, this software is used by a single user on a personal computer, although some microcomputer software is designed for use by multiple users in a network. Some general application software is available on minicomputers and mainframe computers and is designed for use by multiple users, but it is not as common as on microcomputers.

The next four chapters describe the most common general application software for microcomputers. This chapter discusses word processing and related software. The following three chapters describe spreadsheet, data management, graphics, and other software.

WORD PROCESSING

Probably the most common use of microcomputers is for *word processing*, which involves using a computer as a sophisticated typewriter. With word processing, a user can type the text of a document—such as a letter or report—into the computer, make changes electronically, and print one or more copies of the document. The user can save the text in secondary storage and return to it in the future, perhaps to make changes and print another copy.

Almost all work normally done on a typewriter can be done more efficiently by using a computer for word processing. Sometimes short documents that are used only once, such as memos and letters, can be prepared just as easily with a typewriter. But for long reports and documents that may require changes in the future, computerized word processing is much more efficient. The principle advantage of word processing is that a person's *productivity* is improved; that is, a person can do more work in a period of time with word processing than without. Some organizations have stopped using typewriters altogether and instead use computers for preparing all memos, letters, reports, and other documents.

A **word processing system** consists of a computer and **word processing software** (Figure 8–1). Although large computers can be used for word processing, most of the time a microcomputer is used. The word processing software provides the functions needed to accomplish word processing with the computer.

Figure 8–1   A Word Processing System

WORD PROCESSING SOFTWARE FUNCTIONS

When a user uses word processing software, he or she manipulates data that consists of characters, words, paragraphs, and so on. This type of data is called **text**. The user can perform three main functions with text data when using word processing software: enter text into the computer, change or edit text, and print text in different formats. Word processing programs perform these functions in different ways. Some of the features that are common to many types of word processing software are described here.

Entering Text

When a user enters text by using a word processing system, he or she types in the characters just as on a typewriter. The characters, however, are not printed on paper. Rather, they are displayed on the screen and stored in the computer's primary storage. When the user reaches the end of a line, he or she does not press the Enter or Return key. Instead, the user just keeps typing; the computer automatically continues onto the next line, moving any word that does not fit at the end of the line to the beginning of the next line. This feature is called **word wrap**, and it speeds up typing time. The user presses the Enter or Return key only at the end of the paragraph.

Some word processing programs tell the user when a word needs to be hyphenated at the end of a line, a feature called **hyphen help**. The program usually suggests where a hyphen should go and allows the user to insert a hyphen there or someplace else in the word, or to not hyphenate the word at all. Often, this feature as well as others can be turned off if the user does not want to use it.

COMPUTER CLOSE-UP

8—1

SOFTWARE TO HELP YOU WAX POETIC

Shall I compare thee to a perfect word processor?

Mmmm. Michael Newman's Poetry Processor informs me that my first effort at writing a software review in iambic pentameter has gone awry. Fie!

Mr. Newman, a contributing editor of *The Paris Review*, who was a protege of W. H. Auden, has developed three intriguing programs that should delight anyone who loves words.

The programs might even instill a love of words in people who never imagined that creative writing, especially poetry, could be fun.

Just as the electronic calculator and spreadsheet can free the math student from much of the mechanical drudgery of manipulating numbers, the Poetry Processor and its companion programs can free the writer from the mechanical side of prosody, the science and art of versification.

There are three programs, all for IBM PCs and compatibles: The Poetry Processor, which automates the scanning of lines for metrical structure, simple rhyme, cadence and format; Newman's Electronic Rhyming Dictionary, which goes beyond simple rhyme

to suggest internal and slant rhymes; and Orpheus A-B-C, a poetry tutorial that helps the user understand and enjoy the many forms of verse.

The advantages of using a computer for word processing are well known. Yet, Mr. Newman contends, the computer is perhaps even better suited for prosody than for prose.

"A sonnet is an algorithmic system of prompts," he suggested. And what is better suited to deal with prompts, or signals from your computer, and algorithms, or sets of mathematical rules, than a computer?

Using computer algorithms developed by Paul Holzer, a programmer in New York, the software dissects language and displays its sounds, cadence, and form on screen.

The Poetry Processor has the ability to scan a poet's work for meter, assonance and consonance, and to display the results in color-coded highlights, so that even a first-time poet can see how the rhymes and wordplay fit together. There are templates for virtually every poetic style, from sonnets to haiku and sestinas.

"I like to claim that this is the only software that teaches you to write well," Mr. Newman rhapsodized. Word processors do not teach a person to write better, but "poetic forms are self-editing," he noted.

With prosody, Mr. Newman said, "You count every beat, every measure, every line, and that has been a drawback for many people" who might have a poet's soul but the reporter's impatience.

For example, assonance and consonance are the repetitions of vowel and consonant sounds that give poetry much of its aural richness. On paper these aspects are invisible to the casual reader, but on the computer screen the interplay of words stand out in color codes.

"It is really classical poetry in its structured form that is teaching you to write, and the Poetry Processor acts as a midwife," Mr. Newman said. "The forms stimulate you to write."

It was while visiting Silicon Valley, the cradle of cold passionless technology, that

Mr. Newman conceived the idea for the Poetry Processor.

Electronic dictionaries and thesauruses were possible, so why not an electronic rhyming dictionary? In effect, he theorized, the software would automate the type of association processes that occur in a poet's brain, the poet's built-in software.

Next came form. The algorithms were encoded, and the Poetry Processor scanned for syllables, accents, rhyme patterns, number of lines, and other poetic attributes.

On screen, a list of rhyming words appears in one corner; the chosen poetic form is displayed below both in stanza and in meter. For example, a Shakespearean sonnet appears as a form of 14 lines with a certain rhyme scheme, and each line is in iambic pentameter. (An iamb is a two-syllable unit with the accent on the second syllable; five iambs to a line.) The meter is shown as something like Morse code: -/-/-/-/-/.

"The rhymes are there with ease, set up like duck pins waiting to be knocked down, and the poet is thinking only about writing with meter," Mr. Newman said. "The software breaks down everything in steps."

With the mechanics out of the way, the poet is free to concentrate on thought and emotions.

Some poets may contend that the automated poetry processing lessens creativity rather than enhances it. Mr. Newman disagrees. For students, especially, he said, the software allows them to feel as if they were born to be poets. It puts them in touch with a side of their creativity that might otherwise never be tapped.

If the user makes a mistake when entering text, he or she can press the Backspace or Delete kcy to erase the previous characters on the screen and in primary storage. If a mistake is discovered farther back in the document, the user can use the editing feature, discussed later, to correct the error. Any errors in the document can be corrected at any time.

As the user types, he or she can tell the word processing software to do special things with the text. For example, the user can tell the software to center a title or align a column and can specify that certain text should be underlined or printed in bold face. The type style—the font—can also be changed in the middle of a document, and superscripts and subscripts can be entered. These features and others are available with different word processing software.

Sometimes when typing, the user may want to include text from another document. In law offices, for example, standard prewritten paragraphs are often brought together in a legal document. This process can be done with word processing software by copying the required paragraphs from secondary storage into the text being entered. These paragraphs must have been previously stored in secondary storage. Still, this approach can save much typing when the standard paragraphs are used over and over again.

Some word processing software limits the amount of text that can be entered to the amount that can be stored in primary storage. The limit may be as little as ten pages. If a document is longer than the limit, it must be broken up into several sections, each less than the maximum allowed. Other word processing software permits documents to be longer than the amount of text that can be stored in primary storage. This software automatically moves sections of text to secondary storage when primary storage is full. Then a document can be several hundred pages long.

After entering the text, the user must *save* it in secondary storage (Figure 8–2). This step is required even if the word processing software

Figure 8–2 Entering Text

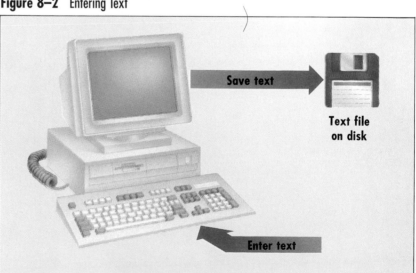

automatically moves sections of text to secondary storage. It is necessary to save the text because primary storage is used only for the text currently being processed. If the user does not save the text, it will be lost when new text is entered into primary storage. In addition, whatever is in primary storage is lost when the computer is turned off, whereas anything stored in secondary storage is not lost. Text is saved by storing it as a **text file** in secondary storage. The text file must be given a name so that the user can refer to it again in the future.

Editing Text

Editing is the process of making changes or corrections in text. With word processing software, a user can easily make changes in a document without having to completely retype it. The user can insert new text, delete old text, and replace existing text with new text. Text can also be moved from one place to another in a document. Any changes the user wants can be made in a document.

Before text can be edited, it must be in primary storage. If the text has just been entered, then it is still in primary storage. If the text was previously saved in secondary storage, however, the user must *retrieve* it from a file before editing it. After editing the text, the user must *save* the new text (Figure 8–3). When the new text is saved, it replaces the old text in the file.

After the text is in primary storage, the user can move the cursor to any place in the text. The cursor can be moved up or down a line, to the left or right of a character or a word, to the beginning or end of a paragraph, to the beginning or end of the text, or to any other desired place.

Once the cursor is in position, there are several choices to be made. The user can *insert* text by typing the new text at that point. The old text moves to the right as the new text is added. Alternatively, the user can

Figure 8–3 Editing Text

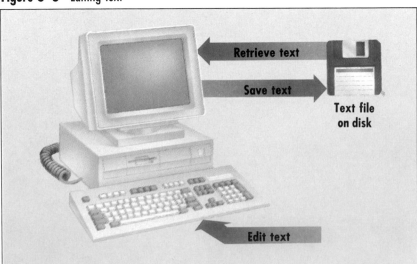

replace the old text with the new text. As the new text is added, the old characters are erased and replaced by the new characters. If the user wants, he or she can *delete* text at the point where the cursor is located without replacing the deleted characters. If the user deletes something in error, he or she can use the **undo** feature to replace the deleted text.

Some of the most useful editing features involve manipulating a large amount of text called a **block**. A block may be a few words, a sentence, a paragraph, or many paragraphs. The user first marks the block in the document by using special keys or a mouse. Then he or she can move or copy the block to another part of the document, delete the block, or save the block separately in secondary storage. Sometimes this feature is called **cut and paste** because it is like cutting a section out of a paper document and pasting it someplace else in the document.

Another useful editing feature is called **search and replace**. With this feature the user can search the document for any text, such as a word or a phrase, and replace it with new text. The user can search for and replace the first occurrence of the word or phrase in the document or can automatically search for and replace all occurrences of the word or phrase. For example, the user could use this feature to change all occurrences of "U.S." to "United States" in a document.

If the text is too long to fit on the screen at one time, it will have to be moved on the screen. Think of the text as a continuous document and the screen as a "window" through which the user looks at just a section of the text (Figure 8–4). Then the user can move the text up or down past the screen to look at different parts of it. This process is called **scrolling**. The user can scroll up or down one line at a time or one screen at a time. If the text is too wide to fit on the screen, he or she can scroll to the right or to the left.

When a user edits a document, he or she makes changes only in the text in primary storage. If the text is retrieved from secondary storage, the original unedited version would appear. Thus, if the user is not satisfied with any changes made, he or she can retrieve the document again and start over. If the editing is satisfactory, however, the user must save the new version of the document in secondary storage.

Formatting and Printing Text

Before printing a document, a user needs to put it into the format in which it will appear on paper. The user must specify how wide the margins should be, how the lines should be spaced (single-spaced, double-spaced, and so on), whether headings should be printed on each page, whether the page numbers should be at the top or at the bottom of the page or omitted altogether, and other characteristics of the output.

Many word processing programs allow the format to be specified before or while the text is entered. Then the text appears on the screen the same as it will be printed, or close to the specified format. This feature is commonly called **WYSIWYG**, which means *what-you-see-is-what-you-get*. Some word processing software requires the user to specify the format after the text is entered. Then the format of the text on the screen may not be the same as the format of the document as it is printed.

Figure 8–4 Scrolling Through a Document

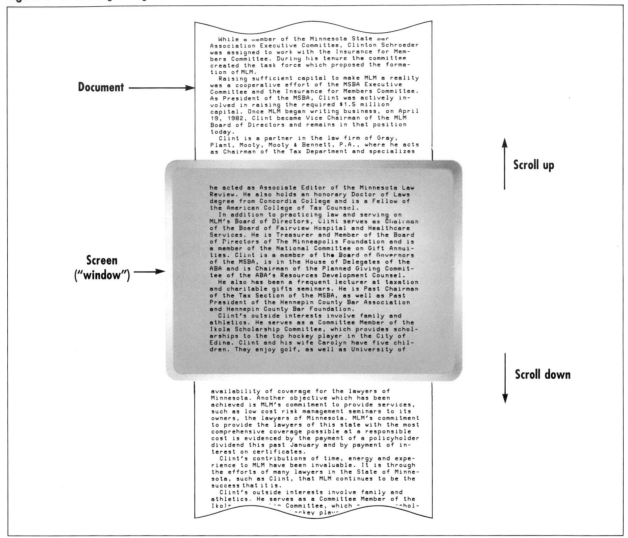

Most computer screens cannot show a full page of a document at one time using regular size characters. Some word processing programs, however, have a feature called **page preview**, which shrinks the size of the characters and displays a complete page on the screen as it will be printed. Using this feature, the user can check the document to see if it will be printed in the exact format he or she wants. Some word processing programs will show more than one page on the screen when page preview is used. This feature can be useful for checking several pages of a document at a time.

After the user has entered, edited, and formatted the text, he or she can print it. If the text is not currently in primary storage, it must be *retrieved* from a file in secondary storage before it can be printed (Figure 8–5). The user can print a single copy or several copies. Because the text

Figure 8–5   Printing Text

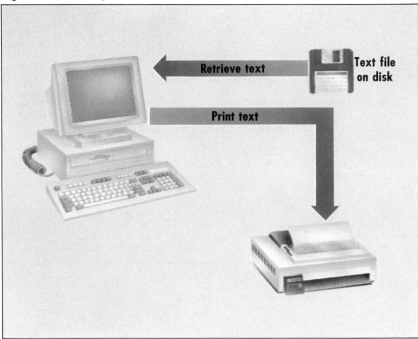

is saved in secondary storage, additional copies can be printed at any time in the future.

Controlling Word Processing Software Functions

Different techniques are used to control the functions performed by a word processing program. Some software uses function keys to perform specific tasks. For example, Figure 8–6 shows a list of the function keys used with WordPerfect, a popular word processing program. This list forms a template that fits over the function keys for easy reference. With this program, a function key may be pressed by itself to perform one function, or it can be pressed in combination with the Control, Shift, or Alternate key to perform other functions. For example, to boldface a word, the user presses F6, but to center a title, the user holds the Shift key and presses F6.

Figure 8–6   List of Function Keys Used in WordPerfect

WordPerfect®
for IBM® Personal Computers

Column Left/Right	Home. · / ·
Compose	2
Delete to End of Ln/Pg	End/PgDn
Delete Word	Backspace
◆Margin Release	Tab
Pull-Down Menus	=
Screen Up/Down	−/+ (num)
Word Left/Right	· / ·
P/N: K6831619	

© WordPerfect Corp. 1989   TMUS/WP51XID–11/89

Shell	Spell	Screen	Move	Ctrl	Text In/Out	Tab Align	Footnote	Font	Ctrl	Merge/Sort	Macro Define		
Thesaurus	Replace	Reveal Codes	Block	Alt	Mark Text	Flush Right	Columns/Right	Style	Alt	Graphics	Macro		
Setup	◆Search	Switch	◆Indent◆	Shift	Date/Outline	Center	Print	Format	Shift	Merge Codes	Retrieve		
Cancel	◆Search	Help	◆Indent		List	Bold	Exit	Underline		End Field	Save	Reveal Codes	Block
F1	F2	F3	F4		F5	F6	F7	F8		F9	F10	F11	F12

Figure 8–7   A WordStar Menu

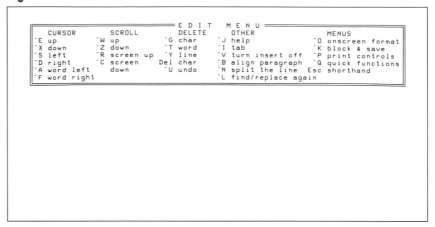

Other software uses character keys in combination with the Control or other keys to perform a task. Often, the keys and tasks are listed in menus. For example, Figure 8–7 shows one menu used with WordStar, another word processing program. To use many of the functions with this software, the Control key must be held down while another key is pressed. For example, to delete a word, the user holds down the Control key and presses the letter T. This combination is called a *Control T* and is shown in the menu as ^T. Some word processing software requires that the Escape key rather than the Control key be pressed before a menu selection is made.

Word processing software used on a computer with a mouse allows the user to make selections by moving the cursor to an item in a menu and clicking the mouse. Often, pull-down menus are used with these types of systems. For example, Figure 8–8 shows a pull-down menu

Figure 8–8   A Microsoft Word Menu

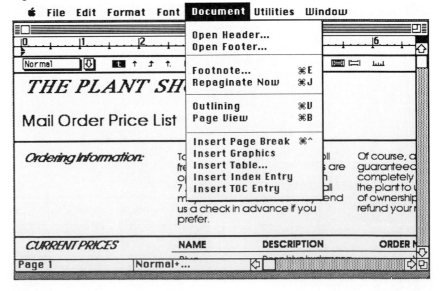

used with Microsoft Word, another popular word processing program. Programs like this one may also have other features of a graphical user interface, including the use of icons for selecting functions, and windows for displaying different documents at the same time.

To move the cursor within the text on a screen, cursor control keys are often used. Pressing the appropriate cursor control key moves the cursor left or right one character, or up or down one line. Sometimes a combination of keys, such as the Control key and a cursor control key, must be pressed to move the cursor a word or several lines at a time. With the appropriate hardware and software, a mouse can be used to move the cursor any place on the screen.

HARDWARE NEEDED FOR WORD PROCESSING

Most microcomputers are capable of doing some word processing. The microcomputer's CPU does not have to be very fast, and a large amount of primary storage is not needed for many word processing programs. Some very powerful word processing programs, however, require much primary storage. Two floppy disk drives are often adequate, although a hard disk drive is needed with some programs.

A good keyboard is essential for word processing. Keys should have a good "feel"; that is, they should not be too soft or too firm, and should give the feeling of a good typewriter when pressed. Special keys and function keys should be easy to reach. Similarly, a screen should be easy to read. A user often spends hours keying text and reading the screen, so these components must be easy to use. If the software requires a mouse, the mouse should roll easily and should feel comfortable to the user.

The most important hardware requirement for word processing is a printer. A draft-quality printer is usually not satisfactory for word processing output. A letter-quality or near–letter-quality printer is essential. A dot-matrix printer, which can be set for near–letter-quality print, may be satisfactory. Laser printers or fully-formed–character printers are good because they produce letter-quality output.

AN EXAMPLE OF WORD PROCESSING SOFTWARE USE

To illustrate the use of word processing software, assume that you are the new national sales manager of a company. Each month you have to send a memo to the vice president of marketing, summarizing the company's sales for the month. You could type a new sales memo each month, but with word processing you can reduce the amount of typing required and save time. The first month's memo will take you about the same amount of time using word processing as it would take using a typewriter, but the memo for each subsequent month will take less time.

At the end of your first month—November—you sit down at your microcomputer and load the operating system and the word processing software. The procedure for loading software depends on which hardware and software you are using. For illustrative purposes, the screens are shown as they would appear using WordPerfect, but the same concepts apply to other word processing software.

After loading the word processing software, the screen will look like the one shown in Figure 8–9. Notice that the screen is blank except for the bottom line. This line shows that you are working on document 1 (Doc 1) and that the cursor is on page 1 (Pg 1) at a line one inch down (Ln 1") from the top of the page and at a position one inch in (Pos 1") from the left edge. As you enter text or move the cursor, the numbers in this line change. The blank screen above this line is the area where the text for the memo you enter will appear.

Next, you type the text for the sales memo. Figure 8–10 shows how the screen will look after the typing is completed. When entering text, you use certain features of the word processing software. For example, you center the word MEMORANDUM in the first line by pressing a function key before typing the word. Also, word wrap automatically occurs while you type the paragraphs, which means you do not press the Enter or Return key at the end of a line unless it is the end of a paragraph.

After typing the memo, you read it on the screen and decide to make several changes. First, instead of using "VP" in the "TO" line, you decide to use "Vice President." You move the cursor to "VP," press the key necessary to delete these letters, and type the words "Vice President." Next, you notice that the word "sales" is misspelled in the first paragraph. Once again, you move the cursor to this word, delete the word, and type it correctly. Finally, you decide to add another sentence at the end of the last paragraph, so you move the cursor to the end of this paragraph and type the new sentence. After this editing is completed, the screen will look like the one shown in Figure 8–11.

The last step is to save the text of the memo in secondary storage, so you press the keys necessary to save it. Before saving the text the word processing program asks for a name for the text file. You decide to give

Figure 8–9 The Word Processing Screen Before the Sales Memo Has Been Entered

Figure 8–10 The Word Processing Screen After the Sales Memo Has Been Entered

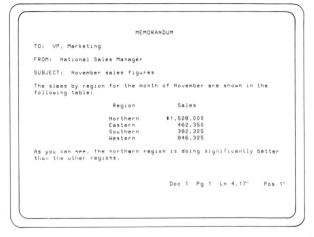

Figure 8–11 The Word Processing Screen After the Sales Memo Has Been Edited

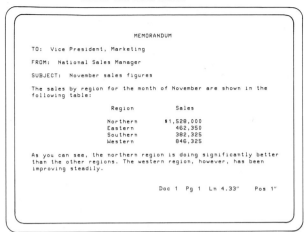

Figure 8–12
The Printed Sales memo

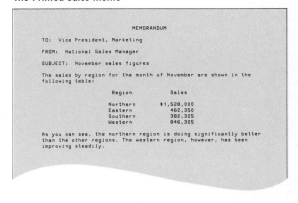

it the name SLSMEMO, which you then enter. The program saves the memo in a file with this name. Now the memo can be printed, so you press the keys required for printing. The output will appear just as it did on the screen but without the extra line at the bottom (Figure 8–12).

At the end of the next month—December—you need to send a similar memo with the sales figures for that month. Instead of retyping the entire sales memo, you decide to edit the current one. Again, you sit down at your microcomputer and load the operating system and word processing software. Then you retrieve the text of the previous month's memo from secondary storage by pressing the appropriate key and entering the name of the file containing the text. At this point the screen will look the same as the one in Figure 8–11 except that the bottom line will include the name of the file. To change the month in the "SUBJECT" line from November to December, you move the cursor to the word "November," delete it, and type the new word. You do the same with the month in the first paragraph. Next, you move the cursor to the sales figure for the northern region, delete it, and type the new figure. You do the same for the sales figures for the other regions. Then, you decide that you need an entirely new final paragraph, so you delete the existing paragraph and type a new one. After making these changes, the screen looks like the one shown in Figure 8–13. After reading it over to be sure there are no errors, you save the text in secondary storage. Finally, you print the new sales memo.

Notice in this example how you have taken advantage of the editing capabilities of the word processing software. These capabilities let you reuse work that you have done previously instead of redoing everything from scratch. By reusing previous work, you can greatly increase your productivity in preparing memos, letters, reports, and other documents.

Figure 8–13   The Word Processing Screen After the Sales
Memo Is Edited for the Next Month

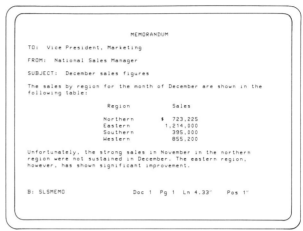

```
                              MEMORANDUM

        TO:  Vice President, Marketing

        FROM:  National Sales Manager

        SUBJECT:  December sales figures

        The sales by region for the month of December are shown in the
        following table:

                          Region           Sales

                        Northern       $   723,225
                        Eastern          1,214,000
                        Southern           395,000
                        Western           855,200

        Unfortunately, the strong sales in November in the northern
        region were not sustained in December. The eastern region,
        however, has shown significant improvement.



        B: SLSMEMO                     Doc 1  Pg 1  Ln 4.33"    Pos 1"
```

ADDITIONAL WORD PROCESSING SOFTWARE FEATURES

In addition to the basic capabilities of entering, editing, formatting, and printing text, word processing software provides other features. Some of the more useful features are described here. Not all these features are available with all word processing programs. When they are not, they may be provided by separate programs.

Spell Checking

Spell checking is a feature that checks for spelling errors within text created by a word processing program. The checking is done by comparing each word in the text with words in a dictionary stored in the computer. If a word cannot be found in the dictionary, the spell checking feature reports it as misspelled (Figure 8–14). Not all words reported this way are misspelled. Sometimes the word is one not commonly used, or it is a technical word not found in the dictionary. The user has the option of leaving the word the way it is or changing its spelling. The spell checking feature itself cannot correct the word, although some programs can suggest possible correct spellings.

Thesaurus

A **thesaurus** feature looks up synonyms for words. The user moves the cursor to a word for which a synonym is desired. Then, he or she presses a special key, and the thesaurus feature provides a list of synonyms (Figure 8–15). One of the words in the list may be selected to replace the original word, or the word can be left unchanged. Some programs allow the user to look up synonyms of synonyms.

Figure 8–14 Spell Checking

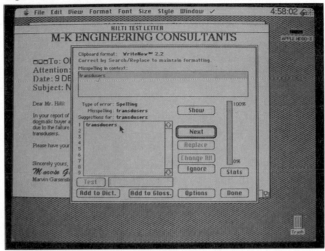

Mail Merge

Mail merge is a feature that merges information from one text file into another text file. A common use of mail merge is to prepare customized form letters. A user creates a file containing the names and addresses of the people to whom letters are to be mailed. Then, another file is created with the letter to be sent, but without the names and addresses. Special codes in the letter file show where the names and addresses are to appear. Finally, the mail merge feature merges each person's name and address with the letter and prints it (Figure 8–16). Thus, a form letter looks like it has been prepared for each person individually.

Figure 8–15 Using a Thesaurus

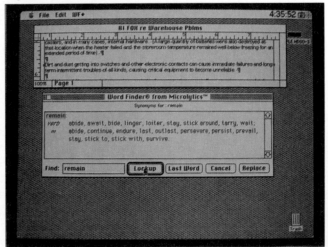

Figure 8–16 Mail Merge

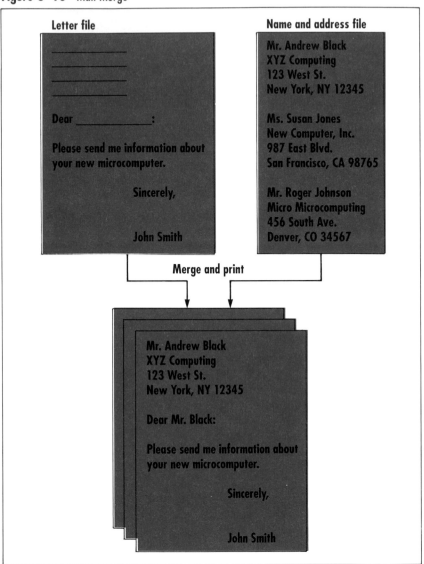

Footnoting

With a **footnoting** feature, the user types footnotes and footnote numbers in the usual way. The word processing program, however, treats the footnotes differently from the rest of the text. When a footnote is added or deleted in the middle of a document, all footnotes that follow are automatically renumbered. If a block of text containing a footnote reference is moved, the corresponding footnote is automatically moved and, if necessary, renumbered. When the text is printed, all footnotes are positioned at the bottom of the pages, and the length of the text on each page is adjusted to compensate for the footnotes. This feature makes it easy to use footnotes in a document.

Figure 8–17 Outlining

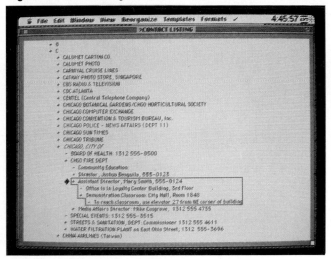

Figure 8–18 Graphics in a Word Processing Document

Outlining

An **outlining** feature makes it easy to create outlines of documents and reports. The user can enter items into an outline, move items around in the outline, and change items easily (Figure 8–17). The user can also print the outline. Some word processing programs allow the user to switch back and forth between an outline and a document on the screen so that he or she can check the outline while entering text.

Graphics

Word processing programs were originally designed to handle only text data—that is, characters. Many times, however, a user wants to include diagrams, charts, and other graphic images in a document. Consequently, some word processing programs allow graphics to be incorporated into the text (Figure 8–18). The graphic image may be created by the word processing program, or it may come from some other program that produces graphic output. With this feature, the user can create documents that convey information more effectively than just text.

Style/Grammar Checking

Style/grammar checking is a feature that checks text for common writing-style and grammatical errors. For example, the feature locates sentences that do not begin with a capital letter or do not end with a period or other appropriate punctuation. In addition, this feature can find common writing-style errors such as the excessive use of passive voice (Figure 8–19). Style/grammar checking is not infallible; it sometimes indicates a writing error when there is none, but it can be useful in locating potential writing problems. Style/grammar checking is often done by a program separate from the word processing program.

COMPUTER CLOSE-UP

8–2

LINCOLN'S SPEECH DOESN'T COMPUTE

Newspaper columnist Mike Royko of the Chicago Tribune decided one day to run Lincoln's Gettysburg Address through a computer program advertised to correct "stylistic errors." This is the speech, with computer advice in parentheses.

Fourscore and seven years ago our fathers brought forth on this continent, a new nation, conceived in Liberty, and dedicated to the proposition that all men are created equal. (#Long sentences can be difficult to read and understand. . . . #Passive voice "are created." Consider revising, using active. See Help for more information. #Usually a paragraph should have more than one sentence.)

Now we are engaged (#Passive voice. . . .) *in a great civil war, testing whether that a nation or any nation so conceived and so dedicated can long enrdure. We are met* (#Passive voice. . . .) *on a great battlefield of that war. We have come to dedicate a portion of that field, as a final resting place for those who here gave their lives that that* (#Delete doubled word or punctuation mark.) *nation might live. It is altogether fitting and proper that we should do this.*

But, (#Use "But" sparingly to start a sentence.) *in a larger sense, we cannot dedicate—we cannot consecrate—we cannot hallow—this ground. The brave men, living and dead, who struggled here, have consecrated it far above our poor power to add or detract. The world will little note nor long remember* (#An adjective "long" is usually not followed by a verb remember." You may need to use an adverbial form of "long" or may need a comma before remember. . . .) *what we say here, but it can never forget what they did here. It is for us, the living, rather* (#This word usually adds little and should be omitted.) *to be dedicated here to an unfinished work which* (#"That" is almost always preferred to "which" in this situation. If you really mean "which," then it usually needs to be preceded by a comma. See Help key for more information.) *they who fought here have thus far so nobly advanced* (#Long sentences are difficult to read and understand.) *It is rather* (#This word usually adds little and should be omitted.) *for us to be here dedicated to the great task remaining before us—that devotion to that cause for which they gave their last full meaure of devotion; that we here highly resolve that these dead* (#Usually "these" should be followed by a plural noun.) *shall not have died in vain; that this nation, under God, shall have a new birth of freedom; and that government of the people, by the people, for the people, shall not perish from the earth.* (Problems marked/detected 13/13).

Royko went on to comment: That's something. As often as I've read this speech, getting a lump in my throat every time, I didn't detect even one stylistic problem, much less 13. . . . But I suppose we really shouldn't expect anything better from someone who grew up in a log cabin, hoofed it to a one-room schoolhouse, and never made it to college. . . . The poor guy didn't have a "Help Key" to push.

Figure 8–19   Style/Grammar Checking

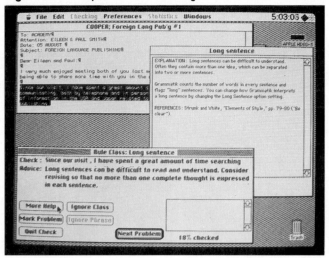

Indexing

An **indexing** feature creates an index for a text file. A user identifies all words in the document that are to be included in the index. Then the feature prepares an index with these words and the numbers of all pages containing each word. An indexing feature can also be used to create a table of contents for a document. This feature can be very useful for long documents such as business reports.

COMMON WORD PROCESSING SOFTWARE

Some word processing systems come with special hardware and software. The software works only with the hardware supplied, and the system can be used only for word processing. These systems are called **dedicated word processors**. Department stores often sell these types of word processors as replacements for typewriters. These systems usually come with special keyboards and other hardware designed for ease of use with the word processing software. A disadvantage of dedicated word processors is that they can be used only for word processing.

Most word processing systems in use today are general-purpose microcomputers with word processing software. These microcomputers can be used for other tasks besides word processing. Many word processing programs are available. Old ones arc constantly being updated, and new ones are continually being developed.

Most word processing programs can be used with several different types of computers. WordPerfect, WordStar, and Microsoft Word, which have already been mentioned, are widely used. All three are available for the IBM personal computers and IBM clones. Microsoft Word and WordPerfect are also available for the Apple Macintosh. Some other commonly used word processing programs are MultiMate, DisplayWrite, and

Ami Professional for IBM computers, and MacWrite, FullWrite, and Write Now for the Apple Macintosh. Word processing programs cost between $50 and $500.

In general, text files created by one word processing program cannot be used by another because the files contain different codes for the word processing features. (For example, different programs may use different codes for underlining.) Some word processing programs come with special *file conversion* software for converting the files created by other programs. This conversion procedure can be cumbersome, however. Most word processing programs have ways of creating files that just contain characters in the ASCII code without any special word processing codes. This type of file is called an **ASCII file**. ASCII files can be retrieved by most word processing programs and therefore can be used for transferring text from one word processing program to another.

DESKTOP PUBLISHING SOFTWARE

An activity related to word processing is **desktop publishing**, which is the use of a microcomputer to prepare high-quality printed output similar to that produced by a printing company. With desktop publishing, professional-looking reports, newsletters, pamphlets, and other printed materials can be prepared directly by the user. Figure 8–20 shows an example of the output produced by desktop publishing.

To do desktop publishing, a user must have **desktop publishing software** designed specifically for this use. This type of software has many word processing capabilities. More importantly, it has the ability to incorporate complex design features, such as graphs, various type styles, and different column widths into the printed output. The user also needs a printer capable of printing high-quality output containing these design features. Usually, a laser printer is required for this purpose. Finally, the user must have the training needed to understand how a well-designed report, newsletter, or other document should look. With

Figure 8–20 Output from Desktop Publishing

these capabilities the user can prepare printed output nearly as good as that produced by professional printing companies.

Desktop Publishing Software Functions

The functions of desktop publishing software are similar to those of word processing programs, except that some capabilities are more sophisticated. A user can enter text using the desktop publishing program in the same way that he or she can enter text with a word processing program. In addition, the user can retrieve text from a file created by another program. For example, the user may enter, edit, and save text using a word processing program and then retrieve the saved text using the desktop publishing program.

In addition to text, the user can retrieve graphic data using the desktop publishing program. Usually, the graphic data is created by another program. (Graphic software is discussed in a later chapter.) The graphic data may consist of charts, diagrams, drawings, and other nontext data.

After text and graphic data is entered, some editing can be done, as with a word processing program. Data can be inserted, deleted, and moved using the desktop publishing program. Many word processing editing capabilities are usually available in desktop publishing software.

The most powerful function of desktop publishing software, however, is its formatting capabilities. After all the text and graphic data has been entered and edited, it can be formatted in numerous ways. This process is called **page layout** because it involves preparing pages of the document in the format in which they will be printed.

In doing page layout, text can be arranged in one or several columns. For example, text can be laid out in multiple columns like a newspaper. Different type styles and sizes can be used for the text. A feature called *kerning*, which adjusts the space between characters based on the shape of the characters, is often available. (For example, the space between the letters "lo" is different from the space between the letters "mo.") Graphic images can be enlarged or reduced to fit with the text, and the text can be rearranged to conform to the shape of the graphics. Horizontal and vertical lines can be included to set off texts and graphics; boxes can be drawn around any text or graphic. Practically any formatting feature that you see in a book, newspaper, or magazine can be incorporated into the document. Using the formatting capabilities, documents that appear to be professionally typeset can be prepared. Figure 8–21 shows the screen for a desktop publishing program.

After the document has been formatted, it can be printed. As noted earlier, a laser printer is usually needed to produce printed output because of the sophisticated formatting capabilities. Usually one copy of the document is printed, which is then reproduced using a copier.

Common Desktop Publishing Software

Most desktop publishing programs are WYSIWYG programs, which means they show the document on the screen as it will be printed. This

Figure 8–21 Screen for a Desktop Publishing Program

way, the user can view the document before printing it. To do so, however, a high-resolution screen is needed.

The first desktop publishing programs were designed for use with the Apple Macintosh because this computer has a high-resolution screen. Numerous programs are available for the Macintosh, including PageMaker and XPress. Some programs are also available for IBM computers, including a version of PageMaker and Ventura Publisher.

Some word processing programs incorporate limited desktop publishing capabilities. For example, some word processing programs provide various type styles, and allow graphics to be included in text. Their features are not as sophisticated as those found in true desktop publishing programs, but these programs can be used for simple publishing needs. Expect the distinction between word processing and desktop publishing software to become less significant in the future as more and more features are added to word processing programs.

TEXT EDITING SOFTWARE

Word processing software is available on some minicomputers and mainframe computers, but its capabilities are usually not as good as word processing software on microcomputers. For processing text on larger computers, programs called **text editors** are usually used. (Text editors are also available for microcomputers.) These programs work somewhat like word processing programs in that text can be entered and edited.

Many word processing features, however, are not available. In addition, formatting and printing capabilities are usually very limited.

A text editor is controlled by commands that are typed in at the keyboard. The commands tell the editor to add text, delete text, change text, and perform other text entry and editing functions. The commands are usually not as easy to use as commands for a microcomputer word processing program.

A user may use a text editor to enter data that is processed by another program. For example, a user may type in data to be analyzed by a statistical program. A knowledgeable user may use a text editor to type in the instructions for a program, although this function is usually performed by experienced data processing personnel. For the preparation of letters and documents, however, a microcomputer word processing system is almost always better.

Chapter Summary

- Using word processing is more efficient than using a typewriter in most typing situations except for those involving short documents that are used only once. For long reports and documents that require changes in the future, word processing is much more efficient.

- A user uses **word processing software** to manipulate **text**. The main functions that the user can perform with word processing software include entering, editing, and printing text. When a user enters text, he or she types the characters just as with a typewriter, except that the user does not have to press the Enter or Return key at the end of each line. When **editing** text, the user makes changes or corrections in the text. Before printing text, the user must put the text into the format in which he or she wants it to appear on paper. Then, the user can print one or more copies of the text. Depending on the software, the user can control these functions by pressing function keys—often in combination with the Control, Shift, or Alternate key—by using character keys in combination with the Control key or another key, or by using a mouse to select functions from a menu.

- Most microcomputers can be used for word processing. Two floppy disk drives are often adequate, although a hard disk drive may be needed. A good keyboard and screen make word processing over a long period of time easier. A mouse is required for some programs. A letter-quality or near–letter-quality printer is essential for printing acceptable output.

- Some word processing programs have a **spell checking** feature for checking spelling of text, a **thesaurus** feature for locating synonyms of words, a **mail merge** feature for merging information from one text file into another, a **footnoting** feature for including footnotes in a document, an **outlining** feature for preparing outlines, the ability to include graphic images within text, a **style/grammar checking** feature for checking the style and grammar of a text file, and an **indexing** feature for preparing an index for a text file.

- Some common word processing programs for IBM personal computers and IBM clones are WordPerfect, WordStar, Microsoft Word, MultiMate, DisplayWrite, and Ami Professional. Microsoft Word and WordPerfect are also available for the Apple Macintosh. Some other word processing programs for the Macintosh are MacWrite, FullWrite, and Write Now.

- **Desktop publishing** is the use of a microcomputer for preparing high-quality printed output similar to that produced by a printing company. With **desktop publishing software**, text and graphics can be incorporated into a complex design that includes various type styles and sizes, different column widths, special headings and titles, and other formatting characteristics seen in books, newspapers, and magazines.

Terms to Remember

ASCII file   p. 220

Block   p. 207

Cut and Paste   p. 207

Dedicated Word Processor
   p. 219

Desktop Publishing   p. 220

Desktop Publishing Software
   p. 220

Editing   p. 206

Footnoting   p. 216

Hyphen Help   p. 202

Indexing   p. 219

Mail Merge   p. 215

Outlining   p. 217

Page Layout   p. 221

Page Preview   p. 208

Scrolling   p. 207

Search and Replace   p. 207

Spell Checking   p. 214

Style/Grammar Checking   p. 217

Text   p. 202

Text Editor   p. 222

Text File   p. 206

Thesaurus   p. 214

Undo   p. 207

Word Processing Software
   p. 201

Word Processing System   p. 201

Word Wrap   p. 202

WYSIWYG   p. 207

Review Questions

Fill-In Questions

1. A feature of word processing software that automatically moves any word that does not fit at the end of a line to the next line is called _____.

2. After entering text when using a word processing program, the user must _____ the text as a file in secondary storage before turning off the computer.

3. The process of making corrections or changes in text is called _____.

4. A(n) _____ is a section of text that has been marked so it can be moved, copied, deleted, or saved.

5. The _____ feature of a word processing program can be used to change all occurrences of a word or phrase to a new word or phrase.

6. WYSIWYG stands for _____.

7. When a user moves text of a document past the computer screen, he or she is _____.

8. A feature of a word processing program that allows a user to display an entire page on the screen exactly as it will be printed is called _____.

9. A(n) _____ is used to look up the synonym of a word in a text file.

10. A word processing program feature used to merge information from one text file into another is_____.

Short-Answer Questions

1. In what situation is word processing more efficient than using a typewriter?

2. What can a user do if he or she makes a mistake while entering text using a word processing program?

3. What can a user do with a block in a text file?

4. What must a user do to a document before printing it?

5. Describe several ways a user can control the functions performed by a word processing program.

6. What microcomputer hardware is needed for word processing?

7. What are some additional capabilities of word processing software beyond entering, editing, and printing text?

8. What are some common word processing programs?

9. How can a text file created by one word processing program be used by another program?

10. What is desktop publishing?

Projects

1. Investigate a word processing program to which you have access. What is the name of the program, and with which microcomputer can it be used? How much does it cost? How does a user control its functions? What features beyond those required for entering, editing, and printing text does it have?

2. Investigate a desktop publishing program. Find out what features the program has and how the user controls the program's functions. Write a brief summary of your findings.

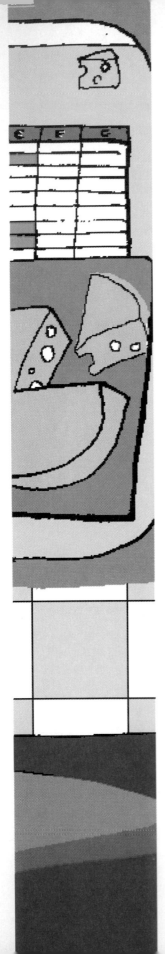

9

SPREADSHEET SOFTWARE

CHAPTER OBJECTIVES

• After completing this chapter you should be able to:

1. Describe the types of situations in which spreadsheet analysis is used and explain why spreadsheet software makes the analysis easy.

2. Identify spreadsheet concepts such as cells and cell addresses, and list the three types of information that can be put into a cell.

3. Explain the main functions that the user can perform with spreadsheet software and describe several techniques used to control these functions.

4. State the microcomputer hardware needed for spreadsheet analysis.

5. Identify several common spreadsheet programs and state the computers with which they can be used.

ONE OF the most widely used types of microcomputer software is **spreadsheet software**. This type of software lets the user easily analyze data with the computer and present the results of the analysis. With spreadsheet software, the user can enter data into the computer, calculate figures using the data, make changes in the data and immediately see the effect of those changes on the calculated figures, and print copies of the results. The user can save the data and calculations in secondary storage and return to them in the future to do further analysis.

This chapter discusses spreadsheet software. First, the chapter explains what spreadsheets are and how they are used to analyze data. Then it examines spreadsheet software and shows how this software makes spreadsheet analysis easy.

SPREADSHEET ANALYSIS

A **spreadsheet** is an arrangement of data into rows and columns. For example, Figure 9–1 shows a hand-prepared spreadsheet that gives the projected income and expenses for a person over several months. The spreadsheet also shows the projected total expenses for each month, which is the sum of the individual expenses, and the projected surplus, which is the amount left over after subtracting the total expenses from the income.

A spreadsheet is used to analyze and present data. Thus, a person would use the spreadsheet in Figure 9–1 to compare projected figures from one month to the next, and to present the results of the analysis to another person (such as a spouse). The results are often used to help in decision making. For example, the spreadsheet in Figure 9–1 could be used to help in a new-car–buying decision by showing whether there is a sufficient surplus each month to make the car payments.

A hand-prepared spreadsheet may be satisfactory if the figures in the spreadsheet do not change. Often, however, you have to change some figures in a spreadsheet, and whenever you do, other figures must be recalculated. For example, certain income or expense figures in the spreadsheet in Figure 9–1 may have to be changed because of new projections. Then, the person using the spreadsheet would have to recalculate all total expense and surplus figures that are affected. Recalculations can be time consuming if changes occur often.

One reason for making changes in figures in a spreadsheet is to see what would happen to other figures when the changes are made. This technique is called **what-if analysis** because you usually ask a question that begins with the words *what if*. For example, using the spreadsheet in Figure 9–1, a person might ask, "What if income increases 10 percent each month and the housing expenses increase 15 percent?" Answering this question involves using new numbers in the spreadsheet and recalculating the total expenses and surplus for each month. This recalculation can be a lot of work for a large spreadsheet and would be especially tedious if you decide to ask several "what-if" questions.

With spreadsheet software, a user creates the equivalent of a spreadsheet in the computer. The user includes with the spreadsheet not only the data but also the rules that describe how totals and other figures are calculated in the spreadsheet. For example, the spreadsheet in Figure 9–1 would include data for the income and expenses, and rules that specify how the total expenses and surplus are to be calculated. The result is called an **electronic spreadsheet** or, simply, a **worksheet**. Once the worksheet is created, the user can easily change data in it, and the computer will automatically recalculate those values determined by the rules. Thus, if a user has an electronic form of the spreadsheet in Figure 9–1, he or she could change any income or expense figure and the computer would calculate the new total expenses and surplus automatically.

Spreadsheet software is useful in many situations. Common uses include income projection, budgeting, sales forecasting, and investment analysis. Almost any problem in which data is put into rows and columns and used in calculations, as well as many other problems, can be solved using spreadsheet software.

Figure 9–1 A Hand-Prepared Spreadsheet

PROJECTED INCOME AND EXPENSES

	1 September	2 October	3 November	4 December
Income	1250 —	1250 —	1300 —	1425 —
Expenses				
Housing	450 —	525 —	525 —	525 —
Food	240 —	240 —	260 —	300 —
Transportation	90 —	90 —	140 —	200 —
Clothing	50 —	50 —	75 —	125 —
Other expenses	160 —	150 —	180 —	210 —
Total expenses	990 —	1055 —	1180 —	1360 —
Surplus	260 —	195 —	120 —	65 —

COMPUTER CLOSE-UP

9–1

HEARTBEAT OF A HOSPITAL

In hospitals across the nation, sophisticated electronic heart monitors absorb enormous amounts of data on the health and progress of patients. A doctor then takes the information about blood pressure and heart rates and records it on a paper chart with a pen.

Much is lost in the translation. Even in the heart of Silicon Valley, the primitive data interpretation methods used by doctors at the Veteran's Affairs Medical Center could not keep up with the wealth of information being supplied by diagnostic equipment.

"The process was error-prone and time-consuming," said Dr. Adam Seiver, chief of general surgery at the center. "We were at the mercy of bad handwriting, errors in math and differing methods of entering data."

In November 1989, the center completed the installation of 23 workstations aimed at supporting clinical activities, including 14 workstations in the intensive care unit. The computers run proprietary applications software and are linked to each other and to diagnostic equipment via a network.

Using the computers, doctors can call up a screen that shows which patients are in which beds. To access patient information,

doctors click a mouse to select the appropriate bed number. A spreadsheet format then appears, with the vertical axis showing up to 48 categories of information such as blood pressure and fluid intake/output. The horizontal axis shows the progression of time, typically in one-hour intervals.

While some information, such as fluid intake, must still be keyed into the system, much is updated automatically from electronic diagnostic machines. The hospital ultimately plans to automate even fluid intake by using infusion pumps that will communicate their activity to the network. Seiver stressed, however, that such information will still be verified by nurses or physicians.

"Before we installed the system, we could never fully trust our intake and output figures," Seiver said. "We frequently had to track as many as 14 intravenous inputs and five outputs on a patient, calculate totals and hope the handwriting was legible. Now the whole process is automatic and accurate."

In addition to automating and standardizing the collection of data, the system gives doctors a better picture of trends in a patient's condition. With a paper-based reporting system, doctors could not get a clear picture of a patient's status from the full range of diagnostic information.

"We were surrounded by all this empirical data, but because we didn't have the tools to interpret it, we had to resort to intuition for many decisions," Seiver said.

The system has also replaced paper filing in storing patient information. Every minute's worth of information is saved on the system for 24 hours; after that it can be saved as designated by doctors—typically at hourly intervals for stable patients. The on-line record gives doctors an easy method of tracking progress and reaction to treatments.

"Previously, we kept patient records at bedside for 48 hours and then stored them in file cabinets," Seiver said. "Digging out those records to review changes in health and treatments was a daunting task, particularly because it was hard to maintain them in chronological order."

SPREADSHEET SOFTWARE CONCEPTS

Spreadsheet software arranges primary storage into a worksheet consisting of rows and columns. The number of rows and columns depends on the software, but one common program provides for a maximum of 8,192 rows and 256 columns. Most spreadsheet programs number the rows (1, 2, 3. . .) and identify the columns by letters (A, B, C. . .), with double letters (AA, AB, AC. . .) used beyond the twenty-sixth column (see Figure 9–2).

Because of the size of a screen, the software can display only part of a worksheet at one time. In other words, the screen is like a "window" through which the user looks at part of the worksheet. For example, Figure 9–3a shows the first part of a blank worksheet, with rows 1 through 20 and columns A through H. Notice that the row numbers and column letters appear on the screen. The user can display a different part of the worksheet by pressing certain keys on the keyboard. For example, Figure 9–3b shows how the screen appears when a user displays rows 75 through 94 and columns M through T.

The intersection of a row and column is called a **cell**. A cell is identified by a **cell address**, which consists of the column letter followed by the row number. For example, Figure 9–4 shows the cell at the cell address B5. A user can enter information into any cell in the worksheet. To enter information, the user moves a **cell pointer** or **cell cursor**, which is usually a highlighted area, to the desired cell by using the cursor control keys on the keyboard. Then, the user types in the information for that cell.

Figure 9–2   Worksheet Rows and Columns

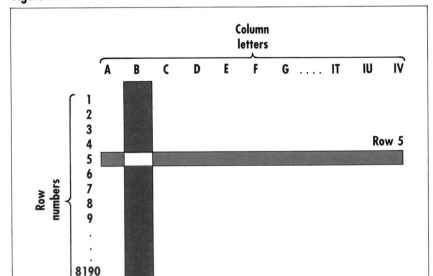

Figure 9–3 Displaying a Worksheet on a Screen

(a) Part of a blank worksheet displayed on a screen

(b) Another part of a blank worksheet displayed on a screen

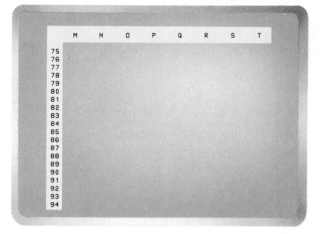

Figure 9–4 A Cell in a Worksheet

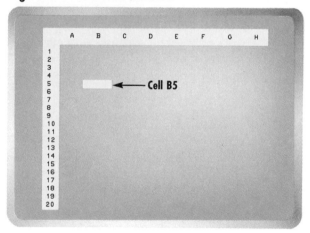

Three types of information can be entered into a cell. One is a number, which is also called a **value**. Any number can be entered into any cell. To enter a number, a user moves the cell pointer to the desired cell and then types the number. After pressing the Enter or Return key the number appears in the cell.

A second type of information that the user can enter into a cell is text, which is called a **label**. Labels are used to provide headings and other descriptions in a worksheet. The user enters labels the same way as numbers. If there is not enough room for a number or a label in a cell, he or she can increase the width of the column containing the cell to accommodate the information. Figure 9–5 shows part of the worksheet for the spreadsheet given in Figure 9–1. Labels have been entered for the columns and rows, numbers have been entered for the income and expenses, and the widths of the columns have been increased.

The third type of information that can be entered into a cell is a **formula**. A formula describes how the quantity or value in a cell is to be computed. In a formula, the user uses addresses of other cells to identify the data in the computation. Mathematical symbols such as + and – are also used to specify what type of computation is to be performed. For example, to find the total expenses for September in the worksheet in Figure 9–5, the user would use the formula +B8+B9+B10+B11+B12. This formula means add the values of cells B8, B9, B10, B11, and B12. The user would enter this formula into cell B13, which is where the total expenses are to appear. After entering the formula, it would *not* appear on the screen in the cell. Instead, the computer would compute the value of the formula and display this value in the cell. As another example, cell B15 (the surplus for September) would contain the formula +B5–B13, which means subtract the value of cell B13 from the value of cell B5. Figure 9–6 shows the complete worksheet for the spreadsheet in Figure 9–1 after the total expenses and surplus formulas have been entered for all months. Notice that the values for each month are correctly calculated and displayed in the worksheet.

Formulas provide a user with the capability of easily recalculating values in a worksheet. Each time a number in a cell is changed in a worksheet, all formulas that use that cell's address are recalculated and the new values are displayed. Thus, in the worksheet shown in Figure 9–6, the user can change any of the income or expense figures, and the corresponding total expenses and surplus will be recalculated because these values are computed using formulas. This capability is one reason spreadsheets are so useful for analyzing data.

SPREADSHEET SOFTWARE FUNCTIONS

When you use spreadsheet software, you always think in terms of the worksheet you are manipulating. A user can perform three main functions with spreadsheet software: create a worksheet, change a worksheet, and print a worksheet.

Figure 9–5
A Partial Worksheet with Labels and Numbers

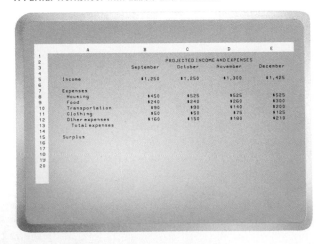

Figure 9–6
A Completed Worksheet After the Formulas Have Been Entered

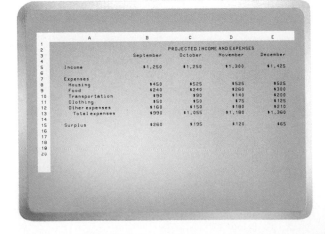

Creating a Worksheet

When the user first loads a spreadsheet program, a blank worksheet appears on the screen (refer back to Figure 9–3a). To create a worksheet, the user enters the labels, numbers, and formulas into the cells that make up the worksheet. When entering this information, the user may change the size of a cell, modify the format used to display numbers, and perform other formatting functions.

After the worksheet is complete, it should be *saved* in secondary storage (Figure 9–7). This step is necessary because the worksheet is created in primary storage and would be lost when a new worksheet was entered or the computer was turned off. The user saves the worksheet by storing it as a **worksheet file** in secondary storage. He or she must give the worksheet file a name so that the worksheet can be retrieved from the file in the future.

Changing a Worksheet

The second main function a user can perform with spreadsheet software is to change information in a worksheet. First, the worksheet must be *retrieved* from the file in secondary storage if it is not already in primary storage (Figure 9–8). Then, the user can change any label, number, or formula. A change is done by moving the cell pointer to the cell containing the information to be changed, and retyping or editing the information. The new information appears in the worksheet immediately, and any affected formulas are recalculated. Changes are made because of changes in data and in how calculations are done, and to do what-if analysis. If the changes are to bc kept permanently, the revised worksheet must be *saved* in secondary storage. When the user saves a revised worksheet the old worksheet in secondary storage is replaced.

Figure 9–7 Creating a Worksheet

Save worksheet

Worksheet
file on
disk

Enter worksheet

Figure 9–8 Changing a Worksheet

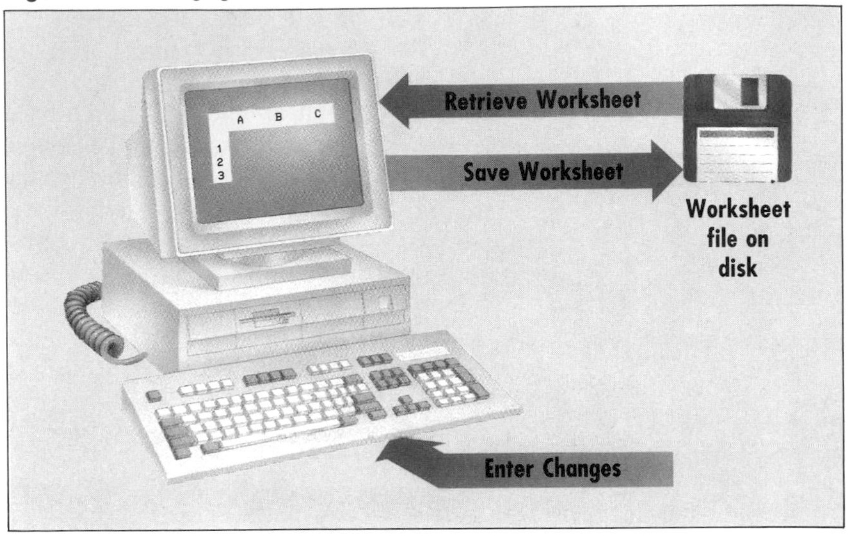

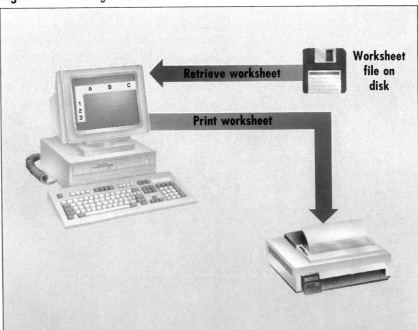

Printing a Worksheet

The final function that a user can perform with spreadsheet software is to print the worksheet. If it is not already in primary storage, the worksheet must be *retrieved* from the file in secondary storage before it can be printed (Figure 9–9). All or part of the worksheet can be printed. For

Figure 9–9 Printing a Worksheet

example, the user could print all four months in the worksheet shown earlier in Figure 9–6, or he or she could just print the information for one month. When a worksheet is printed, the row numbers and column letters are not normally printed; just the information in the worksheet is printed. The printed copy serves as a permanent record.

Controlling Spreadsheet Software Functions

The functions performed by a spreadsheet program are controlled by commands given by the user. With many programs a command is activated by pressing a certain key (often the / key). Then the command can be entered. With some software, the commands are listed in a menu. For example, Figure 9–10 shows the top part of the screen displayed by Lotus 1-2-3, a popular spreadsheet program. The second line is a menu. The user can select an item from the menu by typing the first letter of the item, or he or she can use the cursor control keys to highlight the item and then press the Enter or Return key. Often, selecting a menu item produces a submenu. For example, selecting the File option in the menu in Figure 9–10 produces the submenu shown in Figure 9–11. The user then selects the desired option from this menu.

Spreadsheet software used on a computer with a mouse often allows the user to select a function by moving the cursor to a menu item and clicking the mouse. Often, pull-down menus are used for these types of systems. For example, Figure 9–12 shows a pull-down menu used with Microsoft Excel, another popular spreadsheet program. Programs like this one may have other features of a graphical user interface.

Figure 9–10 A Lotus 1-2-3 Menu

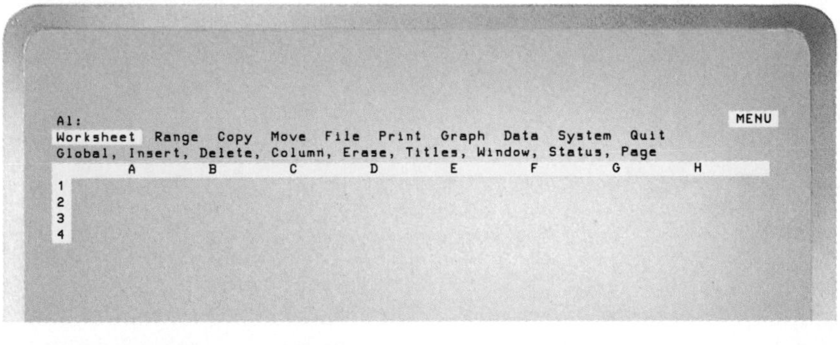

Figure 9–11 A Lotus 1-2-3 Submenu

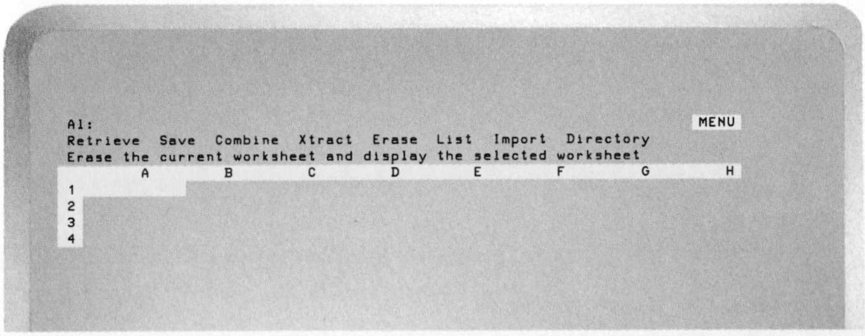

Figure 9–12 A Microsoft Excel Menu

⌘	File	Edit	Formula	Format	**Data**	Options	Macro	Windo

C25		1000			

	A	B	C		E	F
8						
9						
10	Date	Expense	Amo	**Find** ⌘ F		
11	1/1/84	overhead	$1,0	**Extract...** ⌘ E		
12	1/5/84	overhead	$5	**Delete**		
13	1/5/84	overhead	$6	**Set Database**		
14	1/5/84	overhead	$2	**Set Criteria**		
15	1/5/84	overhead	$4			
16	1/6/84	inventory	$16,0	**Sort...**		
17	1/5/84	salary	$1,000	Mary Fuller		
18	1/5/84	salary	$1,270	Carol Stansen		
19	1/5/84	salary	$945	Jim Parsons	**Series...**	
20	1/5/84	salary	$700	Karen Bush	**Table...**	
21	1/5/84	salary	$1,000	James Gregory		
22	1/5/84	salary	$1,160	Lisa La Flamme		
23	1/5/84	salary	$2,000	Andy Lubert		
24	1/15/84	overhead	$5,000	AR Office		
25	1/15/84	salary	$1,000	Mary Fuller		
26	1/15/84	salary	$1,270	Carol Stansen		
27	1/15/84	salary	$945	Jim Parsons		

HARDWARE NEEDED FOR SPREADSHEET ANALYSIS

Most microcomputers are capable of doing some spreadsheet analysis. The most important consideration is the primary storage capacity of the computer. Because a worksheet is stored in primary storage when it is being used, the amount of primary storage determines the maximum size of the worksheet. For large worksheets, the maximum primary storage available with the computer may be needed. It is even possible to use expanded primary storage with certain spreadsheet programs so that very large worksheets can be created.

The amount of secondary storage needed depends on the size of the worksheets to be stored. Often, a floppy disk is adequate, and a microcomputer with two floppy disk drives can be used for most spreadsheet work. For storing large worksheets in secondary storage, however, a hard disk drive is necessary. Use of a hard disk drive also speeds up the loading of the spreadsheet software and the storing and retrieving of worksheets.

The time to calculate all the formulas in a large worksheet can be several minutes. If changes are made often in a worksheet, for purposes such as what-if analysis, the recalculation time can become significant. For large worksheets a computer with a faster CPU should be used. Some spreadsheet software works with special mathematics processors that do calculations very rapidly. Use of these processors can greatly increase the speed of worksheet recalculations.

Most printers can be used to print a worksheet. Usually, a draft-quality printer, such as a dot-matrix printer, is acceptable, although a letter-quality printer may be desirable if the worksheet is to be included with a business letter or report. Because worksheets can be very wide, a printer that can print on wide paper may be needed. Extremely wide worksheets may have to be printed on several pages and taped together. There is even software that allows a worksheet to be printed sideways on several sheets of paper so that the pages do not have to be taped.

AN EXAMPLE OF SPREADSHEET SOFTWARE USE

To illustrate the use of spreadsheet software, assume, as in the word processing example in Chapter 8, that you are the national sales manager of a company. You want to do an analysis each month of the sales in the four regions that you manage. You are interested in how the sales for the current month compare with the sales for the previous month, and you would like to know the percentage increase or decrease in sales for each region and for the total sales of all four regions. This information would be useful in preparing your monthly memo to the vice president of marketing, summarizing the sales (Figure 8–12). You could calculate the values by hand, but because you plan to do the analysis each month, you decide to set up a worksheet to do the work for you.

For the first month, you sit down at your microcomputer and load the operating system and the spreadsheet software. For illustrative purposes, the screens are shown as they would appear using Lotus 1-2-3, but the same concepts apply to other spreadsheet software. After loading the spreadsheet software, the worksheet part of the screen will appear as shown previously in Figure 9–3a.

At this point, labels should be entered for the rows and columns. You move the cell pointer to each cell where a label will appear, and then type the label. Because of the length of some entries, you increase the width of the columns. Also, you specify the format of the sales amounts and totals, and of the percent changes. Figure 9–13 shows what the worksheet will look like after all labels have been entered.

Figure 9–13   The Sales Analysis Worksheet After the Labels Have Been Entered

Next, you enter the sales data by moving the cell pointer to the appropriate cells and typing the data. You type in the sales for each region for last month and for this month, but you do not enter the totals or percentages, because these values will be calculated by the spreadsheet software. After the sales data has been entered, the screen will look like the one shown in Figure 9–14. Notice that no values appear for the totals and percentages because the formulas for these have not yet been entered.

The final step is to enter the formulas. For the total sales last month you enter the formula +B5+B6+B7+B8 in cell B10. This formula finds the sum of the values of the cells from B5 through B8. For the sales this month you enter a similar formula in cell C10 that finds the sum of the values of the cells from C5 through C8. Then you enter formulas for the percent changes—one for each region in cells D5 through D8, and one for the total in cell D10. For example, the formula in cell D5 is (C5–B5)/B5.[1] As each formula is entered, its value is calculated and displayed in the worksheet. Figure 9–15 shows the final worksheet with all values calculated.

At this point you save your worksheet in secondary storage, using the name SLSANLYS to identify the file that contains the worksheet. You also print the worksheet so that you can refer to it when preparing your sales memo.

The next month, you need to perform the same analysis with new data. Again, you sit down at your microcomputer and load the operating system and spreadsheet software. This procedure gives you a blank worksheet. You then retrieve the previous month's worksheet by giving the software the name under which it was stored in secondary storage. At this point the screen will look the same as the one shown in Figure 9–15.

---

[1] The percent changes have been given percentage formats. Consequently, the result of this formula is converted to percentage form (i.e., it is multiplied by 100).

Figure 9–14 The Sales Analysis Worksheet After the Sales Data Has Been Entered

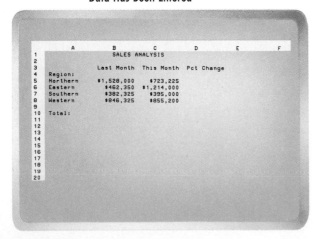

Figure 9–15 The Sales Analysis Worksheet After the Formulas Have Been Entered

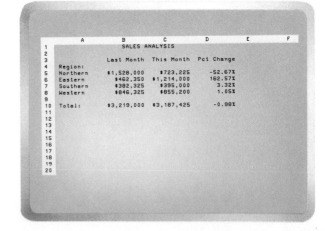

For the new worksheet, the "Last Month" sales data is the same as the "This Month" sales data from the previous month's worksheet. Using the appropriate command, you move the "This Month" sales data to the "Last Month" column. Then, you enter new sales figures for the "This Month" column. The formulas automatically recalculate the totals and the percentages as the changes are made. The result is shown in Figure 9–16. You save the revised worksheet in secondary storage and print a copy for use in preparing the sales memo.

Notice in this example how you have taken advantage of the fact that the worksheet already contains the labels, formulas, and some of the data you needed. Although setting up the worksheet in the first month can be time-consuming, using the worksheet each of the following months can make the analysis much easier.

ADDITIONAL SPREADSHEET SOFTWARE FEATURES

In addition to the basic capabilities of storing numbers, labels, and formulas in the cells of a worksheet, spreadsheet software provides a number of other features. Some of the more useful features are format options, ranges, formula copying, functions, and macros.

Format Options

The format of a worksheet can be changed in several ways. You have already learned that the width of a column can be changed. When starting with a new worksheet, each column has a preset width, such as 9 spaces. The width of any column can be increased or decreased to accommodate long or short numbers and labels.

When labels are entered they are *left-justified* in a column, which means they are positioned as far to the left of a column as possible.

Figure 9–16   The Sales Analysis Worksheet After the Sales Data Has Been Changed for the Next Month

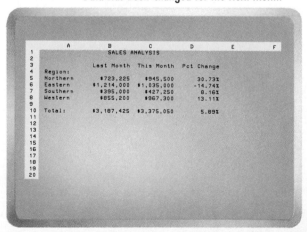

With the appropriate entry, a label may be centered or *right-justified* in a column (positioned as far to the right in a column as possible). If a label is too long for a column, it will be continued into the next column automatically.

Numbers are entered in a general format, usually with a variable number of places to the right of the decimal point and with no other punctuation. The format of any number can be changed to make it more readable. A fixed number of places to the right of the decimal point may be specified. Commas may be included in the number. A currency format may be used that includes a dollar sign, commas, and a fixed number of decimal positions. A percentage format that includes a percent sign may be specified. Using the appropriate format can make a worksheet more readable.

Ranges

To manipulate the data in a *single* cell, a user uses the cell's address. For example, in a formula, the user uses the cell address B5 to process the data in that cell. Sometimes, however, the user needs to manipulate the data in a *group of adjoining cells*. He or she could use the cell address of each cell in the group, or could specify the group as a range.

A **range** is a group of adjoining cells that forms part of a column or row, or a rectangular pattern of rows and columns in a worksheet. For example, Figure 9–17 shows several ranges in a worksheet. Range (a) in this figure is a part of a column, range (b) is a part of a row, and range (c) is a rectangular pattern consisting of rows and columns. Ranges that are columns or rows are specified by giving the cell address of the first and last cell in the range. In Lotus 1-2-3, the cell addresses are separated by two periods. Thus, range (a) in Figure 9–17 is specified by B2..B7 and range (b) is D2..G2. A range that is a rectangle is specified by giving the addresses of the upper-left and lower-right cells in the range. Thus, range (c) in Figure 9–17 is specified by D4..G6.

Using ranges, a user can manipulate a group of data at one time. For example, the user can copy the contents of one range to another range. Similarly, he or she can move data or erase data in a range. With ranges, a great deal of time is saved when manipulating large blocks of data in a worksheet.

Figure 9–17   Ranges in a Worksheet

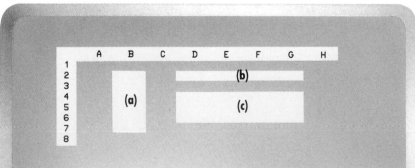

Formula Copying

To save time creating a worksheet, a user can copy the contents of a single cell or a range to other cells. When a cell containing a formula is copied, all cell addresses in the formula are adjusted automatically for the new location. For example, assume that cell B3 contains the formula +B1+B2, meaning add the values of cells B1 and B2. If this formula is copied to cell C3, the formula in C3 becomes +C1+C2. In other words, the formula is changed to reflect its new position in the spreadsheet.

The reason the cell addresses in a formula are changed when the formula is copied is that they are *relative cell addresses*, meaning they represent how far away the cell with the cell address in the formula is from the cell containing the formula. Thus, the formula +B1+B2 in cell B3 really means add the value of the cell two cells up from B3 and the value of the cell one cell up from B3. When this formula is copied to cell C3, it becomes +C1+C2, which means the same thing: Add the value of the cell two cells up from C3 and the value of the cell one cell up from C3.

To keep cell addresses in a formula from being adjusted when the formula is copied, a user can use *absolute cell addresses*. These addresses refer to specific cells. For example, in one spreadsheet program, absolute cell addresses are indicated by using dollar signs in the cell addresses, as in $B$1. Then, if the formula +$B$1+$B$2 in cell B3 is copied to cell C3, the formula does not change.

Functions

As you know, a formula is formed from cell addresses and mathematical symbols such as + and –. A user can also use special **functions**, which are routines built into the spreadsheet software that perform special processing. Each function has a name; in Lotus 1-2-3 each function name begins with the @ symbol. For example, the function that finds the square root of a number is named @SQRT. Each function is followed by one or more *arguments* enclosed in parentheses. An argument may be a number, a cell address, or—for some functions—a range. The arguments identify the data processed by the function. For example, @SQRT(250) finds the square root of the argument 250 and @SQRT(C8) finds the square root of the number at cell C8.

Another example of a function is @SUM. This function finds the sum or total of a group of data. For example, @SUM(250,B5,C8) finds the sum of 250, the value in cell B5, and the value in cell C8. This function also allows a range to be specified as an argument. For example, @SUM(B2..B7) finds the sum of the value in the range consisting of cells B2, B3, B4, B5, B6, and B7.

A function can be used by itself in a cell or as part of a formula. For example, a user can enter @SUM(B2..B7) in cell B8 to have the sum of cells B2 through B7 displayed in cell B8. As another example, the user can use +C7–@SQRT(C8) in cell C9 to have the difference between C7 and the square root of C8 displayed in cell C9.

AN ALTERNATIVE TO SPREADSHEET SOFTWARE

For sophisticated analyses and projections, a variety of dedicated financial-modeling software packages offers an alternative to spreadsheets. The purpose of a financial model is to provide management with accurate projections of future business activity in order to promote informed decision making. By applying a series of calculations to the available data, the model attempts to forecast the results of current business practices and to show the impact of new projects or policies under consideration.

Although spreadsheets let users build customized models by defining the functions that produce the desired calculations, dedicated financial-modeling software includes sophisticated built-in modeling routines.

The programming languages included with many modeling programs are easier to understand and provide more advanced special-purpose functions than do spreadsheet programs, according to vendors. Spreadsheets require the user to place each calculation at a specific cell in the spreadsheet grid, making it difficult to trace the logic used to create the model. By contrast, users of financial-modeling products can develop the model without reference to specific cell locations, often using simple statements that express the model's logic in step-by-step fashion.

These differences make dedicated modeling packages easier to use and far less prone to errors for sophisticated models, according to vendors and users. While conceding that spreadsheets make excellent tools for collecting, viewing, and reporting data and for simple calculations and models, these observers maintain that models of any complexity are better handled by a dedicated product.

"Spreadsheet users are screaming, 'I can't control the thing. I need simplicity, and I don't need seven different fonts—I need the numbers, and I need them to be right or I'm going to lose my job,'" said Michael Chesloff, vice president of marketing for Sinpcr Corp., in North Bergen, New Jersey. The company markets TM/1, a dedicated financial-modeling program.

The biggest problem with using spreadsheets for modeling is that they inspire a tangled web of logic that can be difficult to trace, according to vendors. In a spreadsheet, the results of complex calculations often depend upon previous calculations, which may themselves depend on other calculations, and so on. Since each calculation layer may refer to cells scattered throughout the spreadsheet, a complete understanding of the model's logic may escape even its author after a time, some observers said.

A spreadsheet model "quickly becomes tangled spaghetti, and the possibility for error becomes very high," said Rob Firmin, senior vice president at Information Resources Inc., of Needham, Massachusetts, the publisher of the Javelin Plus modeling package. "I read in The Wall Street Journal that 40 percent of corporate spreadsheets have [errors in referencing data]. That is exactly the problem that financial-modeling packages are addressing."

Unlike spreadsheets, some dedicated financial-modeling products let the user create models in a series of Englishlike statements. Others include features to display or print diagrammatic-model logic trees to minimize errors. "The way to build a model is to write Englishlike statements," Chesloff said. "The modeler can come back to it in a year and understand it, and someone else looking at his model can understand it, too."

"The model is not only good at helping the new modeler to understand where the analysis figures came from, it can give him a clear idea about the business operations. That is a very real advantage that they offer over the spreadsheet," he said.

Firmin said that modeling packages are better suited for complex models because they eliminate the need to reference the locations of specific spreadsheet cells when designing calculations. For example, a user developing a model can refer to data by category and time, such as sales in a certain month, rather than by cell location.

Observers said that the decision to use a spreadsheet or dedicated modeling package should be based on two major factors: the complexity of the model and the length of time it will be used. "Spreadsheets are more appropriate for a throw-away model," such as a list of employees that is used to budget the payroll, said Rusty Luhring, president of Ferox Microsystems Inc., of Arlington, Virginia, maker of Encore Plus modeling software. "But if a system is needed that is reliable and durable for the applications developed, the business should be looking at financial-modeling software."

"It really depends on what their daily work activities include," said William Higgs, vice president of software research at Info-Corp, a Santa Clara, California, marketing-research firm. "If my job is primarily financial analysis, I would go with the modeling package, but the bulk of financial users only use their spreadsheets for a small amount of analysis. For them it doesn't make sense to switch."

Well aware of the market dominance of spreadsheet products, most financial-modeling vendors cast their offerings as spreadsheet enhancement tools rather than spreadsheet competitors.

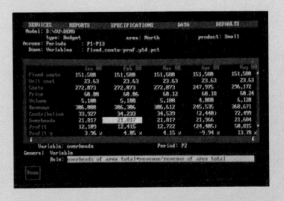

Macros

Sometimes when a user creates or uses a worksheet, he or she enters the same sequence of commands several times. Each time the commands are entered, the user must type them again, which is both tedious and error-prone. An alternative is to use a macro for the commands.

A **macro** is a command or a sequence of commands entered into a cell or group of cells in a worksheet. When the user enters a macro, the commands in the macro are not performed; they are just stored in the worksheet. The user also gives the macro a name to identify it. Then, to execute the commands in the macro, the user just types the name of the macro. The spreadsheet software finds the macro in the worksheet and performs the commands in the macro.

As an example, assume that a user needs to format certain cells in a specific way. He or she could type the commands to do the formatting for each cell separately, but because the commands are the same, the user can create a macro with the necessary formatting commands. Then, to format a cell, the user moves the cell pointer to the cell and types the name of the macro. The commands are performed, and the cell is formatted.

It is possible to have many macros in a worksheet. Macros can be created that display menus, accept input from the keyboard, and perform other sophisticated tasks. Using macros, a user can create a worksheet that automates many functions so that it can be used by other users unfamiliar with the details of spreadsheet use.

COMMON SPREADSHEET SOFTWARE

The first spreadsheet program developed was called VisiCalc. For a while it was the most widely used spreadsheet program and has been credited with changing microcomputers from hobbyists' toys to business tools. VisiCalc is no longer produced but is still used on many computers.

Today, many spreadsheet programs are available. Probably the most widely used one on IBM personal computers and IBM clones is Lotus 1-2-3, and the most popular one on the Apple Macintosh is Excel. There is also a version of Excel for the IBM computers. Other common spreadsheet programs for IBM computers are Quattro Pro, SuperCalc, and VP-Planner Plus. Other spreadsheet programs used on the Macintosh are Full Impact and Wingz. Spreadsheet programs cost between $100 and $500.

In general, worksheets created by one spreadsheet program cannot be used by another. Because of the popularity of Lotus 1-2-3, however, many spreadsheet programs can use worksheets created by Lotus 1-2-3. This feature makes it possible to switch from one spreadsheet program to another without creating a new worksheet. Also, some spreadsheet programs use commands that are very similar to those used in Lotus 1-2-3.

Some spreadsheet programs include other capabilities besides spreadsheet processing. For example, Lotus 1-2-3 and Excel have limited graphics and data-management capabilities. These features are discussed in detail in later chapters.

FINANCIAL MODELING SOFTWARE

Spreadsheet software of the type described for microcomputers is not usually available on minicomputers and mainframe computers. Software that has similar and even more capabilities is available, however. This type of software, called **financial modeling software**, allows a user to create the equivalent of a worksheet by entering formulas and other information to describe the calculations to be done. The software usually includes many more capabilities than microcomputer spreadsheet programs, including the ability to incorporate future uncertainty into the analysis. Some financial modeling programs are available on microcomputers also. Examples are IFPS and Encore Plus.

With modeling software, a user can create a mathematical representation, called a *model*, of a real-world situation in the computer. For example, the user can create a model of possible investments for a business. Then the software can analyze the model to determine how the "real world" may behave in the future. Thus, with an investment model, the user can see how the investments may increase or decrease in value in the future. In so doing, questions can be answered about the potential investments, such as which are most likely to benefit the business.

Spreadsheet software also allows the user to create models. The difference, however, is that spreadsheet software has fewer capabilities and is less versatile than financial modeling software. For example, spreadsheet programs do not have easy ways of incorporating uncertainty about the future, whereas some financial modeling programs do. Consequently, spreadsheet software cannot be used for as complex a model as financial modeling software.

Chapter Summary

- Spreadsheet analysis is used to solve problems in which data is organized in rows and columns—that is, in a **spreadsheet**—and calculations are done with the data. **Spreadsheet software** makes spreadsheet analysis easy because the user can create an **electronic spreadsheet** or **worksheet**. Then, changes can be made in data in the worksheet, and the computer will automatically recalculate values in the worksheet—a procedure called **what-if analysis**.

- A **cell** is the intersection of a row and a column in a worksheet. A cell is identified by a **cell address**, which consists of the column letter followed by the row number. The three types of information that a user can put into a cell are numbers; **labels**, which are text; and **formulas**, which are rules for calculating the values of cells.

- The main functions that the user can perform with spreadsheet software are creating a worksheet, changing a worksheet, and printing a worksheet. When a worksheet is created, the user enters numbers, labels, and formulas into cells in the worksheet. The user changes the information in a worksheet because data changes and because he or she wants to do what-if analysis. All or part of a worksheet may be printed. With some software, the user controls the functions by pressing a special key (such as the / key) followed by a command. Often, the commands are listed in menus and submenus. With other software, the user uses a mouse to select options from a pull-down menu.

- Most microcomputers are capable of doing some spreadsheet analysis. The primary storage capacity of the computer determines the maximum size of the worksheet. Floppy disk drives are often adequate for secondary storage, although a hard disk drive is needed to store large worksheets. A fast CPU or special mathematics processor can make recalculation of large worksheets faster. Most printers can be used to print worksheets.

- Some common spreadsheet programs for IBM personal computers and IBM clones are Lotus 1-2-3, Excel, Quattro Pro, SuperCalc, and VP-Planner Plus. Excel is also available for the Apple Macintosh. Other spreadsheet programs for the Macintosh are Full Impact and Wingz.

Terms to Remember

Cell   p. 230

Cell Address   p. 230

Cell Pointer (Cell Cursor)   p. 230

Financial Modeling Software
   p. 245

Formula   p. 231

Function   p. 241

Label   p. 231

Macro   p. 244

Range   p. 240

Spreadsheet   p. 227

Spreadsheet Software   p. 227

Value   p. 231

What-If Analysis   p. 227

Worksheet (Electronic
   Spreadsheet)   p. 228

Worksheet File   p. 233

Review Questions

Fill-In Questions

1. A(n) _____ is an arrangement of data into rows and columns used for data analysis and presentation.

2. When a user changes certain data in a spreadsheet to see the effect on other data in the spreadsheet, the user is performing _____.

3. A spreadsheet created by spreadsheet software is called a(n) _____.

4. A(n) _____ is the intersection of a row and column in a worksheet.

5. The address of the cell in the third row and fifth column of a worksheet is _____.

6. After creating a worksheet using a spreadsheet program, the user must _____ the worksheet in a file in secondary storage before turning off the computer.

7. A(n) _____ is a group of adjoining cells in a worksheet that forms part of a column or row, or a rectangular pattern of rows and columns.

8. When the formula +D5–D6 in cell D7 is copied to cell D10, the formula becomes _____.

9. A routine built into spreadsheet software that performs special processing and that is invoked by using its name is a(n) _____.

10. A(n) _____ is a named sequence of commands entered into a cell or group of cells in a worksheet.

Short-Answer Questions

1. In what situation is spreadsheet analysis used?

2. Why does spreadsheet software make spreadsheet analysis easy?

3. What are the three types of information that a user can put into a cell of a worksheet?

4. What happens when a user enters a formula into a cell of a worksheet?

5. What are the three main functions a user can perform with a spreadsheet program?

6. Give the cell formulas for each of the following cells in the worksheet in Figure 9–6:

Cell	Formula
B13	+B8+B9+B10+B11+B12
B15	+B5–B13
C13	
C15	
D13	
D15	
E13	
E15	

7. What are several ways a user can control the functions performed by a spreadsheet program?

8. What microcomputer hardware is needed for spreadsheet analysis?

9. Give the cell formula for cell C10 in the worksheet in Figure 9–15 (a) without using a function, and (b) using a function.

10. What are some common spreadsheet programs?

Projects

1. Investigate a spreadsheet program to which you have access. What is the name of the program, and with which microcomputer can it be used? How much does it cost? How does a user control its functions?

What features beyond those required for creating, changing, and printing a worksheet does it have?

2. The spreadsheet software described in this chapter creates two-dimensional worksheets with rows and columns. Some spreadsheet programs can create three-dimensional worksheets. Find out what you can about one of these programs. How are cell addresses formed? How is the worksheet displayed on the screen? What is an example of a problem that requires a three-dimensional worksheet? Write a summary of your findings.

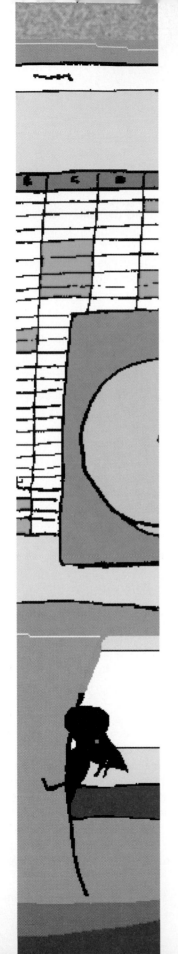

10

DATA MANAGEMENT SOFTWARE

CHAPTER OBJECTIVES

• After completing this chapter you should be able to:

1. Describe the types of situations in which data management is used.

2. Distinguish between file management software and database management software.

3. Explain the main functions that users can perform with data management software and describe several techniques used to control these functions.

4. State the microcomputer hardware needed for data management.

5. Identify several common file management and database management programs and state the computers with which they can be used.

A FTER WORD PROCESSING and spreadsheet software, the most frequently used software on microcomputers is **data management software**. This type of software allows the user to store data in secondary storage, to retrieve the stored data, and to make changes in the data. Although these tasks can be done without the help of data management software, they are much easier to do with this type of software.

This chapter discusses data management software. First, the chapter explains what data management is and describes the types of data management software. Then it examines how data management software is used.

DATA MANAGEMENT

Data management involves organizing and processing data in secondary storage. Recall from Chapter 5 that data is stored in *files* and *databases* in secondary storage. Data management software allows the user to organize stored data into files and databases and then to process the stored data.

Processing stored data involves retrieving data from a file or database. With data management software, a user can retrieve specific data. The retrieved data can then be displayed on a screen, or it can be printed on paper. Processing stored data also involves making changes in the data. The user can add data to a file or database, delete data in a file or database, or change the data in a file or database, using data management software.

Data management software functions differently for files and databases. Recall that a data file consists of a group of *records*. Each record contains several *fields*, and each field has several *characters*. For example, Figure 10–1 shows a file of data about inventory items in a business. (This is the same as Figure 5–21 in Chapter 5.) Each line in this figure is a record containing fields for the item number, item description, unit cost, unit price, and quantity on hand. Each field contains several characters.

A database consists of groups of related data such as groups of files. For example, a database could consist of the inventory item data in the inventory file in Figure 10–1, plus data about customers who have ordered items in the customer-order file in Figure 10–2. The customer-order file has records with fields for the customer number, customer name, item number for the item ordered, and quantity ordered. The data is *related* to the inventory data because the item number in the customer-order file is the same as the item number in the inventory file, meaning that a customer has ordered a particular item. (The common field creates a *relationship* between the data. Relationships are discussed in detail in Chapter 16.)

Figure 10–1 An Inventory File

ITEM NUMBER	ITEM DESCRIPTION	UNIT COST	UNIT PRICE	QUANTITY ON HAND
1208	RACING BICYCLE	205.50	259.95	25
2501	TOURING BICYCLE	184.00	239.95	8
2905	RECREATIONAL BICYCLE	76.25	109.95	41
3504	MOUNTAIN BIKE	188.75	229.95	6
4360	TRICYCLE	51.50	69.95	32
4389	TANDEM BICYCLE	256.00	340.50	12
5124	JUNIOR BICYCLE	69.75	99.95	0
5908	LEARNER BICYCLE	62.00	89.95	17
6531	PORTABLE BICYCLE	112.50	179.95	2

There are two general types of data management software (Figure 10–3). In the first type, called **file management software**, a user can process the data in only one file at a time. If several files are stored in secondary storage, the user can process the data in only one of the files at any moment. For example, if the inventory file in Figure 10–1 and the customer-order file in Figure 10–2 were both stored in secondary storage, the user could process data only about inventory items or about customers, but not about customers and the inventory items they have ordered.

In the second type of data management software, called **database management software**, the user can simultaneously process related data in a database. For example, if a database consisted of the data in the inventory file in Figure 10–1 and the data in the customer-order file in Figure 10–2, the user could simultaneously process related data from both files, using database management software. Thus, the user could process data about customers and the inventory items they have ordered.

Although the difference between these types of data management software may seem small, it is significant. In fact, file management programs are usually much less complex and less expensive than database management programs. Unfortunately, there is much confusion in the terminology used to describe these programs, and often software that is only a file management program is called a database program.

Figure 10–2 A Customer-Order File

CUSTOMER NUMBER	CUSTOMER NAME	ITEM NUMBER	QUANTITY ORDERED
12345	JOE'S BIKE SHOP	3504	4
29636	CITY SPORTS	6531	1
48721	CAMPUS BIKE	2905	10
51387	ABC SPORTING GOODS	4360	8

Figure 10–3 File Versus Database Management Software

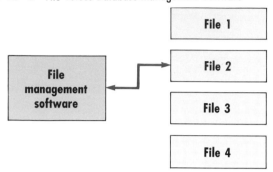

a. File management software

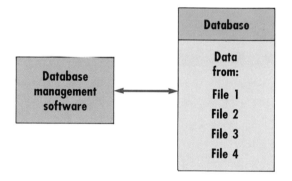

b. Database management software

The basic capabilities of file management and database management software are similar, with the exception, just mentioned, that database programs can process related data in a database. When only a single file needs to be processed, usually either a file management or a database management program can be used. If a database management program is used in this situation, the database consists of the data from a single file. When data from several related files must be manipulated simultaneously, a database management program must be used.

The use of both types of data management software is discussed in this chapter. Because database management software is the more general of the two, it is usually referred to in the examples. The differences between file management software and database management software capabilities are also noted.

DATA MANAGEMENT SOFTWARE FUNCTIONS

When a user uses data management software, he or she manipulates data in a database or file. All data management software allows the user to perform three main functions: create a file or database, retrieve data from a file or database, and change data in a file or database.

DATABASE UNITES VIETNAM VETS

Ernest Hemingway used to wax poetic about the comradeship that develops among brothers in arms. Deafened by exploding shells, their mind numbed by the grinding fear of sudden death, a kinship is born among those who endure the hell of battle that is rarely matched in civilian life.

Larry Horn wasn't about to let those indelible relationships evaporate without a fight. While serving as a medic during the 1968 Tet Offensive in Vietnam, Horn's legs were mangled by an exploding mortar shell. It would be months before he could walk again and a year before he left the hospital, but the memories of the men and women who helped him through those awful months were unforgettable.

Some years ago, Horn tried to organize a reunion of the evacuation unit where he was treated. He soon learned, however, that the Department of Defense keeps precious few records on the 1.2 million soldiers who were shipped off to the steamy jungles of Southeast Asia.

Unable to provide him with the whereabouts of his comrades, Horn soon took on the enormous task of hand-forging the Vietnam Veterans Registry, a computer-based reference tool for veterans like himself who want to rekindle the comradeships borne of a long-gone war.

Armed with about a half-dozen IBM Personal Computer clones, database software and a mountain of persistence, Horn and his wife Fran have created the largest registry of its kind from what was originally intended to be a weekend project.

"It's challenging, but it's very rewarding," said Horn from his home in Sweden, Maine. "There was a large but unfulfilled desire of many veterans to get in touch with their old buddies, and I guess I'm now that vehicle."

Having no computer background, Horn laboriously crafted a multifaceted database that now contains more than 25,000 names. Starting with a scrap of information as small as a person's nickname or a battle in which they fought, Horn can tell the registrant that his ex-Marine Corps buddy is now working as a carpenter in Dubuque. The information is culled from questionnaires filled out by veterans who learn about the service through advertisements and word of mouth.

Although Horn hopes eventually to register as many as 250,000 veterans for the service, he is starting to feel the computational crunch. "No doubt about it, we're already at the point where we could use a small [minicomputer]," Horn said.

Creating a File or Database

Before a file or database can be used, it must be *created*. This process involves two steps (Figure 10–4). First, the user must describe the fields and records in the file or database. The data management software must be told what fields are in each record, what type of data is in each field, and what records are in the file or database. With this information the data management software *initializes* the file or database in secondary storage, which means it reserves space for the data and stores the description of the file or database in this space.

Second, the user must store data in the file or database. Data for each field should be entered in each record. The data entered is stored in secondary storage by the data management software. Notice that

Figure 10–4   Creating a File or Database

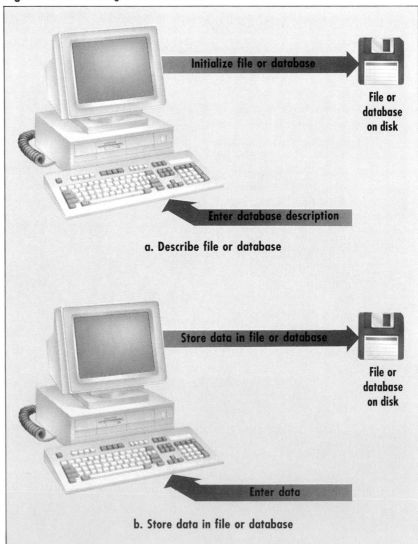

a. Describe file or database

b. Store data in file or database

unlike word processing and spreadsheet software discussed in the last two chapters, the user does *not* have to save the data before turning the computer off; the data management software saves the data for each record automatically after it has been entered.

Accessing a File or Database

The second main function a user can perform with data management software is to retrieve or **access** data in a file or database after it has been created. Accessing data means to bring the data from secondary storage into primary storage (Figure 10–5). The user may retrieve all the data in a file or database, or he or she may retrieve only certain data. With a file management program, only the data in one file can be accessed at a time. With a database management program, the user can access data that comes from several related files simultaneously. After the data has been brought into primary storage, it can be displayed on the screen, printed on paper, or used in some other way.

Accessing data in a file or database is often done to respond to a **query**, which is a request for certain data. The user enters a query, and the data management software locates and retrieves the required data. Accessing data is also done to prepare a **report**, which is a list of data printed on paper or displayed on the screen.

Updating a File or Database

The third main function a user can perform with data management software is to change or **update** data in a file or database. Updating includes three tasks. First, the user can *add* new data to a file or database, which usually involves adding one or more records. Second, the user can *delete* old data in a file or database, which normally involves deleting one or more records. Finally, the user can *modify* the data in any field in any record.

Figure 10–5   Accessing a File or Database

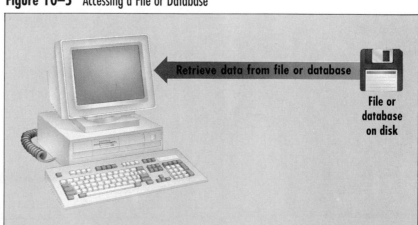

When a file or a database is updated in any of these ways, changes are made in the data stored in secondary storage. The updating process usually involves three steps (Figure 10–6). First, the user must enter information about what changes he or she wishes to make. Then the data management software retrieves the old data—that is, the records that are to be changed. (If new records are to be added, this step is not done.) Finally, the software stores the new data in secondary storage. (If records are to be deleted, this step is not done.)

Controlling Data Management Software Functions

The functions performed by a data management program are controlled in several ways. Most programs use menus to display a list of functions from which a user can select. For example, Figure 10–7 shows a menu used with dBASE III PLUS, a popular database program. Selection of a menu item may be done with function keys, cursor keys, or a mouse, depending on the computer and the software. Some programs also allow the user to type in commands that specify what the software is to do. For example, Table 10–1 lists some of the commands used in dBASE III PLUS. When a program can be controlled both with menus and through commands, the user can choose which approach to use. Sophisticated database management programs have many capabilities and provide complex menus, commands, and other techniques for control. Some of these programs have a graphical user interface.

HARDWARE NEEDED FOR DATA MANAGEMENT

The microcomputer hardware needed for data management depends mainly on the sizes of the files or databases. Because all data is stored

Figure 10–6   Updating a File or Database

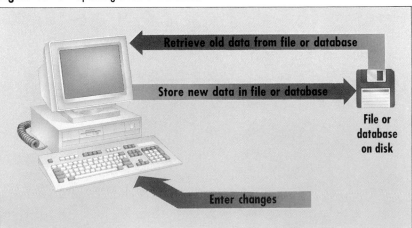

Figure 10–7   A dBASE III PLUS Menu

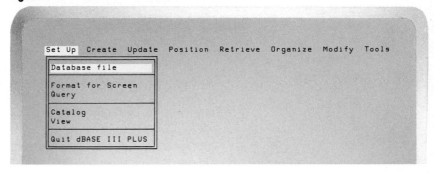

Table 10-1   Commands Used in dBASE III PLUS

Command	Purpose
CREATE	Create a new file
USE	Use an existing file
LIST	Retrieve records from a file and list them on the screen
JOIN	Retrieve related records from two files
APPEND	Add records to a file
DELETE	Delete records in a file
REPLACE	Modify data in records in a file
SUM	Find total of data in records in a file

in secondary storage, the amount of secondary storage determines the amount of data that can be stored. Only relatively small files and databases can be stored on floppy disks. For most data management situations a hard disk drive is needed. The hard disk drive also speeds up the processes of loading the data management software and storing and retrieving data.

Only enough primary storage to store the data management software and a small amount of data is needed. Data management software stores and retrieves one record at a time. Hence, only a small amount of primary storage is needed for data. Some data management programs, however, are very large, and a large amount of primary storage may be needed for the program.

The other hardware found with most microcomputers is usually adequate for data management. No special keyboard or screen features are required. A mouse may be needed with some software. A draft-quality printer is usually adequate, although a letter-quality printer may be needed for printing output to be included in business letters and reports.

EXAMPLES OF DATA MANAGEMENT SOFTWARE USE

To illustrate the use of data management software, continue with the example from the last two chapters, in which you are the national sales manager of a company. You need to keep track of data about each salesperson you manage. You must be able to look up quickly the month's sales for any salesperson, the region in which the person works, and the person's address. Every month, you have to update each salesperson's sales and, occasionally, you have to change a salesperson's address because the person has moved. Also, sometimes you have to delete all information about a salesperson because the person has left the company, or you must add information about a new salesperson who has been hired. You could keep the information for all the salespeople on paper. If there are many salespeople, however, looking up information can be time-consuming, and updating data can involve much erasing and rewriting. You decide to set up a database with the data about all salespeople and let the computer retrieve the required information and do the necessary updating.

File Management

Your first step is to decide what data is to be stored in the database and how the database is to be organized. You have to determine what fields and records make up the database. You decide that you will need the following fields for each salesperson:

> Salesperson name
> Salesperson address
> Salesperson city
> Salesperson state
> Region name
> Salesperson sales

Because all these fields apply to a salesperson, they can be in the same record. Hence, you decide that the database will have one record for each salesperson with these six fields. The records for all salespeople can be in one file. Thus, you do not need a database but just a salesperson file, in which there is one record for each salesperson with the required fields.

Because you have only one file, you could use a file management program. But you think that you may want to add other related data later, so you decide to use a database management program. Nevertheless, you would use the same approach for this file that you would use with file management software. You sit down at your microcomputer and load the operating system and the database management software. For illustrative purposes, the screens are shown as they appear in dBASE III PLUS, but the concepts apply to other database programs.

First, you must create the file. Recall that file creation involves two steps: describing the fields and records in the file, and storing data in the file. You start by selecting a menu item or typing a command that tells the software that you want to create a file. You must give the file a name, which will be used to identify it in secondary storage. You decide to call the salesperson file SLSPERS, and you enter this name. Then, for each field in the records in the file, you must give a field name, the type of data in the field (numeric or character), and the width of the field (that is, the number of characters in the field). You call the salesperson name field SPNAME. This field contains character data. You decide that this field will be 18 characters wide. You enter all this information for the salesperson name field. You go on to enter similar information for the salesperson address field (SPADDR), the salesperson city field (SPCITY), the salesperson state field (SPSTATE), and the region name field (REGNAME). Finally, you decide to call the salesperson sales field SPSALES. This field contains numeric data instead of character data and is 6 digits wide with no decimal places. You enter this information for the sales field. Figure 10–8 shows the screen after all the required information is entered. The database management software uses this information to initialize the file in secondary storage.

At this point you have specified all information about the fields and records in a file. Now you store data in the records. You start by entering the data for each field in the first record. Figure 10–9 shows the screen after the data for the first record has been entered. Then you enter the data for the second record, the third record, and so on, until all data has been entered. After you enter the data for each record, the software stores the record in secondary storage. The data is stored in the file identified by the name you gave it earlier. The fields in the records are identified by the names you specified. After all the data has been entered and stored in secondary storage, the file creation process is complete.

Sometime after creating the file, you need to access data in it to help you with your job. You sit down at your microcomputer and load the operating system and database management software. Then you give the software the name of the file in which the data is stored. First, you want a complete list of all the data in the file. You type a command that

Figure 10–8
Creating a File: Describing the Fields in the Records of the Salesperson File

```
      Field Name   Type        Width   Dec

  1   SPNAME       Character     18
  2   SPADDR       Character     14
  3   SPCITY       Character     14
  4   SPSTATE      Character      2
  5   REGNAME      Character      8
  6   SPSALES      Numeric        6       0
```

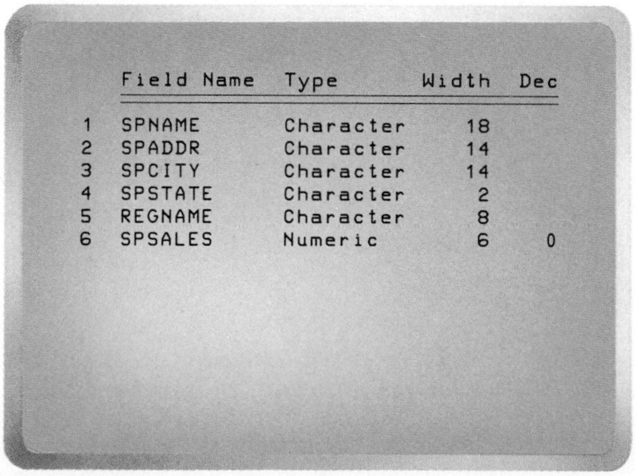

Figure 10–9
Creating a File: Storing Data in a Record of the Salesperson File

```
  SPNAME      John Smith
  SPADDR      45 First St.
  SPCITY      San Francisco
  SPSTATE     CA
  REGNAME     Western
  SPSALES     295700
```

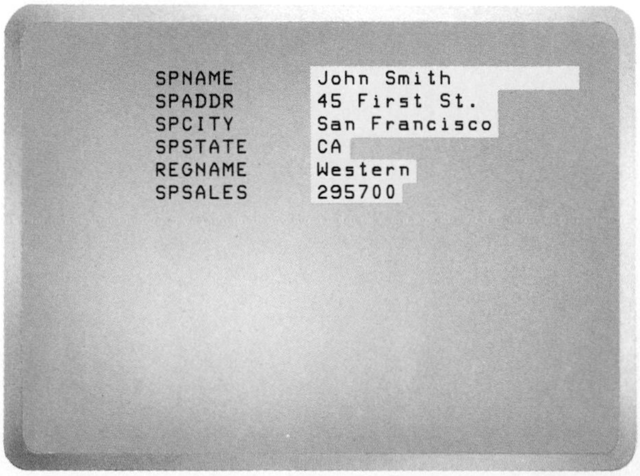

causes the software to retrieve all the data in the salesperson file and to display it on the screen. You also print a copy of this list. Figure 10–10 shows the output. Notice that the data is displayed in rows and columns. Each row is a record in the file, and each column is a field. The name of the field is displayed above its column.

Next, you want to analyze the sales for each of the four sales regions that you manage. You start by typing a command that just retrieves the records for the salespeople in the northern region and lists the salesperson name and sales from these records. Figure 10–11 shows the output. Notice that only five rows are displayed because only five salespeople work in the northern region. From this display you can see who are the best salespeople and who are not doing well. You type another command that gives the sum of the sales from the records of salespeople in the northern region. You print the sum so that you can enter it into your sales analysis worksheet (Figure 9–15) and into your sales memo (Figure 8–11). After analyzing the sales for the northern region, you go through similar steps for each of the other regions.

Finally, you need the address of a certain salesperson. To get this information, you type a command to retrieve the record for the salesperson and to display the address data from the record on the screen. Figure 10–12 shows the output. Notice that this data comes from a single record in the file, whereas the output from the previous examples comes from several records.

Periodically you have to update data in the salesperson file. When a new salesperson is hired, you have to add a record for that salesperson. You use a special command to add a record to the file. You enter the data for the salesperson in the same way that you entered data when creating the database, and the database management software stores the

Figure 10–10 A List of the Data in the Salesperson File

SPNAME	SPADDR	SPCITY	SPSTATE	REGNAME	SPSALES
John Smith	45 First St.	San Francisco	CA	Western	295700
Alan Wood	650 Broadway	Atlanta	GA	Southern	10500
Susan Jenson	62 Lincoln	Cincinnati	OH	Northern	428000
Frank Fuller	280 Winter Rd.	Flint	MI	Northern	120500
Joyce MacAdams	2 Forest Rd	Newark	NJ	Eastern	102150
James Bennett	8 River Way	Eugene	OR	Western	180400
Francis Benton	45 South St.	Birmingham	AL	Southern	36700
Andrew Lee	821 East St.	New York	NY	Eastern	147000
Mary Wong	182 West Blvd.	Seattle	WA	Western	370225
Fred Parks	465 Jefferson	Philadelphia	PA	Eastern	148000
Robert Marshall	312 Main St.	Minneapolis	MN	Northern	315000
Elizabeth Cole	981 Campus Dr.	Boston	MA	Eastern	65200
Paul Napier	28 East Plaza	New Orleans	LA	Southern	121000
Olivia Lock	4871 High St.	Chicago	IL	Northern	405500
Jose Sanchez	7 Bay View	Miami	FL	Southern	214125
Martha Young	405 South Pl.	Indianapolis	IN	Northern	259000

Figure 10–11   A List of Selected Data from the Salesperson File

```
SPNAME              SPSALES
Susan Jenson         428000
Frank Fuller         120500
Robert Marshall      315000
Olivia Lock          405500
Martha Young         259000
```

Figure 10–12   Data Retrieved from a Single Record in the Salesperson File

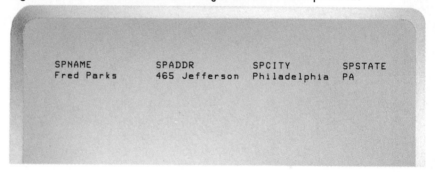

```
SPNAME          SPADDR          SPCITY          SPSTATE
Fred Parks      465 Jefferson   Philadelphia    PA
```

new record in the file. If a salesperson leaves the business, that person's record must be deleted from the file. You use special commands to indicate which record is to be deleted. The database management software finds the record and deletes it. At the end of each month, you have to change the sales figure in each record in the file to reflect the current month's sales. You use special commands to make these changes. You enter the new sales figure for each record, and the database management software modifies the records. Also, you sometimes have to change a salesperson's address in the file because the person has moved. Again, you use commands to make this change. All updating involves making changes in data stored in secondary storage. Figure 10–13 shows a list of the data in the salesperson file after the data has been updated.

Database Management

After you have used the salesperson file for a while, you decide you would like to create another file to keep track of data about each region. You will need the following fields for each region:

Region name
Region total sales
Number of salespeople in the region

Figure 10–13 A List of the Data in the Salesperson File After the Data Has Been Updated

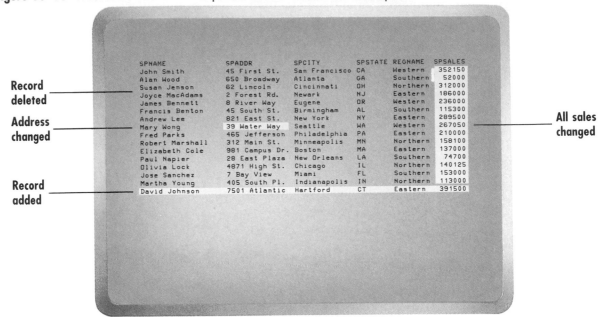

Record deleted

Address changed

Record added

All sales changed

You create a region file by describing these fields (Figure 10–14), but you do not enter data into the file. Instead, you use a series of commands to retrieve data from the salesperson file, compute each region's total sales, count the number of salespeople in each region, and store the required data in the region file. Figure 10–15 shows a list of the data in the region file after these commands have been performed.

You now have two files: the salesperson file and the region file. Notice that each file contains a field for the region name. These files are *related* because they contain this common field. Hence, you have a *database* consisting of two related files. (In dBASE III PLUS, the database management software used in this example, related data in a database is stored separately in distinct files. In other database management software, related data may be stored together in a single, large database file.)

Because you have used database management software to create the files in this database, you can retrieve related data from the files at the same time. For example, say you need a list of the salesperson name and sales data for each salesperson from the salesperson file along with all the data for the region in which the salesperson works from the region file. You enter the necessary commands. The database management software retrieves each salesperson's record and related region record, and displays the required data on the screen. (Figure 10–16 shows the output.) With this information you can determine, among other things, which salespeople are selling below the average for the region. (The average is found by dividing the region's total sales by the number of salespeople in the region.)

Figure 10–14
Describing the Fields in the Records of the Region File

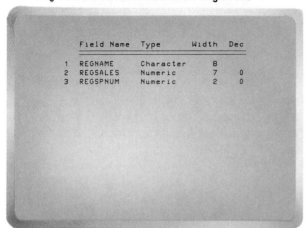

Figure 10–15
A List of the Data in the Region File

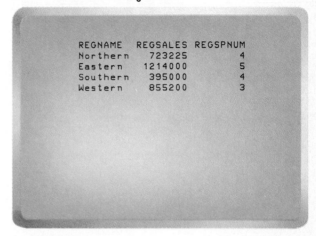

Figure 10–16
A List of Related Data from the Salesperson and Region Files

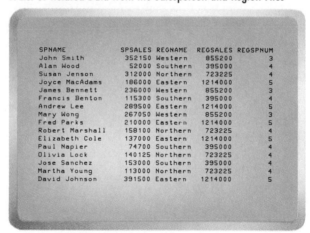

At the end of each month, you need to update the database with each region's total sales. After changing each salesperson's sales in the salesperson file, you enter a series of commands that compute the total sales for each region from the data in the salesperson file and that change this figure in the region file. Then you print the region file and use the printout to enter each region's sales in your sales analysis worksheet and sales memo.

Notice in this example how you have taken advantage of the database program's ability to store, retrieve, and change data. These capabilities allow you to manipulate data in a database more easily than if you kept the same data on paper. The advantages are especially great when there is a large amount of related data in a database.

PLOTTING A NOVEL COURSE

There's no guarantee that with a Plots Unlimited DOS computer program you'll become a John DOS Passos overnight, but those professional authors who've given the database a workout say it can definitely help ease the cramps of writer's block.

Since its introduction in Los Angeles, it has become a big hit among Tinseltown's professional writers. "Screenwriter Steve Hayes, on deadline for a Paramount action-comedy, says he was able to pare his plotting time from his norm of 10 days down to 48 hours," says Tom Sawyer, Plots' co-creator.

Sawyer, a TV/screen writer himself, says there are some 200,000 plot combinations possible through juxtaposing the various themes, conflicts and characters in the database—all there to help one get the creative juices flowing.

Having written scripts for shows as diverse as "All in the Family" and "Murder, She Wrote," he knows Plots' worth.

"I did 10 scripts for 'MSW,' and am currently working on the 11th—and, boy, can you go stale working within a mystery writer-amateur detective format," says Sawyer. "However, with the database I was able to come up with 11 fresh story lines—six of which were salable. 'Murder's' producers loved them all."

The Plots Unlimited program may not only end blockage, he says, but add another resource to the fictionalist's idea bank, heretofore primarily limited to newspaper and periodical articles, chance remarks or happenings in one's own life.

Interested? Boot up and scroll on.

When Sawyer, originally a cartoonist from Chicago, first started thinking about becoming a writer 20 years ago, he was living in New York, and one day bought a used book at Barnes & Noble titled "Plotto."

Published in 1929, it contained fragments of stories, gathered by author William Wallace Cook and presented in a manner that might aid aspiring writers in constructing their fiction works.

"When I got home, I found it too archaic and cumbersome to be of any use. I stuck it in my bookcase, and promptly forgot about it," says Sawyer.

Several years ago, Sawyer, now a successful television/screenwriter living in Malibu, rediscovered "Plotto" while browsing through what had become his very extensive library. "I thought I'd chucked it years ago."

Struck by its potential as a computer program, he called longtime Brooklyn pal Arthur Weingarten, also a successful TV writer, now residing in nearby Beverly Hills.

"Arthur thought it would be a terrific spare-time project, so we took our time and together created a database using 'Plotto' as our starting point—rewriting and restructuring as we went along," says Sawyer.

The result of their labors was Plots Unlimited, published by Ashleywilde, a firm they created and named for Weingarten's cat.

Weingarten is assembling a spoofy romantic potboiler—"Love Summer Hiss"—using the database. But for Weingarten, "Summer Hiss" is merely a romp. In the television industry for 30 years, with scripting credits that include shows for Bob Hope, Dinah Shore, the Smothers Brothers, "The Man from U.N.C.L.E.," "Bonanza" and "Mod

Squad," Weingarten is in the midst of writing a TV series based on Georges Simenon's Inspector Maigret detective novels.

"The opening show presented a problem. It runs two hours, and Simenon never wrote a Maigret story longer than 95 pages. Using a printout of Plots' database—because I still write on a typewriter—I was able to flesh out the Simenon story with a group of subplots I developed with the help of Plots Unlimited," he says.

Explaining how the program works, says Weingarten, is more difficult than actually using it. "Arthur Miller's *Death of a Salesman*," he says, "breaks down into a basic premise: A man who has lived his life with unrealistic expectations—in the end—when reality crashes in, can no longer live that life. With Plots you can have that at your fingertips in 20 different forms from a base of 14,000 fragmentary plot lines. Plug in the characters you want, and conflict situations (subplots), and you've got a whole new ball game—all of your making.

"It's something that the proverbial room of chimps typing could never duplicate. (In theory, 12 chimpanzees at individual typewriters would—if given enough time, through trial-and-error—recreate all of Shakespeare's works.)"

Originally, that "re-creation" concept bothered Weingarten and Sawyer, so to check it out they gave the Plots software to 15 professional writers and 15 "wannabe" writers, set a deadline, and waited.

"Not one of the 30 ever came up with the same story line," says Weingarten.

The database, he says, is programmed so the user has several ways to create a plot: master plot (protagonist, action, termination); through characters, situation, story sub-type (begin with mystery, revenge, etc., then add characters or story types, such as married life); story-type and sub-type (begin with romance, married life, etc., then choose sub-type, such as romance's misadventures); and story type and characters (select a story type, then match with combinations of characters).

The program is designed for fiction writers of all genres. "In fact, right now we're looking for someone capable of rewriting Plots into a broad-based educational program for kids in the five-to-eight group. It would be a bare-bones, create-and-learn database, integrating spelling and grammatical structuring. Later, it could be upgraded for junior and senior high school utilization," says Weingarten, who used to tell his daughter, Tara, fairy tales he spun from news items on the front page of the New York Times.

Tara Weingarten is now a New York Times reporter.

ADDITIONAL DATA MANAGEMENT SOFTWARE FEATURES

In addition to the basic capabilities of creating a file or database, retrieving data from a file or database, and changing data in a file or database, data management software provides other features. Some of the more useful features are SQL, a programming language, report formatting, screen layout, and multiple-user access.

SQL

All data management programs have ways of requesting information from a file or database—that is, ways of *querying* the data. With some programs the user selects queries from a menu, and with others the user enters commands for queries. The forms of the menus or commands, however, vary with different programs, which can make querying difficult to learn for a user who needs to use several programs.

Some database management programs (but not file management programs) use a common language for query commands called **SQL**, which stands for *Structured Query Language*. SQL was originally developed for mainframe computers. It is also available on minicomputers and is becoming more and more common on microcomputers. SQL commands have the same basic form for all types of computers and for all database management programs that use it. Thus, a user does not have to learn new commands to use a different program.

Figure 10–17 shows an example of a query in SQL. This query finds the salesperson number and sales for each salesperson in the northern region. The output from this query would be similar to that shown in Figure 10–11.

SQL can be used for very complex queries. We will describe it in more detail in Chapter 16.

Programming Language

Many database management programs (but not file management programs) have their own programming language. Using this language, the user can prepare programs containing long sequences of commands. For example, Figure 10–18 shows a program written in the programming language used with dBASE III PLUS. Once the program has been prepared, it is stored in secondary storage. Then the user can execute it repeatedly without reentering the instructions in the program. This procedure can save much effort when the same commands have to be used several times.

Complex systems can be created using the data management software's programming language. For example, the user can write a set of programs to do all the payroll processing for a business. Many programs may be needed for this processing, and several files or databases may be used. It may take several months to develop these programs, but once they are finished they can be used over and over again.

Figure 10–17   A Query in SQL

```
SELECT SPNAME, SPSALES
FROM SLSPERS
WHERE REGNAME = "Northern";
```

Figure 10–18   A Program for dBASE III PLUS

```
USE SLSPERS
SUM SPSALES TO NSALES FOR REGNAME = "Northern"
SUM SPSALES TO ESALES FOR REGNAME = "Eastern"
SUM SPSALES TO SSALES FOR REGNAME = "Southern"
SUM SPSALES TO WSALES FOR REGNAME = "Western"
USE REGION
REPLACE REGSALES WITH NSALES FOR REGNAME = "Northern"
REPLACE REGSALES WITH ESALES FOR REGNAME = "Eastern"
REPLACE REGSALES WITH SSALES FOR REGNAME = "Southern"
REPLACE REGSALES WITH WSALES FOR REGNAME = "Western"
```

Report Formatting

Most data management programs provide some way of formatting report output. A user can select which fields are to be printed in a report and where in the report the fields are to be printed. He or she can provide a title for the report and headings for columns of output. Also, the user can specify what fields are to be totaled and where the totals are to be printed. These and other features allow the user to design custom reports.

Once a report is designed, the user can save the report format in secondary storage. Then, anytime a report with new data is needed, the saved format can be used. Thus, the user does not have to specify the report format again.

Screen Layout

Many data management programs provide a way of laying out screens. The user can specify where fields will be displayed on a screen, which fields will be used for input and which for output, what captions or headings go with each field, and other attributes of a screen. With some programs the user can design custom menus for the screen. As with report formats, screen layouts can be saved in secondary storage and used repeatedly.

With preset report formats and screen layouts a data management program can be much easier to use. When the reports and screens have been properly set up, the software can be used by users who are unfamiliar with the details of data management.

Multiple-User Access

Most microcomputer data management software is designed to allow one user at a time to access a database, because most microcomputers are single-user computers. Often, however, several microcomputers are connected in a network. Then multiple users can access a database. In this situation, special network data management software is required.

Single-user data management software cannot be used by several users in a network to access a database simultaneously because there is no way of preventing the users from interfering with each other. For example, assume that one user is updating a record in a database. If, while the user is making the change, another user retrieves the same record, the data this user sees may not be correct because the first user has not completed the update. Because of this type of problem, single-user data management software cannot be used by multiple users in a network to access the same database.

Some microcomputer data management software is designed for use by multiple users in a network. These programs solve the problem of multiple-user access in several ways. One technique is called **record locking**. In this technique, when a record is accessed by a user it is "locked," which means that no other user can access the same record until it is "unlocked." Unlocking occurs when the user who accessed it indicates to the software that he or she no longer needs the record. Through techniques such as this one, multiple users can access the same database without interfering with each other.

COMMON DATA MANAGEMENT SOFTWARE

As noted earlier, there are two main types of data management software: file management software and database management software. The former allows the user to process only a single file at one time, whereas the latter lets the user simultaneously manipulate related groups of data that form a database. Some of the more widely used file management programs for IBM personal computers and IBM clones are Professional File, Reflex, PC File, Rapidfile, and Q & A. Some common file management programs for the Apple Macintosh are FileMaker and Microsoft File. File management programs cost between $70 and $400. Also, some spreadsheet software include file management capabilities. For example, Lotus 1-2-3 and Excel, which are popular spreadsheet programs, have file management features.

The most widely used database management program for IBM computers is dBASE III PLUS. A new version of this program, called dBASE IV, is also available. Some other commonly used database management programs on IBM computers are R:Base for DOS, Paradox, and FoxPro. Some commonly used database management programs for the Apple Macintosh are Fourth Dimension, Double Helix, and Omnis. There is also a program similar, but not identical, to dBASE III PLUS for the Macintosh called dBASE Mac, and one similar to FoxPro for the Macintosh called FoxBase Plus/Mac.

Files and databases created by one data management program may not necessarily be usable by another program. Because of the popularity of dBASE III PLUS, some programs can access dBASE III PLUS databases. This feature makes it possible to switch from one data management program to another without creating a new database. Also, some database management programs use commands that are similar to those in dBASE III PLUS.

Chapter Summary

- Data management is used in situations in which data stored in secondary storage needs to be organized and processed. Stored data is organized into fields, records, files, and databases. Processing stored data involves retrieving and changing data.

- There are two types of **data management software**: file management software and database management software. With **file management software**, the user can process data in one file at a time, whereas with **database management software**, the user can simultaneously process several related groups of data that form a database.

- The main functions that the user can perform with data management software are creating a file or database, accessing a file or database, and updating a file or database. To create a file or database, the user must first describe the fields and records in the file or database and then store data in the file or database in secondary storage. **Accessing** a file or database involves retrieving data from secondary storage to respond to a **query** or to produce a **report**. **Updating** a file or database includes adding new data, deleting old data, and modifying existing data. With some software the user controls these functions by making selections from a menu. The selection may be made by using function keys, cursor keys, or a mouse. Some programs also allow the user to enter commands that specify what function the software is to perform. Some programs provide both menu selection and commands for user control.

- The microcomputer hardware needed for data management depends mainly on the sizes of the files or databases. If only small files and databases are stored, floppy disk drives are satisfactory for secondary storage. For most data management situations, however, a hard disk drive is needed. Primary storage needs to be large enough for the data management software and a small amount of data. The other hardware found with most microcomputers is usually adequate for data management.

- Some common file management programs for the IBM personal computers and IBM clones are Professional File, Reflex, PC File, Rapidfile, and Q & A. Some common file management programs for the Apple Macintosh are FileMaker and Microsoft File. In addition, some spreadsheet programs, such as Lotus 1-2-3 and Excel, have file management features. Some common database management programs for IBM computers are dBASE III PLUS, dBASE IV, R:Base for DOS, Paradox, and FoxPro. Some common database management programs for the Macintosh are Fourth Dimension, Double Helix, Omnis, dBASE Mac, and FoxBase Plus/Mac.

Terms to Remember

Accessing   p. 255

Database Management
  Software   p. 251

Data Management Software
  p. 250

File Management Software
  p. 251

Query   p. 255

Record Locking   p. 268

Report   p. 255

SQL   p. 266

Updating   p. 255

Review Questions

Fill-In Questions

1. Two types of data management software are _____ and
   _____.

2. Unlike word processing and spreadsheet software, the user does not
   have to _____ the data he or she enters into a file or
   database before turning off the computer.

3. The process of retrieving data from a file or database is called
   _____ data.

4. A(n) _____ is a request for information from a file or
   database.

5. The process of changing data in a file or database is called
   _____.

6. Three updating tasks are _____ new data, _____ old
   data, and _____ existing data.

7. A common language for querying a database is _____.

8. A technique that solves the problem of several users accessing the
   same record in a file or database is called _____.

Short-Answer Questions

1. In which situations is data management used?

2. What is the difference between file management software and database management software?

3. What two steps are required to create a file or database?

4. Describe several ways a user can control the functions performed by
   a data management program.

5. What microcomputer hardware is needed for data management?

6. Why are five lines of output displayed in Figure 10–11 but only one
   line displayed in Figure 10–12?

7. What did the user have to enter to describe the region file in Figure 10–14?

8. What are some additional capabilities of data management software
   beyond storing, retrieving, and modifying data in a file or database?

9. What are some common file management programs?

10. What are some common database management programs?

Projects

1. Investigate a data management program to which you have access. What is the name of the program, and with which microcomputers can it be used? How much does it cost? Is it a file management or database management program? How does a user control its functions? What features beyond those required for creating, accessing, and updating a file or database does it have?

2. Libraries can be thought of as large databases. Find out what you can about how libraries currently use computers for data management and how they may use computers in the future. Write a summary of your findings.

GRAPHICS AND OTHER APPLICATION SOFTWARE

CHAPTER TOPICS

Computer Graphics

Basic Graphics Software
- Types of Graphics Software
- Hardware Needed for Graphic Output
- An Example of Graphics Software Use
- Common Graphics Software

Presentation Graphics Software

Computer-Aided Design Software

Integrated Software
- An Example of Integrated Software Use
- Common Integrated Software

Other Application Software
- Personal Information Management Software
- Hypertext Software

CHAPTER OBJECTIVES

- After completing this chapter you should be able to:

1. List several forms of graphic output.

2. Describe two basic types of graphics software.

3. State the microcomputer hardware needed for graphic output.

4. Explain the functions of presentation graphics software and computer-aided design software.

5. Give advantages and disadvantages of integrated software.

6. Explain the functions of personal information management software and hypertext software.

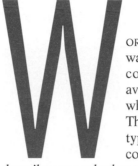

ORD PROCESSING, spreadsheet, and database software are the most widely used software on microcomputers. Other software, however, is also available. One common type is graphics software, which allows the user to produce graphic output. There are many forms of graphic output and several types of graphics software. This chapter covers computer graphics and graphics software. It also describes several other types of application software that users encounter.

COMPUTER GRAPHICS

Computer graphic output comes in a variety of forms. One form is *charts and graphs* (Figure 11–1). The most basic of these are single-color charts in two dimensions. Multiple colors may be used to make a chart more readable. The most complex charts are three-dimensional and multiple-color. These types of computer graphics are often used by business people, scientists, and others to summarize data in an easily understood form.

Another type of computer graphics output is a *diagram* of an object, showing its outline or design (Figure 11–2). These diagrams can be in two or three dimensions, and in a single color or in multiple colors. Architects and engineers use this form of computer graphics when designing buildings, automobiles, and other objects. Often three-dimensional diagrams can be rotated on a screen so that they can be looked at from different angles.

Graphic designs are another type of computer graphics (Figure 11–3). These are almost always in color and often have a three-dimensional effect. You see them many times in advertisements in magazines

Figure 11–1 Computer Graphics: Charts and Graphs

(a)

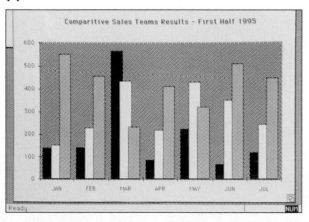

(b)

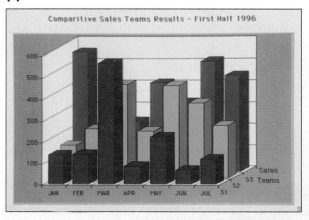

Figure 11–2 Computer Graphics: Diagrams

(a)   **(b)**   **(c)**

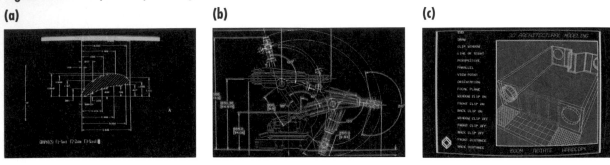

Figure 11–3 Computer Graphics: Graphic Design

(a)   **(b)**   **(c)**

and on television. Movement or animation is often used in this form of computer graphics to enhance the effect.

Another type of computer graphics is a *realistic image* of an object, such as a car or an airplane (Figure 11–4). These are always in color and three-dimensional, and usually move on the screen. One use of this type of image is in machines that simulate real-world situations, such as airplane simulators. Another use is in movies to duplicate visual effects that cannot be created in real life.

A final use of computer graphics is for *computer art* (Figure 11–5). Many artists are finding that they can use computers to create unique works of art. Computer art is almost always in color and three-dimensional. Such art may be abstract or realistic, and it is usually very striking.

BASIC GRAPHICS SOFTWARE

Computer graphic output is produced by **graphics software**. With this type of software the user can create charts, graphs, diagrams, designs, images, art, and other forms of graphic output on a screen or on paper. Some graphics software is very specialized and is used only by certain types of people such as graphics designers and artists. Other graphics software is more basic and can be used by almost anyone. This section describes the basic types of graphics software.

Figure 11–4   Computer Graphics: Realistic Images

(a)

(b)

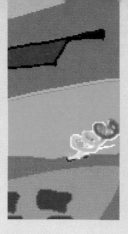

MOVIE-MAKING ABRACADABRA

Motion picture special effects have come a long way since dangling trash can lids passed for attacking alien spacecraft in the cheesy sci-fi movies of the 1950s.

These days, movieland's technicians of trickery can turn out such films as *Who Framed Roger Rabbit*, which transforms a squeaky cartoon rabbit into a reality-bending member of the real world who effortlessly interacts with flesh-and-blood actors. All it takes is a handful of workstations, off-the-shelf software and some of the most creatively warped minds in the business.

"Computer graphics in films are not a novelty anymore," said Nancy St. John, executive producer at Industrial Light and Magic (ILM), one of the foremost practitioners of the art of special effects. The firm, which was created by film director George Lucas, has lent its cinematic phantasms to *Who Framed Roger Rabbit*, *Star Wars* and the trio of *Back to the Future* pictures, among others, and has raked in several Oscars for its efforts.

What is surprising about ILM, however, is that some of the industry's most eye-popping special effects come out of such a relatively simple computer setup. There are no mainframes, minicomputers or elaborate networks in ILM's unassuming creative offices.

Instead, a series of linked workstations run home-grown software packages as well as off-the-shelf graphics applications from companies such as Pixar and Alias Research, Inc.

"We don't want to have a mainframe, because if it goes down, everyone goes down, and that's no way to survive," St. John said.

However, this elementary setup must also handle some very demanding projects. Graphics animation in motion pictures is very computing-intensive. Technical director Lincoln Hu estimated that each frame of a sophisticated animation sequence can demand anywhere from 5M to 20M bytes of system memory and most movies run at 24 frames per second.

Being an industry innovator, ILM's computer jobs also get progressively tougher. "In the special effects business, we've got to beat ourselves every time," Hu said. "But whenever we double the resolution, we quadruple our storage space requirements."

Man-hours are also long. A 30-second ketchup commercial, for instance, which provides an ant-eye view of a picnic, may take eight or nine weeks of computer animation, St. John said.

ILM's newest move to lighten this load is its digital compositing system, which bridges the gap between the computer graphics and film worlds. The system works by using a custom-made scanner to enter the film images into a computer system, where they are then manipulated digitally onto video and then output back onto film. Hu cited several advantages of the digital compositing system over traditional film opticals, including the ability to create multiple images without generational loss or image degradation and the absence of "outlines" like those associated with blue-screen matting.

Digital compositing also allows ILM to create images that cannot be realized by building models. Hu noted that the big change in digital compositing is that it is completely transparent. In *Back to the Future II*, ILM removed visible wires from several scenes and filled in the wire marks with computer-generated imagery.

Figure 11–5   Computer Graphics: Computer Art

(a)

(b)

(c)

Types of Graphics Software

There are two basic types of graphics software. In the first type, sometimes called a **charting program**, the software creates charts and graphs from data supplied to the software. Figure 11–6 shows some of the forms of charts and graphs that can be produced by this type of software. A *bar graph* shows how data is compared by using horizontal or vertical bars. A *pie chart* presents the output in a circle with a different wedge (or "piece of pie") for each set of data. A *line graph* connects dots or other symbols with lines.

The data used by the software to create the chart or graph can come from several sources. One is a worksheet. Data from rows and columns in a worksheet created by a spreadsheet program can be plotted in a chart or graph with the appropriate software. Another source of data for graphic output is a file or database created by a data management program. Charting software can plot the stored data. Finally, the user can enter data directly into a charting program, which can use the data to plot the output.

To use a charting program, a user must specify the source of the data and what type of chart or graph he or she wants created. The software uses the data to figure out how the chart or graph should appear

Figure 11–6   Some Common Forms of Charts and Graphs

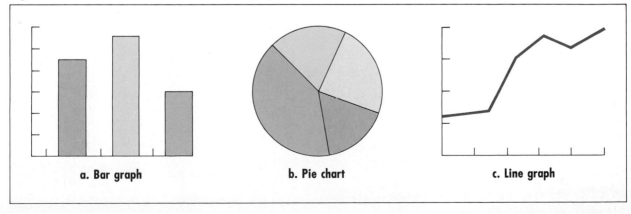

and then produces the output (Figure 11–7). This type of software is often used for producing business charts and graphs, and is sometimes called **business graphics software**.

The second type of graphics software allows the user to draw pictures and diagrams on the screen (Figure 11–8). This type of software usually provides the user with many standard shapes and symbols that can be used to create the output. Boxes, circles, and other shapes may be provided. To use this type of graphics software, the user selects a shape, often by using a mouse to point to it in a menu on the screen. Then the user positions the shape on the screen, changes its size, rotates it, and fills it in with shades and colors. By repeating this process for other shapes and symbols, and by drawing other lines on the screen—usually with a mouse—the user can create complex pictures and diagrams. Because the process is somewhat like painting or drawing, this type of software is sometimes called a **paint program** or a **draw program**. (There are differences in the ways paint and draw programs function and in their capabilities that are beyond the scope of this book.)

Some graphics software includes features of both a charting program and a paint or draw program. Then the software can produce a chart or graph to which the user can add additional items. Sophisticated graphics programs include hundreds of options for the user.

Hardware Needed for Graphic Output

Special output hardware is needed to produce graphic output. A medium- to high-resolution screen is required to display graphs and charts. Very high resolution may be needed for the best graphic output. A monochrome monitor is satisfactory for single-color output, but a color monitor is needed for multiple-color graphics.

Figure 11–7 Charting Program Output

Figure 11–8 Paint Program Output

A printer that can produce graphic output is required if a paper copy is needed. A fully-formed–character printer usually cannot be used for graphic output. Many dot-matrix printers, however, can print graphic output, although the quality may not be very good. Better quality is produced by a laser printer, which can print graphs, charts, and diagrams that are almost as good as those drawn by hand. The best graphic output, however, is produced by a plotter. Some printers and plotters can produce color output.

Graphics software usually requires a powerful computer. A fast CPU is needed because many calculations must be done to produce certain types of graphic output. A large amount of primary storage is necessary to store the output before it is displayed or printed. Workstations, a powerful type of microcomputer discussed in Chapter 2, are often designed for graphic output. To save graphs, charts, and diagrams for future use, a hard disk drive may be needed because a floppy disk may not have sufficient capacity. Some graphics programs require a mouse for user control, whereas other programs work with just a keyboard.

An Example of Graphics Software Use

To illustrate the use of graphics software, consider the example from the previous chapters in which you are the national sales manager of a company. Each month you analyze the sales in the four regions that you manage, using spreadsheet software (Figure 9–16.) You decide that you would like to graph the sales last month and the sales this month for each region. Such a graph will help you analyze the sales when you prepare your sales memo.

You sit down at your microcomputer and load the operating system and the graphics software. For illustrative purposes, the graphics capabilities of Lotus 1-2-3 are used in this example, but the concepts apply to other graphics software. The data for the graph will come from a worksheet you created earlier, so you retrieve that worksheet from secondary storage (Figure 11–9). You decide to display the output in a bar graph. You type commands to indicate this fact to the software. Then you specify what data in the worksheet will be graphed. For this example, you want to graph the sales in each region for both last month and this month, as indicated in Figure 11–9. Finally, you enter titles and legends to make the graphic output easier to read. When these tasks have been done, you display the graph on the screen and print a copy. Figure 11–10 shows the graphic output that is produced.

Notice in this example how you have used the data that already exists in the worksheet to produce the graphic output. You do not have to enter the data again. You need only to specify what type of graph is to be produced and what data in the worksheet is to be used. The graphics software determines how the graph should appear.

Common Graphics Software

Some spreadsheet software includes graphics features. For example, Lotus 1-2-3 and Excel can produce graphic output. Usually, the graphic capabilities of spreadsheet programs are limited to simple charts and graphs. Programs that are designed specifically for producing graphic output are more sophisticated. Such programs can produce many types of charts, graphs, and other forms of output. Examples of charting programs are Chartmaster and Microsoft Chart for IBM personal computers and IBM clones, and Cricket Graph and Delta Graph for the Apple Macintosh. This type of program costs between $100 and $400. Paint and draw

Figure 11–9   Worksheet with Data to be Graphed

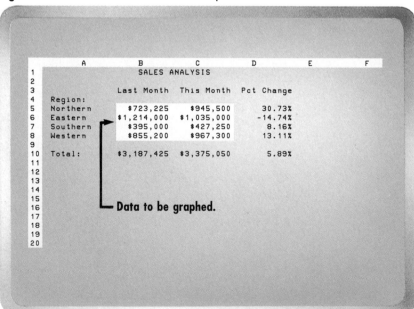

Figure 11–10 The Sales Analysis Graphic Output

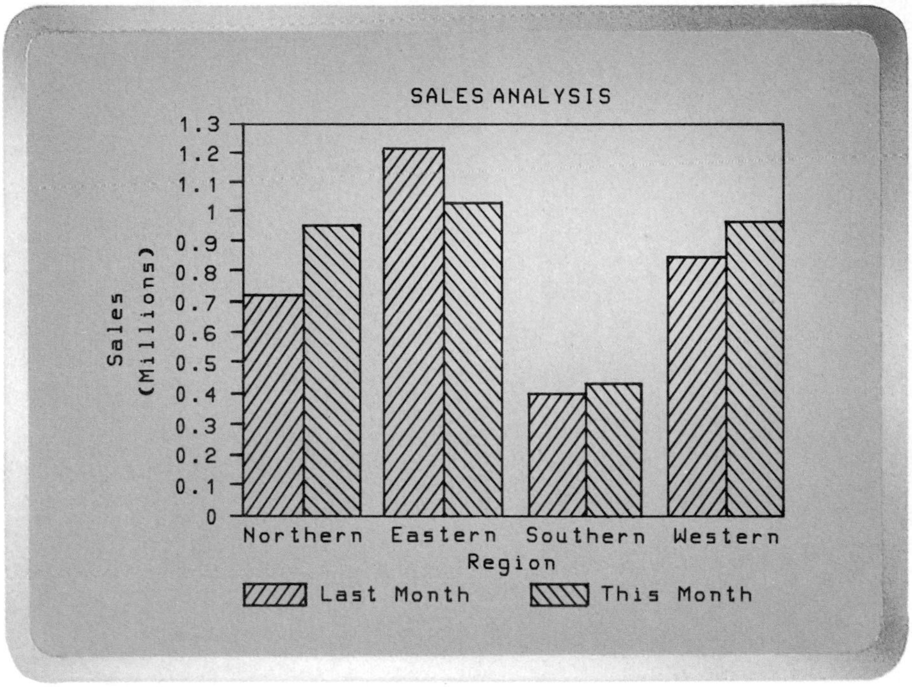

programs include MacPaint, MacDraw, Superpaint, and Freehand for the Apple Macintosh, and PC Paint Plus, Dr. Halo, and PC Paintbrush for the IBM computers. This type of program costs between $100 and $300.

PRESENTATION GRAPHICS SOFTWARE

Graphic output is often used in presentations given to groups of people. To create high-quality graphic output for such presentations, **presentation graphics software** is used. This type of software is usually a combination of a charting program and a drawing program but with additional capabilities. Added capabilities include the ability to prepare different border and background designs, to enter and edit text, and to use graphic images from other files.

The output produced by a presentation graphics program can be produced in several forms suitable for presentations (Figure 11–11). A laser printer can produce presentation graphics output on transparency sheets, which can be projected on a film screen during a presentation. Special hardware is available that records graphic output on photographic film. Slides made from the film can then be used to display the graphic output. Special projectors can be connected directly to a microcomputer to project the screen image on a film screen. These techniques and others make graphics effective in conveying information in a presentation.

Any of the charting programs and paint and draw programs discussed earlier can be used to prepare presentation graphs, but their capabilities

Figure 11–11 Presentation Graphics Output

(a)

(b)

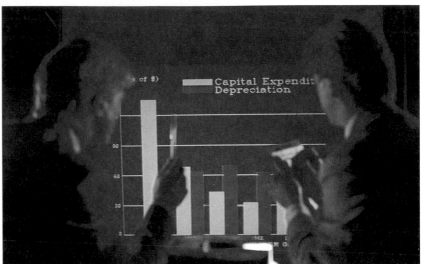

are limited. More powerful presentation graphics programs for the IBM personal computers and IBM clones include Harvard Graphics and Freelance Plus. Programs for the Apple Macintosh include Persuasion and More. This type of program costs between $400 and $500.

COMPUTER-AIDED DESIGN SOFTWARE

Graphics software used for designing objects such as buildings and automobiles is called **computer-aided design**, or **CAD**, software. Using CAD software, a specially trained person can draw the design of an object with a computer, modify the design, try different designs, and perform other design functions. For example, an automotive engineer can use CAD software to design an automobile (Figure 11–12). Using the graphics capability of the software, the engineer draws a car on the screen. Then he or she uses the computer to analyze characteristics of the design. The engineer can change the design easily and analyze the new design. Once a design is finalized, it can be printed with a plotter. Other people who use CAD are aircraft engineers, computer circuit designers, ship builders, and architects.

CAD software usually requires a fast computer with a lot of primary storage and a high-resolution screen. The first CAD programs were developed for mainframe computers and minicomputers because these computers have the necessary capabilities. Today there are a number of CAD programs for the more powerful microcomputers. These include Auto-CAD and VersaCAD for the IBM personal computers and IBM clones. Versions of these programs are also available for the Apple Macintosh. Some other Macintosh CAD programs are Pegasys and Minicad Plus. CAD programs for microcomputers cost between $500 and $3,500.

ART MEETS TECHNOLOGY

Computer-aided design (CAD), once the exclusive province of engineers for use in such industries as auto manufacturing, machining and electronics, is finding its way into new areas ranging from airport design, boat building and landscape layout to the manipulation of molecular models by chemists and the construction of robot hands for use in space.

CAD allows the user to work with the computer to visualize problems, simulate operations, get fast feedback on trial-and-error processes, test theories and get access to information previously hard to get. CAD also allows the user to draft perfectly symmetrical drawings, many of them three-dimensional, and carry out calculations at lightning speed.

Especially intriguing are the applications being developed by nonspecialists, those who are not CAD engineers to begin with, but who discover some previously untried application of CAD technology like education.

CAD and Archaeology

Buried in the jungles of the Yucatan Peninsula in Mexico is a decaying Mayan palace dating to the ninth century A.D. A team of archaeologists seeks to construct a model that will simulate the original appearance of the 44-room structure. Their goal is not only to recreate the model but also to consolidate the current ruins into a recreated palace, based on the model.

In the midst of humid temperatures, hungry mosquitoes, and the cry of exotic birds, the archaeologists have set up a computer loaded with CAD software. Using CAD, they have begun their computer model by reconstructing a particularly well-preserved staircase. Entering fixed X, Y, and Z coordinates, they use CAD to connect the points of the simulated stairway as a starting point. Then, they can now begin the process of reconstructing the whole palace.

The CAD program has enabled the team to bring in a third dimension, depth, as well as fast calculation, aspects that aren't possible in traditional paper-drafting. The team is also able to compare at the site the 3-D model with the palace remains. A "photogrammetric" laser survey technique produces special gridded photos that provide precise measurements of the palace that help create a contour map on the computer. With the palace stones numbered to create the contour map, a wire-frame model is developed and superimposed on the computer design. The result is a re-created model of the original palace.

In an environment worthy of Captain Richard Burton, the dynamic 19th-century English explorer, these innovative archaeologists have found a new way to use computers, not only to preserve the memory of an ancient civilization as represented by this palace, but to bring actual reconstruction of the past one step closer.

Computer-Aided Fashion

Miles away, in the more conventional environment of the University of Tennessee at Knoxville, fashion design students are using CAD to design clothes, plan the apparel production process, and develop schemes for merchandise layout.

The end result is an easy-to-use CAD program that contains customized computer menus, full of icons, that allow the students to load in pre-drawn apparel patterns and use various commands to alter these patterns to create new designs.

The students can also use the apparel CAD to lengthen, shorten, add extra fullness, place and space button holes, add seams, darts, pleats and so on. The patterns are printed out, the students can cut out the fabric according to the pattern and sew the garment.

The students have also learned how to use CAD to plan large-scale apparel production. The goal is to calculate the cost of manufacturing and to streamline production by analyzing such variables as sewing time and plant layout.

In addition, CAD is used to plan the presentation of merchandise to customers, including basic floor plans, furnishings, rack placement, table displays, and even dressing-room size and location.

Figure 11–12 Computer-Aided Design

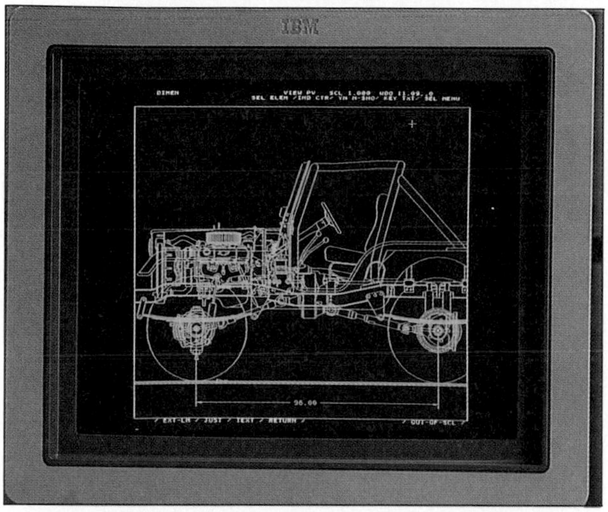

INTEGRATED SOFTWARE

In this and the previous three chapters, four major types of general application software used on microcomputers were described: word processing, spreadsheet, data management, and graphics software. A fifth major type, communications software, was discussed in Chapter 6. There are other types of general application software, such as statistical analysis and project-management software, but the five types just mentioned are the most commonly used. Because of their widespread use, some software is available that combines several of these applications into one package. This type of software is called **integrated software**. For example, one common integrated program includes spreadsheet, data management, and graphics capabilities. Another package includes all five applications, and still another includes all five plus other applications.

There are two main advantages of integrated software. First, because the programs are integrated, the same user interface is used for all applications. Thus, similar menus and commands are used in an integrated program for each application. This characteristic can make the integrated program easier to learn than separate programs, one for each application, in which the menus and commands are different for each program. The second main advantage of integrated software is that it is usually easy to transfer data from one application to another. Thus it is easy with integrated software to incorporate data from a file into a spreadsheet or to use the spreadsheet data in a graph. With separate programs such transferring of data may not be possible or may require special programs to translate the data from one form to another.

There are several disadvantages of integrated software. First, a user may not need all the applications provided by the software. If the user needs only word processing and spreadsheet capabilities, for example, then it probably is not sensible to use a program that includes all five applications. Second, separate programs may be better than their counterparts in integrated software. For example, good word processing programs are usually better for sophisticated word processing tasks than the word processing capabilities of integrated programs. Finally, integrated programs can be complex to use. Because they have so many capabilities, such programs often have many menus and commands, which can make their use difficult.

An Example of Integrated Software Use

Assume that you are the national sales manager of a company and that you have an integrated program that includes word processing, spreadsheet, data management, graphics, and communications capabilities. You can use this program to do all the sales analysis work described in the previous examples, plus more. Figure 11–13 summarizes the process.

First, you use the communications capability of the program to get the sales figures for each salesperson. Each month you need the total sales of each salesperson you manage so that you can update your records. The sales figures are kept in files on minicomputers in the four regional offices. You could have someone at each office retrieve the data from the computer and telephone you with the figures, which you would then have to type into your microcomputer. Alternatively, because you have communications capabilities in your software, you can use your microcomputer to communicate directly with each regional office's minicomputer, retrieve the data yourself, and download it to your microcomputer. This data goes into a salesperson file.

The salesperson file is managed by the data management capability of the program. The data that is downloaded updates each salesperson's sales field in that file. You then use the data management capabilities to

Figure 11–13 Using Integrated Software for Sales Analysis

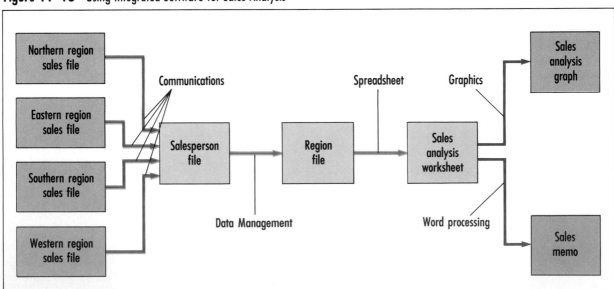

compute the total sales for each region and update the region total sales fields in the region file.

The next step is to update the sales analysis worksheet managed by the spreadsheet capabilities of the program. Among other things you transfer the region total sales figures from the region file to the worksheet. You then graph the sales figures using the graphics capabilities of the program. Also, you transfer the sales figures from the worksheet to the sales memo. Looking at the sales analysis graph and the sales figures you edit the sales memo, using the word processing capabilities of the program.

Common Integrated Software

Many programs that are used primarily for spreadsheet analysis include other capabilities. For example, Lotus 1-2-3 and Excel can do some data management and graphics. These programs are examples of integrated software, although most people think of them just as spreadsheet programs. An integrated program that includes spreadsheet, data management, graphics, word processing, and communications capabilities is Symphony for the IBM personal computers and IBM clones. Another program for IBM computers is Framework. This program has word processing, data management, spreadsheet, graphics, communications, and outline-processing capabilities. First Choice is an integrated program for IBM computers that includes simple word processing, spreadsheet, data management, graphics, and communications capabilities. Microsoft Works is a program for the Apple Macintosh that includes word processing, data management, spreadsheet, graphics, and communications features. Besides these programs, there are many other integrated software packages that include various combinations of applications. Integrated programs cost between $200 and $700.

OTHER APPLICATION SOFTWARE

Although word processing, spreadsheet, data management, graphics, and communications software are the most common, there are many other types of software. Here is a description of two others—personal information management software and hypertext software.

Personal Information Management Software

A **personal information manager,** or **PIM**, is multifunction software that provides many capabilities needed for organizing a person's day or helping with desk work. Some of the common functions of this type of software are the following:

- Calendar. The calendar function lets the user note dates of appointments and other events.
- Notepad. A notepad is a simple word processor for typing quick notes that the user can store and print.

- To-do list. The to-do list function allows the user to create a list of tasks to be done and to keep track of those tasks.
- Calculator. With the calculator function, the user can use the keyboard's numeric keypad as a calculator with the results displayed on the screen.
- Telephone directory. The telephone directory feature lets the user store telephone numbers and addresses for quick reference.

Some personal information managers are **RAM resident**, which means they are always in primary storage even when they are not being used. The program is loaded into an unused section of primary storage when the computer is first turned on. The program can be activated at any time, even when another program is executed. To activate a RAM resident program, the user presses a special combination of keys on the keyboard, such as the Control and Alternate keys. The program then displays its screen, usually a menu screen, on top of the current screen (Figure 11–14). From the menu, the user can use any of the software's functions. When the user is finished, he or she presses a certain key, such as the Escape key. The original screen that the user was working with before activating the RAM resident program then reappears, and the user can continue where he or she left off.

A number of personal information managers are available. The most widely known is Sidekick for IBM personal computers and IBM clones. Some others for IBM computers are Instant Recall, Primetime Personal, and Desktop Set. The Apple Macintosh comes with many personal information management capabilities. This type of program costs between $80 and $130.

Figure 11–14 A Personal Information Manager

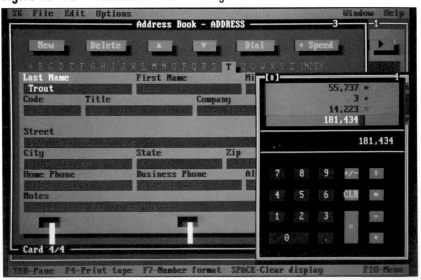

Hypertext Software

Another type of program for microcomputers is called **hypertext software**. This type of program lets you create a document in the computer that consists of text, data, graphics, or anything else that can be stored in the computer. The document is organized into sections, each the size of a screen (Figure 11–15). You can think of these sections as screen-sized index cards, so the entire document is like a stack of large index cards. Also stored with each card is a list of other cards containing related information. For example, there may be a card with general information about the U.S. Congress. This card may also list two other cards with detailed information about the Senate and the House of Representatives. This type of document, consisting of cards with information and lists of related cards, is called **hypertext**.

A hypertext program lets a user create hypertext and then allows him or her to browse through the text. The user creates hypertext by entering information into cards and listing related cards. The user browses through hypertext by displaying the information from a card on the screen and, after reading it, selecting another card from the list of related cards. The information from the selected card replaces the old card's information on the screen. Using a hypertext program, the user can go from card to card, displaying the information that is most important to him or her.

The first hypertext program for microcomputers was HyperCard, which runs on the Apple Macintosh. It sells for under $50. Other hypertext programs are also available for other microcomputers, including Guide for IBM computers.

Figure 11–15   A Hypertext Screen

Chapter Summary

- Graphics output comes in a variety of forms. Some forms are charts and graphs summarizing data, diagrams showing the designs of objects, graphic designs, realistic images of objects, and computer art.

- Two basic types of **graphics software** are **charting programs**, which let the user create charts and graphs from data in worksheets or databases, or from data entered by the user, and **paint** and **draw programs**, which allow the user to create pictures and diagrams from standard shapes and symbols and by drawing lines on the screen.

- The microcomputer hardware needed for graphic output involves special output devices. A medium to very high resolution screen is needed to display graphic output. A printer that can produce graphic output, such as a dot-matrix or laser printer, or a plotter is necessary. A faster CPU and a large amount of primary storage is needed for some graphics software. A hard disk drive may be needed to save graphic output before it is displayed or printed.

- **Presentation graphics software** provides the features of a charting program and a drawing program plus additional capabilities to make it possible to create high-quality graphic output for use in presentations. **Computer-aided design** software has features used by architects and engineers for designing buildings, automobiles, and other items.

- **Integrated software** is software that combines several applications. Two advantages of this type of software are a common user interface for all applications and easy transfer of data between applications. Three disadvantages of integrated software are that the user may not need all the applications, separate programs may be better than their counterparts in the integrated software, and integrated programs can be complex to use.

- A **personal information manager** is multifunction software that provides capabilities associated with organizing a person's day or helping with desk work, including a calendar, notepad, to-do list, calculator, and telephone directory. **Hypertext software** lets the user create and browse through **hypertext**, which is a document stored in the computer that is organized into cards, each containing lists of related cards.

Terms to Remember

Review Questions

Fill-In Questions

1. A graphics program that is used to create charts and graphs from data supplied to the software is called a(n) _____.

2. A graphics program that allows the user to create pictures and diagrams is called a(n) _____ or a(n) _____.

3. Software used to produce graphic output for a presentation to be given to a group of people is called _____.

4. CAD stands for _____.

5. Programs that combine several common applications such as word processing, spreadsheet analysis, and data management are called _____.

6. A(n) _____ is a program that is stored in primary storage whether it is in use or not and that can be activated when needed by the user.

Short-Answer Questions

1. What are some forms of graphic output?

2. What are some common types of charts and graphs produced by charting programs?

3. Where does a charting program get the data that it uses to create a graph or chart?

4. How does a user use a paint or draw program?

5. What microcomputer hardware is needed for graphic output?

6. What are some common graphics programs?

7. What are some advantages and disadvantages of integrated software?

8. What are some common integrated programs, and what applications are included with each?

9. What capabilities do personal information managers provide?

10. What does hypertext software do?

Projects

1. Investigate a graphics program to which you have access. What is the name of the program, and with which microcomputer can it be used? How much does it cost? Is it a charting, paint, or draw program? How does the user control its functions? What hardware is needed to use it? Can it be used for presentation graphics or for computer-aided design?

2. There are other types of microcomputer application software besides those described in Chapters 8 through 11. Investigate one other category of application software. What application is this software used for? How do the programs help the user with the application? What are some common programs used for the application? Write a summary of your findings.

12

DEVELOPING CUSTOM SOFTWARE

CHAPTER OBJECTIVES

• After completing this chapter you should be able to:

1. Explain what an algorithm is and describe several tools for representing algorithms for computer programs.

2. Describe the characteristics of a structured program.

3. Explain what a program module is and describe how a modular program is developed.

4. Describe briefly each of the five steps in the structured programming process.

5. Explain how the user is involved in program development.

A COMPUTER can do nothing by itself. It needs a program—a set of instructions—to tell it what to do. There are two ways you can acquire a program. One is to purchase an existing program, which is called *packaged software*, and the other is to prepare a new program from scratch, in which case it is called *custom software*. The last few chapters discussed common packaged software. Although in many situations packaged software is useful, there are times when no purchased program will be satisfactory. Then you have to develop, or have someone else develop, custom software. This chapter discusses how custom software is developed.

A program is composed of instructions that are arranged in a way that tells the computer how to solve a problem. The arrangement of the instructions must follow a logical pattern for the program to work correctly. In addition, the instructions must be organized so that the program is easy to understand. The first part of this chapter discusses these basic concepts about computer programs.

As you know, programs are developed by people called *programmers*, and the process they follow in developing a program is called *programming*. The second part of this chapter explains the programming process and shows how programmers develop software. Although users do not usually develop programs themselves, they are often involved in different stages of the process. This chapter discusses user involvement in program development.

COMPUTER PROGRAM CONCEPTS

Chapter 2 introduced some basic ideas about programs. There you saw that the instructions in a program are stored in primary storage and executed one after the other in sequence. You also learned that a program is written in a programming language. The following chapter will describe several common programming languages. A language called BASIC is used to illustrate the ideas presented in this chapter. BASIC is widely used on many types of computers, especially microcomputers.

Figure 12–1 shows an example of a BASIC program. This particular program calculates the pay for each employee in a business. The input to the program is an employee's identification number, the number of hours the employee has worked, and the employee's pay rate. This input data is entered at the keyboard. The program calculates the pay based on the number of hours the employee has worked. If the employee has worked 40 hours or less, then the pay is calculated by multiplying the hours worked by the pay rate. If the employee has worked more than 40 hours, then he or she is paid at the regular rate for the first 40 hours and at one and one-half times the regular rate ("time-and-a-half") for all hours worked over 40. The output from the program is the employee's identification number and pay, which are displayed on the screen.

Figure 12–1   The Pay-Calculation Program

```
100 REM - THIS PROGRAM CALCULATES EMPLOYEE PAY
110 PRINT "PAY CALCULATION PROGRAM"
120 PRINT
130 INPUT "ARE THERE EMPLOYEES? ", RESPONSE$
140 WHILE RESPONSE$ = "YES"
150   PRINT
160   INPUT "ENTER EMPLOYEE ID NUMBER: ", ID
170   INPUT "       ENTER HOURS WORKED: ", HOURS
180   INPUT "          ENTER PAY RATE: ", RATE
190   IF HOURS <= 40
         THEN LET PAY = HOURS * RATE
         ELSE LET PAY = 40 * RATE + (HOURS - 40) * (1.5 * RATE)
200   PRINT
210   PRINT "THE PAY FOR EMPLOYEE NUMBER"; ID; "IS $"; PAY
220   PRINT
230   INPUT "ARE THERE MORE EMPLOYEES? ", RESPONSE$
240 WEND
250 PRINT
260 PRINT "END OF PROGRAM"
270 END
```

Figure 12–2 shows how the screen would look as this program executes. First, the program displays a title. Then it asks if there are any employees. The user enters YES to this question. Then the program asks for an employee's ID number, hours worked, and pay rate, which the user enters. Next, the program calculates and displays the pay. Then the program asks if there are any more employees. Again, the user enters YES, so the program asks for another employee's ID number, hours worked, and pay rate, which the user enters. Then it calculates and displays the pay for that employee. Next, the program asks again if there are more employees. The user enters NO, so the program displays an ending message and stops.

Each line in the program in Figure 12–1 is an instruction that tells the computer to do something. You do not have to understand how the instructions in this program are written or how they work. This example will be used only to illustrate some of the concepts about computer programs.

Figure 12–2   Execution of the Pay-Calculation Program

```
PAY CALCULATION PROGRAM

ARE THERE EMPLOYEES? YES

ENTER EMPLOYEE ID NUMBER: 123
      ENTER HOURS WORKED: 30
         ENTER PAY RATE: 5

THE PAY FOR EMPLOYEE NUMBER 123 IS $ 150

ARE THERE MORE EMPLOYEES? YES

ENTER EMPLOYEE ID NUMBER: 345
      ENTER HOURS WORKED: 50
         ENTER PAY RATE: 10

THE PAY FOR EMPLOYEE NUMBER 345 IS $ 550

ARE THERE MORE EMPLOYEES? NO

END OF PROGRAM
```

Problems and Algorithms

Computer programming is a problem-solving process: Given a problem, the programmer prepares a set of instructions that tell the computer what steps to follow to solve the problem. These instructions form the program. In general, a set of steps that, if carried out, results in the solution of a problem is called an **algorithm**. For example, consider the problem of starting a car. Figure 12–3 shows an algorithm that, if carried out, results in a car being started. Another example of an algorithm is a recipe for baking a cake; if you follow the algorithm—the recipe—you get a cake.

The program in Figure 12–1 also is an algorithm. This algorithm solves the problem of calculating the pay for employees in a business. The instructions in the program describe the steps in the algorithm. If the steps are properly carried out—that is, if the instructions are executed correctly—the problem will be solved.

One of the main tasks in programming is to develop an algorithm to solve the required problem. Given a problem, the programmer must figure out what steps the computer has to go through to solve the problem. Only after these steps are determined can the program be written. This task of developing an algorithm can be one of the most difficult in the programming process. More will be said about it later.

Tools for Representing Algorithms

An algorithm can be represented in many forms. It may be written in English, described in mathematical notation, or drawn in a diagram. The algorithm for starting a car, in Figure 12–3, is written in an outline form. An algorithm for baking a cake is in a form a cook can understand. A computer program written in a programming language is also a representation of an algorithm.

When a programmer develops a program, he or she must determine the steps in the program's algorithm. The programmer should represent the algorithm in a form that is clear and easy to understand. For simple programs, brief notes or an outline may be sufficient, but for more

Figure 12–3 An Algorithm for Starting a Car

1. **Insert key in ignition.**
2. **Put car in neutral.**
3. **Repeat the following until car starts or at most 3 times:**
   a. **Turn key to start position.**
   b. **Press accelerator pedal.**
   c. **Release key after car starts or after 5 seconds.**
4. **If car does not start:**
   a. **Put car in park.**
   b. **Take key out of ignition.**
   c. **Call service station to have car started.**

complex programs, formal tools are often needed. Two tools that are commonly used to represent algorithms for programs are *pseudocode* and *flowcharts*.

Pseudocode. **Pseudocode** is a written language that uses English and elements from a programming language to describe the algorithm for a computer program. Actually, there are no rules for pseudocode; any written language for showing a program's algorithm can be thought of as pseudocode. Most programmers, however, use a form of pseudocode that resembles a programming language.

As an example, Figure 12–4 shows the pseudocode for the algorithm used in the pay calculation program in Figure 12–1. In pseudocode, activities such as input, calculations, and output are described by short English phrases. The idea is to summarize what is involved in each step without giving all the details. Sequences of these activities are listed in the pseudocode in the order in which the computer performs them.

To show complex logic in pseudocode, a programmer uses special words that look somewhat like a programming language. In Figure 12–4 the words DO WHILE indicate that the steps that follow are to be repeated as long as a certain condition is true. The end of these steps is marked by a line with the word END-DO. Other special words are used for other types of logic in pseudocode; their uses will be explained later. By reading the pseudocode line for line, you can get an understanding of the algorithm used in the program.

Flowcharts. A **program flowchart**, or simply a **flowchart**, is a diagram of the algorithm for a computer program. The flowchart is drawn using special symbols connected by lines. Figure 12–5 shows the common program flowchart symbols. Within each symbol is written a phrase describing the activity at that step. The symbols are connected by lines that show the sequence in which the steps take place.

Figure 12–6 shows a flowchart of the pay-calculation program in Figure 12–1. In this flowchart the *terminal point symbol* (oval) marks the point where the flowchart logic starts and where it stops. The *input/output symbol* (parallelogram) shows where the input data is accepted and the output is displayed. The *process symbol* (rectangle) is

Figure 12–4 Pseudocode for the Pay-Calculation Program

```
Display program title
Display employees question; accept response
DO WHILE response is "yes"
   Accept employee ID number, hours worked, pay rate
   IF hours ≤ 40 THEN
      Pay = hours × rate
   ELSE
      Pay = 40 × rate + (hours - 40) × (1.5 × rate)
   END-IF
   Display employee ID number, pay
   Display more employees question; accept response
END-DO
Display end of program message
Stop
```

Figure 12–5 Program Flowchart Symbols

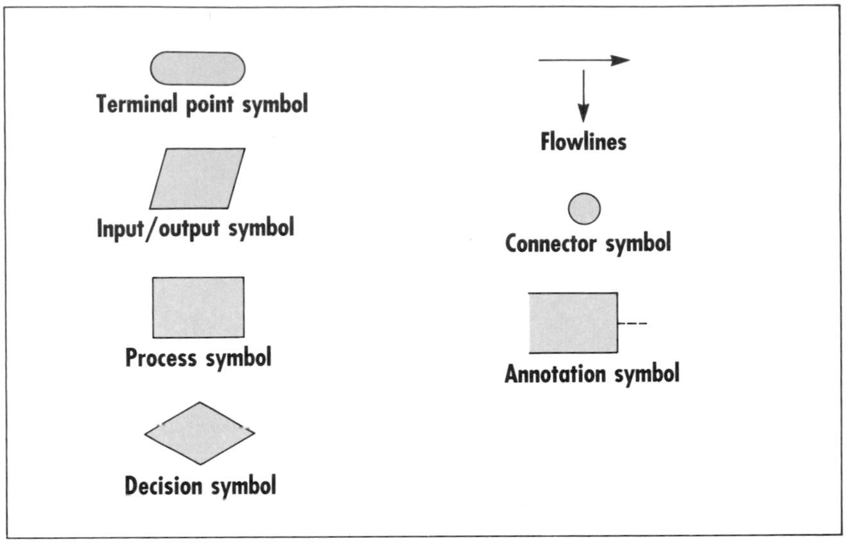

used for the calculation steps. The *decision symbol* (diamond) indicates where the hours worked are checked and where a decision is made to end the program. *Flowlines* (lines with arrowheads) connect the symbols to show the sequence in which the steps are performed. The *connector symbol* (small circle) at the bottom of the flowchart indicates that the flowline there should be connected to the flowline at the connector symbol near the top of the flowchart. The *annotation symbol* (open rectangle) provides additional comments to clarify the processing that takes place. By reading the flowchart beginning with the symbol marked START and following the flowlines to the STOP symbol, you can get an understanding of the algorithm for the program.

Other Tools.   In addition to pseudocode and flowcharts, other tools sometimes are used to represent algorithms. *Nassi-Schneiderman diagrams* and *Chapin charts*, named after their inventors, are two examples. For describing complex decision situations, *decision tables* and *decision trees* are sometimes used. *Warnier-Orr diagrams*, named after their developers, are another tool used to show the flow in an algorithm. Many of these tools as well as others are described in books on computer programming.

Structured Programs

One important concept about programs is that of *program structure*. The structure of a program is the way in which the instructions in the program are organized. When a programmer develops a program, he or she builds a structure of instructions. If the structure is well built, the program is correct, easy to understand, and easily modified. A poorly structured program may have errors that are difficult to detect, may be hard to read, and may be troublesome to change.

Figure 12–6   Flowchart for the Pay-Calculation Program

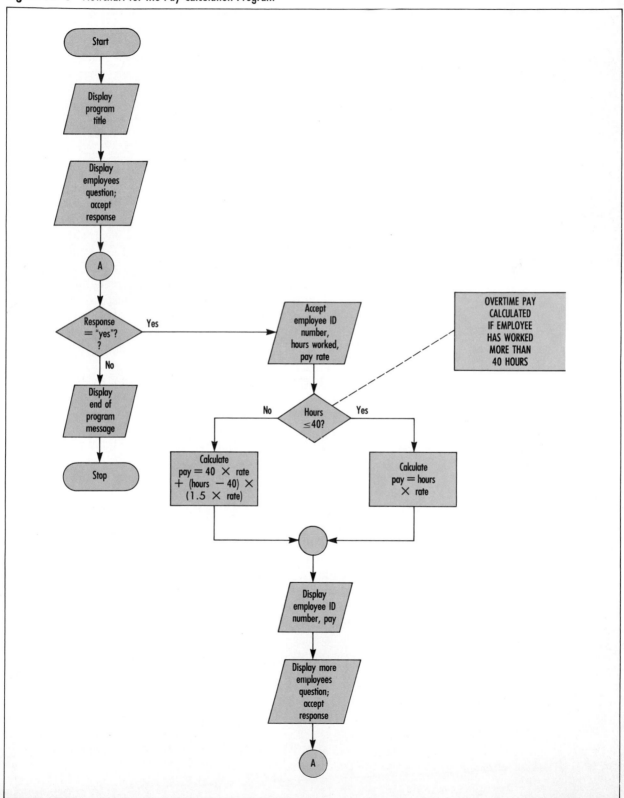

COMPUTER CLOSE-UP

12–1

VAPORWARE

There's a joke going round the computer industry: If Lotus Development Corporation, developer of Lotus 1-2-3, and Ashton-Tate Corporation, developer of dBase, merged, their ticker symbol would be LATE.

Both personal computer software giants recently had trouble shipping products on time. They are not alone. Late programs are endemic to the personal computer software industry. They are a part of the natural—or perhaps unnatural—cycle of doing business in software and are so common that a term has been coined for them, vaporware.

Company executives say there are strong pressures to preannounce products. The idea is to whet the public appetite so buyers will wait a little longer for a product, allowing a company to hold its market turf.

Writing software is very different, say, from casting steel ingots. Manufacturing processes are generally fairly predictable; programming is not so cut and dry. "It's abstract," said Stewart Alsop, editor of P.C. Letter, an industry newsletter. "You can't point to it and say I can build this in a certain time with certain people. It's vapor. It's ideas and concepts implemented in a series of statements."

Basically, programming involves writing long sequences of commands, or code, to the inner machinery of a computer. But it is not enough merely to get the computer to carry out certain tasks. The instructions must be air tight, so the program won't bomb.

Moreover, the software should be straightforward and easy to use, so even casual computer users will find it comprehensible. It's all much harder than it might sound, and professional programmers spend the majority of their time attempting to eliminate defects or "bugs" in the software. The problem is actually getting worse. As personal computers become more powerful and link up to each other in networks, programs grow more complicated.

Computers are capable of automating the office in previously unthinkable ways, but not without software that can take years of torturous effort. Jeff Raikes, general manager of Microsoft's office business unit, said that the first version of its Word software for the IBM PC took 30,000 to 30,500 lines of code. The latest will have between 250,000 and 300,000.

A decade ago, leading software programs such as WordStar and Lotus 1-2-3 resulted from one person's vision and took about a year to develop. As software becomes longer and more unwieldy, the day when one brilliant programmer worked alone to create a product has become unusual. Companies assign a team of programmers to a product, which often requires years to complete. Frequently, a project is divided into separate modules, which must later be merged.

"It's not like one programmer sits down and writes an application," said Andrew Seybold, publisher of the Outlook on Professional Computing, a technology newsletter. "It's done by committee." He said additional personnel don't necessarily add to the quality of a project, but probably increases the time needed to finish it. As a result, the testing of programs has become a key element in the development of software. "We have at least as many testers as programmers," said Raikes at Microsoft, who offers a "Golden Hammer Award" each week to the tester finding the most unusual bug.

In addition, before most software companies release a product they ship it to a test site where people who use the most advanced features of the program put it through its paces with regular use. Lotus, for example, said as many as 10,000 people will use its program before one copy is sold.

Even so, David Bayer, an analyst with brokerage firm Montgomery Securities in San Francisco, said testing is "the key challenge the software industry faces. It's virtually unlimited what you can do with the printed word, so it's virtually impossible to test all the sequences that someone might do with a single product," Bayer said. "If there are subtle errors it's tough to find it during the testing process."

Control Structures. There are three basic **control structures**, or ways of arranging program instructions: the sequence structure, the decision structure, and the loop structure. These structures are summarized in Figure 12–7. In a **sequence structure**, shown in Part *a* of the figure, instructions are executed one after the other in the order in which they are written.

Figure 12–7 Basic Control Structures

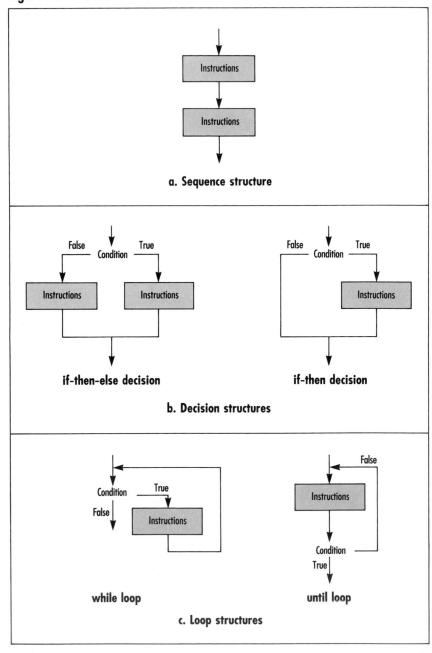

a. Sequence structure

b. Decision structures

c. Loop structures

Decision structures (also called *selection* or *alternation*), shown in Part *b* of Figure 12–7, are used to decide what to do next in a program. The decision is based on a *condition*, which is a statement that is either true or false, such as whether an employee has worked 40 hours or less. In one type of decision structure, often called an *if-then-else decision*, one group of instructions is executed if the condition is true and another group of instructions is executed if the condition is false. In another type of decision structure, called an *if-then decision*, a group of instructions is executed if the condition is true but nothing is done if the condition is false.

In a **loop structure**, or simply a *loop* (also called a *repetition* or an *iteration*), shown in part c of Figure 12–7, a group of instructions is executed repeatedly. In one form of a loop structure, often called a *while loop*, the instructions in the loop are repeated *while* a condition is true. When the condition becomes false, the loop is terminated. In an alternate loop structure, often called an *until loop*, a group of instructions is executed *until* a condition becomes true. As long as a condition is false, the instructions in the loop are repeated. The condition in a while loop is checked at the beginning of the loop, whereas the condition in an until loop is checked at the end.

Other control structures besides sequences, decisions, and loops can appear in a program. *Any* other structure, however, can be created out of these three basic structures. Thus, if a programming language has these structures, no others are needed. A program that is written using just the three basic control structures is called a **structured program**.

Many programming languages have an instruction called a GO TO statement that tells the computer to go from one point in a program to another. For example, Figure 12–8 shows the outline of a very poorly written program with many GO TO statements. A program with unnecessary GO TO statements is not a structured program and can be

Figure 12–8   Outline of a Program with GO TO Statements

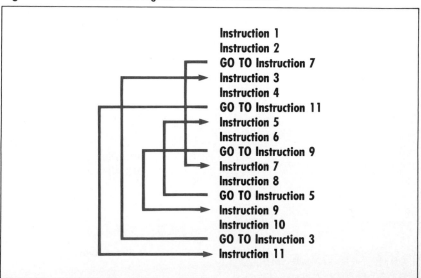

very difficult to understand because the programmer must jump around within the program to see what the program does. Sometimes a program with lots of GO TO statements is referred to as "spaghetti code" because lines drawn on the paper for all the GO TO statements begin to look like a bowl of spaghetti, as in Figure 12–8. GO TO statements should be avoided if possible.

Pseudocode and Flowchart Forms of Control Structures.   All the basic control structures can be represented in pseudocode form and flowchart form. Figure 12–9 shows how a sequence structure is represented in pseudocode and a flowchart. In pseudocode the instructions are listed one after the other; in a flowchart the symbols that represent the instructions are shown in sequence.

Figure 12–10 shows the pseudocode and flowchart forms of the decision structures. In the pseudocode form, the words IF and THEN are used in the first line to indicate that if the condition is *true* then the first group of instructions should be executed. In an if-then-else decision, the word ELSE is used to indicate that if the condition is *false* the second group of instructions should be executed. In an if-then decision, no ELSE is used. The word END-IF marks the end of the structure. (In many programming languages an instruction called an IF statement is used for a decision.) In the flowchart form, the decision symbol is used for the condition. The condition is written inside the symbol, and the words True and False (or Yes and No) are written on two flowlines that leave the symbol. The flowlines indicate which path should be followed if the condition is true and which path if it is false.

Figure 12–11 shows the pseudocode and flowchart forms of the loop structures. In the pseudocode form of a while loop, the words DO WHILE are used in the first line to indicate that the group of instructions that follow are to be executed *while* the condition is *true*. The word END-DO is used after these instructions. (In some programming languages, an instruction called a WHILE statement is used for this type of loop.) In the flowchart form, the decision symbol is used for the condition at the beginning of the loop. The line marked True (or Yes) leaving the

Figure 12–9   Sequence Structure

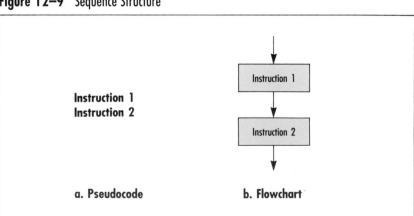

Instruction 1
Instruction 2

a. Pseudocode

Instruction 1

Instruction 2

b. Flowchart

Figure 12–10   Decision Structures

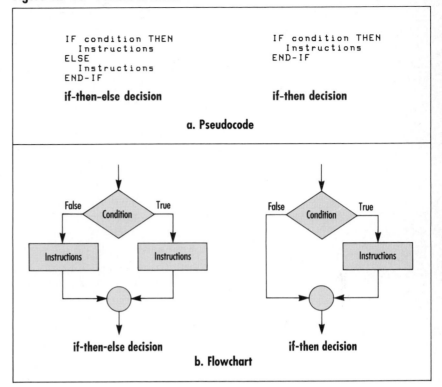

Figure 12–11   Loop Structures

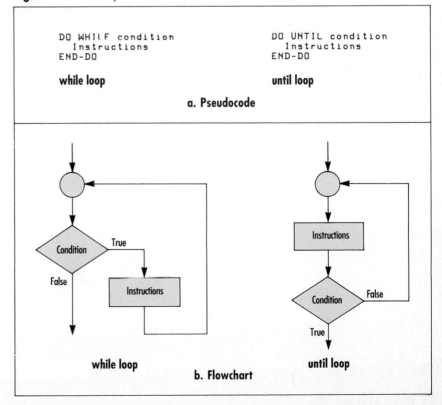

decision symbol goes to the instructions in the loop. A line from the end of these instructions leads back to the beginning of the loop, before the condition. The line marked False (or No) leaving the decision symbol shows the path to follow when the loop is terminated. In the until loop structure, the words DO UNTIL are used in the pseudocode to indicate that the loop is to be repeated *until* a condition is *true*. In the flowchart form, the decision symbol at the end of the loop indicates the condition that, when true, causes the loop to be terminated.

Control Structures in the Pay-Calculation Program.   The pay-calculation program uses the basic control structures. You can see these structures in the pseudocode and flowchart for the program given earlier. For example, Figure 12–12 shows the pseudocode for the program with the structures indicated. The program consists of sequences of instructions, a while loop, and an if-then-else decision within the loop. Reading the pseudocode, you can see that the program first displays the program's title on the screen and asks the user if there are employees for whom the pay needs to be calculated. Then, a while loop is repeated as long as the response to this or another question asked later is yes.

In the while loop, the program accepts the employee's identification number, hours worked, and pay rate from the keyboard. Then a decision is made to determine how to calculate the pay. If the hours worked are less than or equal to 40, the pay is calculated by multiplying the hours worked by the pay rate. If the hours are greater than 40, however, the pay is calculated using the overtime method. After the decision is completed, the employee identification number and the pay are displayed on the

Figure 12–12   Control Structures in the Pay-Calculation Program

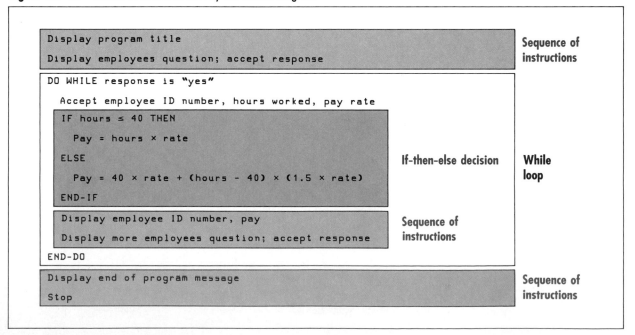

screen. Finally, the last step in the loop asks the user if there are more employees for whom the pay is to be calculated. If the response to this question is yes, the while loop is repeated. If the response is no, however, the loop is terminated and an end-of-program message is displayed on the screen before stopping execution of the program.

Program Modules

Small programs are relatively simple to develop. As programs become larger, however, their development becomes more complex. One way of organizing a large program that makes its development easier is to divide the program into groups of instructions, which are called **modules**. A program that is organized into modules is called a **modular program**. In developing a modular program, a programmer creates each module separately, and then the modules are combined to form a complete program. This procedure can simplify the development of large programs.

Each module in a modular program performs some function related to the processing of the program. To illustrate, assume that a large payroll program gets input data, does payroll calculations with the data, and produces output. This program has three basic functions: input, payroll calculation, and output. The program would include three modules: an input module, a payroll-calculation module, and an output module.

In addition to the modules that perform the program's functions, a modular program has a *main control module* that determines when the other modules are executed. For example, Figure 12–13 shows the outline of a modular program with a main control module and three other modules. The main control module causes each of the other modules to be performed at the appropriate time; we say that the main control module *calls* each module.

The program in Figure 12–13 starts by executing the instruction in the main control module. At the appropriate place, the main control module calls the input module. This causes the instructions in the input

Figure 12–13 Outline of a Modular Program

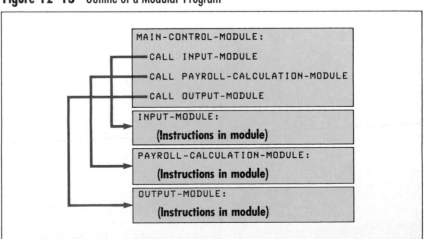

module to be executed. After the instructions in this module have been completed, execution continues in the main control module where it left off. Then the main control module calls the payroll-calculation module. Finally, the main control module calls the output module.

Within each module the programmer arranges the instructions by using the three control structures discussed earlier—sequences, decisions, and loops. Thus, the concepts of control structures and program modules go together. A modular program using the three control structures is a structured program.

Structure Charts.   To show the modular organization of a program, a programmer often uses a diagram called a **structure chart**. Figure 12–14 shows the structure chart for the modular program in Figure 12–13. In a structure chart, each box represents a module in the program. The box at the top represents the main control module. Each box below signifies another module. A line connects two modules if one module calls another module. Thus, Figure 12–14 shows that the main control module calls the input module, the payroll-calculation module, and the output module. This program is organized into two levels; the main control module is at the first level, and the other modules are at the second level.

A structure chart is *not* the same as a flowchart. A structure chart shows how modules are related. The chart does not show, however, the flow in any module of the program; that is the purpose of the flowchart. For each module in the structure chart, the programmer draws a flowchart that shows the flow in that module. Alternatively, the programmer could use pseudocode or some other tool to represent the logic in the module. A tool called *HIPO*, which stands for Hierarchy plus Input-Process-Output, combines a type of structure chart with a form of pseudocode. HIPO is described in books on computer programming.

A module in a modular program may call other modules. For example, the payroll-calculation module in the program in Figure 12–13 may call two other modules to do pay calculation and tax calculation. Figure 12–15 shows how this organization is shown in a structure chart. In

Figure 12–14   A Structure Chart for a Modular Program

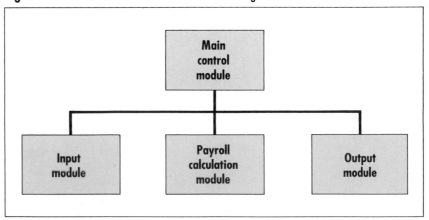

Figure 12–15   A Structure Chart for a More Complex Modular Program

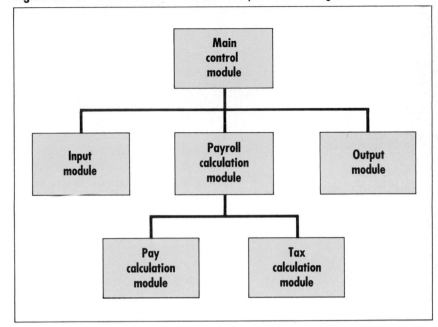

this figure, boxes are used for the pay- and tax-calculation modules. These boxes are connected by lines to the payroll-calculation module because they are called by that module. This adds a third level to the structure chart. Very large programs have many modules that are organized into numerous levels.

THE STRUCTURED PROGRAMMING PROCESS

When preparing a computer program to solve a problem, a programmer performs several tasks. One thing he or she does is to write the instructions in the program. This task, however, is only one activity in the programming process. In fact, there are five main activities that must be completed:

1. Understand and define the problem.
2. Design the program logic.
3. Write the program instructions.
4. Test the program and correct any errors.
5. Document the program.

This section describes each of these activities in detail.

This approach to programming is commonly called **structured programming**. There is some disagreement about what is meant by structured programming; a single definition does not exist. Most people agree, however, that structured programming involves a *systematic process* that results in programs that are *well structured*, that are *easily understood* and *modified*, and that are *correct*.

Structured programming should not be confused with the idea of a structured program. As mentioned earlier, a structured program is one that uses only the three basic control structures. Producing a structured program is one of the goals of structured programming. However, structured programming involves much more than this.

Before structured programming became the normal approach to programming, programmers developed programs in various ways—some very unsystematic. Programs were often poorly structured with many GO TO statements. The resulting programs could be very difficult to understand and modify, and they often had many errors. Structured programming helped overcome these problems.

Problem Definition

The first activity in the programming process is to completely understand and carefully define the problem to be solved. Frequently, the most difficult step is recognizing that a problem exists for which a programmed solution is appropriate. It is usually not the programmer's responsibility, however, to recognize the need for a program to solve a problem. Most often, the programmer receives a general statement of the problem, either orally or in writing, from the user or from the programmer's supervisor. Then the programmer begins the programming process.

At first the programmer should try to understand the problem as a whole. What are the requirements of the problem? Answering this question usually involves determining what output is to be produced. What data is available? This often involves determining what input data is to be processed. What calculations and other processing needs to be done? The programmer tries to get a general understanding of the problem as a whole without going into details about the input, the output, the calculations, and the processing. After the programmer has a general understanding of the problem, he or she should refine the problem definition to include specific information about output layouts, input data-entry formats, calculations, and other processing. The refinement of the problem definition should continue until the programmer obtains sufficient detail to begin designing a solution.

During the problem-definition activity the programmer may have to talk to the user to clarify the problem. The programmer may discuss output layouts and input data-entry formats with the user and ask if they represent what the user wants. The programmer describes what the program will do to be sure it will solve the problem for the user.

Program Design

With an understanding of the problem, the programmer can begin to design the logic of a program to solve the problem. The sequence of steps that is necessary to solve the problem must be carefully planned. This sequence forms the algorithm for the program solution. The programmer may express the algorithm in pseudocode, in a flowchart, or by using some other tool. This program-designing activity does *not* involve writing the instructions for the program. Before the program can be written, the programmer must develop the algorithm to solve the problem.

Developing an algorithm is usually the most difficult task in the programming process, and there are many strategies that can help. The programmer should know common algorithms so that when a problem or a part of a problem requires a known algorithm, the programmer can quickly supply it.

When the algorithm is not known, the programmer must devise one. One technique that is used is called **top-down program design**. In this technique, the programmer starts by designing the overall algorithm for the program. He or she breaks down this algorithm into general functions and then designs the algorithm for each of these functions separately. In designing the algorithm for a program's function, the programmer may break it down into subfunctions and design the algorithm of each subfunction separately. This top-down process continues until all parts of the program have been designed in sufficient detail so that program instructions can be written.

Figure 12–16 illustrates the idea of top-down design for a payroll program. The programmer first determines that to solve a problem the program must perform three main functions:

Get input data
Calculate payroll
Produce output

The overall algorithm for the program involves performing these three functions in sequence. Then the programmer examines each of these functions separately and designs its algorithm using a top-down technique. Thus, in Figure 12–16, the programmer determines that the "Calculate payroll" function involves two subfunctions:

Calculate pay
Calculate tax

The programmer continues to design the program in a top-down fashion, adding more and more detail until all parts of the program algorithm have been designed.

Figure 12–16 Top-Down Program Design

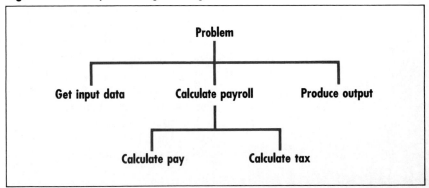

Top-down design leads naturally to a modular program. Each program function in the top-down design forms a program module. As the programmer designs the program in a top-down fashion, he or she draws a structure chart showing the modules. The programmer also prepares pseudocode or a flowchart for each module's logic.

After the programmer completes a program's design, he or she may go over it with other programmers to be sure it is correct. A technique called *structured walkthrough* may be used, in which several programmers examine the program's design to see if it has any errors or inconsistencies. The idea in using this technique is to try to make the design as correct as possible before continuing with the programming process.

The user is involved occasionally in the design process. Sometimes the programmer has to ask questions about the problem definition that he or she did not think of earlier. The programmer may go over some aspects of the design with the user to be sure the program will do what the user wants.

Program Coding

After the programmer has designed the program to solve the problem, the program's instructions can be written. To do this, the programming language to be used must be known. Sometimes the programmer is told what language to use, and at other times the programmer can select the language. (Programming languages and language selection are discussed in Chapter 13.)

The activity of writing the program's instructions in a programming language is called **coding** the program. The programmer uses his or her knowledge of the language, an understanding of the problem to be solved, and the program design determined previously. The programmer usually has the help of various documents, such as layouts of the program's input and output, pseudocode or a flowchart of the program's algorithm, and a structure chart of the program's modular organization. With this information, the programmer codes the program to solve the problem by writing the necessary programming language instructions. The programmer may write the instructions on paper or special coding forms for later entry into the computer (Figure 12–17), or he or she may compose the instructions while keying them into the computer.

In coding the program, the programmer should use only the three control structures explained earlier. Normally, the programmer writes the program in a modular fashion.

Occasionally during the coding activity an error is discovered in the logic of the algorithm. When this happens, the programmer must redesign part of the program. It may even be necessary to return to the problem definition and work forward again if a serious error or misunderstanding is discovered.

The user is normally not involved in the coding activity. Only if the programmer has questions about the problem's definition will it be necessary to contact the user.

Figure 12–17 A COBOL Language Coding Form

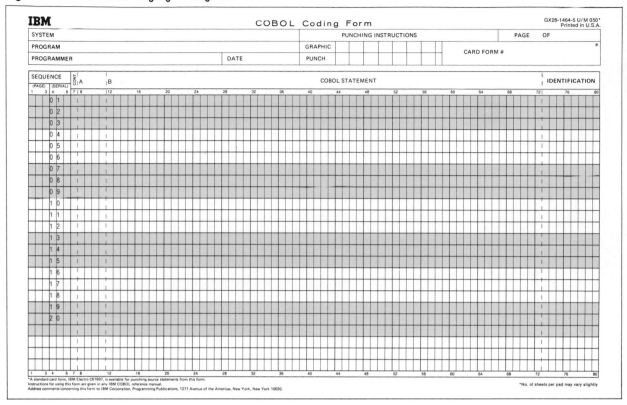

Program Testing and Debugging

Although a programmer may have been very careful in designing and coding a program, the program may not be correct. Programming is a complex activity, and it is easy to make mistakes. Thus, the next step in the programming process is to test the program to see if it has errors and, if it does, to correct the errors.

At this point the programmer enters the program into the computer by keying it in at a keyboard. Before the program can be executed it must go through a translation process, which is done by a special translator program. (Program translation is discussed in Chapter 13.) Then the program can be executed. More often than not, the program does not complete its translation or execution successfully. It is the programmer's responsibility to locate and correct any errors in the program.

Types of Program Errors.   There are three types of errors that can appear in a program: syntax errors, execution errors, and logic errors. *Syntax errors* are errors that the programmer has made in the use of the language. For example, spelling a word in an instruction incorrectly is a syntax error. These errors are detected by the computer before executing the program, and usually a message is displayed on the screen describing each syntax error. Even though a syntax error has been detected, the computer cannot correct it, because the computer cannot figure out what the programmer wants. A program with syntax errors will not execute. The programmer must correct any syntax errors by locating the incorrect instruction and changing it.

If the program has no syntax errors, it can be executed by the computer. During execution, other errors may appear. These are called *execution errors*. For example, an attempt to divide a number by zero causes an execution error. These errors are detected by the computer when it executes the program, and a message is displayed on the screen describing the error. Still, the computer cannot correct the error. The programmer must find the cause of the error and correct it.

The final type of error is detected only after the program has been executed. If the output from the program is not correct, there is a *logic error* in the program. For example, if a program needs to add two numbers but the programmer mistakenly used an instruction to subtract, then no syntax or execution error will be detected. The final output will be incorrect, however, because the logic of the program is wrong. The computer cannot detect such an error because it does not know what the logic should be.

Program Testing.   The procedure that programmers use to find logic errors is called **program testing**. The programmer makes up input data to test the program and figures out what output should be produced by the program using this input test data. Then the program is executed with the test data, and the output that the program produces is compared with the expected output. Any discrepancy indicates a logic error that must be corrected.

A program must be tested thoroughly before putting it to use. The programmer should test typical sets of input to be sure the program works in the usual cases, and also should test unusual sets of input. Some organizations have a different programmer do the testing so that the original programmer is not tempted to overlook possible weaknesses just to finish the job. The objective of program testing is to reveal all errors in the program.

Program Debugging.   An error in a program is commonly called a **bug**. When a bug is detected, the programmer must locate the cause of the error in the program and correct it. This process is called **debugging** the program. *Testing* involves determining if errors are present; *debugging* involves finding and correcting errors.

Debugging logic errors in a program can be difficult. Programmers have developed various strategies to try to find the cause of errors. For example, one technique is to step through the program one instruction at a time, checking the result of each instruction's execution before going on to the next instruction. The idea is to try to locate any instructions that are causing errors. This technique is very time consuming, however. In fact, program testing and debugging often takes as much time as all the other activities of the programming process put together.

FULL CIRCLE

In the beginning, everyone was a programmer. Now, with powerful user languages, everyone is a programmer again.

There was a time when "computer user" and "computer programmer" were synonymous. Ten years ago, if you owned a computer, you almost certainly wrote programs. Buying application programs was originally a way to get around the drudgery of writing your own software. In time, more powerful and flexible applications made it unnecessary—even downright silly—to write your own.

The irony is that the more powerful and flexible an application becomes, the more options you have, and the more useful it becomes to be able to perform diverse functions. If you have commands that can alter the system, conditionals that choose alternate execution pathways, and a method of storing these things, you have a programming language.

Originally, people didn't think of these facilities as languages at all. They were a "macro capability" or a "scripting feature," not a language. In the last few years, however, programmers and users alike have come to recognize that they are, in fact, languages. So there we are—all programmers again. Everything comes full circle in the end. But this time, software developers are consciously trying to make the languages more powerful and easier to use.

What Do You Mean, "User"?

One of the first questions an applications language designer faces is, Who will be using the language? Speaking broadly, there are two answers to this question and, hence, two schools of user-language design.

One school equates "user" with anyone who sits down at the computer. This group tries to make user languages as friendly as possible. The computer's resources ease you into the language and guide you through it. HyperTalk, for instance, was written so that just about anyone could use it.

The other school sees the user as a "power user"—someone who needs to get the most power and flexibility out of an application. The reasoning is that most users are never going to want to get under the hood of the applications, and the ones who do are going to want performance above all else.

Consequently, languages for power users tend toward the complex and difficult. Auto-Lisp, the programming language for AutoCAD, is an excellent example of this approach. Lisp is a notoriously difficult language to learn, mostly because it is so different both from other languages and from the way most people think. But it also offers certain advantages for programming a CAD package.

People can and do make careers out of programming in power-user languages. Programming in dBASE and other database languages is a recognized specialty. In addition to developing custom software, power-user languages lend themselves well to applications that augment the host application. For instance, there are about 700 applications written for AutoCAD, most of them in AutoLisp.

Need to Know

The split between user and power-user languages is not along application lines. In almost every category, from communications programs to word processors, some software companies have opted for easy-to-use languages while others have chosen languages that wring the most power they can out of the machine.

This is especially obvious in database languages. Because databases put such heavy demands on the system, they tend to use power-user languages. In an attempt to make their DBMSs as easy to use as possible, some companies are even willing to sacrifice some power.

One of the more interesting trends in applications is to provide more than one language. In addition to a power-user language, some packages now offer a simpler scripting or macro language for casual use. AutoCAD, for instance, not only has AutoLisp, but it also has a menu-oriented facility that is much easier to use.

You can make too much of the entire question of user versus power-user languages. Most people have a strong ability to learn the information they need to do their jobs, and if they have to, they can master nearly anything.

The User and Program Testing.   During the program-testing process the user may be asked to supply typical data to test the program and then to check the output that results from executing the program with this data. The user would not be involved in debugging the program, however. Sometimes the user uses the program on an experimental basis for a period of time to see if any errors are detected, a process called *beta testing*. The user will also be asked if the program does what he or she wants—in other words, whether the program meets the user's needs.

Program Documentation

The last step in the programming process is to bring together all the material that describes the program. This step results in the program's **documentation**, which is a general term used for any written description of a program or computer application. There are three types of program documentation: user documentation, operator documentation, and programmer documentation.

User Documentation.   **User documentation** of a program provides information so that the user can understand how to use the program. This type of documentation gives instructions for running the program on the computer, including what input to enter and what to expect for output. It describes what keys to press to get the program to perform different functions, what any messages and codes displayed on the screen mean, and what to do if the program does not work. During the preparation of this documentation the user will review it to be sure it is complete and understandable.

Operator Documentation.   Some programs are not used by users directly but are executed by specially trained computer operators. **Operator documentation** provides information that tells the operator how to execute the program. This documentation tells the operator when to execute the program, what input data to supply, what to do with the output, and what to do if any errors occur.

Programmer Documentation.   **Programmer documentation** describes how a program works so that other programmers can correct errors in the program and make modifications in the future. This type of documentation includes any written information about the program prepared during the program's development. Typically, a programmer documentation package contains the following:

- A program summary that provides a brief statement of the purpose of the program and a short description of the program's input, output, and processing.
- Detailed descriptions of the input and output data for the program.
- Pseudocode, flowcharts, structure charts, and any other tools used to describe how the program works.

- Lists of test data used with the program and the output that resulted from each test.
- A printed listing of the instructions in the program.

Program Maintenance

After a program has been in use for a while, it may be necessary to make changes in it—a process called **program maintenance**. Maintenance is necessary to correct errors in a program, to add new features to a program, and to modify a program because of changing requirements. Whenever program maintenance is needed, a programmer must go through the five activities in the programming process. The programmer must (1) understand the change that is needed, (2) design the program logic for the change, (3) code the program instructions for the change, (4) test the program with the change, and (5) document the change. Only after all these activities have been completed will the program maintenance be completed.

Chapter Summary

- An **algorithm** is a set of steps that, if carried out, results in the solution of a problem. Two common tools for representing an algorithm for a computer program are pseudocode and program flowcharts. **Pseudocode** is a written language that uses English and elements from a programming language to describe the algorithm. A **program flowchart** is a diagram that uses special symbols connected by lines to show the algorithm.

- A **structured program** is one that uses only three basic control structures. These control structures are **sequence structures**, in which instructions are executed one after the other; **decision structures**, in which one of two groups of instructions is executed based on a condition; and **loop structures**, in which a group of instructions are repeatedly executed.

- A program **module** is a group of instructions in a program that performs some function related to the processing of the program. A **modular program**, which is one that is organized into modules, is developed by creating each module separately and then combining the modules to form a complete program. A **structure chart** is a diagram that shows the modular organization of a program.

- **Structured programming** is a systematic process that results in programs that are well structured, that are easily understood and modified, and that are correct. The first step in the process is for the programmer to completely understand and carefully define the problem to be solved. Then the programmer designs the algorithm for the program solution to the problem. A technique called **top-down**

program design can be used to help in designing the program. Next, the programmer **codes** the program, which means he or she writes the program's instructions in a programming language. Then the programmer detects and corrects errors in the program. **Program testing** involves executing the program with input test data and checking the output with what was expected in order to detect errors. **Debugging** involves locating and correcting errors, or **bugs**, that are detected in the program. Finally, the programmer prepares the program's **documentation**.

- The user may be involved in certain activities of program development. During problem definition, the user may need to clarify the problem for the programmer and examine output layouts and input data-entry formats. During program design, the user may have to clarify other questions about the problem. During program testing, the user may have to supply typical data to test the program and to check the output from the program. The user may use the program on an experimental basis for a period of time to see if any errors appear. Finally, the user may have to review the user documentation for completeness and understandability.

Terms to Remember

Algorithm   p. 296

Bug   p. 314

Coding   p. 312

Control Structure   p. 302

Debugging   p. 314

Decision Structure   p. 303

Documentation   p. 317

Loop Structure   p. 303

Modular Program   p. 307

Module   p. 307

Operator Documentation   p. 317

Program Flowchart   p. 297

Program Maintenance   p. 318

Program Testing   p. 314

Programmer Documentation
   p. 317

Pseudocode   p. 297

Sequence Structure   p. 302

Structure Chart   p. 308

Structured Program   p. 303

Structured Programming   p. 309

Top-down Program Design
   p. 311

User Documentation   p. 317

Review Questions

Fill-In Questions

1. A(n) _____ is a set of steps that, if carried out, result in the solution of a problem.

2. Two types of decisions are _____ and _____.

3. Two types of loops are _____ and _____.

4. A group of instructions that performs some function related to the processing of the program is called a(n) _____.

5. When a programmer prepares the overall design of a program first and then successively refines the design until a final program is obtained, he or she is using a technique called _____.

6. The process of writing the instructions for a computer program in a programming language is called _____.

7. Three types of errors that can appear in a program are _____, _____, and _____.

8. A common term for an error in a program is a(n) _____.

9. Three types of program documentation are _____, _____, and _____.

10. The process of making changes in a computer program is called _____.

Short-Answer Questions

1. What is the difference between pseudocode and a program flowchart?

2. Describe the three basic control structures used in computer programs.

3. What is a structured program?

4. How is a modular program developed?

5. What is a structure chart used for?

6. What is structured programming?

7. What does a programmer do during the problem-definition activity of the programming process?

8. During which activity of the programming process does the programmer develop the algorithm for the program?

9. What is the difference between program testing and debugging?

10. In which activities of the programming process is the user involved?

Projects

1. Pseudocode, program flowcharts, and structure charts are program design tools. Several other tools were mentioned in the chapter, including Nassi-Schneiderman diagrams, decision tables, and HIPO. Research one of these or some other program design tool. Write a brief description of what the tool is and how it is used in program development.

2. Interview a programmer to find out what he or she does when developing a program. Find out which of the tools and techniques discussed in the chapter the programmer uses. Write a summary of your interview.

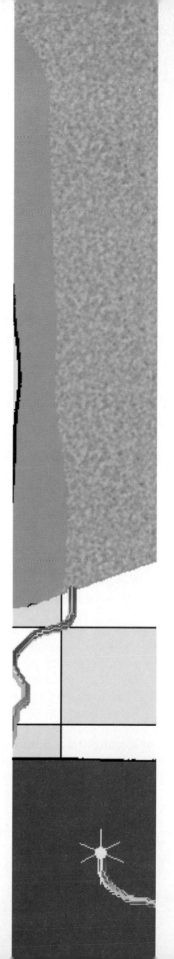

13

COMPUTER PROGRAMMING LANGUAGES

CHAPTER OBJECTIVES
• After completing this chapter you should be able to:

1. Explain what a programming language is, why there are many languages, and how a person selects a language.

2. State the characteristics of programming languages that are good for system programs, for business application programs, and for scientific application programs.

3. Explain the main differences between the five types, or generations, of programming languages.

4. Describe the program translation and execution process.

5. List the main uses of common programming languages.

W HEN A PROGRAMMER develops a program, he or she codes the program's instructions in a computer programming language. But what language does the programmer use? Over the years, hundreds of programming languages have been invented. Most languages were used for a short period of time and then abandoned. Some languages, however, have become popular and are used frequently. Today, a programmer has a choice of a number of widely used programming languages.

This chapter discusses computer programming languages. First it answers some common questions about languages. Then it examines the main types of languages and explains the important process of program translation. Finally, the chapter describes some of the more commonly used programming languages.

SOME COMMON QUESTIONS AND ANSWERS ABOUT PROGRAMMING LANGUAGES

Before describing the different programming languages, we will answer some common questions about languages.

What Is a Programming Language?

English is a natural language. It has words, symbols, and a set of grammatical rules for combining the words and symbols into sentences. When you form a grammatically correct sentence, it has some meaning; that is, someone can understand it. But you can make errors in grammar in a sentence and it still may mean something; that is, a person still may be able to understand it.

A programming language is like a natural language in many ways. It has words, symbols, and rules of grammar. The grammatical rules are called the **syntax** of the language. A programmer forms an instruction by combining the words and symbols according to the syntax rules. Then the instruction has some meaning; that is, it tells the computer to do something. For example, Figure 13–1a shows the syntax of a particular instruction in BASIC, a commonly used programming language. Figure 13–1b gives an example of an instruction that follows this syntax. The meaning of this instruction is to add two numbers identified by the letters B and C and to identify their sum by the letter A.

Figure 13–1 An Instruction in BASIC

LET variable = expression	LET A = B + C
a. Syntax	**b. Example**

Unlike a natural language, if a programmer makes an error in writing an instruction in a programming language, the instruction will not mean anything; the computer will not be able to understand it. To write a program, a programmer must know the syntax rules of the language he or she is using. If the programmer does not abide by these rules, the program will have errors and the computer will not be able to execute it.

Each programming language has a different set of syntax rules. For example, Figure 13–2 shows the syntax and an example of an instruction in COBOL, a common language. The meaning of the example is the same as the one in Figure 13–1b, only the syntax is different. When a new language is invented, the designer of the language determines the syntax rules of the language and the meaning of each instruction. To use a new language, a programmer must learn the syntax and meaning of each instruction.

Why Are There Many Languages?

There are two answers to the question of why there are many languages. First, programming languages have evolved over time as researchers have found better ways of designing them. The first languages were developed in the 1950s and, by today's standards, were poorly designed. Today, researchers know much more about what makes a good language, so modern languages are quite a bit different from the early languages.

The second answer to the question is that different languages are designed for different types of programs. As you know, there are two main types of programs: system programs and application programs. Some languages are designed for writing system programs and some for application programs. There are even different types of application programs, and some languages are designed for certain types of application programs. The characteristics of a language that is good for one type of program may be different from those of a language that is good for another type. Because a computer can be used for many types of programs, there are many programming languages.

System Programming Languages.   System programs, as you know, are general programs that are designed to make the computer easier to use. An example of system software is an operating system, which actually consists of many system programs. To write the programs in an operating system, or other system programs, the programmer needs to have instructions that allow him or her to control the basic circuitry of the computer. For example, the programmer needs to be able to write instructions that move data from specific locations in primary storage

Figure 13–2 An Instruction in COBOL

ADD identifier-1, identifier-2 GIVING identifier-3	ADD B, C GIVING A
a. Syntax	**b. Example**

to certain parts of the CPU. Programming languages that are good for system programs have instructions that give the programmer this type of control over what the computer does.

Application Programming Languages. Application programs are designed for specific computer applications, such as payroll processing. To write programs for payroll processing or other applications, the programmer does not need to control the basic circuitry of the computer. Instead, the programmer needs instructions that make it easy to get input data, produce output, do calculations, and store and retrieve data in secondary storage. Programming languages that are good for application programs have these types of instructions but not the types of instructions needed for system programs.

There are two main types of application programs: business application programs and scientific application programs. Most application programming languages are designed to be good for one type but not the other, although there are some general-purpose languages that are supposed to be good for both types. *Business application programs* are characterized by much processing of input and output data, and a great deal of storage and retrieval of secondary storage data, but few calculations. Languages that are good for writing business programs have instructions that make input, output, and secondary storage operations easy but have comparatively weak instructions for calculations. However, *scientific application programs* require many calculations but relatively little input and output processing or use of secondary storage data. Programming languages that are designed for writing scientific programs have very good instructions for calculations but rather poor instructions for input, output, and secondary storage operations.

How Does a Person Select a Language?

Selecting a language to use for a particular program involves the consideration of several factors. One factor is whether the language is designed for the type of program that needs to be written. As you have seen, some languages are designed for writing system programs, some for writing business application programs, and some for writing scientific application programs. The programmer must select a language that is appropriate for the type of program.

Another factor is the availability of languages on the computer being used. Not all languages can be used on all computers. If a language is just right for the program but will not work with the computer, it cannot be used.

A third factor is the availability of trained programmers to write and maintain the programs using the language. Some languages, although excellent for certain programs, are known by so few programmers that it may be very difficult to find someone qualified to write the program. Also, a program often has to be modified in the future, so the future availability of qualified programmers must be considered.

The next factor is the ease of writing programs in the language. Coding and debugging programs in some languages is easier and takes less time than in others. Because a programmer's time is valuable, a less time-consuming language is usually better than one that requires more time to write programs.

Finally, the efficiency of the program written in the language should be considered. There are two aspects of program efficiency: the speed of execution of the program and the amount of primary storage required for the program. Different languages yield programs with different degrees of efficiency. Sometimes efficiency is not important, but when it is, a language should be selected that produces the most efficient program.

TYPES OF PROGRAMMING LANGUAGES

There are several types of programming languages that have evolved over time. As a consequence, they fall into five generations. This section discusses the five main types—that is, generations—of programming languages.

Machine Languages (First Generation)

Chapter 3 discussed machine language, which is the basic language of a computer. When computers were first invented, this was the only type of language available for them. Hence, machine language forms the first generation of programming languages.

As you know from Chapter 3, a machine language instruction consists of an *operation code* for operations such as addition and subtraction, and one or more *operands* that identify data to be processed. Instructions are represented in a binary form, so they appear as strings of 1s and 0s. For example, Figure 13–3 shows a machine language instruction to add one number to another number.

Each type of computer has its own machine language that may be different from the machine language of other types of computers. Hence, programs written for one computer may not be compatible with another computer; we say machine language is **machine dependent**. Machine language is the only language a computer can understand, however. Any program for a computer must either be written in the machine language of the computer or written in some other language and then translated into machine language, a process that will be discussed in a moment.

With machine language the programmer has control over all the basic circuitry of the computer. In addition, machine language programs can be

Figure 13–3   A Machine Language Instruction

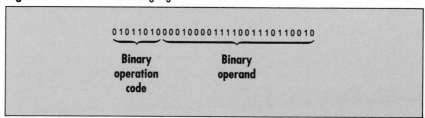

0 1 0 1 1 0 1 0 0 0 0 1 0 0 0 0 1 1 1 0 0 1 1 1 0 1 1 0 0 1 0

Binary operation code   **Binary operand**

very efficient. These characteristics are important in languages used to write system programs. Writing programs in machine language is very difficult, however, because the programmer must remember binary codes and numbers. Hence, machine languages are rarely used today except in special system programming situations.

Assembly Languages (Second Generation)

After using machine languages for a while, computer professionals thought there must be an easier way of writing programs. Their idea was to replace instructions represented in a binary form with words and symbols. Binary operation codes were replaced by symbolic codes that stood for the operation. Thus, instead of using the binary operation code 01011010 for the addition operation, the word ADD was used. In addition, instead of using a binary operand, a symbol such as X was used to stand for the data to be processed by the instruction. Thus, an instruction to add one number to another number would be written as in Figure 13–4. Languages using this form became the second generation of programming languages.

Programs written this way are not in machine language, so they have to be translated into machine language before they are executed. The translation process involves converting each symbol into its equivalent binary form. This translation process is called *assembly*, and these languages are called **assembly languages**. In the assembly language process, each assembly language instruction is translated into one machine language instruction.

Originally, assembly was done by hand; a person would manually translate each assembly language instruction into its equivalent machine language instruction. Then, computer professionals realized that the translation process was largely mechanical, so a computer could do it. People wrote computer programs (in machine language) to translate assembly language programs into equivalent machine language programs. An assembly language translation program is a system program called an **assembler**.

Figure 13–5 shows the process of assembly. First, a program is written in assembly language. This program is called the **source program** because it comes from the source, which is the programmer. Then, the assembler program translates the source program into machine language. The resulting machine language equivalent of the source program is called the **object program**. After translation, the object program is executed.

Because each type of computer has its own machine language, each has its own assembly language, which may be incompatible with the assembly language of other computers. Hence, assembly language is machine dependent. In addition, each type of computer needs its own assembler program to translate its assembly language into its machine language.

As with machine language, the programmer has control over the basic circuitry of the computer with assembly language. Also, programs written in assembly language usually are as efficient as those in machine language. Programming in assembly language is much easier than it is in machine

Figure 13–4
An Assembly Language Instruction

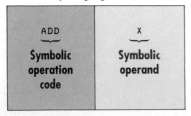

ADD	X
Symbolic operation code	Symbolic operand

Figure 13–5   Assembly and Execution of an Assembly Language Program

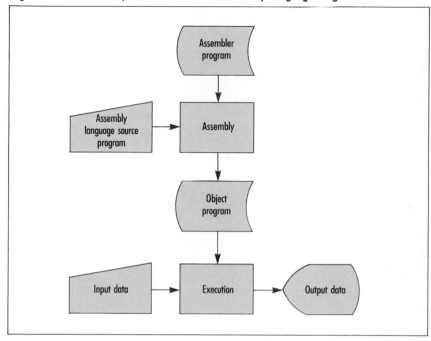

language, however. Assembly language is used to write system programs and other types of programs in which control or efficiency are important. Many general application programs such as word processor, spreadsheet, and data management programs are written in assembly language.

Third-Generation Languages

Although assembly language is better than machine language, it is not very close to human language. The reason for this is that each assembly language instruction is equivalent to one machine language instruction. In fact, both machine and assembly languages are considered to be *low-level languages*. In the mid-1950s computer professionals started to develop *high-level languages*, in which each instruction was equivalent to several machine language instructions. Hence, fewer instructions were required in programs written in these languages than in assembly languages. The high-level languages were closer to human languages. They became the third-generation languages.

The first third-generation languages were similar to simple mathematical notation. Later third-generation languages were closer to English. Still later languages were closer to other notations, such as those used in advanced mathematics. Figure 13–6 shows examples of instructions in several third-generation languages.

Programs written in third-generation languages have to be translated into machine language before they can be executed. There are several processes that are used for the translation. One process is called *compilation*, and it is done by a machine-language system program called a

Figure 13–6 Instructions in Third-Generation Languages

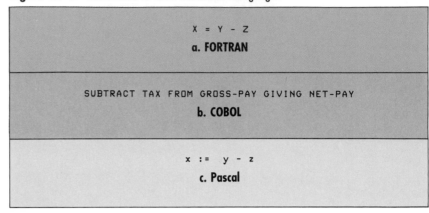

```
                        X = Y - Z
                      a. FORTRAN
```

```
      SUBTRACT TAX FROM GROSS-PAY GIVING NET-PAY
                      b. COBOL
```

```
                       x := y - z
                      c. Pascal
```

compiler. Sometimes third-generation languages are called *compiler languages*. In the compilation process each compiler language instruction is translated into several machine language instructions.

Figure 13–7 shows the compilation process. As with assembly, the programmer prepares a source program, this time in the compiler language (Figure 13–8). Then the compiler program translates the source program into a machine-language–equivalent object program. After translation, the object program is executed.

Another process used to translate third-generation language programs is called *interpretation,* and it is done by a machine language system program called an **interpreter**. The difference between compilation and

Figure 13–7 Compilation and Execution of a Compiler Language Program

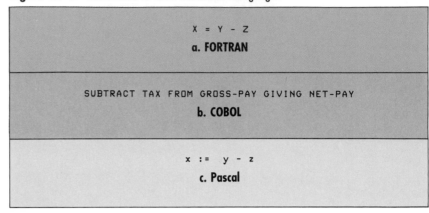

Figure 13–8 A Source Program on a Screen

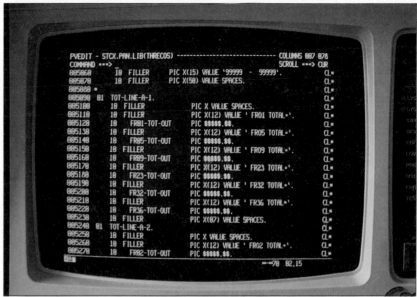

interpretation is as follows: In compilation, the entire source program is translated into machine language before any machine language instructions in the object program are executed. In interpretation, however, each source program instruction is translated into machine language instructions, and then the machine language instructions are executed before going on to translate the next source language instruction. Compiled programs generally execute faster than interpreted programs, but interpreters are less expensive and easier to use than compilers.

Third-generation languages are not tied to particular computers as are assembly and machine languages; we say they are **machine independent**. If a programmer wants to use a third-generation language on a different computer, he or she just needs a compiler or interpreter to translate the language into the machine language of the computer.

With third-generation languages, the programmer has less control over the basic circuitry of the computer than with assembly or machine languages. In addition, third-generation language programs usually are less efficient than assembly or machine language programs. Thus, these languages are not normally used for system programs, although a few are designed for writing this type of software. Most third-generation languages, however, have features that make application programs easier to write; hence, they are used mainly for writing this type of program. In addition, third-generation languages are easier to learn than assembly or machine languages, and many people are familiar with one or more third-generation language. There are many common third-generation languages, some of which will be discussed later in this chapter.

SELECTING A PROGRAMMING LANGUAGE

With such a large selection of programming languages, it can be difficult to choose one for a particular project. Reading the manuals to evaluate the languages is a time-consuming process. On the other hand, most people already have a fairly good idea of how various automobiles compare. So in order to assist those trying to choose a language, here is a chart that matches programming languages with comparable automobiles.

Assembly. A Formula I race car. Very fast, but difficult to drive and expensive to maintain.

FORTRAN II. A Model T Ford. Once it was king of the road.

FORTRAN IV. A Model A Ford.

FORTRAN 77. A six-cylinder 1977 Ford sedan with standard transmission and no seat belts.

COBOL. A delivery van. It's bulky and ugly, but it does the work.

BASIC. A second-hand Datsun with a rebuilt engine and patched upholstery. Your dad bought it for you to learn to drive. You'll ditch the car as soon as you can afford a new one.

RPG. An order form for a simple car. Fill in the blanks for the basic car of your choice.

Pascal. A Volkswagen Beetle. It's small but sturdy. Was once popular with intellectuals.

C. A black Pontiac Firebird, the all-macho car. Comes with optional seat belts and optional fuzz buster.

PL/1. A Cadillac convertible with automatic transmission, a two-tone paint job, white-wall tires, chrome exhaust pipes, and fuzzy dice hanging in the windshield.

Ada. An army-green Mercedes-Benz staff car. Power steering, power brakes, and automatic transmission are all standard. No other colors or options are available. If it's good enough for the generals, it's good enough for you.

Modula-2. A Volkswagen Rabbit with a trailer hitch.

APL. A double-decker bus. It takes rows and columns of passengers to the same place all at the same time. But it drives only in reverse gear, and is instrumented in Greek.

LISP. An electric car. It's simple but slow. Seat belts are not available.

PROLOG. A prototype concept-car.

Smalltalk. Not a car, but a whole new approach to personal transportation.

Fourth-Generation Languages

The fourth generation of programming languages is not so clearly defined as the other generations. Most people feel that a **fourth-generation language**, commonly referred to as a **4GL**, is a high-level language that requires significantly fewer instructions to accomplish a particular task than a third-generation language requires. Thus, a programmer should be able to write a program faster in a fourth-generation language than in a third-generation language.

Most third-generation languages are **procedural languages**, which means that the programmer must specify the steps—that is, the procedure—the computer has to follow in the program. In contrast, most fourth-generation languages are **nonprocedural languages**; the programmer does not have to give the procedure in the program but instead specifies what he or she wants. For example, assume that a program is needed to display some data on a screen, such as the address of a particular employee (Jones) from the personnel file. In a procedural language, the programmer would have to write a series of instructions that do the following:

Get a record from the personnel file.
If this is the record for Jones, display the address.
If this is not the record for Jones, repeat these steps.

In a nonprocedural language, however, the programmer would write a single instruction that says:

Get the address of Jones from the personnel file.

Many 4GLs are used to get information from files and databases, as in the previous example, and to display or print the information. These 4GLs contain a **query language**, which is used to answer queries with data from a database. For example, Figure 13–9 shows an instruction in SQL, a common query language. (Query languages are discussed further in Chapter 16.) Some 4GLs are used to produce complex printed reports. These languages contain **report generators**. With a report generator, the programmer specifies the headings, detailed data, and totals needed in a report. Then the report generator produces the required report, using data from a file or database. Other 4GLs are used to design screens to be used for data input and output and for menus. These languages contain **screen painters**. The programmer designs how he or she wants the screen to look; we say the programmer "paints" the screen. Then the screen painter creates the required screen. Still other 4GLs, called **application generators**, are used to produce entire systems of programs for computer applications. The programmer specifies the queries, reports, and screens needed, and the application generator creates the necessary program. (Application generators are discussed further in Chapter 16.)

Fourth-generation languages are mostly machine independent; usually they can be used on more than one type of computer. They are always used for writing business application programs, not scientific application programs or system programs. Some 4GLs are designed to be easily learned and used by end-users. With these languages, the user can create programs without the aid of a programmer.

Figure 13–9
A Query Language Instruction

```
SELECT ADDRESS
FROM PERSONNEL
WHERE NAME = "JONES"
```

Fifth-Generation Languages

What is the fifth generation of computer languages? There is no clear answer to this question right now. Some people feel that human languages, that is, *natural languages*, are fifth-generation languages. There have been some attempts to create computer programs that understand natural languages such as English. These programs, however, are very limited in their capabilities. Someday we will probably have programs that can understand natural languages. When that happens, we might be able to say definitely what fifth-generation languages are.

COMMON PROGRAMMING LANGUAGES

There are hundreds, perhaps thousands, of programming languages. Only a few, however, are commonly used. The most widely used languages are third-generation languages, although some fourth-generation languages are being used more and more. This section takes a look at some of the more common third-generation programming languages.

Earlier, you learned that third-generation languages are machine independent, which means they can be used on more than one type of computer. Frequently, however, the form a language takes on one computer may be slightly different from the form it takes on another computer. This situation results in different "dialects" or *versions* of the language. Thus, a program written in one version of a language for a particular computer cannot be used on a computer that requires a different version of the language without some, perhaps slight, modification. Some languages have standard versions, developed by the American National Standards Institute, or **ANSI**, which is an organization that determines standards for a number of industries. In theory, an ANSI standard version of a language is the same on all computers; in practice, however, the versions may vary from one computer to another. The discussion and examples of languages that follow will concentrate on each language's common features, but you must keep in mind that variations exist for different versions of the language.

FORTRAN

The first widely used third-generation language was **FORTRAN**, which stands for FORmula TRANslation. It was developed by researchers at IBM Corporation in the mid-1950s and was first available for use on IBM computers in 1957. Since that time, FORTRAN has undergone several modifications and improvements. In 1958 IBM released a version called FORTRAN II, followed by FORTRAN IV in 1962. In 1966 ANSI developed FORTRAN 66, and in 1977 it developed the most recent version, FORTRAN 77.

As its name implies, FORTRAN was designed to make it easy to write programs that include many mathematical formulas. Scientific application programs have numerous formulas, so FORTRAN is commonly used for these types of programs. In fact, FORTRAN is probably the most common third-generation language used today by scientists and engineers. FORTRAN does not have good features for input and output or for storing and retrieving data from secondary storage—characteristics that are needed for business application programs. Hence, it is rarely used for this type of program.

A version of FORTRAN is available for almost all types of computers, from supercomputers down to microcomputers. It is used most frequently, however, on larger computers. On some supercomputers it is the only third-generation language used.

FORTRAN programs consist of instructions that are called *statements*. Figure 13–10 shows an example of a simple FORTRAN program. Each line in this example is a different FORTRAN statement. A programmer codes a FORTRAN program by writing the statements in the program. FORTRAN statements take less time to code than the instructions in some other languages, so writing scientific programs can be done comparatively quickly in FORTRAN. Also, FORTRAN programs execute faster than programs in some other languages.

FORTRAN is fairly easy to learn; it does not have as many instructions as some other languages, and its syntax is not too complex. A science, engineering, or mathematics student can learn FORTRAN in a single college course or by reading a good textbook and doing several practice programs.

COBOL

The second major third-generation language after FORTRAN was **COBOL**. It was developed by a group of computer professionals in 1959. Since then it has evolved through a number of versions. ANSI standard versions became available in 1968, 1974, and 1985. The most recent ANSI version is commonly called COBOL 85.

Figure 13–10 A FORTRAN Program That Finds the Total and Average of Three Test Scores

```
C TEST SCORE AVERAGING PROGRAM
      CHARACTER*18 NAME
      REAL SCORE1,SCORE2,SCORE3,TOTAL,AVE
      PRINT *,'ENTER STUDENT NAME OR TYPE END TO STOP:'
      READ (*,300) NAME
  100 IF (NAME .EQ. 'END') GO TO 200
      PRINT *,'ENTER THREE TEST SCORES:'
      READ *,SCORE1,SCORE2,SCORE3
      TOTAL = SCORE1 + SCORE2 + SCORE3
      AVE = TOTAL / 3.0
      PRINT *
      PRINT *,'STUDENT NAME ',NAME
      PRINT *,'TOTAL SCORE ', TOTAL
      PRINT *,'AVERAGE SCORE ',AVE
      PRINT *
      PRINT *,'ENTER STUDENT NAME OR TYPE END TO STOP:'
      READ (*,300) NAME
      GO TO 100
  200 STOP
  300 FORMAT (A18)
      END
```

COBOL stands for COmmon Business Oriented Language. As the name implies, the language is designed to be *common* to many different computers (that is, machine independent). In addition, it is used most effectively for *business* application programs, not for scientific programs. It has excellent features for storing and retrieving data in files in secondary storage and for printing report output, which are needed in business programs. It does not have good features for doing complex calculations, however. Today COBOL is undoubtedly the most widely used third-generation language for business data processing.

COBOL is available on almost all mainframe computers, minicomputers, and microcomputers. It is most often used, however, on mainframe and minicomputers. Many businesses use it as the only language for business application program development on their medium-sized and large computers.

Figure 13–11 shows an example of a simple COBOL program. All COBOL programs are divided into four main parts, called *divisions*. The divisions are the IDENTIFICATION division, the ENVIRONMENT division, the DATA division, and the PROCEDURE division. The instructions within these divisions are called *entries* and *statements*. A programmer codes a COBOL program by writing the entries and statements in each division. These instructions are very wordy and can be quite long, so coding a COBOL program can be time consuming. Its wordiness, however, often makes COBOL programs read much like English, so they are easy to understand.

COBOL is more difficult to learn than FORTRAN and some other languages. It has many instructions, with numerous options for each instruction, although the syntax of individual instructions is not too complex. A business student can learn much of the COBOL language in two college courses.

BASIC

BASIC, which stands for Beginner's All-purpose Symbolic Instruction Code, was developed in the mid-1960s at Dartmouth College. At that time, the main languages (FORTRAN and COBOL) were used for programs that processed batches of data; it was not easy to write programs in these languages that interacted with the user. The designers of BASIC wanted a simple language in which students could write programs that they could interact with through terminals. They designed BASIC to be used on minicomputers that were shared among many users simultaneously. Today, BASIC is available not only on minicomputers but also on some mainframe computers and all microcomputers. In fact, BASIC is probably the most widely used third-generation language on microcomputers.

BASIC, like FORTRAN and COBOL, has evolved through a number of versions over the years. ANSI has developed some standard versions, but they are not commonly used. Today there are many popular versions for microcomputers. Unfortunately, the versions are often quite different for different microcomputers, and there may be several different versions for one microcomputer. Some popular microcomputer versions are

Figure 13–11 A COBOL Program That Finds the Total and Average of Three Test Scores

```
       IDENTIFICATION DIVISION.
       PROGRAM-ID. AVERAGE.
*
*      THIS PROGRAM CALCULATES THE TOTAL AND AVERAGE OF THREE
*      TEST SCORES FOR EACH STUDENT.
*
       ENVIRONMENT DIVISION.
       CONFIGURATION SECTION.
       SOURCE-COMPUTER. XYZ-1.
       OBJECT-COMPUTER. XYZ-1.
       INPUT-OUTPUT SECTION.
       FILE-CONTROL.
           SELECT STUDENT-FILE
               ASSIGN TO DISK.
           SELECT REPORT-FILE
               ASSIGN TO PRINTER.
*
       DATA DIVISION.
       FILE SECTION.
       FD  STUDENT-FILE
           LABEL RECORDS ARE OMITTED.
       01  STUDENT-DATA               PIC X(27).
       FD  REPORT-FILE
           LABEL RECORDS ARE OMITTED.
       01  REPORT-DATA                PIC X(132).
       WORKING-STORAGE SECTION.
       01  WS-WORKING-FIELDS.
           05  WS-EOF-FLAG            PIC X.
           05  WS-TOTAL               PIC 999.
           05  WS-AVERAGE             PIC 999V9.
       01  STUDENT-RECORD.
           05  ST-NAME                PIC X(18).
           05  ST-SCORE1              PIC 999.
           05  ST-SCORE2              PIC 999.
           05  ST-SCORE3              PIC 999.
       01  HEADING-LINE.
           05  FILLER                 PIC XXX     VALUE SPACES.
           05  FILLER                 PIC X(12)   VALUE "STUDENT NAME".
           05  FILLER                 PIC X(6)    VALUE SPACES.
           05  FILLER                 PIC X(5)    VALUE "TOTAL".
           05  FILLER                 PIC XXX     VALUE SPACES.
           05  FILLER                 PIC X(7)    VALUE "AVERAGE".
           05  FILLER                 PIC X(96)   VALUE SPACES.
       01  DETAIL-LINE.
           05  DL-NAME                PIC X(18).
           05  FILLER                 PIC XXXX    VALUE SPACES.
           05  DL-TOTAL               PIC ZZ9.
           05  FILLER                 PIC X(5)    VALUE SPACES.
           05  DL-AVERAGE             PIC ZZ9.9.
           05  FILLER                 PIC X(97)   VALUE SPACES.
*

       PROCEDURE DIVISION.
*
       A000-MAIN-CONTROL.
           OPEN INPUT STUDENT-FILE
               OUTPUT REPORT-FILE.
           PERFORM B010-WRITE-HEADING.
           MOVE "N" TO WS-EOF-FLAG.
           PERFORM B020-READ-INPUT.
           PERFORM B030-PRODUCE-REPORT-BODY
               UNTIL WS-EOF-FLAG IS EQUAL TO "Y".
           CLOSE STUDENT-FILE, REPORT-FILE.
           STOP RUN.
*
       B010-WRITE-HEADING.
           WRITE REPORT-DATA FROM HEADING-LINE
               AFTER ADVANCING PAGE.
           MOVE SPACES TO REPORT-DATA.
           WRITE REPORT-DATA
               AFTER ADVANCING 1 LINE.
*
       B020-READ-INPUT.
           READ STUDENT-FILE INTO STUDENT-RECORD
               AT END MOVE "Y" TO WS-EOF-FLAG.
*
       B030-PRODUCE-REPORT-BODY.
           PERFORM C010-CALCULATE-TOTAL-AVERAGE.
           PERFORM C020-WRITE-DETAIL-OUTPUT.
           PERFORM B020-READ-INPUT.
*
       C010-CALCULATE-TOTAL-AVERAGE.
           ADD ST-SCORE1, ST-SCORE2, ST-SCORE3
               GIVING WS-TOTAL.
           DIVIDE WS-TOTAL BY 3
               GIVING WS-AVERAGE ROUNDED.
*
       C020-WRITE-DETAIL-OUTPUT.
           MOVE ST-NAME TO DL-NAME.
           MOVE WS-TOTAL TO DL-TOTAL.
           MOVE WS-AVERAGE TO DL-AVERAGE.
           WRITE REPORT-DATA FROM DETAIL-LINE
               AFTER ADVANCING 1 LINE.
```

Microsoft BASIC (called BASICA on IBM computers and GWBASIC on IBM clones), Quick BASIC, and Turbo BASIC.

BASIC has many features that are similar to FORTRAN. Thus, BASIC is sometimes used for scientific application programs. Its features, however, are not as sophisticated as those of FORTRAN, and programs in BASIC usually do not execute as fast as equivalent programs in FORTRAN. Thus, FORTRAN is a better choice for large, complex scientific programs. BASIC is also used to prepare some business application programs, especially on microcomputers. It does not have as many features for business programs as COBOL, so COBOL is usually used for large, sophisticated business programs.

BASIC is good for writing quick programs to solve simple problems, especially in education. For example, a student might write a BASIC program to find the average of the data obtained from an experiment in a class. When a problem requires a quick solution, BASIC is often a good language to use.

Figure 13–12 shows an example of a simple BASIC program. Like FORTRAN, each instruction in a BASIC program is called a *statement*. In most versions of BASIC, including Microsoft BASIC, each statement must begin with a line number. Some versions, such as Quick BASIC and Turbo BASIC, do not require line numbers. A programmer codes a BASIC program by writing the statements in the program, which takes little time because the statements are simple.

BASIC is perhaps the easiest third-generation language to learn; it has few instructions, and the syntax is simple. A student can learn BASIC in a single course or even in part of a course. Many junior and senior high school students learn BASIC as part of their mathematics or science courses. Some students teach themselves BASIC by reading a good textbook and doing practice programs.

RPG

In the mid-1960s IBM introduced a new line of minicomputers designed for use in small–to–medium-sized businesses. To program these computers, the company developed a new language called **RPG**, which stands for Report Program Generator. In the early 1970s RPG II became available, and in the late 1970s RPG III was developed. There is no ANSI standard version of RPG, however.

Figure 13–12 A BASIC Program That Finds the Total and Average of Three Test Scores

```
100 REM - TEST SCORE AVERAGING PROGRAM
110 INPUT "ENTER STUDENT NAME OR TYPE END TO STOP: ", STUNAME$
120 WHILE STUNAME$ < > "END"
130    INPUT "ENTER THREE TEST SCORES: ", SCORE1, SCORE2, SCORE3
140    LET TOTAL = SCORE1 + SCORE2 + SCORE3
150    LET AVE = TOTAL / 3
160    PRINT
170    PRINT "STUDENT NAME "; STUNAME$
180    PRINT "TOTAL SCORE"; TOTAL
190    PRINT "AVERAGE SCORE"; AVE
200    PRINT
210    INPUT "ENTER STUDENT NAME OR TYPE END TO STOP: ", STUNAME$
220 WEND
230 END
```

As its name implies, RPG was designed to write programs that produced reports—specifically, business reports. To go with its report-preparation capabilities, RPG has features for storing and retrieving data in secondary storage. Its computational capabilities, however, are limited. Thus, RPG is used for programs that prepare reports and process business files, which are typical business application programs. It does not have as many features as COBOL, so COBOL is a better language for more complex business programs. RPG is never used for scientific programs.

Although RPG was originally designed for IBM minicomputers, versions of it are available on other minicomputers, as well as on some mainframe computers and some microcomputers. It is used most frequently, however, on IBM minicomputers. Some small and medium-sized businesses use it as their only language for business application programs.

RPG is a nonprocedural language. A programmer does not give the procedure the program must follow, but instead describes the files, inputs, calculations, and outputs for the program. He or she provides these descriptions on special forms called *specification forms*. Figure 13–13, (a) through (d), shows a simple RPG program coded on these forms. The main forms are the File Description Specifications, the Input Specifications, the Calculation Specifications, and the Output-Format Specifications. A programmer codes an RPG program by filling in columns on these forms with the appropriate entries. Writing programs in RPG is relatively easy because the forms guide the programmer. Even though RPG is a nonprocedural language, most people feel it is a third-generation language because of its limited capabilities.

RPG is easier to learn than some other third-generation languages. A business student can learn RPG by taking one or two college courses. A student who already knows COBOL will probably find RPG very easy to learn.

Pascal

By the late 1960s many third-generation languages had been developed. These languages, however, were not designed for writing well-structured programs. About this time, the ideas of structured programming, discussed in Chapter 12, became known. Researchers began to develop languages that included features to make structured programming easier. One researcher, Niklaus Wirth, a Swiss computer scientist, developed a simple third-generation language for teaching structured programming. He called the language **Pascal**, after the French mathematician Blaise Pascal, who invented the first mechanical calculator (see Appendix B).

The use of Pascal spread through colleges and universities around the world until, by the 1980s, it was probably the most commonly taught language in introductory programming courses. During this time, computer programmers discovered that, although Pascal was simple, they could write complex programs with it. Programmers used Pascal for some system programs, such as compilers. In addition, some scientific application programs were developed in Pascal, although it is not as powerful as FORTRAN for these types of programs. Only a few

Figure 13–13 An RPG Program That Finds the Total and Average of Three Test Scores

RPG CONTROL CARD AND FILE DESCRIPTION SPECIFICATIONS

Date _____
Program _____
Programmer _____

Punching Instruction — Graphic / Punch
Page — 1 2
Program Identification — 75 76 77 78 79 80

Control Card Specifications

Line	Form Type	Core Size to Compile	Object Output	Listing Options	Core Size to Execute	Debug	MFCM Stacking Sequence	Input-Shillings	Input-Pence	Output-Shillings	Output-Pence	Inverted Print	360/20 2501 Buffer	Number Of Print Positions	Alternate Collating Sequence	
0 1	H															Refer to the specific System Reference Library manual for actual entries.

File Description Specifications

Line	Form Type	Filename	File Type (I/O/U/C/D)	File Designation (P/S/C/R/T/D)	End of File (E)	Sequence (A/D)	File Format (F/V)	Block Length	Record Length	L/R	Record Address Type (A/K/I)	Type of File Organization or Additional Area (I/D/T or 19)	Overflow Indicator	Key Field Starting Location	Extension Code E/L	Device	Symbolic Device	Labels (S, N, or E)	Name of Label Exit	Extent Exit for DAM / Core Index	A/U	Number of Tracks for Cylinder Overflow / Number of Extents / Tape Rewind / File Condition U1-U8 (N/J)
0 2 Ø	F	STUDENT	I P				F	27	27							DISK						
0 3 Ø	F	REPORT	O				F	132	132							PRINTER						
0 4	F																					
0 5	F																					
0 6	F																					
0 7	F																					
	F																					
	F																					

RPG INPUT SPECIFICATIONS

Date _____
Program _____
Programmer _____

Punching Instruction — Graphic / Punch
Page — 1 2
Program Identification — 75 76 77 78 79 80

Line	Form Type	Filename	Sequence	Number (1/N)	Option (O)	Record Identifying Indicator or **	Position (1)	Not (N)	C/Z/D	Character	Position (2)	Not (N)	C/Z/D	Character	Position (3)	Not (N)	C/Z/D	Stacker Select P = Packed/B = Binary	From	To	Decimal Positions	Field Name	Control Level (L1-L9)	Matching Fields or Chaining Fields	Field Record Relation	Plus	Minus	Zero or Blank	Sterling Sign Position
0 1 Ø	I	STUDENT	AA			Ø1																							
0 2 Ø	I																	1	18		NAME							
0 3 Ø	I																	19	21	Ø	SCORE1							
0 4 Ø	I																	22	24	Ø	SCORE2							
0 5 Ø	I																	25	27	Ø	SCORE3							
0 6	I																											
0 7	I																											
0 8	I																											
0 9	I																											
1 0	I																											
1 1	I																											
1 2	I																											
1 3	I																											
1 4	I																											
1 5	I																											
	I																											
	I																											
	I																											
	I																											

RPG CALCULATION SPECIFICATIONS

Line	Form Type	Control Level	Indicators (Not / And Not / And Not)	Factor 1	Operation	Factor 2	Result Field	Field Length	Decimal Positions	Half Adjust (H)	Resulting Indicators	Comments
01	C		Ø1	SCORE1	ADD	SCORE2	TOTAL	3Ø				
02	C		Ø1	TOTAL	ADD	SCORE3	TOTAL					
03	C		Ø1	TOTAL	DIV	3	AVE	41		H		
04	C											
05	C											
06	C											
07	C											
08	C											
09	C											
10	C											
11	C											
12	C											
13	C											
14	C											
15	C											

RPG OUTPUT - FORMAT SPECIFICATIONS

Line	Form Type	Filename	Type (H/D/T/E)	Space Before	Skip	Output Indicators	Field Name	Edit Codes	End Position in Output Record	Constant or Edit Word
01	O	REPORT	H	2Ø1		1P				
02	O								15	'STUDENT NAME'
03	O								26	'TOTAL'
04	O								36	'AVERAGE'
05	O		D	1		Ø1				
06	O						NAME		18	
07	O						TOTAL		25	' Ø'
08	O						AVE		35	' Ø. '
09	O									
10	O									
11	O									
12	O									
13	O									
14	O									
15	O									

business application programs were written in Pascal, however, because it has limited input and output capabilities. Today, Pascal is widely taught in high schools and colleges and is sometimes used for system and application programs.

As the use of Pascal spread, many versions of the language were developed, but no standard version evolved. Today, a version of Pascal is available for many computers, from mainframe computers down to microcomputers. For some computers, such as most microcomputers, several versions are available. There is no one type of computer on which it is more likely to be used.

Figure 13–14 shows an example of a Pascal program. In Pascal, as in many languages, each instruction is called a *statement*. When a programmer writes a Pascal program, he or she codes the statements in the program. The statements are fairly easy to code, so writing a Pascal program is not too time-consuming.

Pascal is a good first language to learn because it teaches a student how to write well-structured programs. A student can learn Pascal fairly easily in one course because it does not have many instructions and its syntax is simple. Many high schools and colleges teach introductory programming courses using Pascal.

C

Earlier, you learned that system software may be written in assembly language. The problem with assembly language is that it is machine dependent. Thus, an assembly language system program (such as a compiler) cannot be used on a different type of computer without completely rewriting the program. It would be desirable if a language produced the control and efficiency of assembly language but was machine independent. Such a language is **C**.

Figure 13–14 A Pascal Program That Finds the Total and Average of Three Test Scores

```
program TestAve (input,output);
   (Test score averaging program)
var
   Score1,Score2,Score3,Total,Ave: real;
   Name: string[18];
begin
   write ('Enter student name or type end to stop: ');
   readln (Name);
   while Name <> 'end' do
   begin
      write ('Enter three test scores: ');
      readln (Score1,Score2,Score3);
      Total := Score1 + Score2 + Score3;
      Ave := Total / 3;
      writeln;
      writeln ('Student name ',Name);
      writeln ('Total score ',Total);
      writeln ('Average score ',Ave);
      writeln;
      write ('Enter student name or type end to stop: ');
      readln (Name)
   end
end.
```

C was developed by Bell Laboratories in the early 1970s. It is named C because it was developed by Bell after the B language. It includes features that provide the control of assembly language (second generation) but at the same time has third-generation language features. You might think of it as a machine-independent "two and one-half generation" language.

C is used extensively for system programs. For example, the UNIX operating system, discussed in Chapter 7, is written in C. Many microcomputer general application programs—such as word processing, spreadsheet, and database management programs—are written in C. C is used for complex system and application programs that require control of the computer and that must execute rapidly and use primary storage efficiently.

C was originally developed for use on minicomputers. Today, however, versions of C are available on almost all computers from supercomputers to microcomputers. Unfortunately, there is no ANSI standard version of C, so there may be differences between the versions of C on different computers.

Figure 13–15 shows an example of a simple C program. As in other languages, each instruction in C is called a *statement*. The instructions are more difficult to understand than in some other languages.

C is harder to learn than many other languages. Most students should learn another language before studying C. With the right background, however, a student can learn C in a single college course.

Comparison of Languages

Table 13–1 shows a comparison of the languages discussed in this chapter.

Figure 13–15 A C Program That Finds the Total and Average of Three Test Scores

```
main ()    /*Test score averaging program*/
{
   char name[19];
   float score1,score2,score3,total,ave;
   printf ("Enter student name or type end to stop: ");
   scanf ("%s",name);
   while (strcmp(name,"end") != 0)
   {
      printf ("Enter three test scores: ");
      scanf ("%f%f%f",&score1,&score2,&score3);
      total = score1 + score2 + score3;
      ave = total / 3;
      printf ("\n");
      printf ("Student name %s\n",name);
      printf ("Total score %4.0f\n",total);
      printf ("Average score %5.1f\n",ave);
      printf ("\n");
      printf ("Enter student name or type end to stop: ");
      scanf ("%s",name);
   }
}
```

Table 13–1 Comparison of Languages

Language	Generation	Machine dependent	Machine independent	System programs	Application programs Business	Application programs Scientific	Other
Machine language	1	X		X			
Assembly language	2	X		X			General application programs
FORTRAN	3		X			X	
COBOL	3		X		X		
BASIC	3		X		X	X	Education
RPG	3		X		X		
Pascal	3		X	X			Teaching
C	3		X	X			General application programs
4GL	4		X		X		

Other Languages

The programming languages described so far are the most widely used languages. A number of other languages, however, are used occasionally or for specialized purposes. A description of a few of these other languages follows.

PL/1. *PL/1*, which stands for Programming Language 1, was developed by IBM Corporation in the early 1960s. At that time, the two main languages were FORTRAN, used for scientific applications, and COBOL, used for business applications. PL/1 combined features from FORTRAN and COBOL and added new features to create a general-purpose language. As a consequence, the language was very complex and difficult to learn. The language was popular for a while on IBM computers, but few other computer manufacturers adopted it. Today, PL/1 is not very popular; it is used by some businesses for their scientific or business application programming, but its use is very limited.

Ada. In the mid-1970s the U.S. Department of Defense decided it needed a new language for software use in military systems such as missiles. Prior to that time, this type of software, which is called *embedded software*, was written in assembly language and in a variety of third-generation languages. The Department of Defense wanted to have a single language for all embedded software, so it contracted to have a language designed for this purpose. The result, introduced in 1980, was *Ada*. This language is named after Augusta Ada Byron, Countess of Lovelace, who many consider to be the first programmer (see Appendix B).

OOPS

American President Cos., Ltd, the Oakland, California shipper, had an ambitious goal in 1984: doubling its transpacific volume in five years. To do that required access to vast amounts of data: month-by-month figures for each commodity being shipped to different regions in the Pacific Rim. The company's computers weren't up to the task. As for the software that would be needed to manipulate the data, that could have taken years to create, using conventional languages like COBOL.

The dilemma was resolved in early 1986 with a $250,000 purchase from Metaphor Computer Systems. Metaphor sells systems built around a new style of computation called object-oriented programming. Metaphor sells the software tools that make this kind of programming possible.

With Metaphor's workstations in hand, American President's data processing department was able to concoct custom software in a fraction of the time that it would have taken with traditional programming techniques. Derek Williamson, a manager in the department, says the programming time for one market share report was cut from seven months to seven weeks. In the event, American President was able to more than double international volume, from 215,000 containers in 1984 to 491,700 in 1989.

Object-oriented programming (OOPS, they call it) has been around for a number of years, and Metaphor isn't the only firm capitalizing on it. The idea goes back to the computer language Smalltalk, developed by Xerox PARC (Palo Alto Research Center) scientists in the early 1980s. In 1988 Xerox spun off ParcPlace Systems, a Palo Alto, California startup led by former PARC researcher Adele Goldberg, to commercialize Smalltalk. And now OOPS has become a hot concept with the computer set. The operating system on Steven Jobs' NeXT computer is, in part, object-oriented. IBM has begun to sell a version of its Personal System/2 personal computer with Metaphor software.

So what is OOPS? Think of it this way: Object-oriented programming turns software writers from weavers into quiltmakers. Using OOPS, programmers produce programs by stitching together prefabricated modules— "objects"—instead of laboriously weaving threads every time someone orders up a new coverlet.

In the broadest sense modular programming has always been the best kind of programming. You don't tackle a complicated programming project by starting with the first little instruction to the computer. Rather, you conceptually divide the problem into separate and self-contained tasks, or modules, and then write a program for each task. One module may handle the way a customer order is flashed on a screen, another how it is stored in a database, another how it gets printed on paper. The idea is to make it possible to make adjustments to one module without having to redesign them all. Also, later programmers can build on your work by borrowing some of your modules.

In the old days (going back to the FORTRAN computer language of the 1950s) these modules were called "subroutines." But object-oriented programming is more than a new name for an old game. These systems formalize the process of dividing big projects into little "objects"—depicted as boxes on a computer screen that are linked in the way that members of a family are connected to each other in a family tree. The Metaphor system maintains a library of objects on which programmers can build solutions to new programs. Ultimately, a programmer might be able to order up, say, a new report on container traffic merely by moving boxes around on a screen.

The drawback is that an application created using OOPS is slower than an identical application written in a conventional computer language. Because boxes are hierarchical, the object-oriented program ends up being larger—hence, it takes longer to run on a computer. Metaphor Chairman David Liddle says his system uses a hybrid approach and doesn't run as slowly as a pure OOPS system. But, more important, many an end user is willing to sacrifice performance in order to get software that is easy to update and modify. Among the users developing OOPS applications are American Airlines, Boeing and General Dynamics.

Mitchell Oliver is part of a General Dynamics team designing software that will simulate a rocket. Oliver's group is using object-oriented programming tools from ParcPlace Systems. "We had to build a user interface that would allow non–computer-literates to be able to use the system," Oliver explains. "You could do it with traditional languages like FORTRAN, but it's much more difficult." Using object-oriented programming, Oliver and his team could use elements that represented the engineering specifications of the rocket's machinery. These, in turn, could be linked to boxes that represent how each of these parts behaves.

Goldberg, the Xerox PARC alumna who is ParcPlace's president, concedes that object-oriented programming is a technique more suitable for large corporations that write software for their own use than for software companies that create commercial programs. Corporate computer users "need the ability to change their programs more frequently than every two to three years, which is typical for a company selling off-the-shelf packages," Goldberg says. For example, Procter & Gamble uses the Metaphor system to examine product sales cycles; those programs change as new competitors enter the market and others exit. Other factors that might alter sales cycles are new distributors, pricing changes or an advance in technology.

Sacrificing the running speed of a computer program to get more speed out of a programming department makes perfect sense these days. Hardware is cheap. Programmers are expensive.

Ada is like Pascal, but with many additional features. It is a complex language and is difficult to learn. Today, it is used not only for all new embedded software for the U.S. military but also for some scientific and business applications.

Modula-2.   *Modula-2* was invented by Niklaus Wirth, the inventor of Pascal, in the early 1980s. Although Pascal is a good teaching language, it lacks many features needed to make it easy to write real system and application software. Wirth designed Modula-2 to be like Pascal but with additional features not in Pascal in order to make it a more usable language. Among these features was a program organization that made modular programming easy (which is where the name Modula came from). Today, Modula-2 is used for teaching and for some system and application software. It is a little harder to learn than Pascal.

APL.   In 1962 Kenneth Iverson, a Harvard mathematician, published a book called *A Programming Language*, in which he described a language for defining certain mathematical functions. Originally, the language was not intended for use on a computer, but in the late 1960s it became available on IBM computers. Because of the name of the book, the language was called *APL*.

APL uses a set of symbols not found on most computer keyboards. As a result, a special keyboard is needed for using APL. The symbols in the language are very powerful. For example, the symbol ρ (the Greek letter *rho*) tells the computer to determine how many numbers are in a list of numbers. With APL, complex programs can be written in a few lines. APL programs, however, are difficult to read because of the special symbols. Today, APL is used mainly for scientific application programs. It is a difficult language to learn.

LISP and PROLOG.   *LISP*, which stands for LISt Processing, was developed in the late 1950s. It is designed to process lists of data, especially lists of nonnumeric data. This type of processing is common in the field of *artificial intelligence*, or *AI*, which is concerned with using a computer to mimic human intelligence. Using LISP, a programmer can write programs that simulate the way humans think in specific situations, such as in playing a strategy game like chess. LISP is a difficult language to learn and to use.

Another language, called *PROLOG*, which stands for PROgramming LOGic, is also used for artificial intelligence programs. This language was developed in the mid-1970s but has not become popular until recently. It is considered easier to learn and use than LISP.

Smalltalk and C++.   *Smalltalk* was developed in the mid-1970s by Xerox Corporation. It was designed for a new type of programming called **object-oriented programming**, in which the programmer develops a program from *objects*, or combinations of data and instructions to process the data. This approach to programming is considerably different from traditional programming. It is hard to learn Smalltalk because a programmer has to think in an entirely new way, which can take some time to get used to. Once learned, however, it is easier to write complex programs in Smalltalk.

Besides Smalltalk, other languages can be used for object-oriented programming. One of these is C++, which is a version of C that has certain features for object-oriented programming. Object-oriented languages are useful for writing system and application software that have user interfaces with icons, windows, and other graphic features. For example, the operating system for the Apple Macintosh was written in an object-oriented language. You can expect the use of object-oriented languages such as Smalltalk and C++ to increase significantly in the future.

Chapter Summary

- A programming language is a set of words, symbols, and **syntax** or grammatical rules for forming instructions in the language. There are many programming languages because over time, researchers have found better ways of designing languages and because different languages have been designed for different types of programs. A person selects a language by considering whether the language is designed for the type of program that needs to be written, whether it is available on the computer being used, whether trained programmers are available to write and maintain programs using the language, whether programs can be easily written in the language, and whether programs written in the language are efficient.

- Languages that are good for writing system programs have instructions that allow the programmer to control the basic circuitry of the computer. Languages that are good for business application programs have instructions that make input, output, and secondary storage operations easy. Languages that are designed for scientific application programs have good instructions for calculations.

- Machine languages (first generation) have instructions with operation codes and operands in a binary form. **Assembly languages** (second generation) substitute symbols for operation codes and operands, but each instruction still is equivalent to one machine language instruction. In third-generation languages, each instruction is equivalent to several machine language instructions. Programs in these languages require fewer instructions than in assembly languages. Programs in **fourth-generation languages**, or **4GLs**, require even fewer instructions than third-generation languages. Thus, a programmer can write a program faster in a 4GL than in a third-generation language. Also, most fourth-generation languages are **nonprocedural languages**, whereas most third-generation languages are **procedural languages**. Fifth-generation languages may turn out to be natural languages like English.

- An assembly or high-level language program must be translated into machine language before it can be executed. First, the programmer prepares the **source program** in the language. Then, the translator program—which may be an **assembler**, **compiler**, or **interpreter**—translates the source program into the equivalent machine language program, which is called the **object program**. Finally, the object program is executed.

- Machine language is used only for special system programming situations. Assembly language is used for system programs and for some general application programs. **FORTRAN** is used mainly for scientific application programs. **COBOL** is used for business application programs. **BASIC** is used for simpler scientific and business application programs and for quick programs to solve simple problems, especially in education. **RPG** is used only for business application programs. **Pascal** is used to teach programming and is used also for some system and application programs. **C** is used for many system and general application programs.

Terms to Remember

ANSI   p. 332

Application Generator   p. 331

Assembler   p. 326

Assembly Language   p. 326

BASIC   p. 334

C   p. 340

COBOL   p. 333

Compiler   p. 328

FORTRAN   p. 332

Fourth-Generation Language (4GL)   p. 331

Interpreter   p. 328

Machine-Dependent Language p. 325

Machine-Independent Language   p. 329

Nonprocedural Language   p. 331

Object-Oriented Programming p. 345

Object Program   p. 326

Pascal   p. 337

Procedural Language   p. 331

Query Language   p. 331

Report Generator   p. 331

RPG   p. 336

Screen Painter   p. 331

Source Program   p. 326

Syntax   p. 322

Review Questions

Fill-In Questions

1. The grammatical rules for a programming language are called the language's _____.
2. Machine languages are _____ -generation languages.
3. A programming language that can be used on only one type of computer is called _____, whereas one that can be used on several types of computers is called _____.
4. Second-generation languages are _____ languages.
5. A program that translates an assembly language program into an equivalent machine language program is called a(n) _____.

6. A program before it is translated into machine language is called a(n) _____; the equivalent machine language program is called a(n) _____.

7. Third-generation language programs are translated into machine language by a(n) _____ or a(n) _____.

8. A programming language in which the programmer specifies the procedure that the computer must follow in a program is called a(n) _____ language, whereas one in which the programmer specifies what he or she wants but not the procedure is called a(n) _____ language.

9. The first widely used third-generation language was _____.

10. The most widely used third-generation language for business data processing is _____.

11. A third-generation, nonprocedural language used for programs that produce business reports is _____.

12. A third-generation language designed for writing well-structured programs and often used to teach computer programming is _____.

Short-Answer Questions

1. Why is there not just one programming language that can be used for all programs?

2. What are the characteristics of programming languages that are good for writing system programs?

3. What programming language characteristics are important for writing business application programs, and what characteristics are important for writing scientific application programs?

4. List several factors that should be considered in selecting a programming language.

5. What is the difference between assembly and machine language?

6. What must be done to a third-generation language program before it can be executed?

7. What is a fourth-generation language, or 4GL?

8. You have to write a quick program to do simple analysis of data from a chemistry experiment. Which third-generation language would be a good one to use?

9. For what types of programs is the C programming language commonly used?

10. What languages are used for object-oriented programming?

Projects

1. Find out what you can about a programming language not discussed in this chapter. Where did the language come from? What type (generation) of language is it? For what types of programs is it commonly used?

2. Interview a programmer and find out what programming languages he or she uses. Find out what the programmer likes and dislikes about the languages. Write a summary of your interview.

PART FOUR

INFORMATION SYSTEMS

14

INFORMATION SYSTEM CONCEPTS AND APPLICATIONS

CHAPTER OBJECTIVES

• After completing this chapter you should be able to:

1. Explain what an information system is and explain the difference between data and information.

2. Identify the components of an information system.

3. List the main functions of an information system.

4. Explain the difference between batch processing and interactive processing.

5. List several basic business computer applications and give the main purpose of each.

A COMPUTER used in an organization is part of a system that includes hardware, software, data, people, and procedures. The purpose of this system is to process data and provide information to help in the operation and management of the organization. This type of system is called an *information system*. This chapter explains basic concepts about information systems and describes some common applications of information systems.

WHAT IS AN INFORMATION SYSTEM?

A **system** is a collection of parts or *components* that work together for a purpose. For example, an automobile is a system. Its components are an engine, a body, a drive train, and so forth. These components work together for the purpose of providing transportation.

An **information system** is a collection of components that work together to process data and provide information within an organization. For example, a payroll system is an information system. Its components are people, equipment, data, and other elements. The components work together to process payroll data and provide information about payroll costs.

An information system does not have to include the use of a computer; people can process data and provide information manually or by using equipment such as adding machines. Most of the time, however, when people talk about an information system, they mean one that includes a computer. Some people use the phrase **computer information system,** or **CIS,** to emphasize the computer-based characteristics of this type of system.

An Example of an Information System

To illustrate many of the topics in this chapter, we will use a simplified example of an information system in a business that sells bicycles. This system, called an *inventory system*, keeps track of data about the inventory in the business, which is the stock of goods on hand. A bicycle business has an inventory consisting of a stock of bicycles. Each type of bicycle stocked is called an *item* in the inventory.

An inventory system keeps track of data about each item the business has in stock. The quantity of stock the business has on hand is an example of the data that it keeps. Every time the business removes items from stock, usually because of sales, the quantity on hand of the item removed is decreased. Each time the business adds more goods to stock, perhaps because the business purchased them from a manufacturer, the quantity is increased. Periodically, the inventory system must report information about the quantity of stock on hand for each item. This information helps managers in the business decide whether to add more of those items that are low in stock, or to reduce the inventory (perhaps by lowering prices) of those items where there is too much stock. Figure 14–1 illustrates the basic characteristics of an inventory system.

The purpose of an inventory system is to process data about inventory changes and to provide information about inventory quantities. This type of system could be entirely manual. For example, the bicycle business could keep track of each type of bicycle in stock on 3"-x-5" cards (Figure 14–2). Then, when additions to or removals from stock are made, a person could make the changes on the appropriate cards. For each type of bicycle that had stock added or removed, the person would locate the appropriate card, add the amount added to stock to the quantity on hand from the card and subtract the amount removed from stock, and then erase the quantity on hand from the card and replace it with the new quantity. Periodically, a person would go through all the cards and make a list of those types of bicycles for which the quantity on hand is low and those for which the quantity is high.

If the number of different items that the business stocks is small, keeping track of the inventory manually would not be too difficult. If there were many different items, however, using a computer probably would be easier. In a computerized inventory system, the data about the stock of goods for each item would be stored in the computer. Then, data about goods added to or removed from stock would be entered

Figure 14–1 Characteristics of an Inventory System

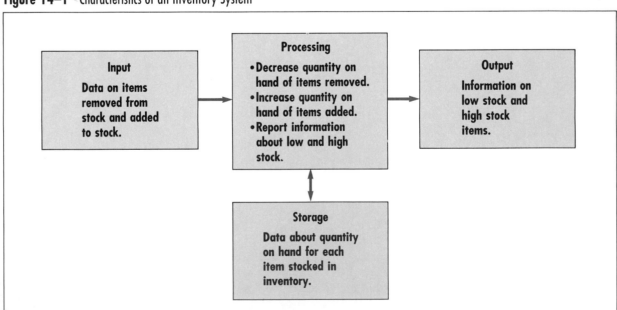

Figure 14–2   A 3"-x-5" Card for Keeping Track of Inventory

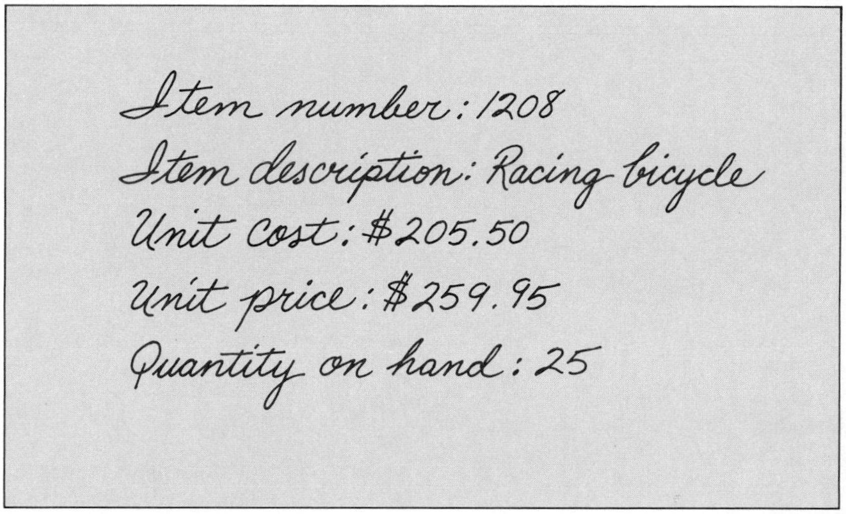

> Item number: 1208
> Item description: Racing bicycle
> Unit cost: $205.50
> Unit price: $259.95
> Quantity on hand: 25

into the computer. The computer would use the entered data to make changes in the stored data. Periodically, the computer would determine which items had low inventory and which had high inventory, and report this information.

Data Versus Information

Although the terms *data* and *information* have been used almost interchangeably, there is a difference between these terms. *Data* is raw facts, figures, numbers, and words. Data is entered into the system, processed by the system, stored in the system, and comes out of the system. **Information**, on the other hand, is data that is meaningful or useful to someone. Information comes out of the system and is used to help run the organization.

In the bicycle business's inventory system, data about each type of bicycle that is added to or removed from stock is entered into the system. This data is processed to make changes in the stored data about the quantity on hand. Out of the system comes data about types of bicycles that are low or high in stock. This data, however, is information to the person who must make decisions about inventory levels.

Data for one person may be information for another. For example, if your job is to decide when to buy more bicycles for inventory, you need information about the current stock of goods. But you do not need data about how many bicycles were sold today. On the other hand, a person who needs to schedule shipments would need information about the items sold today. Thus, whether something is information or data depends on how it is used.

COMPONENTS OF AN INFORMATION SYSTEM

There are five main components of a computer information system:

- Hardware
- Software
- Stored data
- Personnel
- Procedures

These components are summarized in Figure 14–3.

Hardware

The first component of an information system is computer *hardware*. Any type of computer can be used in an information system. Microcomputers, minicomputers, mainframe computers, and even supercomputers can be used. Some information systems include several types of computers and more than one of each type, often in a network. For example, a large system may consist of hundreds of networked microcomputers and several mainframe computers.

The bicycle business's inventory system needs computer hardware to function. Input hardware is needed so that data about stock added and removed can be entered. Secondary storage hardware is needed to store

Figure 14–3 Components of an Information System

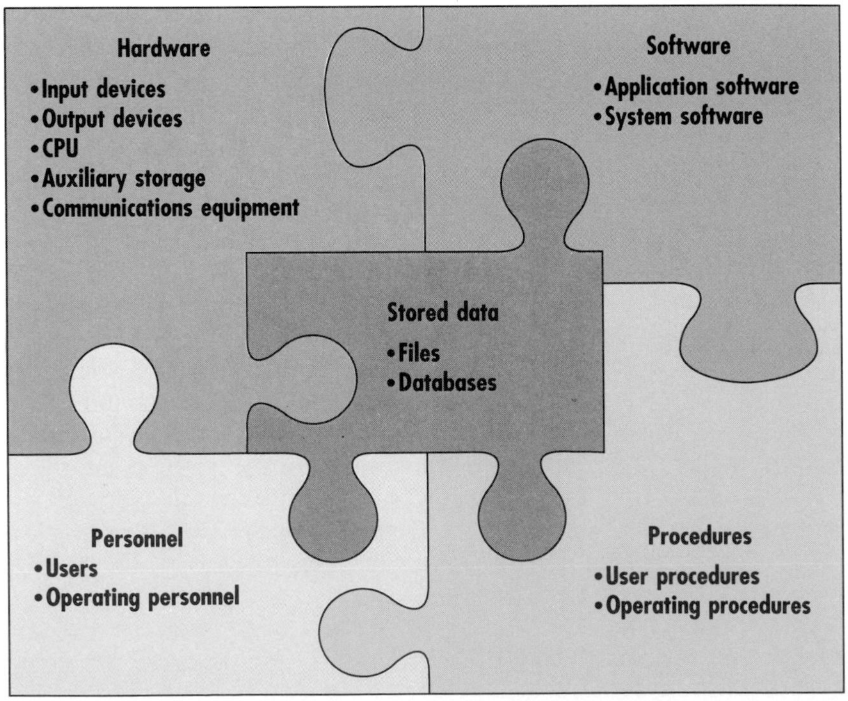

the data about the quantity on hand for each item. Processing hardware is needed to compute new quantities on hand and to make decisions about which items have low or high inventory. Output hardware is needed to produce the information in a form understandable to humans. Other hardware, such as communications hardware, may also be needed in the system.

Software

Software is another component of a computer information system. As you know, there are two main types of software: application software and system software. Both types are needed in a computer information system, but users are most concerned with application software.

For the bicycle business's inventory system, several application programs are needed. One is a program that accepts data from an input device about items that have been added to and removed from stock. This program would have to make changes in the stored data about the quantity on hand so that this data is up to date. Another program is needed to produce output with information about which items are low in stock and which are high. This program would get the information from the stored data. Other programs may also be needed, such as one to look up whether the stock on hand is sufficient to supply an order.

Notice that an information system can include several application programs. This characteristic is common among information systems. The programs in the system are executed at different times depending on the needs of the organization. Some information systems, however, may involve the use of only one application program.

Stored Data

The third component of a computer information system is the data that is stored in the computer system and used by the application software. As you know, files and databases are ways of storing data. The *stored data* component of an information system may be organized as a single file, as several files, or as one or more databases. In any case, this component consists of all the stored data needed by the application programs in the system.

In the bicycle business's inventory system, the stored data component would include data about each item that the business stocks. Each item would be identified by an item number. This data would be stored along with the description of each item, how much each item cost the business to purchase or manufacture (called the *unit cost*), how much the business sells each item for (called the *unit price*), and the quantity that the business has of each item on hand. One way of storing this data is to use a file with one record for each item. Each record would have fields for the item number, item description, unit cost, unit price, and quantity on hand. This file would form an inventory file and would be used by the application programs in the system. The file is the stored data component of the inventory system (Figure 14–4).

Figure 14–4 An Inventory File for a Bicycle Shop

ITEM NUMBER	ITEM DESCRIPTION	UNIT COST	UNIT PRICE	QUANTITY ON HAND
1208	RACING BICYCLE	205.50	259.95	25
2501	TOURING BICYCLE	184.00	239.95	8
2905	RECREATIONAL BICYCLE	76.25	109.95	41
3504	MOUNTAIN BIKE	188.75	229.95	6
4360	TRICYCLE	51.50	69.95	32
4389	TANDEM BICYCLE	256.00	340.50	12
5124	JUNIOR BICYCLE	69.75	99.95	0
5908	LEARNER BICYCLE	62.00	89.95	17
6531	PORTABLE BICYCLE	112.50	179.95	2

Personnel

An information system does not operate by itself; people are needed to make it run. People have to supply input data to the system, receive the output data from the system, operate the computer hardware in the system, and execute the programs that are part of the system. These people, or *personnel*, are the fourth essential component of an information system.

One type of person who is involved with the system is the user. As you know, users are nontechnically oriented people who gain some benefit from using the information system. Users supply input data to the system and receive output data from the system. The output provides information that the user needs in his or her job. Thus, the user is not separate from the system but is part of the personnel component of the system.

Some information systems are used by just one user. Such systems are called *single-user information systems*. For example, a system designed to keep track of customers for one salesperson is a single-user system because the only user of the system is the salesperson. Most information systems are designed to be used by many users. These systems are called *multiple-user information systems*. The bicycle business's inventory system is a multiple-user system because it is used by salespeople, clerical personnel, and business managers.

Other types of people who are part of an information system are *operating* personnel who perform technical functions to run the system. These people prepare input data received from the user, enter the data into the computer, operate the computer to execute programs, and pass the output to the user. If the system involves a microcomputer, the user may operate the computer, but with larger computers, operating personnel are needed. The inventory system needs operating personnel to operate the computer and execute the programs.

Procedures

The final component of an information system is *procedures*. Just as hardware cannot function without software, people do not know what to do unless they have procedures to follow. The procedures tell the users how to use the system, and they tell the operating personnel how to operate the system. The procedures should be in written form so that people can refer back to them.

Procedures are good only if people are trained in their use. Personnel must be trained to follow the procedures to use and operate the system. Thus, when we say personnel is a component of the system, we mean personnel who are trained in the use of the procedures.

The bicycle business's inventory system needs procedures for the personnel to follow. For the user, procedures describe how to enter input and what output to expect from the system. Procedures for the operating personnel describe how to operate the computer and how to execute programs.

FUNCTIONS OF AN INFORMATION SYSTEM

An information system may perform many functions to accomplish its purpose. Figure 14–5 shows the main categories of functions performed by a system. *Input functions* get data from outside the system so that the data can be processed in the system. *Output functions* make the results of processing available outside the system. *Storage functions* maintain data in the system so that it is available for processing. *Processing functions* manipulate data within the system.

Input Functions

Before data can be brought into an information system it must be acquired from its source—a step called *data capture*. Often the data is captured by a person who writes the data on a piece of paper or on a form called a **source document**. Once the data is captured, it must be

Figure 14–5 The Functions of an Information System

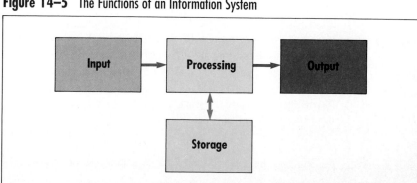

COMPUTER CLOSE-UP
14–1

HIGH-TECH, TRADITION IN CONCERT

The handcrafted Steinway has been the world's piano standard for more than 100 years, according to pianists, music critics, and industry experts. But reputation will not be enough to keep Steinway & Sons, founded by German immigrant Henry Engelhard Steinway in 1853, fine-tuned in the 1990s.

A souring marketplace spurred Steinway's move toward computer technology, said Robert Birmingham, whose Waltham, Massachusetts–based Steinway Musical Properties bought the company from CBS in 1985.

"When the market starts to turn off a little, there's got to be a reason for it," Birmingham said. One such reason, he noted, was inconsistency in quality, a symptom of an antiquated manufacturing process.

Birmingham's remedy has been to "add a little more science to the art of piano making." His continuing goal for Steinway is to harmoniously mesh today's computer-aided manufacturing and research and development techniques with the old-world methods that literally built the company's reputation.

For this tricky task, he has tapped Daniel T. Koenig, a 21-year veteran of General Electric Company and an author and lecturer on computer-integrated manufacturing (CIM).

Koenig, Steinway's director of manufacturing, initiated a ten-step CIM effort and, as the company's self-proclaimed "chief cheerleader," has overseen the development of computer-aided design (CAD) and R&D in acoustics.

After months of seminars and study of the factory's manufacturing flow and production needs, Steinway's "CIM council" of department managers interviewed vendors for an appropriate manufacturing resource planning (MRP II) package. "The MRP system will give us better control of material movement throughout the factory," Koenig said. This is a simple but vital goal for Steinway, which has to coordinate the location of approximately 12,000 different parts—from inch-long pieces of rosewood to 340-pound plates of cast iron—for each of 10 pianos it makes per day across a four-floor, 400,000 square-foot factory.

Steinway is also applying computer technology to its chief selling point—the piano's sound. Koenig's engineering staff has appropriated semiretired virtuoso Vladimir Horowitz's Steinway concert grand—which many experts claim is the best-sounding piano ever made—and wired it up to an HP Dynamic Signal Analyzer.

With electrode-like attachments to piano parts, the machine analyzes sound vibrations and generates printed plots. These are being compared with ones from more "ordinary" pianos in hopes of finding clues to inconsistency in sound quality. Discoveries like this are essential because, Koenig says, "We can't make improvements until we understand the actions."

Such high-tech methods for understanding what old-world artisans intrinsically produced is ironic. But the new blood at the company has high regard for the century-old Steinway traditions that echo in the corners of the dusty, airplane hangar–like expanse of the factory.

For example, the knowledge contained in 6000 original piano design drawings—many dating back to the 19th century—are being painstakingly preserved. Draftsmen are copying these diagrams into a CAD system so that the originals, yellowed and brittle with age, can be displayed as historic artifacts.

Koenig is taking steps to preserve the living knowledge base as well. With the retirement of veteran craftsmen—some of whom are the last of two or three family generations to work at Steinway—the company risks losing lifetimes of accumulated expertise. To guard against this, Koenig is looking into the use of expert systems to "debrief" these human resources.

With such computer-assisted programs implemented and on the way, Steinway has struck a corporate chord by proving that it is possible for a firm to modernize while still maintaining its soul of venerable tradition.

put into the system—a step called *data entry*. Usually, the data is entered by a person who keys in the data on a keyboard.

The bicycle business's inventory system illustrates data capture and entry. For one part of this system, data about sales of bicycles must be captured and entered into the system. The data capture occurs when a salesperson prepares a sales report, which is a source document indicating that certain items have been sold (Figure 14–6a). This document is then sent to a data entry person, who keys the data into a computer, thus entering the data into the system (Figure 14–6b).

Once data is in a system, someone may want to inquire about the data. A **query** is a request for information from a system. Before a system can respond to a query, the query must be entered into the system. Often, the query is entered directly into a computer by the user.

For the inventory system, a salesperson may need to inquire about the availability of stock for a particular type of bicycle. The person enters the query by typing the item number of the bicycle for which the available inventory is needed (Figure 14–7).

Output Functions

Much output from an information system is in the form of **reports**, which are lists of output data printed on paper or displayed on a screen. Several types of reports are commonly produced by an information system. A **detail report** lists detailed information about the results of processing and may contain totals for some of the data. For example, Figure 14–8a shows a detail report produced by the bicycle business's inventory system that lists the value of the inventory on hand for each

Figure 14–6 Data Capture and Entry

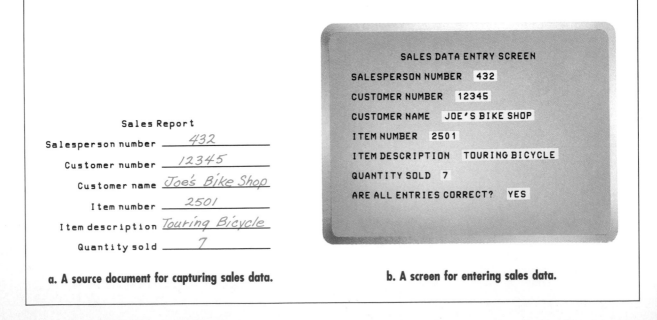

a. A source document for capturing sales data.

b. A screen for entering sales data.

Figure 14–7 Inventory Query Entry

```
STOCK AVAILABILITY QUERY ENTRY SCREEN
ENTER SALESPERSON NUMBER:  432
ENTER ITEM NUMBER:  2501
```

bicycle in stock and gives the total value of all bicycles in stock. A **summary report** contains totals that summarize groups of data but has no detail data. For example, Figure 14–8b shows a summary report that gives the total inventory value for each line of products stocked by the bicycle business. An **exception report** contains data that is an exception to some rule or standard. For example, Figure 14–8c shows a report about bicycles that have a quantity on hand below a certain level and thus should be reordered. Other bicycles with sufficient quantity are not listed in this report.

Reports are prepared by an information system at different times. Some reports are produced periodically and are called **scheduled reports**. For example, a scheduled report may be prepared every month or every week. Other reports are prepared only when requested. These are called **on-demand reports** because someone must request that the report be prepared. A final type of report is one that is prepared only once, for a specific purpose. These are called **ad hoc reports**.

In addition to report output, an information system must provide responses to queries. The response is an output from the system and is usually displayed on a screen, although it may be printed on paper. The response may be just a few lines, or it could be a lengthy report. For example, in the inventory system, a salesperson can enter a query about the available stock for a particular type of bicycle. After determining the stock on hand, the system would respond to the query by displaying the information on the screen (Figure 14–9).

Storage Functions

Data in an information system is stored in files or databases. Before a system can do anything with stored data it must *create* the file or database containing the data, which means it must store initial data. The bicycle business's inventory system must create the inventory file before it can use the stored data. Recall that this file contains one

Figure 14-8 Types of Reports

```
              INVENTORY VALUE REPORT

   ITEM                           INVENTORY
  NUMBER     ITEM DESCRIPTION       VALUE

   1208    RACING BICYCLE         5,137.50
   2501    TOURING BICYCLE        1,472.00
   2905    RECREATIONAL BICYCLE   3,126.25
   3504    MOUNTAIN BIKE          1,132.50
   4360    TRICYCLE               1,648.00
   4389    TANDEM BICYCLE         3,072.00
   5124    JUNIOR BICYCLE              .00
   5908    LEARNER BICYCLE        1,054.00
   6531    PORTABLE BICYCLE         225.00

              TOTAL VALUE        16,867.25
```

a. A detail report

```
   INVENTORY VALUE PER PRODUCT LINE REPORT

   PRODUCT LINE                TOTAL VALUE

    BICYCLES                    16,867.25
    ACCESSORIES                  9,047.78
    CLOTHING                    12,538.60
    PARTS                        8,295.00
    RACKS                        1,587.42

                   TOTAL   48,336.05
```

b. A summary report

```
            INVENTORY RE-ORDER REPORT

   ITEM                           QUANTITY
  NUMBER     ITEM DESCRIPTION     ON HAND

   2501    TOURING BICYCLE           8
   3504    MOUNTAIN BIKE             6
   5124    JUNIOR BICYCLE            0
   6531    PORTABLE BICYCLE          2
```

c. An exception report

record for each type of bicycle in inventory, with fields for the item number, item description, unit cost, unit price, and quantity on hand (see Figure 14–4). To create this file, someone would enter the data for each type of bicycle currently in inventory, and the system would store the data in the inventory file. This file would form the stored data component of the system.

Figure 14-9 A Query Response

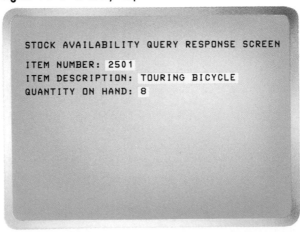

```
STOCK AVAILABILITY QUERY RESPONSE SCREEN

ITEM NUMBER: 2501
ITEM DESCRIPTION: TOURING BICYCLE
QUANTITY ON HAND: 8
```

After the file or database is created, the information system can **access** the stored data, which means that data is retrieved from the file or database. The data that is retrieved is processed to produce a report, to respond to a query, or to create a new file or database. For the inventory system, all records in the inventory file would have to be accessed to produce the Inventory Value Report shown earlier in Figure 14–8a. To respond to a query about the availability of stock for a particular type of bicycle, however, only the record for that item would have to be retrieved.

Sometimes, before a system can access stored data, it must arrange the data in a different way. The process of arranging data into a particular order is called **sorting**. In the inventory system, sorting would be needed if the records in the inventory file were not in the order in which a user wished to see them. For example, he or she may wish the Inventory Value Report to print the bicycles in alphabetical order by their descriptions. If the records were not in this order to begin with, they would have to be sorted into the proper order before preparing the report.

The data put into a file or database when it is created will become out of date over time. **Updating** is the process of bringing the stored data up to date. There are three main updating activities:

1. Existing data can be *changed*.
2. New data can be *added*.
3. Old data can be *deleted*.

In the bicycle business's inventory system, whenever stock is added to or removed from inventory, the quantity on hand for each type of bicycle affected must be changed in the inventory file. If a new type of bicycle— one not currently stocked by the business—is added to the inventory, the item number, name, unit cost, unit price, and quantity on hand for that item must be added to the inventory file. Finally, if an old type of bicycle is dropped from the inventory, all data about that item must be deleted from the file.

Processing Functions

Processing involves manipulating data within the system. In a sense, all the functions already described involve data processing. One function that just involves data processing and does not involve any of the other functions is *computation*, which means doing calculations with data. Before an information system can produce output, the system typically must perform some computations. Input data and stored data are used in the computations to produce the required results that go into the output.

Computation is needed in the bicycle business's inventory system. For example, to produce the total value in the Inventory Value Report, shown earlier in Figure 14–8a, arithmetic computations must be performed with the inventory data.

DATA PROCESSING IN AN INFORMATION SYSTEM

Two basic ways of processing data in an information system are batch processing and interactive processing. In **batch processing**, all the data to be processed is prepared in a form understandable to the computer before the actual processing. Then, the batch of data is processed by the computer, and the resulting output is received in a batch. An example of batch processing is the preparation of the weekly payroll for an organization. At the end of the week, each employee turns in a time sheet. The data from each sheet is keyed into the computer and stored in a payroll file. Once all the data is ready, it is processed in a batch by the payroll program to produce the paychecks.

With **interactive processing**, a person interacts with the computer through a keyboard and screen or other I/O devices at the time the processing is done. Each set of data is entered directly into the computer, where it is processed, and the output is received before the next input data is supplied. Airline reservation processing is an example of this approach. When a customer requests a ticket for a particular flight, the reservation clerk enters the data directly into the computer by using a keyboard. The reservation system checks the data in a flight database and determines if a seat is available on the requested flight. The output goes immediately to the screen so that the customer will know whether the reservation is confirmed (Figure 14–10).

An information system may use batch processing, interactive processing, or, most commonly, both. For example, the bicycle business's inventory system uses both batch and interactive processing. Batch processing is used to prepare the reports. The data in the inventory file is processed

Figure 14–10 An Airline Reservation Screen

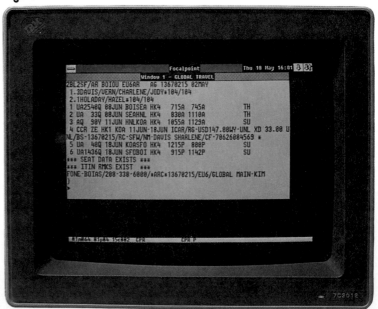

in a batch when each report is printed. Interactive processing is used to determine the response to a salesperson's query about inventory availability. The salesperson interacts with the system when he or she enters the query and receives the response.

Sometimes you hear the terms *on-line* and *off-line* in conjunction with interactive and batch processing. **On-line** means the user is connected to the computer at the time, and **off-line** means the user is not connected. For interactive processing, the user must be on-line so that input can be entered directly into the computer and the output can be received from the computer. Sometimes data for batch processing is prepared off-line with the use of other equipment and then transferred to the computer. For example, data may be keyed onto a disk with the use of special data preparation equipment. Then the data on the disk can be processed in a batch by the computer.

Occasionally, people use the term **real-time processing** instead of *interactive processing. Real-time* means the processing is done immediately after the input is received. This description is not quite accurate for interactive processing. If there are many users of an interactive system, then processing may not begin for some time after the input is received. The amount of time, which can be several seconds to several minutes, depends on how many users there are and the type of computer being used. In real-time processing, a delay is not acceptable. Real-time processing is used when an immediate response is essential. An example is a system that monitors patients in an intensive care unit of a hospital. The system must respond immediately—that is, in real time—to any significant change in a patient's blood pressure, heart rate, and other critical factors. Any delay could result in serious consequences for the patient.

APPLICATIONS OF INFORMATION SYSTEMS

Now that you have an understanding of information system components and functions, you can study applications of information systems in a business. Each use of a computer is a computer application. For example, using a computer to prepare customer bills is a billing application. Within a business, the hardware, software, stored data, personnel, and procedures necessary for an application make up an information system. This system may be separate from other systems or may be part of a more complex information system.

Basic Business Computer Applications

Six basic computer applications used in many businesses are:

- Order entry
- Billing
- Accounts receivable
- Inventory control
- Payroll
- General ledger

Figure 14–11 shows the relationships between these applications. An arrow connects applications in this figure if information flows from one to the other.

Order Entry.   The purpose of the *order entry* application is to accept customer orders for goods or services and to prepare the orders in a form that can be used by the business. This application often is performed by people in the sales department of a business.

In the order entry application, a customer order, which is the input to the application, is received on an order form or over the telephone. The order is entered into the computer, and the inventory file is checked to see if there is sufficient quantity on hand to fill the order. If enough inventory is available, a sales order, which is the output from the application, is prepared (Figure 14–12). This document is sent to the shipping department.

Billing.   The sales order from the order entry application is used by the shipping department to determine what items should be shipped to the customer. As the items are shipped, the shipping department checks them off the sales order and then sends the sales order to the billing department. The billing department uses this copy of the sales order in the *billing* application. The purpose of this application is to prepare the customer's bill, which is called the *invoice*.

The sales order, received from the shipping department, is the input to the billing application. The output is the invoice, which contains information about how much the customer owes for the items ordered (Figure 14–13). To prepare the invoice from the sales order, the billing application looks up the unit price of each item shipped in the inventory file and computes the amount of the purchase by multiplying the quantity shipped by the unit price. This information is printed on the invoice along with the total for all items purchased. A copy of the invoice is sent to the customer, and another copy is sent to the accounts receivable department.

Figure 14–11   Basic Business Computer Applications

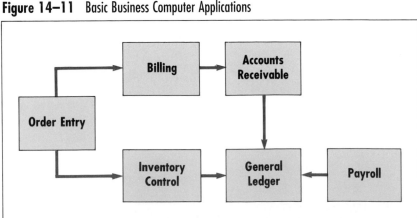

Figure 14–12 A Sales Order

```
                    ACME BICYCLE WHOLESALERS
                         SALES ORDER

   CUSTOMER NUMBER        12345            DATE 11/13/XX
   CUSTOMER NAME          JOE'S BIKE SHOP
   SHIPPING ADDRESS       123 MAIN STREET
                          PORTLAND, OR 97208
```

ITEM NUMBER	ITEM DESCRIPTION	QUANTITY ORDERED
2501	TOURING BICYCLE	7
3504	MOUNTAIN BIKE	14
5124	JUNIOR BICYCLE	12
6531	PORTABLE BICYCLE	3

Accounts Receivable.   The copy of the invoice received by the accounts receivable department is used in the *accounts receivable* application. The purpose of this application is to keep track of money owed to the business by its customers (called *accounts receivable* in accounting terminology) and to record customer payments for invoices.

The inputs to the accounts receivable application are the copy of the invoice received from the billing department and the customer payment. The inputs are entered into the system and are used to produce a statement for each customer that summarizes the invoice charges and payments made recently and gives the current balance due (Figure 14–14). The statement is prepared once a month and sent to the customer.

Figure 14–13 An Invoice

ACME BICYCLE WHOLESALERS

INVOICE

```
SOLD TO                              CUSTOMER NUMBER
   JOE'S BIKE SHOP                         12345
   P.O. BOX 876
   PORTLAND, OR 97208                DATE
                                        11/20/XX
```

ITEM NUMBER	ITEM DESCRIPTION	QUANTITY SHIPPED	UNIT PRICE	AMOUNT
2501	TOURING BICYCLE	7	184.00	1,288.00
3504	MOUNTAIN BIKE	14	188.75	2,642.50
5124	JUNIOR BICYCLE	12	69.75	837.00
6531	PORTABLE BICYCLE	3	112.50	337.50
			TOTAL	5,105.00

Figure 14–14 A Customer Statement

```
                    ACME BICYCLE WHOLESALERS

                           STATEMENT

CUSTOMER NAME                                    CUSTOMER NUMBER
    JOE'S BIKE SHOP                                    12345
    P.O. BOX 876                                  DATE
    PORTLAND, OR 97208                                11/30/XX


            ┌──────────┬──────────────────┬─────────────┐
            │   DATE   │   DESCRIPTION    │   AMOUNT    │
            ├──────────┼──────────────────┼─────────────┤
            │          │ PREVIOUS BALANCE │   4,291.75  │
            │ 11/05/XX │ INVOICE          │   1,273.50  │
            │ 11/07/XX │ PAYMENT          │   4,291.75- │
            │ 11/20/XX │ INVOICE          │   5,105.00  │
            │          │                  │             │
            │          │                  │             │
            │          ├──────────────────┼─────────────┤
            │          │ CURRENT BALANCE  │   6,378.50  │
            └──────────┴──────────────────┴─────────────┘
```

Another output is an accounts receivable report summarizing charges and payments for the month, which is sent to the general accounting department.

Inventory Control. The purpose of the *inventory control* application is to keep track of the business's inventory. The bicycle business's inventory system that was used to illustrate information system concepts in the first part of this chapter is an inventory control application. This application is performed by the inventory control department.

The inputs to the inventory control application are the sales order from the shipping department, giving the quantity of items shipped, and the receiving notice from the receiving department, giving the quantity of items received from vendors or other sources. These inputs are used to update the quantity on hand in the inventory file. The outputs from the application include the inventory reorder report, which lists the items that should be reordered, and the inventory value report, which gives the value of the items in stock. The first report is sent to the purchasing department so that the necessary items can be purchased; the second report is sent to the general accounting department.

Payroll. The purpose of the *payroll* application is to prepare paychecks for employees and to provide reports of payroll for the business. This application is performed by the payroll department.

The inputs to the payroll application are employee time sheets that show how many hours each employee has worked each day. The employee time sheets are used in calculating the pay for each employee. Then the paychecks are printed, which is one output from the application. Another output is the payroll report, which lists for each employee the gross earnings (the amount earned by the employee), the amount deducted for taxes and for other reasons, and the net pay. This report is sent to the general accounting department.

General Ledger.   The last basic business computer application that will be discussed is *general ledger*. This application is central to all businesses. The purpose of the general ledger application is to prepare the business's financial statements, which are reports that summarize information about the financial status of the business. The general ledger application is performed by the general accounting department.

The inputs to the general ledger application are reports on the financial affairs of the business from other applications. For example, the accounts receivable report provides information about accounts receivable. The inventory value report gives the total value of the inventory. The payroll report gives payroll expense information.

The outputs from the general ledger application are financial statements; the two most common are the profit and loss statement and the balance sheet (Figure 14–15). To produce the financial statements, the general ledger application first records financial data from other applications. It then prepares the financial statements from this data.

Other Business Computer Applications

The six computer applications discussed in the last section are basic ones found in many businesses. Other applications, however, are used.

Applications in Accounting.   In accounting, which is responsible for recording and reporting financial information about the business, the basic applications are accounts receivable, payroll, and general ledger. Several other common computer applications in accounting are:

- Accounts payable. The purpose of this application is to pay for items purchased by the business.

- Fixed asset accounting. The purpose of this application is to account for business assets such as buildings, land, and equipment.

- Budgeting. This application prepares projections of revenues and expenses, and compares actual figures with the projected ones.

- Tax accounting. The purpose of this application is to prepare business tax reports and to pay taxes.

Applications in Finance.   None of the applications discussed earlier fall directly into the finance area, which is responsible for planning the use of money in a business. Some common computer applications in finance are:

- Cash management. This application balances the needs of the business for cash with the expected cash availability.

- Capital expenditure analysis. The purpose of this application is to analyze the effect on the business of large expenditures such as those associated with building a new factory or replacing major equipment.

Figure 14–15 Financial Statements

```
              ACME BICYCLE WHOLESALERS
        Profit and Loss Statement, November 30, 19XX

Revenue:
  Sales                                          $76,468

Expenses:
  Cost of goods sold             $48,231
  Salaries                        10,305
  Rent                             3,250
  Advertising                      1,140
  Delivery expense                 3,528
  Supplies                           519
  Depreciation                     1,350
      Total expenses                             $68,323

Net income:                                       $8,145
                                                 =======
```

```
              ACME BICYCLE WHOLESALERS
            Balance Sheet, November 30, 19XX

Assets:
  Cash                           $16,219
  Accounts receivable             12,436
  Inventory                       45,352
  Equipment                        6,750
      Total assets                               $80,757

Liabilities:
  Loans payable                  $31,500
  Accounts payable                24,216
      Total liabilities                          $55,716

Owner's equity:                                  $25,041

Total liabilities & owner's equity               $80,757
                                                 =======
```

- Portfolio management. This application analyzes alternative investment strategies for the business's cash and keeps track of investments.

- Credit analysis. Businesses that extend credit to customers need to determine which customers should receive credit, which is the purpose of this application.

COMPUTER CLOSE-UP

14–2

OUTSTANDING INFORMATION SYSTEMS

Each year, *Computerworld*, a highly regarded publication in the computer field, gives awards for outstanding examples of information systems. Called the Smithsonian Awards, the nominees are judged on their positive impact on society, their success in meeting their goals, and the technological innovation they demonstrate. Here are three winners of recent Smithsonian Awards.

Environment, Energy, and Agriculture

When thousands of gallons of oil spilled into Pennsylvania's Monongahela and Ohio Rivers in 1989, the Emergency Information System was there. When Hurricane Hugo barreled into the Puerto Rican coastline, the Emergency Information System was there. When Jamaicans began rebuilding their lives after the fury of Hurricane Gilbert, the Emergency Information System was there.

Since 1983, emergency workers in these disasters—and hundreds more—have used Research Alternatives, Inc.'s personal computer-based Emergency Information System software to plan, coordinate and track evacuation and relief efforts.

Research Alternatives President James W. Morentz, holder of a Ph.D. in crisis management, founded the Rockville, Maryland–based firm on the idea that information is the critical component in saving lives and protecting the environment during disaster. By combining geographic and demographic data with sophisticated computer modeling of the effects of a disaster, the Emergency Information System acts as the command-and-control center for emergency efforts.

The software is used by more than 100 major chemical and petrochemical companies to do emergency and evacuation planning. Johnson & Johnson has installed the product at most of its manufacturing plants in New Jersey and is in the process of bringing it to Europe.

"We use Emergency Information System for. . . vulnerability assessment, emergency training and as an important tool in a potential emergency," says Lawrence Mondschein, Johnson & Johnson's manager of chemical information and control.

Although a small company with 30 employees, Research Alternatives now boasts more then 1000 installations of Emergency Information Systems in the U.S. and 13 other countries.

Manufacturing

As the first of Raychem Corp.'s manufacturing plants to adopt plantwide computer-integrated manufacturing (CIM), Raychem Advanter has become a showcase for paperless, automated production systems.

Managers at the Richmond, British Columbia, facility have been able to carve out a market niche filling small, custom part orders. Advanter makes and assembles special aluminum adapters used in wiring harnesses. The adapters attach connecting devices to the harness, sealing against moisture, contaminants and interference from electromagnetic or radio frequencies.

Raychem Advanter enables customers to purchase in lot sizes as small as 15 units, instead of hundreds or thousands, says Jim Balcom, a manufacturing consultant at Coopers & Lybrand in Vancouver, British Columbia. Furthermore, lead time is weeks, not months.

The plant hardware consists of 14 workstations that run computer-aided design (CAD) machining and intelligent documentation systems. With these components, Advanter's different manufacturing systems, databases and applications packages interoperate without paper.

For example, an order is faxed and received by a workstation, triggering the CAD system for the job part and quantity. That begins the computer-aided manufacturing (CAM) sequence, which moves the job into a CAM file and then releases it to the shop floor. The order appears in an intelligent documentation form at the tool presetting station, where a technician schedules the task.

Transportation

After Gaylord Evans started using United Parcel Service, Inc.'s international delivery instead of air freight, he never looked back. His company, MCM Distributors, Inc. in Costa Mesa, California, sells miniature car kits made in Europe. By using UPS, he shaved 6% off shipping costs and cut delivery time from 10 days to two.

UPS would credit Evans' satisfaction to its International Shipment Processing System (ISPS), which automates all facets of international package transport and delivery. The system enabled UPS to expand to 180 countries in three years, reports Steven Heit, information services planning manager.

ISPS is built around an IBM mainframe database for on-line transactions and batch processing that is linked to remote personal computers, local-area networks and barcode scanners.

By automating accounting, scheduling and tracking functions and streamlining customs and brokerage tasks, the system lets UPS offer cost-effective, fast international delivery—usually within 48 hours, Heit says. ISPS stores data on customer shipping patterns, automatically generates required forms and schedules optimal use of aircraft.

For exporters and importers, ISPS automates billing, tariff classification and tax and duty calculations.

In addition, customs processing is expedited by two ISPS features: a prealert notification system, which gives agents detailed shipping information before a package arrives, and electronic data interchange, which allows customs agents to enter data directly into government systems.

Applications in Marketing.   In marketing, which is concerned with selling the goods and services of the business, the applications discussed previously are order entry and billing. Other common computer applications in marketing are:

- Sales analysis. This application determines which products are selling well and which are selling poorly, which sales regions have the best and worst sales, which salespeople are selling the most and the least, and so forth.
- Sales forecasting. The purpose of this application is to project sales in the future.
- Direct mail advertising. This application prepares advertising pieces to be mailed directly to potential customers.

Applications in Manufacturing.   Inventory control is the application discussed earlier in manufacturing (also called production), which is responsible for producing the goods that the business sells. Some other common computer applications in manufacturing are:

- Purchasing. The purpose of this application is to purchase items needed by the business.
- Production scheduling. This application schedules the use of manufacturing facilities to produce products most efficiently.
- Material requirements planning (MRP). The purpose of this application is to determine what parts and materials will be needed during the manufacturing process and when they will be needed.

Figure 14–16 A Computer-Controlled Robot

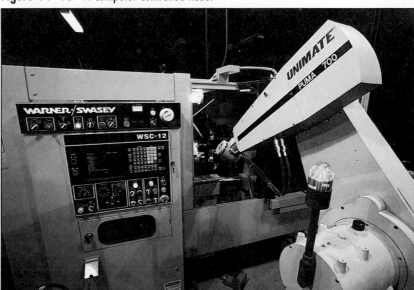

Figure 14–17 Computer-Aided Design

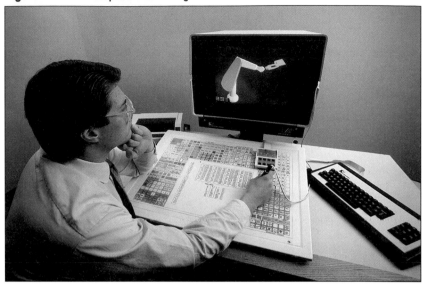

- Just-in-time (JIT) inventory management. This application is a form of inventory control in which parts and materials are scheduled to arrive from suppliers just before they are needed for the manufacturing process.
- Robotics. This application involves using computer-controlled robots in the manufacturing process (Figure 14–16).
- Computer-aided design/computer-aided manufacturing (CAD/CAM). This application involves using computers to help in the design and manufacturing of products (Figure 14–17).
- Computer-integrated manufacturing (CIM). This application combines many of the other manufacturing applications into a single system.

Chapter Summary

- An **information system** is a collection of components that work together to process data and provide information within an organization. Data is raw facts, figures, numbers, and words. **Information** is data that is meaningful or useful to someone.
- The components of an information system are hardware, which is the computer equipment used in the system; software, which are the programs in the system; stored data, which is the files and databases needed by the programs; personnel, which are the people, including the user, who make the system run; and procedures, which are the instructions that tell the people what to do.

- There are four categories of functions of an information system: input, output, storage, and processing. Input functions include capturing data on a **source document** and entering the data into the system. The entry of a **query** (request for information) is also an input function. Output functions include producing **reports** and providing responses to queries. Storage functions include creating files and databases containing stored data, **accessing** stored data, **sorting** stored data, and **updating** stored data. Processing functions involve the manipulation of data, including computation.

- Two ways of processing data in an information system are **batch processing**, in which all data to be processed is brought together and processed in a group; and **interactive processing**, in which a person interacts with the computer at the time the data is processed.

- Several basic business computer applications and their purposes are:

  Order entry: to prepare the customers' orders for goods and services in a form that can be used by the business.

  Billing: to prepare the customers' invoices, which are bills for orders.

  Accounts receivable: to keep track of money owed the business by its customers and to record customer payments.

  Inventory control: to keep track of the business's inventory, which is the stock of goods the business has on hand.

  Payroll: to prepare paychecks for employees and to provide payroll reports for the business.

  General ledger: to prepare the business's financial statements.

Terms to Remember

Accessing p. 365

Ad Hoc Report p. 363

Batch Processing p. 366

Computer Information System (CIS) p. 353

Detail Report p. 362

Exception Report p. 363

Information p. 355

Information System p. 353

Interactive Processing p. 366

Off-line p. 367

On-demand Report p. 363

On-line p. 367

Query p. 362

Real-Time Processing p. 367

Report p. 362

Scheduled Report p. 363

Sorting p. 365

Source Document p. 359

Summary Report p. 363

System p. 353

Updating p. 365

Review Questions

Fill-In Questions

1. An information system that uses a computer is sometimes called a(n) _____.

2. Software are instructions for the hardware in an information system; _____ are instructions for the people in a system.

3. A form used to capture data is called a(n) _____.

4. Two steps that must be performed to get data into an information system are _____ and _____.

5. A(n) _____ is a request for information from an information system.

6. A report that lists totals for groups of data but has no detail data is called a(n) _____.

7. A report that is prepared only once for a specific purpose is called a(n) _____.

8. The process of arranging data into a particular order is called _____.

9. A user who is entering data into a computer is said to be _____, whereas a user who is preparing data with data preparation equipment for later transfer to a computer is said to be _____.

10. A form of processing in which the processing is done immediately after the input is received is called _____.

Short-Answer Questions

1. What is an information system?

2. Explain the difference between data and information.

3. List the components of an information system.

4. What are the main categories of functions performed by an information system?

5. Explain the difference between batch processing and interactive processing.

6. What is the input to the order entry application?

7. What is the output from the billing application?

8. What is the purpose of the accounts receivable application?

9. What updating is done in the inventory control application?

10. What computation is done in the payroll application?

11. State the purpose of the general ledger application.

12. List one application each in accounting, finance, marketing, and manufacturing.

Projects

1. Investigate an information system in an organization or business to which you have access. Find out as much as you can about the components and functions of the system. Write a summary of your findings.

2. Find three computer applications not listed in the chapter. Write a brief description of each application, explaining its purpose and listing its input, output, processing, and data storage requirements.

15

TYPES OF INFORMATION SYSTEMS

CHAPTER OBJECTIVES

- After completing this chapter you should be able to:

1. Describe several types of information systems based on how the functions of the systems are organized.

2. Explain the purpose of a transaction processing system.

3. Describe how the information needs of managers are met by a management information system.

4. Describe decision support systems.

5. Explain how an expert system can provide expert advice.

6. Describe office automation systems.

7. Explain the purpose of executive support systems.

T HE LAST CHAPTER discussed basic concepts about information systems. It explained what an information system is and does. But not all information systems are the same; there are several types. This chapter outlines the main types of information systems.

ORGANIZING THE FUNCTIONS OF AN INFORMATION SYSTEM

Information systems vary in terms of where the functions of the systems are performed. As you know, the information system functions are input, output, storage, and processing. These functions may be performed at one location or at several locations. This section describes the main features of four types of information systems based on how the functions of the system are organized.

Centralized Systems

The first information systems were **centralized systems**, which means that all processing, storage, input, and output are done at a single, central location, usually using a mainframe computer (Figure 15–1). The earliest systems used batch processing, but as technology developed, interactive processing became common. Centralized systems typically involve applications that have an effect on several areas within the organization. An example of a centralized system is payroll, in which all paychecks are prepared by a central computer.

Figure 15–1 Centralized Systems

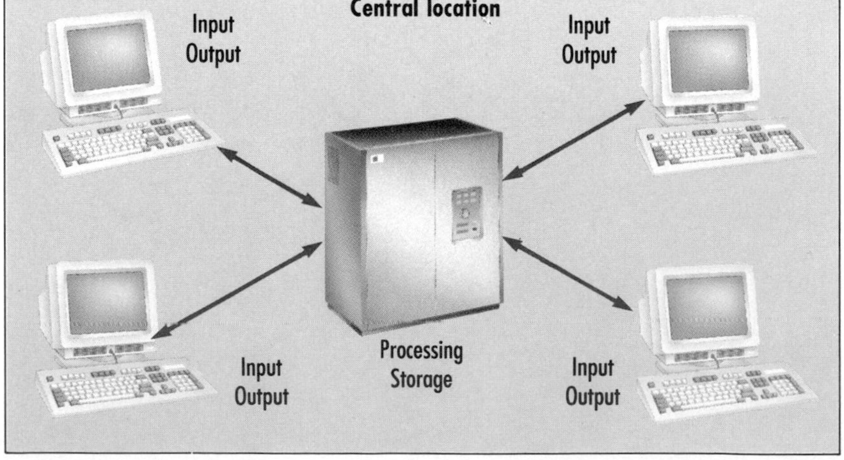

The advantages of centralized systems are economy and control. One large, central computer for all processing is usually the most economical in terms of computer hardware. In addition, with all system functions performed at one location, the computer staff has the most control over what is done and when. The disadvantage of this approach is lack of response to the users. Output may take a long time to be returned to the users. In addition, users must deal with a large, central computer staff when requesting new systems and changes in existing systems, which can be frustrating. Still, many information systems today are centralized.

Teleprocessing Systems

With centralized systems all input data must be sent from the user's location to the central computer location, and all output must be sent back to the user's location. In early systems data was carried manually from one location to another. With the development of data communications it became possible to transmit input and output data electronically between the user's location and the central location. Systems that use this approach are called **teleprocessing systems** (Figure 15–2). The processing and storage functions are still centralized, usually with the use of a mainframe computer; the input and output functions, however, are performed at the users' locations with the use of terminals. Data can be sent to and from the user's location in batches or interactively using data communications. As with centralized systems, teleprocessing systems are usually used for applications that affect a large part of the organization. An example of a teleprocessing system is airline reservation processing, in which a central computer keeps all airline data, but reservation data input and output occurs at terminals located throughout the country.

The advantage of teleprocessing systems is quicker input and output response for the user. Generally, users can send in their input and get

Figure 15–2   Teleprocessing Systems

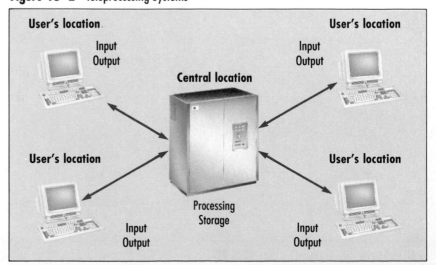

their output back in a short period of time—sometimes almost instantaneously. Still, the user has to deal with a central computer staff to request new or modified systems. Today, many information systems use the teleprocessing approach.

Decentralized Systems

One of the principal disadvantages of centralized and teleprocessing systems is a lack of response to the user's needs for new and modified systems. To overcome this disadvantage, many information systems are **decentralized systems**. In this approach, each department or group of users in the organization uses its own computer to do all processing, storage, input, and output for its applications (Figure 15–3). Furthermore, these separate computers cannot communicate with one another. Thus, the accounting department has a computer that is used for accounting applications, the marketing department has one for marketing applications, and so on, with no communication bctwccn thc departmental computèrs. Usually, minicomputers and microcomputers are used for the applications. There may also be a central minicomputer or mainframe computer used for company-wide applications.

Figure 15–3   Decentralized Systems

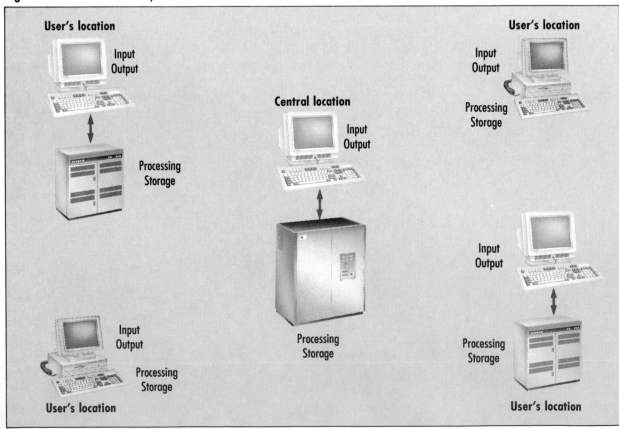

The advantage of decentralization is better response to the user's needs. Because each group of users has a computer for its applications, the users are more likely to get new systems that meet their needs and quicker changes to existing systems. There are several disadvantages to this approach, however. One is hardware cost. Several smaller computers usually cost more than one large computer that is capable of doing all processing. Another disadvantage is lack of control. Each group is responsible for controlling the use of its computer. If the users do not follow appropriate procedures, the system may not perform as desired. Finally, there is often incompatibility between systems in a decentralized approach. One consequence of this is that data from one system may not be transferable to another.

The ultimate form of decentralization is when each user has a personal computer on his or her desk. Then, each user is responsible for input, output, storage, and processing for one or more information systems. If standard procedures for how these systems are to function are not created and enforced, this situation can result in a great deal of incompatibility between systems. Some organizations have set up **information centers** to deal with this problem. An information center consists of computer professionals who establish hardware, software, data, and procedure standards for personal computers in the organization. The center trains users, sets up hardware and software, and provides other assistance to assure that the use of personal computers is in the best interest of the organization.

Distributed Systems

The three approaches for organizing information systems described so far are used for many types of information systems. Some systems, however, need capabilities that are not available in one of these approaches. For these systems, the **distributed systems** approach is used.

Distributed systems are similar to decentralized systems in which each user or group of users has its own computer for processing, storage, input, and output. The computers, however, can communicate with one another because they are linked using data communications to form a network (Figure 15–4). (Networks were discussed in Chapter 6.) The network may be a local area network, contained entirely within a building or group of buildings, or it may be a wide-area network covering a large geographical area. Included in the network may be a centrally located mainframe computer, departmental minicomputers, and personal computers.

With distributed systems, data can be sent from one computer to another by means of data communications. Thus, if one computer needs input data or stored data from another computer, the data can be transferred between the computers. In addition, if a computer does not have the necessary capabilities for a particular processing task, it can send data to another computer where the processing can be done and then the output can be sent back. Thus, with a distributed system, input, output, or stored data at any location can be transferred to any other location. In addition, processing can be done at any location.

Figure 15–4   Distributed Systems

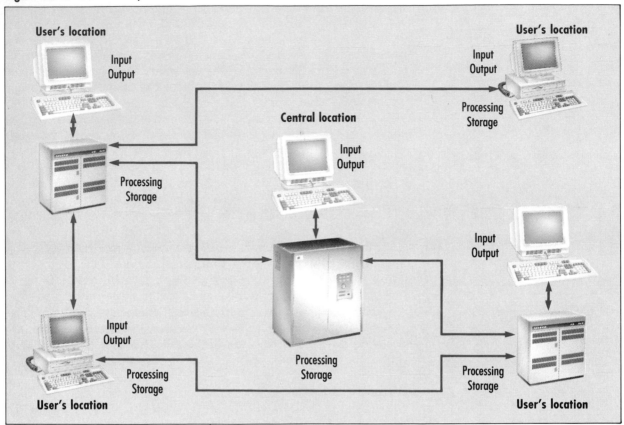

Often, the term **cooperative processing** is heard in conjunction with distributed systems. This means that two or more computers in a network cooperate in performing the functions of an information system. Usually, one computer performs some of the functions and another computer performs other functions. Thus, a microcomputer performing input, output, and processing functions may cooperate with another computer performing data storage functions.

There are several advantages to distributed systems. First, they provide the same response to users' needs as do decentralized systems but with more capabilities. Because system functions can be performed on other computers in the network, the functions are not limited to those of the user's computer. Another advantage is more control because to use the distributed system, the user must follow standard procedures. Finally, there is greater compatibility in distributed systems. For example, to transfer data in a network, the data must be compatible with other computers.

The main disadvantage of distributed systems is their complexity. These systems often involve many computers and a sophisticated network. Hardware must be connected in a network; programs must be developed that function in the network; data must be organized so it is

THE UNITED SYSTEMS OF BENETTON

It's been 25 years since Giuliana and Luciano Benetton sold their first sweater on a street in Northern Italy. Since then, the siblings' clothing franchise company has become a global organization whose retail reach has expanded to more than 5000 shops in 80 countries and whose fashions have graced the likes of Princess Diana and Princess Caroline of Monaco.

While many in the retail industry are struggling, Benetton Group S.p.A.—with the help of networking and electronic data interchange (EDI) technology—has translated its colorful sweaters, shirts and jeans into more than a billion dollars in sales.

Integrating a company of such international scope has taken the efforts of a 100-member information systems (IS) staff and networks that let retail clients worldwide exchange information with Benetton as if they were located on the next strada.

The IS heart of Benetton is located in Ponzano Veneto, a small Italian town just outside of Venice. It is from here than Bruno Zuccaro, the company's 49-year-old IS director, has overseen the organization's IS operations since 1985.

Benetton's international EDI network is one of its key operations. Supplied by General Electric Information Services (GEIS), the network replaced a leased-line setup in 1987 and has since become the IS nexus of Benetton's commercial business, according to Zuccaro. "We were no longer slaves to the old network with its constraints on timing and applications availability," he says.

The GEIS network is at the core of Benetton's ordering cycle, which is initiated by "agents"—Benetton's term for the independent business clients in 73 worldwide locations who act as intermediaries between the Benetton Group and retailers. Working on commission, these agents set up franchises, show twice-yearly collections to retailers and place orders for merchandise with Benetton through the GEIS network.

Interaction between the human and technology networks keeps the highly decentralized Benetton structure together. As a franchiser, Benetton Group has little direct communication with the retail stores, owning only 1% of them. Although the independently owned shops must follow strict marketing, pricing and brand exclusivity guidelines, Benetton cannot legally mandate computer systems use at the retail level, and the majority of shops have no in-store information systems, Zuccaro says.

As a result, Zuccaro relies on agents using the network to bridge the gap between the franchiser's need for information and the franchisee's desire for autonomy.

To order merchandise for his retail clients, an agent dials up the GEIS network from a workstation and places his order using software developed by Benetton. The order handling system collects the orders and routes them to the appropriate factory. It then updates the agent's order portfolio and price lists, Zuccaro says. The system also handles electronic interchange of mail, reports and files between the corporation and agents and among the agents themselves.

"In the past, we used to have to send handwritten orders, which were at the mercy of time and human error," says Francesca Bertelli, the marketing and sales manager for

Manhattan-area stores and assistant to that area's agent. She says the efficiency and fast turnaround of the network are crucial to getting orders right and to the retailers on time.

The data generated in the ordering process enables the Benetton Group to forecast the total number of orders early in the production cycle, Zuccaro says, so it can make faster purchasing decisions on raw material and set up a production schedule.

More importantly, this system allows Benetton to keep inventory low and manufacture only what the franchises are paying for, he explains.

Furthermore, database access to Benetton's corporate IBM mainframe through the network enables agents to track orders by customer and item as well as to find out what is in production, in the warehouse or being distributed. Agents can also track customer credit, which allows them to restrict deliveries to those outlets that have exceeded their credit limits, Zuccaro says.

By analyzing data from point-of-sale (POS) systems installed in a number of Benetton-owned shops in Italy, the company knows what's hot and what's not, Zuccaro says. These shops, located mostly in upscale resort towns, receive merchandise earlier than the rest of Benetton's stores and keep tabs on bar-coded merchandise bought by their fashion-conscious customers.

Based on style, color and size data, the firm notifies its agents of popular items and readies operations to handle the late orders. "Agents can place an order that can be turned around in 11 to 15 days," Zuccaro says.

compatible with the network; procedures must be devised to ensure proper use of the network; users must be trained in the use of the network. Developing a distributed system and ensuring that it works properly is a difficult task.

TRANSACTION PROCESSING SYSTEMS

Many of the computer applications discussed in Chapter 14 form basic information systems called **transaction processing systems** (**TPS**). This type of system processes data about **transactions**, which are events that have occurred that affect the organization or business, such as the sale or purchase of goods. For example, an inventory control application forms an information system that processes data about transactions that affect a business's inventory. These transactions are shipments of inventory due to a sale, and receipt of inventory because of a purchase.

The general purpose of a transaction processing system is threefold: (1) to keep records about the organization; (2) to process data about transactions that affect these records; and (3) to produce outputs that report on transactions that have occurred, that report on the state of the organization, and that cause other transactions to occur. An inventory control system keeps a file of records about the stock of goods that a business has on hand—the inventory—which is one aspect of the state of the business. When items are shipped or received, the state of the business is affected and the inventory control system makes changes in the stored records about the inventory. Periodically, the system prints a report of what shipments and receipts—that is, what transactions—have occurred. It also prints a report giving the quantity on hand for each item in inventory, which is a characteristic of the state of the business. In addition, the system may produce output that causes more inventory to be ordered, which is another type of business transaction.

Figure 15–5 shows the general structure of a transaction processing system. Users of the system typically are clerical personnel. Input, which includes records of transactions, comes from users and other transaction processing systems. Output, which includes reports, goes to users and to other systems. The transaction processing system files store data about the state of the organization. A database could be used instead of files to store the data. The transaction processing system

Figure 15–5 The Structure of Transaction Processing Systems (TPS)

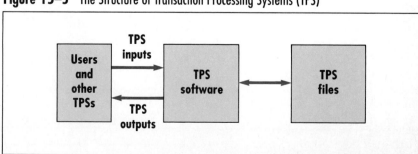

software is application software that accepts the input data about transactions, processes it, updates the files, and produces the outputs.

Transaction processing systems exist in all areas of an organization. Examples include systems for order entry, billing, accounts receivable, and other business computer applications discussed in Chapter 14. In addition, many other transaction processing systems exist. For example, a system in a bank for keeping track of customer deposits and withdrawals is a transaction processing system. These systems are the ones used for the daily data processing of the organization. As you will see, they form the basis for other information systems.

MANAGEMENT INFORMATION SYSTEMS

A **management information system** (**MIS**) is a type of information system that provides information to help in the management of an organization. To understand what an MIS does, you first need to know a little about management decisions and information needs in an organization.

Management Decisions

The main activity of managers in an organization or business is making decisions. For example, a manager in a bicycle business may make the decision to increase the stock of a particular bicycle model. This decision will have an effect on the business because people will have to perform various tasks to order the bicycles, the business's money will have to be spent to buy the bicycles, and equipment will be needed to move the new stock when it arrives.

Decisions are made at several levels in an organization. Figure 15–6 shows the hierarchy of organizational decisions. Starting at the bottom,

Figure 15–6 The Hierarchy of Management Decisions

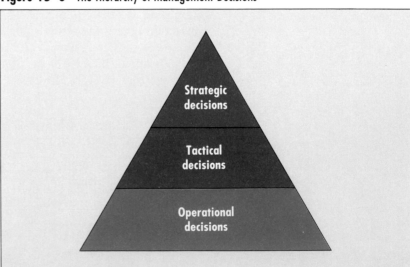

operational decisions are day-to-day decisions needed in the operation of the organization. These decisions affect the organization for a short period of time such as several days or weeks. For example, in a bicycle business, an operational decision is whether to order more racing bicycles today. This decision affects the business for the next few weeks. Operational decisions are made by low-level managers.

On the next level of decisions are *tactical decisions*, which are those that involve implementing policies of the organization. They affect the organization for a longer period of time than operational decisions, usually for several months or years. For example, deciding whether to sell racing bicycles at all is a tactical decision; it has an effect on the organization for a long period of time.

At the highest level of decisions are *strategic decisions*, which are made by top-level managers. These decisions involve setting organization policies, goals, and long-term plans. They affect the organization for many years. For example, a strategic decision is whether the business should sell bicycles at all or should sell some other product. This decision has a long-term effect on the business.

Management Information Needs

When a decision is made, there is uncertainty about what will happen—that is, what the outcome will be. To reduce the uncertainty, a manager needs information. The more information of a relevant nature that the manager has, the more certain the outcome will be.

The information needs are different for different levels of decision making. Figure 15–7 summarizes two characteristics of information needed in management. The first characteristic is the source of information, which means where the information comes from. Most information for operational decisions comes from inside the organization, whereas most information for strategic decisions comes from outside the business. Information for tactical decisions comes from both inside and outside the organization. Thus, to decide whether to order more racing bicycles today (an operational decision), a manager in a bicycle business needs to know the current quantity on hand, which comes from inside the business. To decide whether to stop selling racing bicycles (a tactical decision), the manager needs to know how the business's racing bicycles are selling, which comes from inside the business, and consumer interest in racing bicycles, which comes from outside the business. Finally, to decide whether to stop selling bicycles altogether (a strategic decision), the manager needs to know general trends in bicycle sales compared to sales of other products, which is information that comes from outside the business.

The second characteristic of information needed in management is the degree of detail required in the information. Operational decisions require detailed information, tactical decisions require less detailed and more summarized information, and strategic decisions need summarized information. Thus, to make the operational decision of whether to order racing bicycles today, a manager in a bicycle business may need to know how many racing bicycles were sold yesterday, which is very

Figure 15–7 Characteristics of Information for Management Decisions

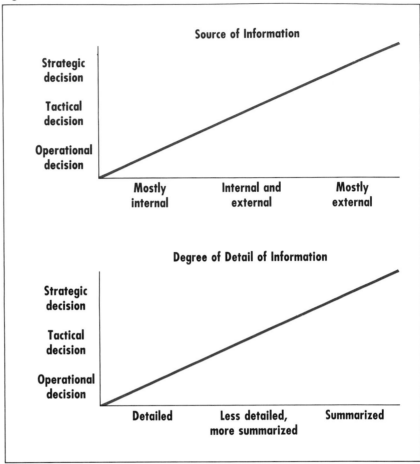

detailed information. To make the tactical decision to stop selling racing bicycles, the manager may need to know the total sales of racing bicycles for each month of the past two years, which is less detailed and more summarized information than daily sales. Finally, to make the strategic decision of whether to stop selling bicycles altogether, the manager may need to know the total sales of all bicycles for each of the past five years, which is summarized information.

Management Information System Structure

With this background on management decisions and information needs, you can understand the structure of a management information system. An MIS provides information to help managers make decisions at each of the three levels of decision making. The information is derived from a database that is maintained by the MIS software. Note that an MIS *helps* the manager make decisions but does not make the decision for the manager.

Figure 15–8 shows the general structure of management information systems and their relationship to transaction processing systems. The users of the MIS are managers at each of the three levels of decision making. The users request information from the system. The information is returned in the form of query responses and reports. The MIS database contains data that is processed to provide the information to the managers. The MIS software consists of application software to manipulate the data in the database. The software accepts requests for information from the managers, accesses data in the database, processes the data, and produces output. The software also updates the data in the database as needed.

The data in the database comes from both inside and outside the organization. Some internal data may be entered by managers, but most comes directly from transaction processing system files, as shown in Figure 15–8. For example, assume that a business has a transaction processing system for inventory control. This system keeps track of the quantity on hand for each item in inventory in an inventory master file. Each day the quantity data in this file is passed to the MIS database. Then, the MIS software uses the data to help make the operational decisions of whether to order more inventory that day. Data at lower levels in the MIS database is passed up through the database where it is summarized for higher-level decisions. Thus, daily inventory quantities used for operational decisions are summarized to get weekly and monthly figures for tactical decisions and summarized again to get yearly figures for strategic decisions.

Figure 15–8   The Structure of Management Information Systems (MIS)

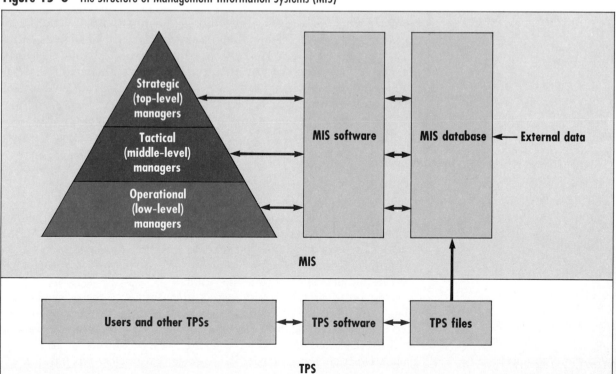

Data from outside the organization comes from many sources. Periodicals, government publications, and research company reports often contain data that is useful in management decision making. This type of data may be entered into the database by managers or their assistants. Another common source of data is *information utilities*, discussed in Chapter 6. Some information utilities, such as Dow Jones News/Retrieval, contain business-related data. The data can be accessed by a microcomputer with the use of data communications. The manager can study the data or copy it to the MIS database for later use.

As an example of a management information system, consider one that supports inventory decisions at all three levels in a bicycle business. This system would contain a database of daily inventory data for each model bicycle the business sells. The inventory control system, a transaction processing system, would supply the data. At the operational level, software would produce output with inventory figures for each model bicycle. These figures would help decision makers determine whether to order more of each model. The inventory data would be summarized for the tactical-level decision makers. This data would be used to decide what models were overstocked so that appropriate actions, such as price reductions, could be taken. Finally, inventory data would be summarized further for strategic managers to help determine inventory storage policies, such as whether more warehouses should be built.

DECISION SUPPORT SYSTEMS

A management information system helps managers make decisions by providing information from a database with little or no analysis. A **decision support system** (**DSS**) is a type of information system that helps managers make decisions by analyzing data from a database and providing the results of the analysis to the manager. An MIS supports all three levels of management by producing reports and query responses. A DSS usually is best for decisions at the middle and top levels of management. As with an MIS, a DSS helps with making decisions but does not actually make decisions; only managers make decisions.

Management Decision Support

To understand decision support systems you need to know something about how data is analyzed to help in management decisions. A DSS includes several ways of analyzing data. Usually, the manager can select what form of analysis he or she wants. The system performs the calculations and displays or prints the results.

One form for analysis is *statistical calculations*. In these calculations, data is manipulated to determine characteristics of the data or to draw conclusions from the data. For example, assume that a manager in a bicycle business has data about the sales of bicycles for each of the last five years. He or she can calculate the average yearly sales, which is one way of characterizing this data. The manager can also use this data to predict sales in future years. Both of these are types of statistical calculations.

Another form of analysis is *mathematical modeling.* A *model* is a representation of reality. For example, a model airplane is a representation of a real airplane. Models used for decision making are not physical things like airplanes, but sets of mathematical equations. A model is used to help predict what will happen with different decisions. For example, a manager can use a model to try different inventory reordering decisions in a bicycle business. The following is a simple inventory model that might be used:

Inventory today = Inventory yesterday – 5

This model says, in equation form, that each day the business sells five bicycles. The manager can also write an equation that calculates the cost of keeping items in inventory. With these equations a manager can compare the cost of ordering a small amount of inventory frequently with the cost of ordering a lot of inventory less frequently. By trying different strategies a manager can use the model to determine the least expensive inventory reordering policy.

Decision Support System Structure

Figure 15–9 shows the general structure of decision support systems. The users of the DSS are managers, usually at the tactical and strategic levels in the organization. Typically, a user uses the system interactively through a keyboard and screen. The user keys in requests for analysis of data. The results of the analysis are displayed on the user's screen. The DSS database contains data that is analyzed to produce the output. The DSS **model base** (analogous to a database) contains the mathematical models and statistical calculation routines that are used to analyze data from the database.

The DSS software provides capabilities for the user to access data in the database and to use models from the model base to analyze the data. The software also displays the results of the analysis on the screen

Figure 15–9 The Structure of Decision Support Systems (DDS)

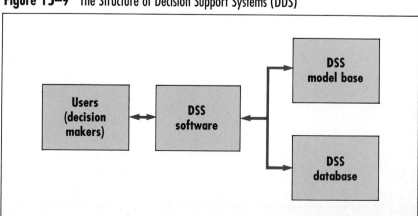

or prints it on paper. Often, the output from a DSS is given in a graphic form, although other forms of output are used. Using the software, the user can try different models and data to see what happens.

The data for the database comes from several sources. The user may enter data into the database, or data may be taken from the MIS database or the TPS files. The results of a previous analysis by the DSS may be stored in the database. External sources, such as information utilities, may also supply data.

An example of a decision support system is one that helps a manager in a bicycle business decide what types of bicycles to advertise. The system would use data from a database containing past sales of different bicycles. The sales data would be analyzed by statistical calculation routines to project sales trends. Then, a mathematical model would be used to estimate the effect of advertising on sales. The manager would try different advertising strategies until he or she found the one that was most likely to increase sales.

A decision support system usually is developed using general software that is adapted for a specific decision. An example of simple decision support system software is spreadsheet software, which was discussed in Chapter 9. This type of software, which is used on microcomputers, usually includes limited data management capabilities, a few built-in statistical calculation routines, and some simple mathematical models. A user can access data, do calculations, use models, and display the results with the software. The capabilities of spreadsheet software are limited; nevertheless, this type of software can be used to create a DSS for some types of decision problems.

More sophisticated decision support system software exists on microcomputers, minicomputers, and mainframe computers. Some of this DSS software is like spreadsheet software but with more complete database and modeling capabilities. Other DSS software is mainly database software with some modeling capabilities, or mathematical modeling and statistical calculation systems with limited database capabilities. Using the appropriate DSS software, a decision support system can be created to help managers make some types of decisions.

EXPERT SYSTEMS

Management information and decision support systems help managers make decisions by providing and analyzing information. They do not, however, advise the decision maker on what to do. An **expert system** (**ES**), on the other hand, is a type of information system that gives expert advice to the decision maker. An expert system mimics the way a human expert would analyze a situation and then recommends a course of action. The system accomplishes this by incorporating human expert knowledge and using this knowledge to analyze specific problems.

Expert systems are best for highly structured problems that involve expertise in very technical areas. They are used for engineering and scientific problems as well as for business problems, usually at the operational or tactical levels. An early example of an expert system is Mycin, which was developed at Stanford University in the 1970s. It is used by doctors to help diagnose certain diseases and to recommend treatment. A recent example is an expert system developed by American Express to decide whether to issue a credit card to a customer. Other expert systems are listed in Figure 15–10.

Expert systems use techniques from the field of **artificial intelligence** (**AI**). The goal of artificial intelligence is to mimic human intelligence by using a computer. For example, artificial intelligence programs have been developed to play complex games of strategy such as chess. Expert systems are just one application of artificial intelligence.

Figure 15–11 shows the general structure of expert systems. The users are decision makers who are not experts in the types of problems that the expert system is designed to solve. A user uses the system interactively. He or she requests advice from the expert system and answers questions asked by the system. The expert system responds to the user's request with advice and recommendations.

The **knowledge base** is like a database of expert knowledge. Different types of expert systems use different techniques for storing knowledge. One technique is to use **rules**. A rule is an *if-then* structure: *if* something is true, *then* something else is true. For example, Figure 15–12 shows three rules that might be used in a simple expert system for deciding whether to hire an applicant for a job. All the rules form the knowledge base for the expert system.

The expert system software consists of a user interface and an inference engine. The user interface receives input from the user and displays output. The **inference engine** analyzes rules in the knowledge base to draw conclusions.

An example of an expert system is one that evaluates a job applicant with the knowledge base given in Figure 15–12. Figure 15–13 shows how the interaction with the user of this system might appear on the screen. The user enters the applicant's name, education, and work experience. Then, the inference engine uses the knowledge base to evaluate this data. The inference engine does the evaluation by deciding which rules apply and by linking the rules together to draw a conclusion. In this example, the inference engine determines that John Doe has the required education (Rule 2) and the required experience (Rule 3). Therefore, he should be hired (Rule 1). The recommendation is then displayed on the screen.

In reality, expert systems are much more complex than this example. Their knowledge base may contain hundreds or thousands of rules, and the inference engine may be very complex. Development of such systems is difficult. Specialists called *knowledge engineers* usually do the development. The knowledge engineer must first contact experts in the problem that the system is trying to solve, and determine what "rules" the experts use. For example, the rules in a hiring expert system would be determined by asking experienced personnel managers in the business how they make hiring decisions. This process can be extremely time-consuming.

After the rules have been determined, the knowledge engineer must construct the knowledge base and the inference engine to evaluate the rules. One way of doing this is to prepare a program in a programming

Figure 15–10 Some Expert Systems

Project/Author	Application Area	System Description
Auditor C. Dungan University of Illinois	Business	Selects procedures to be used by an independent author.
Taxadvisor R. Michaelsen University of Illinois	Business	Provides estate planning recommendations for client.
Xcon J. McDermott Carnegie-Mellon University	Computing	Configures the DEC VAX-11/780 computer system.
Xcel Digital Equipment Corp.	Computing	Extension of Xcon to assist sales-people in selecting appropriate computer systems.
KBVLSI Xerox Corp. Palo Alto Research Center and Stanford University	Engineering	Experimental system to aid in the development of very large-scale integration design.
Sacon J. S. Bennett, R. S. Englemore Stanford Heuristic Programming Project (HPP)	Engineering	Advises structural engineers in using the structural analysis program Marc.
Crib T. R. Addis International Computers Ltd.	Fault diagnosis	Diagnosis of faults of computer hardware and software.
Raffles T. R. Addis International Computers	Fault diagnosis	Diagnosis of faults in computer hardware and software.
Courtier T. Wolf, A. Gershman, R. Strong Cognitive Systems, Inc.	Finance	Provides high-quality investment advice for portfolio management to bank customers in Belgium.
Prospector P. Hart, R. Duda SRI International, Inc.	Geology	Aids geologists in evaluating mineral sites for potential deposits.
Callisto M. S. Fox, A. Sathi, M. Greenburg Robotics Institute, Carnegie-Mellon	Manufacturing	Experimental system that models monitors, schedules and manages large projects.
Mycin E. Shortliffe Stanford HPP	Medicine	Diagnoses certain infectious diseases and recommends appropriate drugs.
Puff J. C. Kunz Stanford HPP	Medicine	Analyzes results of pulmonary function tests for evidence of disorder.
VM L. M. Fagan Stanford HPP	Medicine	Provides care suggestions for patients needing breathing assistance.
Drilling Advisor E. A. Feigenbaum et al Teknowledge, Inc. for Elf-Aquitaine	Resource exploration	Diagnoses oil well problems and recommends corrective and preventive measures.
Genesis Intelligenetics	Science	Helps scientists plan and simulate gene-splicing experiments.
Heuristic Dendral E. A. Feigenbaum et al Stanford HPP	Science	Identification of organic compounds by analysis of mass spectrograms.

Source: *Computerworld*, "Cost of an Expert," July 21, 1986, p. 63

Figure 15–11   The Structure of Expert Systems (ES)

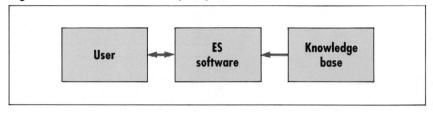

Figure 15–12   Rules in a Knowledge Base

Rule 1:   <u>If</u> applicant has required education and applicant has required experience,
<u>then</u> hire applicant.

Rule 2:   <u>If</u> applicant has BA in business, or applicant has BA in nonbusiness field and MBA,
<u>then</u> applicant has required education.

Rule 3:   <u>If</u> applicant has 2 or more years experience in sales position,
or applicant has 4 or more years experience in any position,
<u>then</u> applicant has required experience.

Figure 15–13   Expert System Use

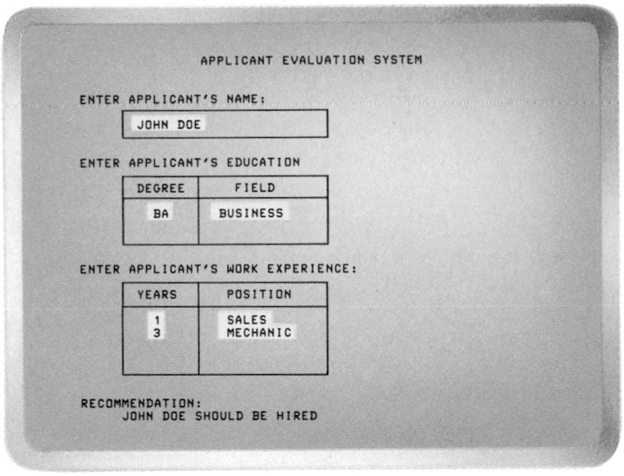

```
                APPLICANT EVALUATION SYSTEM

    ENTER APPLICANT'S NAME:
        JOHN DOE

    ENTER APPLICANT'S EDUCATION
        DEGREE      FIELD
          BA        BUSINESS

    ENTER APPLICANT'S WORK EXPERIENCE:
        YEARS       POSITION
          1         SALES
          3         MECHANIC

    RECOMMENDATION:
        JOHN DOE SHOULD BE HIRED
```

language designed for artificial intelligence, such as LISP or PROLOG (see Chapter 13). Often, however, an existing program is used that provides the skeleton of an expert system. This type of program, called an **expert system shell**, contains an inference engine and a user interface (Figure 15–14). The knowledge engineer has to enter the rules in the knowledge base into the program to form a complete expert system. Expert system shells are available for all types of computers, including microcomputers. Examples of expert system shells for a microcomputer are VP-Expert, Guru, and NeuroSMARTS.

Figure 15–14 An Expert System Shell

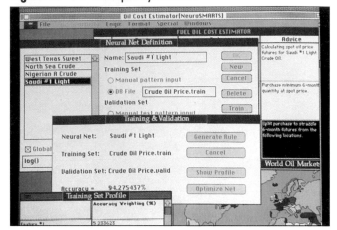

OFFICE AUTOMATION SYSTEMS

People at all levels of an organization or a business need office support to perform their functions. Typing, copying, and filing are some of the office activities they require. Managers at the strategic, tactical, and operational levels utilize office support to assist in decision making. Clerical personnel use office support to help in their work.

Historically, office activities have been performed by secretarial personnel. For example, a manager would dictate a memo to a secretary who would type, copy, mail, and file it. With the introduction of microcomputers, managers and other personnel began doing some of their office work directly. For example, a manager may use word processing (discussed in Chapter 8) to prepare a memo. Still, a secretary would copy, mail, and file the memo. The next step was to link the office microcomputers in a local area network with equipment that performed other office functions. This formed an office automation system.

An **office automation system** (**OAS**) is a type of information system that performs office functions. Some of the functions an OAS can perform are the following:

- Word processing. As explained in Chapter 8, word processing involves using the computer to type a document, make changes in the document, and print copies of the document.
- Electronic mail. Instead of making a paper copy of a document and mailing it, the document can be electronically "mailed" to any person who has access to the OAS. This is done by storing the document in special secondary storage, where it can be retrieved by the recipient of the mail. Electronic mail was discussed in Chapter 6.
- Electronic filing. A paper copy need not be made of a document to save it. Instead, a copy can be "filed" electronically in secondary storage in the OAS. The document can be retrieved in the future and printed if necessary.

- Desktop support. Many common items that are found on a desktop are included in office automation systems, such as appointment and meeting schedules, telephone and address directories, electronic calculators, and notepads.
- Voice processing. With voice processing, a voice message can be recorded and stored in secondary storage in the OAS. Then the message can be "sent" to any person who has access to the system. The person can listen to the voice message by "playing" it back.
- Image processing. In image processing, copies of graphs, charts, photographs, and other images can be stored in secondary storage in the OAS. The images can be viewed by people who have access to the system, or they can be graphed or printed.

Figure 15–15 shows the general structure of office automation systems. Users of the system are managers at all three levels of decision making. In addition, clerical and secretarial personnel are users. The users enter documents, voice messages, images, and other data; request office functions from the system; and receive screen, voice, and paper output. The OAS includes many databases for storing all data including documents, messages, and images. Each computer may have its own database, and several common databases may be stored in the system. The OAS software includes programs to perform all the office functions of the system.

The hardware in an office automation system includes a local area network containing numerous microcomputers and possibly minicomputers and mainframe computers. In addition, the network may contain

Figure 15–15   The Structure of Office Automation Systems (OAS)

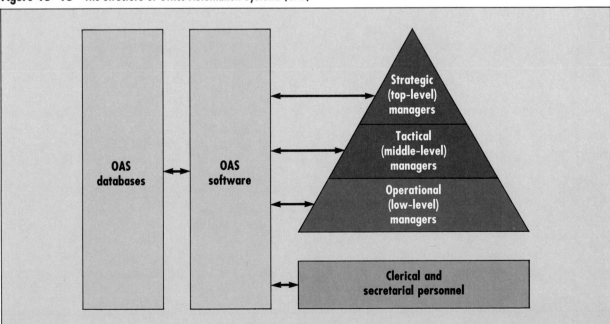

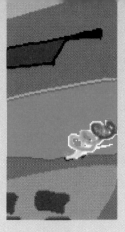

SIMON SAYS SOUP IS GOOD FOOD

How does Campbell Soup Company ensure that its soup is "mm—mm good"? An expert system, chosen and implemented by an end-user department, helps the company determine when something goes wrong with the processing of the soup and what to do about it.

The expert system, dubbed Simon, was installed in 1988 and became fully operational a year later. "We tested it for a year to make sure it's right," said Michael S. Mignogna, corporate process authority at Campbell. "We wanted to make sure that when it decided something, it was the same as if one of our people had made the decision." Thus far, the system has saved Campbell's about $5 million.

Mignogna's department, thermal process development, sets the standards for how soup should be cooked to ensure sterility and to avoid conditions such as botulism. It also makes the calls about what to do if something goes wrong.

For instance, a batch of cream of mushroom needs to be cooked for 50 minutes at 250 degrees, and halfway through the cooking, the plant loses steam pressure or the conveyor belt slows down. Mignogna's group has to decide whether to OK that batch for sale or destroy it. The goal is to destroy as few items as possible while guaranteeing quality. "It's that one can of soup that we worry about," he said.

Before Simon was installed, Mignogna's department used a General Electric Company time-sharing arrangement. Then in 1985, Mignogna and his engineers converted the time-sharing application to run on an IBM Personal Computer. "I wouldn't say it was the most efficient system," Mignogna said, "but it worked." And it saved the approximately $4500 a month that the time-sharing system cost.

All told, Simon has saved Campbell between $2 million and $3 million a year. Most of this is accounted for by products that would have been destroyed under the old system but that were really safe. "That sounds like a lot of money," Mignogna said, "until you realize that Campbell makes five billion to 10 billion cans of soup a year."

With the old PC system, whenever there was a problem the plant would notify Mignogna's people and send data about all the conditions. Thermal process would look at the data and use the PC program to do mathematical simulations to decide whether the product was safe. This process took up to eight weeks, and the product in question needed to be held in a warehouse until a decision was made.

With Simon, however, that decision-making process is cut to about three minutes, and most of the decisions are made by Simon with little human intervention. When something goes wrong at the plant, a quality-control person enters data into Simon on a personal computer. Four plants have PCs that run Simon locally. Mignogna's group also has a PC with Simon on it.

If the expert system determines that the problem will not impact quality, it authorizes the product to be released. "It's the same as if I signed it off," Mignogna said. If the problem is determined to be more serious, the product is put into isolation in a warehouse, and Mignogna's group reviews the paperwork and does a risk analysis.

Simon makes the decisions about 90% of the time, Mignogna said. In the other 10%, all the data may not be immediately available. Nor does Simon contain rules for all the possible combinations—such as container defects, for instance. "These are the sorts of things that are not toxic and won't kill anyone," Mignogna said.

Because the expert system can separate the business rules from the mathematical calculations, Mignogna said, either can be changed without affecting the other. This can come in handy when Campbell adds new products or changes the recipes for old ones. When the company introduced its low-salt soups, for example, Simon needed to be changed to accommodate. "Salt is a preservative, so when you take it out, there's some impact," Mignogna said.

Besides the cost savings, benefits include improved efficiency of the decision-making process and improved morale at the plants, Mignogna said. Plant employees feel more in control of things because they no longer have to wait for his group to make a decision.

a file server or database server for storing data, and a printer and a plotter to produce paper output. Software used in an office automation system includes word processing, electronic mail, and electronic filing software. Software to support desktop functions and for voice and image processing may also be part of an office automation system.

Office automation systems are distributed systems. Input, output, processing, and storage are performed at the users' locations and at central locations. Because of their distributed nature and the many functions they perform, office automation systems can be quite complex.

EXECUTIVE SUPPORT SYSTEMS

Strategic managers have special information system needs that are different from those of other managers. Top-level managers often work in an unstructured way, not knowing in advance what information they will need or what computing functions they will use. These managers need extremely flexible systems that they can easily adapt to their own requirements.

An **executive support system** (**ESS**), also called an *executive information system* (*EIS*), is designed to provide support for the highest level of management in an organization. Unfortunately, it is not clear exactly what functions an ESS should provide. Usually, the functions are similar to those found in management information systems and in office automation systems. They may include:

- On-line access to reports previously received on paper.
- The ability to query the MIS database for information not usually received in reports.
- The ability to access external databases (i.e., information utilities).
- The ability to analyze and summarize data from reports and queries, and to view the results of the analysis graphically.
- Electronic mail to communicate with employees.
- An electronic appointment calendar.
- Basic word processing capabilities for writing notes, memos, and other simple communications.

The users of an ESS are top-level, strategic managers. The user uses the ESS software to access a variety of databases, which may include the MIS database (for reports and queries), the OAS database (for electronic mail, an electronic calendar, and word processing), external databases, and personal databases that they create. The ESS software provides capabilities for analyzing and summarizing data as well as other capabilities listed previously. The user can select the functions to be performed based on his or her needs.

Executive support systems are not widely used yet. Their use should increase in the future as top-level managers become more familiar with their capabilities.

Chapter Summary

- The input, output, storage, and processing functions of an information system are organized in different ways in different types of systems. In a **centralized system**, all functions are performed at a single, central location. In a **teleprocessing system**, the processing and storage functions are centralized, but the input and output functions are performed at the users' locations with data transmitted to the central location. With a **decentralized system**, each group of users has its own computer to perform all functions for the users' applications. A **distributed system** is like a decentralized system but with the computers linked to form a network so that functions can be performed on the user's computer or on other computers in the network.

- The purpose of a **transaction processing system** (**TPS**) is to keep records about the organization, to process data about **transactions**, which are events that have occurred that affect the organization, and to produce output that reports on transactions, reports on the organization, and causes other transactions to occur.

- A manager needs detailed information, mainly from inside the organization, to make day-to-day decisions related to the operation of the organization. To make decisions that involve implementing policies of the organization, a manager needs less detailed, more summarized information from both inside and outside the organization. To make decisions that involve setting organizational policies, goals, and long-term plans, a manager needs summarized information, much of which comes from outside the organization. A **management information system** (**MIS**) provides information to meet the managers' needs at different levels by maintaining a database of internal and external data and processing the data to produce the information at the required level of detail.

- A **decision support system** (**DSS**) helps managers make decisions by analyzing data from a database using statistical calculations and mathematical models, and providing the results of the analysis to the manager. A DSS consists of a database, a **model base**, and software that lets the user access data in the database and use models from the model base to analyze the data.

- An **expert system** (**ES**) provides expert advice by storing human expert knowledge in a **knowledge base** and then using the knowledge to draw conclusions about specific problems.

- An **office automation system** (**OAS**) performs office functions such as word processing, electronic mail, electronic filing, desktop support, voice processing, and image processing. An OAS includes a local area network containing numerous microcomputers, possibly minicomputers or mainframe computers, and other equipment such as file services and printers. An OAS also includes software for the different office functions supported by the system.

■ An **executive support system** (**ESS**) provides top-level managers with support for the functions they perform. These include on-line access to reports and databases, the ability to analyze and summarize data and view the results graphically, and office automation functions such as electronic mail, electronic calendar, and basic word processing.

Terms to Remember

Artificial Intelligence (AI)   p. 395

Centralized System   p. 380

Cooperative Processing   p. 384

Decentralized System   p. 382

Decision Support System (DSS)   p. 392

Distributed System   p. 383

Executive Support System (ESS)   p. 402

Expert System (ES)   p. 394

Expert System Shell   p. 397

Inference Engine   p. 395

Information Center   p. 383

Knowledge Base   p. 395

Management Information System (MIS)   p. 388

Model base   p. 393

Office Automation System (OAS)   p. 398

Rule   p. 395

Teleprocessing System   p. 381

Transaction   p. 387

Transaction Processing System (TPS)   p. 387

Review Questions

Fill-In Questions

1. An information system in which all functions are performed at a single, central location is called a(n) _____.

2. An information system that users use through terminals located around the country but in which all processing and storage are performed at a central location is a(n) _____.

3. Assume that each department in an organization uses its own computer to perform all functions for its information systems. These information systems are called _____.

4. Some organizations have a(n) _____, which consists of computer professionals who assist personal computer users in the organization.

5. A(n) _____ is an event that has occurred that affects an organization or business.

6. Detailed information is required for _____ decisions, whereas summarized information is needed for _____ decisions.

7. A collection of mathematical models and statistical routines stored in a computer is called a(n) _____.

8. The use of a computer to mimic human intelligence is called _____.

9. A collection of expert knowledge stored in a computer is called a(n) _____.

10. A(n) _____ is an *if-then* structure that is used in a knowledge base.

Short-Answer Questions

1. What is a distributed system?

2. What system organizations are usually most responsive to users' needs?

3. State the purpose of a transaction processing system.

4. Describe the levels of decision making in an organization.

5. How does a management information system meet the information needs of managers in an organization?

6. Where does the data in the database of a management information system come from?

7. What is a decision support system?

8. What ways of analyzing data may be included in a decision support system?

9. What is an expert system?

10. Consider an expert system with the knowledge base shown in Figure 15–12. If Mary Roe is a job applicant with a BA in psychology, an MBA, and three years of experience as a teacher, what would the expert system recommend?

11. What office functions are provided by an office automation system?

12. What is the purpose of an executive support system?

Projects

1. Investigate an information system in an organization or business to which you have access. How are the functions of the system organized? Is the system a TPS, MIS, DSS, ES, OAS, or ESS? (Many information systems are combinations of these.) Write a summary of your findings.

2. New expert systems are being developed constantly. Find out what you can about an expert system. What type of expert advice does the system provide? How many rules are in its knowledge base? How long did the system take to develop?

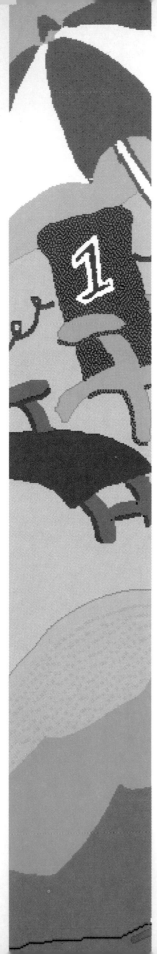

16

DATABASE PROCESSING

CHAPTER OBJECTIVES

• After completing this chapter you should be able to:

1. Explain what a database is and describe the difference between file processing and database processing.

2. List several advantages and several disadvantages of database processing.

3. State why relationships are important in database processing and identify the main types of relationships.

4. Outline the characteristics of the main types of databases.

5. Describe several ways of using a database management system.

6. Describe the use of databases in different types of information systems.

A S YOU KNOW, the stored data component of an information system consists of files and databases. Many information systems process data in files, but more and more systems are using databases. Someday, most information systems may involve database processing. Users will encounter these systems and will have to interact with them. This chapter discusses databases and database processing.

WHAT IS A DATABASE?

In Chapter 5 and again in Chapter 10 you learned that related data are sometimes grouped to form a database. This definition is adequate for a basic understanding of databases, but you need a complete definition for a thorough knowledge of database processing.

A **database** is a collection of *data* and *relationships* between the data stored in secondary storage. The data in a database may be stored in several separate files or in one large file. The actual way the data is stored depends on the database software. To the user, however, the database is viewed as a single set of stored data. The data in the database is arranged into related groups, similar to records, each containing several fields. Groups of data are related to other groups of data, meaning that the groups have something in common. The ways in which the groups of data are related are called **relationships**, and they are part of the database.

To illustrate the idea of a database, consider how data used for inventory control, order entry, and customer billing in a bicycle business can be stored in a database. Figure 16–1 shows a database with the required data. Notice that inventory data, order data, and billing data are grouped separately in the database. The relationships between the data are shown by lines connecting the groups of data. There is a relationship between inventory data and order data if an item in inventory has been ordered. An inventory item can be ordered one or more times or not at all. There is a relationship between billing data and order data if a customer needs to be billed for items ordered. Each customer can order one or more items.

DATABASE VERSUS FILE PROCESSING

Processing data in a database is different from processing data in a file. To illustrate the difference, assume that the bicycle business wants to do inventory control, order entry, and customer billing on a computer. With file processing, the business would need separate files to store the data for each application. For these applications it would need three files: an inventory file, an order file, and a billing file (Figure 16–2). Application programs for inventory control would access the inventory file, order entry programs would access the order file, and customer billing programs would access the billing file.

Figure 16–1 A Database

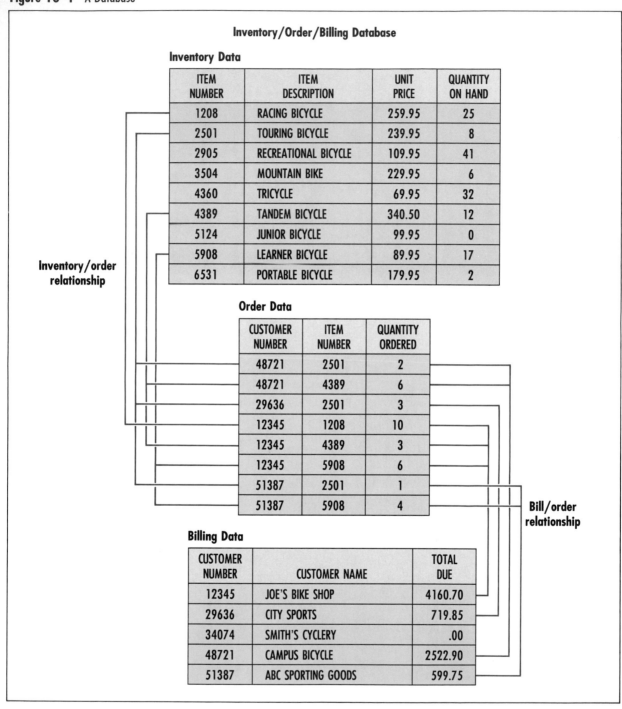

Figure 16–2   File Processing

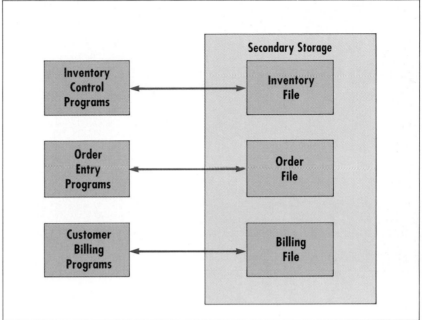

Disadvantages of File Processing

There are several disadvantages of file processing. First, some data may be duplicated in several files. For example, the customer's name and address may appear in both the order file and the billing file. Duplicated data requires extra storage space. More significantly, if duplicated data changes, someone must make sure it is updated every place it is stored. Thus, if a customer moves, his or her address must be updated in all files in which the address is stored. Ensuring that all duplicated data is updated can be a difficult task.

A second disadvantage of file processing is that it is difficult to process data from more than one file. If, for example, the order entry program needs to process data in both the inventory file and the order file, complex programming is required. If a program needs to access three files, the processing is even more complicated.

A final disadvantage of file processing is that there is a dependency between programs and data. Each program must have instructions that tell it how the data in the files it processes are organized. Each program must identify what fields are in the records of each file and how the files are organized. If the record or file organization is changed, every program that processes that file must be modified. Such modification can be time-consuming and expensive.

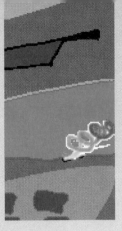

BUT CAN YOU READ IT LIKE A BOOK?

Even though electronic databases contain massive amounts of information, they are more like warehouses than libraries. While all the information is contained under one "roof," it may not be readily apparent where and in what form the information is stored. Walk into a library, on the other hand, and you have a pretty good idea what aisle contains the information you are looking for, and you can expect it to be contained in a book.

That is the basic premise of an "electronic library," which aims to combine the massive amounts of information in an electronic database with the logic and facile use of a library.

About 150 chemistry students and faculty members at Cornell University in Ithaca, New York, are experimenting with such an electronic library, an on-line system that enables users to retrieve information contained in thousands of articles published by the *Journal of the American Chemical Society*. Unlike on-line databases, the electronic library is not limited to textual information: Users are also able to retrieve graphics, illustrations and other images.

It is the first test of its kind, according to officials at Cornell's Albert R. Mann Library, where the Chemistry On-Line Retrieval Experiment (CORE) is being conducted, and Bellcore, where the system's experimental Superbook software interface and database engine was developed.

"Chemists tend not to use or find on-line services that useful because the graphical components are key to understanding," said Howard Curtis, head of the information technology section at the Mann Library. "Take away the schematics, photos, illustrations, and there's not much left."

One objective of CORE will be to determine whether on-line text and image retrieval and reading the material on screen is more practical than actually scouring the shelves for chemistry articles.

"It is not just a question of how willing researchers are to search and browse electronically but also whether they will want to read on their screens," Curtis said.

The database consists of four parts: text stored as ASCII files, an index, graphics that have been extracted from the articles and 300 dot/in. reproductions of complete pages. Text, the index and graphics are stored on magnetic media; the page reproductions are stored on optical discs. Although little of the information contained in the publications is in color, the 70,000 articles and related graphics will take up about 160G bytes of storage space.

Database Processing

In database processing, data is not stored as separate files. Instead, all data is stored together in a database. In our bicycle business example the database would contain inventory, order, and billing data (Figure 16–3). To process the data in the database, another program is needed. This program is called a **database management system** (**DBMS**). The DBMS provides capabilities for creating, accessing, and updating a database. In fact, the DBMS handles all interaction with the database. If an application program, such as an order entry program, needs to process data in the database, the program sends instructions to the DBMS, which then carries out the actions requested by the program.

Advantages of Database Processing

Database processing has important advantages over file processing. First, duplication of data is reduced. Each data value needs to be stored only once in the database because the data is treated as one collection of data rather than as separate files. Thus, in our bicycle business example, each customer's address needs to be stored only once in the database. This characteristic means that extra storage space is not required for duplicate data. More importantly, the updating of data must be done only once.

A second advantage of database processing is that it makes it easier to process different types of data—that is, data that in file processing would be stored in separate files. Because the data in a database is stored as one collection of data, the DBMS can process any data in the database with minimal difficulty. Thus, if, in our example, a program needs to process inventory data and order data, it sends instructions to the DBMS to tell it what to do, and the DBMS handles all details of processing the data.

Figure 16–3 Database Processing

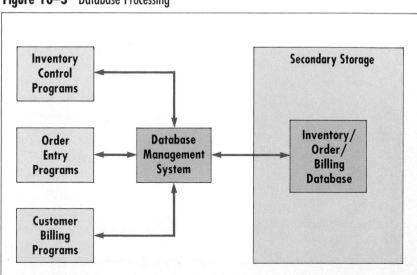

A final advantage of database processing is that programs are not dependent on the organization of the data in the database. The database can be changed without changing every program that uses the database. For example, if fields or records are added to the database, it is necessary only to change those programs that use those fields or records. All other programs can be left unchanged. This characteristic results from the fact that the DBMS handles all database interaction. Because programs do not have to be changed as much, less time and expense is required for programming.

Disadvantages of Database Processing

There are several disadvantages of database processing. First, it can be expensive. One source of expense is the cost of the DBMS. On microcomputers a DBMS typically costs $500 to $700, but on mainframe computers the cost is in the $100,000 to $300,000 range. Another source of expense is that usually a faster computer with more primary and secondary storage is needed for database processing to get the same performance as in file processing. Such a computer is more expensive than one needed for file processing. Finally, programmers' salaries are usually higher with database processing because the programmers are more skilled than those who know only file processing.

Another disadvantage of database processing is that data is more vulnerable than it is in file processing. If several files are used in file processing, each file can be stored on a different disk or tape. If one disk or tape is accidentally destroyed, the files on other disks or tapes are not damaged. In database processing, however, all data must be stored on the same disk. Damage to that disk means all data is lost.

A final disadvantage of database processing is that information systems that use this approach can be complex to develop. Such systems often involve several applications, all using the same database. The development of these information systems usually requires more careful planning and is more time-consuming than file processing systems.

You can see from this discussion that database processing has advantages and disadvantages over file processing. In general, file processing should be used for simpler systems that involve few programs and a single file. Database processing is best for systems that have numerous programs and that use multiple files. In between are many information systems in which the best approach may be either file processing or database processing.

DATA RELATIONSHIPS

The relationships between data are the key to making a database work. Related data are processed in the database through relationships. There are three main types of relationships in databases: one-to-one relationships, one-to-many relationships, and many-to-many relationships. In a **one-to-one relationship**, one group of data is related to only one other group of data, and vice versa. For example, assume that a database contains records of customer data, each with the customer's name, and accounts receivable data, each with the balance due owed by the customer. There is one customer record for each customer and one accounts receivable record for each customer. Then, each customer record is related to one receivables record, and vice versa. Thus, there is a one-to-one relationship between customer records and accounts receivable records.

Figure 16–4 shows a one-to-one relationship between two records. Part *a* of this figure shows the *structure* of the records. The line with a single arrow at each end means that there is a one-to-one relationship between the records. Part *b* of the figure shows data for the two records. The records are connected by a line, meaning they are related. This diagram gives an *occurrence* of the records and the relationship between them.

The second type of relationship is called a **one-to-many relationship**. In this type, one group of data is related to one or more other groups of data, but not vice versa. For example, assume that a database contains customer records and invoice records, each with an invoice date and amount. Each customer can have any number of invoices, but each invoice can be associated with only one customer. Then the relationship between customer records and invoice records is one-to-many.

Figure 16–5a shows the structure of the customer and invoice records and the one-to-many relationship between them. The line with a single arrow at one end and a double arrow at the other signifies a one-to-many relationship. The single arrow points to the "one" record and the double arrow to the "many" record. Figure 16–5b gives an occurrence of these records and the relationship between them. In this example, customer number 12345 has three invoices.

The last type of relationship is a **many-to-many relationship**. In this relationship, one or more groups of data are related to one or more other groups, and vice versa. For example, assume that a database contains vendor records, each with a vendor's name, and inventory records, each with an item description, a unit price, and a quantity on hand. Each vendor can supply several inventory items, and each item can be supplied by several vendors. Then the relationship between vendor records and inventory records is many-to-many.

Figure 16–4   A One-to-One Relationship

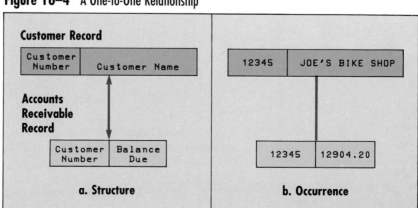

Figure 16–5   A One-to-Many Relationship

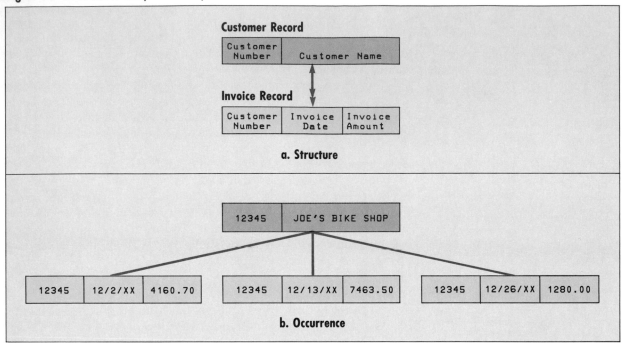

a. Structure

b. Occurrence

Figure 16–6a shows the structure of the inventory and vendor records and the many-to-many relationship between them. The line with a double arrow at each end signifies a many-to-many relationship. Figure 16–6b gives an occurrence of these records and the relationship between them. Notice in this example that vendor number 2147 can supply items number 3504 and 4389, and that item number 3504 can be supplied by all three vendors.

TYPES OF DATABASES

The data in a database is organized in a way that is easy for people to understand. The database organization is based on one of three approaches for arranging data in a database. The three approaches result in three types of databases: hierarchical databases, network databases, and relational databases. Some DBMSs use hierarchical databases, some use network databases, and some use relational databases.

Hierarchical Databases

In a **hierarchical database**, all relationships between groups of data are one-to-one or one-to-many, but no group of data can be on the "many" side of more than one relationship. Figure 16–7 shows an example. Notice that only one-to-many relationships are used in this database and that all the relationships "go in the same direction." (One-to-one relationships could also be used, but many-to-many relationships cannot.)

Figure 16–6 A Many-to-Many Relationship

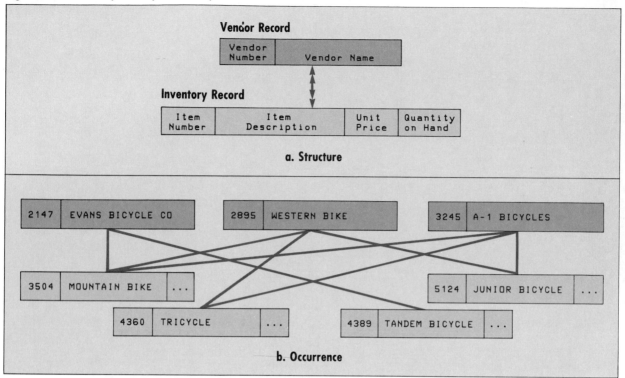

a. Structure

b. Occurrence

The meaning of the database is that each salesperson has any number of customers and that each customer can place any number of orders.

The database in Figure 16–7 looks like a family tree. In fact, this type of database is often called a tree. Going "down" the tree, each record has any number of "children," which are records related to it. Going "up" the tree, however, each record has *only one* "parent." Thus, in Figure 16–7, each salesperson can have any number of customers, but no customer can be served by more than one salesperson.

Network Databases

In a **network database**, all types of relationships are allowed without restriction. Thus, one-to-one, one-to-many, and many-to-many relationships are permitted. (Some DBMSs that use the network approach allow only certain types of relationships in the database or put restrictions on how relationships can be used.)

Figure 16–8 shows an example of a network database. This database has one many-to-many relationship, which is interpreted as meaning that each vendor can supply many inventory items and that each item can be supplied by many vendors. The database also has one one-to-many relationship, which is interpreted as meaning that each warehouse can store any number of inventory items, but that each item can be stored in only one warehouse.

Figure 16–7 A Hierarchical Database

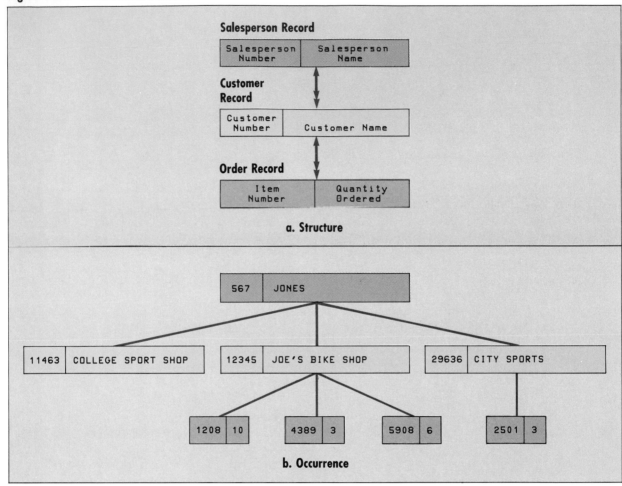

a. Structure

b. Occurrence

Relational Databases

A **relational database** takes an approach to organizing data that is different from that used by hierarchical and network databases. In a relational database, data is arranged in tables that have rows and columns. For example, Figure 16–9 shows a table with nine rows and four columns. In a relational database, a table is called a **relation** (not to be confused with a *relationship*), a row is called a **tuple** (which rhymes with *couple*), and a column is called an **attribute**. Some relational DBMSs use these terms; others use the terms *table*, *row*, and *column*; and still others use *file* (for relation), *record* (for tuple), and *field* (for attribute).

A relational database is a group of related relations. Figure 16–10 shows an example of a relational database with three relations. The structure of the database is indicated by identifying the relations and their attributes. A name is given to each relation and to each attribute in each relation. These names are listed at the top of the relations in Figure 16–10.

Relationships in relational databases exist for a reason different from that of relationships in hierarchical and network databases. In a hierar-

Figure 16–8 A Network Database

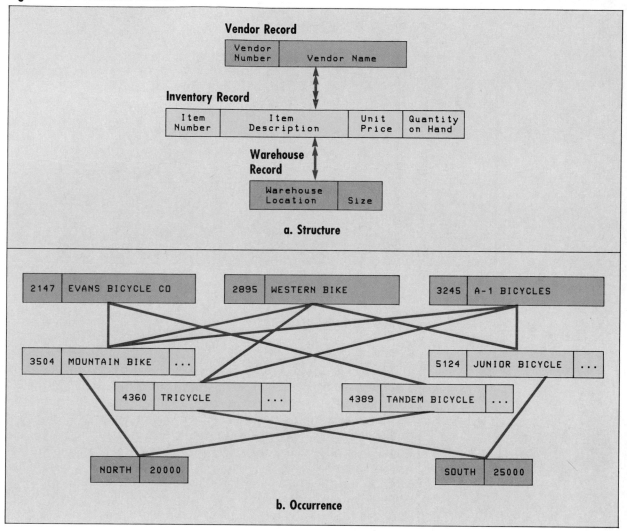

a. Structure

b. Occurrence

chical and network database, relationships exist because connections between records are stored as part of the database. (In other words, the lines in Figure 16–7b and 16–8b between records are actually part of the database, although they are stored in a special way.) In a relational database, however, *relationships* (not to be confused with *relations*) are *not* stored this way. Instead, a relationship exists between two relations because there is a common attribute in the relations. For example, there is a relationship between the INVENTORY relation and the ORDER relation in Figure 16–10 because the ITEM_NUMBER attribute is found in both relations. Similarly, there is a relationship between the BILLING relation and the ORDER relation because the CUST_NUMBER attribute appears in both relations. Any type of relationship—one-to-one, one-to-many, and many-to-many—can be represented in a relational database, although the details of how each is represented are beyond the scope of this book.

Figure 16–9   A Relation

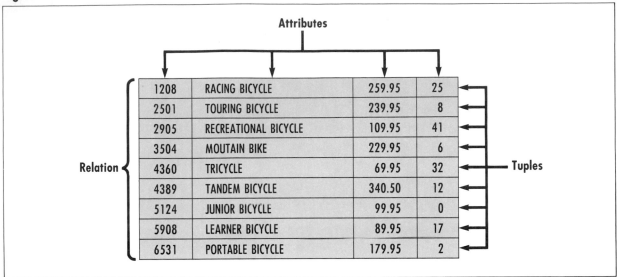

Comparison of Databases

DBMSs for hierarchical databases were developed first, in the 1960s. This type of database is very good for data that is naturally organized in a hierarchical manner, like a family tree. For example, data about products and the parts used in the assembly of the products is organized hierarchically: each product is made up of several main parts, each main part is made up of many subparts, and so on. A hierarchical database would be appropriate for storing this data. Hierarchical databases, however, are not good when data is not organized in a hierarchical way, such as when many-to-many relationships are needed.

DBMSs for network databases were developed in the 1970s. A network database is good for complex data that is not naturally organized in a hierarchical way. For example, data about students, courses, and faculty is complex: each student takes many courses, each course is taken by many students, each faculty member teaches many courses, and each course can be taught by many faculty members. A network database would be appropriate for storing this data.

The relational approach was first proposed in 1970, but DBMSs for relational databases did not become widespread until the 1980s. This type of database is considered to be the easiest for users to understand because all data is presented in relations—tables—which are easy to comprehend. In addition, processing data in relations is relatively simple. A relational database can be used for any type of data, including the product/parts data and the student/course/faculty data described in the previous two paragraphs. If the database is large and complex, however, processing can take more time using the relational approach than with the hierarchical and network approaches.

Figure 16–10 A Relational Database

INVENTORY relation

ITEM_ NUMBER	ITEM_DESC	UNIT_ PRICE	QTY_ON_ HAND
1208	RACING BICYCLE	259.95	25
2501	TOURING BICYCLE	239.95	8
2905	RECREATIONAL BICYCLE	109.95	41
3504	MOUNTAIN BIKE	229.95	6
4360	TRICYCLE	69.95	32
4389	TANDEM BICYCLE	340.50	12
5124	JUNIOR BICYCLE	99.95	0
5908	LEARNER BICYCLE	89.95	17
6531	PORTABLE BICYCLE	179.95	2

ORDER relation

CUST_ NUMBER	ITEM_ NUMBER	QTY_ ORDERED
48721	2501	2
48721	4389	6
29636	2501	3
12345	1208	10
12345	4389	3
12345	5908	6
51387	2501	1
51387	5908	4

BILLING relation

CUST_ NUMBER	CUST_NAME	TOTAL_ DUE
12345	JOE'S BIKE SHOP	4160.70
29636	CITY SPORTS	719.85
34074	SMITH'S CYCLERY	.00
48721	CAMPUS BICYCLE	2522.90
51387	ABC SPORTING GOODS	599.75

COMMON DATABASE MANAGEMENT SYSTEMS

As you know, a database management system is a program that provides capabilities for manipulating data in a database. The DBMS handles all interaction between the application program and the database. It provides capabilities for storing data in the database, retrieving data from the database, and updating data in the database. Without the DBMS, the manipulation of a database would be very complex.

Most DBMSs are based on one of the approaches described previously. Thus, a DBMS may use hierarchical, network, or relational databases. Each DBMS is usually identified by the approach it uses. For example, a relational DBMS uses relational databases.

The first DBMSs were developed for mainframe computers in the late 1960s. In the 1970s, DBMSs were developed for minicomputers, and in the 1980s microcomputer DBMSs appeared.

Mainframe Computer and Minicomputer DBMSs

Database management systems for mainframe computers and minicomputers are large, complex programs that are designed to be used by multiple users at one time. They are expensive, typically costing between $100,000 and $300,000. Because of their complexity, specially trained computer professionals are usually needed to utilize them. Some are hierarchical DBMSs, some are network DBMSs, and some are relational DBMSs. A few of the more widely used mainframe and minicomputer DBMSs are IMS (hierarchical) for large IBM mainframe computers; DL/I (hierarchical) for medium-sized IBM mainframe computers; IDMS (network) for IBM and for some other mainframe computers and some minicomputers; DB2 (relational) for large IBM mainframe computers; SQL/DS (relational) for medium-sized IBM mainframe computers; and ORACLE (relational) for a wide range of mainframe and minicomputers.

Microcomputer DBMSs

Microcomputer database management systems are much less complex than mainframe computer and minicomputer DBMSs. Usually they are designed for use by a single user, although some can be used by multiple users in a network at one time. Microcomputer DBMSs are relatively inexpensive, usually costing between $500 and $700. Almost all are relational DBMSs, although a few use the hierarchical and network approach.

Chapter 10 listed several common microcomputer database programs, including dBASE III PLUS, dBASE IV, R:Base for DOS, Paradox, FoxPro, Fourth Dimension, Double Helix, Omnis, dBASE Mac, and FoxBase Plus/Mac. All these are relational DBMSs. Another relational DBMS is a microcomputer version of ORACLE, which is similar to the mainframe computer and minicomputer versions.

Future DBMSs

Because it is the easiest for users to understand, relational databases are usually preferred over hierarchical and network databases. One trend is away from nonrelational DBMSs and toward relational ones. Almost all new DBMSs are relational. On microcomputers, virtually every new DBMS uses the relational approach. You can expect more relational DBMSs for all types of computers in the future.

Another trend is toward DBMSs that are the same—or very similar—on microcomputers, minicomputers, and mainframe computers. ORACLE is an example of this approach. Other DBMSs should be available in the future that are common to several types of computers. These systems will most likely be relational database management systems.

A third trend is toward distributed databases and distributed database management systems. A **distributed database** is one that is divided into parts with each part stored on a different computer in a network. The database is manipulated through a **distributed database management system**. Each computer in the network has a copy of the distributed DBMS. Using the DBMS, a user at any computer can access data from any part of the database, no matter where it is stored. The user, however, is unaware of where the data is stored. The advantage of distributed databases is that each user has control over the part of the database stored on his or her computer, but all users have access to all parts of the database. With the increase of distributed information systems, you can expect to see more distributed databases and distributed DBMSs.

A final trend is toward a new type of database, called an **object-oriented database**, which is different from hierarchical, network, and relational databases. These older types of databases store only data, whereas an object-oriented database stores *objects*, which are combinations of data and instructions to process the data. An **object-oriented database management system** is used to create, access, and update objects in an object-oriented database. Some people feel that object-oriented databases will be very common in the future.

USING A DATABASE MANAGEMENT SYSTEM

Two main ways of manipulating a database using a database management system are summarized in Figure 16–11. In the first approach an application program sends instructions to the DBMS, which carries out the actions requested by the program. The user interacts with the application program by supplying input and receiving output. In the second approach, the user interacts directly with the DBMS by using a special language called a query language.

Query Languages

A **query language** is a programming language that allows the user to query a database—that is, to retrieve data from a database. This type of

Figure 16–11   Using a Database Management System

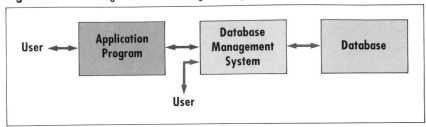

language also allows the user to update the database. Query languages are often included in a fourth generation language or 4GL, discussed in Chapter 13.

The user uses a query language by typing an instruction, usually called a *command*, at the keyboard. The instruction goes directly to the DBMS, which reviews it and performs the requested processing. Depending on the command, the DBMS may display data on the screen or perform an update. Thus, with a query language, the user interacts directly with the database management system to process the data in the database.

To illustrate the idea of a query language, consider examples using **SQL**, which stands for Structured Query Language. SQL is a common query language used with *relational* database management systems. Recall that a relational database consists of relations that are tables of rows and columns, in which the rows are called *tuples* and the columns are called *attributes*. The relations and the attributes have names. With SQL, a user can retrieve selected data from a single relation or several related relations in a database. A user can also update data in one or more relations.

To query a relation, the user gives the name of the relation, a condition that indicates which tuples he or she wishes to display from the relation, and the names of the attributes the user wants to display from those tuples. The form of a query in SQL is:

SELECT attribute names
FROM relation name
WHERE condition

As an example, assume that a user wishes to query the inventory/order/billing relational database discussed earlier and shown again in Figure 16–12. If the user wants to know the item number and description of all items in inventory with a quantity on hand of more than 10, he or she would use the following query in SQL:

SELECT ITEM_NUMBER, ITEM_DESC
FROM INVENTORY
WHERE QTY_ON_HAND > 10

Figure 16–13 shows how the screen would look after executing this command. Notice that several lines are displayed because several items in the INVENTORY relation in Figure 16–12 satisfy the condition that the quantity on hand is greater than 10.

As another example, assume that a user wants to know the names of the customers who ordered item 2501 and the quantity that each customer ordered. Then the user must find the numbers of the customers

Figure 16–12   The Inventory/Order/Billing Database

INVENTORY relation

ITEM_ NUMBER	ITEM_DESC	UNIT_ PRICE	QTY_ON_ HAND
1208	RACING BICYCLE	259.95	25
2501	TOURING BICYCLE	239.95	8
2905	RECREATIONAL BICYCLE	109.95	41
3504	MOUNTAIN BIKE	229.95	6
4360	TRICYCLE	69.95	32
4389	TANDEM BICYCLE	340.50	12
5124	JUNIOR BICYCLE	99.95	0
5908	LEARNER BICYCLE	89.95	17
6531	PORTABLE BICYCLE	179.95	2

ORDER relation

CUST_ NUMBER	ITEM_ NUMBER	QTY_ ORDERED
48721	2501	2
48721	4389	6
29636	2501	3
12345	1208	10
12345	4389	3
12345	5908	6
51387	2501	1
51387	5908	4

BILLING relation

CUST_ NUMBER	CUST_NAME	TOTAL_ DUE
12345	JOE'S BIKE SHOP	4160.70
29636	CITY SPORTS	719.85
34074	SMITH'S CYCLERY	.00
48721	CAMPUS BICYCLE	2522.90
51387	ABC SPORTING GOODS	599.75

who ordered this item and the quantity ordered from the ORDER relation, and the names of the customers with those numbers from the BILLING relation. This query is possible because the customer number is in both the ORDER and BILLING relations; hence there is a relationship between these relations. The following SQL command accomplishes what the user wants:

SELECT BILLING.CUST_NAME, ORDER.QTY_ORDERED
FROM BILLING, ORDER
WHERE BILLING.CUST_NUMBER = ORDER.CUST_NUMBER
    AND ORDER.ITEM_NUMBER = 2501

This command retrieves the CUST_NAME attribute from the BILLING relation (BILLING.CUST_NAME) and the QTY_ORDERED attribute from the ORDER relation (ORDER.QTY_ORDERED), where the CUST_NUMBER in the BILLING relation is the same as the CUST_NUMBER in the ORDER relation and the ITEM_NUMBER in the ORDER relation is 2501. Figure 16–14 shows how the screen would look after executing this command. The operation performed by this query is called a *join,* because it brings together data from two relations based on a relationship. It is the main way of using relationships between data in a relational database.

The examples given here show how SQL can be used to query a relational database. SQL also has commands to update a relational database. With these commands a user can add data to a relation, delete data from a relation, and change data in a relation.

SQL is used with most relational database management systems. In fact, it has become the standard query language for relational databases. A few relational DBMSs use completely different query languages, however. SQL is not used with hierarchical and network DBMSs. These types of database management systems have unique query languages. Finally, some DBMSs have no query language that can be used interactively by the user.

Figure 16–13 The Screen After Executing an SQL Query(1)

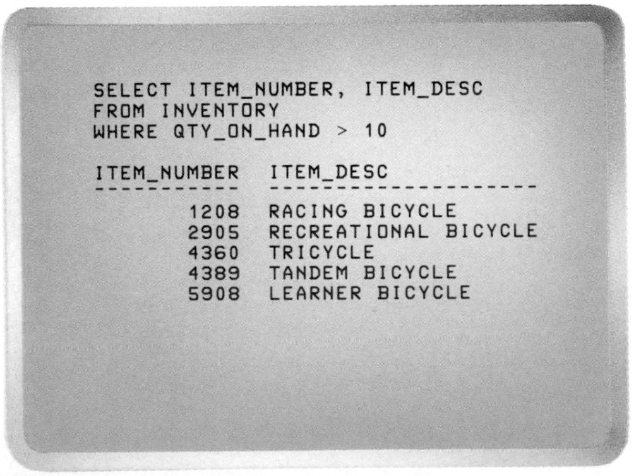

```
SELECT ITEM_NUMBER, ITEM_DESC
FROM INVENTORY
WHERE QTY_ON_HAND > 10

ITEM_NUMBER    ITEM_DESC
-----------    --------------------
       1208    RACING BICYCLE
       2905    RECREATIONAL BICYCLE
       4360    TRICYCLE
       4389    TANDEM BICYCLE
       5908    LEARNER BICYCLE
```

Figure 16–14 The Screen After Executing an SQL Query(2)

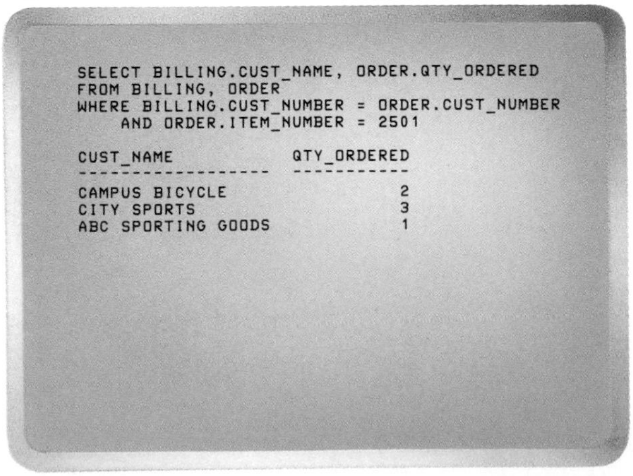

```
SELECT BILLING.CUST_NAME, ORDER.QTY_ORDERED
FROM BILLING, ORDER
WHERE BILLING.CUST_NUMBER = ORDER.CUST_NUMBER
    AND ORDER.ITEM_NUMBER = 2501

CUST_NAME             QTY_ORDERED
------------------    -----------
CAMPUS BICYCLE                  2
CITY SPORTS                     3
ABC SPORTING GOODS              1
```

Host Languages

A **host language** is a programming language for preparing application programs containing commands from a query language. A host language may be a general-purpose programming language that is used for other types of data processing. For example, COBOL is a commonly used host computer language in business. When a programmer uses COBOL as a host language for database processing, he or she places commands from a query language within programs written in COBOL. For example, Figure 16–15 shows part of a COBOL program containing an SQL query. Usually, a programmer can use a host language such as COBOL with several different database management systems. Thus, a programmer can query several databases using the query languages of different DBMSs. To use a general-purpose programming language as a host language requires special training in computer programming and is best left to computer professionals. Using a general-purpose computer language as a host language is a common approach on minicomputers and mainframe computers.

A host language may also be a special-purpose programming language that can be used only with one database management system. In this case, queries are contained within the host language program, but the program can be used only with the particular DBMS for which it is designed. This is the most common approach used on microcomputers. For example, dBASE III PLUS, a microcomputer DBMS, has a host language that can be used only by this DBMS. Figure 16–16 shows part of a dBASE III PLUS program.

Application Generators

An **application generator** is a software system that makes it easy to develop a computer application. With an application generator the user

Figure 16–15   Part of a COBOL Program with an SQL Query

```
DISPLAY "ENTER CUSTOMER NUMBER".
ACCEPT REQUESTED-CUST-NUMBER.
EXEC SQL
    SELECT CUST_NAME, TOTAL_DUE
    INTO :INPUT-CUST-NAME, :INPUT-TOTAL-DUE      } SQL query
    FROM BILLING                                   command
    WHERE CUST_NUMBER = :REQUESTED-CUST-NUMBER
END-EXEC.
MOVE INPUT-CUST-NAME TO OUTPUT-CUST-NAME.
MOVE INPUT-TOTAL-DUE TO OUTPUT-TOTAL-DUE.
DISPLAY OUTPUT-LINE.
```

Figure 16–16   Part of a dBASE III PLUS Program

```
INPUT "ENTER CUSTOMER NUMBER" TO RCUSTNUM
USE BILLING
LIST CUSTNAME, TOTALDUE FOR CUSTNUMBER = RCUSTNUM
```

specifies input and output screen layouts, report formats, menus, and calculations. The user also specifies what data is needed from the database to complete the screens and reports and do the calculations. Then the application generator prepares an application program that accomplishes the required processing. The application program may be in a general-purpose programming language like COBOL, in a special-purpose host language, or in some other form. After the program has been prepared it can be executed on the computer to perform the required processing. Application generators are a type of 4GL, discussed in Chapter 13.

Application generators can be very convenient for developing computer applications. They are used by professional computer personnel and some end-users. They have limits, however, because not all types of processing that can be done with a host language can be done with an application generator.

DATABASE USE IN INFORMATION SYSTEMS

Databases are used in almost all types of information systems. Centralized, teleprocessing, decentralized, and distributed systems can all use databases. They are found in transaction processing systems, management information systems, decision support systems, office automation systems, and executive support systems.

Databases used in single-user information systems are often called **personal databases** because they are used only by one person. Usually, these databases are stored on a microcomputer and processed with a microcomputer database management system. Typically, they are fairly simple databases, with a relatively small amount of data, and are used for only one application. An example is a database of customer and sales data used by only one salesperson. The salesperson creates the database, updates data in it as needed, and accesses data in it to help make sales. It is a personal database for that salesperson.

Multiple-user information systems often require large, complex databases. These databases are used by many users at one time, so we call them **shared databases**. Often, such databases are stored on minicomputers or mainframe computers, where they are processed with a corresponding database management system. Sometimes, shared databases are found on networks of microcomputers. Usually, shared databases are used for several applications. For example, the inventory/order/billing database described earlier could be used for inventory control, order entry, and billing.

Many times with a shared database, each user needs only a part of the database. For example, in processing the inventory/order/billing database, one user may need only inventory and order data and another may need only order and billing data. To prevent users from processing data that they do not need, the database is divided into **views**, which are parts of the database (Figure 16–17). Each user is given access only to his or her view of the database. A user with one view cannot process data in another view.

DATABASE KEEPS THE EARTH'S INVENTORY

The head of the Nature Conservancy's Science Division flashes pictures of rare plants and animals onto a wall of his office, pausing at one of a drab shrub tightly encircled by a fence. "That's the only Pitkin Marsh Paint Brush left on Earth," he says. "That's a depressing thought," someone replies. "It's worse than that," snaps Robert E. Jenkins, Jr. "The plant's a male."

It may be too late for the Nature Conservancy to do anything for the Pitkin Marsh Paint Brush, but aided by an internationally distributed database containing the largest inventory of plants and animals in the world, the Conservancy is quietly and systematically saving endangered species by buying the land on which they live.

The database is the starting point for deciding how the Conservancy will allocate its $100 million-plus annual budget, allowing it to set priorities among thousands of potential land purchases. In the past 40 years, the Conservancy has bought or acquired through gifts some 5 million acres and has built assets worth $619 million.

The database is part of the Conservancy's Biological and Conservation Data System, distributed across 75 data centers in the U.S., Canada, the Caribbean, and Latin America.

The database is actually a collection of some 45 integrated files encompassing 2000 data fields. The key unit of information is an "element occurrence"—one of 65,000 plant or animal species or ecosystems at one of 400,000 locations. Some occurrences are incredibly detailed, with individual plants pinpointed on the globe to within 100 feet. Species and ecosystems are ranked according to their relative endangerment, both regionally and globally.

Each state or region keeps a detailed slice of the database applicable to its area, periodically mailing updates to a database at Conservancy headquarters in Arlington, Virginia. Twice a year, headquarters sends out a software release to the data centers.

The database is an important tool for setting land acquisition priorities. It produces scorecards, one for each state or region, showing conservation priorities in descending order of endangerment.

Not long ago, a scorecard showed that an area in the state of Washington contained two endangered plants and one threatened animal—the extremely rare Oregon Checkermallow, the Green Larkspur and the Larch Mountain Salamander. The Washington area consists of several privately owned parcels and one piece in a national forest. "We're going after them one by one," Jenkins said. "The Green Larkspur is ugly as dirt, but maybe it will cure cancer."

The system began as a centralized mainframe application in 1974. Conservancy officials soon realized the data had to be closer to its source, so each state's offices brought up the application on local minicomputers running a database management system. In the mid-1980s, the remote offices cut over to personal computers running a microcomputer DBMS.

Figure 16–17 User Views of a Database

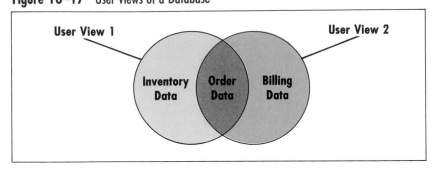

Sometimes a user with a personal database on a microcomputer needs data from a large, shared database on a minicomputer or mainframe computer. To get the data, the user can use micro-to-mainframe data communications techniques (discussed in Chapter 6) to communicate with the larger computer. Then, the user can use the file transfer function of the communications software to download the needed data from the large database to his or her personal database.

DATABASE ADMINISTRATION

Data is an important resource for an organization. With the right data available at the right time, an organization can operate better. To accomplish this goal, organizational data must be managed just like people and money are managed. As data increases in volume and complexity, the management of the data becomes more difficult. With large, complicated databases, the problem of data management is the most severe.

To solve this problem, an organization with large databases often has a person called a **database administrator**, or **DBA**, who is responsible for managing the organization's databases. Some organizations have several database administrators or people with other titles performing the database administration function. As the number, size, and complexity of databases increases, the number of people needed to manage the databases increases.

The database administrator is responsible for the databases. The DBA designs the databases based on the needs of the users. If necessary, he or she changes the databases to meet new requirements. The DBA selects the database management system to process each database. He or she controls the use of the database by giving permission only to specific users to access data in the databases. These tasks and others are performed by the database administrator to manage the database.

Chapter Summary

- A **database** is a collection of data and relationships between data. A **relationship** is a way in which one group of data in a database relates to another group. With file processing, separate files are needed to store the data for each application. In database processing, however, all data is stored together in a database. A **database management system**, or **DBMS**, is a program that provides capabilities for creating, accessing, and updating a database.

- One advantage of database processing over file processing is that duplication of data is reduced. Another advantage is that with database processing, it is easier to process different types of data than with file processing. A third advantage is that programs that do database processing are not dependent on the organization of the data in the database. One disadvantage of database processing is that certain costs are greater than with file processing. Another disadvantage is that data is more vulnerable with database processing than with file processing. A third disadvantage is that information systems that use database processing can be more complex to develop than those that use file processing.

- Relationships are important in database processing because related data are processed through relationships. The three main types of relationships are **one-to-one relationships**, in which one group of data is related to only one other group of data and vice versa; **one-to-many relationships**, in which one group of data is related to many other groups of data but not vice versa; and **many-to-many relationships**, in which many groups of data are related to many other groups of data, and vice versa.

- In a **hierarchical database**, all relationships are one-to-one or one-to-many, but no group of data can be on the "many" side of more than one relationship. In a **network database**, all types of relationships are allowed. In a **relational database**, data is arranged into tables called **relations**. Each table has rows, called **tuples**, and columns, called **attributes**. A relationship exists between two relations when there are common attributes in the relations. Some database management systems use the hierarchical approach, some use the network approach, and some use the relational approach.

- A database management system may be used through a **query language**, which is a programming language that allows the user to query a database—that is, to retrieve data from a database. A database management system may also be used through an application program written in a **host language**, which is a programming language containing commands in a query language. A host language may be a general-purpose programming language, like COBOL, that can be used with several database management systems, or it may be a special-purpose programming language that can be used only with one database management system.

- Databases can be used in almost all types of information systems, including centralized, teleprocessing, decentralized, and distributed systems. Databases can be found in transaction processing, management information, decision support, office automation, and executive support systems. Databases used in single-user information systems are often called **personal databases**. Those found in multiple-user information systems are called **shared databases**. Many times with a shared database each user needs only a part of the database, called a **view**. Sometimes a user with a microcomputer needs to use data communications techniques to transfer data from a shared database to a personal database.

Terms to Remember

Application Generator p. 425

Attribute p. 416

Database p. 407

Database Administrator (DBA)
 p. 428

Database Management System
 (DBMS) p. 411

Distributed Database p. 421

Distributed Database
 Management System p. 421

Hierarchical Database p. 414

Host Language p. 425

Many-to-Many Relationship
 p. 413

Network Database p. 415

Object-Oriented Database p. 421

Object-Oriented Database
 Management System p. 421

One-to-Many Relationship p. 413

One-to-One Relationship p. 412

Personal Database p. 426

Query Language p. 421

Relation p. 416

Relational Database p. 416

Relationship p. 407

Shared Database p. 426

SQL p. 422

Tuple p. 416

View p. 426

Review Questions

Fill-In Questions

1. A database is a collection of data and _____ between the data stored in secondary storage.

2. A(n) _____ is a program used to create, access, and update a database.

3. If each student can have at most one car, and each car can be owned by only one student, then the relationship between students and cars is _____.

4. If each adviser has many students, and each student has only one adviser, then the relationship between advisers and students is _____.

5. If each student can belong to several clubs, and each club can have many student members, then the relationship between students and clubs is _____.

6. Each row in a relation is called a(n) _____, and each column is called a(n) _____.

7. A(n) _____ database is one that is divided into parts, and each part is stored on a different computer in a network.

8. A(n) _____ is a programming language that allows the user to retrieve data from a database. An example is _____.

9. A(n) _____ is a programming language for preparing application programs in which commands from a query language are embedded.

10. A software system that can be used to develop a computer application by specifying screen layouts, report formats, menus, calculations, and database queries is called a(n) _____.

11. A single user would use a(n) _____ database, but multiple users would use a(n) _____ database.

12. The person responsible for managing the databases of an organization is called a(n) _____.

Short-Answer Questions

1. Explain the difference between file processing and database processing.

2. Give several advantages of database processing.

3. Give several disadvantages of database processing.

4. Why are relationships important in database processing?

5. Explain the difference between a hierarchical database and a network database.

6. What is a relational database?

7. What type of database is considered to be the easiest for users to use?

8. Give some trends for future DBMSs.

9. Describe two ways that a user can use a database.

10. What is a *view* of a database?

Projects

1. Investigate a minicomputer or mainframe computer database management system. What is the name of the DBMS, and with which computers can it be used? How much does it cost? Is it a hierarchical, network, or relational DBMS? Does it have a query language? With which host languages can it be used?

2. Find out how an organization or business to which you have access uses databases. What databases does the organization have? For what information systems is each database used? Which databases are used by single users and which by multiple users? Write a summary of your findings.

17

DEVELOPING INFORMATION SYSTEMS

CHAPTER OBJECTIVES

• After completing this chapter you should be able to:

1. List the people who are involved in information system development.

2. Outline the phases in the information system development process.

3. Describe the user's involvement in each phase of the system development process.

4. Explain the purpose of several common tools used for system development.

T

HE LAST THREE CHAPTERS discussed various aspects of information systems. One theme common to these chapters is that information systems are complex: they consist of several components that perform many functions to meet different information processing needs of an organization. Because of their complexity, information systems do not just "appear"; they are developed by people who follow a specific process. This process involves many steps and may take a few days to several years to complete. This chapter discusses the process of information systems development.

PEOPLE IN INFORMATION SYSTEMS DEVELOPMENT

The people who are primarily responsible for developing information systems are called **systems analysts**. In a moment you will learn the step-by-step process that systems analysts go through to develop a system. Other people, such as programmers, also may be involved in the development process. Programming, however, is a special process that was discussed in Chapter 12.

Users of the system are another important group of people involved in the system development process. An information system is designed to meet the needs of its users. To accomplish this goal, the users must explain their needs to the systems analysts. In addition, the users must determine if the system that is developed is what they need. As you will see, users are involved in many steps of the system development process.

Often, systems are developed by a group of people called a **project team**. The team may consist of several systems analysts and programmers. Users also are usually included on the team. One person, usually an experienced systems analyst, is designated as the team leader.

THE SYSTEM DEVELOPMENT PROCESS

There are many ways of describing the system development process, which is sometimes called the *system development life cycle*. This book divides the process into five main phases:

- System planning
- System analysis
- System design
- System implementation
- System maintenance

Each phase involves several steps that are summarized in Figure 17–1 and discussed later.

Figure 17–1 The System Development Process

System Planning
Problem recognition and definition Feasibility analysis
System Analysis
Current system analysis User requirements analysis System specification Alternative identification and evaluation
System Design
Input and output design File or database design Program and procedure design
System Implementation
System acquisition System testing System installation
System Maintenance

System planning is the phase in which the systems analyst decides whether a new information system should be developed. During **system analysis**, the analyst studies the existing system and determines what the new system must do. Then, during **system design**, the analyst specifies how the new system will function. In the next phase, **system implementation**, the systems analyst acquires the components of the system—such as the programs—tests the system, and changes over to the new system. Finally, **system maintenance** involves modifying the system during its life to meet new requirements.

System Planning

In the first phase of the system development process the systems analyst plans what information systems will be developed. To start the planning phase, someone must recognize the need for a new information system. Usually, some type of system already exists in the organization. The existing system may be manual or computerized; it may be formal, with written procedures, or informal, remembered by a few people. In any case, someone must recognize a problem with the existing system and recommend that a new system be developed.

Often, the user of an existing system recognizes the problem. For example, a salesperson using an order entry system may sense a problem with the system when customers complain that orders are being lost. A user may also determine that an entirely new system is needed—one that does things that are not done by any existing system. Even in this case there still is a problem: What is wrong with the existing system that it cannot do everything required? In any case, the user must report the problem to the person responsible for system development.

Next, someone, usually a systems analyst, must carefully define the problem, distinguishing it from its symptoms. For example, lost orders are a symptom of a problem in an order entry system. The actual problem may be inadequate checks for errors in the system, or unreliable hardware. The systems analyst must prepare written documentation of the problem. This documentation establishes the need for the information system.

After the need for an information system has been recognized, the systems analyst must determine if it is feasible to develop the system, a process called **feasibility analysis**. An information system is feasible if it is possible to develop the system using existing technology, if the people in the business will use it, and if it makes economic sense for the business. To evaluate the economic feasibility of the system, the analyst compares the expected costs with the expected benefits of the system, a process called **cost/benefit analysis**. If the total benefits over the life of the system are greater than the total costs over its life, then the system is economically feasible.

After completing the feasibility analysis, the analyst should prepare written documentation of the results. If the system is not feasible, the development process ends at this point. For a feasible system the analyst goes on to the next phase.

System Analysis

After the systems analyst has decided that a new system is feasible, he or she must analyze the system to determine *what* it must do. The analyst starts by analyzing the current system. He or she gathers any written documentation about the current system and collects copies of all forms and documents used in the system. If the current system is computerized, the analyst determines the output (screens and reports) produced by the system, the files or databases used by the system, the input entered into the system, and the processing done by the system. The systems analyst must interview the user to determine what the system actually does. Finally, the analyst prepares written documentation that describes the current system.

Next, the analyst determines what the user requires in the new system. The analyst talks to the user about the user's needs. He or she prepares written **user requirements**, which state what the system will do to help the user in his or her job. The requirements should be such that problems identified earlier are solved by the new system. For example, the following is a requirement for an order processing system:

> The system will allow a salesperson to determine the current status of any sales order at any time.

In the user requirements analysis, the analyst determines what the user needs. Next, the analyst determines what the new system must do to meet the user's needs. The result of this step is called the **system specifications**. For example, to satisfy the requirement for the order processing system just given, the systems analyst may decide that the system will process a query from the salesperson regarding the status of a sales order. To do so, the system will access stored data about sales orders and will supply a response to the salesperson. The systems analyst determines what functions the system will perform to meet each of the user's requirements, and prepares written documentation of these functions. Often, the analyst will review this documentation with the user.

Now that the analyst has an understanding of the functions of the new system, he or she needs to examine alternatives for performing the functions. The alternatives mainly revolve around the hardware and software components of the system, although the other components (stored data, personnel, and procedures) may be considered. The analyst identifies alternatives and estimates the costs and benefits of each alternative. Then, using cost/benefit analysis, the analyst selects the best alternative for the system and prepares written documentation to justify the choice.

Hardware and Software Alternatives.   Figure 17–2 summarizes the common hardware and software alternatives for an information system. If the organization already has a computer in-house, then the decision often is to continue to use it. If the decision is to acquire a new computer, then the choice must be made between a microcomputer, a minicomputer, or a mainframe computer. In addition, networks of computers should be considered. An alternative to in-house hardware is to use a computer operated by a **service bureau**, which is a company that does computer processing for other organizations.

Figure 17–2   Information System Hardware and Software Alternatives

Hardware
Use in-house hardware
Microcomputer
Minicomputer
Mainframe computer
Network
User service bureau's hardware
Software
Develop custom software using in-house programmers
Have custom software developed by software house
Purchase packaged software
Purchase packaged software and modify
Use service bureau's software

The software alternatives depend on the hardware choice. If in-house hardware is used, the organization can develop custom software using its own in-house programmers. This approach yields software that is designed for the exact needs of the organization, but it can be very time-consuming and expensive to develop the software. In addition, the organ-ization must have its own programming staff for this approach. Alternatively, the organization can contract with a type of company called a **software house** to develop the software. This approach also provides for highly customized software, but it may be more expensive than using in-house programmers. Still, the organization is not stuck with a programming staff after the software has been developed.

The next alternative is to purchase packaged software. This alternative is usually the least expensive, but the software may not be exactly what the organization needs. Another alternative is to purchase packaged software and modify the programs to more closely meet the organization's needs. This approach produces software that is closer to the organization's needs than just the packaged programs, but it is more expensive.

If hardware at a service bureau is used for processing, the service bureau usually supplies the software. Sometimes, however, the organization will provide its own software. Then the software can be acquired by any of the methods discussed previously.

Prototyping.   One of the biggest problems in systems analysis is understanding the user's requirements. Often the user cannot state clearly what he or she needs. Many times, after a system has been developed, the user says that the system is not what he or she wanted. All the steps that follow the user requirements analysis step depend on accurate requirements. If the requirements are not accurate, the system will not meet the user's needs.

An alternative approach to systems development that attempts to solve this problem is called **prototyping**. In this approach the systems analyst obtains informal and incomplete requirements from the user. He or she then develops a **prototype** of the system, which is a partial version of the system that acts like the real system for the user but that does not perform all the required functions. The prototype is developed very quickly using special prototyping software. The prototype includes sample screens and reports so that the user can see what the system will do. The user then has a chance to change his or her requirements, and the analyst modifies the prototype to reflect the changes. After several such modifications the prototype reaches a point at which the user is happy with it.

Prototyping replaces the user requirements analysis and system specification steps. Identifying and evaluating alternatives still is necessary, but one of the alternatives now is to continue to develop the prototype into the final system. If this alternative is selected, then prototyping also replaces the system design phase.

System Design

Now that the analyst has an understanding of what the new system must do, he or she can design *how* the system will do it. The steps in this process depend on which alternative is selected. If the software will be developed by in-house programmers, one approach is followed. The result of this approach is a system design that specifies how the information system will work. If a different alternative is selected, another approach may be needed.

System Design for In-House Development.

When the software will be developed in-house, the first step in the system design process is to decide how the functions of the information system will be performed. At this stage the analyst selects the form of the input and output. For example, the analyst decides how input will be entered—by keyboard, by mouse, or by some other method. He or she decides in what form the output will be returned—on a screen, on paper, or in some other form. The analyst also selects the type of secondary storage—disk or tape—and decides whether files or a database will be used. Finally, the analyst identifies the programs and manual procedures that will be involved in the processing and the personnel that will be needed.

Next, the analyst specifies the details of the design. These details include the following:

- Layouts of all screens, reports, and forms.
- Organization of all records, files, and databases.
- Descriptions of all programs.
- Descriptions of all manual procedures.
- Specifications for all hardware.
- Descriptions of all personnel.

The systems analyst will consult with the user while designing the system. For example, the analyst will ask the user about screen, report, and form layouts. In addition, the user may be involved in describing procedures. The systems analyst, however, develops most of the design and prepares written documentation of the design.

Alternative Approaches.

When an alternative other than in-house software development is selected, the system design phase may have to be modified. If a software house is selected to develop the software, then the system design may proceed as described using the organization's analysts, or analysts from the software house may design the system. When packaged software is to be purchased, a system design may not be needed because the software usually determines how the system will function. Requirements that specify what the software packages should do, however, should be prepared at this time. If packaged software is to be modified, then software requirements should be prepared and a system design that specifies what modifications are needed should be developed. When the decision is to have a service bureau do the processing with its own software, a system design is not necessary. Instead, requirements for the service bureau should be prepared.

System Implementation

In the next phase of the system development process the analyst puts together the components of the new system, tests them, and changes over to using the new system. The steps in this phase may vary somewhat, depending on which hardware and software alternatives are selected.

The first step is to acquire the components of the new system. Recall that an information system has five components: hardware, software, stored data, personnel, and procedures. Some of the components may already exist in the organization, some may have to be acquired from outside the organization, and some are constructed within the organization.

For the hardware component, if the system will use existing in-house hardware, then usually nothing needs to be done. If new hardware is to be purchased, however, then alternative equipment that meets the hardware specifications is evaluated and a selection is made. When a service bureau is to be used, various service bureaus are evaluated and one is selected.

For the software component, if in-house programmers are to be used to develop the software, then the programming is done at this time. The programming process can be complex, involving several steps, as discussed in Chapter 12. When a software house will develop the software, the system design is turned over to the software house for programming. If packaged software is to be purchased, then software alternatives are evaluated and a selection is made at this time. Any modifications to the software are done after the software has been acquired.

The stored data component is not completely constructed at this time. Instead, files or databases are created with sample data that can be used to test the software and the system. The actual data is stored later.

Employees are selected for the personnel component during this step. The personnel may already work for the organization, or they may have to be hired from outside the organization. Training, however, usually takes place later.

Finally, the manual procedures that make up the procedures component are developed at this time. Written documentation of any manual procedures required in the system is prepared.

The next step is to make sure that the system works as required, which involves testing the system. Before this step is undertaken the parts of the system are tested individually as they are acquired. For example, all programs are thoroughly tested as they are prepared. During the system testing step, the parts are brought together and the system is tested as a whole. This process involves running the system through all its phases using sample input data and sample data in files or databases. All system functions are checked with what is expected, and any differences mean that there are errors in the system. When an error is detected, the part of the system that caused the error must be modified and tested again. This process continues until no errors are detected in the system.

COMPUTER CLOSE-UP

17–1

A SYSTEM FOR EDUCATION

The company has an annual operating budget of $2 billion.

With that money, it manages the second largest restaurant chain in Illinois after McDonald's, runs one of the state's biggest trucking fleets, does a brisk catalog sideline business and has one million on-line clients—all under the age of 21.

"If you drew up a Fortune 500 list, we'd be smack in the middle," said Clifford E. Cox.

But where computers and academic administration mean business, the Chicago Board of Education heads the list.

"We're in the business of developing students," said Cox, who left a consultant's post at Arthur Anderson & Co. eight years ago to become the assistant superintendent in charge of updating and managing the district's information systems IS needs vis-à-vis its students.

The result is a system that is reducing truancy, giving teachers more classroom time and boosting test scores for 425,000 students in kindergarten through 12th grade in a district composed of minority children from low-income families.

"Vendors come in here all the time thinking we're just a school system they can sell a simple software package to. I tell them they have to think of us as a corporation," Cox said.

Cox has told that to the Board of Education as well, with dramatic results so far.

To date, the board has given him more than $25 million to create a modern on-line system from one that existed on magnetic cards; a system whose IS personnel now work on new applications instead of merely running outmoded programs; and a system that can instantly transmit a student's complete record from any one of 600 schools when it used to take as much as three months to transfer what was often an incomplete paper file.

Along the way, the country's third largest school system has drawn the attention of academia's IS managers from Los Angeles and New York—the nation's first and second largest school districts, respectively—and from as far away as Puerto Rico and Singapore. They come to look at the school's electronic attendance application, whose most talked-about feature is its auto-dialer, which calls the homes of students who are absent without a legitimate excuse.

The function is part of a one-two punch, supplementing teachers' calls to parents. It works from data that teachers enter during the day on the status of students who do not make it to class.

At one high school, 88% of the student body now shows up for classes, nearly a 2% improvement over last year.

They also come to examine an electronic report card application that, in one instance, allows a teacher with 125 students to key in her students' grades in about 20 minutes. Previously, teachers entered grades by hand, taking an entire day to do so—a day in which students did not have to attend class.

"This means I can teach a whole other chapter of math and sometimes more," explained high school teacher Ofelia Solano-Guevara.

Another example of the attention Cox's Comprehensive Student Information System is drawing in academic administration circles is an electronic student record system. When fully implemented, these electronic files will chart students' progress—their grades, attendance, special needs, medical history, transportation needs and awards—from when they enter kindergarten to when they graduate from high school.

Cox characterized the system as "for teachers, by teachers."

One teacher is former high school math and computer programming instructor Laura Spitzbarth, who switched careers to do what she had been teaching. It gave her a huge advantage in being able to design in a fourth-generation language, for example, a 12-computer system that handles scheduling for both teachers and students.

Modernizing the system was done out of sheer necessity because "we were all getting writer's cramp from doing the programs by hand. And we wanted to eliminate redundancy," she said, adding that high schools with more than 600 students need access to a computer for programming enrollment and scheduling.

The last step in the system implementation phase is to install the new system in the business. It is usually at this time that the personnel, including the users, receive their training in the operation and use of the system. In addition, the actual data to be used by the system is stored in the files or databases.

The final activity of this step is to convert from the old system to the new system. The change is usually made gradually by phasing in a part of the new system at a time. Sometimes both the old system and the new system are used simultaneously for a period of time to check for errors in the new system. Eventually, the old system is stopped completely and the conversion is complete.

The steps in the implementation phase are performed under the direction of the systems analyst, although other personnel may do much of the work. Hardware specialists may be involved in acquiring any hardware. Programmers develop the software, create files or databases, and assist with the testing. Managers usually hire personnel, and technical writers prepare written procedures. The training staff train personnel including users. After the system is finished, the user usually is asked to compare the system with the user's requirements and accept or reject it.

System Maintenance

After a system has been operating for a while, it may have to be modified, which is the process of system maintenance. Maintenance is required for three reasons. The first is that errors are found that were not detected when the system was tested. Even though the system was thoroughly tested, errors often appear after the system has been in use for a while. The second reason is that a new function is to be added to the system. For example, the preparation of a new report may be needed. The final reason for system maintenance is that requirements change. For example, programs that produce income tax returns have to be modified almost every year because of changing tax laws.

Whenever maintenance is needed, an abbreviated version of the previous four phases is followed. First, the problem that requires system maintenance must be recognized and defined. Then, the feasibility of performing the maintenance must be examined. In some cases, such as in correcting an error in the system or in meeting new legal requirements, feasibility is not an issue, but in other cases, such as when new functions are requested, a feasibility analysis should be done.

Next, the current system needs to be examined to determine how the change should be made. If not already stated, the user's requirements for the change need to be specified and the specific system function affected by the change must be analyzed. Sometimes alternatives to modifying the existing system are examined. For example, it may be less costly to purchase a new program than to modify an existing one.

System design for the modification should be performed. Then, the programming or other activity necessary to make the change is done. Next, the system is tested with the modification. Finally, the modified system is installed.

Any of the people associated with the development of an information system may be involved in system maintenance. Systems analysts and programmers usually do most of the work, but hardware specialists, managers, technical writers, equipment operators, and trainers may also be involved. The user, too, is included in the process to ensure that the modified system meets the user requirements.

SYSTEM DEVELOPMENT TOOLS

Several tools are used during the system development process to help in the analysis and design of the system. These tools provide a way for the systems analyst to organize his or her thinking about the system and to examine alternative designs. They also serve as documentation of the different steps in the process. The user may have to review some of this documentation during the system development process. A description of several of the more commonly used tools follows.

Data Flow Diagrams

A tool that many analysts use to show the flow of data in an information system is the **data flow diagram**, or **DFD**. Figure 17–3 shows a data flow diagram for an order entry system. In a DFD, a circle is used for a *process*, which is any step that involves manipulating data. The words inside the circle state briefly what the process does. Boxes are used for *data sources*, which are people or organizations who send input data, and *data destinations*, which are receivers of output data. A descriptive name for the person or organization is written inside the box. Two horizontal lines are used for *stored data*, which is any data kept by the system in any form, such as in a file or database. A name that describes the stored data is written between the lines. Finally, lines with arrowheads are used for *data flows*. Data may flow from a data source to a process, between processes, from a process to a data destination, and between a process and stored data. The arrowheads indicate the directions of the data flow. Each data flow line has a name written next to it that describes the data that flows, although data that flows to and from stored data does not need a description because the stored data's name provides the description.

Data flow diagrams are used in several steps of the system development process. They are used in the analysis of the current system to document what the existing system does. In addition, they are used in system specifications to describe the functions of the new system. Finally, they are used in system design to show the design of the new system.

A tool that is used in conjunction with a data flow diagram is the **data dictionary**. The data dictionary describes the data in each data flow and in each set of stored data in the DFD. Figure 17–4 gives part of the data dictionary for the order entry system. This figure describes the customer-order input, the stored order data, and the sales order output. Each description includes the name of the data flow or stored data, an equals sign, and the names of the data items or fields that make up the data.

Figure 17–3 A Data Flow Diagram

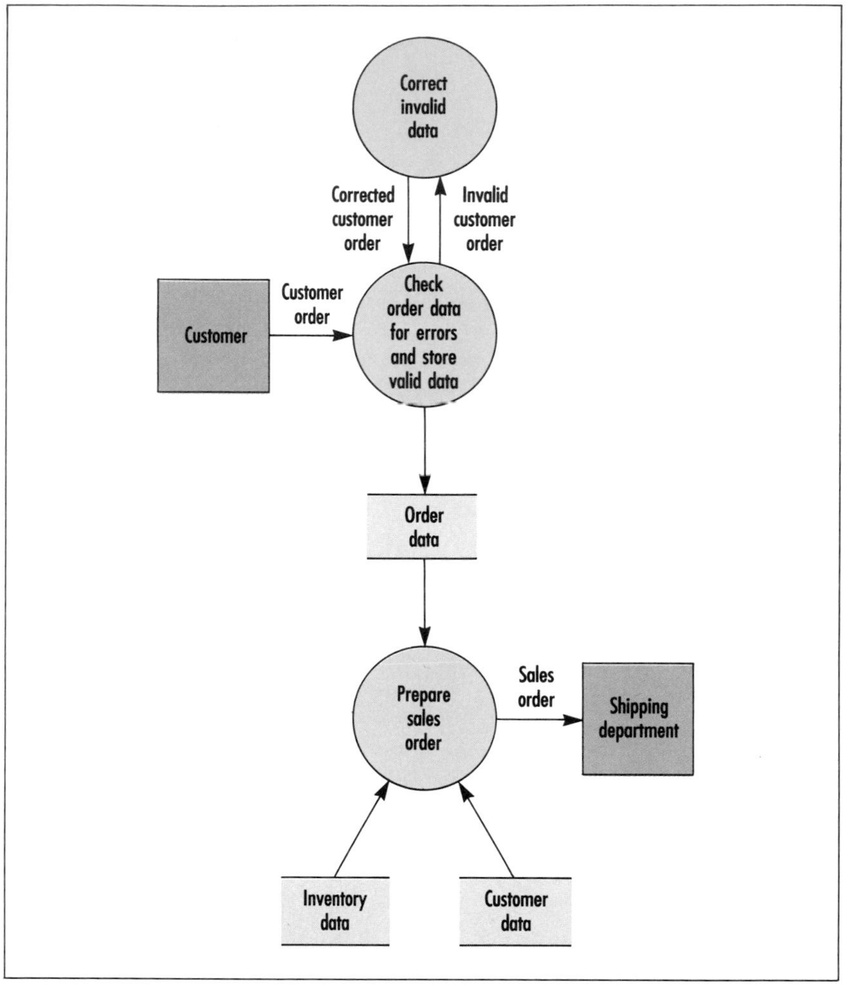

The data names are separated by plus signs to indicate that the item on the left of the equals sign is the "sum" of the items on the right.

The data dictionary describes the data in a data flow diagram. To describe the processes in the DFD, the analyst uses **process descriptions**. There is one process description for each process in the DFD. Several techniques are used for process descriptions, including pseudocode and program flowcharts, which are discussed in Chapter 12. Another technique is *structured English*, which is a simple form of English that uses an outline to describe a process. For example, Figure 17–5 shows the structured English description of one of the processes in the order entry system. This description is a step-by-step outline that uses simple words and data names from the data dictionary to specify the steps in the process. There would be a similar structured English description for each of the other processes in the DFD.

Figure 17–4 Data Dictionary Descriptions

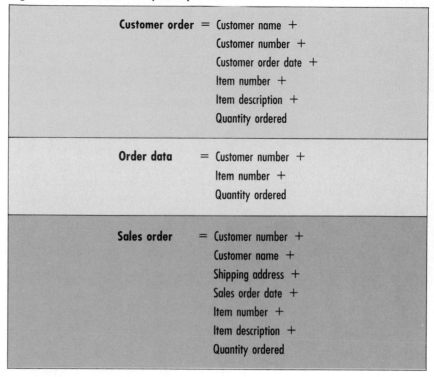

Customer order = Customer name +
Customer number +
Customer order date +
Item number +
Item description +
Quantity ordered

Order data = Customer number +
Item number +
Quantity ordered

Sales order = Customer number +
Customer name +
Shipping address +
Sales order date +
Item number +
Item description +
Quantity ordered

Figure 17–5 A Process Description

Prepare sales order process

For each customer order in the order data do the following:
  1. Determine the customer credit rating from the customer data.
  2. If the customer credit rating is satisfactory, do the following:
     a. Print the customer number, customer name, shipping address, and sales order date on the sales order.
     b. For each item ordered, determine the quantity on hand from the inventory data.
     c. For each item where the quantity ordered is less than or equal to the quantity on hand, print the item number, item description, and quantity ordered on the sales order.

System Flowcharts

Another tool that is used by systems analysts is a **system flowchart**, which is a graphical representation of the functioning of an information system. It is similar to a data flow diagram in that it shows the flow of data in an information system. In addition, a system flowchart shows what type of input data, output data, stored data, and programs will be used in the system. It is different from a program flowchart (discussed in Chapter 12), which shows the flow of logic in a single program.

In a system flowchart the shapes of symbols provide information about the system. Figure 17–6 shows some of the symbols that are used, and Figure 17–7 gives an example of a system flowchart for an order entry system. The *process symbol* is used for any processing function, whether it is done by a computer or manually. If the processing is done by a computer, the symbol corresponds to one or more computer programs. If the processing is done manually, the symbol corresponds to a procedure performed by a person. The *keyboard input symbol*, *screen output symbol*, and *report output symbol* are used for different types of input and output. The *magnetic disk storage symbol* and *magnetic tape storage symbol* are used for different types of data storage. Within each symbol is written a description of the processing, input data, output data, or stored data. The symbols in the flowchart are connected by *flowlines* with arrowheads that show the direction of flow of data within the system. By following the flowlines and reading the symbols in a system flowchart you can get a general understanding of the functioning of an information system.

System flowcharts are used in several steps in the system development process. They are used to document the functioning of the current system and also to show the design of a new system.

Figure 17–6 System Flowchart Symbols

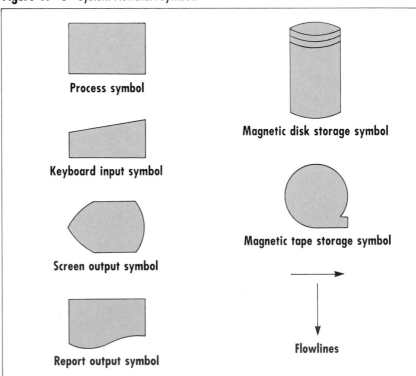

Process symbol

Keyboard input symbol

Screen output symbol

Report output symbol

Magnetic disk storage symbol

Magnetic tape storage symbol

Flowlines

Figure 17–7   A System Flowchart

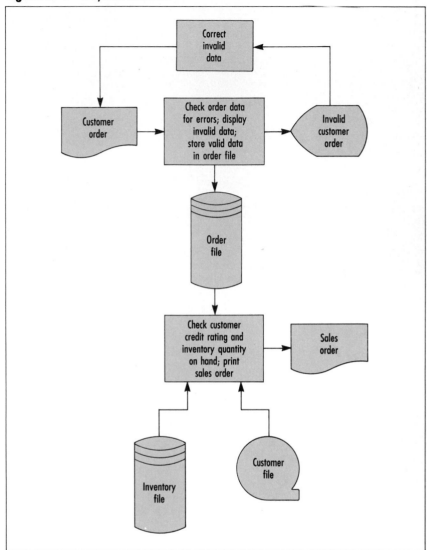

Layout Forms

During the design of the system, the systems analyst prepares the layouts of all input and output, using different forms. For screen I/O, a **screen layout form** is often used. For example, Figure 17–8 shows the layout of a customer order entry screen on such a form. The screen layout form is divided into rows that correspond to lines on a screen and columns that correspond to character positions in each line. The systems analyst writes words or phrases on the form in the exact positions in which they will be displayed on the screen. The analyst uses Xs in the positions where input data will be entered or where variable output data will be displayed.

Figure 17–8   A Screen Layout Form

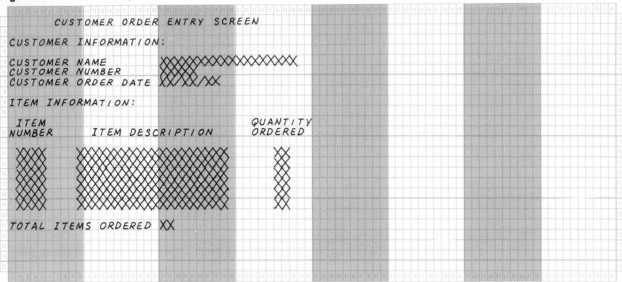

To show the layout of printed output, a **print chart** is used during the design of the system. For example, Figure 17–9 gives the layout of a sales order on such a form. The print chart is divided into rows that correspond to printed lines, and columns that correspond to character positions in each line. As with a screen layout form, the systems analyst writes words or phrases on the form in the exact positions in which they will appear on the printed output, and uses Xs in the positions where variable output data will appear.

Figure 17–9   A Print Chart

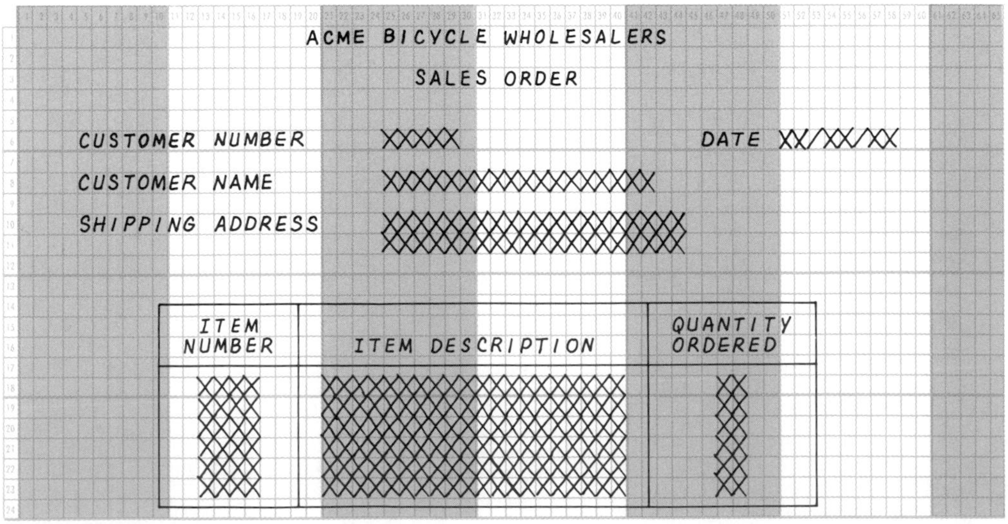

CASE

Some of the tools that are used in systems development are available in computer software. For example, software is available that allows the systems analyst to draw data flow diagrams on a screen (Figure 17–10). The analyst also can develop data dictionaries and process descriptions to accompany the diagrams. Using computer-based tools such as these for systems development is called **CASE**, which stands for Computer-Aided Software Engineering. (The term *software engineering* is sometimes used for the process of developing systems of computer programs.) CASE tools are also available to help in program development.

A CASE STUDY

To illustrate the system development process, let's examine a case study. Acme Bicycle Wholesalers sells bicycles to retail stores throughout the country. It currently has basic information systems for order entry, billing, and so forth. The sales manager, Ann Nelson, feels that the business is not doing the best job it can in selling bicycles because she and other sales personnel do not have good information about how well each bicycle is selling and which regions of the country have high sales and which have low sales. Therefore, she has requested a computerized sales analysis system.

System Planning

Ann has started the system development process by recognizing the need for a new system. She has identified a problem with the existing system. The problem, as she sees it, is that inadequate sales information is available. She has recommended that a new system be developed to

Figure 17–10   A Data Flow Diagram Drawn on a Screen Using a CASE Tool

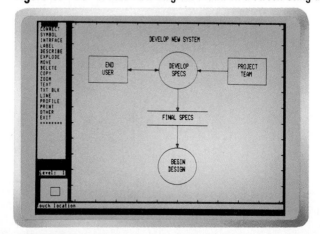

help solve the problem. She will be the user of the system, along with other sales personnel.

A systems analyst, John Boyce, is then assigned to the project. John talks to Ann about the problem and about the idea of a computerized sales analysis system. After a little research into the existing systems, John realizes that the problem is not that sales information is unavailable; the necessary data is stored in various files. The real problem is that no system exists for retrieving the data and making it available for use by sales personnel.

Next, John does a feasibility analysis of the proposed system. He talks to Ann again and to the sales personnel to get a general idea of their requirements for the new system. He realizes that the system involves retrieving data from existing files and preparing appropriate reports. The system is within the technical sophistication of the computer personnel in the business, and the people are likely to use the system because the sales manager has requested it and the sales personnel are enthusiastic about it. John does a cost/benefit analysis to determine the economic feasibility of the new system. He estimates the costs of developing and operating the system and the benefits from increased sales. Because the benefits exceed the costs, the system is economically feasible and the decision is made to proceed with the development of the system.

System Analysis

Now John looks at how sales analysis is currently done. He knows there is no computerized sales analysis system, but there may be a manual system in use. In talking to Ann and the sales personnel, he discovers that a written report is prepared each month listing the best-selling bicycles and the sales regions that have the most sales (Figure 17–11). No information, however, is kept on poor-selling bicycles or on regions with low sales. The current system is very informal and inaccurate. Each month someone in the sales department goes through copies of sales orders for that month and counts the number of orders on which each item appears. This person also determines from the address on each sales order which sales region the customer is in, and counts the number of sales orders in each region. Finally, he or she prepares a list of the five best-selling bicycles and the three top sales regions.

John notices immediately that these lists do not take into consideration the quantity sold or the selling price and that only the best-selling bicycles and top sales regions are listed. He talks to Ann about the current system.

Figure 17–11 Sales Analysis Sheets

```
        THIS MONTH'S
    BEST SELLING BICYCLES

    RACING BICYCLE
    MOUNTAIN BIKE
    TRICYCLE
    RECREATIONAL BICYCLE
    TOURING BICYCLE
```

```
        THIS MONTH'S
     TOP SALES REGIONS

        NORTHWEST
        ATLANTIC
        SOUTHEAST
```

Together they prepare the user requirements for the new system (Figure 17–12). John then discusses these requirements with the other sales personnel to be sure they correctly state what is needed.

Next, John prepares the system specifications for the new system. He knows that order data, inventory data, and customer data are available. By combining these data, the data needed for sales analysis can be produced. Once the sales analysis data is produced, reports listing the total sales of each item (sales by item) and the total sales for each sales region (sales by region) can be prepared. John prepares a data flow diagram for the system (Figure 17–13). He also prepares a data dictionary and process descriptions. He goes over these system specifications with Ann to be sure the new system will meet the users' needs.

The business has adequate computer hardware for the new system. John thinks briefly about packaged software but decides that the system

Figure 17–12 The User Requirements for the New System

Sales analysis system user requirements

1. The system will produce a report each month listing the month's total dollar sales for each item. The items will be listed in decreasing order of sales.

2. The system will produce a report each month listing the month's total dollar sales for each sales region. The regions will be listed in alphabetical order.

Figure 17–13 The Data Flow Diagram for the New System

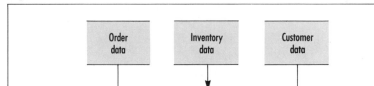

must be customized for the business and that packaged software therefore will not work. The business has in-house programmers who are capable of preparing the programs, so John decides to develop the software using the existing programming staff.

System Design

Now John prepares the system design. The order data, inventory data, and customer data already exist in disk files. He decides that the sales analysis data should be a disk file also. Three programs will be needed in the system: one to produce the sales analysis data, one to prepare the sales by item report, and one to prepare the sales by region report. John draws a system flowchart of the system design (Figure 17–14).

Figure 17–14 The System Flowchart for the New System

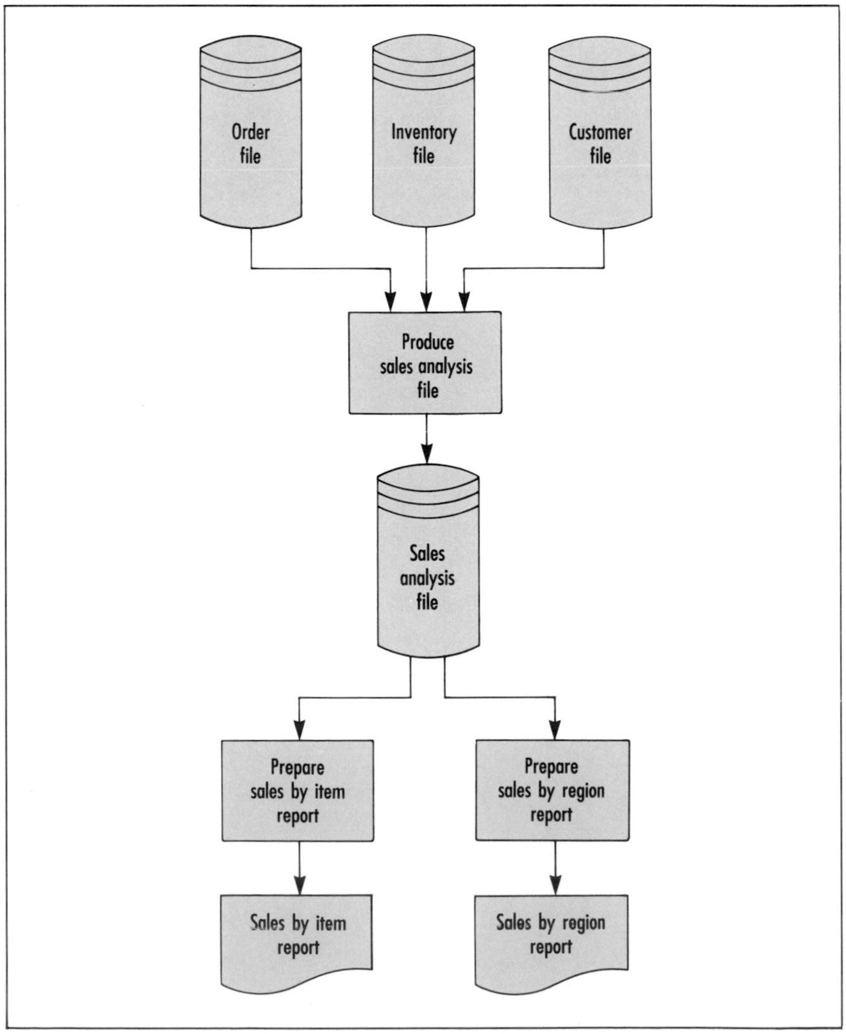

COMPUTER CLOSE-UP

17–2

END-USER SYSTEM DEVELOPMENT

This chapter has emphasized the role of the systems analyst in developing information systems. The user is involved in the process by providing information to the analyst and reviewing the analyst's work. Sometimes, however, the user develops a system without the aid of a systems analyst, a process called *end-user system development.*

Users usually develop only small, single-user information systems that involve a single application on a microcomputer. Large, multiple-user systems that use minicomputers or mainframe computers almost always are developed by systems analysts. Such systems are usually very complex, and special training is required to know how to develop them. Even some microcomputer-based information systems are complex and should be developed only by a systems analyst or other specially trained person.

When the user develops his or her own system, the user is acting as a systems analyst. The same basic phases that are used for large-system development should be followed. Some of the steps can be simplified, however.

End-user system development starts when the user recognizes the need for an information system. The user must identify the problems that a new system will help solve. Then, he or she should investigate the feasibility of developing the system. Many users assume that a computerized solution is the best alternative, but often a manual system is better. The user should quickly analyze whether the desired system is within his or her technical competence and whether he or she will use it. The user should get preliminary estimates of costs and benefits to decide if it is economically beneficial. In analyzing the costs, the user must carefully consider the time he or she will have to spend in developing the system. System development can be very time consuming, and the user has to realize that the time spent developing the system is taken away from other activities.

Next, the user should think about the current system. He or she should gather reports and forms that are currently used. Then, the user should outline his or her requirements for the new system. The requirements analysis is the most important part of the process because without a good understanding of what is needed, the user will not be able to develop a suitable system. Now the user can figure out what functions the new system must perform. An outline of the system specifications might be adequate, or the user may try to sketch a simple data flow diagram. The use of sophisticated DFDs and other tools should be left to computer professionals. Finally, the user should look at alternative approaches for the hardware and software for the system and select the approach he or she feels is best. Most often the approach selected is for the user to acquire his or her own microcomputer (if the user does not already have one) and packaged software.

During the next phase the user should prepare specifications for the hardware and the packaged software. The user should write down details about the hardware, such as how much auxiliary storage is needed, and for the software, such as what features the program should have. When packaged software is used to develop the user's application, a detailed design should be prepared. For example, if the user decides to use database management software, he or she must determine the organization of the records, sketch the layouts of all screens, reports, and forms, and note what calculations are required.

Next, the user can evaluate alternative hardware and software and make a selection. Then, he or she can use the selected packaged software to develop the application for the system. Application development with packaged software involves setting up the software for the user's specific use. Next, the user should make up sample data and thoroughly test the software and the system. He or she should prepare written documentation of how the system works and how it is used in case the user leaves the business and someone else needs to use the system. Finally, the user can set up the actual data and start using the new system. The user should convert gradually to the new system to be sure it works correctly.

After the user has used the system for a while, he or she may have to make modifications in it. The procedure for system maintenance of a single-user information system is basically the same as for larger systems.

You can see from this discussion that system development by end-users follows the same steps as system development by systems analysts. The user may not use the same tools as the systems analyst at each step, and the analysis may not be as formal. The user must follow a systematic approach, however, to ensure that the resulting system meets his or her needs.

Next, John prepares a print chart for each report and shows the print charts to Ann to get her approval (Figure 17–15). The contents of the records in the order, inventory, and customer files are known, but he must decide on the contents of the records in the sales analysis file and how the file will be organized. He also documents what each program must do and notes that a manual procedure will be needed to tell the computer operator how to run the programs and what to do with the output.

System Implementation

Next, a programmer is assigned to prepare the programs for the systems. While the programmer works on the programs, John arranges the other components of the system. The hardware is available, so nothing needs to be done about it. Data files already exist, but John decides to make copies of the files for testing purposes. The computer operator who will run the programs and deliver the output is identified. Finally, John prepares the operator's procedures.

After the programs and other components have been completed, John tests the system with the sample files. He carefully checks the output for errors and has to have some corrections made by the programmer. Once he has determined that the system is working correctly, he takes the sample output to Ann for her approval (Figure 17–16). Ann brings in

Figure 17–15 The Print Charts for the Sales Analysis Reports

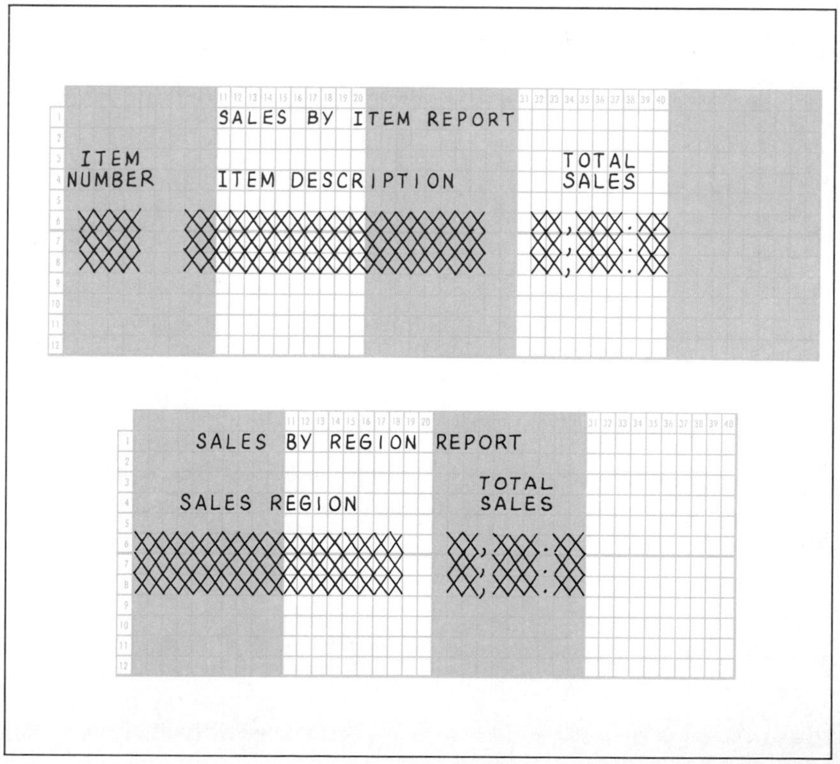

Figure 17–16 The Sales Analysis Reports

```
         SALES BY ITEM REPORT

   ITEM                          TOTAL
  NUMBER   ITEM DESCRIPTION      SALES

   1208   RACING BICYCLE         15,147.50
   3504   MOUNTAIN BIKE          12,370.65
   4360   TRICYCLE               11,094.00
   2905   RECREATIONAL BICYCLE   10,755.25
   2501   TOURING BICYCLE         9,208.00
   5124   JUNIOR BICYCLE          8,541.75
   5908   LEARNER BICYCLE         6,468.50
   6531   PORTABLE BICYCLE        2,370.40
   4389   TANDEM BICYCLE            512.00
```

```
         SALES BY REGION REPORT

                                 TOTAL
         SALES REGION            SALES

   ATLANTIC                      15,242.50
   NORTH CENTRAL                  6,850.20
   NORTHWEST                     18,478.00
   PACIFIC COAST                 12,187.00
   SOUTHEAST                     14,035.75
   SOUTHWEST/CENTRAL              9,674.60
```

sales personnel who will be using the output. After some discussion of the output and of how the system works, she approves the system.

Next, John trains the computer operator in the operation of the new system. He also makes sure that all sales personnel understand their role in the system. He replaces the sample files with actual files. Finally, he decides to phase in the new system. The first month, the system will produce the sales by item report. If all goes well, then during the second month the system will produce both reports.

System Maintenance

The conversion goes smoothly, and after several months of operation John checks with Ann to see if there are any problems. Ann feels that, for the time being, the system is functioning well, but she thinks that modifications may be needed in the future. John assures her that modifications can be handled when requested.

Chapter Summary

- The people who are primarily involved in information system development are **systems analysts**. They follow a step-by-step process to develop the system. In addition, programmers are involved because they write the programs that are part of the system. Users are also involved in system development because the system must be designed to meet the needs of its users. Systems analysts, programmers, and users often work together in a **project team** that is responsible for developing the system.

- The first phase in the information system development process is **system planning**, in which the systems analyst decides whether a new information system should be developed. In this phase, the analyst defines the problem to be solved by the system and performs **feasibility analysis** to determine if it is feasible to develop a system to solve the problem. The next phase is **system analysis**, in which the analyst determines what the new system must do. In this phase, the analyst analyzes the current system, determines the **user requirements**, prepares the **system specifications**, and identifies and evaluates alternative ways of meeting the requirements. In the next phase, **system design**, the analyst specifies how the new system will function. The result of this phase is the design of the new system. The next phase is **system implementation**, in which the analyst acquires the components of the system, tests the system, and changes over to the new system. The last phase, called **system maintenance**, involves modifying the system during its life to meet new requirements.

■ The user is often the one who recognizes the need for a new information system by identifying a problem with the existing system. The user should report the problem to the person responsible for system development, thus beginning the system planning phase. During system analysis, the user is interviewed about how the current system functions. In addition, the user is asked about his or her requirements for the new system. Finally, the user may be asked to review the system specifications with the systems analyst. The user's involvement in system design is mainly in reviewing screen, report, and form layouts and helping to describe procedures. The user has little involvement with system implementation until the system is finished. Then, the user is trained in the use of the system and is asked to compare the system with his or her requirements. Finally, the user is involved in system maintenance to ensure that the modified system meets the user's requirements.

■ A **data flow diagram**, or **DFD**, is used to show the flow of data in an information system. A **data dictionary** is used to describe the data in a data flow diagram, and **process descriptions** are used to describe the processes in a data flow diagram. A **system flowchart** is used to show the flow of data in an information system and what types of input data, output data, stored data, and programs will be used in the system. A **screen layout form** is used to prepare the layout of screen input and output. A **print chart** is used to design the layout of a printed report. **CASE** (Computer-Aided Software Engineering) tools provide computerized versions of other tools.

Terms to Remember

CASE   p. 449

Cost/Benefit Analysis   p. 435

Data Dictionary   p. 443

Data Flow Diagram (DFD)
   p. 443

Feasibility Analysis   p. 435

Print Chart   p. 448

Process Description   p. 444

Project Team   p. 433

Prototype   p. 437

Prototyping   p. 437

Screen Layout Form   p. 447

Service Bureau   p. 436

Software House   p. 437

System Analysis   p. 434

System Design   p. 434

Review Questions

Fill-In Questions

1. The person primarily responsible for developing an information system is called a(n) _____.

2. Determining what a new information system will do is called _____. Determining how the system will do it is called _____.

3. The process of modifying a system to meet new requirements is called _____.

4. The process of determining if it is feasible to develop a new information system is called _____.

5. A technique for evaluating the economic feasibility of an information system is _____.

6. Descriptions of what an information system will do to help a user are called _____.

7. A(n) _____ is a company that does computer processing for other organizations.

8. An alternative approach to developing an information system in which a partial version of the system is developed for the user is called _____.

9. Each data flow and set of stored data in a data flow diagram is described in the _____. Each process is described by a(n) _____.

10. The use of computer-based tools to help in the development of an information system is called _____.

Short-Answer Questions

1. Who are the people that are usually on an information system development project team?

2. List the five main phases of the system development process.

3. How is the user involved in system planning?

4. What steps are involved in system analysis?

5. How is the user involved in system analysis?

6. What are the main software alternatives for an information system?

7. What system details does the systems analyst specify during the system design?

8. What steps are involved in system implementation?

9. Explain the difference between a data flow diagram and a system flowchart.

10. What are two types of layout forms used in system development?

11. In the case study in this chapter, why did Ann Nelson want a new information system?

12. During which phases of the system development process in the case study in this chapter was Ann Nelson most involved, and during which phase was she least involved?

Projects

1. Interview a systems analyst, and find out what he or she does when developing an information system. Which tools discussed in the chapter does the analyst use? Write a summary of your interview.

2. Pick one type of software used to help in information system development, such as prototyping software or CASE software, and find out what you can about it. How is it used? During what phases of the system development process is the software used? Write a summary of your findings.

PART FIVE

COMPUTERS AND SOCIETY

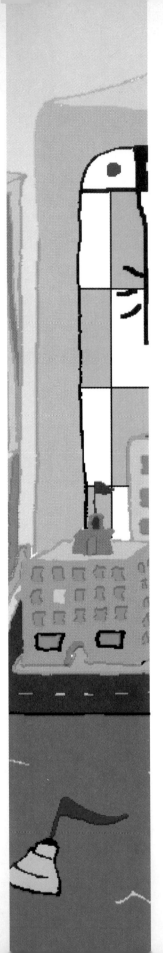

18

THE COMPUTER'S IMPACT ON SOCIETY

CHAPTER TOPICS

Some Benefits of Computers
- Better Information
- Improved Service
- Increased Productivity
- Additional Educational and Recreational Opportunities

Computers and Privacy
- Information and Privacy
- Protection of Privacy

Computers and Employment
- The Effect of Computers on Employment
- Changing Patterns of Work
- Employee Health

Computers and Crime
- Theft of Money
- Theft of Data
- Theft and Destruction of Hardware
- Illegal Copying of Software
- Destruction of Data and Software
- Ethics

The Future of Computers

CHAPTER OBJECTIVES

• After completing this chapter you should be able to:

1. Describe several benefits of computers to society.

2. Explain how computers can reduce people's privacy.

3. Describe some of the effects of computers on employment.

4. List several computer crimes and describe security measures used to help prevent them.

5. Identify some of the trends in the future of computers.

THIS BOOK began by describing how computers affect you every day. But has their effect on you and, more generally, on society been positive, or has society lost more than it has gained from computerization? And what about the future? What will be the impact of computers in coming years? This chapter examines these questions and tries to assess the computer's impact on society, both today and in the future.

The first section of this chapter looks at some of the benefits of computers to society. Although the benefits may be great, they are not without costs. The costs take many forms, and the next three sections of the chapter look at some of the forms. Finally, the last section of the chapter examines some of the trends for the future of computers.

SOME BENEFITS OF COMPUTERS

We can probably all agree that computers provide many benefits to society. Computers are fast and accurate, and they store large volumes of data. These characteristics make computers very useful to people. But the real benefits of computers are much more than just these characteristics.

Better Information

One of the main benefits of computers is *better information*. Computers store and process data, but they also produce information, which is the basis for good decision making. When you make a decision—either a personal or a job-related decision—you select one of several alternative courses of action. Almost always you are uncertain about what exactly will happen with each alternative. Information helps reduce your uncertainty. With better information you are more certain about the outcome from your decision.

Let's take an example in which you want to buy a new car. You have to make a decision: "Which car should I buy?" You could go to several car dealers, pick one car that you like, and buy it. But is it the best car for you? Are there other models with more power, more space, better fuel economy, and more reliability for less money? With more information you might save money and get a better car. So instead of making your decision hastily, you can gather the information you need to help with your decision. For example, you can use a computerized library system to search for articles and reviews of the cars in which you are interested. You can order a computer printout of information about the cars from a popular consumer magazine (Figure 18–1). With this and similar information, you can make a decision that is more likely to result in a better car for you.

Chapter 1 showed a number of examples of the use of computers in our personal lives and in our work lives. Better information was the principal benefit of several of these examples. The use of a home computer for household budgeting provides better information so you can make

Figure 18–1 A Computer Printout of Information About a Car

Make: 1991 BUICK
Model: P69 LE SABRE CUSTOM SEDAN, 4-Door
For last full report on this or similar model, see Consumer Reports, Jan, 1991.

The Consumers Union Auto Test Division recommends the following as the minimum equipment needed for functional reasons:
NONE

CU also recommends the following equipment as desirable for comfort and convenience:
NONE

Equipment recommendations. At the top of each printout is the optional equipment we think necessary for safety and reasonable comfort. The Buick Le Sabre Custom has a wealth of standard equipment, including an overdrive automatic transmission, power steering and brakes, and air-conditioning. There's nothing we would add.

		Dealer Cost	List Price
		14740.00	17080.00
	★★★Selected Standard Equipment★★★		
□ C67	AIR CONDITIONER	0.00	0.000
	BRAKES: POWER		
	Front disc	0.00	0.00
	WIPERS: 2 SPEED	0.00	0.00
	POWER STEERING	0.00	0.00
	TINTED GLASS	0.00	0.00
	CARPETING	0.00	0.00
	SEATS: NOTCHBACK BENCH, CLOTH	0.00	0.00

Base price. The dealer cost (factory invoice) is shown, left; the list price (sticker price), right. The list of standard equipment included in that price follows.

	★★★Optional Equipment★★★		
□ A	STRIPES: BODY SIDE		
	ORDER BY COLOR	38.00	45.00
□ A31	POWER WINDOWS		
	NC/SD,SE	264.00	310.00
□ AM6	SEATS: 55/45 SPLIT BENCH		
	INC/storage armrest	156.00	183.00
□ AU3	POWER DOOR LOCKS		
	NC/SC,SD,SE	196.00	230.00
□ BF9	DELETE FROM PACKAGE: CARPET SAVERS		
	R/SB,SC,SD,SE	– 38.00	– 45.00
□ C09	ROOF: VINYL, FULL		
	NA/Y56	170.00	200.00
□ C47	DELETE REAR DEFOGGER FROM PACKAGE		
	R/SB,SC,SD,SE	– 136.00	– 160.00
□ F79	AXLE RATIO: 2.97		
	R/V08 NC/Y56	0.00	0.00
□ G67	SUSPENSION: AUTOMATIC LEVEL CONTROL		
	NC/Y56	149.00	175.00
☑ JM4	BRAKES: ANTI-LOCK SYSTEM	786.00	925.00
☑ SB	POPULAR OPTION GROUP		
	INC/rear window defogger + speed control + P205/75R14 all season whitewall tires + front & rear floor mats + 2 speed wipers with feature + 55/45 split front seat w/storage armrest	620.00	729.00
□ SC	PREMIUM OPTION GROUP		
	INC/SB + power door locks / w/casette, seek/scan and clock + lock	1117.00	1314.00
□ SD	LUXURY windows + 6/way power driver seat + door edge guards + dual manual seat back recliners	1725.00	2029.00
	PRESTIGE OPTION GROUP		
	INC/SD + electric trunk release + passenger lighted vanity mirror + automatic power antenna + dual power remote control mirrors + concert sound speakers	2019.00	2375.00
□ Y56	GRAN TOURING PACKAGE		
	WO/ANY PACKAGE NA/C09 INC/Gran Touring suspension + 15" aluminum wheels + P215/65R15 blackwall tires + 2.97 axle ratio + heavy duty engine & transmission cooling + leather wrapped steering wheel + automatic level control	627.00	738.00

Copyright 1991, Consumer Reports Auto Price Service.

Individual options. Every piece of optional equipment offered by the factory for the Le Sabre Custom is listed by invoice number, with both dealer cost and list price.

Options packages. Equipment included is listed by name (or, sometimes, by invoice number). On this printout, the full price of the package is given (as it is on window stickers). Also given are all the wrinkles that come with packages. Thus, if you choose the Popular Option Group (as our imaginary buyer did), but you don't want the floor mats or rear defogger that come with the package, you can delete them (items BF9 and C47) and deduct $174 from dealer costs and $205 from list price.

Options availability. Conditions may apply. Here, for example, you find that for reasons known only to the automaker, you can't get a Gran Touring Package if you choose the vinyl roof (invoice number C09).

Sum of optional equipment selected		1,232	1,449
Base Price of Model		14,740	17,080
DESTINATION CHARGES		535.00	535.00
WDV	NEW YORK WARRANTY ENHANCEMENT (LEMON LAW)	55.00	65.00
TOTALS		16,562	19,129

Worksheet. Adding up each column—all the options you selected, the figure for the basic car, and the destination charge—gives a total dealer cost and list price. With the Le Sabre Custom sedan, adding antilock brakes and the Popular Option Group (with the deletions noted above) brings the dealer cost to $15,972 and the list price to $18,529. With the destination charge and warranty enhancement, the totals become $16,562 dealer, $19,129 list. The difference—$2567—represents the room for negotiation.

decisions about personal finances. A database of customer data provides better information for a sales representative so he or she can decide when to contact customers again. A sales analysis system provides better information to a sales manager so he or she can make decisions to help improve sales. Many other examples throughout this book illustrated the benefit of better information provided by computerization.

Improved Service

Another benefit of computers is *improved service*. Computers operate at any time of the day or night and process data faster than humans. Thus, organizations and businesses serve their customers and clients more conveniently and efficiently with computers than without.

You, as a consumer, see the effect of improved service from computers whenever you use an automatic teller machine for your banking transactions or whenever you purchase groceries or merchandise from a store that uses a point-of-sale system. These machines and systems provide service that you would otherwise not have. Consequently, you are able to complete your transactions and your shopping conveniently and quickly.

For businesses, improved service means that customers may be attracted to a certain business because of its service. In fact, many people have come to expect computerized services, and some types of businesses cannot compete without them. For example, automatic teller machines have become so popular that almost all banks now have them just to be competitive.

Increased Productivity

A third benefit of computers is *increased productivity*. Productivity has to do with how much people can accomplish in a given time. With computers, people can do more productive work in a period of time than without computers.

As an example of increased productivity, a typist using a computer for word processing can revise and print a long document faster than if he or she had to retype the document completely on a typewriter. Hence, the typist's productivity is greater with a computer. Another office use of computers, electronic mail, also improves productivity by making it easier and quicker for people to communicate with each other. Similarly, with a point-of-sale system a clerk can check out more customers than with a standard cash register and, by installing automatic teller machines, a bank can handle more customers with the same number of human tellers.

Increased productivity means that it costs less for a business to provide its goods and services. These cost savings may be passed on to the customer in reduced prices. They also result in increased profits for the business.

Additional Educational and Recreational Opportunities

A final benefit of computers discussed here is *additional educational and recreational opportunities*. In many situations a computer can substitute for another person such as a teacher or an opponent in a game. In addition, a computer can simulate situations that would be impossible to experience in reality.

In schools, computer-assisted instruction provides extra opportunities for instruction and practice, adding to what teachers provide. Computer simulation is used in schools to expand the educational experience. Home computers provide many forms of entertainment and other recreational opportunities, including games and simulations. Home computers can also be used for self-improvement without the aid of a teacher. Many of these opportunities for education and recreation were not available before computers became common.

COMPUTERS AND PRIVACY

Now that you have seen some of the benefits of computers, let's examine some of the costs that society must pay for these benefits. One of the main costs of computerization to society is a reduction in people's privacy. Privacy has to do with keeping information about oneself to oneself. People need privacy so that they feel free to do what they want. If people do not have privacy and the things they do are recorded somewhere, they may feel threatened and inhibited. (Read George Orwell's *1984* for some idea about what the world would be like without privacy.)

Information and Privacy

Computerized systems reduce people's privacy by recording information about people. Many government agencies have computer files and databases with information about people. For example, the Social Security Administration has files on practically everyone who has worked in the United States. The Internal Revenue Service has computerized versions of recent tax returns. Figure 18–2 lists some of the government files and databases with information about individuals.

Nongovernment organizations and businesses also have computerized information about people. For example, TRW, the largest credit reporting company in the United States, has computerized credit histories of over 120 million people. Firms that sell mailing lists have large files listing personal characteristics and preferences so that mailing lists can be targeted at certain types of individuals.

There are legitimate uses and benefits of computerized information about people. No one would receive social security checks without the Social Security Administration's system. Credit would be harder to get without computerized credit bureaus. But such information can also be abused. For example, should social security information about you be available to any business that wants to check on your work history?

Figure 18–2   Government Files and Databases with Information About Individuals

Department of Health, Education and Welfare: 693 data systems with 1.3 billion personal records including marital, financial, health and other information on recipients of Social Security, social services, medicaid, medicare and welfare benefits.

Justice Department: 175 data systems with 201 million records including information on criminals and criminal suspects, aliens, persons linked to organized crime, securities-laws violators, and individuals who relate in any manner to official FBI investigations.

Department of Transportation: 263 data systems with 25 million records including information on pilots, aircraft and boat owners, and all motorists whose licenses have been withdrawn, suspended or revoked by any state.

Department of Housing and Urban Development: 58 data systems with 20 million records including data on applicants for housing assistance and federally guaranteed home loans.

Civil Service: 14 data systems with 110 million records, mostly dealing with government employees or applicants for government jobs.

Treasury Department: 910 data systems with 780 million records that include files on taxpayers, foreign travelers, persons deemed by the Secret Service to be potentially harmful to the President, and dealers in alcohol, firearms, and explosives.

Defense Department: 2,219 data systems with 333 million records pertaining to service personnel and persons investigated for such things as employment, security or criminal activity.

Department of Commerce: 95 data systems with 430 million records primarily Census Bureau data but including files on minority businessmen, merchant seamen, and others.

Department of Labor: 97 data systems with 17 million records, many involving people in federally financed work and job training programs.

Source: Office of Management and Budget

Should credit information about you be available to anyone without your permission? To many people, the answer to questions like these is no.

One way that computerized information can be abused is through **matching**. This is a process in which data in one file or database is compared with data in another. Computers can match data in large files or databases very rapidly. Matching can be useful; for example, matching welfare recipient data with social security data can detect welfare fraud. But it can also be used to further reduce people's privacy. For example, matching credit files, mailing list files, work history files, and medical databases would provide detailed descriptions of people.

COMPUTER CLOSE-UP

18–1

IS BIG BROTHER WATCHING?

A right-to-privacy lawsuit brought against Epson America Inc. in the summer of 1990 touched a sensitive nerve for anyone managing a corporate computer system. The suit alleges, among other things, that an Epson systems manager responsible for managing the company's minicomputer systems was systematically reading electronic mail sent from the 700 employees at Epson's headquarters to people outside the facility.

Corporate end-users themselves are blanching at the thought that indiscreet E-mail sent to fellow employees—perhaps making derogatory comments about management, or detailing plans for an upcoming job hunt—could surface during their next performance review. Nonsystems management are concerned that they maintain the right to control and administer their corporate resources as they see fit. And MIS and PC managers see themselves caught in the middle of a sticky situation—one in which they may be requested by their bosses to perform actions they may consider unethical.

"Privacy issues and how they relate to emerging technologies affect more people every year," said Michael Cavanagh, president of the Electronic Mail Association (EMA), in Washington.

Although the facts of the case remain in dispute—with Epson claiming that no such practice of regularly reading employees' electronic communications existed—one thing is clear: It's not so much a question of whether Big Brother is watching you, as it is whether he has warned you first.

In George Orwell's *1984*, there is no question that Big Brother is there, always watching, always listening. Indeed, it would be hard for any inhabitant of that world to be unaware of that fact. Huge two-way television screens are installed in every room of every house, apartment, public building, office complex, and workplace so that every citizen is within both the sight and earshot of officials.

Under current U.S. law, Big Brother's activities—at least those involving the workplace—would probably be legal. This is due to the concept of expectation: If an employer makes it clear that certain ways of communicating are subject to routine supervision—for example, phone calls or the circulation of paper memos—then management has the right to monitor those communications.

If, however, no such policy is made public—if employees have the expectation that such communications are private—then the employer has probably violated the law.

However, much of this is speculation, given the relatively short time that electronic communications have been established in U.S. corporations.

And the issue doesn't apply to electronic mail alone. What about voice mail—personal voice messages stored digitally in a company database? Or faxes, which are merely printed matter transformed into digital information and then turned back into printed material?

In the early 1980s, when PC technology first began to proliferate, a number of individuals and organizations became concerned about the right to privacy involved in these new electronic forms of communication. Thus, the 1986 Electronic Communications Privacy Act (ECPA) was conceived, born, and passed by Congress.

In essence, the ECPA extended the right of privacy protection accorded to users of the U.S. Postal Service and the various telephone companies to the new ways of communicating electronically.

"In the same way that the Wiretap Act was passed to ensure privacy for telephone users not covered by the outdated postal privacy laws, so the ECPA extended that right to privacy to cover new technology," Cavanagh said.

But the ECPA, like the wiretap and postal laws passed before it, did not cover communications within a business organization, Cavanagh said. For example, although it is illegal to put a wiretap on a private individual's phone without a court order, it is not necessarily illegal for an employer to monitor an employee using a company phone. Airline managers do it all the time, checking to see if reservationists are being courteous to customers and efficient using company resources. So do companies dealing with sensitive proprietary data—defense contractors, for example.

"Within organizations, these privacy issues become murky," Cavanagh said. "There is clear U.S. law on outside interception: that you can't steal a letter out of someone's mailbox, or go to the corner telephone pole and steal their conversation. But within the workplace? That raises a whole range of different issues," he said.

As computer systems become larger and more sophisticated, it becomes easier for government agencies and businesses to match information about people from many sources. How would you feel if all the computerized information about you were stored in one central computer and made available to anyone who requested it? This is a far-fetched idea, but it does show the abuse that is possible with large computerized files and databases.

Protection of Privacy

Fortunately, there are safeguards that help prevent the misuse of computerized information. These safeguards are in the form of legislation that limits the use and access of computerized information about individuals. Some of the more important laws are:

- The Freedom of Information Act of 1970. This law lets people find out what information government agencies store about them.
- The Fair Credit Reporting Act of 1970. This law allows people to inspect and challenge information in their credit records.
- The Privacy Act of 1974. This law prohibits government agencies from collecting information about individuals for illegitimate purposes.

Although laws cannot prevent all misuses of computerized information, they can help minimize the problem and thus provide more assurance of privacy to people.

COMPUTERS AND EMPLOYMENT

Another cost of computerization is changes in employment. Some people have lost their jobs to computers, and others have obtained new jobs as a result of computerization. Many, if not most, people's jobs have changed because of computers. Overall, people's work lives have been disrupted by computers.

The Effect of Computers on Employment

Computers sometimes replace workers. When an organization installs a computer for some function, the people who previously performed the function are displaced. Some of these people may lose their jobs, and others may be shifted to other jobs in the organization.

What should be done with workers who are displaced by computers? If people lose their jobs because of computers, they just add to society's social and economic problems. Many organizations offer the option of retraining to the affected workers. People have to adapt in a changing society, and retraining should be expected in one's life. Retrained employees continue as productive members of the organization and of society. Another option is early retirement for older employees. Some workers who are close to retirement may prefer this option to retraining.

It may seem like many jobs have been lost to computers. Some studies have shown, however, that overall this is not the case. While some jobs have been lost, new jobs have been created. Many of these new jobs have been in the computer industry, including jobs in the manufacturing, sales, and repair of computers. Other new jobs have resulted from new functions not performed before computerization. For example, programming and information systems analysis were not needed before computers, but are common jobs today.

Changing Patterns of Work

What is clear is that many people's jobs have changed as a result of computers. The typist now uses a computer for word processing rather than a typewriter for typing. The office manager now communicates with electronic mail rather than with paper memos. The factory worker now checks on the operation of computerized robots rather than working on the assembly line. The jobs are still there; what the employees do is different.

Where and when people work also has changed. With personal computers and data communications it is possible for some people to regularly work away from their office or business. People use computers in their home for office work and then transmit their work to the organization's central computer when they are finished. This way of working is called **telecommuting** because instead of commuting in a car or bus, the employee is "commuting" over telephone lines. In addition, it often does not matter when the work is done because the central computer operates 24 hours a day. Thus, some employees may choose to work in the evenings or on weekends rather than during the regular nine-to-five workday.

Employee Health

In addition to changes in employment patterns, some people worry that computers may affect the physical and mental health of employees. In the past, people have thought that prolonged use of CRT screens may cause cataracts, birth defects, miscarriages, and other serious problems. Most of these concerns have not proven to be true, although the evidence is not conclusive in all cases. Until final proof of safety has been established, some people recommend against prolonged use of CRT screens, especially by pregnant women.

Other physical problems, however, definitely occur in some computer users. Eyestrain, headaches, backaches, neck pain, wrist pain, and similar conditions are common among people who use computers extensively. One way of reducing these problems is through good ergonomic design of both the computer and the employee's work environment (see Chapter 4). Some communities have enacted legislation requiring employers to provide ergonomically sound environments.

In addition to physical health, there is concern that computer use can affect employees' mental health. Because computers work fast, some people feel pressured to work faster than normal just to "keep up" with the computer. This situation can create stress for the employee. In addition, people who work with computers often work alone, creating a feeling of isolation. One potential problem with telecommuting is that the employee does not have the social interaction common in an office environment, again contributing to a feeling of isolation. These concerns are real and need to be considered by employers when determining how employees will work.

COMPUTERS AND CRIME

A third cost of computerization is the emergence of new forms of crime. With computers many criminal activities are possible that could not be done before. To guard against these activities new forms of security are needed. Here we take a look at some types of computer crime and the security measures needed to help prevent them.

Theft of Money

Computers can be used to steal money from organizations and businesses. Computers are used extensively in banks and other financial institutions. Billions of dollars are transferred electronically all over the world every day through a process called **electronic funds transfer,** or **EFT**. There are many opportunities for electronic theft of money in the complex systems needed by financial institutions.

Some examples of the use of computers to steal money are:

- A consultant taps into the electronic funds transfer system of a bank and transfers money to a secret account.
- A computer programmer modifies the interest calculation program for a savings and loan so that fractions of a cent are not rounded correctly but instead are put into a special account. Over time, the fractions build up to thousands of dollars.
- A manager at a credit union modifies computer records of loans to a friend so that the loans appear to have been repaid.

To prevent such crimes, organizations need procedures that detect discrepancies in transactions and files. Financial records should be audited regularly for any inconsistencies. Software should be checked to be sure it performs correctly. Some organizations have one programmer develop a program and another programmer test it. The programmers would have to be in collusion to illegally modify the program. Most important of all, the organization should hire trustworthy employees.

Theft of Data

Data is a valuable resource of an organization. Businesses and other types of organizations store data about their operations in computer systems, and such data is often of interest to competitors. For example, a business may store data about prices of a new product. A competitor would be interested in the prices so that it would know what to charge in order to undersell the business. This type of data must be protected so that others cannot obtain it.

To prevent the improper use of data, data security measures need to be taken. One measure is to use **passwords** to prevent access to the computer system. A password is a word or code given only to those people who have authority to use the system. Whenever someone attempts to retrieve or change data, the system asks for the person's password. If the person cannot supply the correct password, the system does not perform the requested processing. Passwords should be changed frequently to prevent a person with an old password from using the system without authorization. In addition, passwords must be kept secret so that an unauthorized person cannot discover a password.

Some people enjoy gaining access to computer systems not to steal data, but just for the challenge of breaking in. Sometimes the term **hacker** is used for this type of person, although this term is also used for computer programmers in general. Many hackers use personal computers at home to gain access to remote computers operated by businesses and organizations. Most hackers are not interested in doing anything malicious, but just want to investigate the other computer systems. To prevent hackers from accessing their computers, many organizations use sophisticated security procedures. In addition, various laws provide penalties for illegally accessing a computer system.

Another data security measure is to use **data encryption**, which involves changing data to an unintelligible form by using a coding system. Then, even if someone knows the password, he or she cannot understand the data because it is in code. To convert the data back to its normal form, a special *key* is needed, which is a number that must be entered into the computer. If someone does not know the key, he or she cannot understand the data.

As discussed in Chapter 6, data encryption is also used when data is sent over a communication channel. Because channels can be tapped for illegal purposes, data can be intercepted as it is transmitted. If the data is coded, however, the person intercepting the data cannot interpret it without the key.

Data stored on microcomputer floppy disks poses an especially difficult security problem for a business or organization. Often, important data is stored on floppy disks. If the disks are left on a desk, they can be taken by someone with little chance of detection. Many organizations have a policy that no floppy disk may be removed from the organization's property and that all disks must be stored in a locked case when not in use. Also, data encryption can be used for data stored on a floppy disk so that only the person with the key can understand the data.

Theft and Destruction of Hardware

Hardware can be physically damaged or stolen. An unhappy former employee or other person may try to destroy hardware. An unscrupulous employee may steal equipment to use elsewhere or to sell. Security procedures need to be taken to prevent occurrences such as these.

Minicomputer and mainframe computer equipment is usually kept in locked rooms. Only authorized personnel are allowed into the computer rooms. Access to the rooms is controlled by special keys and other security devices (Figure 18–3). Computer rooms often have special fire extinguishing equipment to protect the hardware in case of fire. Precautions such as these are necessary to protect the computer equipment from physical damage.

Microcomputers in an office environment are sometimes easy to steal. To prevent theft, microcomputers are often bolted or chained to the desk. Use by unauthorized personnel is also a potential problem with microcomputers. Consequently, some microcomputers have keys that must be used before they can be turned on. Security procedures such as these are used to protect microcomputer equipment.

Illegal Copying of Software

Most software, especially microcomputer software, is *copyrighted*, just as books, movies, and recordings are copyrighted. This means that it is illegal to make a copy of the software without the permission of the owner of the copyright. When someone works hard developing a program, he or she should be rewarded for the effort. Just as you should not make copies of someone else's book, movie, or recording, you should also not make a copy of someone else's software.

When you purchase a program, you purchase the right to use the program but not the right to give away or sell copies of it. Most programs come with a written **software license agreement** that states what the purchaser can legally do with the software. Most software license agreements allow the purchaser to use the program on only one computer at a time and to make copies only for backup purposes.

Figure 18–3   Computer Room Access Control

When an organization purchases a program, it purchases the right for its employees to use the program. Usually, however, only one employee can legally use the program at a time. Making copies of the program so that more than one person in the organization can use the program is usually illegal. If several people need to use the program, multiple copies must be purchased. Alternatively, some software vendors sell a **site license** for an additional fee, which allows more than one person in the organization to use the program at a time.

To prevent the illegal copying of programs, some software is **copy protected**. This means that a special code has been put on the disk containing the software so that only the original version of the program will work. Any copies of the program will not run on a computer. Many users do not like copy protection because it restricts copying the program to a hard disk so that it can be easily used, or to another disk for backup purposes in case the original is destroyed. Many software vendors have stopped using copy protection because of user complaints.

To prevent the illegal copying of software, many organizations have policies stating that employees who copy software illegally will be disciplined or fired. As an additional measure, employees are usually not allowed to take software disks away from the organization's property.

Some software is not copyrighted. This software, called **public domain software**, can be legally copied and used by anyone. Another kind of software, called **shareware**, is copyrighted but is given away or sold for a very small fee and includes permission to use the software and to make copies for others for evaluation purposes. If, after evaluating the software, the user decides that he or she wants to continue to use it, the user is asked to pay the full price for the software. If the user decides not to use the software, however, he or she owes nothing. Because shareware is copyrighted and is not public domain software, the user must follow the terms specified by the developer. The shareware concept is, however, an inexpensive way of evaluating many programs to decide which is the best for the user's needs.

Occasionally someone will make an illegal copy of a program and try to sell it. This is called **software piracy**, and software developers sue these people. You should always be sure you are buying a legal copy of any program.

Destruction of Data and Software

Some people do not wish to steal data or illegally copy software, but instead destroy or otherwise vandalize it. A disgruntled employee may try to physically damage disks or tapes. A hacker may try to erase programs or data electronically. In addition, data may be destroyed by fire or natural disaster.

To prevent the permanent destruction of data and programs, backup copies are often stored at locations away from the organization. There are even businesses that specialize in storing other organizations' data. Some of these businesses provide computer facilities so that the organization can continue to function after its computers have been destroyed.

COMPUTER CLOSE-UP
18–2

THE MOST COMMON VIRUSES

Scores

This virus originated at Electronic Data Systems in Dallas, Texas. It infects applications on Apple Macintosh computers. It is spread by exchanging infected disks and inserting a disk into an infected system. This virus can slow down the computer, create problems with the printer, cause the computer to crash (stop running), increase file size, and modify icons on the screen.

Lehigh

This virus started at Lehigh University in Bethlehem, Pennsylvania. It infects the operating system on IBM PC's and clones. It activates itself after four infections and destroys data. It is spread by sharing infected disks and inserting a disk into an infected system. It can erase all the data on a hard disk. Because of its short activation period (four infections), the chances of detection before data destruction are slim.

Alameda

This virus began at Merritt College in Oakland, California. It infects the part of the operating system used to boot (start up) the computer on IBM PC's and clones. It spreads by booting the computer from an infected disk or inserting a disk into an infected computer. It slows down the boot sequence, causes the computer to crash, and erases data.

Pakistani Brain

This was one of the first viruses to be spread widely. It was developed by two brothers in Lahore, Pakistan. It infects the part of the operating system used to boot the computer on IBM PC's and clones. It is spread by booting the computer from an infected disk or by any access to an inserted disk. It slows down the boot sequence, causes excessive floppy disk activity for simple tasks, and can cause programs to crash. It spreads very quickly and can cause loss of data.

nVIR

This virus originated in Hamburg, West Germany. It infects applications on Apple Macintosh computers. It appears in many varieties, each with individual characteristics because it was published and modified by programmers. Once a computer is infected, every application executed is infected. It is spread by sharing disks, by inserting a disk into an infected system, and by executing an infected program. Its symptoms vary greatly, but usually result in the computer crashing, a "beep" sound when an application is opened, and files disappearing. It can result in loss of data and programs, and frequent computer crashes. It is particularly virulent.

Israeli

This virus originated at Hebrew University in Jerusalem. It infects programs on IBM PC's and clones. It is spread by transferring infected programs to other disks and by inserting disks into an infected computer. It causes the computer to slow down, programs to disappear on Friday the 13th, and data to be destroyed on hard disks.

A particularly dangerous form of data and program destruction is caused by a computer program called a **virus**. A virus is created by a hacker who puts the virus on floppy disks or on a hard disk on a computer used by several people. Usually, the virus does not do any damage for some period of time, such as several months. During this time people may unknowingly copy the virus to other disks, or the virus may copy itself. At a certain time all the copies of the virus activate themselves and destroy programs and data in many computers.

Sometimes a hacker will put a virus on a computer in a local area network or a wide-area network. Then the virus will copy itself to other computers in the network. This type of virus is sometimes called a *worm* because of the way it moves through the network. After a while, all the copies of the virus in the network begin destroying programs or data in the network.

To prevent viruses, no one should copy a disk from an unreliable source. Backup copies of original software disks should always be kept in case of a virus attack. Virus-detecting programs can be used to check disks for the presence of a virus. Some of these programs are designed so that they check for viruses whenever a new program is executed. Detecting viruses in a network is especially difficult because there are many computers in the network.

Ethics

The computer security measures described here will not prevent all computer crimes. Ultimately, the behavior of the individual determines how secure a computer system is. *Ethics* has to do with the standards of behavior that we follow. For example, people act ethically when they tell the truth even when lying is not against the law. Computer professionals and users must be ethical in their use of computerized systems. Without such ethical behavior, computer security measures would be so strict that the use of computer systems would be almost impossible except by a very few people.

You may confront a number of ethical questions revolving around computers in your life. For example, a friend may ask you to make a copy of a program you bought so that he or she can try it out. You may find out that a co-worker has accessed the company's database and has learned management salary data. Another co-worker, you may discover, has put a seemingly harmless virus on the company's local-area network that causes every computer on the network to play a song at a certain time each day. What would you do in each of these situations? Although these may seem like harmless acts, they involve questions of ethics that you would have to deal with.

THE FUTURE OF COMPUTERS

We have seen that computers have many important benefits that come with certain costs. For most people the benefits outweigh the costs. But even if they did not, we know computers are here to stay. So what about the future? Where are we going with computers? What are the trends we can look for in years to come?

One trend should be obvious: Every day, computers and computer uses become more common. New applications appear constantly. The applications affect our personal lives and our work lives. If you are not now using a computer for something, you will use one in the near future. If you are using computers today, you will use them more next year, and much more in several years. Computer use will do nothing but increase in the future.

But beyond the increased use of computers there are more specific things that we can look for in the future. One is the increased use of graphics and graphical user interfaces. People often find pictures and graphics easier and quicker to understand and use than words. Graphics are very important in certain professions such as engineering design and architecture. But graphics have some role in many other areas, and there will be an increase in graphical computer applications in the future (Figure 18–4). To provide for improved graphics, we will see screens with better resolution and more use of color (especially flat panel screens), printers with better graphic capabilities and color (especially laser printers), and more use of a mouse or similar device for software control.

Another trend is toward more intelligent computer systems. Artificial intelligence and expert systems, discussed in Chapter 15, will become more and more common in the future. Computers will be able to learn from their environment. For example, research is already being done on computer systems, composed of thousands of CPUs, that learn much like a human brain learns. Called **neural networks**, these intelligent computer systems will be used to provide expert advice, run robots, recognize objects, understand human voices, interpret natural languages, and respond by voice.

Figure 18–4 Graphical Computer Applications

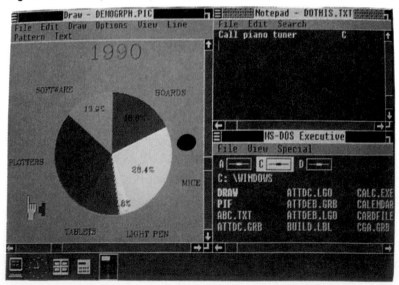

A fourth trend is toward more interconnection of computers and other devices. Networks are here but will become more common in the future. Both local area networks (LANs) and wide-area networks (WANs), discussed in Chapter 6, will become more common. LANs will be connected to WANs so that a user can communicate both locally and over a greater distance. In addition, other devices such as video and music systems (they will not be called TVs and stereos) will be connected to computers. Someday you may be able to tell your computer to play Vivaldi on your music system while you use your video system to scan images of art from the Louvre museum in Paris sent over a wide-area network to your personal computer. (Or maybe you would prefer contemporary music and modern art.)

All these future applications will require more powerful computers than we have today, and so a final trend is toward computers with faster CPUs that have more primary and secondary storage capacity. These computers will not be larger, however, or more expensive; just the opposite will be true. We already have powerful laptop and notebook computers, and inexpensive pocket computers are here. Someday the power of a current supercomputer may be found in a small personal computer, at a fraction of the cost of a supercomputer today. (Today's desktop computers are more powerful than the mainframe computers of ten years ago and cost much less.) Someday you may carry a computer the size of a small notebook with enough power to do any of the things described here and much more. It will, indeed, be an interesting and exciting future.

Chapter Summary

- One benefit of computers to society is better information, which helps people make decisions. Another benefit is improved service, which means customers and clients of organizations and businesses get faster and more convenient service. A third benefit is improved productivity, which means people can accomplish more in a period of time. A final benefit is additional educational and recreational opportunities, which provide people with extra instruction and practice and with new forms of entertainment and recreation.

- Computers can reduce people's privacy by recording information about them. Many government agencies and nongovernment organizations and businesses have files and databases with information about people. Using **matching**, data about people from several files and databases can be brought together. Safeguards, in the form of legislation, help prevent the misuse of computerized information.

- Computers sometimes replace workers in organizations. Some workers may lose their jobs, others may be retrained and shifted to other jobs, and still others may take early retirement. Many people who have not been replaced by computers have had their jobs changed as a result of computers. More and more people are using computers as a normal part of their job functions. Some people have chosen to regularly work away from their office or business and transmit their finished work to a central computer, a process called **telecommuting**. Computers can also affect workers' physical and mental health.

- One computer crime is using a computer to steal money from an organization or business. To help prevent this crime, organizations should follow procedures that detect discrepancies and inconsistencies in computerized data; they should also check software carefully and should hire trustworthy employees. Theft of organizational data is another computer crime. To help prevent this crime, organizations should use **passwords** for accessing data, should have procedures to prevent **hackers** from gaining access to their computers, should use **data encryption** for changing data to an unintelligible form, and should have procedures for securing floppy disks. A third crime is the theft and destruction of hardware. To help prevent this crime, organizations should keep minicomputers and mainframe computers in locked rooms accessible only by authorized personnel and should use security devices with microcomputers. Another crime is the illegal copying of software. To help prevent this crime, organizations should have policies that provide disciplinary actions for employees who copy software illegally and should not allow software disks to be removed from the organization's property. A final crime is the destruction of data and software. To help prevent this crime, organizations should store backup copies of all data and programs away from the organization's location. In addition, organizations should take measures to prevent the destruction of data and programs by a **virus**.

- One trend in the future of computers is that computer use is becoming more and more common. Another trend is toward more use of graphics and graphical interface. A third trend is toward more intelligent computer systems, including **neural networks**. Still another trend is toward more interconnection of computers and other devices in networks. A final trend is toward faster computers with more storage capacity, but which are smaller and less expensive.

Terms to Remember

Copy Protection p. 475

Data Encryption p. 473

Electronic Funds Transfer (EFT) p. 472

Hacker p. 473

Matching p. 467

Neural Network p. 478

Password p. 473

Public Domain Software p. 475

Shareware p. 475

Site License p. 475

Software License Agreement p. 474

Software Piracy p. 475

Telecommuting p. 471

Virus p. 477

Review Questions

Fill-In Questions

1. How much people can accomplish in a period of time is called _____, and computers help to (*increase/decrease*) it.

2. The process of comparing data in several computer files or databases for the purpose of locating common data is called _____.

3. Two options for employees replaced by computers, other than losing their jobs, are _____ and _____.

4. When someone regularly works with a computer away from an office or business and transmits his or her finished work to a central computer, that person is _____.

5. Using a computer to transfer money between bank accounts is an example of _____.

6. One way of helping to prevent the improper use of data is to require that a(n) _____ be entered before someone attempts to retrieve or change data.

7. A(n) _____ is a person who enjoys gaining access to a computer system for the challenge of breaking in and for the purpose of investigating the system.

8. Software that is coded so that only the original version will work is said to be _____.

9. Software that is not copyrighted is called _____.

10. Making illegal copies of software for sale to other people is called _____.

11. A(n) _____ is a computer program that copies itself from one computer system to another and activates itself after a period of time, usually destroying programs and data in many computer systems.

12. A(n) _____ is a computer system consisting of thousands of CPUs that functions similar to a human brain.

Short-Answer Questions

1. How do people benefit from better information?

2. Give an example of improved customer service resulting from the use of computers other than those discussed in the chapter.

3. How can computers reduce people's privacy?

4. Identify some laws that help prevent the misuse of computerized information about individuals.

5. What are some of the physical health problems that can be caused by computers, and how can they be reduced?

6. What can be done to help prevent the theft of money by computers?

7. What is a software license agreement, and what is a site license?

8. What is shareware?

9. How can the permanent destruction of data and programs be prevented?

10. List several trends in the future of computers.

Projects

1. Pick one area in which computers have impacted your life. Write a brief description of how computers have affected you. Has the impact been positive or negative?

2. Identify several emerging or future applications of computers. Find out what you can about each application and its potential impact on people. Write a brief summary of your findings.

19

CAREERS AND COMPUTERS

CHAPTER OBJECTIVES

• After completing this chapter you should be able to:

1. Identify the common jobs found in the information systems department of an organization or business.
2. Describe some of the computer-related jobs found in end-user departments.
3. List some of the jobs in computer hardware and software companies.
4. Outline the educational opportunities available for someone interested in a career in the computer field.
5. Describe the ways computer professionals can keep up with the computer field.

T HIS BOOK has mainly described what end-users do when they use computers. As you know, computer professionals also work with computers. You have already seen what programmers, systems analysts, and database administrators do (see Chapters 12, 17, and 16, respectively). But there are many other types of computer professionals. This chapter takes a look at the jobs that are available in the computer field, the educational requirements for entry-level jobs, and the opportunities that you may find if you pursue a career in this field.

CAREERS IN AN INFORMATION SYSTEMS DEPARTMENT

Most organizations and businesses have a department that is responsible for the development and operation of computer information systems. This department may be called information systems (IS), management information systems (MIS), data processing (DP), or something similar. It is headed by an **information systems manager** who is responsible for the management of the department. In some organizations the information systems manager reports to the **vice president of information systems** (also called the *chief information officer,* or *CIO*). This person is responsible for all computing and information processing in the organization, not just that done by the information systems department.

Figure 19–1 shows how a typical information systems department might be organized. This department has four areas, each with its own manager: systems development, operations, technical support, and end-user computing. Figure 19–2 shows typical salaries for some employees in an information systems department.

Systems Development

The systems development area is concerned with developing and maintaining information systems. *Systems analysts* and *programmers* work in this area. The programmers are often called **application programmers** because they develop application programs. Sometimes a person does both systems analysis and application programming and is therefore called a **programmer/analyst**.

Many organizations classify their systems development employees as trainee, junior, senior, or lead programmers and analysts. A *trainee* usually has little or no experience and works under the careful supervision of a senior person for at least six months. A *junior* person has passed beyond the trainee level but still has limited experience and requires direct supervision. A *senior* programmer or analyst has at least three years of experience and can work largely on his or her own. A *lead* person is the most experienced and may manage a project team of other programmers and analysts.

Figure 19–1   Organization of an Information Systems Department

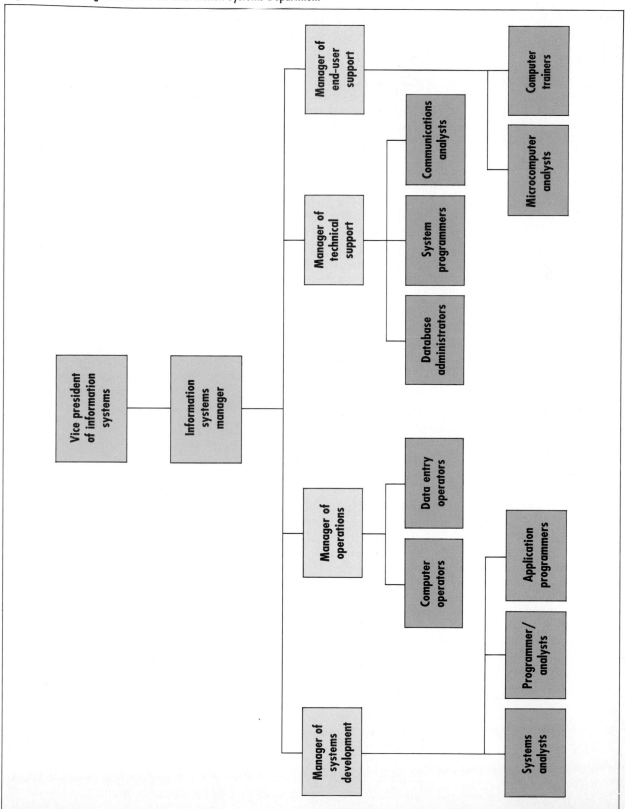

Figure 19–2 Average Annual Salaries in the Computer Field

Vice president of information systems	$75,611
Information systems manager	58,843
Systems analyst	39,617
Application programmer	28,312
Programmer/analyst	34,659
Database administrator	50,938
Operating system programmer	40,196
Communications analyst	38,231
Microcomputer analyst	33,306

Most entry-level jobs in systems development are at the trainee programmer or programmer/analyst level. Usually two to four years of college are required to get started. Advancement depends on skill and education. Many people advance from trainee to lead programmer or analyst and eventually to a management position. Usually, higher-level positions require at least a bachelor's degree and sometimes a master's degree.

Operations

The operations area is concerned with operating the computer and related equipment needed in information systems. **Computer operators** run the computer. They put disks and tapes into the appropriate drives, load paper in printers, start and stop programs, remove output from printers, and monitor the hardware and software for errors and malfunctions. **Data entry operators** run data preparation devices such as key-to-disk and key-to-tape units. They key data into the devices, verify that data has been correctly keyed, and correct errors.

Like the systems development area, many organizations classify their employees in operations as trainee, junior, senior, or lead computer operators. For a computer operator position, two years of college or training in a technical school is usually required. For a data entry position, some college or technical school training is needed. Qualified employees can advance to lead and eventually management positions.

Technical Support

The technical support area provides assistance to the other areas in technical specialties. The *database administrator (DBA)* often works in the technical support area, although some organizations have a separate area just for database administration. **System programmers** are responsible for setting up and maintaining system software such as operating systems and compilers. **Communications analysts** are responsible for the organization's data communications hardware and software.

Because of the technical nature of the jobs in this area, considerable education and experience are required. Usually, a bachelor's degree and sometimes a master's degree is needed. Often, employees move into these technical specialties after gaining experience in other areas. Qualified employees can advance to management positions.

COMPUTERS IN ALL CAREERS

This chapter describes many interesting jobs in the computer field, but you may decide to choose a career in another area. Many careers in non–computer-related fields, however, require a knowledge of computers and computer applications. Chapter 1 described a number of jobs that use computers:

- Salespeople in stores and markets use computerized point-of-sale systems to record sales.

- Office workers use computers for word processing and electronic mail.

- Business managers use computers to store information in a database and to analyze data in a spreadsheet.

- Architects, draftspersons, and engineers use computer-aided design to design buildings and products.

- Graphic designers, advertising layout persons, and television station personnel use computers to design graphic images.

These are just a few of the jobs affected by computers. Many other jobs require the use of computers and computer applications. With your understanding of common computer applications, you can see better what jobs require a knowledge of each application.

Word processing, discussed in Chapter 8, is one of the most common computer applications. Almost any job that involves writing or working with written material makes use of word processing. Typists, secretaries, writers, journalists, editors, business managers, doctors, and teachers are just a few of the people who use word processing. Desktop publishing, a very sophisticated form of word processing, is used by some writers, editors, and people in publishing. So many jobs involve working with written material that it is very likely you will use word processing in your career.

Spreadsheet analysis, described in Chapter 9, is another common computer application. Many jobs require the analysis of data in spreadsheets. Bookkeepers, accountants, financial analysts, stockbrokers, real-estate developers, and insurance agents all make use of spreadsheets. If your job requires the analysis of numbers, it is very likely you will use spreadsheets in your career.

Database management, described in Chapter 10, is a third major computer application. Any job that involves the storage and retrieval of data is likely to use databases. Travel agents, hotel reservation clerks, mail-order telephone operators, sales representatives, business managers, and direct mail advertisers are some of the people who make use of database management. Your job may require that you have easy access to stored data, in which case you will likely use database management in your career.

Graphics, discussed in Chapter 11, is another computer application used in many jobs. Anyone who creates drawings, charts, or graphic images is likely to use computer graphics. Business managers, statisticians, designers, architects, artists, and film special-effects developers use computers for graphic work. More and more jobs will require graphics in the future, so you are likely to use computer graphics in your career.

The jobs listed here are not all that are affected by computers. Practically every job in the future will require some knowledge of computers and computer applications.

End-User Support

Many organizations have an area responsible for 'helping end-users develop and use computer applications, mainly on microcomputers. Sometimes this area is called the **information center**. It is usually part of the information systems department, but in some organizations it is a separate department.

The end-user support area has **microcomputer analysts** who are responsible for evaluating and selecting microcomputer hardware and software for use in the organization. In addition, they help users set up microcomputers, they develop applications for end-users, and they assist users in utilizing application software. For example, the microcomputer analyst may help a user to select and install a microcomputer or to set up a graphics application on his or her microcomputer; this analyst may also show a user how to access data in a mainframe computer database or may develop a spreadsheet application for certain users. In addition, the end-user support area has **computer trainers** who provide users with in-house training courses on hardware and software.

Entry-level positions in this area require two to four years of college. Excellent knowledge of microcomputer hardware and software is essential. Microcomputer analysts need technical training in computer hardware and networks. They must understand numerous microcomputer application programs and may have to know how to use some minicomputer and mainframe computer programs. Computer trainers need to be good teachers. Advancement in this area can lead to management positions.

CAREERS IN END-USER DEPARTMENTS

End-users work in many departments in an organization or business, including the marketing, accounting, finance, and production departments. Sometimes these departments have their own systems development staff, which includes programmers and systems analysts. These people develop information systems just for their own departments. They may use a departmental computer, often a minicomputer, or they may use a central mainframe computer for these systems. Programmers and analysts in end-user departments often need detailed knowledge of the functions performed by the department. For example, a programmer in a marketing department would have to know a lot about the marketing function of a business.

End-user departments that do not have their own systems development staff have to rely on programmers and systems analysts from the information systems department. Many times an end-user department will have a certain individual designated to act as a liaison with the technical specialists. This person not only requires an excellent knowledge of the functions of the department, but must also have a good understanding of the technical aspects of information systems. With this background, he or she can communicate both with the end-users in the department and with the computer professionals in the information systems department.

Many end-user departments have one individual who is in charge of microcomputers in the department. This person helps users to select and set up microcomputer hardware and to develop software applications. He or she not only needs to understand microcomputer hardware and software, but also must be knowledgeable in the functions of the department.

Computer-related entry-level positions in end-user departments often require a background in the functions of the department. Usually a bachelor's degree in a business-related field, such as marketing or finance, is needed, in addition to computer training.

CAREERS IN THE COMPUTER INDUSTRY

In addition to the jobs and careers described so far, there are certain jobs that are found only in businesses that make and sell computer hardware and software. Hardware companies design, manufacture, sell, and service computer hardware. Software companies develop, sell, and support computer software. Many hardware companies also develop and sell software.

In a hardware company, **computer designers** design computer circuits and components of computer systems. **Computer sales representatives** call on potential customers to sell the company's hardware. They may also sell software, developed either by their company or by another, that goes with their hardware. The sales representatives may call on specially trained programmer/analysts, sometimes called **system engineers**, to help with the sale by providing technical support for the customer's applications. After the hardware has been sold and installed, **computer service technicians** maintain and repair the hardware.

In a software company, highly skilled programmers, who are sometimes called **software engineers**, develop software for sale by the company. Depending on the business, they may develop system software or application software. Sales representatives call on customers to sell the software. They may also sell hardware, manufactured by another company, that is needed to use their software. After the software has been sold, **customer support technicians** help customers with problems they may have using the software.

Microcomputers are often sold in retail stores. Salespeople in these stores help customers select appropriate microcomputer hardware and software. A store may also have computer service and customer support technicians to assist the customer with hardware and software problems that he or she may encounter.

Many of the entry-level positions in the computer industry are in sales. Two to four years of college and good sales skills are usually required for a job. Qualified employees can advance to sales management positions.

Other jobs in the computer industry usually require technical training. Computer designers often need at least a bachelor's degree and may need an advanced degree. System and software engineers require the same background as programmers and systems analysts. Computer service technicians need technical training in computer hardware maintenance and repair. Customer support technicians are often programmers with good knowledge of the company's software.

GETTING STARTED IN A CAREER IN THE COMPUTER FIELD

To get started in a career in the computer field you need the proper education. First, you must decide what type of job you are interested in. The education required for a computer programmer is different from that for a microcomputer analyst and still different from that for a computer sales representative.

Many community colleges offer two-year programs in computer information systems. Depending on the courses you take, these programs can prepare you for entry-level positions in computer programming, computer operations, or microcomputer support. Community colleges also offer courses in keyboarding. Basic keyboarding skill is essential for anyone who uses a computer. Advanced keyboarding courses can help you develop the proficiency needed for a data entry operator position. Some community colleges have two-year programs that can prepare you for an entry-level position as a computer service technician. Finally, many community colleges have courses in marketing and sales that may help you secure a position in computer sales.

Four-year colleges and universities often have bachelor's and master's degree programs in computer information systems or management information systems. Often, these programs are part of a business major. Students who complete bachelor's degrees may find employment as trainee programmer/analysts or in end-user support. With a master's degree, graduates may start as systems analysts or in database administration. Students who wish to enter computer sales often major in marketing and take a number of computer-related courses. Students who want to work in the computer field in end-user departments usually major in a business field, such as accounting or finance, and take extra computer courses. Some schools have a minor in computer information systems that can be completed for additional background.

Colleges and universities also offer degrees in computer science, which is different from computer information systems. Computer science is a more technical field and deals with computer hardware and system software, whereas computer information systems deals with application software and information systems. Graduates with bachelor's degrees in computer science often start as software engineers in software companies. Some computer science programs provide extensive education in hardware design. Then the program may be called computer engineering. Graduates start as computer designers in hardware companies.

KEEPING UP WITH THE COMPUTER FIELD

After you get your first job, your education is not over. The computer field changes rapidly, and if you do not keep up, you will quickly be out of date. Some people estimate that after three years, half of what you know about computers will be obsolete. So how do you keep up?

DO COMPUTER SKILLS MAKE COLLEGE GRADS MORE MARKETABLE?

In the mid-1980s when schools like Drexel, Carnegie Mellon University, and Stevens Institute of Technology began introducing undergraduates to microcomputers, the assumption was that computer skills could make students more productive and thus more desirable job candidates. It didn't matter whether they were art, science, or business majors.

Although there's no statistical proof yet that the world's problems will be better solved by students with computer skills, those early assumptions about personal computers in the undergraduate environment have changed little. In fact, microcomputer momentum is gaining force on America's campuses.

Students spent more than $1 billion in a recent year on personal computer products, and colleges spent another $800 million. And these numbers are likely to grow. Hardware and software companies look at colleges and their students as underdeveloped markets with enormous potential. The report said that companies will continue selling directly to students at large discounts while studying other ways to enhance their campus penetration.

One indication of the growth of computer use at the college level is the increase in course-related applications. Software is being developed at a faster rate and is of better quality than before. At many colleges, faculty are designing software for courses where none existed previously. In the philosophy department at Carnegie Mellon, for example, a new program gives students self-paced instruction in symbolic logic.

Colleges have advanced beyond wondering if computers belong on their campuses. According to Kimberly Wiley, a director at the EDUCOM Consulting Group in Princeton, New Jersey, it's now a question of *how*. Do you put them in the dormitories or the libraries? Do you give one to each student or set them up in clusters around campus?

Because there's no statistical validation for the computer as a teaching tool, schools requiring personal computer access or ownership admit they're engaged in what amounts to mighty expensive experiments. But, says Wiley, "The colleges feel they're enhancing their students' learning by offering tools they didn't have before."

The range of hot and cold opinions on computer literacy is remarkable—as expressed by the companies who hire from campuses. After the first large personal computer projects were announced several years ago, campus recruiters began converging on the hottest schools like football talent scouts—all in search of top-round draft picks to fill their entry-level quotas. Yet much of that early corporate enthusiasm appears to have settled.

Though they won't readily admit it, the majority of campus recruiters for non–computer-related jobs only look at computer skills when there's a choice among candidates who otherwise are alike in academics, leadership, and personality. "In general, we just don't consider computer literacy a key hiring criterion," says a recruiting manager with one of the large accounting firms. "But when we're down to a decision over this person or that one, personal computer skills can mean something," she adds

Even Apple Computer ranks computer literacy below experience, leadership skills, and personality as a substantial hiring criterion—particularly for the human-resource type jobs. Explains Apple's college relations coordinator Lynne Capener, "It takes only an afternoon on the average personal computer to acquire many of the necessary skills."

Clarkson University's dean of educational computing, David Bray, maintains that recruiters will always pursue the smart, well-rounded kids. "But it helps if they've been introduced to problem solving on a personal computer. We feel that the computer's presence on campus is a plus, but there's nothing statistical to measure. All we can go by is jobs. . . ."

So why such hype over integrating the computer onto campus if some recruiters aren't sold on its necessity? The answer is that *some* companies apparently *are* sold. And there's growing evidence that students—particularly liberal arts students—with personal computer applications skills are finding better jobs with higher pay. On the campuses with computers, there's a majority opinion that the quality of learning has improved.

The strongest evidence that computer-savvy graduates are going somewhere in the job market comes from an informal research study done by Barbara Kurshan, former director of academic computing at Hollands College, a tiny women's liberal arts institution in Roanoke, Virginia. Kurshan surveyed a cross section of students including approximately 100 who had taken two or more computer courses during their careers at Hollands.

She found that about 70 percent of the students who had taken computer courses were using computers frequently in their jobs. In general, these students perceived that they got their jobs as a result of their computer experience. They also perceived that they were paid more for the same reason.

Burton Nadler, former career advisor at Dartmouth College and now director of recruiting for a Washington, D.C. firm, says employers are impressed by computer literacy. "It's had an impact on job eligibility. Even the leave-term (cooperative semester) employers are looking more and more at computer confidence," he says.

Adds Bray, "In the junior year when our undergrads begin their semester in industry, they know more about computers than the average college graduate does." Bray recalls a special thrill when one of Clarkson's undergrads—a computer science major who studied technical communications as well—became the first bachelor-level job candidate hired at the Mitre Corporation, a Massachusetts High-technology research firm.

Beyond the anecdotes about placement success, there's a belief by most of the campus population at computer-equipped schools that the machines have inspired a rededication to learning. Dr. Joan McCord, a sociologist at Temple University, was teaching at Drexel in 1983 when the university announced that all incoming first-year students would have access to Apple Macintoshes.

In the only known longitudinal study of its kind, McCord looked at the impact of Drexel's decision over the next two years and reported her findings in a paper titled "Computing: Is It a Better Mousetrap?" She found, in general, that students and faculty felt more efficient, more productive, and more interested in learning after the computers hit campus. By the spring of 1985, her report said, only 8 percent of first-year students felt their computers hadn't added value to their courses.

A yet unpublished study done at Stevens Institute turned up the same positive evidence. Sophomores in nonengineering majors used their computers an average of 8 hours a week—in addition to the 18 hours they spent in class, according to Dr. Joseph Moeller, associate provost for computing and information systems. "Our goal was to get students to turn naturally to the computers—and the faculty feels we've done this for most of them," he says.

The idea that personal computers eliminate the drudgery of work in applications such as word processing and spreadsheet analysis suggests that students are then free to reach toward higher levels of learning. One of many who support this theory is Dr. Jan Biros, director of computing services at Drexel. "Students using electronic spreadsheets are climbing more quickly to the 'what if' questions. Using simulations, they're now making judgments. These are skills that normally wouldn't develop until after a year on the job."

Biros discounts criticism that 90 percent of the personal computer work on campus is word processing. "That's not a criticism at all. Especially when we're using it as a tool to teach writing. English majors at Drexel have database, spreadsheet, and programming language software. But even if word processing is all they use it for, the computer still pays for itself."

Is there still hope for the capable non–computer-literate liberal arts graduate? For the time being, yes, says Athena Constantine, career services and placement director at New York's Columbia University. "Employers are willing to train good applicants, but first they want to measure skills and aptitude."

Back to the original question: Do computer skills make college graduates more marketable? Ronald Kutscher, associate commissioner with the U.S. Bureau of Labor Statistics, believes the reply "I know how to use a computer" will be less of a bargaining point for job candidates in the future as more and more applicants gain computer knowledge. But he says that this point won't be reached unless computers become more accessible and easier to use. Stevens Institute's Moeller admits colleges are still just touching the tip of the iceberg as far as integrating personal computers into courses. "But with students now figuring out how to run problem calculations in six minutes instead of six months—I'd say there's all the proof you need!"

First, you need to read professional publications in the computer field. There are many excellent journals, magazines, and other periodicals oriented toward different aspects of the field. Some are published weekly, some monthly, and some quarterly. If you are in programming, you should read publications related to computer languages and programming techniques. If you are in sales, you should read publications related to computer applications and sales techniques. If you are in microcomputer support, you should read microcomputer-oriented publications. There are so many specialized publications in the computer field that they cannot be listed here. After you get a job you should find out what people you work with read and then start your own regular reading program.

Second, you should join one or more professional computer societies. These societies provide members with publications that contain articles on new developments in the field. In addition, these societies hold professional meetings and conferences at which speakers discuss the latest ideas. Members keep abreast of the field by reading the society's publications and attending its conferences and meetings. The two most well-known professional computer societies are the Association for Computing Machinery (ACM) and the Data Processing Management Association (DPMA).

Finally, you should attend classes, seminars, and training programs. Many colleges and universities offer continuing education classes in the computer field. Private companies sponsor many short seminars on various computer-related topics. Although they are expensive, such seminars are worth attending, and often your company will pay the fee. Most organizations and businesses have in-house training programs that you can attend.

Although keeping up in the computer field may seem like a formidable task, it is essential if you are going to grow and advance in your career. By choosing a type of job that you like, getting the proper education, and growing professionally, you can have a rewarding career in the computer field.

Chapter Summary

- The information systems department is responsible for developing and operating computer information systems. A list of some of the jobs in this department follows.
    In the systems development area:
        Systems analyst
        Application programmer
        Programmer/analyst
    In the operations area:
        Computer operator
        Data entry operator
    In the technical support area:

       Database administrator
       System programmer
       Communications analyst
In the end-user support area:
       Microcomputer analyst
       Computer trainer

■ Sometimes programmers and systems analysts work in end-user departments such as marketing, accounting, finance, and production. If not, an end-user department may have a person who acts as a liaison between the users in the department and the technical specialists in the information systems department. Many end-user departments have an individual who is in charge of microcomputers in the department.

■ There are many jobs in the computer industry. Some jobs in hardware companies are:
       Computer designer
       Sales representative
       System engineer
       Computer service technician
Some jobs in software companies are:
       Software engineer
       Sales representative
       Customer support technician
There are also jobs in computer stores as salespeople, computer service technicians, and customer support technicians.

■ The education required for a career in the computer field depends on the type of job. Many community colleges offer programs and courses that can prepare an individual for an entry-level position in computer programming, computer operations, microcomputer support, data entry operations, computer maintenance and repair, and computer sales. Four-year colleges and universities often have bachelor's degree programs in computer information systems or management information systems that can prepare an individual for an entry-level position as a programmer/analyst or in end-user support. Many colleges and universities also have master's degree programs that can prepare an individual for a position as a systems analyst or in database administration. Students interested in computer sales can major in marketing, and those interested in working in an end-user department can major in a business field. Finally, colleges and universities offer degrees in computer science for those interested in software engineering or computer design.

■ Computer professionals must keep up with the rapid changes in the field. They can do this by reading professional computer publications, joining professional computer societies, and attending classes, seminars, and training programs.

Terms to Remember

Application Programmer   p. 484

Communications Analysts   p. 486

Computer Designer   p. 489

Computer Operator   p. 486

Computer Sales Representative
  p. 489

Computer Service Technician
  p. 489

Computer Trainer   p. 488

Customer Support Technician
  p. 489

Data Entry Operator   p. 486

Information Center   p. 488

Information Systems Manager
  p. 484

Microcomputer Analyst   p. 488

Programmer/Analyst   p. 484

Software Engineer   p. 489

System Engineer   p. 489

System Programmer   p. 486

Vice President of Information
  Systems   p. 484

Review Questions

Fill-In Questions

1. The head of the information systems department in an organization or business is called the _____.

2. The person responsible for all computing in an organization or business is called the _____.

3. A(n) _____ does both computer programming and systems analysis.

4. A(n) _____ runs the computer equipment used in an information system.

5. The person responsible for an organization's data communications hardware and software is called a(n) _____.

6. The end-user support area is often called the _____.

7. Computer sales representatives for a hardware company often call on a(n) _____ to help with a sale by providing technical support for the customer's application.

8. Another name for a highly skilled programmer is _____.

Short-Answer Questions

1. What are some of the names used for the department in an organization or business that is responsible for developing and operating computer information systems?

2. What are the common jobs found in the systems development area?

3. Explain the difference between a trainee, junior, senior, and lead programmer.

4. Describe the difference between a system programmer and an application programmer.

5. What are some of the jobs in the end-user support area?

6. In addition to computer knowledge, what background is needed to work in a computer-related job in an end-user department?

7. What is the difference between the fields of computer information systems and computer science in colleges and universities?

8. Describe three ways that computer professionals can keep up with the computer field.

Projects

1. Interview a computer professional about his or her career in the computer field. How did the person get started? What education does the person have? What was his or her first job in the computer field? What promotions has the person had in his or her career? What does the person do now? What computer publications does he or she read? What professional organizations does he or she belong to? Write a summary of your interview.

2. Look through the want ads in your local newspaper for openings in the computer field. What types of jobs are available, and what background is required for different jobs? Many jobs advertised in newspapers list several years of experience as a requirement. Try to find entry-level jobs that do not require experience. Talk to your college or university placement office about how to get a job in the computer field with little or no experience. Write a summary of your findings.

APPENDIXES

APPENDIX A: SELECTING A PERSONAL COMPUTER

You think you would like to buy a personal computer. Several of your friends at school or colleagues at work have computers. They seem to like them and find they help with their work. You think you could use one for your studies or on your job. But which computer do you buy? One friend says buy an IBM clone—it is the least expensive and has the most software. Another friend says buy a Macintosh—it is the easiest to use. A third friend says wait—there will be new models coming out next year. What should you do?

This appendix explains how to go about selecting a personal computer. It gives a step-by-step procedure that guides you through the selection process. It is not an easy process; it will take time and money. But when you are finished you are likely to be happy with the personal computer you have chosen.

STEP 1: EVALUATE NEEDS AND FEASIBILITY

The first step is to determine whether you need a personal computer and whether it is feasible for you to buy one. Do you really need a personal computer, or do you just want one? Some people buy a computer without thinking about whether they need one. After a short period of time, many of these computers end up sitting unused on a desk or stored away in a closet.

Start by making a brief list of what you think you are going to use a computer for. If the only reason on your list is to type letters to relatives, maybe a good typewriter would be better. Write down how much time per week you think you will spend doing each of the things on your list. If it is only a few hours, it might make sense to rent time on a computer. Some businesses have computers that they rent by the hour.

Other businesses rent computers by the month. If you are not sure how much you are going to use a computer, you might rent one for a month or two to try it out.

If you decide that you really do need a computer, then you have to determine if it is feasible for you to buy one. Useful computers are expensive. You cannot do much with a $200 computer. It could cost you several thousand dollars to get what you need. You can read computer publications (see Figure A–1 for a list of publications) or visit a computer store to get a preliminary idea of what the cost may be. You also have to keep in mind that there are not only initial costs, but also ongoing expenses. For example, you have to buy disks for the disk drive and paper and ribbons for the printer. Figure A–2 lists some of the initial and ongoing cost factors of computer ownership.

Another important consideration at this time is where you are going to put the computer. You need a table and chair in a room with good lighting and ventilation. You need storage space for documentation, disks, supplies, and so on. Do you have the necessary space in your home or office?

At this point you can answer the question of buying now or waiting a year or two. It is almost certain that computers in the future will be more sophisticated and will cost less. Some people will say that you should wait so that what you get will not be obsolete or will not cost too much. But then you may always be waiting. A good rule is that if the benefits you expect from the computer outweigh the costs, then you should buy now. If you do not, you will be losing those benefits during the time you wait. However, if the costs are greater than the benefits, you should wait until either the benefits you expect increase or the costs decrease.

Figure A–1   Personal Computer Publications

Personal Computing	(monthly)	**Byte**	(monthly)
PC World	(monthly)	**Infoworld**	(weekly)
PC Magazine	(biweekly)	**PC Week**	(weekly)
PC Computing	(monthly)	**Macworld**	(monthly)
Compute!	(monthly)	**MacGuide**	(monthly)
Home Office Computing	(monthly)	**MacUser**	(monthly)

Figure A–2   Cost Factors of Computer Ownership

Initial costs:	**Ongoing expenses:**
Hardware	Paper
Software	Ribbon
Furniture	Disks
Training	Maintenance and repair

STEP 2: DETERMINE APPLICATION REQUIREMENTS

If you decide you need a personal computer and it is feasible for you, then the next step in the selection process is to determine the requirements of your applications. You are getting a computer to help you with certain computer applications. You have already made a brief list of your computer uses in Step 1. Now you need to determine the requirements for each of your computer applications.

As an example, let's assume that one of your expected uses is to prepare reports and other written documents. You know that this is a word processing application. To determine the requirements for this application, you need to answer questions such as the following:

- How long will typical documents be?
- Will the documents require extensive changes after they are entered?
- Will the output format be simple or complex?
- What quality output is required (letter, near-letter, or draft)?
- How much output will be printed in a period of time, such as a week?

Similar questions will need to be answered to determine the requirements of other applications. Make a complete list of your requirements for each of your applications. (Reread Chapters 8 through 11 for a review of common personal computer applications and their characteristics.)

Additional questions need to be answered about your applications at this point. Do you need to transfer data between applications? Do you need to run more than one application at a time? Do your applications need to be compatible with those of friends or co-workers? Do you need to use your applications at more than one location? Do any of your applications require communicating with other computers? You should determine as many characteristics of your applications as you can at this time.

STEP 3: DETERMINE SOFTWARE AND HARDWARE REQUIREMENTS

Now that you know what your application requirements are, you can determine your software and hardware requirements. Start with software. What type of software do you need for each of your applications? There are many types of software and many variations within each type. You need to determine exactly what type of software will meet your needs. (Again, review Chapters 8 through 11 if you need to refresh your memory about microcomputer software.)

As an example, assume, as before, that one of your applications is word processing to prepare reports and documents. You will need a word processing program for this purpose. Your requirements for this application determine what type of word processing program you need. If your documents are long, if they require extensive changes, and if they are printed in complex formats, you will need a sophisticated word processing program. However, if you prepare only short documents, with few changes and simple output format, you need only a simple (and less expensive) program. Make a list of the general type of program you need for each of your applications.

Other application requirements will influence your software requirements. For example, if you need to transfer data between applications, you may need an integrated program (see Chapter 11). If you need to run more than one application at a time, you need a multitasking operating system, otherwise a single-tasking operating system is satisfactory (see Chapter 7). If your applications need to be compatible with those of friends or co-workers, you may need the same software they use. If any of your applications require communicating with other computers, you will need communications software (see Chapter 6).

After you have determined your software requirements, you can determine your hardware requirements. First, determine any special requirements for input and output devices. You know you will need a keyboard, but do any of your applications have a lot of numeric data entry so that a numeric keypad is desirable? If one of your applications requires graphic output, you may need a different type of screen from what you would need if all you want to display is characters. The quality of output that you need determines what type of printer you require (dot-matrix, laser, and so on). The quantity of output determines how fast a printer you need. If you are going to produce graphic output on paper, you need either a graphics printer or a plotter. (Reread Chapter 4 for a review of microcomputer input and output devices.)

Your applications may also determine specific requirements for secondary storage. For example, a large database application usually requires a hard disk drive. (Reread Chapter 5 for a review of secondary storage devices.) Also, some applications may need large primary storage and fast CPUs. (Reread Chapter 3 for a review of primary storage and CPUs.)

Other application requirements determine more hardware requirements. For example, if you need to use your application at more than one location, you will need a portable computer; otherwise a desktop computer should be satisfactory. If any of your applications require communicating with other computers, you will need a modem and perhaps other hardware. (Reread Chapter 6 for a review of communications hardware.)

Make a list of your software and hardware requirements. You may not know all your hardware requirements at this time, so your list may not be complete. You can always add to your list later, and anything you can write down now will help you in your selection.

STEP 4: IDENTIFY ALTERNATIVES

With your list of software and hardware requirements from the last step, you can identify available programs and computers that are likely to meet your needs. Again, start with software. You need to find programs that will satisfy your software requirements. A good place to begin is friends and co-workers; ask them what programs they use and what they like or dislike about those programs. You can also go to computer stores to find out what software they recommend (but do not plan on buying anything yet). Another source is computer publications (see the list in Figure A–1). Many of these publications describe programs and their characteristics. You can look through recent issues at a local library. You can also request literature about programs from software companies or pick up brochures at computer stores. Make a list of those programs that might satisfy each of your software requirements. (Many of the more common programs are listed in Chapters 8 through 11, but other programs are available and new ones are introduced continually.)

Each program will run on certain types of computers and will have certain hardware requirements. For example, a word processing program may run on an IBM personal computer with 640K of primary storage and two floppy disk drives or a hard disk drive. Some programs require powerful microprocessors found in more expensive computers. A few programs come in several versions for different computers. For each program that meets your software requirements, note its specific hardware requirements.

Now you can go to several computer stores to complete your identification of hardware and software alternatives. Take your application requirements, your software and hardware requirements, and your list of programs that you have identified as likely to meet your software requirements. Go over all requirements with the salesperson, and show him or her your list of software alternatives. Ask the salesperson which programs on your list or which other programs he or she feels will best meet your requirements. Also, ask the salesperson which computers he or she would recommend for your programs. Ask the salesperson to give you a complete list of all hardware and software, with a total price for each alternative he or she is proposing.

At this point you may wish to start a checksheet for each alternative. Figure A–3 shows a model checksheet, but you can list any items on the sheet that you feel are important. You will not be able to fill out everything on the sheet yet, but you can get started, and the sheet will help you organize your notes.

STEP 5: EVALUATE ALTERNATIVES

Now you are ready to evaluate your alternatives. You can start your evaluation when you are at each computer store gathering information in the previous step. Ask for a demonstration of each program on the type of computer the salesperson is proposing. You need to evaluate both the software and the hardware.

It is difficult to evaluate whether a particular program and computer will meet your requirements. You can try different features of a program to see if they work, or you can make up a simple test, such as part of a document that you can enter, edit, and print. Probably, you will have to trust the judgment of others who are experienced with the particular software and hardware you are evaluating.

Figure A–3   Hardware and Software Alternatives Checksheet

Alternatives	A	B	C
Hardware Make			
Model			
CPU type			
Primary storage capacity			
Keyboard Function keys			
Cursor control keys			
Numeric keypad			
"Feel"			
Mouse			
Screen Monochrome/color			
Resolution			
Ease of reading			
Printer Type			
Quality			
Speed			
Secondary storage Type			
Capacity			
Other hardware			
Operating system Name			
Version			
Application software (repeat for each program) Name			
Version			
Type			
User interface			
Help screens			
Ease of use			
Features			
Documentation			
Total price			

Assuming that the proposed software and hardware will satisfy your requirements, your principal basis for evaluation should be ease of use. Try out the user interface for each program. (Reread the section on the user interface in Chapter 7 for a review of this topic.) Does the program use commands, menus, or icons? Does it have Help screens that really are helpful? Can you use it in a way that you like to work, or does it force you to work a certain way? Go through as many features of the program as you can. Also, look at the documentation that goes with each program to see how easy it is to understand.

While trying the software, you can evaluate the hardware. Does the keyboard have a good "feel"? Is the screen easy to read? If the computer comes with a mouse, is the mouse easy to use? How noisy is the computer? (Most computers have fans and make some noise.) Are the quality and speed of the printer satisfactory? Try to get a good sense of how easy the hardware is to operate.

You should repeat the evaluation step for each alternative. You need to look at several programs and computers before making a decision. As you evaluate each alternative you can complete your checksheet (Figure A–3). You can also take notes on what you like and dislike about each program and each computer.

STEP 6: MAKE A DECISION

Now you are ready to make a decision. Gather together all the information that you have about each alternative. You should have information about each program and each computer, the total price of each system proposed by a salesperson, your checksheet, and your notes on your evaluation. In addition to evaluating this information, you may want to consider other factors such as the manufacturer's reputation, the availability of training courses or self-training books, the type of support you can expect from the computer store or the software vendor, the warranty, and the source of hardware repair.

You do not necessarily want to pick the least expensive alternative. Other factors may make a more expensive system preferable. You can make your final decision by using your subjective feeling about all the alternatives, or you can use a more systematic approach. For example, you can assign scores (such as numbers from 1 to 10) to each feature of each system and add the scores to get a total. Then, you can select the system with the greatest total for the least cost. Whatever you do, you should think carefully about your decision before buying.

After you have made your decision, you can return to the computer store to complete the purchase. Make sure you get exactly what you ordered, and check everything carefully when you get it home or to your office. Then you can set up your new computer and begin using it for your applications.

Summary

The steps in selecting a personal computer are:

1. Evaluate needs and feasibility.

List your expected computer uses, and decide if you really need a personal computer.

Estimate your expected costs, and decide if a personal computer is feasible for you.

2. Determine application requirements.

List your requirements for each of your computer applications.

3. Determine software and hardware requirements.

Determine your software requirements for your applications.

Determine your hardware requirements for your applications.

4. Identify alternatives.

Identify available programs that will satisfy your software requirements.

Identify the specific hardware requirements for each program.

Get the total price of each hardware and software alternative.

5. Evaluate alternatives.

Evaluate each program on the proposed hardware.

Evaluate the hardware.

6. Make a decision.

Consider all factors and select the alternative that best meets your needs at the lowest price.

APPENDIX B:
THE HISTORY OF COMPUTERS

Computers have been in use for a relatively short period of time. The first commercial computers became available in the early 1950s. Since then, computers and computer use have gone through a rapid evolution. But before that time, computers and computing devices developed slowly. This appendix takes a brief look at both the early and recent history of computers.

THE EARLY HISTORY OF COMPUTING AND DATA PROCESSING

People have been trying to find easier ways of doing calculations for thousands of years. The abacus, invented over 2500 years ago, was one of the first efforts. The first mechanical calculator was invented by Blaise Pascal, a French mathematician, in 1642 (Figure B–1).

Babbage's Analytical Engine

The first major step toward the development of a computer took place in 1822. A British mathematician, Charles Babbage, designed a machine that he called the **difference engine**, for calculating certain types of mathematical tables (Figure B–2). According to his design, the difference engine would use gears and levers to do calculations. Babbage received several grants from the British government to build the machine, but he was never able to complete it. (A machine based on Babbage's ideas was completed in 1855 and used in the United States and Great Britain.)

In 1834, while working on the difference engine, Babbage conceived the idea of a more powerful calculating machine, which he called the **analytical engine**. As with the difference engine, this machine would

Figure B–1   Pascal and His Calculator

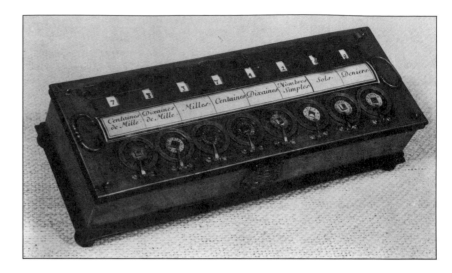

Figure B–2   Babbage and His Difference Engine

use gears and levers for calculations. In addition, it would have the capability of storing up to one thousand numbers and could be programmed for different calculations. Many of the ideas for programming the analytical engine were developed by Augusta Ada Byron, Countess of Lovelace, in 1842. In a way, she was the first programmer.

Babbage never completed the analytical engine, partially because the technology needed to build the machine's parts was not available. The engine, however, had many of the characteristics of a modern computer: a primary storage, an arithmetic unit, and programming capabilities. It lacked the electronic characteristics of current computers, however. Had Babbage lived one hundred years later, he may have invented the first electronic computer.

Hollerith's Punched Cards

To enter programs into his analytical engine, Babbage planned to use cards with patterns of holes in them. He borrowed the idea from a loom invented by Joseph Jacquard in France in 1801. The loom wove patterns into fabric by following instructions given by holes in cards (Figure B–3). In Babbage's analytical engine, the cards would contain instructions to tell the machine what calculations to perform.

Jacquard's cards were also the inspiration for Herman Hollerith, an engineer working for the Census Bureau in the late 1800s. The Census Bureau takes the U.S. census every ten years. The 1880 census required 7½ years to compile. With population growth, the Census Bureau projected that the 1890 census could take more than ten years to tabulate, so something had to be done. Hollerith conceived the idea of recording census data on cards similar to Jacquard's. Patterns of holes in the cards would represent different population characteristics. The cards were called **punched cards**. Hollerith invented two machines for punching

Figure B–3   Jacquard and His Loom

holes in the cards, one machine for sorting cards based on patterns of holes, and another machine for counting or tabulating data from cards (Figure B–4). Using Hollerith's punched card machines, the 1890 census took only 2½ years to compile.

Hollerith saw a commercial value to his ideas, so in 1896 he formed the Tabulating Machine Company to manufacture and sell his machines. His machines were used in the 1900 census as well as by some businesses for data processing. In 1911, the Tabulating Machine Company merged with several other companies to form the Computing-Tabulating-Recording (CTR) Company. In 1924, CTR changed its name to International Business Machines Corporation (IBM), which today is the largest computer manufacturer in the world.

After the 1900 census, the Census Bureau had a disagreement with Hollerith and hired James Powers to develop new punched card machines for the 1910 census. Powers used a different type of card from that used by Hollerith, and his machines had additional capabilities. Like Hollerith, however, Powers saw a commercial value to his machines, so he formed the Powers Accounting Machine Company in 1911. In 1927, his company became a division of Remington Rand Inc., which eventually became Sperry Corporation. Then, in 1986 Sperry merged with Burroughs Corporation to form Unisys Corporation. Today, Unisys is one of the largest computer manufacturers after IBM.

The punched cards of Hollerith and Powers were used for many years after their development. Punched card machines became more and more sophisticated, until many businesses had rooms full of machines used for punched card data processing. For years, computers used punched cards as their main form of input. The modern punched card (Figure B–5) is still available today, but is rarely used.

Figure B–4   Hollerith and His Punched Card Machines

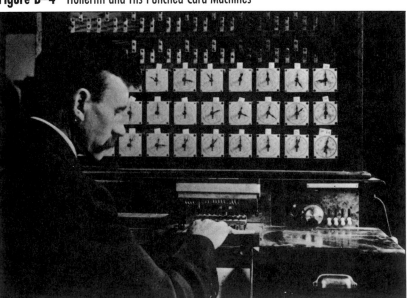

Figure B–5 The Modern Punched Card

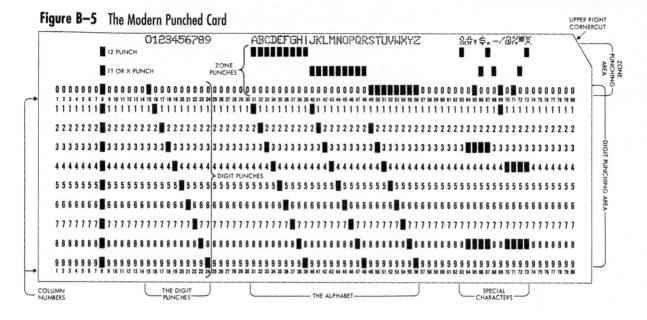

THE INVENTION OF THE COMPUTER

It is hard to say exactly when the modern computer was invented. Starting in the 1930s and through the 1940s, a number of machines were developed that were like a computer. But most of these machines did not have all the characteristics that we associate with computers today. These characteristics are that the machine is *electronic*, that it has a *stored program*, and that it is *general purpose*.

One of the first computerlike devices was developed in Germany by Konrad Zuse in 1941. Called the Z3, it was a general-purpose, stored-program machine with many electronic parts, but it had a mechanical memory. Another electromechanical computing machine was developed by Howard Aiken, with financial assistance from IBM, at Harvard University in 1943. It was called the Automatic Sequence Control Calculator Mark I, or simply the Harvard Mark I. Neither of these machines was a true computer, however, because they were not entirely electronic.

The Atanasoff-Berry Computer

The first fully electronic computerlike device was developed by John Atanasoff and his assistant, Clifford Berry. Atanasoff, a professor at Iowa State College, wanted a machine to help his students solve certain types of equations. In 1937, he conceived the idea of an electronic computing device for this purpose. With Berry's help, Atanasoff worked on the machine until 1942. Called the **Atanasoff-Berry Computer**, or **ABC**, all the components of the machine were never completed, although it was capable of solving some equations (Figure B–6).

Figure B–6   The Atanasoff-Berry Computer or ABC

The ABC was the first electronic, stored-program computing machine, but it was not a general-purpose computer. It was designed only to solve certain types of equations and thus could not be used for other problems. Its existence was not widely known until many years after its invention.

The ENIAC

Perhaps the most influential of the early computerlike devices was the Electronic Numerical Integrator and Computer, or **ENIAC**. It was developed by J. Presper Eckert and John Mauchly at the University of Pennsylvania. The project began in 1943 and was completed in 1946. The machine was huge; it weighed 30 tons and contained over 18,000 vacuum tubes (Figure B–7).

The ENIAC was a major advancement for its time. It was the first general-purpose, electronic computing machine and was capable of performing thousands of operations per second. It was controlled, however, by switches and plugs that had to be manually set. Thus, although it was a general-purpose electronic device, it did not have a stored program. Therefore, it did not have all the characteristics of a computer.

The First Computers

While working on the ENIAC, Eckert and Mauchly were joined by a brilliant mathematician, John von Neuman. Together, they developed the idea of a stored program computer. This machine, called the Electronic Discrete Variable Automatic Computer, or **EDVAC**, was the first machine whose design included all the characteristics of a computer. It was not completed, however, until 1951.

Figure B–7 The ENIAC

Before the EDVAC was finished, several other machines were built that incorporated elements of the EDVAC design of Eckert, Mauchly, and von Neuman. One was the Electronic Delay Storage Automatic Computer, or **EDSAC**, which was developed in Cambridge, England. It first operated in May of 1949 and is probably the world's first electronic, stored-program, general-purpose computer to become operational. The first computer to operate in the United States was the Binary Automatic Computer, or **BINAC**, which became operational in August of 1949.

The UNIVAC I

Like other computing pioneers before them, Eckert and Mauchly formed a company in 1947 to develop a commercial computer. The company was called the Eckert-Mauchly Computer Corporation. Their objective was to design and build the Universal Automatic Computer or **UNIVAC**. Because of difficulties getting financial support, they had to sell the company to Remington Rand in 1950. Eckert and Mauchly continued to work on the UNIVAC at Remington Rand and completed it in 1951. Known as the UNIVAC I, this machine was the first commercially available computer.

The first UNIVAC I was delivered to the Census Bureau and used for the 1950 census. The second UNIVAC I was used to predict that Dwight Eisenhower would win the 1952 presidential election, less than an hour after the polls closed (Figure B–8). The UNIVAC I began the modern era of computer use.

Figure B–8   The UNIVAC I with J. Presper Eckert and Walter Cronkite

COMPUTER GENERATIONS

Since the UNIVAC I, computers have evolved rapidly. Their evolution has been the result of changes in technology that have occurred regularly. These changes have resulted in four main generations of computers.

First-Generation Computers: 1951–1958

First-generation computers were characterized by the use of *vacuum tubes* as their principal electronic component (Figure B–9). Vacuum tubes are bulky and produce a lot of heat, so first-generation computers were large and required extensive air conditioning to keep them cool. In addition, because vacuum tubes do not operate very fast, these computers were relatively slow.

The UNIVAC I was the first commercial computer in this generation. As noted earlier, it was used in the Census Bureau in 1951. It was also the first computer to be used in a business application. In 1954, General Electric took delivery of a UNIVAC I and used it for some of its business data processing.

The UNIVAC I was not the most popular first-generation computer, however. This honor goes to the IBM 650 (Figure B–10). It was first delivered in 1955 before Remington Rand could come out with a successor to the UNIVAC I. With the IBM 650, IBM captured the majority of the computer market, a position it still holds today.

At the same time that hardware was evolving, software was developing. The first computers were programmed in machine language, but during the first computer generation, the idea of programming language translation and high-level languages occurred. Much of the credit for these ideas goes to Grace Hopper, who, as a Navy lieutenant in

Figure B–10   The IBM 650

Figure B–11   Grace Murray Hopper

1945, learned to program the Harvard Mark I (Figure B–11). In 1952, she developed the first programming language translator, followed by others in later years. She also developed a language called Flow-matic in 1957, which formed the basis for COBOL, the most commonly used business programming language today.

Other software developments during the first computer generation include the design of the FORTRAN programming language in 1957. This language became the first widely used high-level language. Also, the first simple operating systems became available with first-generation computers.

Second-Generation Computers: 1959–1963

In the second generation of computers, *transistors* replaced vacuum tubes (Figure B–12). Although invented in 1948, the first all-transistor computer did not become available until 1959. Transistors are smaller and less expensive than vacuum tubes, and they operate faster and produce less heat. Hence, with second-generation computers, the size and cost of computers decreased, their speed increased, and their air-conditioning needs were reduced.

Many companies that had not previously sold computers entered the industry with the second generation. One of these companies that still makes computers is Control Data Corporation (CDC). They were noted for making high-speed computers for scientific work.

Remington Rand, now called Sperry-Rand Corporation, made several second-generation UNIVAC computers. IBM, however, continued to dominate the industry. One of the most popular second-generation computers was the IBM 1401, which was a medium-sized computer used by many businesses.

Figure B–12   A Transistor

All computers at this time were mainframe computers costing over a million dollars. The first minicomputer became available in 1960 and cost about $120,000. This was the PDP-1, manufactured by Digital Equipment Corporation (DEC).

Software also continued to develop during this time. Many new programming languages were designed, including COBOL in 1960. More and more businesses and organizations were beginning to use computers for their data processing needs.

Third-Generation Computers: 1964–1970

The technical development that marks the third generation of computers is the use of *integrated circuits* or *ICs* in computers. An integrated circuit is a piece of silicon (a chip) containing numerous transistors (Figure B–13). One IC replaces many transistors in a computer, resulting in a continuation of the trends begun in the second generation. These trends include reduced size, reduced cost, increased speed, and reduced need for air conditioning.

Although integrated circuits were invented in 1958, the first computers to make extensive use of them were not available until 1964. In that year, IBM introduced a line of mainframe computers called the System/360. The computers in this line became the most widely used third-generation machines. There were many models in the System/360 line, ranging from small, relatively slow, and inexpensive ones, to large, very fast, and costly models. All models, however, were compatible so that programs written for one model could be used on another. This feature of compatibility across many computers in a line was adopted by other manufacturers of third-generation computers.

The third computer generation was also the time when minicomputers became widespread. The most popular model was the PDP-8, manufactured by DEC. Other companies, including Data General Corporation

Figure B–13   An Integrated Circuit

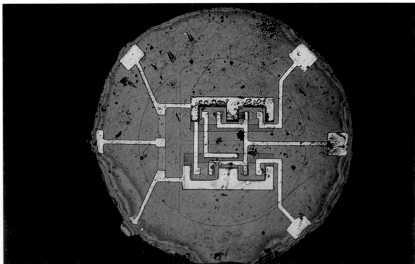

and Hewlett-Packard Company, introduced minicomputers during the third generation.

The principal software development during the third computer generation was the increased sophistication of operating systems. Although simple operating systems were developed for first- and second-generation computers, many of the features of modern operating systems first appeared during the third generation. These include multiprogramming, virtual memory, and time sharing. The first operating systems were mainly batch systems, but during the third generation, interactive systems, especially on minicomputers, became common. The BASIC programming language was designed in 1964 and became popular during the third computer generation because of its interactive nature.

Fourth-Generation Computers: 1971–?

The fourth generation of computers is more difficult to define than the other three generations. This generation is characterized by more and more transistors being contained on a silicon chip. First there was *large scale integration* (*LSI*), with hundreds and thousands of transistors per chip, then came *very large scale integration* (*VLSI*), with tens of thousands and hundreds of thousands of transistors. The trend continues today.

Although not everyone agrees that there is a fourth computer generation, those that do feel that it began in 1971, when IBM introduced its successors to the System/360 line of computers. These mainframe computers were called the System/370, and current-model IBM computers, although not called System/370s, evolved directly from these computers.

Minicomputers also proliferated during the fourth computer generation. The most popular lines were the DEC PDP-11 models and the DEC VAX, both of which are available in various models today.

Supercomputers first became prominent in the fourth generation. Although many companies, including IBM and CDC, developed high-speed computers for scientific work, it was not until Cray Research, Inc., introduced the Cray 1 in 1975 that supercomputers became significant. Today, supercomputers are an important computer classification.

Perhaps the most important trend that began in the fourth generation is the proliferation of microcomputers. As more and more transistors were put on silicon chips, it eventually became possible to put an entire computer processor, called a microprocessor, on a chip. The first computer to use microprocessors became available in the mid-1970s. The first microcomputer designed for personal use was the Altair, which was sold as a kit for hobbyists in 1975. The first Apple computer, the Apple I (Figure B–14), followed shortly. The Apple II was introduced in 1977, and models of it are still made today. IBM entered the microcomputer market with the IBM PC in 1981. Today, microcomputers far outnumber all other types of computers combined.

Software development during the fourth computer generation started off with little change from the third generation. Operating systems were gradually improved, and new languages were designed. Database software became widely used during this time. The most important trend, however, resulted from the microcomputer revolution. Packaged soft-

Figure B–14   The Apple I

ware became widely available for microcomputers so that today most software is purchased, not developed from scratch.

Fifth-Generation Computers

What will be the fifth generation of computers? The answer to this question is difficult to say. New technology could be invented that changes the way computers work. There already is an effort to increase computer speed by using substances other than silicon in chips. Certainly there will be increased numbers of transistors on a chip in the future. Computers that use light for data storage and processing are also being developed.

Some people think fifth-generation computers will be intelligent computers capable of reasoning similar to that of a person. Such a computer would have to be very powerful and would require sophisticated software. Researchers in the United States, Japan, and elsewhere are already designing fifth-generation computers along these lines. It may be many years before we know whether they are successful. We may have to wait a long time for the fifth computer generation.

Summary

- The early history of computing and data processing:

  500 B.C.   Abacus invented.

  1642 A.D.   Blaise Pascal invents first calculator.

  1801   Joseph Jacquard invents loom controlled by punched cards.

1822	Charles Babbage designs difference engine.
1834	Babbage starts design of analytical engine.
1842	Augusta Ada Byron develops program for Babbage's analytical engine.
1890	Herman Hollerith develops punched card and punched card machines to process census data.
1896	Hollerith forms Tabulating Machine Company, later to become the International Business Machines Corporation.
1910	James Powers develops new punched card machines to process census data.
1911	Powers forms Powers Accounting Machine Company, which evolves into Unisys Corporation.

- The invention of the computer:

1937	John Atanasoff designs the Atanasoff-Berry Computer (ABC), the first electronic, stored-program computing device.
1943	J. Presper Eckert and John Mauchly start work on the ENIAC, the first electronic, general-purpose computing device. It is completed in 1946.
1945	Eckert, Mauchly, and John von Neuman develop idea of EDVAC, the first machine whose design includes all the characteristics of a computer.
1947	Eckert and Mauchly form Eckert-Mauchly Computer Corporation to design and build the UNIVAC. The company is sold to Remington Rand in 1950.
1949	EDSAC and BINAC completed; first operational electronic, stored-program, general-purpose computers.
1951	UNIVAC I, the first commercial computer, completed and delivered to Census Bureau.

- The computer generations:

1951–1958	First-generation computers. Characterized by the use of vacuum tubes. Most popular is IBM 650. First use of a computer for a business application. First programming language translator developed by Grace Hopper. FORTRAN designed. First simple operating systems.
1959–1963	Second-generation computers. Characterized by the use of transistors. Most popular is IBM 1401. First minicomputer developed by DEC (PDP-1). COBOL designed.
1964–1970	Third-generation computers. Characterized by the use of integrated circuits. Most popular mainframe computer is IBM System/360. Minicomputers become widespread. Most popular minicomputer is DEC PDP-8. Sophisticated operating systems developed. BASIC designed.

1971–?   Fourth-generation computers. Characterized by large scale and very large scale integrated circuits. Most popular mainframe computer is IBM System/370. Minicomputers proliferate. Most popular minicomputers are DEC PDP-11 and DEC VAX. First supercomputer developed (Cray 1). First microcomputer designed for personal use developed (Altair). Microcomputers proliferate. Database software used widely.

Terms to Remember

Analytical Engine   p. 507
Atanasoff-Berry Computer
   (ABC)   p. 511
BINAC   p. 513
Difference Engine   p. 507
EDSAC   p. 513

EDVAC   p. 512
ENIAC   p. 512
Punched Card   p. 509
UNIVAC   p. 513

APPENDIX C: NUMBER SYSTEMS

A **number system** is a way of expressing quantities. Most people use the **decimal number system**. Computers express quantities by using the **binary number system**. This appendix describes the binary number system and related topics. First, however, you need to understand the decimal number system.

THE DECIMAL NUMBER SYSTEM

Consider the decimal number 285. What does this number really mean? We can think of 285 as 200 plus 80 plus 5. But 200 is 2 times 100, 80 is 8 times 10, and 5 is 5 times 1. Finally, 100 is 10 times 10 or 10^2, 10 is 10^1, and 1 is 10^0. Thus, we can interpret 285 as follows:

$$285 = 200 + 80 + 5$$
$$= (2 \times 100) + (8 \times 10) + (5 \times 1)$$
$$= (2 \times 10^2) + (8 \times 10^1) + (5 \times 10^0)$$

Before going on, let's briefly review the concept of raising a number to a power. Any number raised to a power means *multiply the number by itself the number of times specified in the power*; that is, use the number as a factor the number of times given by the power. For example, 6^4 means *use 6 as a factor 4 times*:

$$6^4 = 6 \times 6 \times 6 \times 6 = 1296$$

The following are other examples:

$$10^2 = 10 \times 10 = 100$$
$$10^3 = 10 \times 10 \times 10 = 1000$$
$$10^4 = 10 \times 10 \times 10 \times 10 = 10,000$$
$$2^2 = 2 \times 2 = 4$$
$$2^3 = 2 \times 2 \times 2 = 8$$
$$2^4 = 2 \times 2 \times 2 \times 2 = 16$$
$$2^5 = 2 \times 2 \times 2 \times 2 \times 2 = 32$$

A number raised to the first power is just that number. For example, 6^1 is 6, 10^1 is 10, and 2^1 is 2. Finally, a number raised to the zero power is one. This fact is true for any number except zero. (0^0 is indeterminate.) For example, 6^0 is 1, 10^0 is 1, and 2^0 is 1.

As another example of a decimal number, consider 4096:

$$4096 = \quad 4000 \quad + \quad 000 \quad + \quad 90 \quad + \quad 6$$
$$= (4 \times 1000) + (0 \times 100) + (9 \times 10) + (6 \times 1)$$
$$= (4 \times 10^3) \quad + (0 \times 10^2) + (9 \times 10^1) + (6 \times 10^0)$$

Notice how the digit zero is used to hold a place in the number without adding value to the number. In this example, zero holds the 100's place. Because zero times any number is zero, it does not increase the value of the number.

These examples illustrate the basic concepts of a number system. A number system is composed of a set of digits. In the decimal number system the digits are 0, 1, 2, 3, 4, 5, 6, 7, 8, and 9. The number of digits is called the **base** of the number system. There are ten digits in the decimal number system because the base of the system is ten. A number is a quantity that is represented by a **numeral** composed of a series of digits. For example, the decimal numeral 285 is composed of digits that are acceptable in the decimal number system. This numeral represents the number two hundred eighty-five. The digits in a numeral occupy positions that have value. The **position values** (also called *place values*) of a number system are successive powers of the base. Considering only whole numbers, the right-most position has a value of the base to the zero power, the next position to the left has a value of the base to the first power, the next position has a value of the base to the second power, and so forth. Thus the position values for the decimal number system are:

$$\ldots 10^5 \ 10^4 \ 10^3 \ 10^2 \ 10^1 \ 10^0$$

A numeral is interpreted in a number system as the sum of the products of the digits in the numeral and their corresponding position values. Thus, 285 is interpreted as a decimal number as follows:

Digits:	2	8	5
Position values:	10^2	10^1	10^0
Interpretation:	$(2 \times 10^2) + (8 \times 10^1) + (5 \times 10^0)$		

The interpretation of the numeral is found by multiplying the digits in the numeral by their corresponding position values and then adding the results. Note that the right-most digit occupies the 10^0 position and that the position values increase to the left.

As another example, consider 4096:

Digits:	4	0	9	6
Position values:	10^3	10^2	10^1	10^0
Interpretation:	$(4 \times 10^3) + (0 \times 10^2) + (9 \times 10^1) + (6 \times 10^0)$			

Notice how the digit zero holds a place in the numeral without adding value to the number.

Although a distinction has been made here between a numeral and a number, the distinction rarely is made in practice. Most often we use the word *number* whether we mean the *quantity* or the representation of the quantity by a *numeral*. This practice will be followed in the remainder of this appendix. The meaning of the term should be clear from the context in which it is used.

THE BINARY NUMBER SYSTEM

Computers do not use the decimal number system to express quantities. Because a computer uses two-state electronic circuits, it requires a number system that has only two digits. Such a system is the binary number system.

The base of the binary number system is two. The digits of the binary number system are 1 and 0. These are the binary digits or bits that correspond to the "on" and "off" states of a computer's circuits. The position values are successive powers of the base:

$$\ldots\, 2^5\ 2^4\ 2^3\ 2^2\ 2^1\ 2^0$$

A number in any number system can be composed only of digits acceptable to the system. Thus, a binary number can be composed only of the digits 1 and 0. For example, 10011 is a binary number (read "one-zero-zero-one-one"). To interpret a binary number, each digit is multiplied by its corresponding position value and the results are totaled. Thus, the binary number 10011 can be interpreted as follows:

Digits:	1	0	0	1	1
Position values:	2^4	2^3	2^2	2^1	2^0
Interpretation:	$(1 \times 2^4) + (0 \times 2^3) + (0 \times 2^2) + (1 \times 2^1) + (1 \times 2^0)$				

Binary to Decimal Conversion

In interpreting a binary number, decimal numbers have been used for the position values (e.g., 2^3). If we carry out the arithmetic, we convert the binary number to its equivalent in the decimal number system:

$$
\begin{aligned}
10011 &= (1 \times 2^4) + (0 \times 2^3) + (0 \times 2^2) + (1 \times 2^1) + (1 \times 2^0) \\
&= (1 \times 16) + (0 \times 8) + (0 \times 4) + (1 \times 2) + (1 \times 1) \\
&= \quad 16 \quad + \quad 0 \quad + \quad 0 \quad + \quad 2 \quad + \quad 1 \\
&= \quad 19
\end{aligned}
$$

Thus, 10011 in the binary system is equivalent to 19 in the decimal number system.

Sometimes we use a special notation to distinguish numbers in different number systems. In this notation the base of the number system is written as a subscript immediately following the number. Thus, 10011_2 is a base 2 or binary number, and 19_{10} is a base 10 or decimal number. This notation, though not required, is important when there may be confusion about the base of the number. For example, consider the number 10. This may represent a decimal number (*ten*) or a binary number (*one-zero*). However, 10_{10} is not equivalent to 10_2 ($10_2 = (1 \times 2^1) + (0 \times 2^0) = 2_{10}$). Therefore, to avoid confusion we use this special notation to indicate what type of number is being expressed.

As a final example, consider the binary number 110101. This number can be interpreted as follows:

Digits:	1	1	0	1	0	1
Position values:	2^5	2^4	2^3	2^2	2^1	2^0
Interpretation:	$(1 \times 2^5) +$	$(1 \times 2^4) +$	$(0 \times 2^3) +$	$(1 \times 2^2) +$	$(0 \times 2^1) +$	(1×2^0)

Carrying out the arithmetic, we can convert the binary number to its decimal equivalent:

$$
\begin{aligned}
110101 &= (1 \times 2^5) + (1 \times 2^4) + (0 \times 2^3) + (1 \times 2^2) + (0 \times 2^1) + (1 \times 2^0) \\
&= (1 \times 32) + (1 \times 16) + (0 \times 8) + (1 \times 4) + (0 \times 2) + (1 \times 1) \\
&= \quad 32 \quad + \quad 16 \quad + \quad 0 \quad + \quad 4 \quad + \quad 0 \quad + \quad 1 \\
&= \quad 53
\end{aligned}
$$

Thus, 110101_2 is equivalent to 53_{10}.

Decimal to Binary Conversion

To convert a decimal number to its binary equivalent, first find the largest power of two that is less than or equal to the decimal number. Then, the maximum significant position value in the binary equivalent of the decimal number is that power of two. Working backward toward 2^0, find the next significant position value. This value is the next power of two that is less than or equal to the original decimal number minus the position value that has already been used. This process continues until you reach the 2^0 position, or until the result from subtracting significant position values from the original number is zero.

For example, consider the decimal number 21. The largest power of two that is less than or equal to 21 is 2^4 or 16. Thus, there is 1×2^4 in 21. Subtracting 2^4 from 21 leaves 5. The largest power of two that is less than or equal to 5 is 2^2 or 4; there is 1×2^2 in 5. Subtracting 2^2 from 5 leaves 1. The largest power of two that is less than or equal to 1 is 2^0 or 1; there is 1×2^0 in 1. Subtracting 1 from 1 leaves 0, and there are no more significant position values. Thus, in 21 there is 1×2^4, 1×2^2, and 1×2^0. The intermediate position values (2^3 and 2^1) are held by the digit 0. Therefore, the binary equivalent of 21_{10} is 10101_2. These calculations can be summarized as follows:

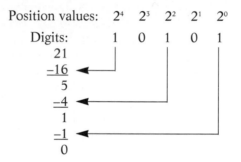

As another example, consider the decimal number 54. The largest power of two that is less than or equal to 54 is 2^5 or 32. Working backward from 2^5 to 2^0, you get the following:

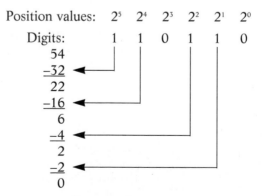

Thus, 54_{10} is equivalent to 110110_2.

HEXADECIMAL NOTATION

One problem that people face when using binary numbers is that these numbers are difficult to read, write, and remember. For example, the binary number

$$1011010100101110$$

is 16 bits in length and is equivalent to the five-digit decimal number 46,382. To try to remember this binary number is difficult. Even copying the number can lead to errors because of the repetitive use of 1s and 0s. You could convert all binary numbers to their decimal equivalents and use these decimal numbers. But, as you have seen, the conversion process takes time and also can lead to errors.

When people work with binary numbers, the usual procedure is to use a shorthand notation for the numbers. The notation is such that it is easy to convert the binary number to its equivalent in the shorthand notation and easy to convert back.

Several shorthand notations are used for binary numbers. One of the most common is **hexadecimal notation**. This notation is based on the *hexadecimal number system*, which has a base of 16 (*hexadecimal* means 16). You do not need to understand the number system, however, to see how it is used as a notation for binary numbers.

There are 16 digits in hexadecimal notation. These digits correspond to the decimal numbers 0 through 15. The first ten hexadecimal digits are the same as the decimal digits 0, 1, . . .9. For the remaining six hexadecimal digits we use the first six letters of the alphabet: A, B, C, D, E, and F. In other words, the hexadecimal digit A corresponds to the decimal number 10, B is equivalent to 11, and so forth up to the hexadecimal digit F, which is equal to the decimal number 15. Notice that we could use any other six symbols for these six hexadecimal digits. We could not use 10, 11, . . .15, however, because these are not individual symbols but rather combinations of other digits. By convention, however, people use the first six letters of the alphabet for the last six hexadecimal digits.

Hexadecimal digits are used as a shorthand notation for binary numbers because any four-bit binary number can be represented by a hexadecimal digit. For example, the four-bit binary number 1010 is equivalent to the decimal number 10, which, as you learned, is equal to the hexadecimal digit A. The largest four-bit binary number is 1111, which is 15 in the decimal number system and F in hexadecimal notation. Some four-bit binary numbers require 0s in the lead positions. For example, 0011 is equal to 3 in the decimal number system and is 3 in hexadecimal notation. The binary number 0000 is 0 in both the decimal and hexadecimal systems. Figure C–1 shows a complete list of hexadecimal digits and their equivalents in the binary and decimal number systems.

Figure C–1   Decimal-Binary-Hexadecimal Equivalence

Decimal	Binary	Hexadecimal
0	0000	0
1	0001	1
2	0010	2
3	0011	3
4	0100	4
5	0101	5
6	0110	6
7	0111	7
8	1000	8
9	1001	9
10	1010	A
11	1011	B
12	1100	C
13	1101	D
14	1110	E
15	1111	F

To use hexadecimal numbers as a shorthand notation for long binary numbers, arrange the bits of the binary number into groups of four. Then, write the equivalent hexadecimal digit for each group. For example, you would convert the binary number given at the beginning of this section to hexadecimal notation as follows:

$$\underbrace{1011}_{B}\underbrace{0101}_{5}\underbrace{0010}_{2}\underbrace{1110}_{E}$$

Thus, B52E is the hexadecimal notation for the 16-bit binary number.

To convert a hexadecimal number to its equivalent binary number you reverse the process. For each hexadecimal digit, write the equivalent four-bit binary number. For example, consider the hexadecimal number 40AF7. This number has five digits, and so the equivalent binary number has five times four or 20 digits. The conversion is as follows:

$$\overbrace{4}\ \overbrace{0}\ \overbrace{A}\ \overbrace{F}\ \overbrace{7}$$
$$01000000101011110111$$

Hexadecimal notation is used by many computers when printing binary numbers. For example, when a computer prints the contents of primary storage (called a *dump*) it usually prints it in hexadecimal notation. In addition, computer reference manuals often use this notation to explain how data is stored in the computer.

Summary

- A **number system** is a way of expressing quantities. It is composed of a set of digits. The **base** of the system is the number of digits that are acceptable in the system. The **position values** are successive powers of the base. A **numeral** is a series of digits that represents a number or quantity. A numeral can be interpreted as the sum of the products of the numeral's digits and their position values.

- The digits in the **decimal number system** are 0, 1, 2, 3, 4, 5, 6, 7, 8, and 9. The base is 10. The position values are:

$$\ldots 10^5 \; 10^4 \; 10^3 \; 10^2 \; 10^1 \; 10^0$$

- The digits in the **binary number system** are 1 and 0. The base is 2. The position values are:

$$\ldots 2^5 \; 2^4 \; 2^3 \; 2^2 \; 2^1 \; 2^0$$

- To convert a binary number to an equivalent decimal number you multiply each binary digit by its position value and add the products. To convert a decimal number to its equivalent binary number you find the largest position value (power of two) that is less than or equal to the decimal number. You subtract this position value from the decimal number and then find the next position value that is less than or equal to the difference. You repeat this step until the difference is zero. All position values found have a 1 binary digit; all others have a 0 binary digit.

- **Hexadecimal notation** is a shorthand notation for long binary numbers. The hexadecimal digits are the digits 0 through 9 and the letters A through F. Each combination of four binary bits has an equivalent hexadecimal digit. To convert a binary number to a hexadecimal number you write the equivalent hexadecimal digit for each group of four bits. To convert a hexadecimal number to its binary number, you write the equivalent four bits for each hexadecimal digit.

Terms to Remember

Base p. 522
Binary Number System p. 521
Decimal Number System p. 521
Hexadecimal Notation p. 526

Number System p. 521
Numeral p. 522
Position Value p. 522

Problems

1. Convert each of the following binary numbers to its equivalent decimal number.

   a. 110

   b. 1001

   c. 1010

   d. 10111

   e. 101001

2. Convert each of the following decimal numbers to its equivalent binary number.

   a. 5

   b. 8

   c. 14

   d. 27

   e. 58

3. Convert each of the following binary numbers to its equivalent hexadecimal number.

   a. 1101

   b. 00110100

   c. 10110001

   d. 00101111101110000

   e. 1101101011101001

4. Convert each of the following hexadecimal numbers to its equivalent binary number.

   a. 8

   b. D1

   c. 55

   d. C3AF

   e. 2BE6

APPENDIX D
STRUCTURED PROGRAMMING IN BASIC

APPENDIX TOPICS

Section 5. Subroutines and Modular Programming
- Subroutines
- Modular Programming
- Functions
- The READ and DATA Statements
- The PRINT USING Statement
- A Sample Program
- Terms to Remember
- Review Questions
- Programming Problems

Section 6. Arrays
- Arrays and Array Elements
- Input and Output of Array Data
- Array Searching
- A Sample Program
- Two-Dimensional Arrays
- Terms to Remember
- Review Questions
- Programming Problems

Summary of BASIC Statements

BASIC Glossary

Answers to Selected BASIC Review Questions

BASIC Index

INTRODUCTION

This appendix is a carefully paced introduction to structured computer programming in the BASIC language. The appendix systematically introduces the features of BASIC as they are needed for various programming situations. Structured programming concepts are incorporated into the discussion of language features. Program examples are drawn from easily recognized problems. As a result, you not only learn the BASIC language, but you also gain an understanding of the need for and use of each language element while you learn how to develop well-structured programs in BASIC to solve a variety of problems.

There are many different versions of BASIC. This appendix covers the features of BASIC found in most versions. Certain details apply specifically to Microsoft BASIC (also called BASICA and GWBASIC). This version of BASIC is commonly used on IBM personal computers and clones, and a similar version is available for Apple Macintoshes. When other versions of BASIC have certain features that are different from those in Microsoft BASIC, this is noted in the text.

SECTION 1
INTRODUCTION TO
PROGRAMMING IN BASIC

This section covers the background necessary to begin learning to program in BASIC. It introduces the BASIC language and describes how programming in BASIC is done on a computer. After completing this section you should have the background needed to begin learning to program in BASIC. Later sections go into detail about programming in the BASIC language.

FUNDAMENTALS OF BASIC

Figure D1–1 shows a sample BASIC program that finds the total and average of three test scores. Later, you will see how this program works, but for now you need to understand only the language concepts it illustrates.

BASIC Statements

Each instruction in a BASIC program is called a **statement**. A BASIC statement tells the computer something about the processing that is to be done in the program. In the sample program in Figure D1–1, each

Figure D1–1   A Sample Program

```
10 REM - TEST SCORE TOTAL AND AVERAGE PROGRAM
20 PRINT "ENTER THREE TEST SCORES"
30 INPUT SCORE1, SCORE2, SCORE3
40 LET TOTAL = SCORE1 + SCORE2 + SCORE3
50 LET AVG = TOTAL / 3
60 PRINT "TOTAL SCORE", TOTAL
70 PRINT "AVERAGE SCORE", AVG
80 END
```

line is a statement. A **BASIC program** is a sequence of BASIC statements that describes some computing process. To prepare a BASIC program, you must know how to form statements in the BASIC language and what each statement means.

In BASIC every statement must begin with a **line number**. The range of acceptable line numbers varies in different versions of BASIC. In Microsoft BASIC, the line numbers can range from 0 to 65529. No two statements can have the same number, and the numbers must be in *increasing* numerical order.

Besides these rules, there are no restrictions on line numbers. Thus, you can number the statements in a program 1, 2, 3, 4. . .; or 10, 20, 30, 40. . . (as in the sample program in Figure D1–1); or 18, 37, 108, 256. . . . The usual practice, however, is to number the statements by tens, as in the sample program, so that it is easy to add statements to the program. For example, if you wish to add a new statement between lines 30 and 40, you can number it 35 and not change any other numbers. Another good practice is to make the line numbers in a program the same length— either two digits (10, 20, 30. . .), three digits (100, 200, 300. . .), or four digits (1000, 2000, 3000. . .). This makes the program easier to read.

Following the line number in a BASIC statement is a special word called a **keyword**. Any number of spaces can be included between the line number and the keyword, and extra spaces are often used to make the program more readable. The keyword identifies the statement and indicates what type of processing is to take place. In the sample program in Figure D1–1, the keywords are REM, INPUT, LET, PRINT, and END. Each has a special meaning in BASIC, which you will learn later.

Constants, Variables, and Expressions

In addition to a keyword, a BASIC statement often contains constants, variables, and expressions. For now, you need only an overview of each of these. Section 2 will explain them in detail.

A **constant** is a fixed data value in a program. For example, 3, 6.5, –37, .0012, and –78.36 are constants that can appear in a program. In the sample program in Figure D1–1, the number 3 in the statement numbered 50 is a constant.

A **variable** is a name that is used to refer to data that can change in a program. In the sample program in Figure D1–1, the variables are SCORE1, SCORE2, SCORE3, TOTAL, and AVG. To understand variables, think of the primary storage of the computer as being composed of boxes or *storage locations*. Each storage location is identified by a name, which is a variable, and can store a single value. Figure D1–2 shows the variables from the sample programs together with their corresponding storage locations and sample values that could be in the storage locations. By using the name (i.e., the variable) for a storage location, you tell the computer to use the value in the location identified by the name. Thus, if you tell the computer to add SCORE1, SCORE2, and SCORE3, you mean add the values found in the storage locations identified by SCORE1, SCORE2, and SCORE3. You can change the value in a location by using the name (variable) for the location in such a way that the value is replaced.

A combination of constants, variables, and other symbols forms an **expression**. An expression is an instruction to the computer to perform some operation with data. Usually, these are arithmetic operations such as addition, subtraction, multiplication, and division. The sample program in Figure D1–1 has two expressions: SCORE1 + SCORE2 + SCORE3 and TOTAL / 3. The first expression tells the computer to add the values of the variables SCORE1, SCORE2, and SCORE3. The second expression tells the computer to divide the value of the variable TOTAL by the constant 3.

A SAMPLE PROGRAM

You can now begin to understand what the sample program in Figure D1–1 does. Its purpose is to find the total and average of three test scores. The input data is the three test scores. The program gets the scores from the keyboard, adds the scores to find the total, calculates the average by dividing the total by three, and sends the results of the calculations to the screen. The results are the output data.

The actual execution of the program on a computer is shown in Figure D1–3. The first line is an instruction to the user. The second line, with the question mark, contains the input data, which is shown in color in this figure. The last two lines contain the output. In figures and other examples

Figure D1–2   Storage Locations and Variables in BASIC for the Sample Program

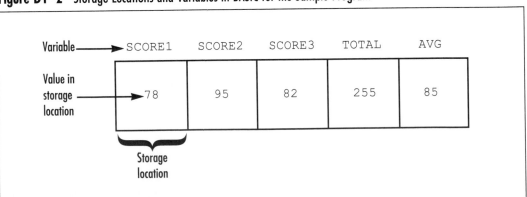

Figure D1–3 The Result of Executing the Sample Program

```
             ENTER THREE TEST SCORES
             ? 78,95,82
             TOTAL SCORE     255
             AVERAGE SCORE   85
```

throughout this appendix, the input data that the user enters is shown in color; the output displayed by the computer is in black.

The first statement in the sample program in Figure D1–1 is a REM statement. This statement is used to put an explanatory comment or remark into a program. As you will see later, REM statements are used often in programs to help explain what a program does and how it works.

The second statement in the program is a PRINT statement. This statement causes the computer to send output data to the screen. You say the program "displays" or "prints" the data on the screen. In this case, the computer displays the words in quotation marks. The first line in Figure D1–3 shows how the words are displayed. These words are instructions to the user of the program.

The next statement is an INPUT statement. This statement instructs the computer to get input data from the keyboard and to store the data in the computer's primary storage. You say that the program "accepts" the data from the keyboard. The input data is typed in and stored in the storage locations that are associated with the variables in the INPUT statement. These are the variables SCORE1, SCORE2, and SCORE3 in the sample program.

The actual effect during execution of the INPUT statement is illustrated in the second line of Figure D1–3. When the INPUT statement is encountered, a question mark is displayed by the computer on the screen. After the question mark appears, the user must type in the input data—in this case, three test scores—separated by commas. For example, in Figure D1–3 the input data that is typed in is the numbers 78, 95, and 82. The computer then stores these numbers in the storage locations in the computer's primary storage identified by the variables SCORE1, SCORE2, and SCORE3. Thus, after execution of the INPUT statement with the input data shown in Figure D1–3, the value of the variable SCORE1 is 78, SCORE2 is 95, and SCORE3 is 82.

Following the INPUT statement in the sample program in Figure D1–1 are two statements that perform calculations. These are called LET statements. The first LET statement instructs the computer to add the values of SCORE1, SCORE2, and SCORE3. The result of the calculation (i.e., the total) is stored in the storage location identified by the variable TOTAL. The next statement then tells the computer to divide the total just calculated by 3 to obtain the average, which becomes the value of the variable AVG.

Figure D1–4 summarizes the execution sequence by showing the values of the variables at different points in the program. Before the program is executed, the values of the variables (SCORE1, SCORE2, SCORE3, TOTAL, and AVG) are all equal to zero (Figure D1–4a). After

Figure D1–4 Values of Variables During the Execution of the Sample Program

(a) Before executing the program

SCORE1	SCORE2	SCORE3	TOTAL	AVG
0	0	0	0	0

(b) After executing statement 30

SCORE1	SCORE2	SCORE3	TOTAL	AVG
78	95	82	0	0

(c) After executing statement 40

SCORE1	SCORE2	SCORE3	TOTAL	AVG
78	95	82	255	0

(d) After executing statement 50

SCORE1	SCORE2	SCORE3	TOTAL	AVG
78	95	82	255	85

statement 30 (the INPUT statement) is executed with the data in Figure D1–3, the values of the variables SCORE1, SCORE2, and SCORE3 are equal to 78, 95, and 82, respectively (i.e., the input data), but the values of TOTAL and AVG are still zero (Figure D1–4b). After the first LET statement (statement 40) is executed, the value of TOTAL is the total of the values of SCORE1, SCORE2, and SCORE3 (Figure D1–4c). With the execution of the second LET statement (statement 50), the average is computed and stored in the storage location identified by the variable AVG (Figure D1–4d).

Statements 60 and 70 in the sample program in Figure D1–1 are PRINT statements. These statements cause the computer to display the words in quotation marks on the screen, followed by the values of the variables given in the statements. Thus, the current values of TOTAL and AVG are displayed on the screen. These values are the output data that result from the calculations in the LET statement. The third and fourth lines in Figure D1–3 shows how the output data is displayed.

There is one final statement in the sample program—the END statement—which contains only the keyword END. Every BASIC program must have an END statement. The END statement indicates the end of the program to the computer and causes the computer to stop execution of a program.

These statements make up a complete BASIC program. The statements are executed in the order in which they are written. Thus, it is important that they be written in a logical order. For example, the order of the two LET statements cannot be reversed, because the total is used in the calculation of the average and therefore must be calculated first.

Notice that most of the statements in the program are fairly easy to understand. This is especially true of the LET statements, which are written very much like a mathematical formula. Beginning with Section 2, you will learn in detail how to write different types of BASIC statements.

RUNNING A BASIC PROGRAM

The BASIC program in Figure D1–1 is complete and can be processed or *run* on a computer. To run a program, you must first enter it into the computer and then execute it. Here you will learn how this is done on microcomputers in general, and specifically using Microsoft BASIC on IBM personal computers and clones.

Booting the Computer

Before using a microcomputer, you must turn on the power to the computer and boot the computer to store part of the operating system in primary storage. (Recall from Chapter 7 that the *operating system* is the set of programs that controls the basic operation of the computer. *Booting* is the process of loading the *supervisor* program from the operating system into primary storage.) The operating system is stored on a floppy disk or on a hard disk, if the computer has one. When there is no hard disk, the floppy disk with the operating system must be inserted into the appropriate disk drive and the power turned on. With a hard disk, the power just needs to be turned on. With some computers a special combination of keys has to be pressed to boot the computer; with other computers this is not necessary. When the computer boots, it usually responds by displaying a prompt on the screen.

To boot an IBM personal computer or clone, you insert the floppy disk with the operating system into disk drive A and turn on the computer. After the computer has booted, the prompt A> will appear on the screen. If the computer does not boot, you must hold the Control and Alternate keys and press the Delete key. If the computer has a hard disk, you just turn the computer on to boot it. Then the prompt on the screen will be C>.

Starting BASIC

After booting the computer, you must indicate that the BASIC language is going to be used. How this is done depends on the computer and on which version of BASIC you want to use. To use Microsoft BASIC on IBM personal computers you type BASICA; to use this version on an IBM clone you usually type GWBASIC. After this is done, the computer will display the prompt "Ok" to indicate that it is ready to proceed.

Various instructions can now be given to the microcomputer. These instructions are called **commands** and are different from BASIC statements. As you have seen, BASIC statements begin with line numbers. BASIC commands, however, do not have line numbers. In addition, BASIC statements are executed only after all statements in the program have been entered, whereas commands are executed immediately. There are many commands, and they vary with different versions of BASIC. An explanation of the more important commands used with Microsoft BASIC follows.

Running an Existing Program

Sometimes you will want to run an existing program. Existing programs are stored in secondary storage, and each is given a unique name to identify it. A program can be executed only if it is in primary storage. Thus, you first have to bring the program into the primary storage of the computer. This is done by typing the command LOAD followed by the name of the program in quotation marks. For example, assume that a program's name is PROGX. You would use the command LOAD "PROGX" to bring this program into the computer's primary storage from secondary storage. You can now run the program by typing the command RUN. During the execution of the program you may have to supply input data. The input data must be separated by commas, and the Enter key must be pressed after the data has been typed.

Entering and Running a New Program

If you wish to enter and run your own program, you begin by typing a command that clears out any existing program in primary storage. This command is the word NEW. If you have just booted the computer, this step is not necessary because no program exists in primary storage.

You can now begin to enter a BASIC program. You type each line of the program exactly as it is written, followed by the Enter key. In most cases it doesn't matter whether upper- or lowercase is used; the computer converts lowercase letters to uppercase. Mistakes in keying are corrected by pressing the Backspace key and then rekeying. If an entire line is wrong, you can simply retype the line with its line number, and the computer will replace the old line with the new one. A line can be erased completely by just typing its line number. Although the line numbers must be in increasing sequence in the program, you can enter the lines out of order and the computer will rearrange them. For example, you can first enter line 10, then line 30, and finally line 20. The computer will arrange the lines in the proper numerical sequence.

After you have entered part or all of the program, you can list the program on the screen by using the command LIST. You can list the program on the printer by using the command LLIST. Any errors that were corrected while the program was being entered will not appear in the listing.

To run the program, you type the command RUN. This causes the computer to execute the statements in the program in sequence, beginning with the first. While the program is running, you may have to supply input data (as in the sample program in Figure D1–1). You can run the program a second time by typing RUN again. In fact, you can run a program as many times as you want. You can stop a program while it is running by holding down the Control key and pressing the Break key (called a *control break*).

Saving a Program

If you wish to save a program for future use, you type the command SAVE followed by a name for the program in quotation marks. The program name must be one to eight characters in length and can contain any alphabetic and numeric characters and many special characters. For example, you may wish to save your program with the name PROGY. This would be accomplished by typing the command SAVE "PROGY." This stores in secondary storage the program that is currently in primary storage and identifies it by the name. (If a program is not saved, it will be lost when you finish using BASIC or when you start a new program.) You can retrieve a saved program at some time in the future by using the LOAD command discussed earlier. You can replace a saved program with the program in primary storage by using the SAVE command. To display the names of all programs that you have previously saved, you can type the command FILES. If you want to erase a previously saved program from secondary storage, you type the command KILL followed by the name of the program in quotation marks. The name must be followed by .BAS. For example, to erase PROGY you use the command KILL "PROGY.BAS."

Ending BASIC

When you have finished, you must indicate that the BASIC language will no longer be used. This is accomplished by the command SYSTEM. Do not forget to save your program, if you wish, before typing this command. Next, the floppy disk containing the operating system should be removed from the disk drive, and then the power should be turned off.

Figure D1–5 Entering and Running a BASIC Program on a Microcomputer

```
A>BASICA

Ok
10 REM - TEST SCORE TOTAL AND AVERAGE PROGRAM
20 PRINT "ENTER THREE TEST SCORES"
30 INPUT SCORE1, SCORE2, SCORE3
40 LET TOTAL = SCORE1 + SCORE2 + SCORE3
50 LET AVG - TOTAL / 3
60 PRINT "TOTAL SCORE", TOTAL
70 PRINT "AVERAGE SCORE", AVG
80 END
RUN
ENTER THREE TEST SCORES
? 78,95,82
Syntax error in 50
Ok
50 LET AVG - TOTAL / 3
50 LET AVG = TOTAL / 3
LIST
10 REM - TEST SCORE TOTAL AND AVERAGE PROGRAM
20 PRINT "ENTER THREE TEST SCORES"
30 INPUT SCORE1, SCORE2, SCORE3
40 LET TOTAL = SCORE1 + SCORE2 + SCORE3
50 LET AVG = TOTAL / 3
60 PRINT "TOTAL SCORE", TOTAL
70 PRINT "AVERAGE SCORE", AVG
80 END
Ok
RUN
ENTER THREE TEST SCORES
? 78,95,82
TOTAL SCORE      255
AVERAGE SCORE   85
Ok
RUN
ENTER THREE TEST SCORES
? 67,39,84
TOTAL SCORE      190
AVERAGE SCORE   63.33333
Ok
SAVE "DEMO1"
Ok
SYSTEM

A>
```

An Example of Running a Program

Figure D1–5 shows an example of the display that results from entering and running a program on a microcomputer. In this figure, items you enter are shown in color; items displayed by the computer are in black. First you indicate that the BASIC language is going to be used by typing the command BASICA. Then you enter a new program. After the program is entered, you run it. While the program is running, an error is detected. (Error detection will be discussed in a moment.) You correct the error and list the corrected version of the program. Next, you run the program, supplying input data and getting output. Then you run the program a second time, supplying different input data and getting different output. Finally, you save the program for future use and end the use of BASIC with the SYSTEM command.

The BASIC commands described here vary from one version of BASIC to another, although their functions are the same. In addition, there are usually many other commands that have not been discussed.

Error Detection

The description of the running of a BASIC program assumes that the program contains no errors. In fact, one of the biggest problems that you face is the detection and correction of errors. More often than not, the program does not complete its run successfully. It is your responsibility to locate and correct any errors in the program.

As you know from Chapter 12, there are three types of errors that can appear in a program: syntax errors, execution errors, and logic errors. The computer can detect the first two types of errors, but you must detect any logic errors.

Syntax errors are usually errors that you have made in the *form* of the language—that is, in the *syntax* of the language. (Programming language syntax was discussed in Chapter 13.) For example, spelling a keyword incorrectly is a syntax error. When such an error is detected, a message that describes the error and the statement with the error are displayed. The message and the erroneous statement appear after the RUN command is typed (see Figure D1–5). Even though an error has been detected, it cannot be corrected by the computer. You must retype the statement to correct any syntax errors that have been detected.

If the program has no syntax errors, the computer can execute it. During execution, *execution errors* may be detected. For example, an attempt to divide a number by zero causes an execution error. Whenever an execution error is detected, the computer displays an error message and stops executing the program. You must correct the error.

The final type of error is detected only after the program has been executed. If the output from the program does not agree with what is expected, there is a *logic error* in the program. For example, if, in the sample program in Figure D1–1, the first LET statement (statement 40) had been incorrectly written as

```
40 LET TOTAL = SCORE1 - SCORE2 - SCORE3
```

then no syntax or execution error would be detected. The final output would be incorrect, however, because the total of three numbers is found by adding the numbers, not by subtracting them. This error is in the logic of the program. The computer cannot detect such an error because it does not know what the logic of the program should be.

It is your responsibility to detect logic errors in the program. You do this by making up input data to test the program and figuring out what output should be produced by the program, using this test data. Then you compare the actual output (from running the program with the test data) with the expected output. Any discrepancy indicates an error that must be corrected. This is the procedure of *program testing*. Finally, after detecting an error or *bug* in a program, you must locate and correct it. This is called *program debugging*.

Terms to Remember

BASIC Program   p. 533   Keyword   p. 533
Command   p. 538   Line Number   p. 533
Constant   p. 533   Statement   p. 532
Expression   p. 534   Variable   p. 533

Review Questions

1. Each instruction in a BASIC program is called a(n) _____.
2. Each statement in a BASIC program must begin with a(n) _____.
3. What are keywords?
4. What is the difference between a constant and a variable?
5. What is the function of BASIC commands?
6. What must you do before executing an existing BASIC program?
7. How do you correct an error in a statement in a BASIC program?
8. What must you do after entering and running a new BASIC program, before you have finished using BASIC?

Computer Exercise

The program shown in Figure D1–1 is complete and can be run on a computer. Doing so will help you to become familiar with the structure of BASIC, the BASIC commands, and the procedures for entering and executing a program.

If you are using a microcomputer, boot the computer. (If you are using a minicomputer, the procedure is different. Consult your instructor.) Then follow the procedure necessary to indicate that the BASIC language is going to be used. Next, enter the sample program exactly as it is shown in Figure D1–1. Any syntax errors that occur are probably the result of keying mistakes and must be corrected. After any errors are corrected, list the program. Then run the program with the input data shown in Figure D1–3. Check the output to be certain it is correct. Finally, run the program several more times with additional sets of input data.

SECTION 2
ESSENTIAL ELEMENTS OF BASIC

This section describes the elements of BASIC that are essential for practically all programs. These elements include the statements necessary for simple input and output, and elementary data processing. After completing this section, you should be able to write programs that involve input, output, and computations.*

NUMERIC CONSTANTS AND VARIABLES

Section 1 introduced the ideas of constants and variables in a program. This section elaborates on these ideas and gives specific rules for constants and variables in BASIC that refer to **numeric data**—that is, data that consists of numbers.

Simple Numeric Constants

A **numeric constant** is a fixed numeric data value that is used in a program. A numeric constant is formed from digits (0 through 9) and may include a decimal point and possibly a plus or minus sign. For example, the following are valid numeric constants in BASIC:

```
    482.59          0.00056
     25              +16
    -18              0.0
   +5.1083         -128.9
      0             5280
```

A numeric constant *cannot* contain a comma or a space. Thus, the number 5,280 is not a valid constant in BASIC.

E-Notation Constants

Sometimes it is necessary to write very large or very small numbers. For example, you may wish to use the following numeric constants in a program:

```
    -128460000000000
  0.000000000008203
```

Although you can use constants such as these, they are tedious to write. Instead, you can use a shorthand notation called *E-notation*.

---

* After completing this section, you can read any of the topics in Section 5 before completing Sections 3 and 4.

E-notation is similar to scientific notation. To write a number in scientific notation, you shift the decimal point until it is just after the first nonzero digit. Then you multiply the number obtained by the power of ten necessary to shift the decimal point back to its correct place. For example, the two numbers just given can be written in scientific notation as follows:

$$-1.2846 \times 10^{14}$$

$$8.203 \times 10^{-12}$$

In BASIC, you write a numeric constant in E-notation by substituting the letter E for the symbols "× 10" in the scientific notation. Then the exponent is written immediately after the E. Thus, the two numbers given earlier are written as follows in E-notation:

```
-1.2846E14
 8.203E-12
```

In writing an E-notation constant, you can place the decimal point anywhere, as long as you adjust the exponent appropriately. For example, the following are all equivalent to the first example given:

```
-0.12846E15
-128.46E12
-12846.0E10
-12846E10
```

In the last of these, the decimal point is omitted, in which case it is assumed to be to the right of the last digit.

Numeric Variables

A **numeric variable** is a name that refers to numeric data in a program. The rules for forming variables vary in different versions of BASIC. Most versions of BASIC allow variables to consist of a letter or a letter followed by other letters, digits, and certain special characters. In Microsoft BASIC variables can be up to 40 letters, digits, and periods, beginning with a letter. Thus, the following are valid variables in Microsoft BASIC:

```
B
AMOUNT
UNIT.PRICE
TOTAL.AMOUNT.DUE
X37Z
```

Some versions of BASIC have other rules for variables. Note that a variable may never contain a blank space and must always begin with a letter.

You should use variables that stand for the data that they identify so that the program is easier to read. For example, instead of using the single-letter variables T and A for the total and average, you should use the longer, more meaningful variables TOTAL and AVG. In Microsoft BASIC, periods may be used where you might want to put a blank space to make the variable easier to read. For example, the variable TOTAL.AMOUNT.DUE is easy to read and to understand.

NUMERIC DATA PROCESSING

Numeric data processing involves computations with numbers. For example, computing an employee's pay involves processing numeric data. The elements of BASIC that are essential for this type of computation are numeric expressions and the LET statement.

Numeric Operators and Simple Numeric Expressions

A **numeric expression** is an instruction to the computer to perform arithmetic. Numeric expressions are formed from numeric constants, numeric variables, and numeric operators. **Numeric operators** are symbols that indicate what form of arithmetic is to be performed. The symbols used in BASIC and their meanings are as follows:

Numeric operator	Meaning
+	add
−	subtract
*	multiply
/	divide
^	exponentiate (i.e., raise to a power)

To form a simple numeric expression using these symbols, you write an unsigned numeric constant or numeric variable on each side of the operator. For example, the following are valid numeric expressions in BASIC:

```
A + B
X - Y
2 * K
C / 5
X ^ 2
```

(Single-letter variables are used in these and other examples for simplicity. As noted earlier, however, you should use longer, more meaningful variables in programs.)

Each of these expressions tells the computer to perform the indicated operation using the values of the variables and constants. For example, A + B means add the value of A and the value of B. If A is 8.3 and B is 5.2, then the value of A + B is 13.5. With subtraction, the value on the right of the subtraction operator is subtracted from the value on the left. Thus, X − Y means subtract the value of Y from the value of X. Notice that multiplication is indicated by the asterisk symbol. Hence, 2 * K means multiply the value of K by the constant 2. With division, the value on the left of the division operator is divided by the value on the right. Thus, C / 5 means divide the value of C by 5. Exponentiation means raise the value on the left of the operator to the power of the value on the right. Hence, X ^ 2 means raise the value of X to the second power (i.e., square the value of X).

Any numeric variable and any type of numeric constant, including E-notation constants, can be used in a numeric expression. For example, the following are valid numeric expressions:

```
AMOUNT.DUE - PAYMENT
VALUE / 3.7E15
3E8 * X37Z
```

The plus and minus signs may be used alone in front of a single numeric variable or constant to form a numeric expression. In fact, a numeric variable or constant by itself is considered to be a numeric expression. Hence, each of the following is a numeric expression:

```
  3
  J
+ 7.5
+ P
- .0063
- A
```

Evaluation of Complex Numeric Expressions

To form more complex numeric expressions, several numeric operators are used. For example, the following are valid numeric expressions:

```
E / F + 2.5
8 - I * J
A * X ^ 2 + B * X - C
3.14159 * R ^ 2
-B + B / 2 / A
```

With complex numeric expressions, the order in which the operations are performed is very important. The order is as follows:

1. All exponentiation is performed.
2. All multiplication and division is performed left-to-right.
3. All addition and subtraction is performed left-to-right.

For example, consider the following expression:

```
8.7 - A * 2.4 / B + C ^ 2 + D
```

Figure D2–1 shows how this expression is evaluated if the value of A is 6.0, B is 4.0, C is 2.0, and D is 1.0. In algebraic notation, the expression is as follows:

$$8.7 - \frac{A \times 2.4}{B} + C^2 + D$$

To change the order of evaluation, numeric expressions can be enclosed in parentheses and combined with other expressions. Then, expressions in parentheses are evaluated before operations outside the parentheses are performed. For example, consider the following modification of the previous expression:

```
8.7 - A * 2.4 / (B + C ^ 2) + D
```

The expression B + C ^ 2 is enclosed in parentheses and is evaluated before any other operations are carried out. Figure D2–2 shows the evaluation sequence for the data given earlier. The equivalent expression in algebraic notation is as follows:

$$8.7 - \frac{A \times 2.4}{B + C^2} + D$$

Numeric expressions in parentheses may be embedded in other parenthetic expressions. Then, the computer evaluates the expression in the innermost parentheses before continuing with the expression in the next level of parentheses. For example, consider the following:

```
8.7 - A * (2.4 / (B + C ^ 2) + D)
```

Figure D2–1   Evaluation of a Numeric Expression

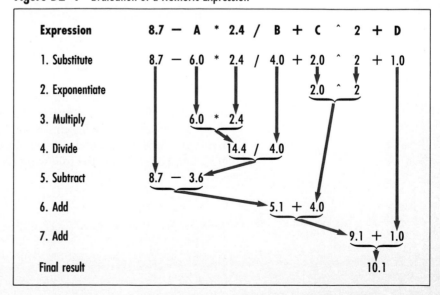

Figure D2–2 Evaluation of a Numeric Expression Containing Parentheses

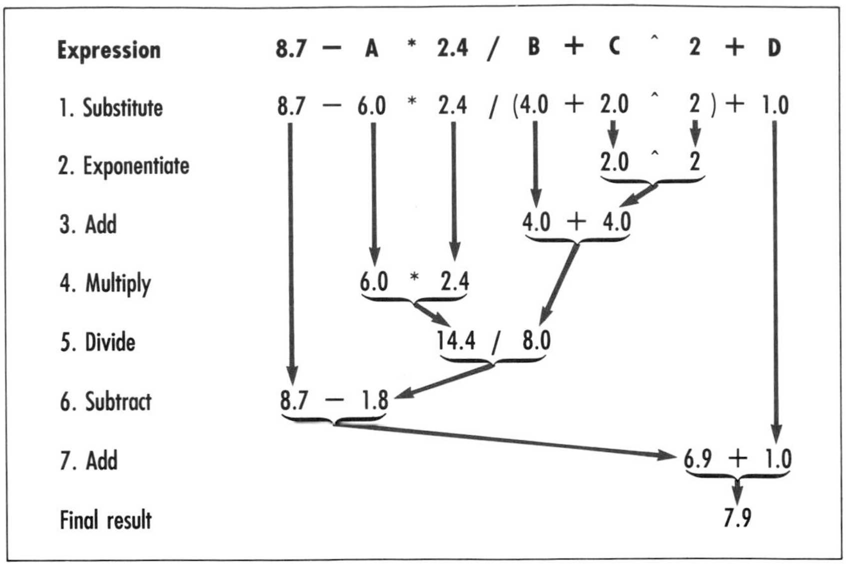

In algebraic notation, this expression is as follows:

$$8.7 - A \times \left[\frac{2.4}{B + C^2} + D \right]$$

The LET statement

A numeric expression by itself is not a BASIC statement, but it is part of several statements. The most common statement in which a numeric expression appears is the LET statement. This statement causes the computer to evaluate a numeric expression and then to assign the result to a numeric variable.

The syntax of the LET statement is as follows:

```
ln LET numeric variable = numeric expression
```

This form shows what must appear in the different parts of the statement. The abbreviation *ln* stands for *line number*, which must be the first thing in the statement. Following this is the keyword LET. Then there must be a *numeric variable*, followed by an equal sign, and finally a *numeric expression*. For example, the following are valid LET statements:

```
40 LET TOTAL = SCORE1 + SCORE2 + SCORE3
50 LET AVG = TOTAL / 3
90 LET Y = A * X ^ 2 + B * X + C
150 LET X = Z - 3.5E15 / Y
160 LET TOTAL.AMOUNT.DUE = AMOUNT.DUE - PAYMENT
```

To execute a LET statement, the computer uses the current values of the variables to evaluate the numeric expression. The result is then stored at the storage location identified by the variable on the left of the equals sign. For example, in the statement

```
40 LET TOTAL = SCORE1 + SCORE2 + SCORE3
```

if the value of SCORE1 is 78, SCORE2 is 95, and SCORE3 is 82, then after the execution of this statement, the value of TOTAL is 255. This value replaces the previous value of TOTAL. The values of SCORE1, SCORE2, and SCORE3 are unchanged by the execution of this statement.

The equals sign in a LET statement does not mean equality; it means *assignment.* That is, the equals sign tells the computer that the value of the expression on the right is to be *assigned* to the left-hand variable (i.e., stored in the storage location identified by the variable). Consequently, some algebraically invalid equations become valid statements in BASIC. For example, the following statement is valid and often useful:

```
70 LET K = K + 1
```

The meaning of this statement is that 1 is added to the current value of K and the result is returned to the storage location reserved for K. Thus, the value of K is increased by 1.

As you know, a numeric constant or variable, with or without a sign, is considered to be a numeric expression. Hence, you can use the LET statement to assign a constant or the value of a variable to a variable. For example, the statement

```
120 LET M = 3
```

assigns the value 3 to the variable M, and the statement

```
130 LET N = -M
```

assigns the negative of the value of M to N.

In many versions of BASIC, including Microsoft BASIC, the keyword LET is optional in the LET statement. For example, in these versions, the following statements are equivalent:

```
40 LET TOTAL = SCORE1 + SCORE2 + SCORE3
40 TOTAL = SCORE1 + SCORE2 + SCORE3
```

WRITING COMPLETE PROGRAMS

You can now begin to write complete programs in BASIC. Using sequences of LET statements, you can develop programs that perform numeric computations.

As an example, suppose you want to compute the amount of interest that a bank deposit will earn in a year. Assume that, at the beginning of the year, you put $500 into a bank account at an interest rate of 6%. How much interest do you earn in a year, and what is the total amount you have in the bank at the end of the year?

The following statements show part of a program to solve this problem:

```
10 LET BEGINBAL = 500
20 LET RATE = .06
30 LET INTEREST = BEGINBAL * RATE
40 LET ENDBAL = BEGINBAL + INTEREST
```

In this example, BEGINBAL is a variable that stands for the beginning bank balance ($500), and RATE is a variable for the interest rate expressed in decimal form (.06). These variables are assigned values in statements 10 and 20, respectively. Statement 30 then computes the interest earned, INTEREST, by multiplying BEGINBAL by RATE. Finally, statement 40 adds the interest to the initial bank balance to obtain the balance at the end of the year, ENDBAL.

Notice the sequential order of the execution of the statements in this example. The statements are always executed in the order in which they are written, one statement after another. This order must be carefully planned when the program is designed so that it correctly solves the problem.

The END Statement

This example is not a complete program because it does not have an END statement. The last statement executed in a BASIC program must be an END statement with the following syntax:

> *ln* END

When the END statement is reached, execution of the program stops. Adding the statement

```
50 END
```

to the previous LET statements would make a complete interest-calculation program.

The PRINT Statement

The interest-calculation program developed so far is not a very useful program because there is no way to determine the answer to the problem. What are the interest and the end-of-year balance? To obtain this information the program needs to display the values of INTEREST and ENDBAL. This is accomplished with the PRINT statement.

The syntax of the PRINT statement is as follows:

> *ln* PRINT *output list*

Several different types of items can appear in the *output list* in the PRINT statement. For the time being, you will just use numeric variables separated by commas. For example, the following are valid PRINT statements:

```
75 PRINT A
85 PRINT P, Q, R
95 PRINT B, X, Z, D, C
```

   The effect of the PRINT statement is to cause the computer to display on the screen the values of all variables listed in the statement. In the examples just given, statement 75 causes the value of A to be displayed; statement 85 causes the values of P, Q, and R to be displayed; statement 95 displays the values of five variables. Those values currently assigned to the variables in the computer's primary storage are displayed.
   Each PRINT statement causes a line to be displayed. A line on a screen has a fixed number of *print positions,* usually 80, for displaying output. The print positions are divided into areas called **print zones.** Each print zone contains a certain number of print positions that depends on the version of BASIC. In Microsoft BASIC there are five print zones in a line, each 14 print positions wide, as shown in Figure D2–3.
   When a PRINT statement executes, the values of the variables are displayed in successive zones. For example, assume that the value of X is 10, Y is –75.5, and Z is .003, and that the following PRINT statement is executed:

```
105 PRINT X, Y, Z
```

Then the output appears as follows:

(Print Zone 1)	(Print Zone 2)	(Print Zone 3)	(Print Zone 4)	(Print Zone 5)
10	-75.5	.003		

Because there are three variables in the PRINT statement, the values are displayed in the first three print zones. The remaining print zones are left blank. (Of course, just the numbers appear in the output; the vertical lines and the words identifying the print zones are not displayed.)
   Each PRINT statement starts a new line. If there are more variables in the PRINT statement than there are print zones in a line, a new line is started after the last print zone is filled. The form of the output depends on the number being displayed. If the number is an integer (i.e., a whole number), such as 10 or –385, the number is displayed without a decimal point. A negative sign is displayed before a negative number; a blank space precedes a positive number. Most numbers with fractional parts are displayed with a decimal point as you would normally write them. For example, the numbers 289.372 and .000461 would be displayed in these forms. If the number is very large or very small, however, it is displayed in E-notation.

Figure D2–3   Print Zones on a Screen

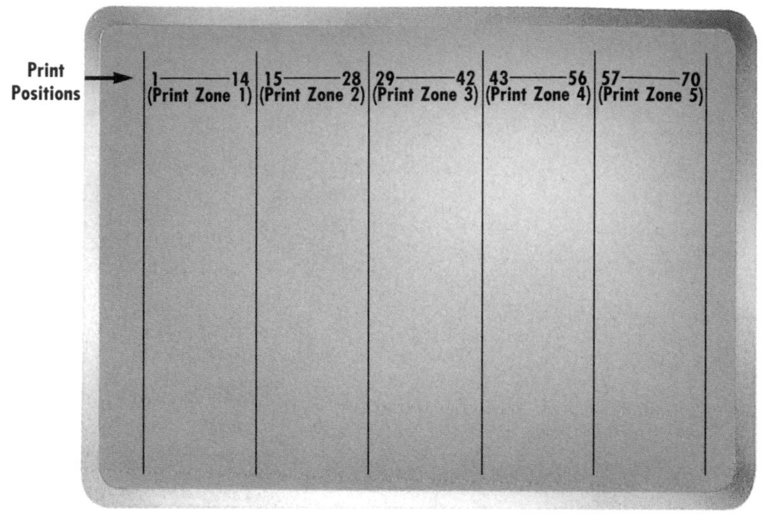

You can now write a more complete version of the interest-calculation program. Assume that you want the program to display the beginning bank balance, the year's interest, and the end-of-year balance. The program in Figure D2–4a accomplishes this. The output from running this program is shown in Figure D2–4b.

In addition to numeric variables, the output list of a PRINT statement can also contain numeric constants and expressions. For example, the following statement is valid:

```
115 PRINT A, 1, A + 1
```

The effect of this statement is to print the value of the variable A, the constant 1, and the value of the expression A + 1. Thus, if A is 5, this statement displays the output:

```
5               1               6
```

The PRINT statement is used to display output on a screen. With some versions of BASIC, this statement is used also to print output on

Figure D2–4   The Interest-Calculation Program with a PRINT Statement

(a) The Program

(b) Output

```
10 LET BEGINBAL = 500
20 LET RATE = .06
30 LET INTEREST = BEGINBAL * RATE
40 LET ENDBAL = BEGINBAL + INTEREST        500        30        530
50 PRINT BEGINBAL, INTEREST, ENDBAL
60 END
```

paper with a printer. In Microsoft BASIC, however, the LPRINT statement is used for printing on the printer. The syntax of the LPRINT statement is the same as that of the PRINT statement except that the keyword LPRINT is used instead of PRINT. For example, the program in Figure D2–4 can be modified to print the output on the printer by replacing statement 50 with the following:

```
50 LPRINT BEGINBAL, INTEREST, ENDBAL
```

The output is the same except that it is printed with the printer and is not displayed on the screen.

The INPUT Statement

The program in Figure D2–4 is not very useful. The difficulty is that it solves the interest problem for only one bank balance ($500) and one interest rate (6%). If you wish to change either of these, you must change the program. A better approach is to design the program so that the values of BEGINBAL and RATE can be supplied when the program is run without modifying the actual program. This is accomplished with the INPUT statement.

The purpose of the INPUT statement is to accept input data from the keyboard. The syntax of this statement is as follows:

ln INPUT *list of variables*

The variables in the list must be separated by commas. The following are valid INPUT statements:

```
15 INPUT A
25 INPUT P, Q, R
35 INPUT B, X, Z, D, C
```

When an INPUT statement is encountered during the execution of a program, the computer displays a question mark on the screen and waits for input data to be typed. The question mark is a prompt that indicates that input data must be entered. The user must type one number after the question mark for each variable in the INPUT statement. The numbers must be separated by commas. After the input data is typed, the Enter key must be pressed.

For example, assume that a user is running a program that contains the following INPUT statement:

```
45 INPUT X, Y, Z
```

When the statement executes, a question mark prompt is displayed and the user must type three numbers, separated by commas, because there are three variables in the statement. Thus, the user could enter the data after the prompt as follows:

```
? 10,-75.5,.003
```

After the Enter key is pressed, the computer accepts these numbers and assigns them in order to the variables in the INPUT statement. Thus, 10 would be assigned to X, –75.5 would be assigned to Y, and .003 would be assigned to Z.

The input data that is entered must follow the rules for constants in BASIC. The numbers can be positive or negative, they can contain decimal points or they can be whole numbers, or they can be written in E-notation. A comma cannot appear in an input value because commas are used to separate the data.

With the addition of an INPUT statement, the interest-calculation program can be designed to compute the interest for any bank balance and any interest rate. The program is shown in Figure D2–5a. Notice that the program no longer assigns values to BEGINBAL and RATE; these variables appear in the INPUT statement. Whatever values are entered when the program is run are used in the calculation. Thus, if the user types the data

```
? 500,.06
```

after the prompt, the program gives the same answer as before (i.e., the interest on $500 at 6%). However, if the user types

```
b
```

the program computes the interest on $2000 at 7.5% (Figure D2–5b).

The REM Statement

A statement that is not required but is usually used in BASIC programs is the REM, or remarks, statement. The syntax of the REM statement is as follows:

```
ln REM remark
```

Figure D2–5 The Interest-Calculation Program with an INPUT Statement

(a) The Program

(b) Input and Output

```
10 INPUT BEGINBAL, RATE
20 LET INTEREST = BEGINBAL * RATE
30 LET ENDBAL = BEGINBAL + INTEREST
40 PRINT BEGINBAL, INTEREST, ENDBAL
50 END
```

```
? 2000,.075
  2000          150            2150
```

You can include any remarks or comments that you want in a REM statement. For example, the following is a valid REM statement:

```
10 REM - INTEREST CALCULATION PROGRAM
```

REM statements can go anywhere in the program. During execution of the program, the computer ignores all REM statements. They are included in any listing of the program, however.

The purpose of the REM statement is to include explanatory comments or remarks in the program. Such remarks are often used to identify the program, to describe the variables used in the program, and to explain the processing that is done. REM statements with no comments in them are sometimes used to separate parts of a program. Figure D2–6 shows the interest-calculation program with REM statements.

In Microsoft BASIC, remarks may also be included in a program by beginning them with an apostrophe ('). A remark in this form may be on a line by itself or may come at the end of a line following a statement. The following are examples of this form of a remark:

```
10 'INTEREST CALCULATION PROGRAM
20 INPUT BEGINBAL, RATE 'ACCEPT BALANCE AND RATE
```

Pseudocode of Complete Programs

Chapter 12 describes *pseudocode* as a tool for representing the logic of a computer program. Figure D2–7 shows the pseudocode of the interest-calculation program in Figure D2–6. The pseudocode uses short English phrases to describe the input, calculations, and output steps in the program. The phrases are listed in the order in which the computer performs the steps.

Figure D2–6 The Interest-Calculation Program with REM Statements

```
100 REM - INTEREST CALCULATION PROGRAM
110 REM - VARIABLES:
120 REM        BEGINBAL = BEGINNING BANK BALANCE
130 REM        RATE     = INTEREST RATE
140 REM        INTEREST = INTEREST EARNED
150 REM        ENDBAL   = ENDING BANK BALANCE
160 REM
170 INPUT BEGINBAL, RATE
180 LET INTEREST = BEGINBAL * RATE
190 LET ENDBAL = BEGINBAL + INTEREST
200 PRINT BEGINBAL, INTEREST, ENDBAL
210 END
```

Figure D2–7 Pseudocode of the Interest-Calculation Program

```
Accept beginning balance, interest rate
Compute interest, ending balance
Display beginning balance, interest, ending balance
End
```

Figure D2–8 Flowchart of the Interest-Calculation Program

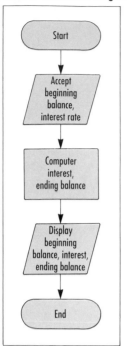

Flowcharts of Complete Programs

Chapter 12 also describes *flowcharts* as a tool for representing the logic in a computer program. Figure D2–8 shows the flowchart of the interest-calculation program. The flowchart uses the terminal point symbol (oval) for the beginning and end of the flowchart logic, the input/output symbol (parallelogram) for the steps where the input is accepted and the output is displayed, the process symbol (rectangle) for the calculation step, and flowlines (lines with arrowheads) to connect the symbols in the proper sequence. (See Figure 12–5 for a list of the symbols used in flowcharts.)

MAKING INPUT AND OUTPUT UNDERSTANDABLE

The program in Figure D2–6 uses simple input and output. A user, however, would find the execution of this program difficult to understand. This section describes several ways of making the input and output for a program more understandable.

Positioning Output

On a screen, the cursor indicates where the next output will be displayed. You can position the cursor on a line by using certain features of the PRINT statement.

The Comma.   If a comma is used in a PRINT statement to separate variables, the output is displayed in fixed print zones. The effect of the comma is to move the cursor to the next print zone. Thus the statement

```
70 PRINT X, Y
```

displays the value of X in the first print zone, then moves the cursor to the second print zone and displays the value of Y. Extra commas can be used in the PRINT statement to space over print zones. Each extra comma, in effect, skips one zone. For example, the following statement displays the value of X in the second print zone and the value of Y in the fourth print zone:

```
170 PRINT ,X,, Y
```

The first comma causes the cursor to be moved to the second print zone, thus skipping the first print zone. The extra comma between the variables causes the third print zone to be skipped.

If you put a comma at the end of a list of variables in a PRINT statement, a new line is not started when the next PRINT statement is executed. For example, consider the following statements:

```
270 PRINT X, Y,
275 PRINT Z
```

The comma at the end of line 270 means that the value of Z will be displayed in the next print zone on the same line as the values of X and Y.

The Semicolon.   When commas are used in a PRINT statement, the output is widely spaced and may be difficult to read. To display the output closer together you can use semicolons instead of commas to separate the items in the PRINT statement. For example, consider the following statement:

```
80 PRINT X; Y; Z
```

Notice that semicolons separate the variables in the PRINT statement. Each semicolon causes the cursor to be left where it is after displaying a value, rather than being advanced to the next print zone. Thus, in this statement the values of X, Y, and Z are displayed close together, with only one or two blank spaces between them, not in successive print zones. As with a comma, a semicolon at the end of a PRINT statement causes the next output to appear on the same line as the previous output.

The TAB Function.   Occasionally you want to display the output beginning at a specific print position on the screen. This can be done by using the TAB function in the PRINT statement. The TAB function consists of the word TAB followed by a numeric constant, numeric variable, or more complex numeric expression in parentheses. For example, the following statement uses the TAB function twice:

```
570 PRINT TAB(10); X; TAB(20); Y
```

The effect of the TAB function is to cause the cursor to move or tabulate to the print position given in parentheses. Then, output begins at that position. In the example, the value of X is displayed beginning at position 10, and the value of Y is displayed beginning at position 20. It is not possible to tabulate backward with the TAB function.

Notice in this example that a semicolon is used before and after the TAB function. If commas are used instead, the cursor is moved to the next print zone whenever a comma is encountered. This usually results in output completely different from what you want.

Clearing the Screen

To make the screen easier to read, it is often desirable to erase everything on the screen before displaying any output. In Microsoft BASIC this is accomplished with the clear screen statement, which has the following syntax:

```
ln CLS
```

For example, the following is a clear screen statement:

```
10 CLS
```

The effect of this statement is to erase everything on the screen and to move the cursor to the upper left-hand corner.

Describing Output

A program should display not only the results of processing but also words and phrases that describe the output. This helps the user know what the data represents.

To produce descriptions in the output, you put in quotation marks the words to be displayed in the PRINT statement, as in the following statement:

```
80 PRINT "THE ANSWER IS", X
```

Execution of this statement causes the computer to display the phrase THE ANSWER IS, followed by the value of the variable X. For example, if X is 125.25, the output appears as follows:

```
THE ANSWER IS  125.25
```

There may be as many words or phrases in a PRINT statement as are needed. For example, the following statement displays two separate phrases and the values of two variables:

```
180 PRINT "AMOUNT =", A, "COUNT =", C
```

If A is 250 and C is 9, the output is as follows:

(Print Zone 1)	(Print Zone 2)	(Print Zone 3)	(Print Zone 4)
AMOUNT =	250	COUNT =	9

Notice that the output in this example is spread out because each value begins in the next print zone. To print the output closer together you can use semicolons, as in the following statement:

```
180 PRINT "AMOUNT" ="; A; "COUNT ="; C
```

Then the output will be as follows:

```
AMOUNT = 250 COUNT = 9
```

You can also use the TAB function to position descriptive output, as in the following example:

```
180 PRINT TAB(10); "AMOUNT ="; A; TAB(30); "COUNT ="; C
```

You can use the PRINT statement to display just a word or a phrase without displaying any other data, as in the following statement:

```
280 PRINT "STATISTICAL DATA"
```

This approach is often used to display a heading to describe the output that follows.

Print zones can be used to arrange headings above columns of output. For example, if you wish to display two columns of data in the first two print zones with the titles AMOUNT and COUNT, the following statement can be used:

```
380 PRINT "AMOUNT", "COUNT"
```

You can display a line that contains nothing by using a PRINT statement with nothing following the keyword PRINT, as in the following example:

```
580 PRINT
```

This technique is often used to double-space output.

Prompting Input

As you know, the INPUT statement displays a question mark to prompt the user. Usually, however, you want to provide additional prompting in the form of a message that explains what input is required. For example, if a test score is to be entered, you may display the message ENTER TEST SCORE just before the appropriate INPUT statement is executed. The following statements accomplish this:

```
20 PRINT "ENTER TEST SCORE"
30 INPUT SCORE
```

On the screen, the sequence appears as follows:

```
ENTER TEST SCORE
? 85
```

The user sees the message and the question mark, and types the appropriate data (85 in this example).

In Microsoft BASIC, the input prompt can be included in the INPUT statement. The syntax is as follows:

```
ln INPUT "prompt", list of variables
```

For example, the following INPUT statement includes a prompt:

```
60 INPUT "ENTER TEST SCORE: ", SCORE
```

The effect of this statement is to display the phrase enclosed in the quotation marks. Then the computer waits for input to be entered after the phrase. The blank space at the end of the phrase provides a space before the input data. The sequence appears on the screen as follows:

```
ENTER TEST SCORE: 85
```

Notice that no question mark prompt is displayed in this example. A question mark can be displayed by including it within the quotation marks. Alternatively, a question mark will be displayed if a semicolon is used instead of a comma after the prompt, as in the following example:

```
60 INPUT "ENTER TEST SCORE"; SCORE
```

Figure D2–9a shows the interest-calculation program with input prompts and output descriptions. The program first clears the screen and displays a heading with the program's title. Then it requests input from the user with appropriate prompts. After doing the calculations, the program displays three lines of output with descriptive phrases. Finally, the program displays a message indicating the end of the program. Notice that blank lines are displayed to make the output easier to read. The input and output that result from running the program are shown in Figure D2–9b.

STRING DATA PROCESSING

Many programs process data that consists of letters and symbols, not just numbers. Data of this type is called **string data**, or simply a **string.** This section describes several features of BASIC that are used for processing string data.

Figure D2–9 The Interest-Calculation Program with Input Prompts and Output Descriptions

(a) The Program

(b) Input and Output

```
100 REM - INTEREST CALCULATION PROGRAM
110 REM - VARIABLES:
120 REM       BEGINBAL = BEGINNING BANK BALANCE
130 REM       RATE     = INTEREST RATE
140 REM       INTEREST = INTEREST EARNED
150 REM       ENDBAL   = ENDING BANK BALANCE
160 REM
170 CLS
180 PRINT "INTEREST CALCULATION"
190 PRINT
200 INPUT "ENTER BEGINNING BANK BALANCE: ", BEGINBAL
210 INPUT "ENTER INTEREST RATE: ", RATE
220 LET INTEREST = BEGINBAL * RATE
230 LET ENDBAL = BEGINBAL + INTEREST
240 PRINT
250 PRINT "BEGINNING BANK BALANCE:"; BEGINBAL
260 PRINT "INTEREST EARNED:"; INTEREST
270 PRINT "ENDING BANK BALANCE:"; ENDBAL
280 PRINT
290 PRINT "END OF PROGRAM"
300 END
```

```
INTEREST CALCULATION

ENTER BEGINNING BANK BALANCE: 500
ENTER INTEREST RATE: .06

BEGINNING BANK BALANCE: 500
INTEREST EARNED: 30
ENDING BANK BALANCE: 530

END OF PROGRAM
```

String Constants and Variables

A **string constant** is a group of characters enclosed in quotation marks. For example, the following are string constants:

```
"ABC"
"X37Z$"
"JOHN'S"
"New York"
"1881"
" "
```

Both upper- and lowercase letters can be included in a string constant. Digits can be used in a string constant. In fact, a group of digits alone enclosed in quotation marks is a string constant. A blank space can be part of a string constant because it is a character. In fact, one or more blanks enclosed in quotation marks without any other characters forms a string constant. The only character not allowed in a string constant is a quotation mark. The maximum length of a string constant depends on the version of BASIC. In Microsoft BASIC, the limit is 255 characters.

You have already seen one use of string constants in a program. Output descriptions can be displayed by enclosing words and symbols in quotation marks in a PRINT statement. In fact, such a description in the PRINT statement is a string constant. For example, the following statement contains a string constant:

```
80 PRINT "THE ANSWER IS"; X
```

Execution of this statement causes the string THE ANSWER IS to be displayed followed by the value of X. Notice that the quotation marks are not part of the string and are not displayed. You will see other uses of string constants in this section.

A **string variable** is a variable that is used to refer to a string. A string variable is formed from a variable followed by a dollar sign. For example, A$, N3$, and FIRST$ are string variables. Note that A$ is a variable that identifies string data, whereas A is a variable that refers to numeric data. Both can be used in the same program.

String Expressions

String constants and variables are types of **string expressions.** In general, a string expression is an instruction to the computer to perform operations with string data. An example of a string operation is *concatenation,* which involves combining two strings to form one string. In Microsoft BASIC, the plus sign (+) is used in a string expression to mean concatenation. Thus,

```
"ABC" + A$
```

is a string expression that means concatenate the string constant "ABC" and the value of the string variable A$. If A$ equals XYZ, then the result of this expression is the string ABCXYZ. Other examples of string expressions involving concatenation are:

```
A$ + B$
C$ + "XYZ" + D$
```

The LET Statement with String Data

The LET statement can be used to assign the value of a string expression to a string variable. The syntax is:

```
ln LET string variable = string expression
```

Since a string constant and a string variable are string expressions, they can be assigned to string variables with a LET statement. For example, the following LET statement assigns a string constant to a string variable:

```
70 LET A$ = "THE ANSWER IS"
```

After execution of this statement, the value of the string variable A$ will be the string THE ANSWER IS. As another example, the following statement assigns the value of the string variable A$ to B$:

```
80 LET B$ = A$
```

As a final example, the following statement uses a string expression to concatenate two strings, and assigns the result to a string variable:

```
90 LET C$ = A$ + B$
```

It is important to distinguish between numeric variables and string variables and between numeric constants and string constants when using the LET statement. For example, consider the following statements:

```
210 LET X = 15
220 LET X$ = "15"
```

The first statement assigns a numeric constant to a numeric variable; the second assigns a string constant to a string variable. Even though the characters in the constants are the same (i.e., 15), they represent different types of data. The string constant ("15") can be assigned only to a string variable, and the numeric constant (15) can be assigned only to a numeric variable. In addition, string constants and variables cannot be used in numeric expressions; only numeric constants and variables can be used. Similarly, numeric constants and variables cannot be used in a string expression.

Input and Output of String Data

As you know, the value of a string can be displayed by using a string constant in a PRINT statement. You can also use a string variable in a PRINT statement. For example, consider the following statement:

```
80 PRINT A$; X
```

The effect of execution of this statement is that the value of the string variable A$ is displayed followed by the value of the numeric variable X. If A$ is assigned the string THE ANSWER IS, then this string is displayed when this statement is executed.

A string can be accepted as input data when you use a string variable in an INPUT statement. For example, consider the following statement:

```
10 INPUT N$
```

When this statement is executed, a question mark prompt is displayed on the screen. A string must be entered following the question mark. In most cases, the string may be enclosed in quotation marks or the marks may be omitted. For example, the following input can be entered;

```
? JOHN
```

After the Enter key is pressed, the computer accepts the data and assigns it to the string variable N$.

Quotation marks are optional around the string input except when the data contains a comma or when spaces to the left or right are part of the string. For example, assume that the following statement is executed:

```
20 INPUT D$
```

The string input that is to be entered is a date that begins with two spaces and ends with three spaces. In addition, a comma separates the day and the year. The data must then be enclosed in quotation marks, as shown in the following example:

```
? "  SEPT. 1, 1993   "
```

Note that quotation marks can be used even when they are not required.

PROGRAM STYLE

The most important objective during the programming process is to produce a program that correctly solves the required problem. The process of program testing, discussed in Section 1, is designed to help locate errors in a program. More will be covered about program testing and debugging in later sections.

After correctness, the most important characteristic of a program is its understandability. This means the qualities of the program that make it understandable or readable to others. Program understandability is important because programs are often reviewed by people other than the original programmer. For example, the programming manager may review a program to check for completeness and consistency with the problem definition. Other programmers may have to read the program to correct errors that are not detected until after the program has been in use for a while. Often, modifications are necessary in the program because of changing requirements. For example, payroll programs have to be modified regularly because of changing tax structures. Sometimes a program is enhanced to do more than was originally planned. In all these situations, someone must look at the program months or even years after it was first coded. Even if the original programmer is given the task, he or she may have difficulty remembering the program's logic unless the program is easily understood.

Program style deals with those characteristics of a program that make it more understandable. Even though you know only a few features of the BASIC language, it is possible to begin incorporating good style into your programs. One good style rule is to use variables that symbolize the data to which they refer. For example, the program in Figure D2–6 used BEGINBAL for the beginning bank balance, RATE for the interest rate, INTEREST for the interest, and ENDBAL for the ending bank balance.

Another style rule is to use line numbers that are all the same length so that all the statements are aligned in the program. Usually, this means using line numbers that are three or four digits each. In addition, line numbers should increase by ten to make the program easier to change.

Sometimes long numeric expressions are difficult to understand because of the order in which the operations are performed. When this is the case, it is often useful to include extra sets of parentheses around parts of the expression to make the expression easier to understand.

Finally, remarks should be used to help explain the program. At a minimum, the program should be identified at its beginning in a remark, and all variables that are difficult to understand should be described. Remarks should also be used to explain complex parts of the program.

The style rules discussed here are just a few of the ways that a program can be made more understandable. As you learn about other features of the BASIC language, you will learn more rules for program style.

A SAMPLE PROGRAM

This section develops a program for a problem using the language features discussed so far. We will follow the structured programming process discussed in Chapter 12. Recall that this process involves five activities:

1. Define the problem.
2. Design the program.
3. Code the program.
4. Test the program.
5. Document the program.

The goal of this process is to produce a well-structured program that is easy to understand and that is correct. Here a program to compute the payroll for an organization is developed.

Problem Definition

A program is needed to compute the gross pay, withholding tax, and net pay for each of the employees in an organization. The program should display the results of these computations along with the employee's identification number and name. Input to the program consists of an employee's identification number, name, and hours worked. Figure D2–10 shows how the input and output should appear for one employee. (In this figure, Xs indicate where variable data will be displayed.) The gross pay is computed at $6.50 per hour. The withholding tax is 16% of the gross pay. The net pay is the gross pay less the withholding tax.

Program Design

Recall from Chapter 12 that an algorithm is a set of steps that, if carried out, results in the solution of a problem. The algorithm that solves the payroll problem involves accepting the input data; computing the gross pay, withholding tax, and net pay; and displaying the results. Hence, the algorithm has a similar structure to that of the interest-calculation program. The algorithm is shown in pseudocode in Figure D2–11 and in a flowchart in Figure D2–12.

Figure D2–10   Input and Output Layout for the Payroll Program

```
              PAYROLL CALCULATION

         ENTER EMPLOYEE ID: XXX
         ENTER EMPLOYEE NAME: XXXXXXXXXX
         ENTER HOURS WORKED: XX

         PAYROLL DATA FOR EMPLOYEE XXX

           NAME: XXXXXXXXXX
           GROSS PAY: XXXXX
           TAX: XXXXX
           NET PAY: XXXXX

         END OF PROGRAM
```

Figure D2–11   Pseudocode for the Payroll Program

```
      Display program title
      Accept employee ID, name, hours worked
      Compute gross pay, tax, net pay
      Display employee ID, name, gross pay, tax, net pay
      Display end of program message
      End
```

Program Coding

The program is shown in Figure D2–13. The program logic follows the algorithm in the pseudocode and the flowchart. The first PRINT statement displays the program title. The INPUT statements accept the input data. Notice that a string variable is used for the employee's name. The three LET statements do the computations. The order of these statements is important. The gross pay must be computed first because it is needed in the calculation of the withholding tax. The tax must be computed before the net pay can be found. The next PRINT statements display the output in the form shown in Figure D2–10. The last PRINT statement displays the end-of-program message. REM statements have been included at the beginning to describe the program and the variables used in the program. In addition, REM statements have been included within the program to explain the input, output, and processing.

Program Testing

To test the program, it should be run several times with input test data for which the output has been computed by hand. Then the output from each run of the program using the test data should be compared with the hand-computed output.

Table D2–1 gives three sets of input test data and the expected output for each set. Figure D2–14 shows the input and output from

Figure D2–12
Flowchart for the Payroll Program

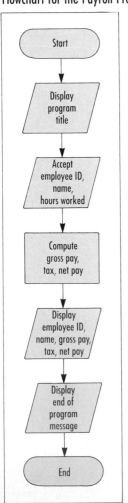

Figure D2–13 The Payroll Program

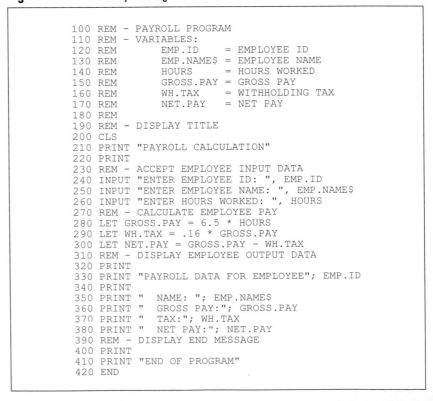

```
100 REM - PAYROLL PROGRAM
110 REM - VARIABLES:
120 REM        EMP.ID    = EMPLOYEE ID
130 REM        EMP.NAME$ = EMPLOYEE NAME
140 REM        HOURS     = HOURS WORKED
150 REM        GROSS.PAY = GROSS PAY
160 REM        WH.TAX    = WITHHOLDING TAX
170 REM        NET.PAY   = NET PAY
180 REM
190 REM - DISPLAY TITLE
200 CLS
210 PRINT "PAYROLL CALCULATION"
220 PRINT
230 REM - ACCEPT EMPLOYEE INPUT DATA
240 INPUT "ENTER EMPLOYEE ID: ", EMP.ID
250 INPUT "ENTER EMPLOYEE NAME: ", EMP.NAME$
260 INPUT "ENTER HOURS WORKED: ", HOURS
270 REM - CALCULATE EMPLOYEE PAY
280 LET GROSS.PAY = 6.5 * HOURS
290 LET WH.TAX = .16 * GROSS.PAY
300 LET NET.PAY = GROSS.PAY - WH.TAX
310 REM - DISPLAY EMPLOYEE OUTPUT DATA
320 PRINT
330 PRINT "PAYROLL DATA FOR EMPLOYEE"; EMP.ID
340 PRINT
350 PRINT "  NAME: "; EMP.NAME$
360 PRINT "  GROSS PAY:"; GROSS.PAY
370 PRINT "  TAX:"; WH.TAX
380 PRINT "  NET PAY:"; NET.PAY
390 REM - DISPLAY END MESSAGE
400 PRINT
410 PRINT "END OF PROGRAM"
420 END
```

running the program using each set of input data in Table D2–1. As you can see, all test runs give the correct results. Had any run given incorrect results, it would be necessary to debug the program.

Program Documentation

Part of the documentation for the program is included in the program in the form of remarks. The complete set of documentation for the program would include the listing of the program (Figure D2–13) and the sample runs of the program (Figure D2–14). The documentation may also include the input and output layout (Figure D2–10), the pseudocode (Figure D2–11), the flowchart (Figure D2–12), and the input test data and expected output (Table D2–1).

Terms to Remember

Numeric Constant p. 543

Numeric Data p. 543

Numeric Expression p. 545

Numeric Operator p. 545

Numeric Variable p. 544

Print Zone p. 551

String Constant p. 561

String Data p. 560

String Expression p. 561

String Variable p. 561

Review Questions

1. Indicate whether each of the following is a valid or invalid numeric constant in BASIC:
   a. -.004385
   b. 83,250
   c. 16.5%
   d. 273.51E-12
2. Convert the following E-notation constants to simple numeric constants:
   a. -8031E+2
   b. .1234E-6

Table D2–1   Input Test Data and Expected Output for the Payroll Program

Input Test Data			Expected Output		
Employee ID	Name	Hours	Gross Pay	Tax	Net Pay
234	JOHNSON	32	208	33.28	174.72
456	SMITH	48	312	49.92	262.08
678	JONES	36	234	37.44	196.56

Figure D2–14 Input and Output for Three Test Runs of the Payroll Program

```
                    PAYROLL CALCULATION

        ENTER EMPLOYEE ID: 234
        ENTER EMPLOYEE NAME: JOHNSON
        ENTER HOURS WORKED: 32

        PAYROLL DATA FOR EMPLOYEE 234

           NAME: JOHNSON
           GROSS PAY: 208
           TAX: 33.28
           NET PAY: 174.72

        END OF PROGRAM

                    PAYROLL CALCULATION

        ENTER EMPLOYEE ID: 456
        ENTER EMPLOYEE NAME: SMITH
        ENTER HOURS WORKED: 48

        PAYROLL DATA FOR EMPLOYEE 456

           NAME: SMITH
           GROSS PAY: 312
           TAX: 49.92
           NET PAY: 262.08

        END OF PROGRAM

                    PAYROLL CALCULATION

        ENTER EMPLOYEE ID: 678
        ENTER EMPLOYEE NAME: JONES
        ENTER HOURS WORKED: 36

        PAYROLL DATA FOR EMPLOYEE 678

           NAME: JONES
           GROSS PAY: 234
           TAX: 37.44
           NET PAY: 196.56

        END OF PROGRAM
```

3. Convert the following simple numeric constants to E-notation constants:

   a. $-.0000456$

   b. 7.8316

4. Code a numeric expression that is equivalent to each of the following algebraic expressions:

   a. $x^2 - 2x + 3$

   b. $\dfrac{4x}{y} + \dfrac{a}{3}$

5. Assume that the value of A is 2, B is 3, and C is 4. What is the value of each of the following numeric expressions?

   a. `A - B * C / A + B / C`

   b. `(B - A) * (C / ((B + A) / C))`

6. What is the effect of the following statement?

```
50 LET X = X / 2
```

7. The last statement executed in a BASIC program must be a(n) _____ statement.

8. Consider the following statement:

```
80 PRINT X, A, Z, P, Q, R, V
```

How many lines of output are displayed when this statement is executed, assuming each line contains five print zones?

9. How are remarks included in a BASIC program?

10. What is the difference between the effects of a comma and a semicolon in a PRINT statement?

11. What statement is used to clear the screen?

12. Code a statement that displays the heading TUITION CALCULATION on the screen.

13. Code a statement that displays the prompt ENTER PAYMENT on the screen, and then accepts the value of a variable for the payment.

14. Code a statement that assigns the string MY NAME IS to a variable.

15. Code a statement that accepts two numbers and three strings from the keyboard.

16. Why is good program style important?

Programming Problems

Each of the following problems gives the requirements for a computer program. Prepare a complete BASIC program according to the requirements given in the problem. The program should request all input with appropriate prompts and identify all output with appropriate headings or descriptions. The program should be fully debugged and tested on a computer, using the test data given.

1. Fahrenheit temperature is converted to Celsius temperature by the following formula:

$$C = \frac{5}{9} \times (F - 32)$$

In this formula, F is the temperature in degrees Fahrenheit, and C is the temperature in degrees Celsius. Write a BASIC program to accept the temperature in Fahrenheit, calculate the equivalent temperature in Celsius using this formula, and display the result. To test the program, run the program with each of the following Fahrenheit temperatures as input data:

```
78.4
-50
98.6
0
32
212
```

2. The present value, P, of income, I, received N years in the future is given by the following formula:

$$P = \frac{I}{(1+R)^N}$$

In this formula, R is the discount rate expressed as a fraction (e.g., if the discount rate is 5%, then R is .05). Write a BASIC program that computes the present value—given the income, number of years, and discount rate—and displays the result. Test the program by running it with each of the following sets of input data:

Income	Number of Years	Discount Rate
$10,000	5	10%
$1,200	2	5%
$42,365	18	12.5%
$6,000	20	8%

3. The final score for a particular test is equal to the number of questions answered correctly minus one-fourth of the number answered incorrectly. Assume that test data available for input includes the student's identification number, name, number correct on the test, and number incorrect. Write a BASIC program to calculate the final score from this data and to display the results along with the input data. Test the program by running it with each of the following sets of input data:

Student Number	Student Name	Number Correct	Number Incorrect
1	BENNETT	90	10
2	LOCK	75	20
3	HAINES	84	0
4	WONG	57	35
5	REDDING	10	50

4. The interest and maturity value of a promissory note can be calculated as follows:

$$\text{Interest} = \frac{\text{Principal} \times \text{Rate} \times \text{Time}}{360}$$

$$\text{Maturity value} = \text{Principal} + \text{Interest}$$

Write a BASIC program that accepts the loan number, principal, rate (percent), and time (days); calculates the interest and maturity value; and displays the loan number, rate (percent), time, interest, and maturity value. Note that the rate is expressed in percent for input and output purposes, but must be converted to decimal form for the calculation. Thus, if the input value for the rate is 5 (meaning 5%), this must be converted to .05 for use in the calculation. The conversion from percent to decimal form must be done within the program; the input and output of the rate should be in percent. Use the program to find the interest and maturity value of each of the following loans:

Loan Number	Rate	Time
1875	6%	60
2134	8%	180
3906	7.5%	360
4521	9%	90

5. The payroll in a particular business is calculated as follows:

a. Gross pay is the hours worked times the pay rate.

b. Withholding tax is found by subtracting 13 times the number of exemptions from the gross pay and multiplying the result by the tax rate.

c. Social security tax is 7.65% of the gross pay.

d. Net pay is the gross pay less all taxes.

Write a BASIC program that accepts an employee's identification number, name, hours worked, pay rate, tax rate, and number of exemptions. Then the program should calculate the employee's gross pay, withholding and social security taxes, and net pay, and display these results along with the employee's identification number.

Test the program by running it with each of the following sets of input data:

Employee Number	Employee Name	Hours Worked	Pay Rate	Tax Rate	Number of Exemptions
1001	ROBINSON	40	4.50	28%	3
1002	HOLT	36	3.75	15%	4
1003	TAYLOR	47	6.50	31%	0
1004	ADAMS	25	5.25	15%	2

SECTION 3
PROGRAMMING FOR DECISIONS

This section describes BASIC statements and program logic for decision making. A *decision* involves selecting among alternative sequences of statements based on a *condition* that occurs during the execution of the program. After completing this section, you should be able to write programs that use various patterns of decision making.

IF STATEMENTS

The fundamental decision-making statement in BASIC is the IF statement. There are several forms of this statement, depending upon the version of BASIC. In Microsoft BASIC, two forms are the IF-THEN statement and the IF-THEN-ELSE statement.

The IF-THEN Statement

The syntax of the IF-THEN statement is as follows:

```
ln IF relational expression THEN statement
```

Following the keyword IF is a **relational expression** that determines whether a particular relationship holds between two values. For example, A > B is a relational expression that determines whether the value of A is greater than that of B. (Relational expressions are described in detail later.) Following the word THEN is another statement in the program. The following is an example of an IF-THEN statement:

```
50 IF A > B THEN PRINT A
```

Execution of an IF-THEN statement causes the computer to evaluate the relational expression and determine whether it is true or false—that is, whether or not the relationship holds. If the expression is true, the computer executes the statement following the word THEN. If the expression is false, the computer does *not* execute the statement; rather, it continues with the next statement after the IF-THEN statement. In the previous example, if the value of A is greater than the value of B, the computer executes the PRINT statement and then goes on to the next statement in sequence following the IF-THEN statement. If A is *not* greater than B, the computer goes on to the next statement following the IF-THEN statement without executing the PRINT statement.

The IF-THEN-ELSE Statement

The syntax of the IF-THEN-ELSE statement is:

```
ln IF relational expression THEN statement ELSE statement
```

A relational expression follows the keyword IF. Then comes the word THEN and another statement. Following this statement is the word ELSE and still another statement. For example, the following is an IF-THEN-ELSE statement:

```
60 IF A > B THEN PRINT A ELSE LET C = B - A
```

The effect of the IF-THEN-ELSE statement is that if the relational expression is true, the statement following the word THEN is executed, but the statement following the word ELSE is *not* executed. If, however, the relational expression is false, the computer bypasses the statement following the word THEN and executes the statement following the word ELSE. Thus, in the previous example, if the value of A is greater than that of B, the computer executes the PRINT statement. If A is *not* greater than B, the computer executes the LET statement. After executing either the PRINT statement or the LET statement, the computer goes on to the next statement in sequence after the IF-THEN-ELSE statement.

Relational Expressions

A relational expression compares the values of two numeric expressions. The relational expression has a **truth value** of *true* or *false*, depending on the result of the comparison. The comparison made is determined by a **relational operator**. The relational operators in BASIC and their meanings are as follows:

Relational operator	Meaning
<	Less than
<=	Less than or equal to
>	Greater than
>=	Greater than or equal to
=	Equal to
<>	Not equal to

The simplest form of a relational expression is a numeric constant or variable, followed by a relational operator and then another numeric constant or variable. For example, the following are valid relational expressions:

```
J < K
6 <= C
Q > 5.6
```

```
K >= -5
A = B
7 <> J
```

To evaluate each of these, the values of the variables and constants are compared according to the relational operator. For example, if J is 6 and K is 5, the first expression is *false*. Similarly, if both J and K are equal to 6, this expression is *false*. However, if J is 6 and K is 7, the expression is *true*.

A more complicated form of a relational expression involves comparing the values of complex numeric expressions. For example, the following relational expressions are valid:

```
Q > P - 5.6
K + 8 >= -5 - L
X + Y / (4.56 - Z) = Z - M
(A - I) <> (K - 5)
```

Notice that parentheses can be used to enclose part or all of either numeric expression in a relational expression.

In evaluating a relational expression containing numeric expressions, the current values of the variables are used to evaluate each numeric expression. The resulting values of the numeric expressions are then compared according to the relational operator to determine the truth value of the relational expression. For example, consider the following relational expression:

```
N - 3 >= 5
```

If the value of N is 10, then N – 3 is 7. Because 7 is greater than 5, the relational expression is *true*. However, if N is 4, then N – 3 is 1. Because 1 is not greater than or equal to 5, the expression is *false*. Finally, if N is 8, then N – 3 is 5, and the relational expression is *true*.

Relational expressions can also be used to compare string constants, variables, and complex expressions. This topic is discussed later in this section.

Illustrative Programs

To illustrate the use of the IF statement and relational expressions in a program, assume that you need to write a program that calculates the tuition for a college student. The input data is the student's identification number and the number of units (credits) for which the student is enrolled. The tuition is $350 if the student is taking twelve or fewer units. If the student is taking more than twelve units, the tuition is $350 plus $20 per unit for all units over twelve. The program must display the student's identification number and tuition for any valid input.

The program to accomplish this requires decision making. First, the program must accept the input data. Then, the program must examine the number of units to determine the tuition. This decision-making step can be stated as follows: If the number of units is less than or equal to twelve, the tuition is $350; otherwise, the tuition is $350 plus $20 per unit for all units over twelve. After the tuition is calculated, the computer must display the output.

The program in Figure D3–1 solves this problem. The INPUT statements accept the student's identification number (ID) and number of units (UNITS). The IF-THEN-ELSE statement then compares the number of units with 12. If the value of UNITS is less than or equal to 12, the computer sets the tuition (TUIT) equal to $350 with the first LET statement. If, however, the value of UNITS is greater than 12, the tuition (TUIT) is calculated at $350 plus $20 per unit for all units over 12 (UNITS – 12) with the LET statement. Finally, the output is displayed.

An alternative way of writing this program is shown in Figure D3–2. In this example, the INPUT statements accept the input, and then the tuition is set equal to $350. Next, an IF-THEN statement determines if the units are greater than 12. If this is the case, the tuition is calculated at $350 plus $20 per unit over 12. This new value of the tuition replaces the previous value. Then the computer goes on to the PRINT statements. Although this program is slightly different from the one in Figure D3–1, the output is identical for the same input.

Pseudocode of Programs with Decisions

Figure D3–3 shows the pseudocode for the first tuition-calculation program (Figure D3–1). In the pseudocode, the decision is indicated by using the word IF, followed by the condition that the units are less than or equal to 12. If this condition is true, the tuition is set equal to $350; otherwise, it is calculated by the formula given in the pseudocode. The word ELSE is used between the true and false steps, and the word END-IF comes at the end of the decision.

Figure D3–1   The Tuition-Calculation Program (Part 1 of 2)

(a)   The Program

```
100 REM - TUITION CALCULATION PROGRAM
110 REM - VARIABLES:
120 REM        ID    = STUDENT ID
130 REM        UNITS = NUMBER OF UNITS
140 REM        TUIT  = TUITION
150 REM
160 CLS
170 PRINT "TUITION CALCULATION"
180 PRINT
190 INPUT "ENTER STUDENT ID: ", ID
200 INPUT "ENTER NUMBER OF UNITS: ", UNITS
210 IF UNITS <= 12 THEN LET TUIT = 350 ELSE LET TUIT = 350 + 20 * (UNITS - 12)
220 PRINT
230 PRINT "STUDENT ID:"; ID
240 PRINT "TUITION:"; TUIT
250 PRINT
260 PRINT "END OF PROGRAM"
270 END
```

Figure D3–1 The Tuition-Calculation Program (Part 2 of 2)

(b) Input and Output for Two Runs

```
TUITION CALCULATION

ENTER STUDENT ID: 1234
ENTER NUMBER OF UNITS: 6

STUDENT ID: 1234
TUITION: 350

END OF PROGRAM


TUITION CALCULATION

ENTER STUDENT ID: 3456
ENTER NUMBER OF UNITS: 15

STUDENT ID: 3456
TUITION: 410

END OF PROGRAM
```

Figure D3–4 shows the pseudocode for the alternative tuition-calculation program (Figure D3–2). In this pseudocode, the tuition is set equal to $350 before the decision, which is indicated by the word IF, followed by the condition that the units are greater than 12. If this condition is true, a new value for the tuition is calculated by the formula. No ELSE is used, but END-IF comes at the end of the decision.

Figure D3–2 The Alternative Tuition-Calculation Program

```
100 REM - TUITION CALCULATION PROGRAM
110 REM - VARIABLES:
120 REM        ID    = STUDENT ID
130 REM        UNITS = NUMBER OF UNITS
140 REM        TUIT  = TUITION
150 REM
160 CLS
170 PRINT "TUITION CALCULATION"
180 PRINT
190 INPUT "ENTER STUDENT ID: ", ID
200 INPUT "ENTER NUMBER OF UNITS: ", UNITS
210 LET TUIT = 350
220 IF UNITS > 12 THEN LET TUIT = 350 + 20 * (UNITS - 12)
230 PRINT
240 PRINT "STUDENT ID:"; ID
250 PRINT "TUITION:"; TUIT
260 PRINT
270 PRINT "END OF PROGRAM"
280 END
```

Figure D3–3 Pseudocode of the Tuition-Calculation Program

```
Display program title
Accept student ID, units
IF units ≤ 12 THEN
   Tuition = $350
ELSE
   Tuition = $350 + $20 x (units - 12)
END-IF
Display student ID, tuition
Display end of program message
End
```

Figure D3–4 Pseudocode of the Alternative Tuition-Calculation Program

```
Display program title
Accept student ID, units
Tuition = $350
IF units > 12 THEN
   Tuition = $350 + $20 x (units - 12)
END-IF
Display student ID, tuition
Display end of program message
End
```

Flowcharts of Programs with Decisions

Figure D3–5 shows the flowchart for the first tuition-calculation program (Figure D3–1). The decision symbol (diamond) is used for the condition that the units are less than or equal to 12. The condition is written as a question within the symbol, and the flowlines leaving the symbol are labeled with the answers to the question. These lines go to the processing steps that determine the tuition. After the processing steps, the flowlines come together before the output step.

Figure D3–5   Flowchart of the Tuition-Calculation Program

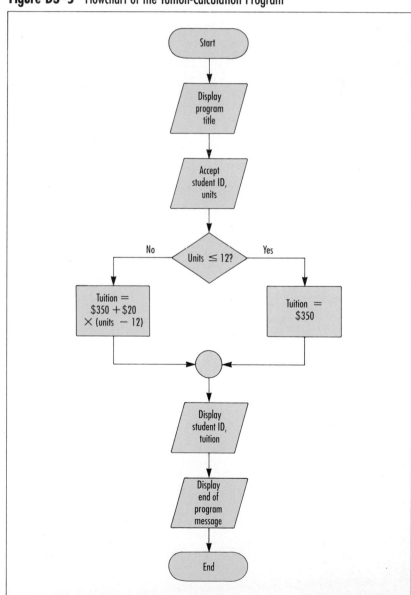

Figure D3–6 gives the flowchart of the alternative tuition-calculation program (Figure D3–2). The flowchart shows that, before the decision step, the tuition is set equal to $350. Then the decision symbol is used to test whether the units are greater than 12. If this is the case, a new value for the tuition is calculated before going on to the output step. If the units are less than or equal to 12, the logic flows directly to the output step.

Figure D3–6 Flowchart of the Alternative Tuition-Calculation Program

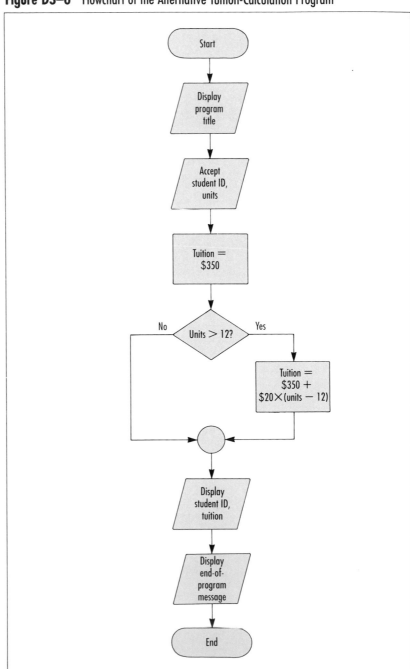

Multiple-Statement Decisions

In the examples of IF-THEN and IF-THEN-ELSE statements so far, only one statement is executed if the relational expression is true or false. Often, however, more than one statement needs to be executed. This can be accomplished by putting multiple statements in the IF-THEN or IF-THEN-ELSE statement, separated by colons (:). For example, consider the following IF-THEN statement:

```
100 IF A > B THEN LET C = A - B: PRINT C
```

In this example, if A is greater than B, the LET statement is executed first, and then the PRINT statement is executed. If A is not greater than B, *both* of these statements are bypassed. The following example illustrates this approach with an IF-THEN-ELSE statement:

```
110 IF A > B THEN LET C = A - B: PRINT C ELSE LET D = B - A: PRINT D
```

Here, if A is greater than B, the first LET and PRINT statements are executed. If A is *not* greater than B, the second LET and PRINT statements are executed.

Often, when multiple statements are used in an IF-THEN or IF-THEN-ELSE statement, the statement becomes longer than one line. In this case, with Microsoft BASIC, you can type beyond the end of the line and the typing will continue onto the next line. The Enter key must not be pressed until all lines in the statement have been typed. A line number is used only on the first line. The complete statement should not exceed 254 characters (including all blank spaces), which is a little more than three lines. Any characters in the statement beyond this limit will be ignored by the computer.

You can continue onto the next line without typing to the end of the line by holding the Control key and pressing the Enter key. For example, the previous IF-THEN statement can be entered on two lines as follows:

```
100 IF A > B                        <Control/Enter>
      THEN LET C = A - B: PRINT C    <Enter>
```

Notice that the second line, which gives what is to be done if the condition is true, has been indented. This is a common program style that makes the statement easier to read.

The following example shows this technique for an IF-THEN-ELSE statement:

```
110 IF A > B                        <Control/Enter>
      THEN LET C = A - B: PRINT C    <Control/Enter>
      ELSE LET D = B - A: PRINT D    <Enter>
```

Notice that the second and third lines, which show what is to be done if the condition is true and false, have been indented to make the program easier to read.

The limit of 254 characters in a statement must be considered when continuing a statement onto the next line, using this technique. Depending on the version of Microsoft BASIC, the blank spaces at the end of the line, after the Control/Enter, may or may not be counted in the total. In BASICA, they are counted, and the statement should not be more than a little over three lines. In GWBASIC, they are not counted, and the statement can be more than three lines as long as the total number of characters does not exceed 254.

Logical Operators

Most versions of BASIC, including Microsoft BASIC, have **logical operators** that can be used to combine several relational expressions. The two main logical operators are AND and OR. For example, the following IF statements use these logical operators:

```
120 IF A >= B AND C <= 5 THEN PRINT C
130 IF K = 5 OR X <> Y THEN LET Z = X + Y
```

The AND logical operator compares the truth values of two relational expressions to determine if both are true at the same time. First, the computer determines whether each relational expression is true or false. Thus, in the first example just given, the computer would first determine if A is greater than or equal to B and if C is less than or equal to 5. Then, if both relational expressions are true, the combined expression is *true*. If, however, one or the other or both of the relational expressions is false, the combined expression is *false*. Thus, in the first example, the combined expression is true if A is greater than or equal to B and if C is less than or equal to 5, but it is false if A is less than B or if C is greater than 5 or if both A is less than B and C is greater than 5. In this example, the PRINT statement in the IF statement would be executed only if the combined expression is true.

The OR logical operator compares the truth value of two relational expressions to determine if one or the other or both are true. First, the computer determines the truth values of the relational expressions. Thus, in the second example given earlier, the computer first determines if K equals 5 and X does not equal Y. Then, if one or the other of the relational expressions is true or if both are true, the combined expression is *true*, but if both are false, the combined expression is *false*. Thus, in the second example, the combined condition is true if K equals 5 or if X does not equal Y or if both K equals 5 and X does not equal Y, but it is false if K does not equal 5 and X equals Y. In this example, the LET statement in the IF statement would be executed only if the combined expression is true.

It is permissible to have more than two relational expressions combined with the AND and OR logical operators, and even to mix these operators with several relational expressions. The rules, however, can be complex, and thus these situations should be avoided.

DECISION STRUCTURES IN BASIC

Recall from Chapter 12 that two types of decision structures are *if-then-else decisions* and *if-then decisions*. In an if-then-else decision, the computer selects between two alternative groups of instructions based on some condition. The alternatives are called the *true part* and the *false part* of the decision. In an if-then decision, the computer either executes one group of instructions or bypasses them based on some condition. These decision structures are represented diagrammatically in Figure D3–7.

Decision Structures in Microsoft BASIC

Decision structures are easily created in Microsoft Basic and in other versions that have the IF-THEN-ELSE and IF-THEN statements described here. The IF-THEN-ELSE statement is used for an if-then-else decision, and the IF-THEN statement is used for an if-then decision. Figure D3–8 shows how the decision structures are created using these statements. The tuition-calculation program in Figure D3–1 illustrates an if-then-else decision using the IF-THEN-ELSE statement. The alternative tuition-calculation program in Figure D3–2 illustrates an if-then decision using the IF-THEN statement.

Figure D3–7   Decision Structures

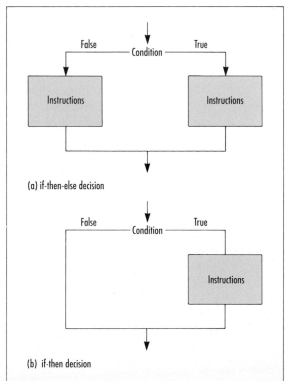

(a) if-then-else decision

(b) if-then decision

Figure D3–8 Decision Structures in BASIC Using the IF-THEN-ELSE and IF-THEN Statements

(a) If-then-else Decision

```
IF condition
   THEN statements to be executed if condition is true
   ELSE statements to be executed if condition is false
```

(b) If-then Decision

```
IF condition
   THEN statements to be executed if condition is true
```

Decision Structures in Other Versions of BASIC

If the IF-THEN-ELSE and IF-THEN statements are available, they should be used for all decisions. In some versions of BASIC, however, these statements are not provided. In these versions, the IF statement has the following syntax:

```
ln IF relational expression THEN ln
```

Notice that following the word THEN is a line number, not another statement. For example, the following is an IF statement of this type:

```
50 IF A > B THEN 200
```

Execution of this type of IF statement causes the computer to determine whether the relational expression is true or false. If the expression is true, the computer continues execution with the statement whose number is given after the word THEN. You say that the program *branches* to that statement. If, however, the expression is false, the computer does not branch; rather, it continues with the next statement in sequence. In the previous example, if A is greater than B, the computer branches to statement 200. If A is not greater than B, the computer goes on to the next statement in sequence following the IF statement.

To create if-then-else and if-then decisions using this form of the IF statement, one more statement is needed: the GOTO statement. *This statement should never be used unless no other alternative is available, and then it should be used only in the restricted ways that are described here.* The syntax of this statement is as follows:

```
ln GOTO ln
```

For example, the following is a GOTO statement:

```
75 GOTO 150
```

The effect of the GOTO statement is to branch to the statement whose number is given after the word GOTO. In the previous example, the computer would branch to statement 150.

Figure D3–9 shows how the decision structures are created using the IF and GOTO statements. To create these decisions requires a little rearrangement in the way you usually think about decisions. All that the IF statement can do is branch to another statement or continue with the next statement in sequence, depending upon the truth or falsity of a relational expression. Hence, to create an if-then-else decision, you must code the IF statement so that it branches to the true part of the condition. The false part must follow the IF statement and end with a GOTO statement that branches around the true part. This pattern is shown in Figure D3–9a. To create an if-then decision, you must code the IF statement using the *complement* of the condition. This is the condition that is true if the original condition is false, and vice versa. For example, the complement of A > B is A <= B. Then the IF statement branches around the true part, which follows the IF statement, if the complement is true. This pattern is shown in Figure D3–9b.

The decisions in the tuition-calculation programs in Figures D3–1 and D3–2 can be rewritten using IF and GOTO statements. Figure D3–10 shows the results. In Figure D3–10a, which illustrates the if-then-else decision, if the condition that the number of units is less than or equal to 12 is true, the computer branches to the second tuition calculation (the true part). If the condition is false, the computer goes on (you say that it "falls through") to the next statement in sequence (the false part). The statement GOTO 210 between the false and the true parts is necessary to branch around the true part. In Figure D3–10b, which illustrates the if-then decision, the tuition calculation (the true part) is to be done if the condition that the units are greater than 12 is true. Therefore, the complement of this condition is used in the IF statement to branch around the true part if the complement is true.

Figure D3–9   Decision Structures in BASIC Using the IF and GOTO Statements

(a)   If-then-else Decision   **(b)**   If-then Decision

```
      IF condition THEN ln1                        IF complement of condition THEN ln

                  Statements to be                             Statements to be
                  executed if                                  executed if
                  condition is false                           condition is true
                                                               (i.e., complement is false)
      GOTO ln2
                                                 ln (next statement)
ln1               Statements to be
                  executed if
                  condition is true

ln2 (next statement)
```

Figure D3–10 Examples of Decision Structures Using the IF and GOTO Statements

(a) If-then-else Decision

(b) If-then Decision

```
200 IF UNITS <= 12 THEN 207
202    LET TUIT = 350 + 20 * (UNITS - 12)
205 GOTO 210
207    LET TUIT = 350
210 (next statement)
```

```
200 IF UNITS <= 12 THEN 210
205    LET TUIT = 350 + 20 * (UNITS - 12)
210 (next statement)
```

As a final reminder, the IF and GOTO statements described here should *not* be used for decisions unless no alternative is available. If they are used, they should be used only in the patterns shown in Figure D3–9. They will not be used in future examples.

NESTED DECISIONS

Within the true or false parts of a decision structure there may be any type of instructions. In fact, there may be instructions for decision making in the true and false parts. Then you say there are **nested decisions**. In BASIC, nested decisions are created by putting an IF statement within another IF statement to form *nested IF statements*.

As an example of nested decisions using nested IF statements, assume that the tuition charged a college student is based not only on the number of units for which the student is enrolled but also on whether the student is a resident of the state. If the student is a state resident and the number of units is less than or equal to 12, the tuition is $350. If the units are greater than 12 (and the student is a state resident), the tuition is $350 plus $20 for each unit over 12. If the student is not a resident and the number of units is less than or equal to 12, the tuition is $800. For a nonresident with more than 12 units, the tuition is $800 plus $45 for each additional unit.

This problem involves determining first whether the student is a state resident and then whether the number of units is less than or equal to 12. Assume that the input data is the student's identification number (ID), the number of units (UNITS), and a resident code (RES)—which is 1 if the student is a state resident and 0 otherwise. A program to solve this problem is shown in Figure D3–11. After accepting the input data, the program compares RES with 1 in the first IF statement. If RES is equal to 1, the computer compares UNITS with 12 in the second IF statement, which is nested in the true part of the first IF statement. If RES is not equal to 1, the computer checks UNITS in the third IF statement, nested in the false part of the first IF statement. The actual tuition depends on both the residence code and the number of units. After the tuition is calculated, the output is displayed.

The pseudocode for this program is shown in Figure D3–12, and the flowchart is given in Figure D3–13. The nested decisions show up very clearly in both the pseudocode and the flowchart.

Within a nested decision may be other nested decisions, as long as the statement is within the length limit. Usually, however, nesting several decisions makes the program difficult to understand.

Figure D3–11 The Tuition-Calculation Program with Nested Decisions

(a) The Program

```
100 REM - TUITION CALCULATION PROGRAM
110 REM - VARIABLES:
120 REM      ID   = STUDENT ID
130 REM      UNITS = NUMBER OF UNITS
140 REM      RES  = RESIDENT CODE
150 REM      TUIT = TUITION
160 REM      .
170 CLS
180 PRINT "TUITION CALCULATION"
190 PRINT
200 INPUT "ENTER STUDENT ID: ", ID
210 INPUT "ENTER NUMBER OF UNITS: ", UNITS
220 INPUT "ENTER RESIDENT CODE: ", RES
230 IF RES = 1
        THEN IF UNITS <= 12 THEN LET TUIT = 350 ELSE LET TUIT = 350+20*(UNITS-12)
        ELSE IF UNITS <= 12 THEN LET TUIT = 800 ELSE LET TUIT = 800+45*(UNITS-12)
240 PRINT
250 PRINT "STUDENT ID:"; ID
260 PRINT "TUITION:"; TUIT
270 PRINT
280 PRINT "END OF PROGRAM"
290 END
```

(b) Input and Output for Four Runs

```
TUITION CALCULATION                    TUITION CALCULATION

ENTER STUDENT ID: 2345                 ENTER STUDENT ID: 6789
ENTER NUMBER OF UNITS: 8               ENTER NUMBER OF UNITS: 18
ENTER RESIDENT CODE: 0                 ENTER RESIDENT CODE: 0

STUDENT ID: 2345                       STUDENT ID: 6789
TUITION: 800                           TUITION: 1070

END OF PROGRAM                         END OF PROGRAM


TUITION CALCULATION                    TUITION CALCULATION

ENTER STUDENT ID: 4567                 ENTER STUDENT ID: 8901
ENTER NUMBER OF UNITS: 13              ENTER NUMBER OF UNITS: 10
ENTER RESIDENT CODE: 1                 ENTER RESIDENT CODE: 1

STUDENT ID: 4567                       STUDENT ID: 8901
TUITION: 370                           TUITION: 350

END OF PROGRAM                         END OF PROGRAM
```

COMPARING STRING DATA

So far, relational expressions have compared only numeric data. String data, however, may also be compared in relational expressions. String constants, variables, and complex expressions can appear on both sides of a relational operator. The result is that the string data is compared to determine the truth value of the relational expression. All six of the relational operators discussed earlier can be used with string data. For

Figure D3–12 Pseudocode of the Tuition-Calculation Program with Nested Decisions

```
Display program title
Accept student ID, units, resident code
IF resident code = 1 THEN
  IF units ≤ 12 THEN
    Tuition = $350
  ELSE
    Tuition = $350 + $20 x (units - 12)
  END-IF
ELSE
  IF units ≤ 12 THEN
    Tuition = $800
  ELSE
    Tuition = $800 + $45 x (units - 12)
  END-IF
END-IF
Display student ID, tuition
Display end of program message
End
```

example, the following are valid relational expressions involving string data comparison:

```
N$ = "JOHN"
RES$ <> "YES"
X$ < Y$
"A" <= B$
"WXYZ" > U$ + V$
V$ >= "AA"
```

Equal Comparison

When the = or <> relational operator is used with string data, a comparison is made to determine if the data consists of identical characters in identical positions. If it does, the values are equal. If the string data is not identical, the values are not equal. For example, in the expression

```
N$ = "JOHN"
```

if the value of N$ is JOHN, the expression is true, but if N$ is JEAN, the expression is false.

Figure D3–14 shows an example of the use of this type of comparison in a program that determines tuition for a college student. In this example, the input consists of each student's identification number (ID) and his or her state of residence (STATE$), which is a two-character code. Tuition is based on whether or not the student is a California resident. If the student is a California resident, the tuition is $350. Out-of-state residents pay a tuition of $800. The IF statement compares the string variable STATE$ with the string constant "CA," which is the code for California. The value assigned to the tuition (TUIT) is based on whether this comparison is true or false. A string equal to the word RESIDENT or NONRESIDENT is assigned to the string variable STATUS$ based on this comparison. The value of this string variable is displayed along with the other output.

Figure D3–13   Flowchart of the Tuition-Calculation Program with Nested Decisions

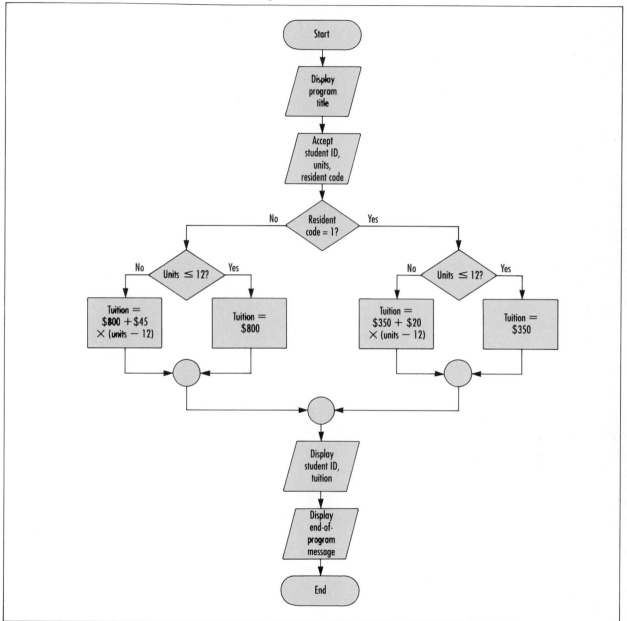

All types of characters—letters, digits, and special characters including blanks—can be compared. Upper- and lowercase letters can be compared. An uppercase letter, however, is not equal to its corresponding lowercase letter. If the strings being compared are not the same length, the evaluation depends on the version of BASIC. In Microsoft BASIC, strings that are not the same length are not equal. This is true even if the strings are the same except for extra blank spaces at the end of one string.

When comparing string data, it is important to use only string constants, string variables, and string expressions. You cannot compare

Figure D3–14   A Tuition-Calculation Program with String Comparison

(a)   The Program

```
100 REM - TUITION CALCULATION PROGRAM
110 REM - VARIABLES:
120 REM      ID      = STUDENT ID
130 REM      STATE$  = STATE OF RESIDENCE
140 REM      STATUS$ = RESIDENT STATUS
150 REM      TUIT    = TUITION
160 REM
170 CLS
180 PRINT "TUITION CALCULATION"
190 PRINT
200 INPUT "ENTER STUDENT ID: ", ID
210 INPUT "ENTER STATE OF RESIDENCE: ", STATE$
220 IF STATE$ = "CA"
       THEN LET TUIT = 350: LET STATUS$ = "RESIDENT"
       ELSE LET TUIT = 800: LET STATUS$ = "NONRESIDENT"
230 PRINT
240 PRINT "STUDENT ID:"; ID
250 PRINT "TUITION:"; TUIT
260 PRINT "STATUS: "; STATUS$
270 PRINT
280 PRINT "END OF PROGRAM"
290 END
```

(b)   Input and Output for Two Runs

```
TUITION CALCULATION

ENTER STUDENT ID: 2345
ENTER STATE OF RESIDENCE: CA

STUDENT ID: 2345
TUITION: 350
STATUS: RESIDENT

END OF PROGRAM



TUITION CALCULATION

ENTER STUDENT ID: 4567
ENTER STATE OF RESIDENCE: IL

STUDENT ID: 4567
TUITION: 800
STATUS: NONRESIDENT

END OF PROGRAM
```

string data with numeric data. For example, the following relational expression is invalid because 123 is a numeric constant:

$$123 = A\$$$

This does not mean, however, that you cannot determine if A\$ equals 123. To do this you must make 123 a string constant by putting quotation marks around it. Hence, the following relational expression is valid:

$$"123" = A\$$$

Greater-Than and Less-Than Comparison

When string data is compared using one of the relational operators (<, <=, >, or >=) the evaluation of the relational expression is based on the ordering of the characters for the computer being used. This ordering is called the **collating sequence** and depends on the internal code used for the characters by the computer. Many computers, including all microcomputers, use *ASCII*, discussed in Chapter 3. The ASCII collating sequence is as follows:

Blank space
Special characters
Digits in numerical order
Special characters
Uppercase letters in alphabetical order
Special characters
Lowercase letters in alphabetical order
Special characters

When two characters are compared, one is less than the other if it is earlier in the ASCII collating sequence. Thus, uppercase A is less than B, which is less than C, and so forth, and lowercase a is less than b, which is less than c, and so on. All uppercase letters, however, come before the lowercase letters in the collating sequence. Hence, A is less than a, B is less than b, and so on. The collating sequence for the digits is the same as the numerical sequence. Thus, 0 is less than 1, which is less than 2, and so on, as you would expect. All digits, however, are less than all letters. Special characters appear at various positions in the collating sequence.

When two strings of several characters each are compared, the evaluation is done by comparing strings character-for-character, left-to-right. As soon as two corresponding characters are not equal to each other, the computer determines which string is the lesser based on which of the unequal characters comes earlier in the ASCII collating sequence. Thus, in comparing JEAN and JOHN, the computer examines the first character of each and determines that they are equal. It then compares the second character of each and determines that they are not equal. Then, because E is earlier in the collating sequence than O, the computer would indicate that JEAN is less than JOHN.

Considering the uppercase letters, one string is less than the other if it appears before the other in an alphabetical list. Thus, as you have just seen, the string JEAN is less than JOHN. Also, JOHN is less than MARY. When there are both upper- and lowercase letters in the strings, the results may be different. Jean is less than John, as you would expect, but greater than JOHN because lowercase e is greater than uppercase O. Thus, in comparing alphabetic strings, you need to be careful about the case of the letters in the strings. It is usually best if the letters are either all uppercase or all lowercase.

If a string contains a blank space, the blank is less than any other character. Hence, JOHN SMITH is less than JOHNNY JONES because the fifth character in the first string is a blank space, which is less than the fifth character in the second string—an N.

A string of digits is evaluated in the same way as a string of letters. Thus, 123 is less than 456, as you would expect. But because a blank space is less than any other character, *b*9 is less than 8*b* (where *b* stands for a blank). Notice that comparing strings of digits can yield results different from those of comparing the corresponding numbers.

When a string contains a mixture of letters, digits, and special characters, the evaluation is done based on the collating sequence. For example, X37Z is less than XM7Z because the digit 3 is less than the letter M. Similarly, AB#5 is less than AB12 because the # symbol is less than the digit 1.

If one string is shorter than another, and if all characters are the same up to the end of the string, the shorter string is less than the longer one. Thus, JOHN is less than JOHNNY. Note, however, that the longer string can be less than the shorter one if the characters are not the same. Thus, JOANNE is less than JOHN because the third character of JOANNE is less than the third character of JOHN. Table D3–1 shows other examples of string comparison.

Table D3–1 Examples of String Comparison

Relational Expression	Truth Value
`"ED JONES" < "ED SMITH"`	true
`"EDWARD JONES" < "ED SMITH"`	false
`"ED JONES" < "ED JON"`	false
`"1234" > "4567"`	false
`"1234" > " 4567"`	true
`" 1234" > "4567"`	false
`"MARY" = "MARY"`	true
`"MARY" = "MARY "`	false
`"MARY" = "MAR Y"`	false
`"    " <> "  "`	true
`"X37Z <> "2AY7"`	true
`"abc" <> "ABC"`	true

PROGRAM TESTING

As you know, a program must be thoroughly tested to see if there are any logic errors. The basic process of program testing involves making up input test data, determining the expected output using the test data, running the program with the test data, and comparing the actual output with the expected output. Any discrepancy between the actual output and the expected output indicates an error.

The first tests of the program should be simple to ensure that the program works in the simplest cases. Obvious errors, such as misspellings of headings or non-alignment of columns, can be corrected at this point. Then more complex tests can be performed.

Every statement in the program should be executed at least once, and usually several times, with test data. If a statement includes variables that are used for input data, test cases that represent a range of values for each variable should be provided. For example, consider the following statement from the interest-calculation program in Section 2 (Figure D2–9):

```
210 LET INTEREST = BEGINBAL * RATE
```

In that program, BEGINBAL and RATE were input variables. Several different values for these variables should be used to test this statement in the program. What happens if BEGINBAL is 0? RATE is 0? Both are 0? What happens if either or both BEGINBAL and RATE are large values (e.g., 1000000 for BEGINBAL and 1 for RATE)? What happens with typical values of these variables (e.g., 20000 for BEGINBAL and .08 for RATE)? Test data that represents extreme cases as well as common cases should be used.

Testing a decision requires special care. At a minimum, every statement in the decision should be executed at least once, using the test data. This strategy, however, will not catch all errors. For example, consider a tuition-calculation program in which the tuition should be $350 if the units are less than or equal to 12, and $800 if the units are greater than 12. The decision in this program should be coded as follows:

```
200 IF UNITS <= 12 THEN LET TUIT = 350 ELSE LET TUIT = 800
```

To test this decision, you might supply two sets of test data, one in which UNITS is equal to 9 and the other in which UNITS is equal to 15. These data would cause both LET statements to be executed at least once. The data would not catch certain errors, however. For example, if the relational expression in the IF statement had been incorrectly coded as UNITS < 12, testing with only the two sets of input data would not detect this error. You must also test the case in which UNITS is equal to 12.

You now have three sets of test data for this program. Even with this data, however, errors may still not be detected. For example, if the relational expression in the IF statement had been coded as UNITS <= 13, these data would not detect this error. You need a test case that is just greater than 12, such as 12.5 or 13, depending on whether partial units are allowed.

You can see from this example a general strategy for testing decisions. For this program, the input value for the units ranges from 0 to some practical limit, such as 20. This range is divided into two subranges based on the decision. If the units are between 0 and 12, one tuition applies. If the units are greater than 12 but less than or equal to 20, another tuition applies. For each subrange, test the decision with the minimum and maximum values of the subrange and with some representative value in between. Applying this strategy to the tuition example, you would test the program with the units each to 0, 9, 12, 13, 15, and 20. If the program works for each of these cases, it is likely to work for others.

The testing strategy described here will not detect all errors. For example, the tests will not detect errors that result from using invalid input data. In the previous example, no test is done to see what happens with a negative value for the units. You should make up special tests for the worst possible cases. Every case that can be thought of should be tested.

A SAMPLE PROGRAM

This section develops a program for a problem that involves decision making. The problem is to compute the charges for orders that customers place.

Problem Definition

A program is needed to compute the purchase amount, the tax, the shipping charge, and the total due for an order made by a customer. The program should display the results of these computations along with the customer's number and name. Input to the program is the customer number, the customer name, the quantity ordered, and the price for the item ordered (called the *unit price*). Figure D3–15 shows how the input and output should appear.

The purchase amount is the quantity ordered times the unit price less the discount. The discount depends on the quantity ordered. If the quantity is less than 10 units, there is no discount. If the quantity ordered is 10 to 19 units, the discount is 10% of the basic purchase amount, which is the purchase amount before the discount is taken. If the quantity ordered is 20 or more units, the discount is 20% of the basic purchase amount.

The tax is 6% of the purchase amount. The shipping charge is $5 if the purchase amount is less than $100. There is no shipping charge if the purchase amount is $100 or more. The total due is the sum of the purchase amount, the tax, and the shipping charge.

Program Design

The pseudocode for the program is given in Figure D3–16, and the flowchart is shown in Figure D3–17. To compute the purchase amount, the program must first multiply the quantity purchased by the unit price and then subtract the discount. The discount depends on the quantity ordered. A nested decision is needed to find the discount because there are three cases. The shipping charge depends on the purchase amount. A simple decision (nonnested) is needed to find the shipping charge because there are only two cases.

Program Coding

The program to solve this problem is shown in Figure D3–18. The logic of the program follows that of the pseudocode and the flowchart. Notice that the computation of the purchase amount requires several

Figure D3–15   Input and Output Layout for the Customer-Order Program

```
            CUSTOMER ORDER PROCESSING

            ENTER CUSTOMER NUMBER:   XXXX
            ENTER CUSTOMER NAME:     XXXXXXXXXX
            ENTER QUANTITY ORDERED:  XX
            ENTER UNIT PRICE:        XX

            CUSTOMER NUMBER:         XXXX
            CUSTOMER NAME:           XXXXXXXXXX
            PURCHASE AMOUNT:         XXXX
            TAX:                     XXXX
            SHIPPING CHARGE:         XXXX
            TOTAL DUE:               XXXX

            END OF PROCESSING
```

Figure D3–16   Pseudocode for the Customer-Order Program

```
Display program title
Accept customer number, name, quantity, price
Basic purchase amount = quantity x price
IF quantity < 10 THEN
   Discount = $0
ELSE
   IF quantity < 20 THEN
      Discount = 10% of basic purchase amount
   ELSE
      Discount = 20% of basic purchase amount
   END-IF
END-IF
Purchase amount = basic purchase amount - discount
Tax = 6% of purchase amount
IF purchase amount < 100 THEN
   Shipping charge = $5
ELSE
   Shipping charge = $0
END-IF
Total due = purchase amount + tax + shipping charge
Display customer number, name, purchase amount,
        tax, shipping charge, total due
Display end of program message
End
```

steps, including a nested decision. A simple decision is needed for the computation of the shipping charge.

Program Testing

To test a program with decisions, all possible cases for all decisions should be tested. For this program, test cases are needed with the quantity ordered less than 10, between 10 and 19, and greater than 19. Similarly, test cases are needed in which the purchase amount is less than $100 and in which it is $100 or more.

Table D3–2 shows several sets of input test data and the expected output for each set. The different cases discussed in the previous paragraph are represented in this data, although other test cases should also be used. The input and output from running the program with this data are shown in Figure D3–19. As you can see, all test runs give correct results.

Program Documentation

The program in Figure D3–18 contains numerous remarks that help document the program. In addition to the program description and list of variables, remarks are included at various points in the program to identify the processing being performed.

The complete set of documentation for this program would include a listing of the program (Figure D3–18) and the input and output from running the program (Figure D3–19). The documentation may also include the input and output layout (Figure D3–15), the pseudocode (Figure D3–16), the flowchart (Figure D3–17), and the input test data and expected output (Table D3–2).

Figure D3–17 Flowchart for the Customer-Order Program (Part 1 of 2)

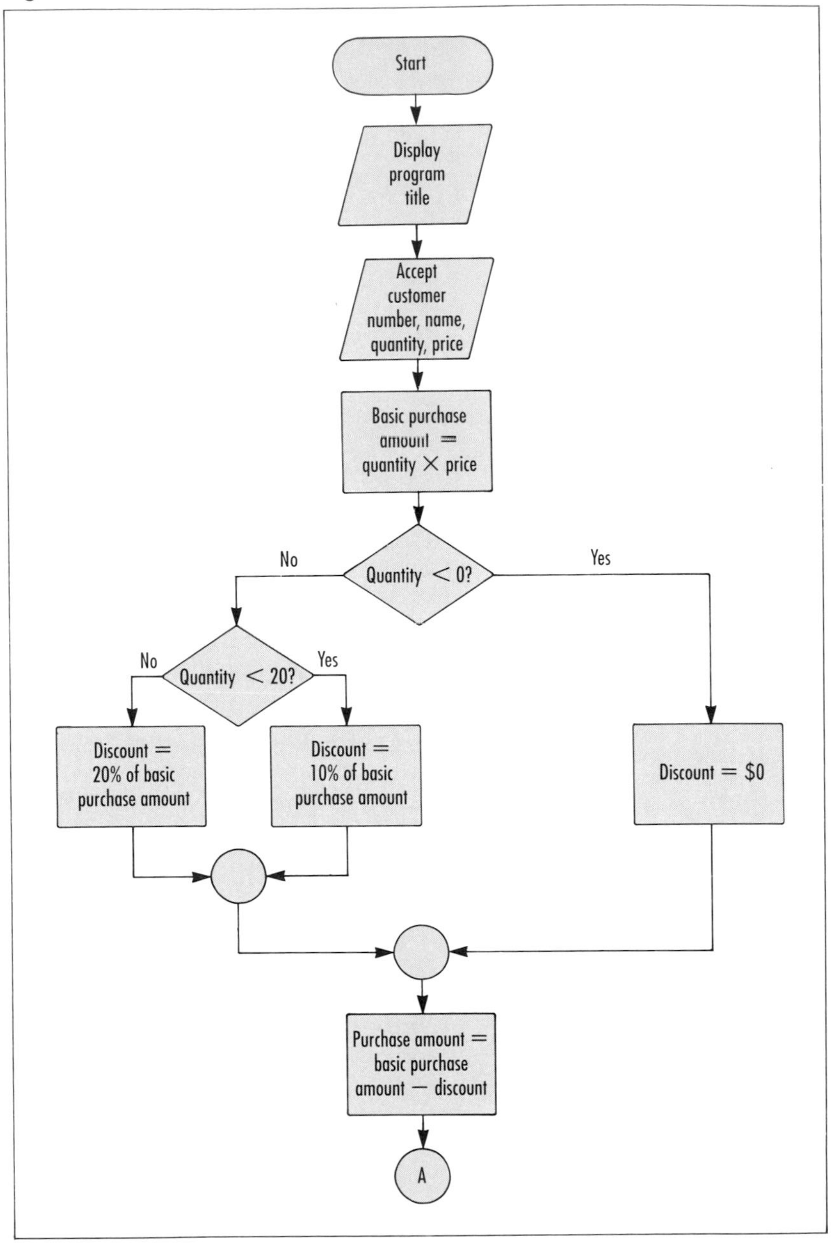

Terms to Remember

Collating Sequence   p. 588

Logical Operator   p. 580

Nested Decisions   p. 584

Relational Expression   p. 572

Relational Operator   p. 573

Truth Value   p. 573

Figure D3–17   Flowchart for the Customer-Order Program (Part 2 of 2)

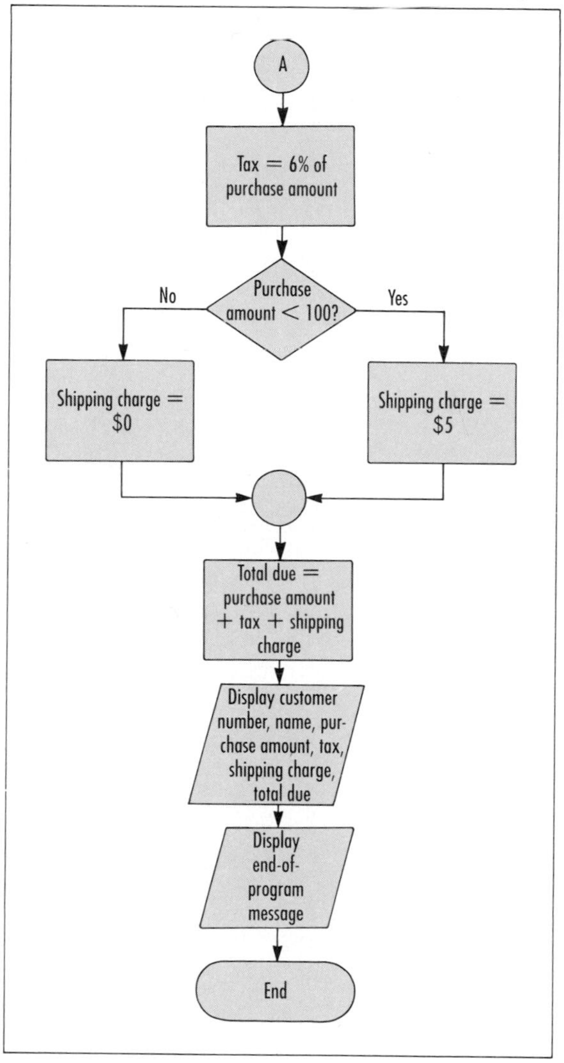

Review Questions

1. What is the meaning of each of the following relational operators?

  a. <=

  b. <>

  c. =

  d. >

2. Assume that the value of I is 2, J is 3, and K is 4. What is the truth value of each of the following relational expressions?

  a. I > J

  b. K <= J + 1

  c. 12 / I + 3 = J ^ 2

  d. I * J <> K + 2

Figure D3–18 The Customer-Order Program

```
100 REM - CUSTOMER ORDER PROGRAM
110 REM - VARIABLES:
120 REM       CUS.NUM     = CUSTOMER NUMBER
130 REM       CUS.NAME$   = CUSTOMER NAME
140 REM       QTY.ORD     = QUANTITY ORDERED
150 REM       UNIT.PRICE  = UNIT PRICE
160 REM       BAS.PUR.AMT = BASIC PURCHASE AMOUNT
170 REM       DISC        = DISCOUNT
180 REM       PUR.AMT     = PURCHASE AMOUNT
190 REM       TAX         = TAX
200 REM       SHP.CHRG    = SHIPPING CHARGE
210 REM       TOTAL       = TOTAL DUE
220 REM
230 REM - DISPLAY TITLE
240 CLS
250 PRINT "CUSTOMER ORDER PROCESSING"
260 PRINT
270 REM - ACCEPT CUSTOMER ORDER DATA
280 INPUT "ENTER CUSTOMER NUMBER: ", CUS.NUM
290 INPUT "ENTER CUSTOMER NAME: ", CUS.NAME$
300 INPUT "ENTER QUANTITY ORDERED: ", QTY.ORD
310 INPUT "ENTER UNIT PRICE: ", UNIT.PRICE
320 REM - COMPUTE PURCHASE AMOUNT
330 LET BAS.PUR.AMT = QTY.ORD * UNIT.PRICE
340 IF QTY.ORD < 10 THEN LET DISC = 0
        ELSE IF QTY.ORD < 20 THEN LET DISC = .1 * BAS.PUR.AMT
        ELSE LET DISC = .2 * BAS.PUR.AMT
350 LET PUR.AMT = BAS.PUR.AMT - DISC
360 REM - COMPUTE TAX
370 LET TAX = .06 * PUR.AMT
380 REM - COMPUTE SHIPPING CHARGE
390 IF PUR.AMT < 100
        THEN LET SHP.CHRG = 5
        ELSE LET SHP.CHRG = 0
400 REM - COMPUTE TOTAL DUE
410 LET TOTAL = PUR.AMT + TAX + SHP.CHRG
420 REM - DISPLAY CHARGE DATA
430 PRINT
440 PRINT "CUSTOMER NUMBER:"; CUS.NUM
450 PRINT "CUSTOMER NAME:    "; CUS.NAME$
460 PRINT "PURCHASE AMOUNT:"; PUR.AMT
470 PRINT "TAX:            "; TAX
480 PRINT "SHIPPING CHARGE:"; SHP.CHRG
490 PRINT "TOTAL DUE:      "; TOTAL
500 REM - DISPLAY END MESSAGE
510 PRINT
520 PRINT "END OF PROCESSING"
530 END
```

3. Consider the following statement:

```
100 IF X >= Y THEN LET Z = 20 ELSE LET Z = 10
```

What is the value of Z after execution of these statements

a. if X is 20 and Y is 10?

b. if X is 20 and Y is 20?

4. Code a statement to add 5 to C if A is greater than B; otherwise add 6 to C.

5. Code a statement that accepts and displays the values of D and E if F is not equal to 100.

Table D3–2   Input Test Data and Expected Output for the Customer-Order Program

Input Test Data				Expected Output			
Customer Number	Customer Name	Quantity Ordered	Unit Price	Purchase Amount	Tax	Shipping Charge	Total Due
1234	JONES	9	11	99	5.94	5	109.94
2345	SMITH	15	8	108	6.48	0	114.48
3456	ANDREWS	30	1	24	1.44	5	30.44
4567	JOHNSON	6	17	102	6.12	0	108.12
5678	BROWN	20	8	128	7.68	0	135.68
6789	ADAMS	19	10	171	10.26	0	181.26

Figure D3–19   Input and Output for Six Test Runs of the Customer-Order Program

```
CUSTOMER ORDER PROCESSING

ENTER CUSTOMER NUMBER: 1234
ENTER CUSTOMER NAME: JONES
ENTER QUANTITY ORDERED: 9
ENTER UNIT PRICE: 11

CUSTOMER NUMBER: 1234
CUSTOMER NAME:    JONES
PURCHASE AMOUNT: 99
TAX:              5.94
SHIPPING CHARGE: 5
TOTAL DUE:        109.94

END OF PROCESSING


CUSTOMER ORDER PROCESSING

ENTER CUSTOMER NUMBER: 2345
ENTER CUSTOMER NAME: SMITH
ENTER QUANTITY ORDERED: 15
ENTER UNIT PRICE: 8

CUSTOMER NUMBER: 2345
CUSTOMER NAME:    SMITH
PURCHASE AMOUNT: 108
TAX:              6.48
SHIPPING CHARGE: 0
TOTAL DUE:        114.48

END OF PROCESSING
```

```
CUSTOMER ORDER PROCESSING

ENTER CUSTOMER NUMBER: 3456
ENTER CUSTOMER NAME: ANDREWS
ENTER QUANTITY ORDERED: 30
ENTER UNIT PRICE: 1

CUSTOMER NUMBER: 3456
CUSTOMER NAME:    ANDREWS
PURCHASE AMOUNT: 24
TAX:              1.44
SHIPPING CHARGE: 5
TOTAL DUE:        30.44

END OF PROCESSING


CUSTOMER ORDER PROCESSING

ENTER CUSTOMER NUMBER: 4567
ENTER CUSTOMER NAME: JOHNSON
ENTER QUANTITY ORDERED: 6
ENTER UNIT PRICE: 17

CUSTOMER NUMBER: 4567
CUSTOMER NAME:    JOHNSON
PURCHASE AMOUNT: 102
TAX:              6.12
SHIPPING CHARGE: 0
TOTAL DUE:        108.12

END OF PROCESSING
```

```
CUSTOMER ORDER PROCESSING

ENTER CUSTOMER NUMBER: 5678
ENTER CUSTOMER NAME: BROWN
ENTER QUANTITY ORDERED: 20
ENTER UNIT PRICE: 8

CUSTOMER NUMBER: 5678
CUSTOMER NAME:    BROWN
PURCHASE AMOUNT: 128
TAX:              7.68
SHIPPING CHARGE: 0
TOTAL DUE:        135.68

END OF PROCESSING


CUSTOMER ORDER PROCESSING

ENTER CUSTOMER NUMBER: 6789
ENTER CUSTOMER NAME: ADAMS
ENTER QUANTITY ORDERED: 19
ENTER UNIT PRICE: 10

CUSTOMER NUMBER: 6789
CUSTOMER NAME:    ADAMS
PURCHASE AMOUNT: 171
TAX:              10.26
SHIPPING CHARGE: 0
TOTAL DUE:        181.26

END OF PROCESSING
```

6. Code one or more statements that assign the larger of X and Y to Z. Did you use an if-then or if-then-else decision? Code another group of statements using the other approach.

7. A program pattern in which one decision is contained in another is called _____.

8. Code a statement that assigns 0, 1, 2, or 3 to I depending on the values of J and K as given in the following table:

		K	
		Less than 5	**5 or More**
J	**Equal to 10**	0	1
	Not Equal to 10	2	3

9. Assume that the value of A\$ is AL, B\$ is ALLAN, and C\$ is ALFRED. What is the truth value of each of the following relational expressions?

a. A\$ = B\$

b. B\$ <> C\$

c. C\$ = "ALFRED "

10. Assume that A\$, B\$, and C\$ have the values given in Question 9. What is the truth value of each of the following relational expressions?

a. A\$ < B\$

b. B\$ <= C\$

c. A\$ >= "AL"

11. Code a statement that increases N by 1 if M\$ equals M, decreases N by 1 if M\$ equals D, and assigns 0 to N if M\$ equals anything else.

12. The input to a program is a whole number that can range from 100 to 200. If the input is 125 or less, the program should print the word YES. If the input is greater than 125, the program should print the word NO. Design input test data, using the strategy discussed in this section, that tests this program.

Programming Problems

1. Commission paid to a salesperson is often based on the amount sold by the person. Assume that the commission rate is 7½% if a person's sales total less than $10,000 and 9% if sales total $10,000 or more. The commission is calculated by multiplying the person's sales by the appropriate commission rate.

   Write a BASIC program that accepts the salesperson's identification number and total sales, calculates the commission, and displays the result along with the identification number. Test the program with data for salesperson number 18735, with sales of $11,250; data for salesperson number 27630, whose sales total $6500; and data for salesperson 31084, whose sales were $10,000.

2. A telephone company's charge for long-distance calls is based not only on the distance but also on the length of time of a call. Assume that between two cities the rate is $1.10 for the first three minutes or fraction

thereof, and $.40 for each additional minute. Data for a customer who made calls between these two cities consists of the customer's number and the length of call.

Write a BASIC program to accept the customer's number and length of call, calculate the charge, and display the customer's number, length of call, and the charge. Test the program by running it with each of the following sets of input data:

Customer Number	Length of Call
9606	8
9735	3
2802	2
7921	5
1509	4
5371	1

3. A real estate office employs several salespeople. At the end of each month the total value of all property sold by each salesperson is used to calculate the person's commission. If total sales exceed $600,000, the commission is 3½% of the sales. If the sales are greater than $300,000 but not more than $600,000, the commission is 3% of the sales. Otherwise, the commission is 2½% of the sales.

Write a BASIC program that accepts the salesperson's number, name, and total sales, performs the necessary commission calculation, and displays the result along with the salesperson's number and total sales.

Test the program by running it with each of the following sets of input data:

Salesperson's Number	Name	Total Sales
1085	WOOD	$652,350
1720	BROWN	$142,500
2531	SHORE	$295,000
3007	KRAFT	$455,500
3219	SADLER	$173,250
4806	MARTINEZ	$682,950
6111	ROSS	$310,000
7932	CAMPBELL	$518,000

4. An electric company charges its customers 5 cents per kilowatt-hour for electricity used, up to the first 100 kilowatt-hours; 4 cents per kilowatt-hour for each of the next 200 kilowatt-hours (up to 300 kilowatt-hours); and 3 cents per kilowatt-hour for all electricity used over 300 kilowatt-hours. Write a BASIC program to calculate the total charge for each customer. Input to the program consists of the customer's number and kilowatt-hours used. Output from the program should give the customer's number, the kilowatt-hours used, and the total charge. Test the program by running it with each of the following sets of input data:

Customer Number	Kilowatt-Hours Used
1065	640
2837	85
3832	220
6721	300
8475	100

5. Write a BASIC program to determine whether a student is a freshman, sophomore, junior, or senior, based on the number of units (credits) that the student has completed. Input to the program consists of the student's number, name, and number of units completed.

A student's classification is based on his or her units completed according to the following schedule:

Units Completed	Classification
Less than 30 units	Freshman
30 units or more but less than 60 units	Sophomore
60 units or more but less than 90 units	Junior
90 units or more	Senior

The output from the program should give the student's number, name, units completed, and the classification (FRESHMAN, SOPHOMORE, JUNIOR, or SENIOR). Test the program by running it with each of the following sets of input data:

Student Number	Name	Units Completed
2352	FULLER	38.0
3639	LARISON	15.5
4007	BRYANT	29.5
4560	MCKAY	67.0
4915	JENSON	103.5
8473	HOLMES	89.0

6. A credit card company bases its evaluation of card applicants on four factors: the applicant's age, how long the applicant has lived at his or her current address, the annual income of the applicant, and how long the applicant has been working at the same job. For each factor, points are added to a total as follows:

Factor	Value	Points Added
Age	20 and under	−10
	21–30	0
	31–50	20
	Over 50	25
At current address	Less than 1 year	−5
	1–3 years	5
	4–8 years	12
	9 or more years	20
Annual income	$15000 or less	0
	$15001–$25000	12
	$25001–$40000	24
	Over $40000	30
At same job	Less than 2 years	−4
	2–4 years	8
	More than 4 years	15

On the basis of the point total, the following action is taken by the company:

Points	Action
−19 to 20	No card issued
21 to 35	Card issued with $500 credit limit
36 to 60	Card issued with $2000 credit limit
61 to 90	Card issued with $5000 credit limit

Write a BASIC program that accepts an applicant's number, age, years at current address, annual income, and years at the same job. Then the program should evaluate the applicant's credit worthiness and display the applicant's number plus a phrase describing the action taken by the company. Test the program by running it with each of the following sets of input data:

Applicant Number	Age	Years at Current Address	Annual Income	Years at Same Job
1234	55	10	$42,000	15
2345	18	0	$10,000	1
3456	35	2	$32,000	4
4567	22	5	$21,500	1
5678	50	1	$25,000	2
6789	31	4	$40,000	5

7. Write a BASIC program to compute final grades for a course. Input to the program is the student's identification number, name, and five letter grades. In the program, convert each letter grade to its equivalent numerical grade according to the following table:

A+	4.3	C	2.0
A	4.0	C–	1.7
A–	3.7	D+	1.3
B+	3.3	D	1.0
B	3.0	D–	0.7
B–	2.7	F+	0.3
C+	2.3	F	0.0

The lowest of the five grades should be dropped, and the remaining four should be averaged (weighted equally). Compute the numeric average, and determine the final letter grade according to the following scale (where G is the numerical grade):

$3.5 \leq G$	A
$2.5 \leq G < 3.5$	B
$1.5 \leq G < 2.5$	C
$0.5 \leq G < 1.5$	D
$G < 0.5$	F

Output from the program should give the student's identification number, name, numerical grade, and letter grade. Test the program by running it with each of the following sets of input data:

Student Number	Name	Grades
1015	SMITH	B,C+,B+,A–,C–
1130	MILLER	A,C–,C,D,D+
1426	LEE	B–,A–,B+,A+,A
1703	JACKSON	C,F+,D,F,D–
1933	EDWARDS	A+,A+,A,A,A+

SECTION 4
PROGRAMMING FOR REPETITION

Each program example you have seen so far has solved a problem for one set of input data. For example, the tuition-calculation program in the last section (Figure D3–1) solved the tuition problem with the data for one student. If you want to use this program to compute the tuition for more than one student, you have to run the program again with different data. An easier approach, however, is to design the program so that it automatically repeats.

This example illustrates one situation in which program repetition is useful. In this section you will see several other situations, and you will learn BASIC statements and programming techniques for repetition. Repetition is accomplished by a *loop*, which is a group of statements that is repeatedly executed. Loops can be created in several ways in BASIC. The biggest problem with loops, however, is not how to create a loop but, rather, how to stop repeating the loop. *Loop control* involves techniques to get the computer to stop looping. After completing this section you should be able to write programs that have loops and that use a variety of loop-control techniques.

THE WHILE STATEMENT

One BASIC statement used for loop control is the WIIILE statement. The form of this statement varies with different versions of BASIC. This section describes the form of the WHILE statement found in Microsoft BASIC. It is used with the WEND statement to form a **WHILE loop.**

WHILE Loops

The syntax of the WHILE and WEND statements and their pattern of use in a WHILE loop are as follows:

```
ln WHILE relational expression
          .
          .
          .
       statements
          .
          .
          .
ln WEND
```

The WHILE statement contains a relational expression; any relational expression like those used in IF statements can be used in WHILE statements. Several relational expressions combined with logical operators (AND and OR) can also be used. Following the WHILE statement comes the sequence of statements that is to be repeatedly executed—that is, the statements in the loop. At the end of the loop must be a WEND statement. For example, the following is a valid WHILE loop:

```
40 WHILE I <= 10
50    PRINT I
60    LET I = I + 1
70 WEND
```

The effect of the WHILE and WEND statements is to execute repeatedly the statements in between—that is, the statements in the loop—as long as the relational expression in the WHILE statement is true. In the previous example, the PRINT and LET statements form the loop and are repeatedly executed as long as the value of I is less than or equal to ten. As soon as the relational expression becomes false, the computer stops repeating the loop and continues with the next statement after the WEND statement.

The relational expression is tested at the *beginning* of each execution of the loop. As a consequence, the loop may not be executed at all. For example, if the value of I before execution of the previous WHILE loop were 11, the relational expression would be false at the beginning and the loop would not be executed.

Notice in the example that the statements in the loop have been indented. This is a common program style that makes it easier to see the loop in a program.

An Illustrative Program

To illustrate the use of WHILE loops, consider the tuition-calculation program discussed in Section 3 (Figure D3–1). A loop that repeats statements that process the data for one student can be added to this program. The main concern is how to stop the loop from repeating when there is no more student data to process.

One technique for stopping this type of loop is to use an input data value to indicate the end of the regular data. Each time input data is accepted, the program checks whether the special end-of-data input has been entered. If not, the program continues with the normal execution of the statements in the loop. When the end-of-data input has been entered, the program ends the loop.

Usually the end-of-data input is a value for one of the variables that is not used for any other input data. This is called a **trailer value**. In the tuition-calculation program, the input consists of the student's identification number and number of units. You can use a special identification number as a trailer value. The value would have to be one that is not used as an actual student's identification number. Then, each time input data is accepted, the program can test for this value.

Assume that the trailer value for the tuition data is the identification number 9999. Figure D4–1a shows the program with this form of loop control. Figure D4–1b shows the input and output from one run of this program. Notice that the last input is the trailer value.

The program in Figure D4–1 first accepts the identification number (ID). Then it checks the value of ID in a relational expression in the WHILE statement. If ID is *not* equal to 9999, the program executes the statements in the loop. If the value of ID equals 9999, the program stops the loop.

The statements in the loop in this program first accept the number of units, then find the tuition, and finally display the results. At the end of the loop, just before the WEND statement, is an INPUT statement

Figure D4–1   The Tuition-Calculation Program with a Loop

(a)   The Program

```
100 REM - TUITION CALCULATION PROGRAM
110 REM - VARIABLES:
120 REM        ID    = STUDENT ID
130 REM        UNITS = NUMBER OF UNITS
140 REM        TUIT  = TUITION
150 REM
160 CLS
170 PRINT "TUITION CALCULATION"
180 PRINT
190 INPUT "ENTER STUDENT ID OR 9999 TO STOP: ", ID
200 WHILE ID <> 9999
210   INPUT "ENTER NUMBER OF UNITS: ", UNITS
220   IF UNITS <= 12 THEN LET TUIT = 350 ELSE LET TUIT = 350 + 20 * (UNITS - 12)
230   PRINT
240   PRINT "STUDENT ID:"; ID
250   PRINT "TUITION:"; TUIT
260   PRINT
270   INPUT "ENTER STUDENT ID OR 9999 TO STOP: ", ID
280 WEND
290 PRINT
300 PRINT "END OF PROGRAM"
310 END
```

(b)   Input and Output

```
TUITION CALCULATION

ENTER STUDENT ID OR 9999 TO STOP: 1234
ENTER NUMBER OF UNITS: 6

STUDENT ID: 1234
TUITION: 350

ENTER STUDENT ID OR 9999 TO STOP: 3456
ENTER NUMBER OF UNITS: 15

STUDENT ID: 3456
TUITION: 410

ENTER STUDENT ID OR 9999 TO STOP: 9999

END OF PROGRAM
```

that accepts the next identification number (ID). Thus, this program accepts the value of ID, which is the variable used for the trailer value, in two places: one just before the WHILE statement, and the other at the end of the loop, just before the WEND statement. The WHILE statement checks that the value of ID is *not* equal to the trailer value.

It is important to understand why there are two INPUT statements for ID and why they are placed where they are in this program. The first INPUT statement, before the loop, accepts the *first* value for ID. The WHILE statement then tests that this value is not equal to 9999 and executes the loop if this condition is true. The second INPUT statement, at the end of the loop, accepts the *next* value for ID. Immediately after doing this, the computer goes back to the WHILE statement and tests that the value is not equal to 9999. If 9999 had not been entered, the loop would be repeated, but if 9999 were entered, the loop would be terminated. By placing this INPUT statement at the *end* of the loop, the next thing the computer does after the input data is accepted is to check for the trailer value. The first INPUT statement, before the loop, is necessary to start the loop going.

Pseudocode of Programs with Loops

Figure D4–2 shows the pseudocode for this program. In the pseudocode, the loop is indicated by using the words DO WHILE, followed by the condition that the student ID is not equal to 9999. The steps in the loop follow this line, and the word END-DO comes after these steps.

Flowcharts of Programs with Loops

Figure D4–3 shows the flowchart of this program. A loop is shown in a flowchart by a flowline that extends from the end of the loop to its beginning. The decision symbol is used at the beginning of the loop for the test that repeats the loop. In Figure D4–3, this test checks that the student ID is not equal to 9999. If this is true, the loop repeats; otherwise, the loop terminates.

Figure D4–2   Pseudocode of the Tuition-Calculation Program with a Loop

```
Display program title
Accept student ID
DO WHILE student ID not equal to 9999
  Accept units
  IF units ≤ 12 THEN
    Tuition = $350
  ELSE
    Tuition = $350 + $20 x (units - 12)
  END-IF
  Display student ID, tuition
  Accept student ID
END-DO
Display end-of-program message
End
```

Figure D4–3   Flowchart of the Tuition-Calculation Program with a Loop

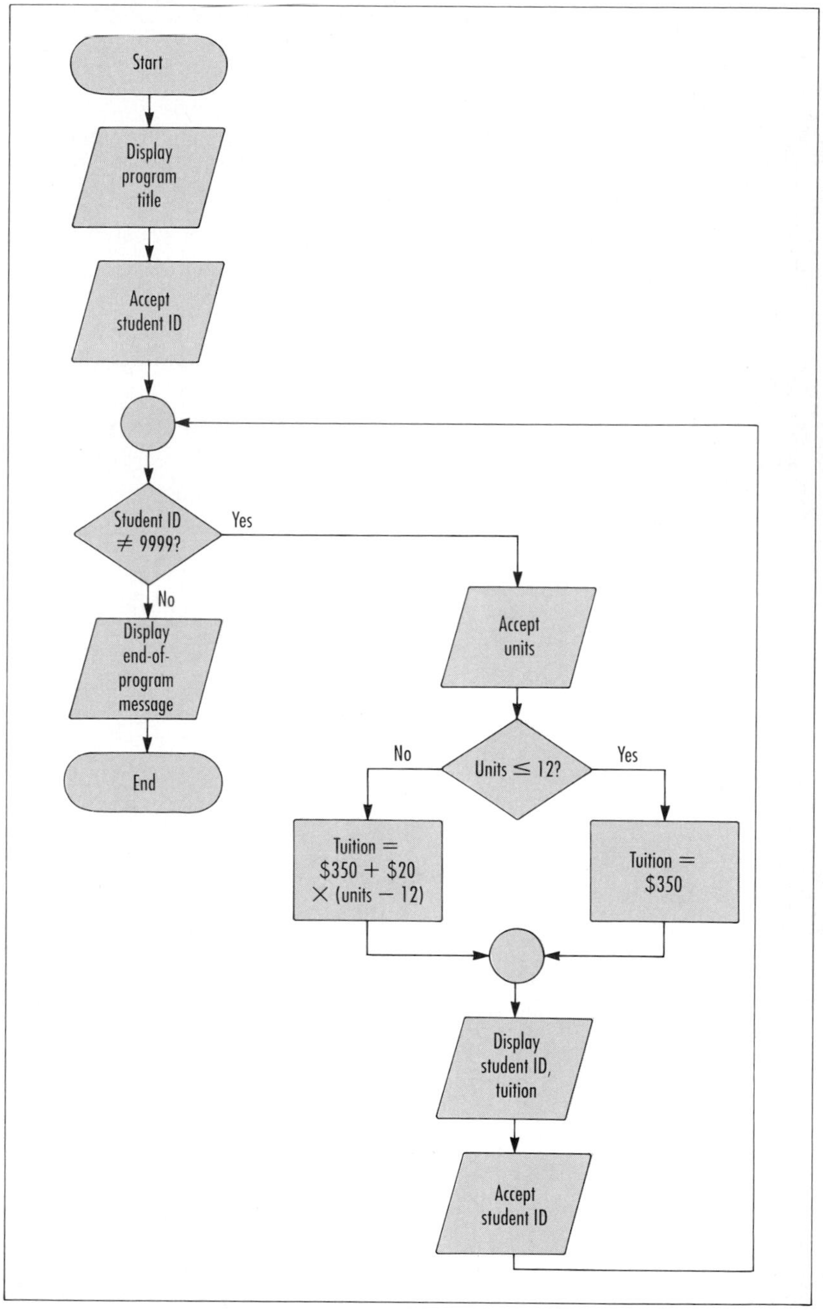

LOOP STRUCTURES IN BASIC

Recall from Chapter 12 that two types of loop structures are *while loops* and *until loops*. A while loop is repeated as long as a condition is true, and an until loop is repeated until a condition becomes true. In addition, the condition in a while loop is checked at the beginning of the loop, whereas the condition in an until loop is checked at the end. These structures are represented graphically in Figure D4–4.

Loop Structures in Microsoft BASIC

A while loop is easily created in Microsoft BASIC, using WHILE and WEND statements. Figure D4–5 shows how this is done. The tuition-calculation program (Figure D4–1) demonstrated this type of loop. An until loop cannot be created in Microsoft BASIC except by using IF and GOTO statements, as we are about to describe. This technique, however, should be avoided when other loop structures are available. Because while loops are available with Microsoft BASIC, it is unnecessary to have until loops (although in some situations it may be convenient).

Loop Structures in Other Versions of BASIC

If statements such as the WHILE and WEND statements are available, they should be used for looping. In some versions of BASIC, however,

Figure D4–4   Loop Structures

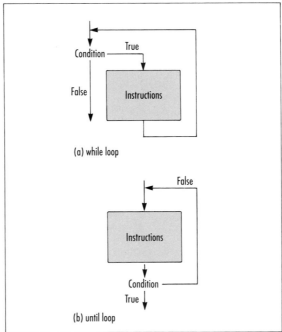

Figure D4–5   While Loop in BASIC Using the WHILE and WEND Statements

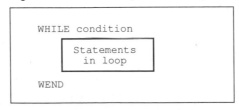

these statements are not provided. Then the IF and GOTO statements, discussed in Section 3, can be used for looping.

Figure D4–6 shows how the loop structures are created in BASIC using IF and GOTO statements. To create a while loop, an IF statement is used at the beginning to branch out of the loop if the complement of the while loop's condition is true. A GOTO statement is used at the end to repeat the loop. To create an until loop, an IF statement is used at the end of the loop to repeat the loop if the complement of the until loop's condition is true. No GOTO statement is used in the until loop.

The while loop in the tuition-calculation program in Figure D4–1 can be rewritten using IF and GOTO statements. Figure D4–7 shows the result. (This loop also uses the IF and GOTO statements for the decision because if a version of BASIC does not have a WHILE statement it usually does not have an IF-THEN-ELSE statement.) In this example, the IF statement at the beginning of the loop branches out of the loop if the value of ID is 9999. The GOTO statement at the end of the loop branches to the IF statement to cause the loop to be repeated.

As a final reminder, the IF and GOTO statements should not be used for loops unless no alternative is available. If they are used, they should be used only in the patterns shown in Figure D4–6. They will not be used in future examples.

PROGRAM LOGIC FOR LOOP CONTROL

The WHILE statement can be used for several different types of looping structures. These types of loops and how they are controlled with the WHILE statement are discussed here.

Input Loops

An **input loop** is a loop that has an input operation within it that is used to control the loop. The tuition-calculation program discussed earlier (Figure D4–1) contained an input loop. There are several techniques that can be used for input loop control. One technique is to use a trailer value to signal the end of the input data. This technique was used in the tuition-calculation program.

Figure D4–6   Decision Structures in BASIC Using the IF and GOTO Statements

(a)   While Loop   **(b)**   Until Loop

```
ln1 IF complement of condition THEN ln2
        ┌─────────────────┐
        │   Statements    │
        │    in loop      │
        └─────────────────┘
      GOTO ln1
ln2 (next statement)
```

```
ln  ┌─────────────────┐
    │   Statements    │
    │    in loop      │
    └─────────────────┘
    IF complement of condition THEN ln
    (next statement)
```

Figure D4–7   A While Loop Using IF and GOTO Statements

```
200 IF ID = 9999 THEN 290
210   INPUT "ENTER NUMBER OF UNITS: ", UNITS
220   IF UNITS <= 12 THEN 227
222     LET TUIT = 350 + 20 * (UNITS - 12)
225   GOTO 230
227     LET TUIT = 350
230   PRINT
240   PRINT "STUDENT ID:"; ID
250   PRINT "TUITION:"; TUIT
260   PRINT
270   INPUT "ENTER STUDENT ID OR 9999 TO STOP: ", ID
280 GOTO 200
290 (next statement)
```

Another technique used to control an input loop is to ask the user whether he or she wishes to repeat the loop. The question is usually asked in a prompt in an INPUT statement that accepts the response from the user. The response is usually a string (YES or NO), and the WHILE statement compares this string response with a string constant to decide whether to repeat the loop.

Figure D4–8 shows how this technique can be used in the tuition-calculation program. The string variable RES$ is used for the user response. The user answers YES or NO to the question of whether he or she wants to compute the tuition for a student. The WHILE statement compares the value of RES$ with the string constant "YES," and repeats the loop as long as the condition is true. As soon as the user enters NO to the question, the loop ends.

Notice that, as with the tuition-calculation program using a trailer value (Figure D4–1), there are two INPUT statements for the variable (RES$) that controls the loop. One is just before the WHILE statement, and the other is at the end of the loop, just before the WEND statement. The INPUT statement for the student ID, however, appears only once, at the beginning of the loop, because it is not used for loop control in this program.

Processing Loops

A **processing loop** is one that is controlled by some condition of the data that is processed in the loop, not by an input value. Usually, computations take place within the loop that affect the value of some variable. Each time the loop is executed, the variable is used to test whether the loop should be terminated. If the loop is properly designed, the test will eventually become true and the program will end the loop.

As an example, consider the problem of determining the amount of time that it takes for a bank deposit to double at a given interest rate. Assume that $1000 is put into a bank at 8% interest compounded annually. This means that at the end of the first year, the interest is 8% of $1000, or $80, which is added to the original deposit to give a balance of $1080. At the end of the second year, the interest is 8% of $1080, or $86.40. The balance is then $1166.40. Thus, the interest is added to the balance at the end of each year and is used in the next year's interest

Figure D4–8   The Tuition-Calculation Program with an Input Loop Controlled by a User Response Test

(a) The Program

```
100 REM - TUITION CALCULATION PROGRAM
110 REM - VARIABLES:
120 REM        RES$  = RESPONSE TO QUESTION
130 REM        ID    = STUDENT ID
140 REM        UNITS = NUMBER OF UNITS
150 REM        TUIT  = TUITION
160 REM
170 CLS
180 PRINT "TUITION CALCULATION"
190 PRINT
200 INPUT "DO YOU WANT TO COMPUTE THE TUITION FOR A STUDENT? ", RES$
210 WHILE RES$ = "YES"
220   PRINT
230   INPUT "ENTER STUDENT ID: ", ID
240   INPUT "ENTER NUMBER OF UNITS: ", UNITS
250   IF UNITS <= 12 THEN LET TUIT = 350 ELSE LET TUIT = 350 + 20 * (UNITS - 12)
260   PRINT
270   PRINT "STUDENT ID:"; ID
280   PRINT "TUITION:"; TUIT
290   PRINT
300   INPUT "DO YOU WANT TO COMPUTE THE TUITION FOR ANOTHER STUDENT? ", RES$
310 WEND
320 PRINT
330 PRINT "END OF PROGRAM"
340 END
```

(b) Input and Output

```
TUITION CALCULATION

DO YOU WANT TO COMPUTE THE TUITION FOR A STUDENT? YES

ENTER STUDENT ID: 1234
ENTER NUMBER OF UNITS: 6

STUDENT ID: 1234
TUITION: 350

DO YOU WANT TO COMPUTE THE TUITION FOR ANOTHER STUDENT? YES

ENTER STUDENT ID: 3456
ENTER NUMBER OF UNITS: 15

STUDENT ID: 3456
TUITION: 410

DO YOU WANT TO COMPUTE THE TUITION FOR ANOTHER STUDENT? NO

END OF PROGRAM
```

calculation. The problem is to write a program that displays a table of yearly interest and balance until the deposit has doubled to $2000.

Figure D4–9 shows a program that accomplishes this. There are no INPUT statements in this program because the program does not require any input data. The variable BAL is the bank balance; initially, BAL is 1000. YEAR is a variable that counts the number of years; for the first year's calculation, YEAR is 1. The loop is controlled by a WHILE statement that repeats the loop as long as BAL is less than 2000. Within the loop, the current year's interest (INTEREST) is calculated by multiplying

BAL by .08. The value of INTEREST is then added to BAL to give the new balance. The output is then displayed, and YEAR is increased by 1 for the next year. The loop stops repeating when BAL is greater than or equal to 2000. (The output from this program, shown in Figure D4–5b, is not exact for some years because of the way the computer represents numbers internally. The error, however, is very small.)

The program in Figure D4–9 shows how headings can be displayed above columns of output. The PRINT statement at line 190 causes the headings to be displayed in successive print zones. Notice that this PRINT statement is outside the loop. If it were in the loop, the headings would be displayed each time the loop is repeated.

The program also demonstrates the need for *initializing* variables, which means assigning beginning values to variables. You can never assume that a variable has any known value unless you assign a value to it. Thus, in the program in Figure D4–9, you cannot assume that BAL equals 1000 or that YEAR is 1. These values must be assigned to the variables at the beginning of the program, before the loop. If this is not done, zero will be used for these variables. (Even if the initial value of a variable is supposed to be zero, it is a good idea to initialize it in the program just to be sure.)

Counting Loops

A special type of processing loop, called a **counting loop**, is controlled by counting the number of times that the loop is repeated and ending the loop when the count reaches some desired number. This approach uses a variable as a *counter*. Before entering the loop, the counter is *initialized* to some beginning value. Each time the loop is executed, the value of the counter is *modified*, usually by increasing its value by 1. Also, each time the loop is executed, the counter is *tested* to determine whether its value has exceeded some final value.

Figure D4–9 The Interest-Calculation Program

(a) The Program

(b) Output

```
100 REM - INTEREST CALCULATION PROGRAM
110 REM - VARIABLES:
120 REM      BAL      = BANK BALANCE
130 REM      YEAR     = YEAR
140 REM      INTEREST = INTEREST EARNED
150 REM
160 CLS
170 PRINT "         INTEREST CALCULATION"
180 PRINT
190 PRINT "YEAR", "INTEREST", "BALANCE"
200 PRINT
210 LET BAL = 1000
220 LET YEAR = 1
230 WHILE BAL < 2000
240    LET INTEREST = .08 * BAL
250    LET BAL = BAL + INTEREST
260    PRINT YEAR, INTEREST, BAL
270    LET YEAR = YEAR + 1
280 WEND
290 END
```

```
          INTEREST CALCULATION

YEAR          INTEREST        BALANCE

1               80            1080
2               86.39999      1166.4
3               93.31199      1259.712
4               100.777       1360.489
5               108.8391      1469.328
6               117.5463      1586.874
7               126.95        1713.824
8               137.1059      1850.93
9               148.0744      1999.005
10              159.9204      2158.925
```

As an example, the statements in Figure D4–10 show the general form of a loop that is executed 100 times. In this example, the counter is the variable K. Initially, K is assigned the value 1 with a LET statement. Then K is tested in a WHILE statement to see if it is less than or equal to 100. If this is the case, the computer executes the loop. If K is greater than 100, the loop is terminated. At the end of the loop, just before the WEND statement, the value of K is increased by 1 with a LET statement.

Notice that the WHILE statement in Figure D4–10 is such that the loop is repeated as long as K is less than *or equal to* 100. This is necessary to ensure that the loop is executed exactly 100 times. If the WHILE statement were coded so that the computer repeated the loop only when the counter was less than 100, the loop would be executed just 99 times.

The interest-calculation program in Figure D4–9 can be modified to use this technique. Assume that you want to display a table of interest and bank balance for five years. The variable YEAR may be used to count the number of years and, at the same time, the number of times that the loop is executed. The modified program is shown in Figure D4–11. In this program, YEAR is initialized to 1 before the loop. Each time through the loop, YEAR is increased by 1. The loop is repeated as long as YEAR is less than or equal to 5.

Figure D4–10   A Counting Loop

```
25 LET K = 1                    (initialize counter)
35 WHILE K <= 100               (test counter)

        ┌─────────────┐
        │  Statements │
        │  in loop    │
        └─────────────┘

75   LET K = K + 1              (modify counter)
85 WEND
```

Figure D4–11   The Interest-Calculation Program with a Counting Loop

(a)   The Program

(b)   Output

```
100 REM - INTEREST CALCULATION PROGRAM
110 REM - VARIABLES:
120 REM      BAL       = BANK BALANCE
130 REM      YEAR      = YEAR
140 REM      INTEREST  = INTEREST EARNED
150 REM
160 CLS
170 PRINT "         INTEREST CALCULATION"
180 PRINT
190 PRINT "YEAR", "INTEREST", "BALANCE"
200 PRINT
210 LET BAL = 1000
220 LET YEAR = 1
230 WHILE YEAR <= 5
240   LET INTEREST = .08 * BAL
250   LET BAL = BAL  + INTEREST
260   PRINT YEAR, INTEREST, BAL
270   LET YEAR = YEAR + 1
280 WEND
290 END
```

	INTEREST CALCULATION	
YEAR	INTEREST	BALANCE
1	80	1080
2	86.39999	1166.4
3	93.31199	1259.712
4	100.777	1360.489
5	108.8391	1469.328

As another example of this form of loop control, consider the problem of finding the total and average of ten test scores. Assume that the test scores are to be entered one at a time at the keyboard and that there is no trailer value. The program must accept the data, calculate the total and average, and display the results.

The program is shown in Figure D4–12. The variable TOTAL is used to accumulate the total of the test scores. Each time through the loop, the INPUT statement accepts a test score (SCORE). The value of SCORE is then added to TOTAL, and the result is assigned to TOTAL. Notice that initially TOTAL is set equal to zero outside the loop so that, with the first execution of the loop, the first test score is added to zero. Each successive time through the loop, TOTAL is increased by the value of another test score until all ten scores have been entered and added.

The loop in this program is controlled by using the variable I as a counter. Initially, I is set equal to 1. Each time through the loop, I is increased by 1 and tested to see whether it is less than or equal to 10. When I exceeds 10, the program ends the loop and calculates the average by dividing TOTAL by 10. Then the output is displayed and the program terminates.

In these examples, the counter is initialized to 1 and modified by 1 each time the loop is repeated. This is not essential, however; you can also vary the way in which counting is done. The initial value of the counter can be any value, depending on the problem. You can modify the counter by adding or subtracting any reasonable value. The test condition is determined by the initial value of the counter, how it is modified each time through the loop, and the number of times you wish to execute the loop.

Figure D4–12   A Program That Finds the Total and Average of Ten Test Scores

(a)   The Program

(b)   Input and Output

```
100 REM - TEST SCORE AVERAGING PROGRAM
110 REM - VARIABLES:
120 REM       SCORE    = TEST SCORE
130 REM       TOTAL    = TOTAL OF TEST SCORES
140 REM       AVG      = AVERAGE TEST SCORE
150 REM       I        = COUNTER
160 REM
170 CLS
180 PRINT "TEST SCORE AVERAGING"
190 PRINT
200 PRINT "ENTER 10 TEST SCORES - ONE PER LINE"
210 LET TOTAL = 0
220 LET I = 1
230 WHILE I <= 10
240    INPUT SCORE
250    LET TOTAL = TOTAL + SCORE
260    LET I = I + 1
270 WEND
280 LET AVG = TOTAL / 10
290 PRINT
300 PRINT "THE TOTAL IS"; TOTAL
310 PRINT "THE AVERAGE IS"; AVG
320 END
```

```
TEST SCORE AVERAGING

ENTER 10 TEST SCORES - ONE PER LINE
? 85
? 92
? 77
? 54
? 89
? 100
? 72
? 78
? 82
? 53

THE TOTAL IS 782
THE AVERAGE IS 78.2
```

NESTED LOOPS

Within a loop there may be other loops. Such a combination is referred to as **nested loops**. Any type of loop may be nested in another loop. Thus, a processing loop may be nested in another processing loop or in an input loop, and an input loop may be nested in another input loop or in a processing loop. Loops can be nested within nested loops. For example, a processing loop may be nested in another processing loop, which is nested in an input loop. There is no limit to the number of loops that can be nested.

When one loop is nested within another, you think of the most encompassing loop as the *outer loop* and the loop that is nested as the *inner loop*. During execution of the program, each repetition of the outer loop causes the statements in the inner loop to be repeated as many times as the inner loop requires.

In BASIC, nested loops can be created by putting one WHILE loop within another to form *nested WHILE loops*. The only restriction is that each WHILE statement must have a corresponding WEND statement.

To illustrate the use of nested WHILE loops, assume that you want to determine the amount of time it will take for a $1000 bank deposit to double at interest rates varying from 6% to 10% in 1% increments. One approach is to run the program in Figure D4–9 five times, each time using a different interest rate in the interest calculation. A better approach is to put another loop into the program that repeats the interest calculation five times, each with a different rate. The resulting program is shown in Figure D4–13.

In this program, the outer WHILE loop is repeated once for each interest rate, which is the variable, RATE. The inner WHILE loop calculates the interest, accumulates the bank balance, and counts the years. Notice that each WHILE statement has a matching WEND statement. All output is displayed after the inner loop is terminated. The variable for the year (YEAR) is decreased by 1 before the results are displayed to compensate for the extra year that is added to YEAR just before the inner loop is terminated.

This program uses indentation to show the loops and the nesting. All the statements that are in the outer loop (except the WHILE and WEND statements) are indented. All the statements that are in the inner loop (except the WHILE and WEND statements) are indented further. This style gives a visual clue to the program's organization.

The pseudocode for this program is shown in Figure D4–14. Notice that each loop is clearly shown in the pseudocode with its own DO WHILE and END-DO lines.

The flowchart for this program is given in Figure D4–15. The nested loops appear clearly in the flowchart. Each begins with a decision symbol that indicates the condition under which the loop is to be repeated, and ends with a flowline that returns to the beginning of the loop.

Nested loops can be difficult to understand, especially when loops are nested within other nested loops. In general, it is best to nest no more than two or three loops so that the program's logic is not too complex.

Figure D4–13 The Interest-Calculation Program with Nested Loops

(a) The Program   **(b)** Output

```
                              100 REM - INTEREST CALCULATION PROGRAM       INTEREST CALCULATION
                              110 REM - VARIABLES:
                              120 REM      BAL      = BANK BALANCE          INTEREST RATE   6
                              130 REM      RATE     = INTEREST RATE         FINAL YEAR      12
                              140 REM      YEAR     = YEAR                  FINAL BALANCE   2012.197
                              150 REM         INTEREST = INTEREST EARNED
                              160 REM                                       INTEREST RATE   7
                              170 CLS                                       FINAL YEAR      11
                              180 PRINT "INTEREST CALCULATION"              FINAL BALANCE   2104.852
                              190 PRINT
                              200 LET RATE = 6                              INTEREST RATE   8
                        ┌──── 210 WHILE RATE <= 10                         FINAL YEAR      10
                        │     220   LET BAL = 1000                          FINAL BALANCE   2158.925
                        │     230   LET YEAR = 1
                        │ ┌── 240   WHILE BAL < 2000                       INTEREST RATE   9
                        │ │   250     LET INTEREST = (RATE / 100) * BAL     FINAL YEAR      9
Outer      Inner        │ │   260     LET BAL = BAL + INTEREST              FINAL BALANCE   2171.893
loop       loop         │ │   270     LET YEAR = YEAR + 1
                        │ └── 280   WEND                                   INTEREST RATE   10
                        │     290   LET YEAR = YEAR - 1                     FINAL YEAR      8
                        │     300   PRINT "INTEREST RATE", RATE             FINAL BALANCE   2143.589
                        │     310   PRINT "FINAL YEAR", YEAR
                        │     320   PRINT "FINAL BALANCE", BAL
                        │     330   PRINT
                        │     340   LET RATE = RATE + 1
                        └──── 350 WEND
                              360 END
```

THE FOR STATEMENT

Counting loops plays an important role in programming. Because of the importance of this type of loop, BASIC provides two special statements—the FOR statement and the NEXT statement—for the control of counting loops. A loop that is controlled by these statements is called a **FOR loop**.

Figure D4–14 Pseudocode of the Interest-Calculation Program with Nested Loops

```
Display program title
Rate = 6%
DO WHILE rate ≤ 10%
  Balance = $1000
  Year = 1
  DO WHILE balance < $2000
    Interest = (rate / 100) x balance
    Add interest to balance
    Increase year by 1
  END-DO
  Decrease year by 1
  Display rate, year, balance
  Increase rate by 1%
END-DO
End
```

Figure D4–15   Flowchart of the Interest-Calculation Program with Nested Loops

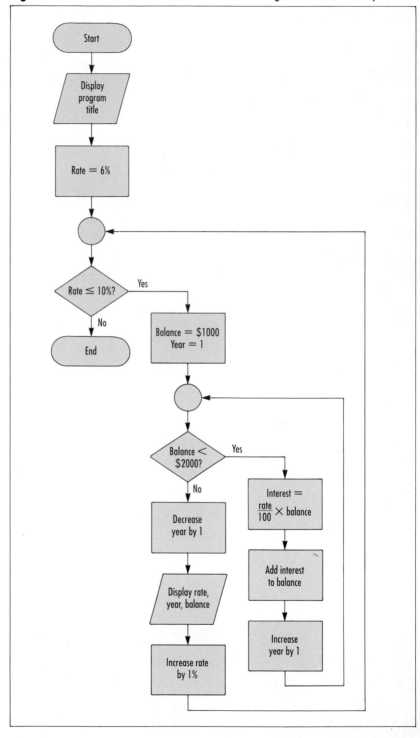

FOR Loops

The syntax of the FOR and NEXT statements and their pattern of use in a FOR loop are as follows:

```
ln FOR control variable = initial value TO limit STEP increment
     .
     .
     statements
     .
     .
     .
ln NEXT control variable
```

The FOR and NEXT statements always appear in pairs; there can never be a FOR statement without a corresponding NEXT statement, and vice versa. A FOR loop begins with a FOR statement, contains any number of BASIC statements, and ends with a NEXT statement. In the FOR statement, the *control variable* is a numeric variable that serves as a counter. The NEXT statement must contain the same control variable as the FOR statement. The *initial value*, *limit*, and *increment* in the FOR statement are each a numeric constant, variable, or complex expression. They determine how many times the loop is executed.

As an example, consider the following FOR and NEXT statements:

```
10 FOR J = 1 TO 50 STEP 1
     .
     .
     .
70 NEXT J
```

The control variable is J, which is the same in the FOR statement and the NEXT statement. The initial value is 1, the limit is 50, and the increment is 1.

The effect of a FOR loop is to execute repeatedly the statements between the FOR and NEXT statements. The first time the statements are executed, the control variable is assigned the initial value. Each succeeding time, when the NEXT statement is reached, the increment is added to the value of the control variable. When the value of the control variable becomes *greater than* the limit, the computer stops the loop and continues with the statement immediately following the NEXT statement.

In the previous example, the control variable, J, is assigned the initial value, 1, for the first execution of the loop. When the NEXT statement is executed, the increment, 1, is added to J to make it equal to 2. Each succeeding time through the loop, J is increased by 1 until its value is greater than the limit, 50. Then the computer stops repeating the loop and goes on to the statement following statement 70 (the NEXT statement). Thus, this loop is executed exactly 50 times.

As another example, consider the following FOR loop:

```
15 FOR K = 10 TO 20 STEP 3
                .
                .
                .
75 NEXT K
```

The control variable is K, the initial value is 10, the limit is 20, and the increment is 3. This loop is executed four times. The first time it is executed, K is 10. Then the control variable is incremented by 3 and assigned the value 13, and the loop is executed a second time. Next, K is incremented again by 3 to get 16, and the loop is executed a third time. Then 3 is added to K to obtain 19 for the fourth repetition of the loop. After this, the increment is added to K to get 22. But because 22 is greater than the limit, 20, the loop is *not* repeated again. Instead, the computer continues with the statement following the NEXT statement.

With many FOR loops, the increment is 1. When this is the case, the word STEP and the increment can be omitted. For example, the following FOR statement is valid:

```
10 FOR J = 1 TO 50
```

Because no increment is given, the computer assumes it is 1. If any increment other than 1 is needed, the STEP must be included.

Besides constants, variables can be used for the initial value, limit, and increment. For example, the following FOR statement uses variables for the initial value and limit:

```
20 FOR K = I TO L STEP 5
```

The values of the variables when the program is run determine the initial value and limit.

When a FOR loop is used, you do *not* use separate statements to initialize, test, and modify the counter and to repeat the loop. These operations are implied by the FOR and NEXT statements. Still, you must be aware of the order in which the computer performs these operations. First, the control variable is initialized. Then the test is made to determine whether the control variable is greater than the limit. Next, the statements in the loop are executed. Then the increment is added to the control variable. Finally, the loop is repeated.

Notice that test of the control variable is at the beginning of the loop, and that it is therefore possible to code a FOR loop that is never executed. For example, consider the following loop:

```
25 FOR M = A TO B
            .
            .
            .
65 NEXT M
```

If A has a value of 50, and B is 40, the initial value is greater than the limit. Hence, the loop will not be executed at all.

The initial value, limit, and increment may be any reasonable values. This means that any of these may be positive, negative, or zero (although the increment should not be zero). For example, the following FOR statement is valid:

```
30 FOR I = -10 TO 0 STEP 1
```

The first time the FOR loop for this statement is executed, the value of I is –10. Then 1 is added to I, making it –9 for the second execution of the loop. The value of I is incremented by 1 for each successive time through the loop. The last time the loop is executed, I is zero.

If the increment is negative, the FOR loop, in effect, counts backward. For example, the following FOR statement causes the value of J to be decreased by 1 each time the loop is executed:

```
40 FOR J = 10 TO 1 STEP -1
```

When the increment is negative, the loop terminates when the value of the control variable is *less than* the test value. In this example, the value of J is 1 during the last execution of the loop. Then –1 is added to J, decreasing its value to zero. Because J is now less than 1, the limit, the loop is not repeated again.

The initial value, limit, and increment need not be whole numbers. For example, the following FOR statement is acceptable:

```
50 FOR X = .05 TO 1 STEP .01
```

The initial value is .05, the limit is 1, and the increment is .01. Thus, the control variable, X, varies from .05 to 1 in increments of .01.

Besides constants and variables, complex numeric expressions can be used for the initial value, limit, and increment in a FOR loop. The value of any expression is evaluated at the time the FOR statement is encountered. The resulting value is then used for loop control. For example, consider the following FOR statement:

```
60 FOR Y = A TO A + B STEP 2 * C
```

If A is 5, B is 20, and C is 3 when this statement is executed, the initial value of Y is 5, the limit is 25, and the increment is 6.

Illustrative Programs

A program to find the total and average of ten test scores illustrates the use of a FOR loop. The complete program is shown in Figure D4–16. After initializing the total to zero, the program uses a FOR loop to accumulate the total of the ten test scores by accepting each score and adding it to the total. The FOR loop's control variable, I, is a counter that counts the number of times the loop is executed. After the FOR loop is completely executed, the average is calculated and the results are displayed.

Figure D4–16 A Program That Finds the Total and Average of Ten Test Scores, Using a FOR Loop

```
100 REM - TEST SCORE AVERAGING PROGRAM
110 REM - VARIABLES:
120 REM       SCORE  = TEST SCORE
130 REM       TOTAL  = TOTAL OF TEST SCORES
140 REM       AVG    = AVERAGE TEST SCORE
150 REM       I      = COUNTER
160 REM
170 CLS
180 PRINT "TEST SCORE AVERAGING"
190 PRINT
200 PRINT "ENTER 10 TEST SCORES - ONE PER LINE"
210 LET TOTAL = 0
220 FOR I = 1 TO 10
230   INPUT SCORE
240   LET TOTAL = TOTAL + SCORE
250 NEXT I
260 LET AVG = TOTAL / 10
270 PRINT
280 PRINT "THE TOTAL IS"; TOTAL
290 PRINT "THE AVERAGE IS"; AVG
300 END
```

Notice in this example that the statements between the FOR and NEXT statements have been indented. This is a common program style that helps set off the statements in the loop so that the program is easier to understand.

Figure D4–17 shows the pseudocode for this program. The pseudocode of a FOR loop starts with the words DO FOR, followed by a description of how the counter will be varied. Then come the steps in the loop. At the end of the loop is the word END-DO.

Figure D4–18 gives the flowchart of the program. The flowchart shows the steps in the FOR loop separately. Before entering the loop, the counter is initialized. Then the first step in the loop is a decision that tests the counter. Next come the steps in the loop. At the end of the loop, the counter is modified, and then the loop is repeated.

A modification of the program in Figure D4–16 is to accept the number of test scores to be averaged before the other data. This value determines the number of times the loop is to be executed. The program in Figure D4–19 illustrates this technique. Notice that the value

Figure D4–17 Pseudocode of a Program That Finds the Total and Average of Ten Test Scores, Using a FOR Loop

```
Display program title
Display test score prompt
Total = 0
DO FOR counter varying from 1 to 10
  Accept test score
  Add test score to total
END-DO
Average = total / 10
Display total, average
End
```

Figure D4–18 Flowchart of a Program That Finds the Total and Average of Ten Test Scores, Using a FOR Loop

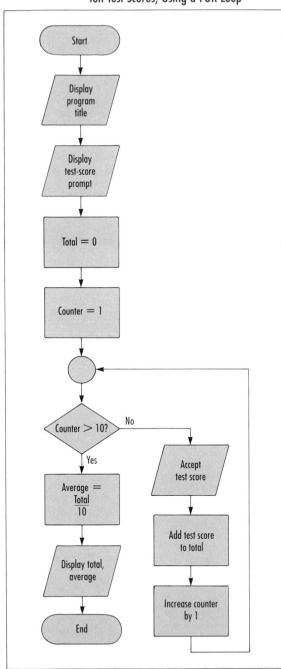

of NUM is accepted with the first INPUT statement. NUM is then used as the limit in the FOR statement.

Figure D4–11 showed a program that displays the interest and balance on an original deposit of $1000 at 8% interest compounded annually for five years. The program required a counting loop and thus can

Figure D4–19 A Program That Finds the Total and Average of a Variable Number of Test Scores, Using a FOR Loop

```
100 REM - TEST SCORE AVERAGING PROGRAM
110 REM - VARIABLES:
120 REM        NUM   = NUMBER OF TEST SCORES
130 REM        SCORE = TEST SCORE
140 REM        TOTAL = TOTAL OF TEST SCORES
150 REM        AVG   = AVERAGE TEST SCORE
160 REM        I     = COUNTER
170 REM
180 CLS
190 PRINT "TEST SCORE AVERAGING"
200 PRINT
210 INPUT "ENTER THE NUMBER OF SCORES TO BE AVERAGED"; NUM
220 PRINT
230 PRINT "ENTER"; NUM; "TEST SCORES - ONE PER LINE"
240 LET TOTAL = 0
250 FOR I = 1 TO NUM
260   INPUT SCORE
270   LET TOTAL = TOTAL + SCORE
280 NEXT I
290 LET AVG = TOTAL / NUM
300 PRINT
310 PRINT "THE TOTAL IS"; TOTAL
320 PRINT "THE AVERAGE IS"; AVG
330 END
```

be written with a FOR loop. The equivalent program with a FOR loop is shown in Figure D4–20. Notice that the value of YEAR is controlled with the FOR and NEXT statements. In addition, the value of this variable is displayed each time through the loop. This example illustrates the use of the control variable within the FOR loop. Whenever the control variable is used in the loop, its value depends on the initial value, the increment, and the number of times the loop has been executed.

Figure D4–20 The Interest-Calculation Program with a FOR Loop

```
100 REM - INTEREST CALCULATION PROGRAM
110 REM - VARIABLES:
120 REM        BAL      = BANK BALANCE
130 REM        YEAR     = YEAR
140 REM        INTEREST = INTEREST EARNED
150 REM
160 CLS
170 PRINT "          INTEREST CALCULATION"
180 PRINT
190 PRINT "YEAR", "INTEREST", "BALANCE"
200 PRINT
210 LET BAL = 1000
220 FOR YEAR = 1 TO 5
230   LET INTEREST = .08 * BAL
240   LET BAL = BAL + INTEREST
250   PRINT YEAR, INTEREST, BAL
260 NEXT YEAR
270 END
```

Nested FOR Loops

Within a FOR loop may be another FOR loop to form *nested FOR loops*. As an example of the use of nested FOR loops, consider the problem of finding the total and average of five groups of ten test scores each. One approach would be to execute the program in Figure D4–16 five times. Each time, a different set of input data would be processed by the program. A better approach is to put another loop into the program to repeat the totaling and averaging statements five times. The resulting program is shown in Figure D4–21. With this program all data can be processed at one time.

In this program the first FOR statement initializes the control variable CLASS to 1. The variable TOTAL is then assigned the value zero. The second FOR statement initializes the control variable I to 1. Next, the inner FOR loop is executed. When the NEXT statement for the inner FOR loop is encountered, I is incremented. The inner loop is repeated until its control variable exceeds the limit. At that point the computer executes the statements following the NEXT statement of the inner FOR loop. In this case, the average is computed and the output is displayed. Then the NEXT statement for the outer loop is encountered, and the control variable CLASS is incremented.

With the second execution of the outer FOR loop, the value of the variable TOTAL is reset to zero. The inner FOR statement is then encountered. This causes I to be set to 1, and the inner loop is executed ten times. Next, the average is calculated, and the PRINT statements are executed. Then the outer loop's control variable is incremented.

Figure D4–21 A Program with Nested FOR Loops

```
100 REM - TEST SCORE AVERAGING PROGRAM
110 REM - VARIABLES:
120 REM        CLASS = CLASS NUMBER
130 REM        SCORE = TEST SCORE
140 REM        TOTAL = TOTAL OF TEST SCORES
150 REM        AVG   = AVERAGE TEST SCORE
160 REM        I     = COUNTER
170 REM
180 CLS
190 PRINT "TEST SCORE AVERAGING"
200 PRINT
210 FOR CLASS = 1 TO 5
220   PRINT "ENTER 10 TEST SCORES - ONE PER LINE - FOR CLASS"; CLASS
230   LET TOTAL = 0
240   FOR I = 1 TO 10
250     INPUT SCORE
260     LET TOTAL = TOTAL + SCORE
270   NEXT I
280   LET AVG = TOTAL / 10
290   PRINT
300   PRINT "THE CLASS IS"; CLASS
310   PRINT "THE TOTAL IS"; TOTAL
320   PRINT "THE AVERAGE IS"; AVG
330   PRINT
340 NEXT CLASS
350 END
```

This continues for a total of five times. Each time the outer loop is executed, the statements in the inner loop are performed ten times.

You can nest a FOR loop in another nested FOR loop. For example, consider the following outline of nested FOR loops:

```
100 FOR L = 11 TO 20
110    FOR M = 1 TO 5
120       FOR N = 2 TO 6 STEP 2
               .
               .
               .
200       NEXT N
210    NEXT M
220 NEXT L
```

In this example, the innermost loop is executed three times for each execution of the intermediate loop. The intermediate loop is executed five times for each execution of the outermost loop. Because the outermost loop is executed ten times, the intermediate loop is executed a total of 50 times (10×5) and the innermost loop is performed 150 times ($10 \times 5 \times 3$).

Notice that each nested FOR loop is indented beyond the loop in which it is nested. This is a common style for nested FOR loops that helps show the organization of the program.

PROGRAM DEBUGGING

As you know, program testing is the process of checking for logic errors in a program. Once an error has been detected, however, the cause of the error must be found and the error corrected. This is the process of program debugging.

Some errors are the result of incorrect input data. Therefore, a good practice while debugging is to display all input data immediately after it is entered. A simple PRINT statement after each input operation can be used for this. Then you can check that the desired input data has been entered.

Another technique is to display the values of variables that are not used for input or output, called *intermediate values*. Usually this is done by putting a PRINT statement after each statement that changes the value of such a variable. This lets you check the results of intermediate calculations.

A common technique is called **tracing**, the purpose of which is to show the order of execution of the statements in the program. This can be done by putting a PRINT statement into each alternative of a decision and into each loop in the program. Each PRINT statement should display a simple phrase that identifies where in the program the statement is located. The resulting output lets you compare the actual execution sequence with what was expected.

To illustrate these techniques, Figure D4–22 shows the program that finds the total and average of ten test scores from Figure D4–12, with several errors in it. PRINT statements have been added to display the input for the variable SCORE, along with the intermediate values of the variables I and TOTAL, and to trace the execution sequence of the program. You can see from the output that the input is not correct, that the total is not computed correctly, and that the loop is executed nine times instead of ten. This gives you clues about the possible errors in the program.

Tracing is such a useful technique that some versions of BASIC have special commands just for that purpose. In Microsoft BASIC, these are the TRON and TROFF commands. If you enter the command TRON to turn the trace on just before you run a program, the computer will display the line number of each statement as it is executed. Figure D4–23 shows how the screen appears when this is done for the interest-calculation program in Figure D4–11. The numbers in brackets are the line numbers of the statements in the order in which they are executed. The normal output is also displayed, although it is not aligned properly. Had there been an error in this program, the trace would provide a clue to its location. After the trace is completed, you must enter the command TROFF to turn the trace off. Otherwise, the next program that you execute will also be traced. The TRON and TROFF commands can also be put into the program by giving them line numbers.

A SAMPLE PROGRAM

This section develops a program for a problem that involves loop control. The problem is to compute the pay for the employees in a business.

Problem Definition

A program is needed to compute the week's regular pay, overtime pay, and total pay for each employee in a business. The program should display the results of the computations together with the employee's identification number. Input to the program for each employee is the employee's identification number and name, the number of days that the employee worked during the week (0 to 7), and the hours worked each day. Figure D4–24 shows how the input and output should appear for one employee. The program title, PAYROLL CALCULATION, should be displayed at the beginning, before any input is entered, and the phrase ALL EMPLOYEE DATA PROCESSED should be displayed at the end, after all the output for all employees has been produced.

The number of days worked during the week varies with each employee. Therefore, the number of data entries for the hours worked varies. To handle this, the program should first accept the employee ID, name, and number of days worked. Then the program should accept the hours worked for each day that the employee worked. The number of employees is unknown. The program should stop when an employee ID of 999 is entered.

Figure D4–22   A Program with Extra PRINT Statements for Debugging (Part 1 of 2)

(a)   The Program

```
100 REM - TEST SCORE AVERAGING PROGRAM
110 REM - VARIABLES:
120 REM      SCORE = TEST SCORE
130 REM      TOTAL = TOTAL OF TEST SCORES
140 REM      AVG   = AVERAGE TEST SCORE
150 REM      I     = COUNTER
160 REM
170 CLS
180 PRINT "TEST SCORE AVERAGING"
190 PRINT
200 PRINT "ENTER 10 TEST SCORES - ONE PER LINE"
210 LET TOTAL = 0
220 LET I = 1
225 PRINT "***BEGINNING OF LOOP"              'DEBUGGING
230 WHILE I < 10
235   PRINT "***LOOP REPEATED WITH I ="; I    'DEBUGGING
240   INPUT SCOR
245   PRINT "***SCORE ="; SCORE               'DEBUGGING
250   LET TOTAL = TOTL + SCOR
255   PRINT "***TOTAL ="; TOTAL               'DEBUGGING
260   LET I = I + 1
270 WEND
275 PRINT "***END OF LOOP"                    'DEBUGGING
280 LET AVG = TOTAL / 10
290 PRINT
300 PRINT "THE TOTAL IS"; TOTAL
310 PRINT "THE AVERAGE IS"; AVG
320 END
```

The pay is based on the total regular hours worked and the total overtime hours worked during the week. Regular hours are all hours worked up to eight in a day. Hours worked over eight in a day are overtime hours. The regular pay is $6.50 times the week's total regular hours; the overtime pay is $9.75 times the week's total overtime hours. The total pay is the sum of the regular pay and the overtime pay.

Program Design

The program that solves this problem needs an input loop to process the data for an employee. To accumulate the total regular and overtime hours for an employee, another loop must be nested in the input loop. Within the nested loop, the regular and overtime hours are added to their respective totals. This step requires a decision. If the hours worked are less than or equal to eight, all hours are added to the total regular hours. If the hours worked are greater than eight, only eight hours are added to the total regular hours and all hours over eight are added to the total overtime hours. Figure D4–25 gives the pseudocode for the program, and Figure D4–26 shows the flowchart.

Program Coding

The program to solve this problem is shown in Figure D4–27. The input loop, which is controlled by a WHILE statement, is repeated as long as the employee ID is not equal to 999. The counting loop is controlled by

Figure D4–22 A Program with Extra PRINT Statements for Debugging (Part 2 of 2)

(b) Input and Output

```
              TEST-SCORE AVERAGING

              ENTER 10 TEST SCORES - ONE PER LINE
              ***BEGINNING OF LOOP
              ***LOOP REPEATED WITH I = 1
              ? 85
              ***SCORE = 0
              ***TOTAL = 85
              ***LOOP REPEATED WITH I = 2
              ? 92
              ***SCORE = 0
              ***TOTAL = 92
              ***LOOP REPEATED WITH I = 3
              ? 77
              ***SCORE = 0
              ***TOTAL = 77
              ***LOOP REPEATED WITH I = 4
              ? 54
              ***SCORE = 0
              ***TOTAL = 54
              ***LOOP REPEATED WITH I = 5
              ? 89
              ***SCORE = 0
              ***TOTAL = 89
              ***LOOP REPEATED WITH I = 6
              ? 100
              ***SCORE = 0
              ***TOTAL = 100
              ***LOOP REPEATED WITH I = 7
              ? 72
              ***SCORE = 0
              ***TOTAL = 72
              ***LOOP REPEATED WITH I = 8
              ? 78
              ***SCORE = 0
              ***TOTAL = 78
              ***LOOP REPEATED WITH I = 9
              ? 82
              ***SCORE = 0
              ***TOTAL = 82
              ***END OF LOOP

              THE TOTAL IS 82
              THE AVERAGE IS 8.2
```

a FOR statement that uses the day number (DAY.NUM) to count from 1 to the number of days worked (DAYS). Within the FOR loop is a decision that adds the regular and overtime hours to their respective totals.

Program Testing

To test this program, test data for all cases of the decision and for all loop cases should be used. For the decision, cases in which the hours worked in a day are less than eight, equal to eight, and greater than eight should be tested. The input loop should be tested for the case in which input data is supplied and in which a trailer value is entered. The counting loop should be tested with several values for the number of days worked, including one and seven.

Figure D4–23   A Example of the Use of the TRON and TROFF Commands

```
TRON
Ok
RUN
[170]          INTEREST CALCULATION
[180]
[190]YEAR       INTEREST       BALANCE
[200]
[210][220][230][240][250][260] 1          80          1080
[270][280][240][250][260] 2          86.39999    1166.4
[270][280][240][250][260] 3          93.31199    1259.712
[270][280][240][250][260] 4          100.777     1360.489
[270][280][240][250][260] 5          108.8391    1469.328
[270][280][290]
Ok
TROFF
Ok
```

Figure D4–24   Input and Output Layout for the Payroll Program

```
          PAYROLL CALCULATION

          ENTER EMPLOYEE ID: XXX
          ENTER EMPLOYEE NAME: XXXXXXXXXX
          ENTER NUMBER OF DAYS WORKED: X

          ENTER NUMBER OF HOURS WORKED EACH DAY
          ? XX
          ? XX
          ? XX
          ? XX

          EMPLOYEE ID: XXX    EMPLOYEE NAME: XXXXXXXXXX
          REGULAR PAY    OVERTIME PAY   TOTAL PAY
           XXXXX          XXXXX          XXXXX

          ALL EMPLOYEE DATA PROCESSED
```

Figure D4–25   Pseudocode for the Payroll Program

```
Display program title
Accept employee ID
DO WHILE employee ID not equal to 999
  Accept employee name
  Accept number of days worked
  Display hours worked prompt
  Total regular hours = 0
  Total overtime hours = 0
  DO FOR day number varying from 1 to number of days worked
    Accept hours worked
    IF hours worked ≤ 8 THEN
      Add hours worked to total regular hours
    ELSE
      Add 8 to total regular hours
      Add hours worked over 8 to total overtime hours
    END-IF
  END-DO
  Regular pay = $6.50 x total regular hours
  Overtime pay = $9.75 x total overtime hours
  Total pay = regular pay + overtime pay
  Display employee ID, name, regular pay, overtime pay, total pay
  Accept employee ID
END-DO
Display end-of-program message
End
```

Figure D4–26 Flowchart for the Payroll Program

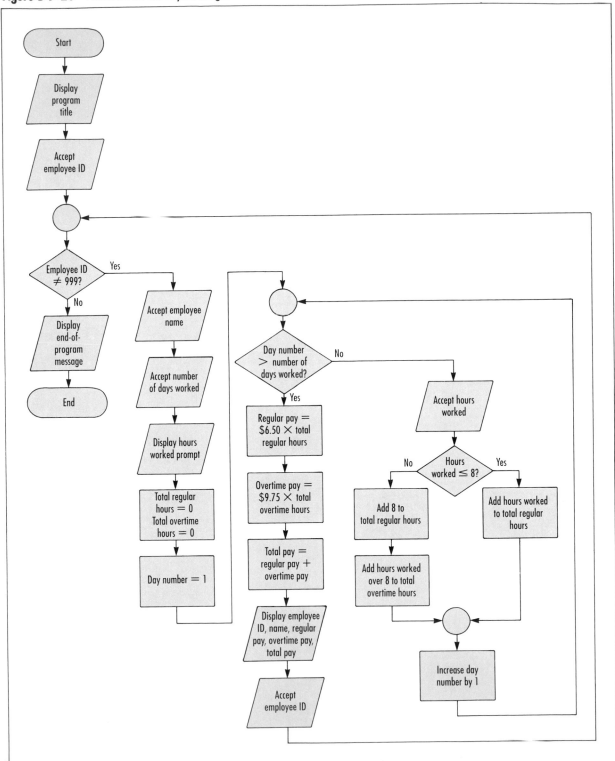

Figure D4–27   The Payroll Program

```
100 REM - PAYROLL PROGRAM
110 REM - VARIABLES:
120 REM        EMP.ID      = EMPLOYEE ID
130 REM        EMP.NAME$   = EMPLOYEE NAME
140 REM        DAYS        = NUMBER OF DAYS WORKED
150 REM        HOURS       = HOURS WORKED
160 REM        REG.HRS     = TOTAL REGULAR HOURS WORKED
170 REM        OVT.HRS     = TOTAL OVERTIME HOURS WORKED
180 REM        DAY.NUM     = DAY NUMBER
190 REM        REG.PAY     = REGULAR PAY
200 REM        OVT.PAY     = OVERTIME PAY
210 REM        TOT.PAY     = TOTAL PAY
220 REM
230 REM - DISPLAY TITLE
240 CLS
250 PRINT "PAYROLL CALCULATION"
260 PRINT
270 REM - ACCEPT FIRST EMPLOYEE ID
280 INPUT "ENTER EMPLOYEE ID: ", EMP.ID
290 WHILE EMP.ID <> 999
300   REM - ACCEPT EMPLOYEE NAME AND DAYS WORKED
310   INPUT "ENTER EMPLOYEE NAME: ", EMP.NAME$
320   INPUT "ENTER NUMBER OF DAYS WORKED: ", DAYS
330   PRINT
340   REM - ACCUMULATE TOTAL HOURS WORKED
350   PRINT "ENTER NUMBER OF HOURS WORKED EACH DAY"
360   LET REG.HRS = 0
370   LET OVT.HRS = 0
380   FOR DAY.NUM = 1 TO DAYS
390     INPUT HOURS
400     IF HOURS <= 8
            THEN LET REG.HRS = REG.HRS + HOURS
            ELSE LET REG.HRS = REG.HRS + 8: LET OVT.HRS = OVT.HRS + (HOURS - 8)
410   NEXT DAY.NUM
420   REM - COMPUTE PAY
430   LET REG.PAY = 6.5 * REG.HRS
440   LET OVT.PAY = 9.75 * OVT.HRS
450   LET TOT.PAY = REG.PAY + OVT.PAY
460   REM - DISPLAY EMPLOYEE PAY DATA
470   PRINT
480   PRINT "EMPLOYEE ID:"; EMP.ID; "  EMPLOYEE NAME: "; EMP.NAME$
490   PRINT "REGULAR PAY", "OVERTIME PAY", "TOTAL PAY"
500   PRINT REG.PAY, OVT.PAY, TOT.PAY
510   PRINT
520   REM - ACCEPT NEXT EMPLOYEE ID
530   INPUT "ENTER EMPLOYEE ID: ", EMP.ID
540 WEND
550 REM - DISPLAY END MESSAGE
560 PRINT
570 PRINT "ALL EMPLOYEE DATA PROCESSED"
580 END
```

Table D4–1 shows several sets of input test data and the expected output for each set. The input and output from running the program with this data are shown in Figure D4–28. As you can see, all test cases give the correct results.

Program Documentation

The program in Figure D4–27 contains remarks to help document it. This listing of the program along with the input and output from running the program (Figure D4–28) should be included in the documentation.

Table D4–1 Input Test Data and Expected Output for the Payroll Program

| | Input Test Data | | | | Expected Output | | |
Employee ID	Employee Name	Days Worked	Hours Worked		Regular Pay	Overtime Pay	Total Pay
123	JONES	4	8,11,6,9		195	39	234
234	SMITH	2	4,8		78	0	78
345	JOHNSON	3	9,12,15		156	117	273
456	ANDREWS	7	11,3,8,13,6,2,7		273	78	351
567	BROWN	1	16		52	78	130
999	---	---	---		---	---	---

The documentation may also include the input and output layout (Figure D4–24), the pseudocode (Figure D4–25), the flowchart (Figure D4–26), and the input test data and expected output (Table D4–1).

Terms to Remember

Counting Loop   p. 612
FOR Loop   p. 616
Input Loop   p. 609
Nested Loops   p. 615

Processing Loop   p. 610
Tracing   p. 625
Trailer Value   p. 604
WHILE Loop   p. 603

Review Questions

1. During the execution of a WHILE loop, when is the relational expression tested?

2. Code a WHILE loop to display the numbers 21, 18, 15. . .3 in a column.

3. Consider the following group of statements:

```
40 INPUT A, B, C
50 PRINT A, B, C
```

These statements are supposed to form a loop that is to be repeated until the input data contains a zero for the last value. All input should be printed, including the zero input. What additional statements are needed?

4. What is the difference between an input loop and a processing loop?

Figure D4–28   Input and Output for the Payroll Program

```
PAYROLL CALCULATION

ENTER EMPLOYEE ID: 123
ENTER EMPLOYEE NAME: JONES
ENTER NUMBER OF DAYS WORKED: 4

ENTER NUMBER OF HOURS WORKED EACH DAY
? 8
? 11
? 6
? 9

EMPLOYEE ID: 123   EMPLOYEE NAME: JONES
REGULAR PAY   OVERTIME PAY   TOTAL PAY
 195            39            234

ENTER EMPLOYEE ID: 234
ENTER EMPLOYEE NAME: SMITH
ENTER NUMBER OF DAYS WORKED: 2

ENTER NUMBER OF HOURS WORKED EACH DAY
? 4
? 8

EMPLOYEE ID: 234   EMPLOYEE NAME: SMITH
REGULAR PAY   OVERTIME PAY   TOTAL PAY
 78             0             78

ENTER EMPLOYEE ID: 345
ENTER EMPLOYEE NAME: JOHNSON
ENTER NUMBER OF DAYS WORKED: 3

ENTER NUMBER OF HOURS WORKED EACH DAY
? 9
? 12
? 15

EMPLOYEE ID: 345   EMPLOYEE NAME: JOHNSON
REGULAR PAY   OVERTIME PAY   TOTAL PAY
 156           117            273

ENTER EMPLOYEE ID: 456
ENTER EMPLOYEE NAME: ANDREWS
ENTER NUMBER OF DAYS WORKED: 7

ENTER NUMBER OF HOURS WORKED EACH DAY
? 11
? 3
? 8
? 13
? 6
? 2
? 7

EMPLOYEE ID: 456   EMPLOYEE NAME: ANDREWS
REGULAR PAY   OVERTIME PAY   TOTAL PAY
 273            78            351

ENTER EMPLOYEE ID: 567
ENTER EMPLOYEE NAME: BROWN
ENTER NUMBER OF DAYS WORKED: 1

ENTER NUMBER OF HOURS WORKED EACH DAY
? 16

EMPLOYEE ID: 567   EMPLOYEE NAME: BROWN
REGULAR PAY   OVERTIME PAY   TOTAL PAY
 52             78            130

ENTER EMPLOYEE ID: 999

ALL EMPLOYEE DATA PROCESSED
```

5. What is wrong with the following program?

```
10 WHILE RES$ = "Y"
20   INPUT "DO YOU WANT TO TOTAL SCORES? ", RES$
30   INPUT "ENTER TEST SCORES: ", SCORE1, SCORE2
40   LET TOTAL = SCORE1 + SCORE2
50   PRINT "THE TOTAL IS: ", TOTAL
60 WEND
70 END
```

6. How many lines will be displayed when the following group of statements is executed?

```
100 LET J = 20
110 WHILE J > 3
120   PRINT J
130   LET J = J - 4
140 WEND
150 (next statement)
```

7. Code a group of statements that accepts and displays 25 numbers entered at the keyboard. Do not use a FOR statement.

8. A program pattern in which one loop is contained within another loop is called a(n)_____.

9. Consider the following program:

```
100 LET J = 1
110 WHILE J <= 5
120   LET K = 20
130   WHILE K >= 10
140     LET K = K - 2
150     PRINT J, K
160   WEND
170   LET J = J + 1
180 WEND
190 END
```

How many times will each of the following statements in this program be executed?

a. statement 100

b. statement 120

c. statement 150

d. statement 170

10. During the execution of a FOR loop, when is the control variable tested and when is it modified?

11. Rewrite the following group of statements using a FOR loop:

```
100 LET K = 5
110 WHILE K <= 15
120   LET X = X + K
130   LET K = K + 3
140 WEND
150 (next statement)
```

12. Rewrite the following group of statements without using a FOR loop:

```
200 FOR L = 150 TO 100 STEP -5
210    LET Y = Y + L
220 NEXT L
```

13. Code a FOR loop that displays the numbers 21, 18, 15. . .3 in a column.

14. How many lines are displayed by each of the following groups of statements?

a.
```
310 FOR K = 1 TO 10
320    PRINT K
330 NEXT K
```

b.
```
340 FOR L = 4 TO 15 STEP 2
350    PRINT L
360 NEXT L
```

c.
```
370 FOR M = 9 TO -9 STEP -3
380    PRINT M
390 NEXT M
```

d.
```
400 FOR X = 5 TO 7 STEP .25
410    PRINT X
420 NEXT X
```

Programming Problems

1. Write the program for Problem 2 or Problem 4 in Section 3 with the additional requirement that the program has an input loop that terminates when the customer number is 9999.

2. Write the program for Problem 5 or 7 in Section 3 with the additional requirement that the program has an input loop controlled by a user response to a prompt asking whether to repeat the processing for another student.

3. A classic exercise in computer programming is called the "Manhattan Problem." It is based on the historical fact that in 1627 the Dutch purchased Manhattan Island from the Indians for the equivalent of $24. Did the Dutch make a good investment, or would it have been better to have deposited the original $24 in a bank at a fixed interest rate and left it for all these years?

Assume that the original $24 used to purchase Manhattan Island was deposited in a bank that paid 3% interest compounded annually. Write a BASIC program to determine the account total at the end of 1992 (366 years later). Do not use an interest formula to calculate the amount at the end of the time period; instead, accumulate the total one year at a time.

4. A company agrees to pay one of its employees in grains of rice instead of in money. The employee receives one grain on the first day, two grains the second day, four grains the third day, eight grains the fourth day, and so forth. In other words, on each succeeding day the employee receives twice as many grains as he or she did the day before. The employee works for the company for 15 days.

Write a BASIC program to determine the number of grains of rice that the employee receives on each day that he or she works. Also, accumulate the total of the rice earnings. There is no input for this program. Output should consist of 15 lines each with the day number, the number of grains received on that day, and the accumulated number of grains received to date.

5. Write a BASIC program that displays a table of Fahrenheit and equivalent Celsius temperature. The conversion formula is

$$C = \frac{5}{9} \times (F - 32)$$

The program should be designed to begin the table at any initial Fahrenheit temperature, end at any final temperature, and increase in increments between the initial and final temperatures by any given value. Input for the program is the initial Fahrenheit temperature, the final temperature, and the increment. Use the following sets of input data to test the program:

Initial	Final	Increment
32	212	10
70	71	.1
40	30	−1
−10	0	2
0	0	0

The program should terminate if the increment is 0.

6. A problem in timber management is to determine how much of an area to leave uncut so that the harvested area is reforested in a certain period of time. It is assumed that reforestation takes place at a known rate per year, depending on climate and soil conditions. The reforestation rate expresses this growth as a function of the amount of timber standing. For example, if 100 acres are left standing and the reforestation rate is .05, then at the end of the first year there are $100 + .05 \times 100$, or 105 acres forested. At the end of the second year the number of acres forested is $105 + .05 \times 105$, or 110.25 acres.

Assume that the total area to be forested, the uncut area, and the reforestation rate are known. Write a BASIC program to determine the percent of the total area that is forested after 20 years. Output should give the input data plus the number of acres forested after 20 years and the percentage of the total area that this represents. Use the following input data to test the program:

Area Number	Total Area	Uncut Area	Reforestation Rate
045	10,000	100	.05
083	1,000	50	.08
153	20,000	500	.10
192	14,000	3,000	.02
234	6,000	1,000	.01
416	18,000	1,500	.05
999 (trailer value)			

SECTION 5
SUBROUTINES AND MODULAR PROGRAMMING

A common way of organizing programs is to arrange groups of statements into subroutines. A subroutine consists of one or more BASIC statements that can be referred to at different points in a program. Each time that a subroutine is referenced, you say it is *called*. A program can call a subroutine from the main part of a program, which is called the *main program*, or from another subroutine. The effect of calling a subroutine is the same as if the statements in the subroutine were coded in the program at the calling point.

Subroutines let you organize a program into sections or modules. Each module is coded as a separate subroutine. The main program then performs the modules (calls the subroutines) in the order in which the modules should be executed. Such modular programming makes the program easier to develop, understand, and modify.

This section describes the programming of subroutines and their use in modular programs. After completing this section you should be able to write BASIC programs with subroutines and to develop modular BASIC programs. This section also covers several other useful topics.*

SUBROUTINES

A **subroutine** is a group of statements that can be executed from different points in a program. A subroutine begins with any BASIC statement and ends with a RETURN statement. The form of a subroutine is as follows:

```
ln first statement in subroutine
       .
       .
       .
    statements
       .
       .
       .
ln RETURN
```

---

*Any of the topics in this section can be read after Section 2 has been completed.

For example, the following is a simple subroutine that finds the total and average of three numbers:

```
250 REM - TOTAL AND AVERAGE SUBROUTINE
260 LET TOTAL = SCORE1 + SCORE2 + SCORE3
270 LET AVG = TOTAL / 3
280 RETURN
```

As a matter of style, you should always begin a subroutine with a REM statement containing a phrase that identifies the subroutine. Although not required by the syntax, this sets off the subroutines more clearly from the rest of the program. The example just given illustrates this style.

A subroutine can begin at any statement in a program. The subroutine is identified by the *number* of the first statement in the subroutine. In the example, the subroutine begins at statement 250. There can be any number of statements in a subroutine. The last statement executed in a subroutine must be a RETURN statement, which consists of just the keyword RETURN. When executed, the RETURN statement causes the computer to return to the point where the subroutine was called.

You can have as many subroutines as you need in a program. Each subroutine begins at a unique line number and ends with a RETURN statement. A subroutine can do any type of processing required. Often, subroutines contain sets of input or output statements, or statements for complex computations.

The GOSUB Statement

To call a subroutine, you use a GOSUB statement. The syntax of the GOSUB statement is as follows:

```
ln GOSUB ln
```

The effect of this statement is to execute the statements in the subroutine that begin at the line number given after the keyword GOSUB. For example, to call the subroutine at line 250, you would use the following GOSUB statement:

```
140 GOSUB 250 'CALL TOTAL AND AVERAGE SUBROUTINE
```

Again for style purposes, you should identify which subroutine is called with a remark, which may be either in a REM statement on the line before the GOSUB statement or on the same line as the GOSUB statement, beginning with an apostrophe. The second approach is used in the previous GOSUB statement.

The GOSUB statement causes the computer to execute the subroutine whose number is given in the statement. The computer starts with the first statement in the subroutine and executes the subroutine's statements in sequence. When the RETURN statement is reached, the computer continues on to the *next statement following* the GOSUB statement. This is illustrated in Figure D5–1. Notice that execution of the subroutine starts with a REM statement, which has no effect; the computer simply continues with the next statement in sequence.

One advantage of using a subroutine is that it can be called from several points in the program; that is, you can have more than one GOSUB statement that calls the same subroutine. When a RETURN statement in a subroutine is executed, the computer returns to the next statement following the GOSUB statement that called the subroutine. This is illustrated in Figure D5–2, in which a subroutine is called twice in a program.

You can call a subroutine from any point in a program. You can even call one subroutine from another. This situation is illustrated in Figure D5–3. All that is needed to call a subroutine is a GOSUB statement with the number of the first statement of the subroutine. When the RETURN statement of the called subroutine is reached, the computer returns to the point where the subroutine was called.

Writing Complete Programs with Subroutines

All subroutines in a program are normally placed at the end of the program. The first part of the program forms the main program that calls the subroutines. So that the subroutines are not executed in the normal sequential processing of the program, an END statement must come at the end of the main program, just ahead of the first subroutine.

Figure D5–1   Calling a Subroutine

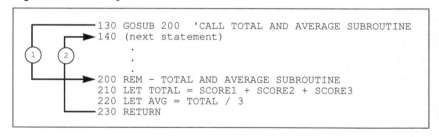

Figure D5–2   Calling a Subroutine Twice

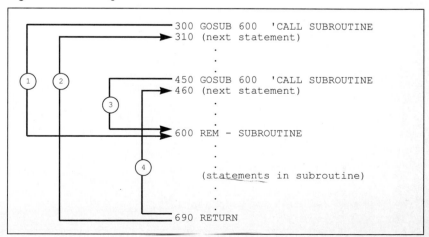

Figure D5–3 Calling a Subroutine from Another Subroutine

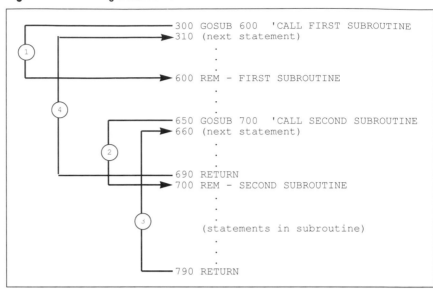

```
300 GOSUB 600   'CALL FIRST SUBROUTINE
310 (next statement)
        .
        .
        .
600 REM - FIRST SUBROUTINE
        .
        .
        .
650 GOSUB 700   'CALL SECOND SUBROUTINE
660 (next statement)
        .
        .
        .
690 RETURN
700 REM - SECOND SUBROUTINE
        .
        .
    (statements in subroutine)
        .
        .
790 RETURN
```

Figure D5–4 shows a complete program that includes a subroutine. The subroutine is called twice in this program. Notice that the subroutine comes after the END statement.

Pseudocode of Programs with Subroutines

If a program has subroutines, separate pseudocode is written for each subroutine and for the main program. To illustrate, Figure D5–5 shows the pseudocode for the program in Figure D5–4. The pseudocode of the subroutine begins with a title to identify it. Following this come the steps in the subroutine. The pseudocode of the main program also has a title. The points where the subroutine is called are indicated in the main program.

Figure D5–4 A Program That Includes a Subroutine

(a) The Program   **(b)** Input and Output

```
100 REM - TEST SCORE TOTAL AND AVERAGE PROGRAM
110 REM - MAIN PROGRAM
120 PRINT "ENTER THREE TEST SCORES"
130 INPUT SCORE1, SCORE2, SCORE3
140 GOSUB 250   'CALL TOTAL AND AVERAGE SUBROUTINE
150 PRINT "TOTAL SCORE", TOTAL
160 PRINT "AVERAGE SCORE", AVG
170 PRINT
180 PRINT "ENTER THREE TEST SCORES"
190 INPUT SCORE1, SCORE2, SCORE3
200 GOSUB 250   'CALL TOTAL AND AVERAGE SUBROUTINE
210 PRINT "TOTAL SCORE", TOTAL
220 PRINT "AVERAGE SCORE", AVG
230 END
240 REM
250 REM - TOTAL AND AVERAGE SUBROUTINE
260 LET TOTAL = SCORE1 + SCORE2 + SCORE3
270 LET AVG = TOTAL / 3
280 RETURN
```

```
ENTER THREE TEST SCORES
? 78,95,82
TOTAL SCORE     255
AVERAGE SCORE   85

ENTER THREE TEST SCORES
? 100,84,92
TOTAL SCORE     276
AVERAGE SCORE   92
```

Figure D5–5 Pseudocode of a Main Program and a Subroutine

(a) Main Program   **(b)** Subroutine

```
Main program:                      Total and average subroutine:
  Accept three test scores           Add three test scores to get total
  Call total and average subroutine  Divide total by three to get average
  Display total and average          Return
  Accept three test scores
  Call total and average subroutine
  Display total and average
  End
```

Flowcharts of Programs with Subroutines

For a program with subroutines, a separate flowchart is drawn of each subroutine, and a flowchart is drawn of the main program. For example, Figure D5–6 shows a set of flowcharts for the program in Figure D5–4. The flowchart of the main program begins with a terminal point symbol (oval) marked Start and ends with one marked End. To show where a subroutine is called, a process symbol (rectangle) is used with a vertical line on each side. Within the symbol is written a phrase that identifies the subroutine.

The flowchart of each subroutine begins with a terminal point symbol containing a phrase that identifies the subroutine. The flowchart ends with a terminal point symbol marked Return. Between these symbols, standard flowchart symbols are used to show the logic of the subroutine.

MODULAR PROGRAMMING

As programs become large, their development becomes complex. As discussed in Chapter 12, a way of organizing a large program that helps in its development is to divide the program into *modules*. Each module performs some function related to the overall processing of the program. The modules for a program can be developed separately and then combined to form a complete program after all modules are finished.

Subroutines are used in BASIC for modular programming. Each module is coded as a separate subroutine. Then the main program is composed of a series of calls of the subroutines.

An Illustrative Program

To illustrate this approach, consider the payroll program discussed in Section 2 (Figure D2–13). This program was not modular but can easily be modularized using subroutines. The first step is to determine the basic functions this program performs. At the beginning, the program displays the program's title. Then it accepts the input for an employee, calculates the employee's pay, and displays the output for the employee. At the end, the program displays an end-of-program message. Thus the program performs five separate functions:

Figure D5–6   Flowchart of a Main Program and a Subroutine

(a) Main Program   **(b)** Subroutine

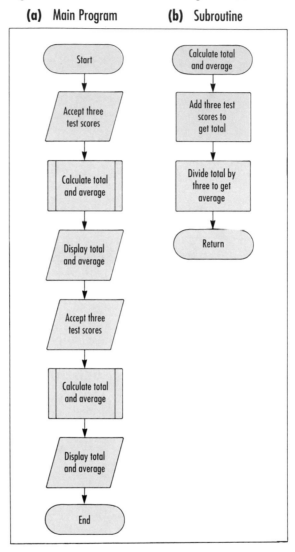

1. Display title
2. Accept employee input
3. Calculate employee pay
4. Display employee output
5. Display end message

The statements to perform each of these functions form the modules in the program. Following the approach of using subroutines to modularize the program, each of these modules is coded as a separate subroutine.

Assume that you have coded the five subroutines corresponding to these functions and that they begin at lines 300, 400, 500, 600, and 700, respectively. The main program to call the subroutines in the proper sequence is shown in the first part of Figure D5–7, up to the END statement (lines 190 to 250). Notice the simplicity of this part of the program; it is basically a sequence of five GOSUB statements. Each GOSUB statement has a remark to document further which subroutine is called at each point. Notice also that the main program ends with an END statement.

The subroutines are shown in the second part of Figure D5–7, after the END statement (lines 300 to 730). Each subroutine begins with a REM statement to identify it and ends with a RETURN statement. The statements in each subroutine are the same as those in the payroll program in Section 2.

Figure D5–7   The Modular Payroll Program

```
100 REM - PAYROLL PROGRAM
110 REM - VARIABLES:
120 REM        EMP.ID    = EMPLOYEE ID
130 REM        EMP.NAME$ = EMPLOYEE NAME
140 REM        HOURS     = HOURS WORKED
150 REM        GROSS.PAY = GROSS PAY
160 REM        WH.TAX    = WITHHOLDING TAX
170 REM        NET.PAY   = NET PAY
180 REM
190 REM - MAIN PROGRAM
200 GOSUB 300   'CALL DISPLAY TITLE SUBROUTINE
210 GOSUB 400   'CALL ACCEPT EMPLOYEE INPUT DATA SUBROUTINE
220 GOSUB 500   'CALL CALCULATE EMPLOYEE PAY SUBROUTINE
230 GOSUB 600   'CALL DISPLAY EMPLOYEE OUTPUT DATA SUBROUTINE
240 GOSUB 700   'CALL DISPLAY END MESSAGE SUBROUTINE
250 END
260 REM
300 REM - DISPLAY TITLE SUBROUTINE
310 CLS
320 PRINT "PAYROLL CALCULATION"
330 PRINT
340 RETURN
350 REM
400 REM - ACCEPT EMPLOYEE INPUT DATA SUBROUTINE
410 INPUT "ENTER EMPLOYEE ID: ", EMP.ID
420 INPUT "ENTER EMPLOYEE NAME: ", EMP.NAME$
430 INPUT "ENTER HOURS WORKED: ", HOURS
440 RETURN
450 REM
500 REM - CALCULATE EMPLOYEE PAY SUBROUTINE
510 LET GROSS.PAY = 6.5 * HOURS
520 LET WH.TAX = .16 * GROSS.PAY
530 LET NET.PAY = GROSS.PAY - WH.TAX
540 RETURN
550 REM
600 REM - DISPLAY EMPLOYEE OUTPUT DATA SUBROUTINE
612 PRINT
620 PRINT "PAYROLL DATA FOR EMPLOYEE"; EMP.ID
630 PRINT
640 PRINT "  NAME: "; EMP.NAME$
650 PRINT "  GROSS PAY:"; GROSS.PAY
660 PRINT "  TAX:"; WH.TAX
670 PRINT "  NET PAY:"; NET.PAY
680 RETURN
690 REM
700 REM - DISPLAY END MESSAGE SUBROUTINE
710 PRINT
720 PRINT "END OF PROGRAM"
730 RETURN
```

Structure Charts

A way of showing the modular organization of a program is with a *structure chart*, which is discussed in Chapter 12. In a structure chart, each subroutine is represented by a box; the main program is also represented by a box. A line connects two boxes if one part of the program calls the other.

Figure D5–8 shows the structure chart for the modular payroll program. The box at the top represents the main program. Each box below signifies a subroutine. Because the main program calls each subroutine, a line connects the box for the main program with the box for each subroutine.

In the modular payroll program, only the main program calls subroutines. Therefore, the structure chart for this program has only two levels—one for the main program and one for the subroutines. Many times, however, a program has subroutines that call other subroutines. Then the structure chart has more than two levels. (Figure 12-15 in Chapter 12 shows an example of a structure chart with three levels.)

A structure chart shows how the subroutines and the main program are related—that is, what part of the program calls what other parts. The structure chart does not show the flow of logic in any part of the program; that is the purpose of the pseudocode or the flowchart. For each box in the structure chart, pseudocode is written, or a flowchart is drawn, that shows the logic flow in the part of the program that the box represents. Figure D5–9 shows the pseudocode for the modular payroll program. Notice that there are six sections of pseudocode—one for the main program and five for the subroutines. Figure D5–10 gives the flowcharts for this program. There are six flowcharts—one for the main program and one for each of the five subroutines.

Top-Down Program Design

One advantage of using subroutines to modularize a program is that you can design the program in a top-down fashion. In *top-down program design*, a topic discussed in Chapter 12, you start by designing the

Figure D5–8   Structure Chart of the Modular Payroll Program

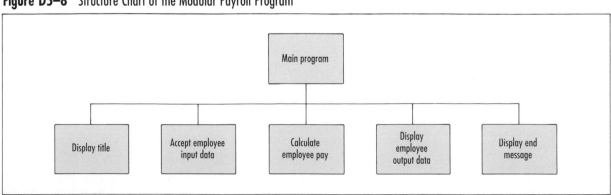

Figure D5–9 Pseudocode of the Modular Payroll Program

```
Main program:
  Call display title subroutine
  Call accept employee input data subroutine
  Call calculate employee pay subroutine
  Call display employee output data subroutine
  Call display end message subroutine
  End


Display title subroutine:
  Display program title
  Return


Accept employee input data subroutine:
  Accept employee ID, name, hours worked
  Return


Calculate employee pay subroutine:
  Compute gross pay, tax, net pay
  Return


Display employee output data subroutine:
  Display employee ID, name, gross pay, tax, net pay
  Return


Display end message subroutine:
  Display end-of-program message
  Return
```

overall logic of the program. Each basic operation that the program is to perform becomes a subroutine. The main program contains a series of calls to the subroutines. (There may be other statements in the main program besides those that call subroutines.) You then design each subroutine in a similar top-down fashion. Eventually you reach the point where the detailed operations of the program can be coded.

A structure chart shows clearly the top-down design of a program. At the top of the chart is the box for the main program, which contains the overall program logic. Below this are the boxes for the subroutines called by the main program. These subroutines contain the logic for the basic processing in the program. Below these may be more boxes for additional subroutines called by the first subroutines. These called subroutines contain more detailed logic. Thus, working down the structure chart leads from the overall logic to the detailed logic of the program.

Menu-Driven Programs

Many programs allow the user to control the processing of the program through a *menu*, which is a list of the functions a program can perform displayed on the screen. For example, Figure D5–11 shows the menu for a program that performs several payroll-processing functions. Notice that one of the menu items is to end the program. A *menu-driven program* is one that is controlled through a menu.

Figure D5–10 Flowcharts of the Modular Payroll Program

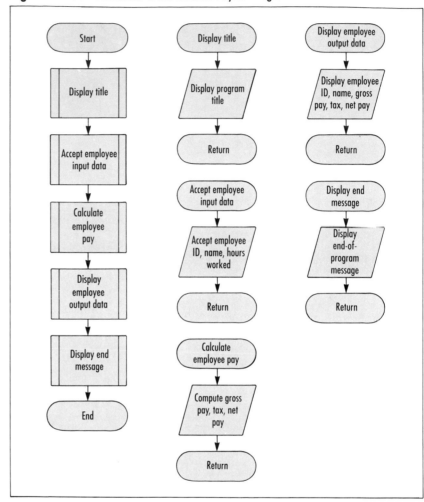

In a menu-driven program, each menu function is performed by a subroutine. Thus, for the program that is driven by the menu in Figure D5–11, subroutines would be needed to calculate the pay, calculate the tax, and print a check. In addition, the program would have a subroutine to display the menu and accept the user's selection. Finally, the main program would use decision and loop-control techniques from Sections 3 and 4 to control the order of execution of the program.

To illustrate, Figure D5–12 shows part of a menu-driven payroll program, including the main program and the display-menu subroutine. The main program first calls the display-menu subroutine to get the user's first menu selection. It then executes a WHILE loop that is repeated if the menu selection is not equal to 9. In the loop, the program uses IF-THEN statements to decide which subroutine should be called to do the selected processing. At the end of the loop, the display-menu subroutine is displayed again to get the next menu selection from the user. Then the loop is repeated if the user did not select 9. When 9 is entered by the user, the loop is terminated and the program ends.

Figure D5–11   A Menu for a Menu-Driven Payroll Program

```
                    PAYROLL-PROCESSING MENU

                    1.   CALCULATE PAY
                    2.   CALCULATE TAX
                    3.   PRINT PAYCHECK
                    9.   END PROGRAM

                    ENTER NUMBER OF SELECTION:
```

Figure D5–12   Part of a Menu-Driven Payroll Program

```
100 REM - PAYROLL PROGRAM
110 REM - VARIABLES:
120 REM       SEL      = MENU SELECTION
       .
       .
       .
200 REM - MAIN PROGRAM
210 GOSUB 300  'CALL DISPLAY MENU SUBROUTINE
220 WHILE SEL <> 9
230   IF SEL = 1 THEN GOSUB 500  'CALL CALCULATE PAY SUBROUTINE
240   IF SEL = 2 THEN GOSUB 600  'CALL CALCULATE TAX SUBROUTINE
250   IF SEL = 3 THEN GOSUB 700  'CALL PRINT PAYCHECK SUBROUTINE
260   GOSUB 300  'CALL DISPLAY MENU SUBROUTINE
270 WEND
280 END
290 REM
       .
       .
       .
300 REM - DISPLAY MENU SUBROUTINE
310 CLS
320 PRINT "PAYROLL PROCESSING MENU"
330 PRINT
340 PRINT "1.   CALCULATE PAY"
350 PRINT "2.   CALCULATE TAX"
360 PRINT "3.   PRINT PAYCHECK"
370 PRINT "9.   END PROGRAM"
380 PRINT
390 INPUT "ENTER NUMBER OF SELECTION: ", SEL
410 RETURN
420 REM
500 REM - CALCULATE PAY SUBROUTINE
       .
       .
       .
580 RETURN
590 REM
600 REM - CALCULATE TAX SUBROUTINE
       .
       .
       .
680 RETURN
690 REM
700 REM - PRINT PAYCHECK SUBROUTINE
       .
       .
       .
780 RETURN
```

FUNCTIONS

Many standard processing activities are commonly required in BASIC programs. For example, it is often necessary to find the square root of a number or to perform various mathematical computations. In order to relieve the programmer of the responsibility of preparing the instructions necessary for such processing, BASIC supplies special built-in routines called **functions**. A function is a separate set of instructions that performs a specific task.

Each function is identified by a name. You use a function in a program by coding the name of the function, usually followed by an expression in parentheses. The resulting reference to the function forms an expression that can be used by itself in a statement or as part of a more complex expression. (You can also create your own functions using the DEF statement, which is not covered in this book.)

Most BASIC functions process numeric data and are called *numeric functions*. Some functions process string data and are called *string functions*.

Numeric Functions

Most BASIC functions process numeric data. Table D5–1 lists the numeric functions common to most versions of BASIC. Notice that some of the functions correspond to mathematical functions, such as those used in trigonometry. Many versions of BASIC have additional numeric functions.

To illustrate the characteristics of numeric functions, consider the square-root function. The name of this function is SQR. You use this function by coding its name followed by a numeric expression enclosed in parentheses. You then use the combination of function name and

Table D5–1   Common BASIC Numeric Functions

Function	Meaning
ABS(X)	Absolute value of X
ATN(X)	Arctangent (in radians) of X
COS(X)	Cosine of X (X must be in radians)
EXP(X)	Exponential of X (that is, e^x)
INT(X)	Largest integer less than or equal to X
LOG(X)	Natural logarithm of X (that is, ln X)
RND	Random number between 0 and 1
SGN(X)	Sign of X (that is, -1 if X < 0, 0 if X = 0, $+1$ if X > 0)
SIN(X)	Sine of X (X must be in radians)
SQR(X)	Square root of X
TAN (X)	Tangent of X (X must be in radians)

expression in a statement in a program. For example, the following LET statement shows the use of the square-root function:

```
20 LET C = SQR(A + B)
```

In evaluating this function, the computer first determines the value of the numeric expression in parentheses. Then the SQR function finds the square root of the value. For example, if A is 9 and B is 7 in the previous statement, then A + B is 16 and SQR(A + B) is 4. This value is then assigned to C by the LET statement.

The expression in parentheses may be a constant, a variable, or a more complex numeric expression with a nonnegative value. All the following statements are valid examples of the use of the square-root function:

```
30 LET X = SQR(Y)
40 PRINT SQR(100)
50 LET R = (-B + SQR(B ^ 2 - 4 * A * C)) / (2 * A)
60 IF SQR(P) <= 3 * SQR(Q) THEN PRINT SQR(P)
```

Note that the function cannot be used by itself, but only as part of a statement. In fact, the SQR function can be used only in place of a numeric expression in a statement or as part of a more complex numeric expression.

The program in Figure D5–13 demonstrates the use of the square-root function. The input to this program is the length (LNGTH) and width (WDTH) of a piece of carpet purchased to cover a floor. The problem is to compute the length of the side (SIDE) of the largest square floor that can be covered by this amount of carpet. To do this, the program must first compute the area (AREA) of carpet purchased. This is done by the LET statement at line 220. Then the square root of the area is computed by the LET statement at line 230 to give the length of the side (SIDE). Notice that because the value of AREA is not needed for output, the LET statement at line 220 can be eliminated and the statement at line 230 can be written as follows:

```
230 LET SIDE = SQR(LNGTH * WDTH)
```

A useful numeric function is the integer, or INT, function. This function finds the largest integer (i.e., whole number) that is less than or equal to the value of the expression in parentheses. For example, consider the following statement:

```
110 LET A = INT(B)
```

If B is 5.8, the INT function finds the largest integer that is less than or equal to 5.8. This integer is 5, which is assigned to A in the LET statement. Notice that the value is *not* rounded; the largest integer *less than or equal to* the value in parentheses is found. If the value is negative, the same rule applies. Thus, if B is –5.8 in the previous example, INT(B) is –6, the largest integer less than or equal to –5.8.

Figure D5–13 A Program That Calculates Floor Dimensions

(a) The Program

```
100 REM - FLOOR DIMENSION PROGRAM
110 REM - VARIABLES:
120 REM      LNGTH = LENGTH OF CARPET
130 REM      WDTH  = WIDTH OF CARPET
140 REM      AREA  = AREA OF CARPET
150 REM      SIDE  = LENGTH OF SIDE OF SQUARE FLOOR
160 REM
170 CLS
180 PRINT "FLOOR DIMENSION CALCULATION"
190 PRINT
200 INPUT "ENTER LENGTH OF CARPET: ", LNGTH
210 INPUT "ENTER WIDTH OF CARPET: ", WDTH
220 LET AREA = LNGTH * WDTH
230 LET SIDE = SQR(AREA)
240 PRINT
250 PRINT "THE LENGTH OF THE SQUARE FLOOR SIDE IS"; SIDE
260 PRINT
270 PRINT "END OF PROGRAM"
280 END
```

(b) Input and Output

```
FLOOR DIMENSION CALCULATION

ENTER LENGTH OF CARPET: 10
ENTER WIDTH OF CARPET: 16

THE LENGTH OF THE SQUARE FLOOR SIDE IS 12.64911

END OF PROGRAM
```

As with other functions, any numeric expression can be used with the INT function. For example, the following statements are valid:

```
130 LET X = INT(2.5 * Y - 7.3)
140 PRINT INT(N)
150 LET C = 3.5 * INT(D / E) + 8.4
160 IF INT(P) * INT(Q) <= R THEN PRINT INT(P)
```

Any expression in parentheses is first evaluated before the INT function is used. Thus, if Y is 4 in statement 130, 2.5 * Y – 7.3 is 2.7 and INT(2.5 * Y – 7.3) is 2, which is the value assigned to X. Note also that the INT function can be used in a statement only in place of a numeric expression or as part of a more complex expression, as shown in these examples.

There are many uses for the INT function. As an example, the program in Figure D5–14 calculates the number of dozen in a given number of eggs (NUM.EGGS). After accepting the input, the program computes the number of dozen (NUM.DOZ) by dividing NUM.EGGS by 12. The INT function converts the result to a whole number. Then statement 220 finds the number remaining (NUM.REM) after the dozens are removed. If the input value is 226 eggs, the output is 18 dozen with 10 eggs remaining.

Figure D5-14 The Egg Program

(a) The Program

```
100 REM - EGG PROGRAM
110 REM - VARIABLES:
120 REM       NUM.EGGS = NUMBER OF EGGS
130 REM       NUM.DOZ  = NUMBER OF DOZEN EGGS
140 REM       NUM.REM  = NUMBER OF EGGS REMAINING
150 REM
160 CLS
170 PRINT "EGG CALCULATION"
180 PRINT
190 INPUT "ENTER NUMBER OF EGGS: ", NUM.EGGS
200 LET NUM.DOZ = INT(NUM.EGGS / 12)
210 LET NUM.REM = NUM.EGGS - NUM.DOZ * 12
220 PRINT
230 PRINT "THERE ARE"; NUM.DOZ; "DOZEN WITH"; NUM.REM; "REMAINING ";
240 PRINT "IN"; NUM.EGGS; "EGGS."
250 PRINT
260 PRINT "END OF PROGRAM"
270 END
```

(b) Input and Output

```
EGG CALCULATION

ENTER NUMBER OF EGGS: 226

THERE ARE 18 DOZEN WITH 10 REMAINING IN 226 EGGS.

END OF PROGRAM
```

String Functions

In addition to numeric functions, BASIC provides string functions that process string data. Table D5-2 lists some of the common string functions. Many versions of BASIC have other string functions.

To illustrate the characteristics of string functions, consider the MID$ function. This function produces the middle characters from a string. The form of the function is MID$(A$, M, N). The function produces the N characters from A$, beginning with character M. For example, if A$ is ABCDEF, then MID$(A$, 2, 3) is BCD. These are the three characters, beginning with the second character in the string.

The MID$ function cannot be used by itself, but must be part of a statement. It may be used anyplace a string expression can appear. For example, the following LET statement assigns the result produced by the MID$ function to a string variable.

```
50 LET B$ = MID$(A$, 2, 3)
```

The MID$ function may use string and numeric expressions within its parentheses. For example, consider the following statement:

```
LET C$ = MID$(A$ + B$, I, J + 1)
```

Table D5–2 Common BASIC String Functions

Function	Meaning
LEFTS(AS, N)	Left N characters of AS
MIDS(AS, M, N)	Middle N characters of AS beginning with character M
RIGHTS(AS, N)	Right N characters of AS
LEN(AS)	Number of characters (i.e., length) of AS
INSTR(AS, BS)	Beginning position of BS in AS

In this statement, the MID$ function produces characters from the string formed from concatenating A$ and B$. The string produced begins at character I and contains J + 1 characters.

Figure D5–15 shows a program that illustrates the use of the MID$ function. In this program, the user enters his or her telephone number (ten digits including area code). Then the program displays the area code (the first three digits), the prefix (the next three digits), and the number (the last four digits). Notice that the input data is assigned to a string variable in the INPUT statement rather than to a numeric variable, even though the input data is a number, because the program treats the data as a string. The MID$ function is used to separate the parts of the telephone number.

Figure D5–15 A Program That Processes Telephone Numbers

(a) The Program

```
100 REM - TELEPHONE NUMBER PROGRAM
110 REM - VARIABLES:
120 REM        PHONE.NUM$ = COMPLETE TELEPHONE NUMBER
130 REM
140 CLS
150 PRINT "TELEPHONE NUMBER PROGRAM"
160 PRINT
170 INPUT "ENTER COMPLETE TELEPHONE NUMBER: ", PHONE.NUM$
180 PRINT
190 PRINT "AREA CODE: "; MID$(PHONE.NUM$, 1, 3)
200 PRINT "PREFIX:    "; MID$(PHONE.NUM$, 4, 3)
210 PRINT "NUMBER:    "; MID$(PHONE.NUM$, 7, 4)
220 PRINT
230 PRINT "END OF PROGRAM"
240 END
```

(b) Input and Output

```
TELEPHONE NUMBER PROGRAM

ENTER COMPLETE TELEPHONE NUMBER: 2122077000

AREA CODE: 212
PREFIX:    207
NUMBER:    7000

END OF PROGRAM
```

THE READ AND DATA STATEMENTS

The INPUT statement is the main statement used for data input in BASIC. Its primary application is in interactive data processing. There are situations, however, in which a batch of data needs to be processed. This can be done by using the INPUT statement to accept all the data from the keyboard. Another approach is to put the data into the program by using a DATA statement and then to accept, or "read," the data with a READ statement.

The READ and DATA statements are always used together in a program. The syntax of the READ statement is as follows:

```
ln READ list of variables
```

The variables in the list must be separated by commas. The following is an example of a READ statement:

```
10 READ X, Y, Z
```

Notice that the syntax is the same as that of the INPUT statement with the exception of the keyword. The syntax of the DATA statement is as follows:

```
ln DATA list of constants
```

The following is an example of a DATA statement:

```
15 DATA 78,95,82
```

Any valid constants can appear in a DATA statement, including constants in E-notation. The constants must be separated by commas.

When a READ statement is executed, data is read from a DATA statement. Each variable in the READ statement is assigned a value from a DATA statement. The data is read in sequence, left-to-right. If the READ and DATA statements just given appear in a program, then after execution of the READ statement, X is 78, Y is 95, and Z is 82.

There may be any number of DATA statements in a program, and they may be placed anywhere in the program. When a DATA statement is encountered during the sequential execution of a program, the computer ignores it. A DATA statement is used only when a READ statement is executed.

When there is more than one DATA statement in a program, input begins with the data in the first statement and continues sequentially through the data in the other statements. For example, consider the following statements:

```
10 READ X
11 READ Y, Z
15 DATA 78,95
16 DATA 82
```

The first READ statement reads the first value in the first DATA statement. Thus, X is assigned the value 78. Then the second READ statement is executed. Input continues where the previous READ statement left off. Thus, 95 is read and assigned to Y. Now, because there are no more values in the first DATA statement, the computer automatically goes on to the second DATA statement. Hence, the value 82 is read for Z.

The READ and DATA statements can be used for string input. When this is done, a string variable is used in the READ statement and a string, either with or without quotation marks, is used in the DATA statement. For example, consider the following statements:

```
140 READ N$
145 DATA JOHN
```

When the READ statement is executed, the string JOHN is read from the DATA statement and assigned to N$.

Quotation marks around the string in the DATA statement are optional unless the string contains a comma, leading spaces, or trailer spaces. For example, consider the following statements:

```
150 READ D$
155 DATA "  SEPT. 1, 1993   "
```

In this case, quotation marks must be used around the string input in the DATA statement.

As a simple example of the use of the READ and DATA statements in a program, consider the interest-calculation program in Section 2 (Figure D2–9). This program can be modified to use the READ and DATA statements instead of the INPUT statements. Figure D5–16 shows the result. Notice that the READ statement has replaced two INPUT statements in the original program, and a DATA statement comes at the end of the program, just before the END statement. This is a common place in which to put DATA statements so that data can be easily located and changed. A REM statement comes before the DATA statement to identify the input data.

When this program executes, the user does not enter any input data (see Figure D5–16b). All data has already been put into a DATA statement. This is an example of *batch processing*, in which all input data is prepared in a batch prior to executing the program. In contrast, the interest-calculation program in Section 2 was an example of *interactive processing* because the user interacted with the program by supplying input as the program executed.

As a more complex example of a batch-processing program, consider the tuition-calculation program with a loop, discussed in Section 4 (see Figure D4–1). A similar program using READ and DATA statements for batch processing is shown in Figure D5–17. Each time a READ statement is executed, the next two values are read from the DATA statements. The first value read is a student's identification number, and the second is the number of units. The data appears in pairs in the DATA statements; the last pair contains the trailer value (9999) for ID

Figure D5–16 The Interest-Calculation Program, Using the READ and DATA Statements

(a) The Program   **(b)** Output

```
100 REM - INTEREST CALCULATION PROGRAM          INTEREST CALCULATION
110 REM - VARIABLES:
120 REM       BEGINBAL = BEGINNING BANK BALANCE  BEGINNING BANK BALANCE: 500
130 REM       RATE     = INTEREST RATE           INTEREST EARNED: 30
140 REM       INTEREST = INTEREST EARNED          ENDING BANK BALANCE: 530
150 REM       ENDBAL   = ENDING BANK BALANCE
160 REM                                          END OF PROGRAM
170 CLS
180 PRINT "INTEREST CALCULATION"
190 PRINT
200 READ BEGINBAL, RATE
210 LET INTEREST = BEGINBAL * RATE
220 LET ENDBAL = BEGINBAL + INTEREST
230 PRINT "BEGINNING BANK BALANCE:"; BEGINBAL
240 PRINT "INTEREST EARNED:"; INTEREST
250 PRINT "ENDING BANK BALANCE:"; ENDBAL
260 PRINT
270 PRINT "END OF PROGRAM"
280 REM - INPUT DATA
290 DATA 500,.06
300 END
```

and an arbitrary value (0) for UNITS. Because all data is prepared in advance in a batch, this is a batch-processing program. Notice in Figure D5–17b that the user does not enter any input data and that the program prints the output in columns below headings.

THE PRINT USING STATEMENT

With the PRINT statement, the value of a variable is displayed in a standard format determined by the computer. You do not have control over how the output appears, although the output would sometimes look better in a different format. Improvements in the output format can be made with the PRINT USING statement.

The PRINT USING statement is not available in all versions of BASIC, and its syntax varies somewhat from one version of the language to another. Here is a description of the form used in Microsoft BASIC. The syntax of this form is as follows:

```
ln PRINT USING "format"; list of variables
```

The variables in the list must be separated by commas. The following is an example of a PRINT USING statement:

```
50 PRINT USING "#### ###.###"; I, T
```

The PRINT USING statement consists of the keywords PRINT USING, followed by the *format*, which must be enclosed in quotation marks. In the format, special symbols are used to describe the arrangement of the

Figure D5—17   The Tuition-Calculation Program with a Loop, Using the READ and DATA Statements

(a)   The Program

```
100 REM - TUITION CALCULATION PROGRAM
110 REM - VARIABLES:
120 REM       ID    = STUDENT ID
130 REM       UNITS = NUMBER OF UNITS
140 REM       TUIT  = TUITION
150 REM
160 CLS
170 PRINT "          TUITION REPORT"
180 PRINT
190 PRINT "STUDENT ID", "UNITS", "TUITION"
200 PRINT
210 READ ID, UNITS
220 WHILE ID <> 9999
230   IF UNITS <= 12 THEN LET TUIT = 350 ELSE LET TUIT = 350 + 20 * (UNITS - 12)
240   PRINT ID, UNITS, TUIT
250   READ ID, UNITS
260 WEND
270 PRINT
280 PRINT "ALL DATA PROCESSED"
290 REM - INPUT DATA
300 DATA 1001,15,1013,18,1025,8
310 DATA 1085,12,1117,20,1130,6
320 DATA 1147,3,1165,13.5,1207,11
330 DATA 1229,12.5,9999,0
340 END
```

(b)   Output

```
          TUITION REPORT

STUDENT ID     UNITS          TUITION

  1001          15             410
  1013          18             470
  1025          8              350
  1085          12             350
  1117          20             510
  1130          6              350
  1147          3              350
  1165          13.5           380
  1207          11             350
  1229          12.5           360

ALL DATA PROCESSED
```

output data. Following the format is a semicolon and then a list of variables just as in a simple PRINT statement. When the PRINT USING statement is executed, the values of the variables are displayed according to the specifications given in the format. The symbols used in the format determine how the output appears.

Numeric Output

To display a number, the # symbol is used in the format for each digit position in the number. For example, consider the following PRINT USING statement:

```
60 PRINT USING "###"; X
```

This statement tells the computer to display the value of X using the format ###. This means that the value is to be displayed in the first three print positions. If X is 128, this number is displayed at the beginning of the output line. If the value of X requires fewer than three print positions, the number is displayed so that it is aligned on the right; that is, the value is *right-justified*. For example, if X is 9, the output consists of two blank spaces and then the digit 9. When not enough print positions are provided in the format, an error occurs. In this case the % symbol is displayed, followed by the value. For example, if X is 1024, the output appears as %1024.

Minus Sign.   If the output value is negative, a minus sign is displayed to the left of the first digit, provided there are enough print positions. Thus, if X is –4 in the previous example, the output consists of a space, the minus sign, and the digit 4. If the number is positive, no plus sign is displayed.

Sometimes it is desirable to have the minus sign displayed after the number. This is accomplished by putting a minus sign after the # symbols in the format, as in the following example:

```
70 PRINT USING "###-"; X
```

If the value to be displayed is positive, a blank space replaces the minus sign. If the value is negative, the minus sign is displayed. Thus, the value 128 is displayed as 128 followed by a blank space, and –4 appears as 4–.

Decimal Point.   For a decimal point to be included in the output, the decimal point is used in the format in the appropriate position as illustrated in the following statement:

```
80 PRINT USING "###.##"; Y
```

If Y is 486.37 in this example, the output consists of this number displayed in the first six print positions, with a decimal point in the fourth print position. (Notice that six print positions are needed because the decimal point requires one print position.) If the value has more places to the right of the decimal point than are indicated in the format, the output is rounded. Thus, if X is 486.376, the number displayed is 486.38. When the value has fewer places to the right than indicated in the format, zeros are added to fill out the decimal positions. Thus, if Y is 486.3, then 486.30 is displayed.

Comma.   If a comma is inserted *anywhere* to the left of the decimal point in the format, commas are displayed every three digits in the output. For example, consider the following statement:

```
90 PRINT USING "#,#######"; Z
```

If the value of Z is 5000000, the output appears as 5,000,000. Notice that two commas are displayed even though only one comma appears in the format. Each comma that is displayed requires a print position.

Dollar Sign.   A dollar sign can be displayed immediately preceding the first digit of a number by using *two* dollar signs at the beginning of the format. For example, consider the following statement:

```
100 PRINT USING "$$##.##"; P
```

If the value of P is 500, the output displayed is $500.00. If the value of P is 5, the output consists of two blank spaces and then $5.00. In effect, the double dollar sign causes one dollar sign to be displayed just ahead of the first digit in the number. Note that two dollar signs are required in the format to cause the output to be displayed as described.

A minus sign cannot be displayed before or after a dollar sign. Thus, if the value of P is negative in the previous example, an error will occur. A minus sign will be displayed on the right if the sign is used in the format. For example, the previous statement could be written as follows:

```
100 PRINT USING "$$##.##-"; P
```

If P is –8, the output is displayed as $8.00–.

Asterisk.   If *two* asterisks are used at the beginning of a format, any blank print positions to the left of the number are filled with asterisks. The following statement illustrates this:

```
110 PRINT USING "**##.##"; P
```

If P is 500, the output displayed is *500.00. If P is 5, the output appears as ***5.00. Asterisks are often used in this way to protect dollar amounts on checks from alterations. Notice that two asterisks are required in the format to cause the output to be displayed as described. Table D5–3 shows other examples using the special symbols described here.

Positioning Output

In the examples given so far, the output has begun in the first print position. For the output to start in a different print position, blank spaces are used at the beginning of the format. For example, the following PRINT USING statement has four blanks at the beginning of the format:

```
120 PRINT USING "    ###"; X
```

This causes the first four print positions to be skipped, and the output begins in the fifth print position. Note that the TAB function cannot be used with the PRINT USING statement.

When more than one number is to be displayed on a line, the format must contain the appropriate symbols to describe the arrangement of each number with the necessary blanks to spread out the values. For example, consider the following statement:

```
130 PRINT USING "  ##   ##.##   #,###.##"; A, B, C
```

Table D5–3 Examples of Formats

Format	Value	Output
"####"	1234	1234
"####"	56	56
"####"	-789	-789
"####-"	1234	1234
"####-"	56	56
"####-"	-789	789-
"##.###"	12.345	12.345
"##.###"	12.3456	12.346
"##.###	12	12.000
"#,###"	1234	1,234
"#,###"	56	56
"$$###"	1234	$1234
"$$###"	56	$56
"**###"	1234	*1234
"**###"	56	***56
"$$#,###.##-"	1234.56	$1,234.56
"$$#,###.##-"	-78.90	$78.90-
"**#,###.##-"	1234.56	**1,234.56
"**#,###.##-"	-78.90	*****78.90-

This statement tells the computer to display the values of A, B, and C in the specified format. The output line contains two blank spaces, then the value of A in the format ##, then three spaces followed by the value of B in the format ##.##, then three more spaces and the value of C in the format #,###.##. If A is 20, B is 25.95, and C is 1482.38, the output appears as follows:

```
20    25.95    1,482.38
```

Notice that the horizontal positioning of the output is controlled by the format, not by the punctuation in the list of variables. Commas and semicolons in the variable list have no effect on the placement of the output.

String Output

String constants that are to be displayed on the same line as the values of variables are included in the format. Any characters that are used in the format, except for characters with special meaning, such as the # symbol, are displayed exactly as they appear. For example, consider the following statement:

```
140 PRINT USING "TOTAL = ###, AVERAGE = ##.#"; T, A
```

If T is 252 and A is 84, the output line appears as follows:

```
TOTAL = 252, AVERAGE = 84.0
```

To display the value of a string variable, the backslash symbol (\) is used in the format to mark the beginning and end of the string output. For example, consider the following statement:

```
100 PRINT USING "\  \"; N$
```

The format in this statement is \ \ with two blank spaces between the backslash symbols. This causes the value of N$ to be displayed in the first four print positions. If the value of N$ is JOHN, this name is displayed at the beginning of the output line.

Notice that the backslashes mark the beginning and the end of the output. The number of characters to be displayed is determined by counting the number of spaces between the backslashes and adding two for the backslashes. Thus, in the previous example there are two spaces between the backslashes; hence, four characters are displayed.

If the output string is longer than the number of characters specified in the format, only the left part of the string is displayed. For example, if N$ is ROBERT when the previous statement is executed, only ROBE is displayed. When the string is shorter than the number of characters in the format, the string is displayed so that it is aligned on the left; that is, the string is *left-justified*. Extra spaces are added on the right. For example, if N$ is ED when the previous statement is executed, the output displayed is the string ED followed by two blank spaces.

The shortest string that can be displayed using backslashes in the format is two characters because backslashes must always appear in pairs. To display a one-character string, the exclamation point (!) is used. For example, consider the following statement:

```
110 PRINT USING "!"; N$
```

In this case, the first character in the string assigned to N$ is displayed. If N$ is JOHN, only the letter J is displayed.

You can combine string output and numeric output in the same PRINT USING statement. For example, assume that F$, M$, and L$ are equal to an employee's first name, middle name, and last name, respectively, and that S is the employee's salary. Then the following statement displays the employee's first initial, middle initial, last name, and salary:

```
120 PRINT USING "! ! \          \ $$#,###.##"; F$, M$, L$, S
```

This example uses exclamation points in the format for the initials, backslashes for the last name, and the # and other symbols for the salary.

Illustrative Programs

As a simple example of the PRINT USING statement, consider the interest-calculation program in Section 2 (Figure D2–9). This program can use the PRINT USING statement to make its output easier to read. Figure D5–18 shows the result. In this program, the values of the beginning bank balance, interest earned, and ending bank balance are displayed with the PRINT USING statements. Dollar signs, commas, and decimal points are used in the format.

As a more complex example, consider the interest-calculation program with a loop, in Section 4 (Figure D4–9). Figure D5–19 shows this program with PRINT USING statements. In this program, the values of YEAR, INTEREST, and BAL are displayed in the format given in the PRINT USING statement at line 260. This format is designed to align the columns under the headings displayed by the PRINT statement at line 190. Notice that dollar signs, a comma, and decimal points are used in the format in the PRINT USING statement. The program also displays a final output line with the PRINT USING statement at line 310.

Figure D5–18   The Interest-Calculation Program, Using the PRINT USING Statement

(a)   The Program

```
100 REM - INTEREST CALCULATION PROGRAM
110 REM - VARIABLES:
120 REM        BEGINBAL = BEGINNING BANK BALANCE
130 REM        RATE     = INTEREST RATE
140 REM        INTEREST = INTEREST EARNED
150 REM        ENDBAL   = ENDING BANK BALANCE
160 REM
170 CLS
180 PRINT "INTEREST CALCULATION"
190 PRINT
200 INPUT "ENTER BEGINNING BANK BALANCE: ", BEGINBAL
210 INPUT "ENTER INTEREST RATE: ", RATE
220 LET INTEREST = BEGINBAL * RATE
230 LET ENDBAL = BEGINBAL + INTEREST
240 PRINT
250 PRINT USING "BEGINNING BANK BALANCE: $$#,###.##"; BEGINBAL
260 PRINT USING "INTEREST EARNED:           $$###.##"; INTEREST
270 PRINT USING "ENDING BANK BALANCE:   $$##,###.##"; ENDBAL
280 PRINT
290 PRINT "END OF PROGRAM"
300 END
```

(b)   Input and Output

```
INTEREST CALCULATION

ENTER BEGINNING BANK BALANCE: 1500
ENTER INTEREST RATE: .08

BEGINNING BANK BALANCE:   $1,500.00
INTEREST EARNED:            $120.00
ENDING BANK BALANCE:      $1,620.00

END OF PROGRAM
```

Figure D5–19 An Interest-Calculation Program with Loop, Using the PRINT USING Statement

(a) The Program

```
100 REM - INTEREST CALCULATION PROGRAM
110 REM - VARIABLES:
120 REM       BAL       = BANK BALANCE
130 REM       YEAR      = YEAR
140 REM       INTEREST  = INTEREST EARNED
150 REM
160 CLS
170 PRINT "   INTEREST CALCULATION"
180 PRINT
190 PRINT "YEAR    INTEREST     BALANCE"
200 PRINT
210 LET BAL = 1000
220 LET YEAR = 1
230 WHILE BAL < 2000
240   LET INTEREST = .08 * BAL
250   LET BAL = BAL + INTEREST
260   PRINT USING " ##     $$##.##     $$,###.##"; YEAR, INTEREST, BAL
270   LET YEAR = YEAR + 1
280 WEND
290 LET YEAR - YEAR - 1
300 PRINT
310 PRINT USING "BALANCE DOUBLES IN ## YEARS"; YEAR
320 END
```

(b) Output

```
     INTEREST CALCULATION

YEAR    INTEREST     BALANCE

  1      $80.00     $1,080.00
  2      $86.40     $1,166.40
  3      $93.31     $1,259.71
  4     $100.78     $1,360.49
  5     $108.84     $1,469.33
  6     $117.55     $1,586.87
  7     $126.95     $1,713.82
  8     $137.11     $1,850.93
  9     $148.07     $1,999.00
 10     $159.92     $2,158.93

BALANCE DOUBLES IN 10 YEARS
```

Printer Output

To produce printer output, the LPRINT USING statement can be used. The syntax and format rules for this statement are the same as for the PRINT USING statement, with the exception that the first keyword must be LPRINT. For example, the following is an LPRINT USING statement:

```
140 LPRINT USING "TOTAL = ###, AVERAGE = ##.#"; T, A
```

The result is the same as an equivalent PRINT USING statement, except that the output is printed on the printer, rather than displayed on the screen.

A SAMPLE PROGRAM

This section develops a program that uses several of the topics just covered. The program solves a problem that involves determining averages and grades for students in a course and producing a course grade report.

Problem Definition

A program is needed to calculate the weighted average of three test scores for each student in a course. The first test score is weighted 15%, the second test score is weighted 35%, and the last score is weighted 50%. The program must also determine the student's letter grade based on a straight percentage scale (that is, 90% to 100% is an A; 80% to 89% is a B; 70% to 79% is a C; 60% to 69% is a D; and 59% or less is an F). Finally, the program must determine the overall course average score for all students in the course.

The input to the program consists of an identification number and three test scores for each student in the course. The number of students is unknown, but the data for all students will be prepared in a batch for processing by the program. To end the processing, the last input will contain 9999 for the student identification number and 0 for each test score.

The output from the program is a course grade report in the layout shown in Figure D5–20. Notice that the student number, average score, and letter grade are printed in columns below headings. The overall course average is printed at the end.

Program Design

This program will be designed in a modular fashion using subroutines. Figure D5–21 shows the structure chart for the program. Notice that the structure chart has three levels. The first level is the main program. The main program calls three subroutines at the second level to display the report headings, produce the body of the report, and compute and display the overall course average.

The subroutine that produces the report body calls six subroutines at the third level. It calls subroutines to read a student's test score data, compute a student's average score, determine a student's letter grade,

Figure D5–20 Output Layout for the Grade-Report Program

```
                     COURSE GRADE REPORT

          STUDENT          AVERAGE          LETTER
          NUMBER            SCORE           GRADE

           XXXX              XXX              X
           XXXX              XXX              X
           XXXX              XXX              X

        COURSE AVERAGE XXX.X
```

Figure D5–21 Structure Chart for the Grade-Report Program

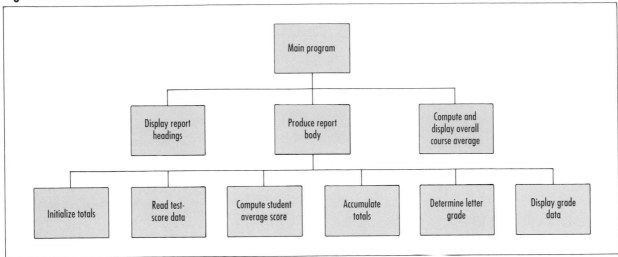

and display a student's grade data. It also calls a subroutine to initialize variables used to find the total number of students and total average score, and a subroutine to accumulate the totals. These totals are needed to compute the overall course average.

Figure D5–22 gives the pseudocode for the program. Separate pseudocode is shown for the main program and the nine subroutines. Notice that the pseudocode of the subroutine that produces the report body has an input loop and that the pseudocode of the subroutine that determines the letter grade requires decisions.

Figure D5–23 shows the flowcharts for the program. There is a separate flowchart for each of the nine subroutines and for the main program. The flowchart of the subroutine that produces the report body has an input loop, and the flowchart of the subroutine that determines the letter grade has decisions.

Program Coding

Figure D5–24 shows the complete grade-report program. The program is organized in a modular fashion, as given in the structure chart. The logic of the main program and of each subroutine follows that of its pseudocode and flowchart.

The main program consists of three GOSUB statements to call three subroutines. The produce-report-body subroutine has a number of GOSUB statements and a WHILE loop that forms the input loop. The read-test-score-data subroutine uses a READ statement to read the input data from DATA statements. The determine-letter-grade subroutine uses IF statements to decide what the letter grade should be. The display-grade-data subroutine uses the PRINT USING statement to format the output as does the compute-and-display-overall-average subroutine.

Figure D5–22   Pseudocode for the Grade-Report Program

```
   Main program:
     Call display report headings subroutine
     Call produce report body subroutine
     Call compute and display overall average subroutine
     End

   Display report headings subroutine:
     Display report title
     Display column headings
     Return

   Produce report body subroutine:
     Call initialize totals subroutine
     Call read test score data subroutine
     DO WHILE student ID not equal to 9999
        Call compute student average score subroutine
        Call accumulate totals subroutine
        Call determine letter grade subroutine
        Call display grade data subroutine
        Call read test score data subroutine
     END-DO
     Return

   Compute and display overall average subroutine:
     Overall average = total average / number of students
     Display overall average
     Return

   Initialize totals subroutine:
     Initialize number of students to 0
     Initialize total average to 0
     Return

   Read test score data subroutine:
     Read student ID, three test scores
     Return

   Compute student average score subroutine:
     Student average = 15% of first test score +
                       35% of second test score +
                       50% of third test score
     Return

   Accumulate totals subroutine:
     Add 1 to number of students
     Add student average to total average
     Return

   Determine letter grade subroutine:
     IF student average ≥ 90 THEN
       Letter grade is A
     ELSE
       IF student average ≥ 80 THEN
         Letter grade is B
       ELSE
         IF student average ≥ 70 THEN
           Letter grade is C
         ELSE
           IF student average ≥ 60 THEN
             Letter grade is D
           ELSE
             Letter grade is F
           END-IF
         END-IF
       END-IF
     END-IF
     Return

   Display grade data subroutine:
     Display student ID, student average, letter grade
     Return
```

Figure D5–23 Flowcharts for the Grade-Report Program (Part 1 of 3)

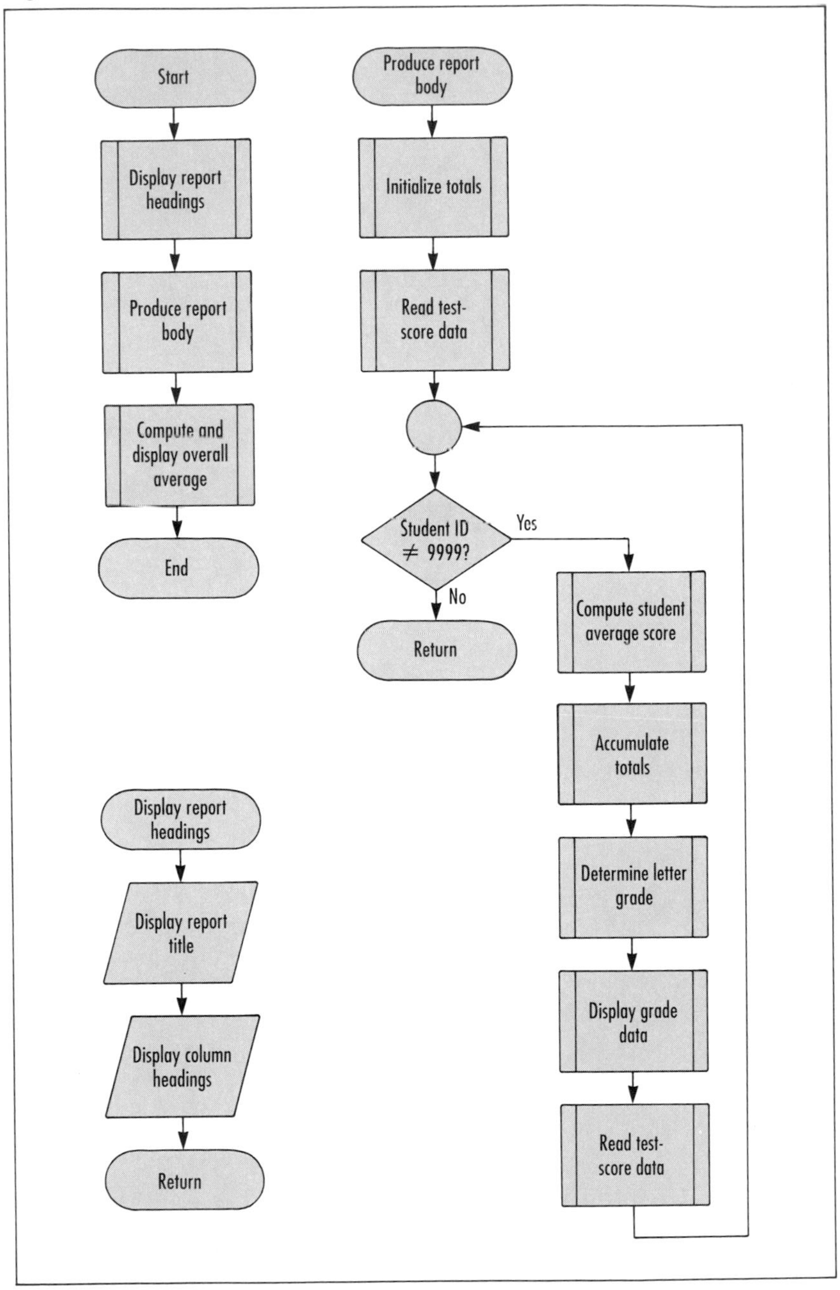

Program Testing

To test this program, test data should be provided that produces a range of values for the students' average scores. This data will provide a thorough test of the determine-letter-grade subroutine and also check the computation of the student's average score. Table D5–4 shows several

Figure D5–23   Flowcharts for the Grade-Report Program (Part 2 of 3)

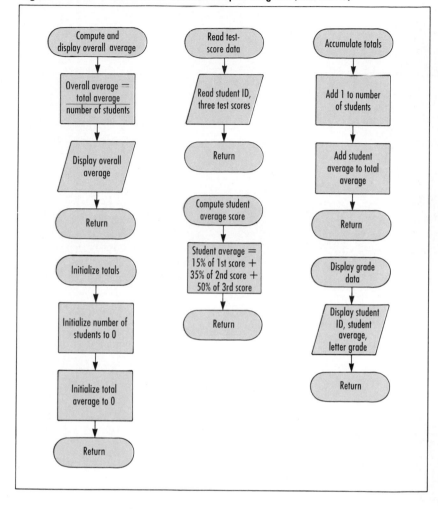

sets of input test data and the expected output. The data should be arranged in random order before it is tested with the program. Figure
D5–25 shows the output from running the program with this data. As
you can see, all test cases give the correct results, and the overall course
average is correct.

Program Documentation

A modular program should be well documented with remarks for each
subroutine and each subroutine call. The program in Figure D5–24 illustrates these remarks. The complete set of documentation should include a listing of the program (Figure D–24) and the output from
running the program (Figure D5–25). The documentation may also include the output layout (Figure D5–20), the structure chart (Figure
D5–21), the pseudocode (Figure D5–22), the flowcharts (Figure
D5–23), and the input test data and expected output (Table D5–4).

Figure D5–23 Flowcharts for the Grade-Report Program (Part 3 of 3)

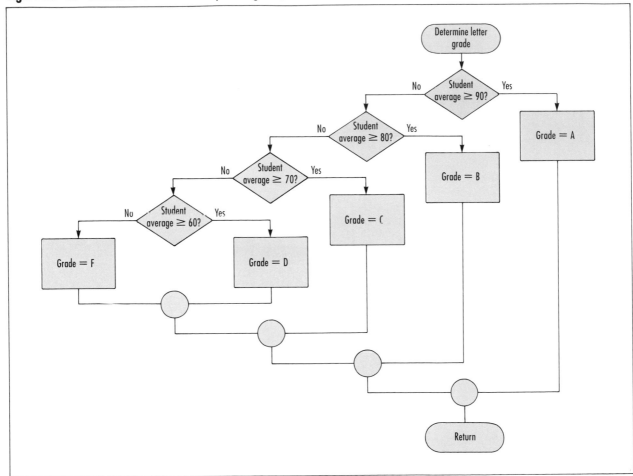

Terms to Remember

Function p. 648
Subroutine p. 637

Review Questions

1. When a subroutine is referenced in a program, you say it is

     _____.

2. The last statement executed in a subroutine must be a(n)
     _____ statement.

3. Code a statement to call a subroutine that begins at line 500.

4. What is the next statement executed after a RETURN statement is
    executed?

Figure D5–24 The Grade-Report Program (Part 1 of 2)

```
100 REM - GRADE REPORT PROGRAM
110 REM - VARIABLES:
120 REM      ID        = STUDENT ID
130 REM      SCORE1    = SCORE ON FIRST TEST
140 REM      SCORE2    = SCORE ON SECOND TEST
150 REM      SCORE3    = SCORE ON THIRD TEST
160 REM      STU.AVG   = STUDENT AVERAGE SCORE
170 REM      GRADE$    = STUDENT GRADE
180 REM      NUM.STU   = NUMBER OF STUDENTS
190 REM      TOTAL.AVG = TOTAL AVERAGE SCORE
200 REM      ALL.AVG   = OVERALL AVERAGE SCORE
210 REM
220 REM - MAIN PROGRAM
230 GOSUB 280  'CALL DISPLAY REPORT HEADINGS SUBROUTINE
240 GOSUB 370  'CALL PRODUCE REPORT BODY SUBROUTINE
250 GOSUB 490  'CALL COMPUTE AND DISPLAY OVERALL AVERAGE SUBROUTINE
260 END
270 REM
280 REM - DISPLAY REPORT HEADINGS SUBROUTINE
290 CLS
300 PRINT "        COURSE GRADE REPORT"
310 PRINT
320 PRINT "STUDENT         AVERAGE        LETTER"
330 PRINT "NUMBER           SCORE         GRADE"
340 PRINT
350 RETURN
360 REM
370 REM - PRODUCE REPORT BODY SUBROUTINE
380 GOSUB 540  'CALL INITIALIZE TOTALS SUBROUTINE
390 GOSUB 590  'CALL READ TEST SCORE DATA SUBROUTINE
400 WHILE ID <> 9999
410    GOSUB 700  'CALL COMPUTE STUDENT AVERAGE SCORE SUBROUTINE
420    GOSUB 740  'CALL ACCUMULATE TOTALS SUBROUTINE
430    GOSUB 790  'CALL DETERMINE LETTER GRADE SUBROUTINE
440    GOSUB 830  'CALL DISPLAY GRADE DATA SUBROUTINE
450    GOSUB 590  'CALL READ TEST SCORE DATA SUBROUTINE
460 WEND
470 RETURN
480 REM
490 REM - COMPUTE AND DISPLAY OVERALL AVERAGE SUBROUTINE
500 LET ALL.AVG = TOTAL.AVG / NUM.STU
510 PRINT
520 PRINT USING "COURSE AVERAGE ###.#"; ALL.AVG
530 REM
540 REM - INITIALIZE TOTALS SUBROUTINE
550 LET NUM.STU = 0
560 LET TOTAL.AVG = 0
570 RETURN
580 REM
```

5. What is wrong with the following program?

```
10 INPUT X
20 GOSUB 40
30 PRINT Y
40 LET Y = 2 * X
50 RETURN
60 END
```

6. How is a modular program coded in BASIC?

7. How are subroutines used in top-down design?

8. How is a menu-driven program organized in BASIC?

Figure D5–24 The Grade-Report Program (Part 2 of 2)

```
590 REM - READ TEST SCORE DATA SUBROUTINE
600 READ ID, SCORE1, SCORE2, SCORE3
610 REM - INPUT DATA
620 DATA 1006,86,76,81,1011,80,50,71,1002,83,93,100
630 DATA 1009,50,70,76,1015,0,0,0,1004,88,88,90
640 DATA 1005,82,79,90,1013,18,48,79,1008,73,80,72
650 DATA 1001,100,100,100,1012,45,75,54,1010,68,68,70
660 DATA 1003,76,96,90,1007,78,78,80,1014,40,40,70
670 DATA 9999,0,0,0
680 RETURN
690 REM
700 REM - COMPUTE STUDENT AVERAGE SCORE SUBROUTINE
710 LET STU.AVG = .15 * SCORE1 + .35 * SCORE2 + .5 * SCORE3
720 RETURN
730 REM
740 REM - ACCUMULATE TOTALS SUBROUTINE
750 LET NUM.STU = NUM.STU + 1
760 LET TOTAL.AVG = TOTAL.AVG + STU.AVG
770 RETURN
780 REM
790 REM - DETERMINE LETTER GRADE SUBROUTINE
800 IF STU.AVG >= 90 THEN LET GRADE$ = "A"
       ELSE IF STU.AVG >= 80 THEN LET CRADE$ = "B"
       ELSE IF STU.AVG >= 70 THEN LET GRADE$ = "C"
       ELSE IF STU.AVG >= 60 THEN LET GRADE$ = "D"
       ELSE LET GRADE$ = "F"
810 RETURN
820 REM
830 REM - DISPLAY GRADE DATA SUBROUTINE
840 PRINT USING " ####          ###              !"; ID,
STU.AVG, GRADE$
850 RETURN
```

9. Code a statement that is equivalent to the following algebraic equation:

$$c = \sqrt{a^2 + b^2}$$

Use a function.

10. Assume that X is 6.8, Y is 4.6, and Z is 2.1. What is the value of each of the following?

   a. INT(X)

   b. INT(Y / Z)

   c. INT(Z - X)

   d. INT(Y + .3333)

11. Assume that FIRST.NAME\$, MIDDLE.NAME\$, and LAST.NAME\$ equal a person's first name, middle name, and last name, respectively. Code a statement that prints the person's three initials. Use functions.

12. What is the value of each variable after the following group of statements is executed?

```
10 READ P, Q, R
20 READ S, T
30 DATA 8,4,7,3,6
```

13. How can a batch processing program be created in BASIC?

Table D5–4 Input Test Data and Expected Output for the Grade-Report Program

	Input Test Data				Expected Output	
Student Number	First Score	Second Score	Third Score		Average Score	Letter Grade
1001	100	100	100		100	A
1002	83	93	100		95	A
1003	76	96	90		90	A
1004	88	88	90		89	B
1005	82	79	90		85	B
1006	86	76	81		80	B
1007	78	78	80		79	C
1008	73	80	72		75	C
1009	50	70	76		70	C
1010	68	68	70		69	D
1011	80	50	71		65	D
1012	45	75	54		60	D
1013	18	48	79		59	F
1014	40	40	70		55	F
1015	0	0	0		0	F

Course average: 71.4

Figure D5–25 Output from the Grade-Report Program

```
                    COURSE GRADE REPORT

        STUDENT           AVERAGE          LETTER
        NUMBER            SCORE            GRADE

          1006              80               B
          1011              65               D
          1002              95               A
          1009              70               C
          1015               0               F
          1004              89               B
          1005              85               B
          1013              59               F
          1008              75               C
          1001             100               A
          1012              60               D
          1010              69               D
          1003              90               A
          1007              79               C
          1014              55               F

        COURSE AVERAGE   71.4
```

14. Code a PRINT USING statement that displays the values of S, T, and U. All values should be displayed with three places to the left of the decimal point and one to the right. Two blank spaces should separate the output values.

15. Code a PRINT USING statement that displays the word AMOUNT followed by the value of A. The value of A should be displayed with five places to the left of the decimal point and two places to the right, a comma, a dollar sign, and a minus sign on the right if A is negative.

16. Assume that your name and date of birth are assigned to string variables N$ and D$, respectively. Code a PRINT USING statement to display this data.

Programming Problems

Any of the programs for problems in previous sections can be organized in a modular fashion using subroutines. In addition, any previous program can use the PRINT USING statement instead of the PRINT statement.

1. The tuition charged a student at a small private college is based on the number of units (credits) that the student takes during a quarter. The tuition charge is $200 plus $25 per unit for each of the first eight units and $32.50 per unit for all units taken over eight. Write a subroutine in BASIC to determine the tuition charge given the number of units.

   Write a main program in BASIC that accepts student data consisting of the student number, the units taken during the fall quarter, the units taken during the winter quarter, and the units taken during the spring quarter. Then, the main program should use the subroutine described in the previous paragraph, to calculate the tuition for each quarter. Finally, the main program should display these results along with the student number.

   Use the following input data to test the program:

Student Number	Units Taken		
	Fall Quarter	**Winter Quarter**	**Spring Quarter**
1018	7.0	18.0	15.0
1205	15.0	12.5	6.0
1214	15.5	15.5	15.5
1218	8.0	7.0	5.0
1293	8.5	7.5	4.0
1304	6.0	6.0	6.0
1351	10.5	18.5	0.0
1354	0.0	15.0	6.0
0000 (trailer value)			

2. Write the following subroutines in BASIC:

   a. *Calculate charge.* This subroutine determines the total gas utility charge based on the number of gas therms used. (Gas consumption is measured in therms.) The charge is $.09 per therm for the first

200 therms, $.08 per therm for the next 300 therms, $.07 per therm for the next 500 therms, and $.065 per therm for all gas used over 1000 therms.

b. *Display output.* This subroutine displays the customer number, the gas used in therms, and the charge for one month.

Write a main program in BASIC that accepts the customer number and the gas consumed for three separate months. Then, through three calls of the first subroutine, the main program should calculate the charge for each of the three months. Finally, the main program should display the results for each month, using three calls of the second subroutine.

Use the following data to test the program:

Customer Number	Month 1	Month 2	Month 3
11825	425	172	253
13972	665	892	1283
14821	45	572	313
19213	1562	973	865
28416	200	500	1000
31082	0	300	600
99999 (trailer value)			

3. A classic problem in computer programming is the "automatic change-maker" problem. The problem involves determining the breakdown of a customer's change into various denominations.

Write a BASIC program that solves the automatic change-maker problem. The program should accept a customer's number, the amount of the customer's bill, and the cash payment. Then the program should display the customer's number, the amount of the bill, the payment, and the change, if any. If there is no change, an appropriate message should be displayed. Similarly, if the payment is less than the bill, a message should be displayed.

For each transaction in which there is change, the program should display the number and kind of each denomination in the change. The total number of bills and coins should be kept to a minimum. Assume that only pennies ($.01), nickels ($.05), dimes ($.10), quarters ($.25), and one-dollar bills are available for change.

Use the following data to test the program:

Customer's Number	Customer's Bill	Payment
1234	$ 3.59	$ 5.00
2345	8.00	8.00
3456	14.95	14.00
4567	21.03	25.00
5678	9.95	50.00
6789	.29	1.00

4. Write a BASIC program to grade a six-question multiple-choice test. Each question on the test can be answered A, B, C, D, or E. The first input is the correct answers. Assign the correct answers to a single string variable. Each successive set of input consists of a student's name and his or her answers to the six questions. Assign the student's answers to a single string variable. The program should determine the number of correct answers for each student. The output should give each student's name, his or her answers, and the number of correct answers.

Use the following data to test the program:

Correct Answers: BECADC

Student's Name	Student's Answers
JONES	AECBDC
SMITH	BECADC
JOHNSON	EABADC
DOE	BCDEAB
ANDREWS	EDACBD
COLE	CECADC
EMERY	BEEADC

5. Complete the program for Problem 6 in Section 4 with the additional requirement that all input data is read from DATA statements and all output is printed with PRINT USING statements.

SECTION 6
ARRAYS

Many times you need to store and process a large amount of data in a program. For example, you may need to process a list of 50 numbers, all of which must be available in the program at the same time. With the techniques discussed so far, you would have to use a separate variable for each number in the list. Another approach to this type of problem is to identify the entire list of data by a single variable. Then you could refer to each list value by indicating its position in the list. A list of data like this is called an *array*. This section explains the use of arrays in BASIC. After completing this section you should be able to write programs that process arrays of data.

ARRAYS AND ARRAY ELEMENTS

An **array** is a group of data values that is identified in a program by a single name. You can think of an array as a list or table of data. For example, Figure D6–1 shows an array of 10 numbers identified by the name A. The name that refers to an array is called an **array variable**. An array variable must follow the same syntax rules as a simple variable.

Each value in an array is called an **array element**. In the array in Figure D6–1, the number 23.2 is an array element. Similarly, 17.5, –10.8, and so forth are elements of the array A. There are 10 elements in this array.

The elements of an array are numbered; the first element is numbered 1, the second element is numbered 2, and so forth. Figure D6–1 shows numbers of the elements of the array A. Element number 1 in this array is 23.2, element number 2 is 17.5, and so on, up to element number 10, which is 16.2. The element numbers do not actually appear in the array, but the computer keeps track of the elements by their numbers.

Figure D6–1   An Array

Element numbers	The array A
1 →	23.2
2 →	17.5
3 →	– 10.8
4 →	6.3
5 →	31.5
6 →	– 4.3
7 →	5.7
8 →	13.8
9 →	20.5
10 →	16.2

Subscripted Variables

In a program, you identify an array element by using the array variable followed by the number of the element in parentheses. Figure D6–2 shows how this is done for the array A. The first element in this array is identified by A(1), the fifth element is A(5), and the last element is A(10). The number in parentheses following the array variable is called a **subscript**. An array variable with a subscript is called a **subscripted variable**. A subscripted variable such as A(5) is read "A sub five."

The data in an array is referred to collectively by the array variable. An array variable, however, cannot be used by itself in a BASIC program. An array variable must always be followed by a subscript to identify an element of the array. A subscripted variable may be used like any other variable. Thus, subscripted variables may be used in INPUT and PRINT statements and in numeric expressions. For example, assume that X and Y identify arrays of ten elements each. Then the following statements are valid examples of the use of subscripted variables:

```
110 INPUT X(1), Y(1)
140 IF Y(5) > X(10) THEN PRINT Y(5)
180 LET W = X(3) + X(5) + X(7)
190 PRINT W, X(7), X(5), X(3)
```

Dimensioning Arrays

To use an array in a program, you must specify the array in a DIM statement. This is called **dimensioning the array**. The syntax of the DIM statement is as follows:

```
ln DIM list of array declarations
```

Figure D6–2 Subscripted Variables for an Array

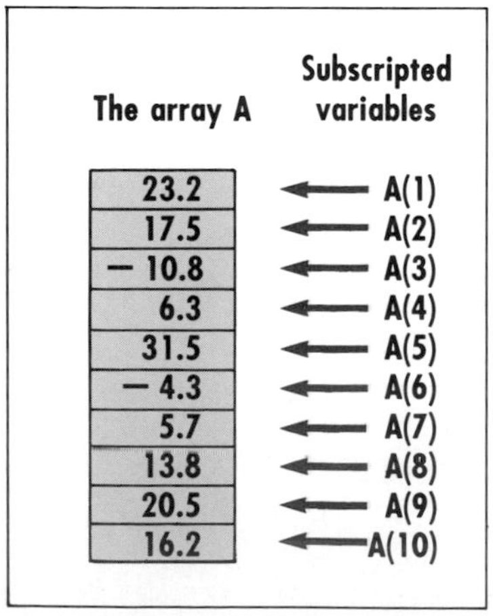

In the DIM statement, each array declaration consists of an array variable followed by a whole number enclosed in parenthcses. The array declarations must be separated by commas. The following statement contains two array declarations:

```
100 DIM B(50), C(25)
```

The number in parentheses is *not* a subscript, but rather specifies the maximum element number for the array. In this example, the elements of array B are numbered 1 to 50, and the elements for array C are numbered 1 to 25. (Actually, each array has an element numbered 0, but most people don't use it. It will be ignored in this book.)

As many arrays as arc needed can be dimensioned in a DIM statement. All arrays can be dimensioned in one DIM statement, or several statements can be used. For example, the following statements could be used in a program:

```
10 DIM Z(100)
20 DIM S(50), T(200), U(84)
30 DIM W(320), D(39)
```

DIM statements may appear anywhere in a program, as long as each array is dimensioned before it is used. It is usually best to group all DIM statements together at the beginning of the program so that it is easier to refer to the statements to check whether an array has been dimensioned.

Subscripts

A subscript indicates which element of an array is being identified. As you have seen, a subscript may be a numeric constant. A subscript may also be a numeric variable. For example, A(I) is a valid subscripted variable. This is read "A sub I." The element of the array A identified by this variable depends on the value of I. For example, if the value of I is 3, then A(I) identifies the third element of the array.

The use of a variable as a subscript is a powerful technique in BASIC programming. As an example, assume that the input to a program consists of ten numbers. The program must store the numbers in an array, compute the total of the numbers, display the array data, and then display the total. The program in Figure D6–3 shows how this can be done. The program is complete except for the input and output of the array data. (Array input and output are discussed later.)

At the beginning of the program is a DIM statement for the array A. Processing in the program begins with the input of the array data. The total of the array elements is then found by successively adding each element to the variable TOTAL. This is accomplished in a FOR loop by using the FOR statement control variable as the subscript to identify an array element. Initially, the value of TOTAL is set to zero. With the first execution of the loop, the control variable I is 1, and hence the value of A(1) is added to TOTAL. The second execution of the loop causes the value of A(2) to be added to TOTAL. This continues for the remaining executions of the loop. Upon completion of the FOR loop,

Figure D6–3 An Array-Processing Program

```
100 REM - ARRAY DATA TOTALING PROGRAM
110 REM - VARIABLES:
120 REM       A     = ARRAY DATA
130 REM       TOTAL = TOTAL OF ARRAY DATA
140 REM       I     = COUNTER
150 REM
160 DIM A(10)
170 REM - ACCEPT DATA FOR ARRAY
        .
        .
        .
230 REM - FIND TOTAL OF ARRAY DATA
240 LET TOTAL = 0
250 FOR I = 1 TO 10
260    LET TOTAL = TOTAL + A(I)
270 NEXT I
280 REM - DISPLAY ARRAY DATA
        .
        .
        .
340 REM - DISPLAY TOTAL
350 PRINT
360 PRINT "TOTAL"; TOTAL
370 END
```

the value of TOTAL is 0+A(1)+A(2)+. . .+A(10). The program terminates after displaying the array data and the total.

In addition to constants and variables, numeric expressions can be used as subscripts. For example, A(2*I–1) is a valid subscripted variable. If I is 5, this variable refers to the ninth element of A. Any valid numeric expression can be used as a subscript.

The value of a subscript, whether a constant, a variable, or a more complex expression, must be between 1 and the maximum element number declared in the DIM statement. Thus, a subscript cannot be negative. (A zero subscript is valid but rarely used.) Similarly, if A has a maximum element number of 10, A(15) is invalid.

The value of a subscript need not be a whole number. For example, A(X), where the value of X is 3.25, is acceptable. When the subscript is not a whole number, its value depends on the version of BASIC. In Microsoft BASIC, the value is rounded. Thus, if X is 3.25, A(X) is interpreted as A(3), but if X is 3.75, A(X) is A(4).

String Arrays

An array may contain string data, in which case it is called a *string array*. Each element of a string array is a string. An array variable that identifies a string array is called a *string array variable*. A string array variable must end with a dollar sign. For example, A$ can be used as a string array variable. A *subscripted string variable* is a string array variable followed by a subscript in parentheses. For example, A$(1) is the first element (i.e., the first string) in the A$ array, A$(2) is the second element, and so forth. A string array must be declared in a DIM statement. Thus, if the array A$ is to contain 20 elements, the following DIM statement must be used in the program:

```
100 DIM A$(20)
```

A subscripted string variable can be used in statements just like a simple string variable. For example, the following statements use subscripted string variables:

```
120 LET A$(5) = A$(4)
140 IF A$(I) = "END" THEN PRINT "END OF DATA"
150 PRINT A$(18), A$(19), A$(20)
160 LET A$(I+2) = A$(I+1) + A$(I)
```

INPUT AND OUTPUT OF ARRAY DATA

Several techniques can be used for input and output of array data. One technique is to list each subscripted variable in an INPUT, READ, or PRINT statement. For example, assume that B is an array with five elements. You can use the following statement to accept five input values and assign them to the elements of B:

```
110 INPUT B(1), B(2), B(3), B(4), B(5)
```

When this statement is executed, five values must be entered after the question-mark prompt. You can use the same technique with the READ and PRINT statements.

The problem with this technique is that if the array is very large, the list of subscripted variables in the INPUT, READ, or PRINT statement is long and tiresome to code. A better approach is to use a loop to control the input or output operation. For example, the following sequence of statements uses a FOR loop to control the input process:

```
110 FOR I = 1 TO 5
120    INPUT B(I)
130 NEXT I
```

The control variable in this loop is used as a subscript for the array. With each execution of the loop, the INPUT statement is executed and a new value is accepted. Thus, with the first execution of the loop, the value of B(1) is accepted. Then the control variable is incremented and the value of B(2) is accepted during the second execution of the loop. This continues until the loop is terminated. Notice that because the INPUT statement is executed five times, five question-mark prompts are displayed. Thus, each value is entered on a separate line.

You can use this technique with a READ statement or a PRINT statement. For example, the following program segment reads the five values for B from a DATA statement and then displays the values:

```
110 FOR I = 1 TO 5
120    READ B(I)
130 NEXT I
140 FOR I = 1 TO 5
150    PRINT B(I)
160 NEXT I
170 DATA 78,95,84,36,67
```

The output is displayed with one value per line on five lines because the PRINT statement is in a loop that is executed five times.

Using a loop to control the input and output of array data is most useful for large arrays or when there is an unusual arrangement of the data. For example, assume that X and Y are two 20-element arrays that need to be displayed in adjacent columns. The following statements cause the data in the arrays to be displayed in two columns along with another column for the value of the FOR loop-control variable:

```
170 FOR J = 1 TO 20
180    PRINT J, X(J), Y(J)
190 NEXT J
```

You can now complete the program shown in Figure D6–3. Recall that this program finds the total of ten numbers. The program is not complete because the array input and output are not included. Figure D6–4 shows the program with the array input and output. The array input is accepted using a loop. Notice in Figure D6–4b that ten numbers are entered, one on each line. A loop is also used to display the array data with one element per line.

ARRAY SEARCHING

One common computer problem is to locate a specific value in a group of data—a process called *searching*. When the data is in an array, the problem involves searching through the array for a specific value.

As an example of array searching, assume that X is an array with 20 elements. The following statements search this array for the first element whose value is equal to that of V:

```
110 LET I = 1
120 WHILE X(I) <> V
130    LET I = I + 1
140 WEND
150 PRINT "VALUE FOUND AT ELEMENT"; I
```

Figure D6–4 A Complete Array-Processing Program

(a) The Program   **(b)** Input and Output

```
100 REM - ARRAY DATA TOTALING PROGRAM          ENTER ARRAY DATA
110 REM - VARIABLES:                           ? 23.2
120 REM      A     = ARRAY DATA                ? 17.5
130 REM      TOTAL = TOTAL OF ARRAY DATA       ? -10.8
140 REM      I     = COUNTER                   ? 6.3
150 REM                                        ? 31.5
160 DIM A(10)                                  ? -4.3
170 REM - ACCEPT DATA FOR ARRAY                ? 5.7
180 CLS                                        ? 13.8
190 PRINT "ENTER ARRAY DATA"                   ? 20.5
200 FOR I = 1 TO 10                            ? 16.2
210    INPUT A(I)
220 NEXT I                                     ARRAY DATA
230 REM - FIND TOTAL OF ARRAY DATA              23.2
240 LET TOTAL = 0                               17.5
250 FOR I = 1 TO 10                            -10.8
260    LET TOTAL = TOTAL + A(I)                  6.3
270 NEXT I                                      31.5
280 REM - DISPLAY ARRAY DATA                    -4.3
290 PRINT                                        5.7
300 PRINT "ARRAY DATA"                          13.8
310 FOR I = 1 TO 10                             20.5
320    PRINT A(I)                               16.2
330 NEXT I
340 REM - DISPLAY TOTAL                        TOTAL 119.6
350 PRINT
360 PRINT "TOTAL"; TOTAL
370 END
```

In this sequence, I is used as a subscript. Initially, the value of I is 1. Each time through the loop, I is increased by 1. The loop is repeated as long as X(I) is not equal to V. As soon as X(I) equals V, the loop is terminated. Then the value of I at that time is the number of the first element in X that has a value equal to V. This value of I is displayed along with an appropriate message when the loop is terminated.

The problem with this sequence of statements is that it does not take into account the case in which the value of V is not in the array. The sequence of statements shown in Figure D6–5 includes this case. In this sequence, the loop is repeated as long as X(I) is not equal to V *and* I is less than 20. As soon as either of these conditions is false, the loop is terminated. The latter case becomes false when the end of the array is reached. After ending the loop, the program must see if the value was actually found or if the loop was terminated without finding the value. If X(I) is equal to V, the value was found and the corresponding array element

Figure D6–5 Searching an Array

```
210 LET I = 1
220 WHILE X(I) <> V AND I < 20
230    LET I = I + 1
240 WEND
250 IF X(I) = V
       THEN PRINT "VALUE FOUND AT ELEMENT"; I
       ELSE PRINT "VALUE NOT FOUND"
```

number is displayed. If X(I) is not equal to V when the loop is terminated, the value was not found and an appropriate message is displayed.

Frequently, you need to search one array and retrieve the corresponding element of another array. For example, you may wish to search array X for value V and display the corresponding value of another array, Y, when V is found. The only modification in the sequence of statements in Figure D6–5 that is necessary is that Y(I) is displayed instead of I in the true part of statement 250.

A SAMPLE PROGRAM

This section develops a program for a problem that involves processing a table of data. The problem is to locate the price of an item ordered in a pricing table and to compute the cost of the order.

Problem Definition

Table D6–1 shows a table of item numbers, item descriptions, and prices. A program is needed to find the description and price of an item from this table when the item number is given, and to compute the order cost by multiplying the price by the quantity ordered. The input to the program is the customer number, the item number ordered, and the quantity ordered. The program should display the customer number, item number, item description, quantity ordered, price from the table, and order cost. Figure D6–6 shows how the input and output should appear. The program should display the message ITEM NOT FOUND IN PRICING TABLE if the requested item is not in the table.

Table D6–1 A Pricing Table

Item Number	Item Description	Price
1001	SCREWS	$2.95
1023	NAILS	$3.64
1045	BOLTS	$2.25
1172	WASHERS	$1.75
1185	NUTS	$1.52
1201	HOOKS	$1.95
1235	GLUE	$4.85
1278	CLAMP	$9.95
1384	HANGER	$6.28
1400	TAPE	$4.75

Figure D6–6   Input and Output Layout for the Order-Cost Calculation Program

```
CUSTOMER ORDER COST CALCULATION

DO YOU WANT TO COMPUTE ORDER COSTS? XXX

ENTER CUSTOMER NUMBER: XXXX
ENTER ITEM NUMBER ORDERED: XXXX
ENTER QUANTITY ORDERED: XXX

CUSTOMER NUMBER: XXXX
ITEM NUMBER: XXXX
ITEM DESCRIPTION: XXXXXXXX
QUANTITY ORDERED: XXX
PRICE: XX.XX
ORDER COST: XXX.XX

DO YOU WANT TO COMPUTE ANOTHER ORDER COST? XXX

END OF PROGRAM
```

Program Design

The pricing table for this problem has three columns of data: a column for the item numbers, a column for the item descriptions, and a column for the prices. These columns can be stored in three arrays in the program. The program must first read the pricing-table data and store it in the arrays. Then it must accept the customer-order data and determine the order costs. The program must also display the order-cost data. Figure D6–7 shows the structure chart that incorporates these functions. Notice that the structure chart has three levels.

As the structure chart indicates, the program will have a main program and four subroutines. Figure D6–8 shows the pseudocode for this program. Separate pseudocode is given for the main program and each subroutine. The subroutine for determining the order cost uses the array-searching logic discussed earlier to locate the price in the table.

Figure D6–7   Structure Chart for the Order-Cost Calculation Program

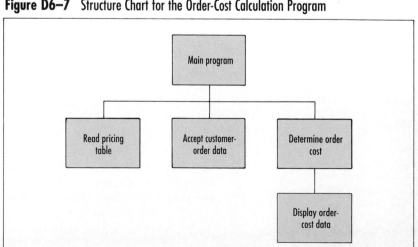

Figure D6–8 Pseudocode for the Order-Cost Calculation Program

```
Main program:
  Call read pricing table subroutine
  Display program title
  Display program repetition question; accept response
  DO WHILE response equals YES
    Call accept customer order data subroutine
    Call determine order cost subroutine
    Display program repetition question; accept response
  END-DO
  Display end of program message
  End

Read pricing table subroutine:
  DO FOR I varying from 1 to 10
    Read item number (I), item description (I), price (I)
  END-DO
  Return

Accept customer order data subroutine:
  Accept customer number, item number ordered, quantity ordered
  Return

Determine order cost subroutine:
  I = 1
  DO WHILE item number (I) not equal to item number ordered and I < 10
    Increase I by 1
  END-DO
  IF item number (I) = item number ordered
    Order cost = quantity ordered x price (I)
    Call display order cost data subroutine
  ELSE
    Display item not found message
  END-IF
  Return

Display order cost data subroutine:
  Display customer number, item number (I), item description (I),
          quantity ordered, price (I), order cost
  Return
```

Figure D6–9 gives the flowcharts for the program. There is a separate flowchart for each subroutine and for the main program.

Program Coding

The program to solve this problem is shown in Figure D6–10. The program is organized in a modular fashion as given in the structure chart. The logic of the main program and of each subroutine follows that of the pseudocode and flowcharts.

Notice in the read–pricing-table subroutine that the data for the three arrays is read from DATA statements. A FOR loop with a READ statement accomplishes this. Each execution of the READ statement in the loop reads the next three values from a DATA statement, and assigns the values to the next three elements of the item number, item description, and price arrays. Notice that a string array is used for the item descriptions. The data appears in groups of three in the DATA statement. The first group of three is the first item number, description, and price; then comes the second item number, description, and price; and so on.

Figure D6–9   Flowcharts for the Order-Cost Calculation Program (Part 1 of 2)

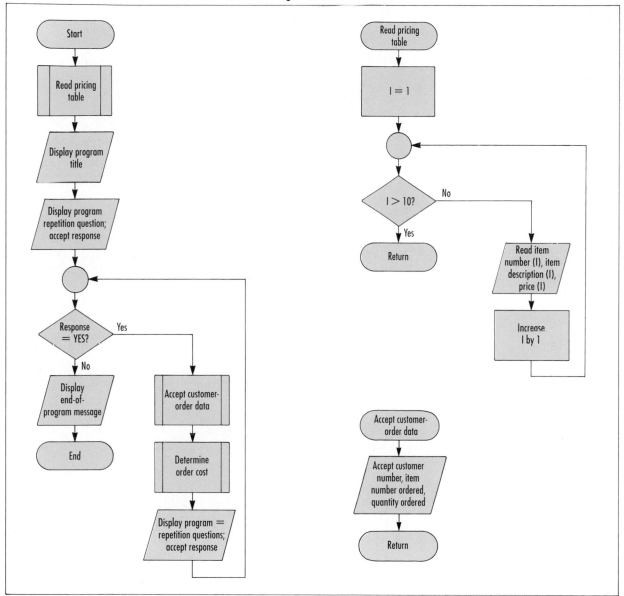

The determine–order-cost subroutine must first find the price from the pricing table. To do so, it uses the array-searching logic discussed earlier to find the item number or to search the entire array without finding the item number. Then the subroutine checks to see if the item number has been found. If it has, it computes the order cost by multiplying the quantity ordered by the corresponding price from the table, and calls the display–order-cost-data subroutine. Otherwise, it displays an error message.

Figure D6–9   Flowcharts for the Order-Cost Calculation Program (Part 2 of 2)

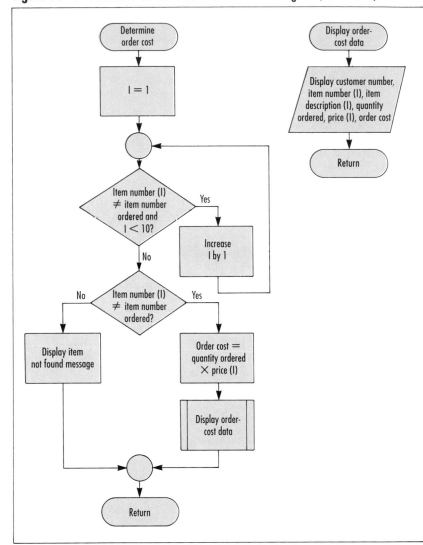

Program Testing

To test this program, item numbers should be used that correspond to the first item in the table, the last item in the table, and items in between. In addition, item numbers not in the table should be included in the test data. A range of values for the quantity ordered should be used. Table D6–2 shows several sets of input test data and the expected output from each case. The input and output from running the program with this data are shown in Figure D6–11. As you can see, all test cases give the correct results.

Figure D6–10   The Order-Cost Calculation Program

```
100 REM - ORDER COST CALCULATION PROGRAM
110 REM - VARIABLES:
120 REM        ITEM.NUM   = ITEM NUMBER ARRAY
130 REM        ITEM.DESC$ = ITEM DESCRIPTION ARRAY
140 REM        PRICE      = PRICE ARRAY
150 REM        RES$       = RESPONSE TO QUESTION
160 REM        CUS.NUM    = CUSTOMER NUMBER
170 REM        ITEM.ORD   = ITEM NUMBER ORDERED
180 REM        QTY.ORD    = QUANTITY ORDERED
190 REM        ORD.COST   = ORDER COST
200 REM        I          = COUNTER
210 REM
220 DIM ITEM.NUM(10), ITEM.DESC$(10), PRICE(10)
230 REM - MAIN PROGRAM
240 GOSUB 390  'CALL READ PRICING TABLE SUBROUTINE
250 CLS
260 PRINT "CUSTOMER ORDER COST CALCULATION"
270 PRINT
280 INPUT "DO YOU WANT TO COMPUTE ORDER COSTS? ",RES$
290 WHILE RES$ = "YES"
300   GOSUB 500  'CALL ACCEPT CUSTOMER ORDER DATA SUBROUTINE
310   GOSUB 580  'CALL DETERMINE ORDER COST SUBROUTINE
320   PRINT
330   INPUT "DO YOU WANT TO COMPUTE ANOTHER ORDER COST? ", RES$
340 WEND
350 PRINT
360 PRINT "END OF PROGRAM"
370 END
380 REM
390 REM - READ PRICING TABLE SUBROUTINE
400 FOR I = 1 TO 10
410   READ ITEM.NUM(I), ITEM.DESC$(I), PRICE(I)
420 NEXT I
430 REM - PRICING TABLE DATA
440 DATA 1001,SCREWS,2.95,1023,NAILS,3.64,1045,BOLTS,2.25
450 DATA 1172,WASHERS,1.75,1185,NUTS,1.52,1201,HOOKS,1.95
460 DATA 1235,GLUE,4.85,1278,CLAMP,9.95,1384,HANGER,6.28
470 DATA 1400,TAPE,4.75
480 RETURN
490 REM
500 REM - ACCEPT CUSTOMER ORDER DATA SUBROUTINE
510 PRINT
520 INPUT "ENTER CUSTOMER NUMBER: ", CUS.NUM
530 INPUT "ENTER ITEM NUMBER ORDERED: ", ITEM.ORD
540 INPUT "ENTER QUANTITY ORDERED: ", QTY.ORD
550 PRINT
560 RETURN
570 REM
580 REM - DETERMINE ORDER COST SUBROUTINE
590 LET I = 1
600 WHILE ITEM.NUM(I) <> ITEM.ORD AND I < 10
610   LET I = I + 1
620 WEND
630 IF ITEM.NUM(I) = ITEM.ORD
       THEN LET ORD.COST = QTY.ORD * PRICE(I): GOSUB 660
       ELSE PRINT "ITEM NOT FOUND IN PRICING TABLE"
640 RETURN
650 REM
660 REM - DISPLAY ORDER COST DATA SUBROUTINE
670 PRINT "CUSTOMER NUMBER:"; CUS.NUM
680 PRINT "ITEM NUMBER:"; ITEM.NUM(I)
690 PRINT "ITEM DESCRIPTION: "; ITEM.DESC$(I)
700 PRINT "QUANTITY ORDERED:"; QTY.ORD
710 PRINT "PRICE:"; PRICE(I)
720 PRINT "ORDER COST:"; ORD.COST
730 RETURN
```

Table D6–2 Input Test Data and Expected Output for the Order-Cost
Calculation Program

Input Test Data			Expected Output		
Customer Number	Item Number	Quantity Ordered	Item Description	Price	Order Cost
4321	1185	8	NUTS	1.52	12.16
5432	1001	5	SCREWS	2.95	14.75
6543	1225	10	ITEM NOT FOUND IN PRICING TABLE		
7654	1400	7	TAPE	4.75	33.25
8765	1484	12	ITEM NOT FOUND IN PRICING TABLE		
9876	1023	6	NAILS	3.64	21.84

Program Documentation

The program in Figure D6–10 has many remarks to document the program logic and modular organization. The complete set of documentation should include a listing of the program (Figure D6–10) and the input and output from running the program (Figure D6–11). In addition, the documentation may include the input and output layout (Figure D6–6), the structure chart (Figure D6–7), the pseudocode (Figure D6–8), the flowchart (Figure D6–9), and the input test data and expected output (Table D6–2).

TWO-DIMENSIONAL ARRAYS

The type of arrays described so far are called *one-dimensional arrays* because you think of the data in the array as being organized in one direction, like a column. BASIC also allows two-dimensional arrays.

A *two-dimensional array* is thought of as a table of data organized into rows and columns. Figure D6–12 shows a two-dimensional array of four rows and three columns. This data could represent the test scores of four students on three different exams. For example, the data in row 1 represents the three test scores of student number 1. The score on the first test for this student is 91; this score is found in column 1 of row 1. In row 1, column 2, is the score of this student on the second test (78). The third test score for this student is found in row 1, column 3. Similarly, test scores for the other students are found in the other rows.

Like a one-dimensional array, a two-dimensional array is identified by an array variable. A two-dimensional array variable must follow the same syntax rules as a one-dimensional array variable. The same array variable cannot be used in a program to identify both a one-dimensional array and a two-dimensional array.

Figure D6–11   Input and Output for the Order-Cost Calculation Program

```
             CUSTOMER ORDER COST CALCULATION

             DO YOU WANT TO COMPUTE ORDER COSTS? YES

             ENTER CUSTOMER NUMBER: 4321
             ENTER ITEM NUMBER ORDERED: 1185
             ENTER QUANTITY ORDERED: 8

             CUSTOMER NUMBER: 4321
             ITEM NUMBER: 1185
             ITEM DESCRIPTION: NUTS
             QUANTITY ORDERED: 8
             PRICE: 1.52
             ORDER COST: 12.16

             DO YOU WANT TO COMPUTE ANOTHER ORDER COST? YES

             ENTER CUSTOMER NUMBER: 5432
             ENTER ITEM NUMBER ORDERED: 1001
             ENTER QUANTITY ORDERED: 5

             CUSTOMER NUMBER: 5432
             ITEM NUMBER: 1001
             ITEM DESCRIPTION: SCREWS
             QUANTITY ORDERED: 5
             PRICE: 2.95
             ORDER COST: 14.75

             DO YOU WANT TO COMPUTE ANOTHER ORDER COST? YES

             ENTER CUSTOMER NUMBER: 6543
             ENTER ITEM NUMBER ORDERED: 1225
             ENTER QUANTITY ORDERED: 10

             ITEM NOT FOUND IN PRICING TABLE

             DO YOU WANT TO COMPUTE ANOTHER ORDER COST? YES

             ENTER CUSTOMER NUMBER: 7654
             ENTER ITEM NUMBER ORDERED: 1400
             ENTER QUANTITY ORDERED: 7

             CUSTOMER NUMBER: 7654
             ITEM NUMBER: 1400
             ITEM DESCRIPTION: TAPE
             QUANTITY ORDERED: 7
             PRICE: 4.75
             ORDER COST: 33.25
             DO YOU WANT TO COMPUTE ANOTHER ORDER COST? YES

             ENTER CUSTOMER NUMBER: 8765
             ENTER ITEM NUMBER ORDERED: 1484
             ENTER QUANTITY ORDERED: 12

             ITEM NOT FOUND IN PRICING TABLE

             DO YOU WANT TO COMPUTE ANOTHER ORDER COST? YES

             ENTER CUSTOMER NUMBER: 9876
             ENTER ITEM NUMBER ORDERED: 1023
             ENTER QUANTITY ORDERED: 6

             CUSTOMER NUMBER: 9876
             ITEM NUMBER: 1023
             ITEM DESCRIPTION: NAILS
             QUANTITY ORDERED: 6
             PRICE: 3.64
             ORDER COST: 21.84

             DO YOU WANT TO COMPUTE ANOTHER ORDER COST? NO

             END OF PROGRAM
```

Figure D6–12 A Two-Dimensional Array

		Column numbers	
	1	2	3
1	91	78	85
2	95	90	96
3	85	100	89
4	69	75	68

Row numbers

Subscripted Variables for Two-Dimensional Arrays

To identify an element of a two-dimensional array, both the row number and the column number of the element must be given; that is, a subscripted variable is formed from the array variable and *two* subscripts. The subscripts are separated by a comma and enclosed in parentheses. The first subscript is the row number, and the second subscript is the column number. For example, assume that the array in Figure D6–12 is identified by the array variable S. Then the element in row 1, column 2, is referred to by the subscripted variable $S(1,2)$. The element in row 3, column 1, is $S(3,1)$. Figure D6–13 shows the subscripted variables for all elements in this two-dimensional array.

Dimensioning Two-Dimensional Arrays

As with one-dimensional arrays, you must dimension two-dimensional arrays in a DIM statement. For example, assume that the array T has 25 rows and 8 columns. The following DIM statement dimensions this array:

```
110 DIM T(25,8)
```

The numbers in parentheses are the maximum row number and column number, respectively. The array T in this example is said to be a "25-by-8" array.

Figure D6–13 Subscripted Variables for a Two-Dimensional Array

		Column numbers	
	1	2	3
1	S(1, 1)	S,(1, 2)	S(1, 3)
2	S(2, 1)	S(2, 2)	S(2, 3)
3	S(3, 1)	S(3, 2)	S(3, 3)
4	S(4, 1)	S(4, 2)	S(4, 3)

Row numbers

You can use one- and two-dimensional arrays in the same program as long as each array is identified by a different array variable. In addition, the same DIM statement can be used for both one- and two-dimensional arrays. For example, the following statement declares three arrays:

```
130 DIM X(20,20), Y(50), Z(5,100)
```

The first array is a 20-by-20 two-dimensional array, the second array is a 50-element one-dimensional array, and the third array is a 5-by-100 two-dimensional array.

Subscripts for Two-Dimensional Arrays

Subscripts for two-dimensional arrays may be numeric constants, variables, or more complex expressions. For example, S(I,J) refers to the element in the "Ith" row and "Jth" column. Similarly, S(3,K+2) refers to the element in row 3 and column K+2. The value of each subscript must be between 1 and the maximum row and column number, respectively, specified in the DIM statement. (Either or both subscripts may be zero, although a zero subscript is rarely used.) As with one-dimensional arrays, if the subscript is not a whole number, its value is rounded to locate the array element.

You can use a two-dimensional subscripted variable like any other variable. For example, all the following statements are acceptable in BASIC:

```
100 INPUT S(1,1), S(1,2), S(1,3)
130 LET A = S(I,J) + S(I,K)
160 PRINT S(X+3,2*Y-1)
190 IF S(I,3) > 90 THEN PRINT S(I,3)
```

To illustrate the processing of a two-dimensional array in a program, assume that you need to find the total of all elements in the test-score array S discussed earlier. Figure D6–14 shows a program that does this. The program is complete except for the input and output of the array data, which will be discussed later.

In this program, the two-dimensional array is processed using nested FOR loops. The control variable of the outer loop is used as the subscript that indicates the row number. This control variable is incremented from 1 to 4. The control variable of the inner loop is used as the subscript for the column number. This control variable is incremented from 1 to 3. In the inner loop, an element of the array is added to the total (which is initially zero). For each repetition of the outer loop, the inner loop is executed three times, causing the elements of one row of the array to be added to the total. After four repetitions of the outer loop, the elements in all four rows will have been added to the total.

Input and Output of Two-Dimensional Array Data

Input and output of two-dimensional array data can be accomplished by listing the subscripted variables for the array in an INPUT, READ, or PRINT statement. For example, assume that X is a 2-by-3 array. The

Figure D6–14 A Two-Dimensional Array-Processing Program

```
100 REM - TWO-DIMENSIONAL ARRAY DATA TOTALING PROGRAM
110 REM - VARIABLES:
120 REM        S     = TEST SCORE ARRAY
130 REM        TOTAL = TOTAL SCORE
140 REM        I,J   = COUNTERS
150 REM
160 DIM S(4,3)
170 REM - READ DATA FOR ARRAY
        .
        .
        .
230 REM - FIND TOTAL OF ARRAY DATA
240 LET TOTAL = 0
250 FOR I = 1 TO 4
260   FOR J = 1 TO 3
270     LET TOTAL = TOTAL + S(I,J)
280   NEXT J
290 NEXT I
300 REM - DISPLAY ARRAY DATA
        .
        .
        .
430 REM - DISPLAY TOTAL
440 PRINT
450 PRINT "TOTAL OF ALL SCORES:"; TOTAL
460 REM - ARRAY DATA
        .
        .
        .
490 END
```

following statements can be used to accept input data for X and then to display the array data:

```
10 INPUT X(1,1), X(1,2), X(1,3), X(2,1), X(2,2), X(2,3)
20 PRINT X(1,1); X(1,2); X(1,3); X(2,1); X(2,2); X(2,3)
```

The problem with this technique is that if the array is large, the list of subscripted variables will be long. The usual approach, therefore, is to use some sort of looping technique. For example, assume that the data for the 4-by-3 test-score array S is to be entered one row at a time. The following loop can be used to accept the data:

```
100 FOR I = 1 TO 4
110   INPUT S(I,1), S(I,2), S(I,3)
120 NEXT I
```

Execution of this loop causes the INPUT statement to be executed four times. Each time the statement is executed, a question-mark prompt is displayed on the screen. Three test scores must be entered after each prompt. Each set of input data is stored in one row of the array.

You can use nested FOR loops for the input operation. The following statements show how this is done for the test-score array:

```
200 FOR I = 1 TO 4
210   FOR J = 1 TO 3
220     INPUT S(I,J)
230   NEXT J
240 NEXT I
```

In this case the INPUT statement is executed 12 times. Hence, 12 prompts are displayed on the screen. Following each prompt, one test score must be entered. The first three scores entered must be the data for the first row; then the data for the second row must be entered, and so forth.

Nested FOR loops are often used to read data for a two-dimensional array using READ and DATA statements. For example, the following statements can be used to read the test-score data:

```
110 FOR I = 1 TO 4
120   FOR J = 1 TO 3
130     READ S(I,J)
140   NEXT J
150 NEXT I
160 DATA 91,78,85,95,90,96
170 DATA 85,100,89,69,75,68
```

Notice that the data is recorded in the DATA statements in order by rows because this is the order in which the data is read in the nested FOR loops.

To display a two-dimensional array, you can use a FOR loop. For example, the following statements display the test-score array with each row on a separate line:

```
200 FOR I = 1 TO 4
210   PRINT S(I,1), S(I,2), S(I,3)
220 NEXT I
```

You can also use nested FOR loops as in the following example:

```
280 FOR I = 1 TO 4
290   FOR J = 1 TO 3
300     PRINT S(I,J)
310   NEXT J
320 NEXT I
```

In this case, however, the elements of the array are displayed one per line on 12 lines.

To display a two-dimensional array with one row per line using nested FOR loops requires a special technique. Recall that a comma or a semicolon at the end of a PRINT statement causes the next value displayed to appear on the same line as the previous value. You can use this fact in the previous example to display the data in rows. You start by modifying the PRINT statement at line 300 as follows:

```
300 PRINT S(I,J),
```

Notice that a comma has been added to the PRINT statement after the subscripted variable. Thus, each time the PRINT statement is executed, the array element is displayed on the same line as the previous element, provided there is room on the line. Once a line is full, the next value is automatically displayed at the beginning of the next line. In this case, five values are displayed on each line because there are five print zones.

(If a semicolon is used instead of a comma, the values are displayed closer together, and more data will appear on a line.)

This approach still does not display one row per line unless there are five elements in each row. By including a PRINT statement with no variables between the two NEXT statements, you obtain the desired result. The following statements show the complete sequence:

```
280 FOR I = 1 TO 4
290   FOR J = 1 TO 3
300     PRINT S(I,J),
310   NEXT J
320   PRINT
330 NEXT I
```

In this sequence, the comma in the PRINT statement at line 300 causes each value in a row to be displayed on the same line as the previous value. But after a complete row is displayed, the PRINT statement at line 320 causes a new line to be started. Thus, each row is displayed on a separate line.

You can now complete the program shown in Figure D6–14. Recall that this program finds the total of all elements in the 4-by-3 test-score array S. To complete the program, you need to include the statements necessary for the array data input and output.

The final program is shown in Figure D6–15. Nested FOR loops are used to read the array data from DATA statements. Nested FOR loops are also used to display the array data. The PRINT statement at line 370 displays the value of the outer FOR loop's control variable. This corresponds to the student's number. The comma at the end of this PRINT statement prevents a new line from being started. Thus, when the PRINT statement at line 390 is executed, the output is displayed on the same line as the previous output. The comma at the end of this PRINT statement causes all elements in one row of the array to be displayed on the same line. The PRINT statement at line 410 starts a new line for the next row of the array.

An Illustrative Program

To illustrate some of the two-dimensional array-processing techniques discussed in this section, consider the problem of tabulating test scores. Assume that there are 12 students in a class and that each student took four tests. The problem is to count, for each test, the number of students who scored between 90 and 100, between 80 and 89, between 70 and 79, and between 0 and 69. In addition, you need the total number of test scores that fall into each range for all tests.

Figure D6–16 shows the program that accomplishes this. In this program, SCORE is a 12-by-4 array that contains the test-score data. The rows correspond to the students, and the columns correspond to the tests. The 4-by-4 array COUNT is used to keep count of the number of test scores in each range for each test. The first row of this array is used for

Figure D6–15   A Two-Dimensional Array-Processing Program

(a) The Program

```
100 REM - TWO-DIMENSIONAL ARRAY DATA TOTALING PROGRAM
110 REM - VARIABLES:
120 REM        S     = TEST SCORE ARRAY
130 REM        TOTAL = TOTAL SCORE
140 REM        I,J   = COUNTERS
150 REM
160 DIM S(4,3)
170 REM - READ DATA FOR ARRAY
180 FOR I = 1 TO 4
190   FOR J = 1 TO 3
200     READ S(I,J)
210   NEXT J
220 NEXT I
230 REM - FIND TOTAL OF ARRAY DATA
240 LET TOTAL = 0
250 FOR I = 1 TO 4
260   FOR J = 1 TO 3
270     LET TOTAL = TOTAL + S(I,J)
280   NEXT J
290 NEXT I
300 REM - DISPLAY ARRAY DATA
310 CLS
320 PRINT TAB(19); "TEST SCORES"
330 PRINT
340 PRINT "STUDENT", "TEST 1", "TEST 2", "TEST 3"
350 PRINT
360 FOR I = 1 TO 4
370   PRINT I,
380   FOR J = 1 TO 3
390     PRINT S(I,J),
400   NEXT J
410   PRINT
420 NEXT I
430 REM - DISPLAY TOTAL
440 PRINT
450 PRINT "TOTAL OF ALL SCORES:"; TOTAL
460 REM - ARRAY DATA
470 DATA 91,78,85,95,90,96
480 DATA 85,100,89,69,75,68
```

(b) Output

```
                   TEST SCORES

STUDENT         TEST 1         TEST 2         TEST 3

   1              91             78             85
   2              95             90             96
   3              85            100             89
   4              69             75             68

TOTAL OF ALL SCORES: 1021
```

Figure D6–16 The Test-Score Tabulation Program (Part 1 of 2)

(a) The Program

```
100 REM - TEST SCORE TABULATION PROGRAM
110 REM - VARIABLES:
120 REM        SCORE = TEST SCORE ARRAY
130 REM        COUNT = ARRAY FOR COUNT OF TEST SCORES
140 REM                IN EACH RANGE FOR EACH TEST
150 REM        TOTAL = ARRAY FOR TOTAL NUMBER OF TEST SCORES
160 REM                IN EACH RANGE
170 REM        I, J  = COUNTERS
180 REM
190 DIM SCORE(12,4), COUNT(4,4), TOTAL(4)
200 REM - MAIN PROGRAM
210 GOSUB 270  'CALL READ TEST SCORE ARRAY DATA SUBROUTINE
220 GOSUB 420  'CALL COUNT TEST SCORES SUBROUTINE
230 GOSUB 550  'CALL ACCUMULATE TOTALS SUBROUTINE
240 GOSUB 660  'CALL DISPLAY OUTPUT SUBROUTINE
250 END
260 REM
270 REM - READ TEST SCORE ARRAY DATA SUBROUTINE
280 FOR I = 1 TO 12
290    FOR J = 1 TO 4
300       READ SCORE(I,J)
310    NEXT J
320 NEXT I
330 REM - TEST SCORE ARRAY DATA
340 DATA 74,84,86,77,100,94,95,89
350 DATA 82,87,87,91,35,48,52,63
360 DATA 85,84,75,72,91,84,72,95
370 DATA 72,78,81,69,84,75,80,79
380 DATA 70,69,72,73,55,72,70,38
390 DATA 90,95,91,82,75,81,78,72
400 RETURN
410 REM
420 REM - COUNT TEST SCORES SUBROUTINE
430 FOR I = 1 TO 4
440    FOR J = 1 TO 4
450       LET COUNT(I,J) = 0
460    NEXT J
470 NEXT I
480 FOR I = 1 TO 12
490    FOR J = 1 TO 4
500       IF SCORE(I,J) >= 90 THEN LET COUNT(1,J) = COUNT(1,J) + 1
              ELSE IF SCORE(I,J) >= 80 THEN LET COUNT(2,J) = COUNT(2,J) + 1
              ELSE IF SCORE(I,J) >= 70 THEN LET COUNT(3,J) = COUNT(3,J) + 1
              ELSE LET COUNT(4,J) = COUNT(4,J) + 1
510    NEXT J
520 NEXT I
530 RETURN
540 REM
```

the number of scores between 90 and 100 on each of the four tests, the second row is used for the number of scores between 80 and 89 on each test, and so on. Finally, the four-element, one-dimensional array TOTAL is used for the total number of test scores in each range on all tests.

The program is written in a modular fashion. First, the program calls a subroutine to read the test-score array data. This subroutine reads the data into the SCORE array, using nested FOR loops. Then the program calls a subroutine to count the test scores. First, this subroutine initializes the COUNT array to zero. This is necessary because these elements are used to count the number of test scores in each range. Next, the subroutine uses nested FOR loops to check the elements of the SCORE array one at a time. Within the FOR loops, IF statements are used to

Figure D6–16 The Test-Score Tabulation Program (Part 2 of 2)

(a) The Program (continued)

```
550 REM - ACCUMULATE TOTALS SUBROUTINE
560 FOR I = 1 TO 4
570   LET TOTAL(I) = 0
580 NEXT I
590 FOR I = 1 TO 4
600   FOR J = 1 TO 4
610     LET TOTAL(I) = TOTAL(I) + COUNT(I,J)
620   NEXT J
630 NEXT I
640 RETURN
650 REM
660 REM - DISPLAY OUTPUT SUBROUTINE
670 CLS
680 PRINT TAB(30); "TEST SCORE SUMMARY"
690 PRINT
700 PRINT , "90-100", "80-89", "70-79", "0-69"
710 PRINT
720 FOR J = 1 TO 4
730   PRINT "TEST"; J,
740   FOR I = 1 TO 4
750     PRINT COUNT(I,J),
760   NEXT I
770 NEXT J
780 PRINT
790 PRINT "TOTALS",
800 FOR I = 1 TO 4
810   PRINT TOTAL(I),
820 NEXT I
830 RETURN
```

(b) Output

	TEST SCORE SUMMARY			
	90-100	80-89	70-79	0-69
TEST 1	3	3	4	2
TEST 2	2	5	3	2
TEST 3	2	4	5	1
TEST 4	2	2	5	3
TOTALS	9	14	17	8

determine into which range a test score falls. Once this is determined, 1 is added to the appropriate element of the COUNT array.

After all elements of the SCORE array have been checked, the program calls a subroutine to accumulate the totals of the counts in each range. This is done by totaling the elements in each row of the COUNT array. The TOTAL array is used to accumulate the totals. Notice that the elements of the TOTAL array are first initialized to zero in the subroutine.

Finally, the program calls a subroutine to display the output. First, the subroutine displays headings. Then it displays the elements of the COUNT array by using nested FOR loops. Each column of the array is displayed on a separate line. A column of this array represents the counts of the number of test scores in each range on one test. The test number is displayed on the left by using the control variable of the outer FOR loop in a PRINT statement at the beginning of the outer loop. The elements in a column are displayed by using a PRINT statement in the inner FOR loop. A comma at the end of the PRINT statement causes the output to be displayed on one line. Because there are five print zones and a value is displayed in each zone, a new line will begin after the last value is displayed in a line. Hence, an extra PRINT statement between the two NEXT statements is not needed to start a new line. Finally, the subroutine displays the elements of the TOTAL array at the end of the output.

Terms to Remember

Array   p. 675

Array Element   p. 675

Array Cariable   p. 675

Dimensioning an Array   p. 676

Subscript   p. 676

Subscripted Variable   p. 676

Review Questions

1. Consider the array A, shown in Figure D6–1. Assume that the value of J is 4 and the value of K is 3. What is the value of each of the following subscripted variables?

   a. A(9)

   b. A(J)

   c. A(J+K)

   d. A(J/K)

2. Code a statement to declare that D and E are each 50-element arrays.

3. Code a statement that multiplies the first two elements of the array D defined in Question 2, and assigns the result to the last element of the array E.

4. Code a group of statements to read the data for the array D defined in Question 2 from DATA statements.

5. Code a group of statements to accept the data for the array E defined in Question 2 from the keyboard.

6. Code a group of statements to display in two columns the elements of the arrays D and E defined in Question 2.

7. Code a group of statements to find the total of all the elements of the arrays D and E defined in Question 2.

8. Consider the arrays D and E defined in Question 2. Code a group of statements to search the array D for all elements equal to R. Each time an element of D equal to R is found, display the corresponding element from the array E.

9. Consider the two-dimensional array S, shown in Figure D6–12. Assume that the value of I is 2, J is 3, and K is 4. What is the value of each of the following subscripted variables?

   a. S(3,2)

   b. S(K,1)

   c. S(I,J)

   d. S(I*J-4,K/2)

10. Code a statement to specify that X is a two-dimensional array with four rows and 20 columns.

11. Consider the array X defined in Question 10. Code a statement that adds the first element of the first row of this array and the third element of the second row, and assigns the result to the last element of the fourth row.

12. Code a group of statements to read data for the array X defined in Question 10. Assume that the data is recorded in order by rows in DATA statements.

Programming Problems

1. Write a BASIC program that reads hourly temperatures for a day into a 24-element array. The first element of the array gives the temperature at 1:00 a.m., the second gives the temperature at 2:00 a.m., and so forth. Note that the thirteenth element is the temperature at 1:00 p.m. Then search the array for the maximum and minimum temperatures. Display these temperatures along with the times that they occur. Supply appropriate input data to test the program.

2. An inventory table contains information about the quantity of inventory on hand for each item stocked. Assume that there are 15 items in the inventory. The inventory table contains 15 entries, each consisting of an item number and the quantity of the item that is in stock.
   Write a BASIC program to do the following:

   a. Read the inventory table data into two arrays—one for the item numbers and one for the quantities. Then display the inventory data in columns below appropriate headings.

   b. Accept an item number, an amount received, and an amount sold. Search the inventory table for the corresponding item. Then update the quantity on hand by adding the amount received to the amount from the table and subtracting the amount sold. Repeat this step until 9999 is entered for an item number. Be sure to account for the case in which the item is not in the table.

   c. After all items have been updated, display the inventory data in columns below appropriate headings.

Use the following data for the inventory table:

Item Number	Quantity on Hand
1102	100
1113	25
1147	37
1158	95
1196	225
1230	150
1237	15
1239	105
1245	84
1275	97
1276	350
1284	82
1289	125
1351	138
1362	64

Use the following data to update the inventory table:

Item Number	Quantity Received	Quantity Sold
1230	25	100
1113	0	15
1255	16	42
1289	50	0
1405	26	5
1102	100	75
1239	25	25

3. This problem involves analyzing product sales information. Input consists of the identification number and quantity sold for each of 25 products. Write a BASIC program to do the following:

   a. Read the identification numbers and quantities into two arrays. After all data has been read, display the arrays in columns below appropriate headings.

   b. Calculate and display the average of the quantities sold.

   c. Determine the number of products whose sales fall into each of the following categories:

   500 or more

   250 to 499

   100 to 249

   0 to 99

   Display the results with appropriate headings.

   Use the following data to test the program:

Identification Number	Quantity Sold
208	295
137	152
485	825
217	100
945	250
607	435
642	500
735	36
300	163
299	255
435	501
116	75
189	0
218	63
830	617
695	825
708	416
325	99
339	249
418	237
225	712
180	328
925	499
455	240
347	378

4. Each state has a two-letter abbreviation authorized by the U.S. Postal Service. For example, the abbreviation for California is CA; the abbreviation for New York is NY. (See a zip code directory for a complete list.)

   Write a BASIC program that reads a complete table of state abbreviations and corresponding state names. Use one array for the abbreviations and another array for the names. Then display the arrays below appropriate headings. Next, accept a state abbreviation, and search the table for the corresponding state's name. Display the abbreviation and the name. Repeat this part of the program until an abbreviation of XX is entered. Supply appropriate input data to test the program.

5. A company sells five products with four models for each product. The following table gives the price of each model of each product:

		Model Number			
		1	2	3	4
	1	10.50	16.25	21.00	23.75
	2	4.95	5.95	6.50	6.95
Product Number	3	.38	.47	.59	.62
	4	8.75	8.95	9.10	9.22
	5	1.52	1.75	1.95	2.25

Write a BASIC program to read the pricing table and store it in a two-dimensional array. Then display the pricing table with appropriate headings. Next, accept from the keyboard a customer number, a product number, a model number, and the quantity sold. From this information calculate the sales amount for each customer by multiplying the price from the table by the quantity sold. Display the customer number, product number, model number, quantity sold, price, and sales amount.

To test the program, use the data in the preceding pricing table and the following sales data:

Customer Number	Product Number	Model Number	Quantity
10113	1	1	10
11305	5	4	35
11412	1	1	100
22516	2	3	125
11603	4	2	75
11625	4	1	65
11735	3	3	50
11895	1	3	130
11899	2	4	20
11907	5	2	82
00000 (trailer value)			

6. The data gathered from scouting a football team can be analyzed by a computer. In a simple system, assume that four characteristics of each offensive play are recorded by the scout. The characteristics are the down, the yards to go for a first down, the type of play (in which 0 identifies a pass and 1 indicates a run), and the number of yards gained or lost (in which a negative value indicates lost yardage). The information for each play can be recorded in one row of a two-dimensional array. The first element in the row is the down, the second element is the yards to go, the third element is the type of play, and the final element is the yards gained or lost. In all, 25 plays are to be analyzed.

Write a BASIC program to read the scouting data and store it in a two-dimensional array. Display the data in columns with appropriate headings. Then find and display the answers to the following questions:

a. What was the average yards gained per play?

b. What was the average yards gained per running play?

c. Of all running plays, what percent gained yardage, what percent lost yardage, and what percent gained zero yardage?

d. What was the average yards gained per passing play?

e. What percent of the plays were passes?

f. What percent of first-down plays were passes?

g. What percent of second-down plays were passes?

h. What percent of third-down plays were passes?

i. Of third-down plays with less than five yards to go, what percent were passes?

Use the following data to test the program:

Down	Yards to Go	Play	Gain (+) or Loss(−)
1	10	1	+4
2	6	0	0
3	6	0	+8
1	10	1	−3
2	13	1	+8
1	10	1	0
2	10	0	+8
3	2	0	+15
1	10	0	+12
1	10	1	−15
2	25	0	+5
3	20	0	0
1	10	1	+2
2	8	1	+4
3	4	1	+1
1	10	0	0
2	10	1	+6
3	4	0	+12
1	10	0	0
2	10	1	+6
3	4	1	+2
1	10	0	−3
2	13	1	−5
1	10	1	+2
2	10	1	−16

Summary of BASIC Statements

Statement	Syntax	Example	Section
CLS	*ln* CLS	100 CLS	2
DATA	*ln* DATA *list of constants*	800 DATA 1,2,3	5
DIM	*ln* DIM *list of array declarations*	100 DIM A(20), B(15,5)	6
END	*ln* END	900 END	2
FOR/NEXT	*ln* FOR *control variable=initial value* TO *limit* STEP *increment statements* *ln* NEXT *control variable*	300 FOR I=1 TO 20 STEP 2 310 PRINT I 320 NEXT I	4
GOSUB	*ln* GOSUB *ln*	350 GOSUB 400	5
GOTO	*ln* GOTO *ln*	140 GOTO 110	3
IF	*ln* IF *relational expression* THEN *ln*	160 IF A>B THEN 200	3
IF-THEN	*ln* IF *relational expression* THEN *statement*	170 IF A>B THEN LET C=A−B	3
IF-THEN-ELSE	*ln* IF *relational expression* THEN *statement* ELSE *statement*	180 IF A>B THEN LET C=A−B ELSE LET C=B−A	3
INPUT	*ln* INPUT *list of variables*	110 INPUT B,C	2
INPUT	*ln* INPUT *"prompt", list of variables*	120 INPUT "ENTER DATA"; B,C	2
LET	*ln* LET *numeric variable=numeric expression*	150 LET A=B+C	2
LET	*ln* LET *string variable=string expression*	240 LET S$="ABC"+T$	2
LPRINT	*ln* LPRINT *output list*	130 LPRINT A,B,C	2
LPRINT USING	*ln* LPRINT USING "format"; list of variables*	360 LPRINT USING "### ###"; A,B	5
PRINT	*ln* PRINT *output list*	130 PRINT A,B,C	2
PRINT USING	*ln* PRINT USING "format"; list of variables*	360 PRINT USING "### ###"; A,B	5
READ	*ln* READ *list of variables*	130 READ A,B,C	5
REM	*ln* REM *remark*	100 REM - ADD TWO NUMBERS	2
RETURN	*ln* RETURN	790 RETURN	5
WHILE/WEND	*ln* WHILE *relational expression statements* *ln* WEND	270 WHILE A>B 280 LET A=A−1 290 WEND	4

BASIC GLOSSARY

Array A group of data values that is identified by a single name in a BASIC program. (6)

Array element A value in an array. (6)

Array variable A variable that refers to an array in a BASIC program. (6)

BASIC program A sequence of BASIC statements that describes some computer process. (1)

Collating sequence The ordering of the characters in a computer. (3)

Command An instruction to the computer to perform some action with a BASIC program. (1)

Constant A fixed data value in a BASIC program. May be a numeric constant or a string constant. (1)

Counting loop A loop that is controlled by counting the number of times that the loop is repeated. (4)

Dimensioning an array Specifying the size of an array in a BASIC program. (6)

Expression An instruction to the computer to perform some operation with data. May be a numeric expression, a relational expression, or a string expression. (1)

FOR loop A loop that is controlled by a FOR statement. (4)

Function A predefined set of instructions that can be used in a BASIC program. (5)

Input loop A loop that is controlled by an input operation. (4)

Keyword A word that identifies a statement in a BASIC program. (1)

Line number A number that begins a statement in a BASIC program. (1)

Logical operator A word used between relational expressions to create a combined expression. May be AND or OR. (3)

Nested decisions A program pattern in which one decision is contained within another. (3)

Nested loops A program pattern in which one loop is contained within another. (4)

Numeric constant A constant that consists of numeric data. (2)

Numeric data Data that consists of numeric values. (2)

Numeric expression An instruction to the computer to perform arithmetic. (2)

Numeric operator A symbol that indicates what form of arithmetic is to be performed in a numeric expression. May be +, −, *, /, or ^. (2)

Numeric variable A variable that is used to refer to numeric data. (2)

Print zone An area on a screen or on paper containing a certain number of print positions and in which one value is displayed or printed. (2)

Processing loop A loop that is controlled by some condition of the data that is processed in the loop. (4)

Relational expression An instruction to the computer to compare two values. (3)

Relational operator A symbol that indicates what form of comparison is to be performed in a relational expression. May be <, <=, >, >=, =, or <>. (3)

Statement An instruction in a BASIC program. (1)

String constant A constant that consists of string data enclosed in quotation marks. (2)

String data Data that consists of letters, digits, and other symbols. (2)

String expression An instruction to the computer to perform operations with string data. (2)

String variable A variable that is used to refer to string data. (2)

Subroutine A group of statements that can be executed from different points in a BASIC program. (5)

Subscript A numeric constant, variable, or expression that identifies an element of an array. (6)

Subscripted variable An array variable followed by one or more subscripts enclosed in parentheses. (6)

Tracing A debugging technique in which the order of execution of the statements in a program is displayed. (4)

Trailer value A value for a variable that is used to signal the end of the input data. (4)

Truth value The value of a relational expression. May be *true* or *false*. (3)

Variable A name that refers to data that can change in a BASIC program. May be a numeric variable, string variable, array variable, or subscripted variable. (1)

WHILE loop A loop that is controlled by a WHILE statement. (4)

The number in parentheses following each entry indicates the section in the BASIC appendix in which the term is located.

ANSWERS TO SELECTED BASIC REVIEW QUESTIONS

SECTION 1

1. statement
3. Keywords are words that identify statements in a BASIC program.
5. BASIC commands tell the computer what to do when processing a BASIC program.
7. An error in a statement in a BASIC program is corrected by retyping the statement with its line number.

SECTION 2

1. **a.** valid
   b. invalid
   c. invalid
   d. valid
3. **a.** -4.56E-5
   b. 7.8316E0
5. **a.** -3.25
   b. 3.2
7. END
9. Remarks are included in a BASIC program by using REM statements.
11. The CLS statement is used to clear the screen.
13. `110 INPUT "ENTER PAYMENT ",PAY`
15. `130 INPUT X, Y, A$, B$, C$`

SECTION 3

1. **a.** less than or equal to
   b. not equal to
   c. equal to
   d. greater than

3. **a.** 20
   b. 20
5. `100 IF F <> 100`
   `        THEN INPUT D, E: PRINT D, E`
7. nested decisions
9. **a.** false
   b. true
   c. false
11. `100 IF M$ = "M"`
    `        THEN LET N = N + 1`
    `        ELSE IF M$ = "D" LET N = N - 1`
    `                ELSE LET N = 0`

SECTION 4

1. The relational expression is tested at the beginning of each execution of the loop.
3. The additional statements needed are
   ```
   30 WHILE C <> 0
   60 WEND
   ```
5. The INPUT statement that controls the loop is at the beginning of the loop. The value of RES$ will not be tested until the loop is completely executed. The INPUT statement for RES$ should be put at the end of the loop and another INPUT statement for RES$ should be put before the loop.
7.
   ```
   10 LET I = 1
   20 WHILE I <= 25
   30    INPUT A
   40    PRINT A
   50    LET I = I + 1
   60 WEND
   ```
9. **a.** 1
   b. 5
   c. 30
   d. 5

11.
```
100 FOR K = 5 TO 15 STEP -3
110    LET X = X + K
120 NEXT K
```
13.
```
300 FOR I = 21 TO 3 STEP -3
310    PRINT I
320 NEXT I
```

9. a. 100

b. 69

c. 96

d. 90

11. `110 LET X(4,20) = X(1,1) + X(2,3)`

SECTION 5

1. called

3. `200 GOSUB 500`

5. There is no statement to terminate execution before the subroutine. Between statements 30 and 40 there must be an END statement.

7. Subroutines are used in top-down design to perform the basic operations of the program.

9. `100 LET C = SQR(A ^ 2 + B ^ 2)`

11. `200 PRINT MID$(FIRST.NAME$, 1, 1); MID$(LAST.NAME$, 1, 1)`

13. A batch processing program can be created in BASIC by putting all data to be processed by the program into DATA statements and using READ statements to read the data.

15. `110 PRINT USING "AMOUNT $$#,###.##-"; A`

SECTION 6

1. a. 20.5

b. 6.3

c. 5.7

d. 23.2

3. `110 LET E(50) = D(1) * D(2)`

5.
```
150 FOR I = 1 TO 50
160    INPUT E(I)
170 NEXT I
```

7.
```
210 LET TOTAL = 0
220 FOR I = 1 TO 50
230    LET TOTAL = TOTAL + D(I) + E(I)
240 NEXT I
```

BASIC INDEX

A

Algorithm, 565
Apple Macintosh, 532
Array, 675
    dimensioning, 676–677
    input and output, 679–680
    searching, 680–681
    string, 678–679
    subscript, 676, 677–678
    two-dimensional, 688–698
Array element, 675
Array variable, 675
ASCII, 588
Assignment, 549. *See also* LET
    statement

B

BASIC, 532
BASICA, 532, 538
BASIC program, 533
    running, 537–541
BASIC statement. *See* Statement
Batch processing, 654
Booting, 537
Branching, 582
Bug, 541

C

Calling (a subroutine), 637–638. *See also* GOSUB statement
CLS statement, 557–558
Coding a program. *See* Program coding
Collating sequence, 588
Comma (in PRINT statement), 556–557
Comment. *See* Remark

Command, 538. *See also command name*
Complement (of a condition), 583
Concatenation, 561–562
Condition, 572, 581
Constant, 533, 543–545. *See also* Numeric constant; String constant
Continuing a statement, 579
Control variable, 613
Counter, 612
Counting loop, 612–614
Cursor, 556

D

DATA statement, 653–655
Debugging. *See* Program debugging
Decision, 572
    if-then, 581, 583
    if-then-else, 581, 583
    nested, 584
Decision structure, 581–584
Design. *See* Program design
Dimensioning an array, 676–677
    two-dimensional array, 690–691
DIM statement, 676–677
    with two-dimensional array, 690–691
Documenting a program. *See* Program documenting

E

END statement, 537, 550
E-notation, 543–544
Error detection, 541
Execution error, 541
Expression, 534. *See also* Numeric expression; Relational expression; String expression

F

False part of a decision, 581
FILES command, 539
Flowchart, 556
    of complete programs, 556
    of programs with decisions, 577–558
    of programs with loops, 606
    of programs with subroutines, 641
FOR loop, 616–620
FOR statement, 618–620
Format. *See* PRINT USING statement format
Function, 648
    numeric, 648–650
    string, 651–652

G

GOSUB statement, 638–639
GOTO statement, 582–583, 609
GWBASIC, 532, 538

I

IBM clone, 532
IBM PC, 532
IF statement, 582, 583, 609
If-then decision, 581, 583
IF-THEN statement, 572
If-then-else decision, 581, 583
IF-THEN-ELSE statement, 573
Increment, 618
Indentation
    in decisions, 579
    in FOR loops, 621, 625
    in WHILE loops, 604, 615
Initial value, 618
Input loop, 609–610

GLOSSARY

ABC Atanasoff-Berry Computer. (B)*

Accessing The process of retrieving data from a file or database. (10, 14)

Address A unique number used to identify a storage location. (3)

Ad hoc report A report that is prepared only once, for a specific purpose. (14)

AI Artificial intelligence. (15)

Algorithm A set of steps that, if carried out, results in the solution of a problem. (12)

ALU Arithmetic-logic unit. (3)

Analog signal A signal that transmits data by a wave pattern that varies continuously. (6)

Analytical engine A general-purpose mechanical calculating machine designed by Charles Babbage in the mid-1800s. (B)

ANSI An organization that determines standards for a number of industries in the United States, including the computer industry. Stands for American National Standards Institute. (13)

Application generator A program that is used to develop a computer application containing menus, screen input and output, report output, file and database processing, and other forms of processing. (13, 16)

Application programmer A programmer who develops application programs. (19)

Application software Programs designed for specific computer applications. (2)

Arithmetic-logic unit (ALU) The unit in the CPU that does arithmetic and performs logical operations. (3)

Artificial intelligence (AI) The use of a computer to mimic human intelligence. (15)

ASCII An industry standard code for representing characters using seven bits per character. Stands for American Standard Code for Information Interchange. (3)

ASCII file A file containing text using only the ASCII code. (8)

Assembler A program that translates assembly language programs into equivalent machine language programs. (13)

Assembly language A programming language in which each instruction consists of a symbolic operation code and one or more symbolic operands. (13)

Asynchronous transmission Transmission of data in a channel one character at a time. (6)

Atanasoff-Berry Computer (ABC) The first electronic, stored-program computing device. It was a special-purpose machine designed by John Atanasoff in 1937 and built with the assistance of Clifford Berry. (B)

ATM Automatic teller machine. (1)

Attribute A column in a relation. (16)

Automated teller machine (ATM) A device connected to a bank's computer that allows a person to perform a banking transaction without the aid of a human teller. (1)

Auxiliary storage *See* Secondary storage. (2)

Backup copy A copy of data stored separately in case the original data is lost or destroyed. (5)

Bar code scanner A device that recognizes a bar code, which is a series of parallel lines of different widths. (4)

Base The number of digits in a number system. (C)

BASIC A programming language used mainly for simple scientific and business application programs and for education-related programs. Stands for Beginner's All-Purpose Symbolic Instruction Code. (13)

*Numbers or letters following each entry indicate the chapter or appendix in which a term is located.

Batch processing A form of data processing in which all the data to be processed is prepared in a form understandable to the computer before processing, then processed in a batch to produce the output. (14)

Baud rate The rate at which the signal on a communications channel changes. (6)

BINAC The first electronic, stored-program, general purpose computer to become operational in the United States. It was operational in August 1949. (B)

Binary digit A 1 or 0. (3)

Binary number A type of number that uses only the binary digits. (3)

Binary number system A base 2 number system. (C)

Bit *See* Binary digit. (3)

Block A section of text that has been marked so it can be moved, copied, deleted, or saved. (8)

Booting The process of loading the supervisor of an operating system. (7)

Bridge A connection between two networks of the same type. (6)

Bug An error in a computer program. (12)

Bus A set of wires through which parts of a computer communicate. (3)

Business graphics software Graphics software used to create charts and graphs used in businesses and organizations. (11)

Bus network A network in which each node is connected to a single, common communications channel. (6)

Byte A group of bits capable of storing one character. (3)

C

C A programming language used mainly for system programs and microcomputer general application programs. (13)

CAD Computer-aided design. (1, 11)

CAI Computer-assisted instruction. (1)

CASE The use of computer-based tools to help in the development of an information system. Stands for Computer-Aided Software Engineering. (17)

CD Compact disk. (5)

CD-ROM A type of optical disk system that can only retrieve data from compact disks but cannot store data on disks. Stands for Compact Disk–Read Only Memory. (5)

Cell The intersection of a row and column in a worksheet. (9)

Cell address The identifier for a cell in a worksheet. Usually consists of a column letter followed by a row number. (9)

Cell cursor *See* Cell pointer. (9)

Cell pointer A highlighted area on a screen that can be moved to any cell in a worksheet. (9)

Centralized system An information system in which all functions are performed at a single, central location. (15)

Central processing unit (CPU) The central component of a computer that carries out instructions in a program. Sometimes just called the processor. (2)

Character A symbol such as a digit, letter, or special symbol. (3, 5)

Charting program Graphics software used to create charts and graphs. (11)

Chip A piece of silicon containing electronic circuits. (3)

CIS Computer information system. (14)

COBOL A programming language used mainly for business application programs. Stands for COmmon Business Oriented Language. (13)

Coding The process of writing the instructions for a computer program in a programming language. (12)

COM Computer output microfilm. (4)

Command A word or phrase entered into a computer that tells a program to perform a function. (7)

Communications analyst A person who is responsible for an organization's data communications hardware and software. (19)

Communications channel A link between computer devices used for data communications. (6)

Communications control unit A device that controls communications traffic over a channel. Includes multiplexors, controllers, and front-end processors. (6)

Communications software Software used to control data communications in a computer. (6)

Compact disk (CD) A small optical disk. (5)

Compiler A program that translates high-level language programs into equivalent machine language programs. (13)

Computer An electronic device that processes data by following instructions in a program. (1)

Computer-aided design (CAD) The use of a computer to aid in a design process. (1, 11)

Computer application A use of a computer. (1)

Computer-assisted instruction (CAI) The use of a computer to provide instruction and practice in a subject. (1)

Computer designer A person who designs computer circuits and components. (19)

Computer information system (CIS) An information system that uses one or more computers. (14)

Computer operator A person who operates computer equipment. (19)

Computer output microfilm (COM) A system for recording output directly on microfilm. (4)

Computer sales representative A person who sells computer hardware and/or software. (19)

Computer service technician A person who maintains and repairs computer hardware. (19)

Computer simulation The use of a computer to represent how something else will function. (1)

Computer trainer A person who trains end-users in the use of computer hardware and software. (19)

Control structure A way of arranging instructions in a computer program. (12)

Control unit The unit in the CPU that analyzes and executes instructions. (3)

Cooperative processing Computer processing in which two or more computers in a network cooperate in performing the functions of an information system. (15)

Copy protection A method for preventing the copying of software, in which a code is placed on the original disk so that the software cannot be copied to other disks. (18)

Cost/benefit analysis The process of comparing the expected costs and benefits of an information system to determine its economic feasibility. (17)

CPU Central processing unit. (2)

CRT A screen that is made from a tube similar to a television tube. Stands for Cathode Ray Tube. (4)

Cursor A mark on a screen that indicates where the next output will be displayed or the next input will be entered. (4)

Cursor control key A key on a keyboard used for moving the cursor on the screen. (4)

Customer support technician A person who assists customers with problems they are having using software sold by a software company. (19)

Custom software Programs that are prepared "from scratch" for a specific person, organization, or business. (2)

Cut and paste A feature of a word processing program that allows the user to move blocks of text within a document. (8)

D

Data Facts, figures, numbers, and words that are used by a computer. (1)

Database A collection of data and relationships between the data stored in secondary storage. (1, 5, 16)

Database administrator (DBA) A person responsible for managing an organization's databases. (16)

Database management software A type of data management software that allows the user to simultaneously process several related groups of data that form a database. Also called a database management system or DBMS. (10)

Database management system (DBMS) A program that provides capabilities for creating, accessing, and updating a database. (16)

Database server A server with a secondary storage device, usually a large hard disk, that can be used for database processing by other computers in the network. (6)

Data dictionary A description of the data in a data flow diagram. (17)

Data encryption The process of changing data to a form that is unintelligible unless a special key is known. (6, 18)

Data entry operator A person who operates data preparation devices. (19)

Data file A collection of related records stored in secondary storage. Also just called a file. (2, 5)

Data flow diagram (DFD) A diagram of the flow of data in an information system. (17)

Data management software Software used to store, retrieve, and change data in files and databases. (10)

DBA Database administrator. (16)

DBMS Database management system. (16)

Debugging The process of locating and correcting bugs in a computer program. (12)

Decentralized system An information system in which each user or group of users in an organization performs all processing, storage, input, and output functions for its applications on its own computer. (15)

Decimal number system A base 10 number system. (C)

Decision structure A control structure in which one of two groups of program instructions is executed based on a condition. (12)

Decision support system (DSS) An information system that helps managers make decisions by analyzing data from a database and providing the results of the analysis to the manager. (15)

Dedicated line *See* Leased line. (6)

Dedicated word processor Computer hardware and software that can be used only for word processing. (8)

Desktop computer A microcomputer designed to sit on a desk and not be moved. (2)

Desktop publishing The use of a microcomputer to prepare high-quality printed output similar to that produced by a printing company. (8)

Desktop publishing software Software used for desktop publishing. (8)

Detail report A report that lists detailed information resulting from data processing. (14)

DFD Data flow diagram. (17)

Dial-up line *See* Switched line. (6)

Difference engine A mechanical device designed by Charles Babbage in the early 1800s for calculating certain types of mathematical tables. (B)

Digital signal A signal that transmits bits as high and low pulses. (6)

Digitizer tablet A desktop tablet that can sense where it is touched by a stylus. (4)

Direct access *See* Random access. (5)

Direct file A file in which the records are stored at locations determined directly from the record's key field. (5)

Disk *See* Magnetic disk. (2)

Disk drive A device for storing data on and retrieving data from magnetic disk. (2)

Disk pack A stack of several hard disks with spaces between the disks. (5)

Distributed database A database that is divided into parts, with each part stored on a different computer in a network. (16)

Distributed database management system A database management system for manipulating a distributed database. (16)

Distributed system An information system in which each user or group of users performs processing, storage, input, and output functions on its own or other computers in a network. (15)

Documentation Any written description of a program or information system. Includes user documentation, operator documentation, and programmer documentation. (12)

Dot-matrix printer A printer that prints each character by striking a ribbon and the paper with a group of pins arranged in a rectangular pattern or matrix. (4)

Downloading Transferring data from a remote computer to a local computer. (6)

Draft-quality printer A printer that produces output that is of low-to-medium quality. (4)

Draw program Graphics software that allows the user to create pictures and diagrams. (11)

DSS Decision support system. (15)

E

EBCDIC A code developed by IBM for representing characters using eight bits per character. Stands for Extended Binary Coded Decimal Interchange Code. (3)

Editing The process of making changes or corrections in text using a word processing program or a text editor. (8)

EDSAC The first electronic, stored-program, general-purpose computer to become operational in the world. It was operational in May 1949, in England. (B)

EDVAC The first electronic, stored-program, general-purpose computer to be invented. It was invented in 1945 and completed in 1951. It was not the first such computer to become operational, however. Stands for Electronic Discrete Variable Automatic Computer. (B)

EFT Electronic funds transfer. (18)

Electronic bulletin board A microcomputer system that is accessible using data communications and that stores information of interest to certain types of users. (6)

Electronic funds transfer (EFT) A technique for transferring funds electronically between accounts. (18)

Electronic mail (E mail) A use of computers to transmit messages electronically from one computer to another. Also refers to the messages that are sent. (1, 6)

Electronic spreadsheet *See* Worksheet (9)

E mail Electronic mail. (1, 6)

End-user *See* User. (1)

ENIAC The first electronic, general-purpose computing device. It did not have a stored program, however. It was designed by J. Presper Eckert and John Mauchly and completed in 1946. Stands for Electronic Numerical Integrator and Computer. (B)

Erasable optical disk A form of secondary storage that consists of a disk on which data is recorded magnetically with the aid of a laser. The recorded data can be erased and changed. (5)

Ergonomics The study of how machines should be designed for effective human use. (4)

ES Expert system. (15)

ESS Executive support system. (15)

Exception report A report that contains data that is an exception to some rule or standard. (14)

Executive support system An information system that provides support for the top-level managers in an organization. (15)

Expert system (ES) An information system that provides expert advice. (15)

Expert system shell Software that contains an inference engine and a user interface for an expert system. (15)

External command A system command for an operating system that causes another program in the operating system to be loaded and executed. (7)

F

Feasibility analysis The process of determining if it is feasible to develop an information system. (17)

Field A group of related characters. (5)

File A collection of related items stored in secondary storage. Also refers specifically to a data file. (2, 5)

File management software A type of data management software that allows the user to process the data in only one file at a time. (10)

File server A server with a secondary storage device, usually a hard disk drive, that can be used for file storage by other computers in a network. (6)

File transfer A function provided by communications software that allows files to be transferred between computers. (6)

File transfer protocol Protocols that specify how files of data will be transferred between computers and how error checking will be provided. (6)

Financial modeling software Software, often used with minicomputers or mainframe computers but also available on microcomputers, that provides capabilities for financial analysis beyond those of spreadsheet software. (9)

Flat panel screen A screen that is thin and lightweight. (4)

Floppy disk A magnetic disk made of flexible plastic with a metallic coating. (5)

Flowchart *See* Program flowchart. (12)

Font A type style used by a printer. (4)

Footnoting A feature of a word processing program for creating footnotes. (8)

Format a disk The process of marking the tracks and sectors on a magnetic disk using a special computer program. (5)

Formula An expression entered into a cell in a worksheet that describes how the value of the cell is to be computed. (9)

FORTRAN A programming language used mainly for scientific application programs. Stands for FORmula TRANslation. (13)

4GL Fourth-generation language. (13)

Fourth-generation language (4GL) A programming language that requires significantly fewer instructions to accomplish a particular task than a third-generation language. (13)

Full-duplex transmission Transmission of data in a channel in both directions simultaneously. (6)

Fully formed character printer A printer that prints each character by striking a ribbon and the paper with an element shaped like a character. (4)

Function A routine built into spreadsheet software that performs special processing and that is invoked by using its name in a formula. (9)

Function key A key on a keyboard that, when pressed, causes a program to perform a certain function. (4)

G

Gateway A connection between two networks of different types. (6)

GB Gigabyte. (3)

G byte Gigabyte. (3)

Gigabyte (GB, G byte) 1,073,741,824 bytes; commonly thought of as one billion bytes. (3)

Graphical user interface (GUI) A software interface that usually includes icons, a desktop or similar display, pull-down menus, and windows. (7)

Graphic output Output that consists of diagrams, charts, and pictures. (4)

Graphics software Software used to create graphic output. (11)

GUI Graphical user interface. (7)

H

Hacker A person who gains access to a computer system not to steal data, but for the challenge of breaking in and for the purpose of investigating the system. Also, a term used for computer programmers in general. (18)

Half-duplex transmission Transmission of data in a channel in both directions, but only in one direction at a time. (6)

Hard disk A magnetic disk made of a nonflexible material such as aluminum. (5)

Hardware The physical equipment that makes up a computer. (2)

Help screen An explanation, displayed on a screen, of how to use some function of a program. (7)

Hexadecimal notation A notation for representing binary numbers in which each group of four bits is represented by a hexadecimal digit. (C)

Hierarchical database A database in which all relationships are one-to-one or one-to-many, but no group of data can be on the "many" side of more than one relationship. (16)

Hierarchical network A network in which the nodes are organized in a hierarchical fashion like a family tree. (6)

Host language A programming language for preparing application programs in which commands from a query language are embedded. (16)

Hypertext A document stored in the computer that is organized into cards, each containing text, data, graphics, or other information. Each card also contains a list of other cards with related information. (11)

Hypertext software Software that is used to create and browse through hypertext. (11)

Hyphen help A feature of a word processing program that suggests hyphenation of a word that does not fit at the end of a line. (8)

I

Icon A small picture, displayed on a screen, that represents a function that a program can perform or a file stored in secondary storage. (7)

Impact printer A printer that makes an image by striking paper with a metal or plastic mechanism. (4)

Indexed file A system of two files, one a sequential data file and the other an index file containing the key field of each record in the data file and the location of the corresponding record in the data file. (5)

Indexed sequential file *See* Indexed file. (5)

Indexing A feature of a word processing program that creates an index for a text file. (8)

Inference engine Software that analyzes rules in a knowledge base to draw conclusions. (15)

Information Data that is meaningful or useful to someone. (14)

Information center A department or group in an organization that helps end-users develop and use computer applications, mainly on microcomputers. (15, 19)

Information system A system that processes data and provides information within an organization. (14)

Information systems manager The person responsible for the management of the information systems or similar department in an organization. (19)

Information utility A company that supplies access to information stored in a mainframe computer for a variety of users using data communications. (6)

Ink-jet printer A printer that prints each character by spraying drops of ink on the paper. (4)

Input data Data entered into a computer from outside the computer. (1)

Input device A device that accepts data from outside the computer and converts it into an electronic form that the computer can understand. (2)

Input-process-output cycle The cycle in which input data is entered into a computer and then stored and processed by the computer to produce the output data. (1)

Integrated software Software that provides multiple applications with a common user interface. (11)

Interactive processing A form of data processing in which the user interacts with the computer at the time the processing is done. Each set of data is entered into the computer and then processed, and the output is received before the next input data is entered. (14)

Internal command A system command for an operating system that is interpreted and executed by the supervisor. (7)

Internal storage *See* Primary storage. (2)

Interpreter A program that translates and immediately executes instructions in a high-level language program. (13)

J

JCL Job control language. (7)

Job control language (JCL) The set of system commands used with a mainframe computer operating system. (7)

K

KB Kilobyte. (3)

K byte Kilobyte. (3)

Keyboard An input device that accepts keyed input data. (2)

Key field A field that identifies a record in a file. (5)

Kilobyte (KB, K byte) 1,024 bytes; commonly thought of as one thousand bytes. (3)

Knowledge base A collection of expert knowledge stored in a computer. (15)

L

Label Text entered into a cell in a worksheet. (9)

LAN Local area network. (6)

Laptop computer A small, portable microcomputer. (2)

Laser printer A printer that prints each page by recording an image of the page on the surface of a metal drum with a laser, then transferring the image to the paper. (4)

Leased line A telephone line that is used by only one customer. (6)

Letter-quality printer A printer that produces output that is the quality of a good typewriter. (4)

Light pen A pen-light device with a light-sensitive tip that, when touched to a screen, causes the computer to sense where it has been touched. (4)

Line printer A printer that prints one line at a time. (4)

Local area network (LAN) A network that covers a small area such as a single building or several nearby buildings. (6)

Loop structure A control structure in which a group of program instructions is executed repeatedly. (12)

M

Machine-dependent language A programming language that can be used on only one type of computer. (13)

Machine-independent language A programming language that can be used on several types of computers. (13)

Machine language The basic language of a computer. (3)

Macro A named sequence of commands entered into a cell or group of cells in a worksheet. (9)

Magnetic disk A form of secondary storage that consists of a disk with a metallic coating on which data is recorded magnetically. (2)

Magnetic ink character recognition (MICR) A technique used by the banking industry for processing checks imprinted with special characters. (4)

Magnetic strip reader A device that can recognize data recorded in a magnetic strip. (4)

Magnetic tape A form of secondary storage that consists of tape similar to audio recording tape on which data is recorded magnetically. (2)

Mail merge A feature of a word processing program that merges information from one text file into another text file. (8)

Mainframe computer A large, multiple-user computer. (2)

Management information system (MIS) An information system that provides information to assist in the management of an organization. (15)

Many-to-many relationship A relationship in which many groups of data are related to many other groups of data. (16)

Mark-sense reader A device that can sense marks made on special forms. (4)

Mass storage system A system consisting of thousands of magnetic tapes that can be accessed mechanically. (5)

Matching The process of comparing data in several files or databases for the purpose of locating common data. (18)

MB Megabyte. (3)

M byte Megabyte. (3)

Megabyte (MB, M byte) 1,048,576 bytes; commonly thought of as one million bytes. (3)

Megahertz (MHz) The units used to measure the internal clock speed of a computer; one megahertz is one million cycles per second. (3)

Menu A list of options for a program displayed on a screen. (7)

MHz Megahertz. (3)

MICR Magnetic ink character recognition. (4)

Microcomputer A small, single-user computer. Also called a personal computer or PC. (2)

Microcomputer analyst A person responsible for evaluating, selecting, and setting up microcomputer hardware and software for use in an organization, and for assisting end-users in developing and utilizing computer applications. (19)

Microprocessor A CPU contained on one chip. (3)

Microsecond One-millionth of a second. (3)

Millisecond One-thousandth of a second. (3)

Minicomputer A medium-sized computer. (2)

MIPS The units used to express the number of instructions that can be executed per second by a computer; one MIPS is one million instructions per second. (3)

MIS Management information system. (15)

Model base A collection of mathematical models and statistical calculation routines stored in a computer. (15)

Modem A device that converts digital signals to analog signals (modulation) and analog signals to digital signals (demodulation). (6)

Modular program A program that is organized into modules. (12)

Module A group of instructions that performs some function related to the processing of the program. (12)

Monitor A CRT designed for computer use. (4)

Motherboard The main circuit board of a microcomputer containing the microprocessor chip and memory chips. (3)

Mouse A hand-held device that is rolled on a table top to move the cursor on the screen and that is used to select program functions by pressing buttons on its top. (4)

Multiple-user computer A computer used by several people at a time. (1)

Multiprocessing The use of several CPUs simultaneously in a computer to increase speed. (3)

Multiprogramming A technique for accomplishing multitasking, in which each program is given a priority level and lower priority programs are executed only when higher priority programs have to wait for some other process to be completed. (7)

Multitasking The process of executing more than one program at a time by switching between programs. (7)

N

Nanosecond One-billionth of a second. (3)

Near–letter-quality printer A printer that produces output that is almost as good as that of a letter-quality printer. (4)

Network A configuration of several computer devices connected so that all can communicate with each other. (2)

Network database A database in which all types of relationships are allowed. (16)

Network interface device A device that connects a computer to a network. (6)

Neural network A computer system, consisting of thousands of CPUs, that functions similar to a human brain. (18)

Nonimpact printer A printer that makes an image in some way other than by striking the paper. (4)

Nonprocedural language A programming language in which the programmer specifies what is wanted from the computer in a program. (13)

Nonvolatile storage A storage medium that does not lose its contents when the power to the computer is turned off. (3)

Notebook computer A small microcomputer that folds to the size of a notebook. (2)

Number system A way of expressing quantities. (C)

Numeral A series of digits that represents a number or quantity in a number system. (C)

Numeric keypad A set of keys on a keyboard for entering numbers. (4)

O

OAS Office automation system. (15)

Object-oriented database A database that stores objects, which are combinations of data and instructions to process the data. (16)

Object-oriented database management system A database management system for manipulating an object-oriented database. (16)

Object-oriented programming A form of computer programming in which the programmer develops a program from objects, which are combinations of data and instructions to process the data. (13)

Object program The machine-language equivalent of a source program that is produced by an assembler or compiler. (13)

OCR Optical character reader. (4)

Office automation system (OAS) An information system that performs office functions. (15)

Off-line Not connected to a computer. (14)

On-demand report A report that is prepared only when requested. (14)

One-to-many relationship A relationship in which one group of data is related to many other groups of data, but not vice versa. (16)

One-to-one relationship A relationship in which one group of data is related to only one other group of data and vice versa. (16)

On-line Connected to a computer. (14)

Operating system A set of programs that controls the basic operation of a computer. (2)

Operator documentation Documentation that provides information for a computer operator on how to execute a computer program. (12)

Optical character reader (OCR) A device that can recognize OCR characters, which are symbols printed in a special style. (4)

Optical disk A form of secondary storage that consists of a disk on which data is recorded by small holes that are created and sensed by a laser. The recorded data cannot be erased or changed. (5)

Optical disk drive A device for storing data on and retrieving data from an optical disk. (5)

Outlining A feature of a word processing program used to create, edit, and print outlines. (8)

Output data Data resulting from computer processing that is made available outside the computer. (1)

Output device A device that converts data from an electronic form inside the computer to a form that can be used outside the computer. (2)

P

Packaged software Programs that are purchased. (2)

Page layout The process of preparing pages of a document in the format in which they will be printed. (8)

Page preview A feature of a word processing program that allows a user to display an entire page or several pages on the screen as they will be printed. (8)

Page printer A printer that prints one page at a time. (4)

Page scanner A device that can sense the image on an entire page and transfer it into a computer. (4)

Paint program Graphics software that allows the user to create pictures and diagrams. (11)

Parity bit An extra bit in a group of bits used to check if there are errors in the other bits. (3)

Pascal A programming language used mainly for teaching computer programming and for some system and application programs. (13)

Password A word or code that must be entered into a computer system to gain access to the system. (18)

PC Personal computer. (1)

Peripheral equipment Any device used with a computer other than the primary storage or CPU, such as secondary storage and input and output devices. (2)

Personal computer (PC) A computer used by one person at a time. (1)

Personal database A database used by only one user. (16)

Personal information manager (PIM) A multifunction program that provides capabilities associated with organizing a person's day or helping with desk work. (11)

PIM Personal information manager. (11)

Pixel The smallest mark or dot on a screen; short for picture element. (4)

Plotter A device that draws graphic output on paper. (4)

Pocket computer A very small microcomputer that folds to a size that will fit into a coat pocket. (2)

Point-of-sale (POS) system A computerized system for recording sales as customers pay for their merchandise. (1)

Pop-up menu *See* Pull-down menu. (7)

Port A socket for connecting certain devices, such as printers, with the computer. (4)

Position value The values of the positions held by digits in a numeral; successive powers of the base of a number system. (C)

POS system Point-of-sale system. (1)

Power user A computer user who is very familiar with computers and programs, and who develops sophisticated uses of the computer. (1)

Presentation graphics software Software used to produce graphic output for presentations. (11)

Primary storage The part of a computer that stores data currently being processed and instructions in programs currently being performed. (2)

Print chart A form used to show the layout of printed output. (17)

Printer An output device that produces output data on paper. (2)

Print server A server with a printer that can be used for printing by other computers in a network. (6)

Procedural language A programming language in which the programmer specifies the procedure the computer has to follow in a program. (13)

Process description A description of a process in a data flow diagram. (17)

Processor *See* Central processing unit. (2)

Program A set of instructions that is stored in a computer and performed automatically by the computer. (1)

Program file A file for a program stored in secondary storage. (2)

Program flowchart A diagram that uses special symbols connected by lines to show the algorithm for a computer program. (12)

Program maintenance The process of making changes in a computer program. (12)

Programmer A person who prepares computer programs. (2)

Programmer/analyst A person who functions as both a systems analyst and an application programmer. (19)

Programmer documentation Documentation that provides information for a computer programmer about how a computer program works. (12)

Programming The process of preparing a program. (2)

Programming language A set of rules for preparing instructions for a program. (2)

Program testing The process of detecting errors in a program by executing it with test data and comparing the output with what was expected. (12)

Project team A group of systems analysts, programmers, and users that work together to develop an information system. (17)

Prompt A symbol, word, or phrase, displayed on a screen, that indicates that a program is ready to accept input. (7)

Protocol converter A device that converts the protocols of one computer device to those of another computer device. (6)

Protocols Rules that describe how computer devices communicate. (6)

Prototype A partial version of an information system that acts like the system for the user but does not perform all the system's functions. (17)

Prototyping The process of developing a prototype of an information system. (17)

Pseudocode A written language that uses English and elements from a programming language to describe the algorithm for a computer program. (12)

Public domain software Software that is not copyrighted. (18)

Pull-down menu A menu that appears on a screen when the menu's title is selected from a list of titles displayed on the screen. (7)

Punched card A card in which holes have been punched to represent data. (B)

Q

Query A request for information from a file or database. (10, 14)

Query language A programming language that is used to answer queries or questions by retrieving data from a database. May also be used to update a database. (13, 16)

R

RAM Random access memory. (3)

RAM resident program A program that is stored in primary storage whether it is in use or not, and that is activated when needed by the user. (11)

Random access The process of reading or writing records in a file in any order. (5)

Random access memory (RAM) A type of primary storage in which programs and data can be stored and retrieved in any order as often as needed. (3)

Random file *See* Direct file. (5)

Range A group of adjoining cells in a worksheet that forms part of a column or row, or a rectangular pattern of rows and columns. (9)

Read only memory (ROM) A type of primary storage in which programs and data, stored once by the manufacturer, can be retrieved as many times as needed, but in which new programs and data cannot be stored. (3)

Real-time processing A form of data processing in which processing is done immediately after the input is received rather than possibly being delayed while other processing is completed. (14)

Record A group of related fields. (5)

Record locking A technique for controlling multiple-user access to a file or database, in which a record accessed by one user is locked so that no other user can access it until the first user unlocks the record. (10)

Relation A table of data arranged in rows and columns. (16)

Relational database A database that consists of one or more related relations. (16)

Relationship A way in which groups of data in a database are related. (16)

Report A list of output data printed on paper or displayed on a screen. (10, 14)

Report generator A program that is used to produce reports from data in a file or database. (13)

Ring network A network in which the nodes are connected to form a loop. (6)

ROM Read only memory. (3)

RPG A programming language used mainly for programs that produce business reports and that process secondary storage data. Stands for Report Program Generator. (13)

Rule An *if-then* structure that is used in a knowledge base. (15)

S

Scheduled report A report that is produced periodically. (14)

Screen An output device that displays output data as video images. (2)

Screen layout form A form used to show the layout of screen input and output. (17)

Screen painter A program that is used to create screens for input, output, and menus. (13)

Screen resolution The number of pixels that can be displayed on a screen at one time. (4)

Scrolling The process of moving text past the computer screen. (8)

Search and replace A feature of a word processing program that allows the user to search text for a certain word or phrase and replace it with a new word or phrase. (8)

Secondary storage A device that stores data not currently being processed by the computer and programs not currently being performed. (2)

Sector A section of a track on a disk. (5)

Sequence structure A control structure in which program instructions are executed one after the other in the order in which they appear in the program. (12)

Sequential access The process of reading or writing records in a file in sequence. (5)

Sequential file A file in which the records are organized in sequence one after the other in the order in which they are stored in the file. (5)

Serial printer A printer that prints one character at a time. (4)

Server A computer connected to a network that operates a resource, such as a printer or a disk drive, which is shared by other computers in the network. (16)

Service bureau A company that does computer processing for other organizations. (17)

Shared database A database used by many users. (16)

Shareware Inexpensive or free copyrighted software that comes with permission to use and make copies for evaluation purposes, but which must be paid for in full if the user wishes to use it after evaluating it. (18)

Simplex transmission Transmission of data in a channel in one direction only. (6)

Site license A software license agreement that allows the use of the software by more than one person at a time within an organization. (18)

Software A computer program or set of programs. (2)

Software engineer A programmer who develops software for sale by a software company. Also used for any programmer or programmer/analyst. (19)

Software house A company that develops software for other organizations. (17)

Software license agreement A written statement of what the purchaser of certain software can legally do with that software. (18)

Software piracy The process of making illegal copies of software in order to sell those copies to other people. (18)

Sorting The process of arranging data into a particular order. (14)

Source document A document in which data is captured at its source. (14)

Source program A program written in a language other than machine language. (13)

Spell checking A feature of a word processing program that checks the spelling of a text file. (8)

Spreadsheet An arrangement of data in rows and columns used for data analysis and presentation. (1)

Spreadsheet software Software used to create, modify, and print electronic spreadsheets. (9)

SQL A commonly used query language. Stands for Structured Query Language. (10, 16)

Star network A network in which each node is connected to a central computer node. (6)

Storage location A group of bits in primary storage used to store a certain amount of data. (3)

Structure chart A diagram of the modular organization of a program. (12)

Structured program A program that uses only sequence, decision, and loop structures. Often, a structured program is written in a modular fashion. (12)

Structured programming A systematic process for developing computer programs that results in programs that are well structured, that are easily understood and modified, and that are correct. (12)

Style/grammar checking A feature of a word processing program that checks text for common writing style and grammar errors. Often done by a program separate from the word processing program. (8)

Summary report A report that contains totals that summarize groups of data but that has no detail data. (14)

Supercomputer A computer designed for high-speed processing. (2)

Supervisor A program in an operating system that is stored in primary storage and that is in control of the computer when another program is not executing. Also called monitor, executive, or kernel. (7)

Switched line A telephone line that can be used by any customer. (6)

Synchronous transmission Transmission of data in a channel in blocks of characters. (6)

Syntax The grammatical rules of a programming language. (13)

System A collection of components that work together for a purpose. (14)

System analysis The phase in the system development process in which the systems analyst studies the existing system and determines what the new system must do. (17)

System command A command given to an operating system. (7)

System design The phase in the system development process in which the systems analyst specifies how the new system will function. (17)

System engineer A programmer/analyst who works for a computer hardware company and provides technical support for the company's customers. (19)

System flowchart A diagram that uses special symbols connected by lines to show the functioning of an information system. (17)

System implementation The phase in the system development process in which the systems analyst acquires the system components, tests the system, and changes over to the new system. (17)

System maintenance The process of modifying an information system. (17)

System planning The phase in the system development process in which the systems analyst decides whether a new information system should be developed. (17)

System programmer A programmer who sets up and maintains system software. (19)

Systems analyst A person who develops information systems. (17)

System software General programs designed to make a computer easier to use. (2)

System specifications A description of what a new system must do to satisfy the user's requirements. (17)

T

Tape *See* Magnetic tape. (2)

Tape drive A device for storing data on and retrieving data from magnetic tape. (2)

Telecommuting Regularly working with a computer away from an office or business and then transmitting finished work to a central computer. (18)

Teleprocessing system An information system in which processing and storage functions are performed at a central location, input and output functions are performed at the users' locations, and data are sent between locations, using data communications. (15)

Terminal A device that is a combination of an input and an output device; often a keyboard combined with a screen. (2)

Terminal emulation A function provided by communications software that makes a microcomputer appear as if it is a terminal to another computer. (6)

Text Data consisting of characters, words, paragraphs, and so on. (8)

Text editor A program, often used with minicomputers or mainframe computers but also available on microcomputers, for entering and editing text. It provides fewer capabilities than a word processing program. (8)

Text file A file for text stored in secondary storage. (8)

Thermal printer A printer that prints each character by using wires to apply heat to special paper or to a special ribbon. (4)

Thesaurus A feature of a word processing program that looks up synonyms for words. (8)

Time sharing A technique used by an operating system for allowing multiple users to use a computer by giving each user a small amount of time to execute his or her program before going on to the next user. (7)

Top-down program design A program design technique in which the programmer starts with the overall design for a program and then successively refines the design until the final program is obtained. (12)

Touch pad A desktop pad that can sense where it is touched by a person's finger or a special pen. (4)

Touch screen A screen that can sense where it is touched by a person's finger. (4)

TPS Transaction processing system. (15)

Track A concentric circle on a magnetic disk or a line on a magnetic tape along which bits are recorded. (5)

Trackball A device with a ball on top to move the cursor on the screen and buttons to select program functions. (4)

Transaction An event that has occurred that affects an organization or business. (15)

Transaction processing system (TPS) An information system that keeps records about the organization, processes data about transactions, and produces output that reports on transactions, reports on the organization, and causes other transactions to occur. (15)

Tuple A row in a relation. (16)

U

Undo A feature of a word processing program that allows the user to replace text that is erroneously deleted. (8)

UNIVAC The first commercially available computer. It was completed in 1951. (B)

Updating The process of changing data in a file or database to bring it up to date. (10, 14)

Uploading Transferring data from a local computer to a remote computer. (6)

User A nontechnically oriented person who gains some benefit from using a computer in his or her personal or work life. (1)

User documentation Documentation that provides information for a computer user about how to use a computer program. (12)

User requirements A description of what an information system will do to help a user in his or her job. (17)

Utility program A program that provides additional capabilities beyond those of an operating system, such as sorting and merging. (7)

V

Value A number entered into a cell or the result of a formula in a cell in a worksheet. (9)

VDT Video display terminal. (4)

Vice president of information systems The person responsible for all computing and information processing in an organization. May also be called chief information officer (CIO). (19)

Video display terminal (VDT) A terminal consisting of a keyboard and a screen. (4)

View Part of a database to which a user has access. (16)

Virtual memory The memory that a computer appears to have, consisting of primary storage and some secondary storage. It is created by the operating system so that programs that are larger than primary storage can be executed without modification. (7)

Virus A computer program that copies itself from one disk to another and that activates itself after a period of time, usually destroying programs and data in many computer systems. (18)

Volatile storage A storage medium that loses its contents when the power to the computer is turned off. (3)

W

WAN Wide area network. (6)

What-if analysis The process of changing certain data in a spreadsheet to see the effect on other data in the spreadsheet. (9)

Wide area network (WAN) A network that covers a large geographic area. (6)

Window A section of a screen surrounded by a border and containing one type of display. (7)

Word A group of bytes used together. (3)

Word processing The use of a computer to prepare written documents such as letters and reports. (1)

Word processing software   Software used for word processing. (8)

Word processing system   A computer with word processing software. (8)

Word wrap   A feature of a word processing program that allows the user to continue entering text when the end of a line is reached without pressing the Enter or Return key, and that automatically moves to the next line any word that does not fit at the end of the line. (8)

Worksheet   A spreadsheet created by spreadsheet software. (9)

Worksheet file   A file for a worksheet stored in secondary storage. (9)

Workstation   A powerful microcomputer. (2)

WYSIWYG   A feature of a program that shows on the screen an exact image of what will be printed. Stands for what-you-see-is-what-you-get. (8)

ANSWERS TO SELECTED REVIEW QUESTIONS

CHAPTER 1

Fill-In Questions

1. input data; output data
3. automated teller machine or ATM
5. point-of-sale or POS system
7. user or end-user

Short-Answer Questions

1. A computer is an electronic device that stores data and programs, and that processes data by following instructions in a program.
3. Computers are used in homes for entertainment, self-improvement, and personal financial management.
5. Computers are used by architects, draftspersons, and engineers for computer-aided design (CAD). Graphic designers use computers to design product packaging, company symbols, book covers, and so forth.
7. People use computers because of their speed, their accuracy, and their capacity to handle large amounts of information.

CHAPTER 2

Fill-In Questions

1. input device; output device
3. central processing unit or CPU; primary storage
5. file
7. network
9. primary
11. operating system

Short-Answer Questions

1. The five basic components of a computer are the input device, the output device, primary storage, the CPU, and secondary storage.
3. The central processing unit carries out instructions in a program. It does arithmetic and performs logical operations. It controls the other parts of the computer.
5. When the power to the computer is turned off, anything stored in primary storage is lost, but anything stored in secondary storage remains.
7. The four general types of computers are microcomputers, minicomputers, mainframe computers, and supercomputers.
9. Application software are programs that are designed for specific computer applications. System software are general programs that are designed to make the computer easier to use.

CHAPTER 3

Fill-In Questions

1. chip
3. bus
5. ASCII; 7; EBCDIC; 8
7. byte
9. one thousand; one million; one billion
11. one-thousandth; one-millionth; one-billionth

Short-Answer Questions

1. Three processing problems that a user should be aware of when evaluating a computer are primary storage capacity, CPU speed, and data and program compatibility.

3. The contents of volatile storage are lost when the power to the computer is turned off, whereas the contents of nonvolatile storage are not lost.

5. a. 1001101 1000001 1010010 1011001

   b. 0110010 0110111

7. a. JOE

   b. 36

9. When we say that data is stored in a binary representation, we mean that the data is stored in a two-state manner with patterns of on/off states representing the data.

11. Two CPUs are compatible if the machine language instructions used with one are identical to those used with the other. One CPU is upward compatible with another if the instructions in the first CPU may be used on the second, but not necessarily vice versa.

13. An internal clock governs the speed of the CPU. In a 10 MHz CPU the clock ticks 10 million times per second, whereas in a 20 MHz CPU the clock ticks 20 million times per second. All other things being equal, the 20 MHz CPU will be twice as fast as the 10 MHz CPU.

CHAPTER 4

Fill-In Questions

1. cursor

3. pixels

5. characters per second or cps; lines per minute or lpm; pages per minute or ppm

7. laser printer

9. port

11. page scanner

13. plotter

Short-Answer Questions

1. Some of the special-purpose keys on a computer keyboard are the Control key, the Escape key, the Break key, and the Alternate key.

3. Two purposes of a mouse are to move the cursor and to select what the computer does next.

5. An impact printer makes an image by striking paper with a metal or plastic mechanism, whereas a nonimpact printer makes an image without striking the paper.

7. A video display terminal (VDT) is a combination of a keyboard and a screen.

9. The two main types of high-volume printers are line printers and laser printers.

11. A data preparation device is used to prepare data in a form accessible to the computer. The data is entered into the device, which converts the data into a code such as EBCDIC or ASCII. The coded data is stored until it is transferred to the computer.

CHAPTER 5

Fill-In Questions

1. tracks

3. disk pack

5. sequentially; randomly

7. backup copy

9. optical disk

11. sequential; direct; indexed

13. direct file organization

Short-Answer Questions

1. Secondary storage is used because, unlike primary storage, data and programs can be stored permanently in it and because it costs less than primary storage.

3. Data is recorded on a magnetic disk by spots of magnetism representing bits. The bits are grouped to form bytes, which are recorded along tracks on the disk's surface.

5. An advantage of removable disks is that they allow unlimited storage capacity. Advantages of nonremovable disks are that they are more reliable, faster at transferring data, and greater in storage capacity than removable disks.

7. Sequential access is the process of reading or writing records in a file in the order in which the records are stored, whereas random access is the process of reading or writing records in a file in any order.

9. Data is recorded on a magnetic tape by spots of magnetism representing bits. The bits are recorded along tracks on the tape's surface. A

byte is formed from a group of bits recorded across the tracks.

11. A tape drive stores data on a magnetic tape by moving the tape past a read/write head and writing the data on the tape. It retrieves data from a tape by moving the tape past a read/write head and reading the data recorded on the tape.

13. Key fields are usually numeric code fields rather than names or descriptions, because numbers usually are unique, whereas names and descriptions often are duplicated in a file.

CHAPTER 6

Fill-In Questions

1. communications channel

3. simplex transmission; half-duplex transmission; full-duplex transmission

5. switched or dial-up line; leased or dedicated line

7. data encryption

9. uploading; downloading

11. star; hierarchical; bus; ring

Short-Answer Questions

1. Three situations in which a user needs data communications are I/O device-to-computer communications (terminal communications), computer-to-computer communications (micro-to-micro and micro-to-mainframe), and computer-to-shared resources communications (network communications).

3. Baud rate is the number of times per second that the signal on a communications channel changes. It may or may not be the same as bits per second or bps.

5. A modem converts digital signals to analog signals (modulation) and converts analog signals to digital signals (demodulation).

7. For a terminal to communicate with a distant computer, a modem and possibly a protocol converter, a data encryption device, and various communication control units are needed. No communications software is needed, however.

9. For a microcomputer to communicate with a mainframe computer, a modem, possibly a pro-

tocol converter and a data encryption device, and a communications program are needed.

11. For a microcomputer to use a local area network, a network interface device and LAN communications software are needed.

CHAPTER 7

Fill-In Questions

1. booting the computer

3. job control language or JCL

5. time sharing

7. command

9. help screen

Short-Answer Questions

1. The three main functions of an operating system are process management (managing the execution of programs), resource management (managing primary storage, I/O devices, and secondary storage), and data management (managing the flow of data between the main components of a computer).

3. An internal system command is one that is interpreted and executed by the supervisor. An external system command is one that causes another program in the operating system to be loaded and executed.

5. Some common microcomputer operating systems are PC DOS for the IBM personal computers, MS DOS for IBM clones, and the Apple Macintosh operating system.

7. User-friendly software is software that is designed to be very easy for someone to use.

9. A menu is a list of options for a program displayed on a screen. A pull-down menu is a menu that appears on a screen when the menu's title is selected from a list of titles displayed on the screen.

11. Users can receive output from a program in the form of a short screen display, as a long report printed on paper or displayed on a screen, and in graphic form displayed on a screen or produced on paper by a printer or a plotter.

CHAPTER 8

Fill-In Questions

1. word wrap
3. editing
5. search and replace
7. scrolling
9. thesaurus

Short-Answer Questions

1. Word processing is more efficient than using a typewriter in most typing situations except those involving short documents that are used only once. For long reports and documents that require changes in the future, word processing is much more efficient.

3. A user can move or copy a block to another part of a document, delete a block, and save a block separately in secondary storage.

5. A user can control the functions performed by a word processing program by pressing function keys, often in combination with the Control, Shift, and Alternate keys, by using character keys in combination with the Control or another key, and by using a mouse to select functions from a menu.

7. Some additional capabilities of word processing software are spell checking, a thesaurus, mail merge, footnoting, outlining, graphics included in documents, style/grammar checking, and indexing.

9. A text file created by one word processing program can be used by another by using a file conversion program to convert the file. Alternatively, one word processing program can create an ASCII file that can be retrieved by the other program.

CHAPTER 9

Fill-In Questions

1. spreadsheet
3. electronic spreadsheet or worksheet
5. E3

7. range
9. function

Short-Answer Questions

1. Spreadsheet analysis is used to solve problems in which data is organized in rows and columns and calculations are done with the data.

3. The three types of information that a user can put into a cell of a worksheet are numbers (values); labels, which are texts; and formulas, which are rules for calculating the values of cells.

5. The three main functions a user can perform with a spreadsheet program are creating a worksheet, changing a worksheet, and printing a worksheet.

7. With some spreadsheet software, the user can control the functions performed by the program by pressing a special key followed by a command. With other software the user uses a mouse to select options from a pull-down menu.

9. a. +C5+C6+C7+C8
   b. @SUM (C5..C8)

CHAPTER 10

Fill-In Questions

1. file management software; database management software
3. accessing
5. updating
7. SQL

Short-Answer Questions

1. Data management is used in situations in which data in secondary storage needs to be stored, retrieved, and changed.

3. To create a file or database, the user must first describe the fields and records in the file or database and then enter data for each field in each record.

5. A microcomputer used for data management must have adequate secondary storage for storing files or databases. Floppy disk drives may be satisfactory for small files and databases, but in

most data management situations a hard disk drive is needed. Primary storage needs to be large enough to store the data management software and a small amount of data. The other hardware found with most microcomputers is usually adequate for data management.

7. To describe the region file in Figure 10–14, the user had to enter the name of each field (REGNAME, REGSALES, REGSPNUM), the type of data in each field (character or numeric), the width of each field, and, for numeric fields, the number of decimal positions.

9. Some common file management programs are:

For the IBM personal computers and IBM clones:

Professional File
Reflex
PC File
Rapidfile
Q & A

For the Apple Macintosh:
File Maker
Microsoft File

CHAPTER 11

Fill-In Questions

1. charting program
3. presentation graphics software
5. integrated software

Short-Answer Questions

1. Some forms of graphic output are charts and graphs, diagrams, graphic designs, realistic images, and computer art.

3. A charting program can get data that it uses to create a chart or graph from a spreadsheet or database, or it can use data entered by the user.

5. The microcomputer hardware needed for graphic output includes a medium- to very-high-resolution screen, a printer capable of producing graphic output or a plotter, a fast CPU, a large amount of primary storage, and a hard disk drive.

7. Two advantages of integrated software are a common user interface for all applications and easy transfer of data between applications. Three disadvantages are that the user may not need all the applications provided by the integrated software, that separate programs may be better than their counterparts in the integrated software, and that integrated programs can be complex to use.

9. A personal information manager provides capabilities associated with organizing a person's day and helping with desk work, including a calendar, notepad, to-do list, calculator, and telephone directory.

CHAPTER 12

Fill-In Questions

1. algorithm
3. while loops; until loops
5. top-down program design
7. syntax errors; execution errors; logic errors
9. user documentation; operator documentation; programmer documentation

Short-Answer Questions

1. Pseudocode is a written language that uses English and elements from a programming language to describe an algorithm, whereas a program flowchart is a diagram that uses special symbols connected by lines to show the algorithm.

3. A structured program is one that uses only the three basic control structures (sequences, decisions, and loops).

5. A structure chart is used to show the organization of a modular program.

7. During the problem definition activity the programmer tries to understand the problem to be solved and determines output layouts, input data-entry formats, calculations, and other processing for the program.

9. Program testing involves determining if errors are present in a program, whereas debugging involves finding and correcting errors in a program.

CHAPTER 13

Fill-In Questions

1. syntax
3. machine-dependent; machine-independent
5. assembler
7. compiler; interpreter
9. FORTRAN
11. RPG

Short-Answer Questions

1. There is not just one programming language that can be used for all programs because different types of programs require different language characteristics.
3. Programming languages that are good for writing business application programs have instructions that make input, output, and secondary storage operations easy. Programming languages that are good for writing scientific application programs have good instructions for calculations.
5. In machine language, instructions consist of binary operation codes and operands, whereas in assembly language, instructions consist of symbolic operation codes and operands.
7. A fourth-generation language or 4GL is a high-level language that requires significantly fewer instructions to accomplish a particular task than a third-generation language requires.
9. The C programming language is commonly used for writing system programs and microcomputer general application programs.

CHAPTER 14

Fill-In Questions

1. computer information system or CIS
3. source document
5. query
7. ad hoc report
9. on-line; off-line

Short-Answer Questions

1. An information system is a collection of components that work together to process data and to provide information within an organization.
3. The components of an information system are hardware, software, stored data, personnel, and procedures.
5. In batch processing, all data to be processed is brought together and processed in a group, whereas in interactive processing, each set of data is entered into the computer by the user, and then processed, and the output is received before the next input is entered.
7. The output from the billing application is the customer's bill or invoice.
9. The inventory control application updates the quantity on hand in the inventory file.
11. The purpose of the general ledger application is to prepare the business's financial statements.

CHAPTER 15

Fill-In Questions

1. centralized system
3. decentralized systems
5. transaction
7. model base
9. knowledge base

Short-Answer Questions

1. A distributed system is an information system in which each user or group of users in an organization performs processing, storage, input, and output functions on its own computer and on other computers in a network.
3. The purposes of a transaction processing system are to keep records about an organization, to process transactions, and to produce output that reports on transactions, reports on the organization, and causes other transactions to occur.
5. A management information system meets the information needs of managers of an organization by maintaining a database of internal and

external data and processing the data to produce information at the required level of detail.

7. A decision support system is an information system that helps managers make decisions by analyzing data from a database and providing the results of the analysis to the manager.

9. An expert system is a system that provides expert advice by using knowledge from a knowledge base to draw conclusions about specific problems.

11. Office functions provided by an office automation system include word processing, electronic mail, electronic filing, desktop support, voice processing, and image processing.

CHAPTER 16

Fill-In Questions

1. relationships
3. one-to-one
5. many-to-many
7. distributed
9. host language
11. personal; shared

Short-Answer Questions

1. With file processing, separate files are needed to store the data for each application, whereas with database processing, all data is stored together in a database.

3. Disadvantages of database processing compared to file processing are greater cost, increased vulnerability, and more complex development of information systems.

5. A hierarchical database can have only one-to-one and one-to-many relationships organized in a "tree" fashion, whereas a network database can have all types of relationships organized in any way.

7. A relational database is considered to be the easiest for users to use.

9. Two ways a user can use a database are through a query language and through an application program written in a host language.

CHAPTER 17

Fill-In Questions

1. systems analyst
3. system maintenance
5. cost/benefit analysis
7. service bureau
9. data dictionary; process description

Short-Answer Questions

1. The people who usually are on an information system development project team are systems analysts, programmers, and users.

3. The user is often the one who recognizes a problem with an existing information system. Reporting this problem starts the system planning phase.

5. During systems analysis, the user is interviewed about how the current system functions, is asked about his or her requirements for a new system, and is asked to review system specifications.

7. During system design the analyst specifies the layouts of all screens, reports, and forms; the organization of all records, files, and databases; the description of all programs and manual procedures; the specification of all hardware; and the description of all personnel.

9. Both a data flow diagram and a system flowchart show the flow of data in an information system. In addition, a system flowchart shows what type of input data, output data, stored data, and programs will be used in the system.

11. Ann Nelson wanted a new information system to do sales analysis because she felt she and other sales personnel were not getting good information about how well each bicycle was selling and about which regions of the country had high sales and which had low sales.

CHAPTER 18

Fill-In Questions

1. productivity; increase
3. retraining; early retirement

5. electronic funds transfer or EFT

7. hacker

9. public domain software

11. virus

Short-Answer Questions

1. People benefit from better information because the information helps them make better decisions.

3. Computers can reduce people's privacy by recording information about them.

5. Computer use can cause physical health problems such as eyestrain, headaches, backaches, wrist pain, and neck pain. These problems can be reduced by good ergonomic design of the computer and of the work environment.

7. A software license agreement is a written statement of what the purchaser of certain software can legally do with that software. A site license is a software license agreement that allows the use of the software by more than one person at a time in an organization.

9. To help prevent the permanent destruction of data and programs, backup copies should be kept away from the organization's location.

CHAPTER 19

Fill-In Questions

1. information systems manager

3. programmer/analyst

5. communications analyst

7. system engineer

Short-Answer Questions

1. The department in an organization or business responsible for developing and operating computer information systems may be called information systems (IS), management information systems (MIS), data processing (DP), or something similar.

3. A trainee programmer has little or no experience and works under the careful supervision of a senior programmer for at least six months. A junior programmer has passed beyond the trainee level but still has limited experience and requires direct supervision. A senior programmer has at least three years of experience and can work largely on his or her own. A lead programmer has the most experience and may manage a project team.

5. Some of the jobs in the end-user support area are microcomputer analyst and computer trainer.

7. The field of computer information systems is concerned with application software and information systems, whereas the field of computer science deals with computer hardware and system software.

APPENDIX C

Problems

1. a. 6
   b. 9
   c. 10
   d. 23
   e. 41

3. a. D
   b. 34
   c. B1
   d. 2F70
   e. DAE9

ACKNOWLEDGMENTS

Photo Credits

Unless otherwise acknowledged, all photographs are the property of ScottForesman. Page abbreviations are as follows: (T)top, (C)center, (B)bottom, (L)left, (R)right.

6TL: Richard Megna/Fundamental Photographs
6BR: Courtesy of IBM
7: Courtesy of IBM
8T: Courtesy of Hewlett-Packard Company
8B: David R. Frazier Photolibrary
10TL: Brownie Harris/The Stock Market
10TR: Hank Morgan/Rainbow
10CR: Milt & Joan Mann/Cameramann International, Ltd.
10B: Dan McCoy/Rainbow
11ALL: Courtesy of IBM
12: Milt & Joan Mann/Cameramann International, Ltd.
13T: Milt & Joan Mann/Cameramann International, Ltd.
13B: Courtesy Steelcase Inc.
15T: Milt & Joan Mann/Cameramann International, Ltd.
17: Lightscapes/The Stock Market
19: Gabe Palmer/The Stock Market
20: Hank Morgan/Rainbow
29ALL: Courtesy of IBM
30: David Bishop/Phototake
32TL: Courtesy of IBM
32TR: Dan McCoy/Rainbow
37ALL: Milt & Joan Mann/Cameramann International, Ltd.
38TL: Courtesy NEC Home Electronics/
38TR: Milt & Joan Mann/Cameramann International, Ltd.
38B: Courtesy NeXT Corporation
39: Courtesy Digital Equipment Corp.
40L: Courtesy of IBM
40R: Courtesy of Cray Research Center, Minneapolis
54C: Louis Bencze/ALLSTOCK, INC.
54B: Chuck O'Rear/ALLSTOCK, INC.
55L: David Bishop/Phototake
55T&B: Courtesy of IBM
56: Courtesy of IBM
71: Courtesy of Intel Corporation
72: Courtesy of Motorola, Inc.
82: Dan McCoy/Rainbow
84B: Courtesy of Key Tronic, Spokane, WA.
85T: Milt & Joan Mann/Cameramann International, Ltd.
86: Courtesy Micro Express, Santa Ana, CA.

88L: Courtesy NEC Home Electronics/U.S.A. Inc.
88R: Courtesy Grid Systems Corporation
90: Dan McCoy/Rainbow
91: Courtesy of IBM
92: Courtesy of IBM
94: Courtesy Sperry Corporation
96TL: Milt & Joan Mann/Cameramann International, Ltd.
96TR: Courtesy of IBM
96BL: Milt & Joan Mann/Cameramann International, Ltd.
96BR: Milt & Joan Mann/Cameramann International, Ltd.
99: Richard Pasley/Stock Boston
101L: Courtesy of IBM
101R: Courtesy PrintaColor Corporation
106TL: Courtesy Sperry Corporation
106TR: David R. Frazier Photolibrary
117B: Courtesy of IBM
119T&BL: Courtesy of IBM
119BR: Milt & Joan Mann/Cameramann International, Ltd.
126R: Milt & Joan Mann/Cameramann International, Ltd.
127L: Milt & Joan Mann/Cameramann International, Ltd.
127R: Milt & Joan Mann/Cameramann International, Ltd.
130: Courtesy of IBM
131R: Hitachi America, Ltd.
148R: Bob Burch/Bruce Coleman, Inc.
148L: Stuart L. Craig, Jr./Bruce Coleman, Inc.
151: Hayes Microcomputer Products
166: Mark Brownstein/Los Angeles Times Photo
196: Microsoft
202: Courtesy of IBM
208: Peter H. Lewis/THE NEW YORK TIMES
212T: Milt & Joan Mann/Cameramann International, Ltd.
212B: Milt & Joan Mann/Cameramann International, Ltd.
214B: Courtesy of IBM
215Both: Milt & Joan Mann/Cameramann International, Ltd.
217T: Milt & Joan Mann/Cameramann International, Ltd.
219: Milt & Joan Mann/Cameramann International, Ltd.
220: Courtesy Apple Computer Inc
222: Courtesy Letraset USA
239: Susan V. Steinkamp
274TL: Dan McCoy/Rainbow
274TR: Precision Visuals

274BL: Computer Support Corporation
274BC: Computer Support Corporation
274TL: Milt & Joan Mann/Cameramann International, Ltd.
275B: 1989 John Paul Endress/The Stock Market
275T: Courtesy of Frasca International
277L: Karen Sundheim, Dicomed Corporation
277C: Ann Cook, Dicomed Corporation
277R: Karen Sundheim, Dicomed Corporation
282L: 1989 Jeff Smith/The Image Bank
282R: 1984 Walter Bibikow/The Image Bank
310: Nina Lisowski
316: Milt & Joan Mann/Cameramann International, Ltd.
319: Milt & Joan Mann/Cameramann International, Ltd.
329: Milt & Joan Mann/Cameramann International, Ltd.
331: Ellen Schuster/The Image Bank
361: Richard Pastore, Steinway & Sons/Computerworld, March 29, 1989, p.29
366: David R. Frazier Photolibrary
375: Milt & Joan Mann/Cameramann International, Ltd.
376: Milt & Joan Mann/Cameramann International, Ltd.
398: Milt & Joan Mann/Cameramann International, Ltd.
508ALL: Library of Congress
509: The Bettmann Archive
510: Library of Congress
512: Information Services/Iowa State University
513: University of Pennsylvania
514T: Sperry Corporation
514B: Dan McCoy/Rainbow
515T: Courtesy of IBM Archives
515B: AP/Wide World
516T: Dan McCoy/Rainbow
516B: Fairchild Camera & Instrument Corp./A Schlumb Company
518: Courtesy Apple Computer Inc.

Literary Credits

16: From "A day in Your Life Without Computers" by Eric Brand, *Datamation*, September 15, 1987. Copyright (c) 1987 Cahners Publishing Company. Reprinted by permission.
22: From "No escape from computers" by Harvey P. Newquist III, *Computerworld*,

September 11, 1989. Copyright (c) 1989 by CW Publishing, Inc., Framingham, MA 01701. Reprinted from Computerworld.

34: From "Programmers write right on cue" by James Daly, *Computerworld*, May 7, 1990. Copyright (c) 1990 by CW Publishing, Inc., Framingham, MA 01701. Reprinted by permission from Computerworld.

41: "Creating a 'Virtual Chicken'" by Carl Malamud, *InfoWorld*, December 3, 1990. Copyright (c) 1990 by InfoWorld. Reprinted by permission of InfoWorld.

41: "Visualizing a Cure for Alzheimer's Disease" by Carl Malamud, *InfoWorld*, December 3, 1990. Copyright (c) 1990 by InfoWorld. Reprinted by permission of InfoWorld.

41: "Some Modeling Taxes Even Supercomputers" by Carl Malamud, *InfoWorld*, December 3, 1990. Copyright (c) 1990 by InfoWorld. Reprinted by permission of InfoWorld.

60: "Universal Computer Language Due" by Andrew Pollack from *The New York Times*, February 20, 1991. Copyright (c) 1991 by The New York Times Company. Reprinted by permission.

68: From "The Computer with Many Heads" by William F. Allman, *U.S. News and World Report*, May 2, 1988. Copyright (c) 1988 U.S. News and World Report. Reprinted by permission.

83: "Is It Taps for QWERTY?" by T.R. Reid, *San Francisco Chronicle*, April 1, 1985. Copyright (c) 1985 by Washington Post Writers Group. Reprinted by permission.

102: "Computer Gaining a Way With Words" by Don Clark, *San Francisco Chronicle*, June 13, 1991. Copyright (c) 1991 San Francisco Chronicle. Reprinted by permission.

132: From "Molecules light up path to enhanced optical storage" by Michael Alexander, *Computerworld*, January 22, 1990. Copyright (c) 1990 by CW Publishing, Inc., Framingham, MA 01701. Reprinted by permission from Computerworld.

159: From "IS: The hottest thing to hit Hollywood since the phone" by Jim Nash, *Computerworld*, December 24, 1990, January 1, 1991. Copyright (c) 1990, 1991 CW Publishing, Inc., Framingham, MA 01701. Reprinted by permission of Computerworld.

166: Abridgment of "L.A. Times Uses Wide Area Network to Link Its Bureaus" by Mark Brownstein, *InfoWorld*, February 15, 1988. Copyright (c) 1988 by InfoWorld. Reprinted by permission of InfoWorld.

184: From "Mindreading Software" by David Churbuck from *Forbes Magazine*, October 15, 1990, page 198. Reprinted by permission of Forbes magazine (c) Forbes Inc., 1990.

195: From "Macs talk to visually impaired" by Jean S. Bozman, *Computerworld*, June 4, 1990. Copyright (c) 1990 by CW Publishing, Inc., Framingham, MA 01701.

Reprinted by permission from Computerworld.

203: Abridgment of "Software to Help You Wax Poetic" by Peter H. Lewis from *The New York Times*, September 27, 1988. Copyright (c) 1988 by The New York Times Company. Reprinted by permission.

218: Abridgment of "If Lincoln Had Used a Computer" by Mike Royko, *The Chicago Tribune*, March 8, 1990. Copyright (c) 1990 by The Chicago Tribune. Reprinted by permission of Tribune Media Services.

229: From "Heartbeat of hospital lies in diagnostic system" by Charles Von Simson, *Computerworld*, June 18, 1990. Copyright (c) 1990 by CW Publishing, Inc., Framingham, MA 01701. Reprinted by permission of Computerworld.

242: Abridgment of "Financial Modeling: A Powerful Alternative" by Steve Cummings and Marshall Cummings from *PC Week*, April 3, 1989, page 97. Copyright (c) 1989 by Steve Cummings and Marshall Cummings. Reprinted by permission.

253: From "Database unites Vietnam vets" by James Daly, *Computerworld*, October 23, 1989. Copyright (c) 1989 by CW Publishing, Inc., Framingham, MA 01701. Reprinted by permission of Computerworld.

264: From "Plotting a Novel Course to Release Writer's Block" by Al Morch, *San Francisco Examiner*, October 28, 1990, page E5. Copyright (c) 1991 San Francisco Examiner. Reprinted with permission from the San Francisco Examiner.

276: From "Movie-making abracadabra" by James Daly, *Computerworld*, June 25, 1990. Copyright (c) 1990 by CW Abridgment of "L.A. Times Uses Wide Area Network to Link Its Bureaus" by Mark Brownstein, *InfoWorld*, February 15, 1988. Copyright (c) 1988 by InfoWorld. Reprinted by permission of InfoWorld.

283: From "Art Meets Technology" by Michael C. Perkins and Kelly Rivers from *San Francisco Examiner*, January 20, 1991, pages D-13 and D-14. Reprinted by permission of the authors.

300: From "'Vaporware' Inventories on the Rise" by Paul Freiberger, *San Francisco Examiner*, March 12, 1989. Copyright (c) 1989 The San Francisco Examiner. Reprinted with permission of The San Francisco Examiner.

315: From "Full Circle" by Rick Cook, *Byte Magazine*, August 1990. Copyright (c) 1990 McGraw-Hill, Inc., New York, N.Y. Reprinted with permission. All rights reserved.

330: From "Selecting a Programming Language Made Easy" by Daniel Salomon and David Rosenbleuth, *SIGPLAN Notices*, September 1986. Reprinted by permission of the author.

343: From "OOPS" by Julie Pitta from *Forbes Magazine*, March 19, 1990, pages 162 and 164. Reprinted by permission of Forbes magazine (c) Forbes Inc., 1990.

360: From "High-Tech, Tradition in Concert at Steinway" by Richard Pastore, *Computerworld*, March 20, 1989. Copyright (c) 1989 by CW Publishing Inc., Framingham, MA 01701. Reprinted by permission.

372: From "Awards praise the human touch" by Nell Margolis, Clinton Wilder, Maryfran Johnson and Susan Nykamp, *Computerworld*, June 17, 1991. Copyright (c) 1991 by CW Publishing, Inc., Framingham, MA 01701. Reprinted by permission of Computerworld.

385: From "The united systems of Benetton" by Lory Zottola, *Computerworld*, April 2, 1990. Copyright (c) 1990 by CW Publishing, Inc., Framingham, MA 01701. Reprinted by permission of Computerworld.

400: From "Simon says soup is good food" by Johanna Ambrosio, *Computerworld*, September 17, 1990. Copyright (c) 1990 by CW Publishing, Inc., Framingham, MA 01701. Reprinted by permission of Computerworld.

410: From "But can you read it like a book?" by Michael Alexander, *Computerworld*, November 19, 1990. Copyright (c) 1990 by CW Publishing, Inc., Framingham, MA 01701. Reprinted by permission of Computerworld.

427: From "Database keeps the Earth's inventory" by Gary H. Anthes, *Computerworld*, July 23, 1990. Copyright (c) 1990 by CW Publishing, Inc., Framingham, MA 01701. Reprinted by permission of Computerworld.

440: From "An educational smorgas-board" by Helen Pike, *Computerworld*, June 15, 1989. Copyright (c) 1989 by CW Publishing, Inc., Framingham, MA 01701. Reprinted by permission of Computerworld.

468: Abridgment of "Is Big Brother Watching?" by Alice LaPlante, *InfoWorld*, October 22, 1990. Copyright (c) 1990 by InfoWorld. Reprinted by permission of InfoWorld.

476: "The Most Common Computer Viruses," *Computerworld*, February 13, 1989. Copyright (c) 1989 by CW Publishing, Inc., Framingham, MA 01701. Reprinted by permission.

487: From "The envelope, please" by David A. Ludlum, *Computerworld*, September 3, 1990. Copyright (c) 1990 by CW Publishing, Inc., Framingham, MA 01701. Reprinted by permission of Computerworld.

491: "Do Computer Skills Make College Grads More Marketable?" by Jack Hayes, *Family and Home-Office Computing*, April 1988. Copyright (c) 1988 Home-Office Computing Magazine. Reprinted by permission.

INDEX